Uniquely Kosher

Written and Illustrated by

Chasya Katriela Eshkol

Tovim Press
TovimPress.com

Published by Tovim Press, LLC.

Phoenix, Arizona, USA

Library of Congress Control Number: 2022940601

ISBN: 9781643940014

UniquelyKosher.com

Published by Tovim Press, LLC.

Phoenix, Arizona, USA

TovimPress.com

Table of Contents

Section 2

Section 3

Section 4

Section 5

Section 6

Section 7

This Book is

Dedicated to Klal Yisrael,

and In Memory of

Mr. Herbert M. Pollock z"l.

Introduction

"You can't have milk and meat together", say the books. "What?!? No more cheeseburgers or pepperoni pizzas?!" There's an old saying that "there is no substitute for the real thing." ... Well, I'm happily here to say, "Oh yes there is!" Some of the strangest things can create authentic tasting counterfeits. Believe it or not, the way in which foods are prepared can make them taste just like the real thing.

Uniquely Kosher is a must for any Jewish home. More than just a cookbook, there is something for everyone including many handy guides, kids' projects, herbal gifts, extensive sections on equivalencies, substitutions, and educational kosher topics. For the person first starting out, it will ease you into Jewish dietary laws without giving up the flavors in which you have been accustomed to. Even a person who's been kosher their whole life will appreciate tasting foods that they had never dreamed of! Choose from over 613 tested recipes and thousands of variations, or adapt virtually any non-kosher recipe into a completely kosher dish. This book helps to teach you the ways in order to accomplish this. If you're unsure as to what ingredient to use, look it up in the Substitutions section. Designed to be multifunctional, you'll never outgrow *Uniquely Kosher*, since there's so much more included.

Virtually anyone with special dietary needs will find *Uniquely Kosher* helpful. Heart patients can make cholesterol-free imitations (such as cheesecake or country ham) without giving up that "dangerously delicious" taste. Vegetarians or those who are lactose intolerant should be particularly fond of this book, because every recipe has the option to be fixed without meat or milk!

For the first time in history, a system has been devised for listing three different alternatives of cooking in one recipe. I like to call it, the "Tri-Optional Ingredient System". There are thousands of possible combinations throughout this book, with over 248 containing the Tri-Optional Ingredient alternatives, and at least 365 that are totally meat-and-dairy-free. The alternative ingredients can be utilized to create a delicacy compatible with anything else that you're eating. If you want your meat "cheesy", this book makes keeping kosher so easy! Using this book, you can actually not only have delicious kosher cheeseburgers, but they can also be fixed in one of three different ways!

It's simple… when it is *Uniquely Kosher*.

— *Chasya Katriela Eshkol*

Acknowledgments

Sometimes there are far too many "coincidences" for something to be accidental. For instance, after deciding to write this book, unusual things started happening. Although the project was a complete secret, people new to keeping kosher would ask me questions, leading me to better address their concerns. Many times, at classes completely unrelated to keeping kosher, a subject pertaining to what was being written about would come up "out of the blue". This would remind me to add something, initiated new issues that needed addressing, or uncannily answered specific (yet unasked) questions! Could all these things have happened of their own accord? I don't believe it's by chance. Therefore, it is with much gratitude to Hashem our Creator, for all His extraordinary help. I recognize that He has given me a unique perspective: Being someone who can relate to the issues of newcomers, yet provide helpful resources even those who are kosher from birth, due to a love of in-depth research. I thank Him from the bottom of my heart for allowing me the privilege of writing this book. There are many seemingly confusing rules of *kashrut* found in books on *Halachah*, but it is my sincerest hope that by streamlining the major issues and implementing them in a simplified manner, that even the most "clueless" of newcomers can learn how to keep kosher like a pro!

This book was originally started back in May 2005. Ultimately, many people helped add to it in different ways over the years, whether through *shiurim*, advice, suggestions, or recipes. Many are mentioned below...

I'm so grateful to Mum, who aside from giving me life and raising me, (no small task!), gave me an appreciation for a wide variety of foods. Her independence and determination with life's many challenges has always been an inspiration to me. She has always helped me with an unwavering support.

A note of appreciation to Rabbi Moshe Heigh (A rebbe at Atara High School) for help on *Halachic* sources. I also owe so much to his wife Rebbetzin Heigh (my best friend), who I know in her great humility won't want to be mentioned. (Sorry Pnina, I must give credit where it is due!) First, her suggestion to write for a local Jewish magazine led me to rediscover a love of writing. Her constant encouragement never fails to cheer me on. Secondly, it was due to one of her creative recipes that tasted amazingly like something from my childhood, which was the actual catalyst for the creation of this book (and ultimately giving me the idea for the "Tri-Optional Ingredient System"). Without her, this book may not have been written!

Many thanks to Daveed Henn for help with general editing, organization, and confirmation of sources with his *chavrutot* [study partners] at the Cincinnati Community Kollel, early-on in this project. He had invaluable input and suggestions, but his clever analogies that created the *brachot* section truly made it distinct. It was great fun to try to capture his "little world" in picture form for the "Kingdom of Brachot" section.

Much gratitude to Rabbi Daniel J. Raccah (Sefardic Posek of Chicago, Rav of the Sephardic Community Shaare Mizrach, and a Dayan of the Chicago Rabbinical Council), for answering many questions on *Sefardic kashrut* issues.

I'm very thankful to Rabbi Zelig Sharfstein z"l (Rav of the Vaad Hoier of Cincinnati– now called "Cincinnati Kosher") and Rabbi Ya'acov Toron (Former Rabbinic Administrator of the Vaad), both for clarifying many *kashrut* questions and answering questions on some *Chassidic kashrut* issues.

Great appreciation to my first *chavrutah* [study partner] Mrs. Bracha Schutz (a former *mashgichah* [kosher supervisor] for the Vaad), for instilling a love of *kashrut* and the details that go into it.

I have such gratitude to Rabbi Moshe Berlove (*mashgiach* [kosher supervisor] and Former Senior Rabbi of Wellington, New Zealand), for answering questions, and checking the Glossary's accuracy. Also, to his wife Rebbetzin Janet Berlove for her many helpful tips over the years. They are both wellsprings of knowledge!

Much deference to Mr. Herbert Pollock HaKohen z"l who did some preliminary editing. I'll always cherish his funny jokes and stories, and many fond memories. Also, to his wife Mrs. Ellen Pollock (who often acted as my "Jewish mother"), for helping look it over as well. Her incredible tenacity, unending caring, kindness, and perseverance in the most formidable of tasks is truly extraordinary.

Special thanks go to Rabbi Moshe Heinemann (Rabbinic Administrator of the Star-K), for sharing his valuable time. (I never expected him to suddenly call me!) He made sure to explain all the details of white veal that bothered me so that I understood all the issues.

A note of recognition to Rabbi Hanan Balk (Rabbi Emeritus of Golf Manor Synagogue), for proof-reading the original parts of this book in its very infancy, and his helpful suggestions and encouragement.

I also would like to express my appreciation for the advice, help and/or clarifying questions from:

Rabbis Mordechai Frankel & Dovid Heber (Rabbis of Star-K Kosher Certification),

Rabbi Yitzchak Preis (Outreach Director of the Cincinnati Community Kollel),

Rabbi Meir Minster (Rosh Kollel of the Cincinnati Community Kollel), and of course his wife Rebbetzin Aviva Minster, my great (former) next-door neighbors.

A note of thanks must go to the local Jewish community of Cincinnati. Most especially, I am so thankful to the Berloves, Hagages, Heighs, and Pollocks, (my adopted "families"), for their never-ending warmth, hospitality and unconditional positive support. They are the ones who taught me what it really means to be Jewish.

Section 1
Exploring the World of Kashrut
A Food Foundation

Kosher Fundamentals

WHAT DOES "KOSHER" MEAN? Literally, fit or proper. "Kosher" is not an ethnic style of cooking, nor does it mean that a rabbi "blessed" the food. It simply means food is "fit for consumption", or that utensils are "safe for food contact", both being in compliance with *kashrut* [Jewish dietary laws]. Genuine *kashrut* can't be changed nor compromised, but it can certainly be made easy!

WHERE DOES KEEPING KOSHER COME FROM? The basis of *kashrut* is in the *Torah* [Jewish Bible or Written Tradition]. We are instructed to discern between kosher and non-kosher species, and not to eat "creepy" things (*Vayikra* [Leviticus] 20:25). As the old saying goes, "You are what you eat".

Every word in the *Torah* can have a deeper meaning. Sometimes the depth is obvious, but it can also be hidden in *kabbalah* [tradition or secret inner meaning] or coded in *gematria* [numerical value]. More significantly, it is said that the *Torah* doesn't use words unnecessarily. It only reiterates important topics, and most *kashrut* laws are mentioned multiple times. The specific sources are elaborated on below:

Kosher Animals: Mammals that can be eaten must have two combined distinctions: Completely split hooves, plus bringing up and chewing the cud. Kosher meats include beef, veal (baby cattle), buffalo, bison, sheep, lamb, mutton (older sheep), venison (deer), goat and antelope. Giraffe are kosher but too costly to slaughter and difficult to restrain. (*Vayikra* 11:3 and *Devarim* [Deuteronomy] 14:4-6.)

Kosher Birds: No birds of prey or scavengers are eaten. Kosher birds include pigeon, squab (baby pigeons), Cornish hen, chicken, quail, duck, and goose. Turkey is accepted as kosher. The status of pheasant and partridge is unclear, so these are avoided. (*Vayikra* 11: 13-19 and *Devarim* 14:11-18, 20.)

(Note that the above kosher animals and birds can only be eaten if they have been farm-raised and if they are slaughtered humanely, according to very precise *Torah* laws.)

Kosher Fish: Only fish having both fins and scales can be eaten. Scales must be removable without tearing the skin. Fish eggs (roe or caviar) must be from kosher fish. Fortunately, the vast majority of fish are kosher, so non-kosher ones are listed later in "Fish Laws" on page 11. (*Vayikra* 11:9-12 and *Devarim* 14:9-10.)

Kosher Insects: The tradition for identifying kosher locusts has been lost except by a minority of *Yemenites* [Jews originally from Yemen] and Moroccan Jews. Consuming any other bugs is prohibited. That's right, no more chocolate-covered ants! Therefore, we make every effort to avoid consuming insects. Most "creepy things" are referred to as an abomination. (*Vayikra* 11:21-22.)

The Prohibition of Eating Non-Kosher Creatures: Worms, snakes, creeping things, and swarming things are considered inedible. Among others listed are pigs, rabbits and hares, rodents, and other small critters. As an interesting note, rodents and rabbits often carry an infection called tularemia, a highly contagious plague-like disease. Similarly, pork can contain trichinosis. Why eat them? People who eat them say they taste like chicken anyway! (*Vayikra* 11:4-8, 20, 23, 29-31, 41-42, and *Devarim* 14:7-8, 19.)

The Prohibition of Eating Previously Dead Animals: Any animals that have died naturally are prohibited for eating. The animal is likely to have died from a disease (which could often render it non-kosher), as well as not having been slaughtered properly. (*Vayikra* 7:24, 17: 15-16 and *Devarim* 14:21.)

The Prohibition of Eating "Torn" Meat: Meat that has been torn or cut in any way other than proper slaughter is prohibited for eating. Although the Hebrew word "*treifah*" [torn] pertains to meat that has been torn by another animal that killed it, this has become the accepted term used for any non-kosher or unfit food. Hunting can also tear the flesh, mixing impurities with the meat. (*Vayikra* 7:24 and 17: 15-16.)

The Prohibition of Eating Blood: Everyone is aware of how blood can carry disease or viruses. According to the *Torah*, life is in the blood, and is forbidden to consume. One's own blood (such as from gums) and juices that come out of rare meat do not apply. Also, fish blood is permissible if scales are present, but it's not eaten due to appearance. (*Vayikra* 7:26-27, 17:10-14 and *Devarim* 12:16 and 15:23.)

The Prohibition of Eating Fat: Only certain fats from some animals are prohibited, so don't panic if you find fat in your roast! The kosher butcher does the removal of forbidden fats. (*Vayikra* 7:23-25.)

The Prohibition of Eating the Sciatic Nerve: The prohibition includes the inner and outer sinews, the sciatic nerve, the fat surrounding it and six other nerves, plus many specific veins. This is a specific *Torah* commandment pertaining to Ya'akov [Jacob] injuring his "sinew". (*Bereshit* [Genesis] 32:33.)

The Prohibition of Combining Milk and Meat: "You shall not cook a kid in its mother's milk." Aside from the esoteric explanations, it is unethical to cook a baby in the very liquid meant to sustain it. One view says it's akin to the prohibition of slaughtering a cow and its young on the same day. There is another view that idol worshippers cooked meat with milk so the law was put in effect to keep us from being like them. The rabbis point out that this phrase is mentioned three times, one for each facet of the prohibition— one is for **cooking** them together, one for **eating** a mixture of milk and meat, and the last for **benefiting** from their having been combined. "Benefit" would be feeding the mixture (especially if cooked together) to any animal- pet or wildlife, or giving it to humans- be it a Jew or a non-Jew. Such a combination must be discarded. (*Shemot* [Exodus] 23:19 and 34:26, and *Devarim* 14:21.)

WHY SHOULD I KEEP KOSHER? For one thing, it is healthier. Kosher foods have been proven to be beneficial, often preventing many ailments and diseases. For example, both pork and shrimp, which are forbidden by the *Torah*, are proven to be high in cholesterol. The body in general, as well as the mind performs better in every aspect of life. It is said to have spiritual benefits as well, enabling the mind to see things more clearly. Another good reason for keeping kosher is that it is much more humane to animals.

WHAT IS INVOLVED IN KEEPING KOSHER? We will cover the different factors involved in keeping kosher as we go. Of course, one can only eat the animals and fish outlined in the *Torah*, and foods which have been properly processed and/or prepared. Another large part of *kashrut* is keeping meat and milk separate, including their residues on seemingly clean items.

Absorption plays a large role in *kashrut*, especially concerning hotter temperatures. The reason behind this is actually very scientific, but the *Torah* taught this concept long before science explained it. When food is heated, it is absorbed into the vessel it is being cooked in on a microscopic level. This is illustrated in the following true example: A local rabbi had been working with a food processing plant that was concerned about absorption. The company had just gotten a huge new vat, and had hired a scientist to calculate the loss upon its first use. After the initial heating, hundreds of gallons of food had literally soaked into the vat's stainless-steel walls! The same thing happens with your own cookware. If meat were cooked in a dairy pot, some of the dairy residue would leach out into the meat, making it a prohibited mixture. This is why we have two different sets of dishes and vessels for cooking and serving. Just remember this simple rule— "Dairy is dairy and meat is meat, and never the two of them shall meet!"

Although to the newcomer it may seem somewhat restrictive, it really isn't. You can still enjoy the same food flavors you used to eat, via a new format. This is where the role of "imitation" food comes in, and as you'll see in the recipes, it's not really all that hard. After a while, it becomes totally natural once you learn the basics. Nowadays, keeping kosher is easier than ever!

CAN I USE MY OLD DISHES AND COOKWARE? Depending on how items were used, and what they are made of, one can *kasher* [make fit for use or consumption] some materials (such as metals). *Kashering* is a process that purges the absorbed food flavor from a vessel, making it virtually like new. The majority of kitchen items (even major appliances) can easily be made usable again. Synthetic materials (such as plastics) when heated, absorb food flavor in such a way that it is difficult to totally remove, and therefore are usually not *kasherable*. (Try storing water in a clean empty plastic soda or juice bottle— the water will taste and smell much like the product that the bottle had once contained!) Fortunately, most plastic gadgets are inexpensive and easily replaced. A competent rabbi can determine if questionable items can be *kashered* or not. We shall cover all the details of *kashering* in Section 2.

7

CAN I EAT MEAT OR DAIRY ONE AFTER THE OTHER? It depends on which comes first:

Eating Meat After Dairy: For most people, it's usually not a problem to eat meat after having had dairy— as long as and bit of non-dairy or non-meat food is eaten, followed by a drink in-between to clean the mouth. Hands should be washed if they touched dairy. In some communities *minhagim* [customs] vary. Some have a tradition to wait ½-hour in-between, and a few others will wait an hour.

The only real exception to this rule is for "hard" cheeses that have been aged for 6 months or longer in any form (plain, powdered or liquid). Some examples of these are Swiss, Sharp Cheddar, Romano and Parmesan. With these, one will have to wait 6-hours before eating meat. Check to see if the cheese is indeed aged. (There is a guide on p. 444.) If you're not sure, ask a reliable *kashrut* agency or rabbi.

Eating Dairy After Meat: The majority of Jews wait six hours before eating dairy after the last bite of meat. Some families have a *mesorah* [unbroken tradition] to wait less time some for all meat, others only after poultry or ground meat, but this is rare. The waiting period also applies to these examples:

1. Non-meat items that have been cooked in the same pot along with meat.
2. Non-meat items baked in an oven at the same time as uncovered meat.
3. Non-meat items fried in the same oil that had been used to fry meat.

For ease, many people have dairy during the day and eat meat at night. Time passes quickly when you're sleeping. If someone waited the proper amount of time and wanted to eat dairy, but found meat in their teeth, it's no big deal. Just remove the meat, (it couldn't hurt to brush your teeth if you are really picky), eat a bit of non-meat/non-dairy food and drink a little. You're now ready for dairy. (Note: Separate toothbrushes aren't needed; one will suffice. Also, it's perfectly fine to kiss your spouse who just had an opposite food as long as it's at an appropriate time!) Ideally, people shouldn't eat opposite foods at one table. If they do, one should use different colored place mats as a reminder on the table.

HOW DO I KNOW WHEN A PRODUCT IS KOSHER? A commercially manufactured product will display a *hechsher* [a *kashrut* supervising agency's symbol] on the package or label, proving that it has indeed been supervised and is certified to be kosher. This must not be confused with "K" or "Kosher" listed on a product, which is not a *hechsher* at all. *Hechsherim* [*hechsher* plural] usually look something like a registered trademark ®, and each agency will have a different symbol for their "seal of approval". Most often a *hechsher* is found on the front of a label, but occasionally you will find one at the end of an ingredient list, though sometimes it will be very small. (One of the exceptions to this is the three major soft drink producers, whose products are under supervision but do not always display a *hechsher* on the product.) Thousands of certified items can be found at regular supermarkets. Proper supervision is very important. The vast majority of foods need an acceptable *hechsher*. Exceptions are covered in Section 2.

Parve Foods

WHAT ARE "PARVE" FOODS? It's not a fancy French word listed on a package. *Parve* or *pareve* [neither meat nor dairy] means foods that are neutral ("on the fence" if you will), and can be eaten either by themselves or at the same time with either meat or dairy. (Meat and Dairy are considered "opposite genders".)

All nuts, grains, flour, legumes, mushrooms, coffees, fruits, and vegetables are automatically *parve* in their unaltered form. Most dried fruits are *parve* as well, but they must have a *hechsher*.

Oddly enough, eggs are *parve* (unless they happen to be found inside a chicken— those eggs are considered meat and actually have to be *kashered* like meat).

Even stranger than this is the fact that fish are considered *parve*, even though they are categorized as animals. Although they don't need to be slaughtered, they are enough like meat that some stringencies apply. This will be discussed later in *"Fish Laws"*.

It is very helpful to have *parve* utensils and cutting boards for vegetables. This enables a portion of the vegetable you are preparing to be used in a meat dish, while the other part can be used in a dairy dish. It's quite handy to chop several vegetables at once and freeze them for later use in all kinds of recipes. However, you can only do this if it is prepared with *parve* utensils.

Parve items will sometimes say *"Parve"* or *"Pareve"* next to the *hechsher*, but generally it will just have a plain *hechsher* on it. This is not to be confused with a "P" listed next to the *hechsher*, which means it is "Kosher for Passover", and does not necessarily mean that it is *parve*.

Sharp Foods

WHAT ARE "SHARP" FOODS? "Sharp" foods are not just some good-looking garnishes. They are treacherous *parve* foods, which can pick up meat or dairy status simply by a touch. Whatever a sharp ("*charif*" in Hebrew) item comes in contact with, it becomes. For example, virtually every marinating recipe contains something sharp in order to pick up flavor quickly. The same thing happens when a few red pepper flakes have been sitting on or in a food; inevitably the whole dish picks up the spicy flavor.

Generally tangy, strong flavored, or hot and spicy foods which would not normally be eaten alone are sharp. Some examples are horseradish, radishes, onions or garlic and their relatives, lemons, limes, hot peppers, and anything containing these items. In addition, anything containing vinegar such as condiments (ketchup, mustard) and pickled foods (herring, olives, pickles, peppers, etc.) are all considered sharp. Highly salted foods and foods packed in brine (salt water) can also have this status. With some items such as onion leaves, it can depend on how potent the flavor. Very potent will be sharp.

It is important to have *parve* utensils such as forks for removing food from jars, and knives and cutting boards for cutting these items. If you used a meat fork to take one pickle slice out of a brand-new jar of pickles, that would make that whole jar of pickles "meat"! Then if you then wanted to have those pickles on a dairy grilled cheese sandwich, you'd be out of luck. If an onion were cut with a dairy knife, that onion would be rendered "dairy", and it could never be used with a meat meal. Another scenario is if the condiment bottle were to be touched by the food. For instance, someone was trying to squeeze some horseradish sauce out onto a beef bologna sandwich. Their fingers slipped and they dropped the bottle nozzle right onto the bologna. The horseradish is now considered "meat".

When onions and garlic are thoroughly cooked, they lose the sharp characteristic and become mild. It's no problem if a cooked meat onion falls on a clean dairy table as long as they are both cold. Just clean it up well.

10

Fish Laws

WHAT ARE THE FISH LAWS? Before your fish gets stewed, you need to know the laws. Even though fish is *parve*, there are guidelines for serving it. "Fish" is sometimes found next to the *hechsher*, but not always. (If in doubt, one should check the ingredients.) Here are the details:

Fish and Meat: Fish is never mixed with meat, as it is said by our Sages that it can be detrimental. However, many use clean "meat-designated" cookware to prepare, serve and eat fish as long as the fish is never allowed to touch any actual meat or meat by-products. A minority of people only use *parve* items for fish. Details on serving fish at a meat meal are covered in Section 2.

Fish and Dairy: The laws on mixing fish with dairy depend on your *minhag* [custom].

Many *Ashkenazim* [Jews of European descent] will be able to mix the two. A very common fish and dairy combination is bagels and lox with cream cheese, which is often served after a *Brit Milah* [ritual circumcision eight days after a boy's birth].

Some *Sefardim* [Jews of Spanish, Middle Eastern, Asian, or North African descent] and *Chassidim* [ultra-Orthodox *Ashkenazim*—most originating from Poland and areas around the Ukraine] will keep fish and dairy separate. (*Parve* imitation cheese can always be substituted for the real thing.) As a general rule, one should let their hosts know their *minhag* ahead of time if fish is to be served at a dairy meal.

WHAT FISH ARE NOT KOSHER? Anything in the water that does not have fins and scales. This shows that it not only includes fish, but all seafood, even reptiles and mammals. Interestingly enough, these are usually scavengers or live in very dirty water. There's a big fad in some oriental restaurants to eat puffers. Evidently people get a thrill from the danger of eating them, since they're toxic! If the following lists repulse you, then you can easily keep kosher!

Fish: Catfish, Dogfish, Eelpout, Eels, Fiddlefish, Frog-fish, Glake, Goosefish, Huss, Lungfish, Marlin, Monkfish, Puffers (blowfish), Rays, Rigg, Rockfish, Roker, Sea Devils, Sea Pout, Sailfish, Skate, Swordfish and Triggerfish. Lumpfish and Sturgeon are non-kosher species, which most roe or caviar comes from. Sharks are not kosher and have tiny sharp indistinct scales and lack traditional style fins.

Mollusks: Abalone, Clams, Conk or Conch, Mussels, Nautilus, Oysters, Octopus, Scallops, Squid (Calamari), Cuttlefish, Cockles or Periwinkles, Limpets, and Snails (Escargot)— which for some bizarre reason are considered seafood even though they live on land.

Invertebrates: Anemones, Sea Urchins, Sea Pincushions, and Starfish.

Crustaceans: Crab, Crayfish (Crawfish, Crawdad, Écrevisses, Rock Lobster or Langouste), Lobster (Langoustine or Scampo), Prawns, and Shrimp.

Reptiles: Alligators, Crocodiles, Lizards (all types), Snakes, Terrapins, Tortoises, and Turtles.

Amphibians: Frogs, Salamanders, Tadpoles (Pollywogs), and Toads (which are poisonous).

Marine Mammals: Manatees, Porpoises and Whales. This also includes Dolphins— not to be confused with "Dolphinfish" or "Mahi-mahi", which are kosher and often served on Thanksgiving in Hawaii.

WHAT DO I LOOK FOR WHEN BUYING FISH? All fish that is processed in any way must have a reliable *hechsher*. This especially goes for roe or caviar, since it is indiscernible as to whether it was a kosher fish that laid the eggs! Some fish (especially canned and breaded) can be processed with dairy ingredients or derivatives and will have a "D" next to the *hechsher*. Breaded fish can pose a problem because they can be processed with non-kosher oils, or the breading could contain non-kosher ingredients.

Fresh fish must be cut with a kosher knife, as well as packaged, refrigerated, and frozen fillets. Even though it's cold, a *treifah* knife could transfer juices or particles of non-kosher seafood into your fish! It is best to buy fresh fish only at a kosher store or a grocery store that offers supervised "kosher-cut-fish".

One can buy a whole fish— head and all. Wash it thoroughly and trim away any cut areas with a kosher knife. Some hold that fresh fillets (or frozen in a bag) can be bought without a *hechsher*, as long as one can see that some skin is visibly attached as proof of it having scales. It should also be rinsed well.

Dairy Foods

ARE ALL DAIRY FOODS KOSHER? No, it's not so simple these days to just go out and milk a cow. All milk or dairy (called *"chalav"* in Hebrew, and *"milchig"* in Yiddish) must be derived from a kosher mammal. Dairy products have a "D" next to the *hechsher*. There are two levels, as explained below:

"Chalav Stam": The lower level is known as *Chalav Stam* [plain milk]. Many years ago, non-Jewish farmers would add milk from pigs or horses to cow's milk. Nowadays, Federal regulations stipulate that anything labeled "milk" must be from a cow. Many rabbis consider the governmental USDA standards for milk and cream (but not other dairy products) as good enough; however, this is not necessarily the case in other countries. In a sense, the USDA becomes the *mashgiach* [kosher supervisor], since anyone daring to add anything to the milk is risking a hefty fine and a bad reputation. Therefore, U.S. *Chalav Stam* milk does not need a *hechsher* according to some, although there are brands of milk that carry one.

All other dairy products must have a *hechsher* such as canned, powdered or flavored milk, buttermilk, yogurt and especially cheese— due to non-kosher additives or processing equipment. Hard cheese made by non-Jews is not permitted.

"Chalav Yisrael": The higher standard is known as *Chalav Yisrael* [dairy products supervised by a Jew from milking to packaging]. In addition to being supervised, the cows are checked for health prior to milking. It is said to have spiritual benefits, especially for children. It is consumed by all *Chassidim*, most *Sefardim* and some *Ashkenazim*. All *Chalav Yisrael* products including milk need a *hechsher*, and will have "Chalav Yisrael" (often spelled *"cholov"*) stated in English or Hebrew somewhere on the label.

13

Kosher Meat

IS KOSHER MEAT MORE HUMANE? Yes. It is quite impressive how the welfare of animals is taken into consideration. For example, there is a *Halachah* [Jewish Law] stipulating that Jewish farmers cannot eat until they feed their animals first. The *Torah* also prohibits cruelty to animals, and Jews are to make every effort to ensure that animals do not suffer in any way.

Many farms that supply kosher meat feed their animals organic food, and don't use growth hormones or antibiotics. In addition, their animals are often free ranging and happy—the way it was intended to be. If you are into animal welfare, it is very easy to find these good companies on the Internet to order from, because they are proud of the way they raise their animals. They don't need antibiotics, because their animals are not overcrowded or sick.

When the time comes to prepare the animal for "processing", if properly done according to *Torah* law, the animal feels little or no pain, may get a little woozy, and simply goes to sleep before it has a chance to feel anything. The process is likened to getting a paper cut—most of the time a person doesn't even notice a paper cut until well after it has happened.

Unfortunately, meat is sometimes raised on non-kosher farms but sold to kosher companies for slaughter. In these cases, the animals may not have been raised properly according to *Torah* law. There are two particular meats that should be avoided due to inhumane treatment: Goose liver and "white veal". For those interested, "*Prohibition of Cruelty to Animals*" is discussed in Section 7 on p. 626.

WHAT MAKES MEAT KOSHER? For meat (called "*basar*" in Hebrew, and "*fleishig*" in Yiddish) to be considered kosher, the animal must have been slaughtered properly, examined internally ascertaining that it was completely healthy, and then prepared very precisely. All must be done under reliable supervision in a meticulously clean facility. "Meat" (or "Glatt") is found next to the *hechsher*. Below are the details:

Proper Slaughter: Proper *sh'chitah* [kosher slaughter according to Jewish Law] must be done by a professional, certified *shochet* [kosher slaughterer]. The *shochet* has a special knife, which is examined thoroughly before every single use. It must be razor-sharp; the slightest flaw renders it unfit for use. The knife is taken and with one swift motion the throat is cut. The animal or bird simply loses consciousness within seconds from the loss of blood, before it feels any pain.

Examination: In accordance to Torah law, an animal or bird must have been perfectly healthy in order to be considered kosher. After *sh'chitah*, it is thoroughly examined for any signs of internal illnesses, disease, broken bones, or defects. One small adhesion on a lung can render a whole animal *treifah*. As a result, many animals are rejected and sold as non-kosher. Only the best, healthiest stock can be used.

Preparation of Meat: To become kosher, depending on the meat, many procedures must take place. Certain fats and veins must be removed from beef, buffalo, lamb and goat. The forbidden fats surrounding specific organs and other areas are removed. Additional veins and arteries are removed to enable proper blood removal. Since the removal of sinews and surrounding parts of the thighs are time consuming and costly, the entire hindquarters are sold as *treifah* in the U.S.

All meat has to go through a *kashering* process to remove any remaining blood. It must be done quickly and completely before it can congeal. This is accomplished by way of soaking in cool water for half an hour, salting on a special rack for an hour, and triple rinsing. For poultry, the inner cavity is salted as well. Fortunately, nowadays, most butcher shops sell pre-*kashered* meat that is completely ready for cooking so you won't need to deal with it. With all this, it's amazing how kosher meat is affordable!

Preparation of Liver: All liver must go through a different process to remove blood, since it is so concentrated. It must be washed, salted, slit, and broiled on a special rack, then triple-rinsed. It is very important to know that any bagged livers (not to be confused with the harder permissible gizzards) found inside whole poultry have **not** been *kashered*. The liver juices still contain blood and must **not** be exposed to any food, or cooked inside the bird. They have to be discarded or given to someone who *kashers* liver. Even some packaged frozen chicken livers have not been *kashered*, so be sure to read the labels carefully. It's advisable to buy only pre-*kashered* liver. There's no need to cook it, just heat and eat! Fortunately, ready-to-serve kosher chopped liver is often available fresh or frozen at kosher groceries or butcher shops.

ARE THERE DIFFERENT LEVELS OF KOSHER MEAT? Yes. When determining the health of the animal, there are varying levels of strictness. All kosher meat, as well as butcher shops need reliable *hashgachah* [supervision for *kashrut*] from slaughter to selling. Also, all pre-packaged meat must have a good *hechsher* from a reliable *kashrut* agency. Here is information on the different levels:

Regular "Kosher" Meat: Just because meat is called "kosher", doesn't mean that it is acceptable. Sometimes there are misleading brand names that lead one to believe it is. The meat may have been kosher-slaughtered, but might not have passed the internal inspections. These may even have a *hechsher*, but are often under unreliable supervision. Ask a competent rabbi or a reliable *kashrut* agency.

"Glatt" Kosher Beef: *Glatt* ["smooth" in Yiddish] is eaten by *Ashkenazim* and *Chassidim*. It is for beef only, the term referring to checking the lungs, which if the animal is healthy, should be smooth. The requirements for examinations are stringent, however, there is a leniency that if an adhesion on the lung can be peeled off, in some instances it still can pass as "*glatt* kosher". Products need a reliable *hechsher*.

Unfortunately, non-meat products are often incorrectly marked "glatt" in an attempt to imply a higher level of *kashrut*. Although soy or dairy foods may be "smooth", they do not have lungs to check!

"Bet Yosef" Kosher Beef: *Chalak Bet Yosef* ["smooth" as according to Rabbi Yosef Cairo] is eaten by *Sefardim*. It is a level that is stricter in the U.S. than "*glatt*" in that any adhesions on the lungs renders it non-kosher. However, in other countries *Bet Yosef* has leniencies that might make it forbidden to *Ashkenazim*. Products need a reliable *hechsher*. If *Bet Yosef* is unavailable, *Sefardim* may be able to eat *Glatt* kosher.

Kosher Lamb, Venison, and Veal: These types of meat are either kosher or *treifah* because the lungs must have no adhesions at all (the "*glatt*" leniencies apply to full-grown beef only). Therefore, if they are marked "glatt", don't assume you're getting anything special. Just be sure it has a reliable *hechsher*.

Kosher Poultry: Poultry is either kosher or *treifah*. *Kashrut* standards for fowl are entirely different from mammals in that the lungs aren't checked unless a problem is believed to exist. If it is marked "glatt", ignore it and look for a reliable *hechsher*. Note: Consult a rabbi for these rare problems— Broken bones surrounded by congealed blood; re-knit broken bones; dislocated bones, especially with bad discoloration.

WHERE CAN I GET KOSHER MEAT? For fresh meat, see if there is a kosher butcher or kosher grocery in your area or a neighboring city. Frozen poultry and refrigerated lunch meats can sometimes be found at your regular local grocery store if it has a kosher section. There are web sites that sell to individuals; some offer discounts for bulk purchases and many have toll-free phone numbers.

Imitation Foods

WHY USE IMITATION FOODS? Don't be too "chicken" to try out these wonderful foods in disguise.

In the Talmud (a *Gemarah* in *Chullin* 109b*)*, a Sage's wife noted that every non-kosher food has a kosher equivalent that tastes just like it, a fact recorded long before the invention of soy ice cream! Since imitation products are often *parve*, they can be substituted in a variety of recipes which would otherwise be *treifah*. Modern technology provides even more diversity due to vegan products which have the taste and texture of the imitated food. Tips on working with *parve* imitation substitutes can be found on p. 574.

There are all kinds of kosher-certified imitation items readily available at grocery stores in the refrigerated or frozen vegetarian sections. You can also find many products in health food stores, but be sure they have a good *hechsher*. For those items that aren't available, this book lists many excellent imitation recipes. You can also look up the dairy, meat or *treifah* substitutes in the end of the "*Substitutions*" section on pp. 579-580.

A note about the history of "food forgeries": Back in the time of the *Talmud*, the sages said one must display some almonds when one had almond milk with meat. Therefore, when *parve* creamer first came out, it was advised to display the carton so others would know that it wasn't real milk. Today, with so many imitation foods, wrongdoing is not suspected and people no longer have to display the container.

With all the options available, there's virtually an endless array of flavors to work with:

Imitation Dairy: Imitation dairy has come a long way! When I was at an event serving chicken fajitas, they served *parve* sour cream off to the side. Being a dairy connoisseur of sorts, I am very picky and wasn't sure how it would taste. Reluctantly, I tried some, and could not believe how great it was! I even went up to the caterer and asked, "are you sure this is *parve*?" He replied, "absolutely—and so is the whipped cream over there. I like to eat it plain." After that, my fears were relieved.

There are all kinds of *parve* milk alternatives made from soy, rice, oats, almonds, and coconut. Also, non-dairy creamers, whipped creams, ice creams, cheeses, cream cheeses, and sour creams that are all totally *parve*. This means you can have them with meat meals. For instance, imitation cheese can be used to make kosher meat cheeseburgers, as well as other delectable meat recipes. Although some imitation cheeses may not taste as good when eaten plain, they become perfectly delicious when fixed with other flavors as outlined in the *Uniquely Kosher* recipes. Ironically, many of the imitation cheese recipes turned out to taste even better than the real cheese dish!

Imitation Meat: These *parve* items range from hot dogs and cold cuts to chicken breasts and chunks. They are generally soy or wheat-based and contain no actual meat and can be served at dairy meals. For example, real dairy cheese can be used with *parve* "meat" to make kosher dairy cheeseburgers, and other delicious recipes containing dairy. Most products have an identical flavor and texture to the real thing, and you can't taste any difference when mixed in recipes. One exception is some *parve* soy-based hot dogs tend to have the "Israeli-style hot dog" texture, which is softer than the traditional American type.

Also, there is a great product that can be used exactly like ground beef, called "TVP®" (Textured Vegetable Protein). It is sold dry in bags—just add water, or for extra flavor it can be soaked in a *parve* soup "broth" (either beef or chicken flavor). It can be found in the dry goods section of supermarkets, often with specialty and organic flours. It can even be ordered over the Internet in various forms. Seitan is another meat-like product made from wheat gluten, which can be made as very large chunks.

Imitation "Treifah" Foods: The majority of imitation *treifah* foods are *parve* such as pepperoni, ham, bacon, (and of course) bacon bits. These are basically used in the same manner as imitation meats.

For *parve* imitation seafood, there are great kosher versions such as shrimp, crab and lobster, which are available at kosher grocery stores. (Made with real fish, you still have to follow the rules for fish.)

For those die-hard "meat-eaters", you can buy turkey bacon and beef salami that is kosher. They can be purchased at kosher grocery stores, supermarkets, kosher butcher shops or delis. These of course, can only be eaten in meat meals, but with so many imitation dairy foods available, it's not a problem. As far as other things that taste like pork, I've found smoked whitefish salad tastes very similar to deviled ham, and smoked chicken or turkey tastes every bit as good as (and is healthier than) an actual ham.

Now that you know all the kosher basics, it's time to start— *"Putting It into Practice"…*

Section 2
Putting It into Practice
Achieving the Goal

Getting Started

WHERE DO I START? Sometimes becoming kosher is a slow process. Nobody expects you to know or do everything instantly. Just go at your own pace and don't rush things. Everyone has their own way of doing things, but here is a technique to help you become kosher in six easy steps:

☑ **Familiarization:** Reading the details in this section as to the different foods, kosher products and what affects *kashrut*, etc. helps give you a good working knowledge of what you are doing. Having just read "*Kosher Fundamentals*", you're already well on your way to becoming kosher.

☑ **Foods:** Start buying only strictly kosher food items. Hunting for *hechsherim* can be a fun activity for kids, and favorite foods become real treasures when you find them with kosher certification. *Treifah* foods can be given to non-Jews or a food pantry, but meat and dairy mixtures should be discarded.

☑ **Practice:** You may want try a "mock kosher run" to just get the feel of it. Even if it's just temporary, you can designate certain pots, pans, and silverware etc. to start learning how to separate things. The best way to learn something is to actually do it. Try it out, it's not that hard!

☑ **Planning:** Figure out which cabinets will contain what, etc. Determine which old items you want to keep and *kasher*, and what they will be used for. It will be helpful to have easily identifiable sets of cookware, dishes, and utensils used for preparation and eating. If you buy new items, store them until you are totally changed over. Mixing the old with the new would defeat the purpose.

☑ **Transitioning:** You can use paper plates and disposable cookware when in a transitionary stage, enabling you to eat totally kosher. Ideally, you should use different colored plasticware (blue for dairy, red for meat, etc.), so that identification becomes natural. You can also buy prepackaged foods or kosher take out (if you have that luxury) during this temporary stage. Many people have said that by this time they noticed that they felt better and could think more clearly.

☑ **Switching Over:** Once you feel comfortable enough that you know what you're doing, you are ready for the final stage. You can *kasher* your kitchen and cookware either by yourself, or with the help of a rabbi. After the preliminary cleaning process, the entire kitchen will become kosher within just a few hours.

Kosher Certification

בהשגחת הבד"ץ
ירושלם
העדה החר

HOW DO I KNOW IF A KOSHER SYMBOL IS GOOD? If you find a mysterious *hechsher*, follow the clues below, or ask a knowledgeable rabbi or reliable *kashrut* agency, and the case will be solved.

It is very important to check every food label for a good certified *hechsher*. Some examples of nationally known and well-respected *kashrut* certifying agencies are shown above, just to illustrate a few. These are good on all products, since their reliability guarantees that the food has had proper *hashgachah*.

Just because a "kosher-looking" *hechsher* appears often, it doesn't mean it's kosher. One should be aware of which *hechsherim* are reliable, since acceptability of lesser-known agencies can change over time. Occasionally, some questionable *hechsherim* are good on some items but not others.

Often companies know that a kosher symbol will improve the sale of a given product, since many people buy kosher food simply because they feel it is healthier or more trustworthy. However, supervision costs money, so some companies just display a "K" to avoid the expense. An ordinary "K" on a package, or a label saying "kosher" or "kosher pareve" is not a *hechsher*. The people involved in making the product generally aren't Jewish and simply do not realize the complex laws that *kashrut* involves. Always investigate before purchasing these products, since they may not be kosher at all.

A bit of shopping advice: "Scan your brand!" Sometimes a store can carry a kosher product and next to it will be a different variety that isn't, but they may look alike. Also, a brand may drop *hashgachah* on a certain variety and it's no longer kosher. Although identical otherwise, the new batch's label reflects this. Once at a store, there was a favorite brand of mushroom spaghetti sauce that had a *hechsher* on some labels but not all. I promptly cleared them out of the ones that did! Thankfully, this doesn't happen often.

WHY DO SEEMINGLY KOSHER PRODUCTS NEED CERTIFICATION? Although one might think that they can tell whether a product is kosher (or not) simply by reading the ingredient list, so much is involved with modern-day food production that it is impossible to know for sure!

A *kashrut* agency's *mashgiach* must supervise more than just the food itself. Any equipment from start to finish must be kosher already, or it must be *kashered* specifically for that product. Even before ingredients arrive at the processing plant, their origins, handling, equipment history, and shipping must be reviewed to determine that they are truly kosher. Many food additives such as colorings, flavors, enzymes, and emulsifiers can be derived from either kosher or non-kosher sources. The rabbi must also ascertain that any papers or plastics used in packaging don't contain any non-kosher substances that could leach into the product.

The following list gives some specific examples of why certain products need certification:

Baked Goods: Even if the ingredients in a baked product are kosher, the pans could have been greased with lard or other non-kosher animal derivatives. Since the grease is technically not an ingredient, it does not legally have to be listed on the package. A reliable *hechsher* will guarantee a totally kosher product.

Canned Foods: Even if canned fruits and vegetables have only pure ingredients, it doesn't mean they are automatically kosher. Steel cans can be coated with non-kosher oils. Many canneries process non-kosher foods such as pork and beans, clams, etc. on the same equipment without *kashering* between runs. No big deal? Consider people with nut allergies. Violent allergic reactions can be triggered by nut-free foods merely processed on equipment which previously contained nuts. Food residues can be transferred!

Dried Fruits and Raisins: Dried fruits (especially raisins) need a reliable *hechsher*, because they may have been coated with non-kosher fats to assist in the dehydration process.

Dried Herbs and Spices: These can contain non-kosher anti-caking and/or anti-dusting additives, and processing equipment could have been lubricated with *treifah* oils. All should have a reliable *hechsher*.

Produce From Israel: Special *Torah* laws apply to any produce grown in Israel. A *hechsher* will be displayed proudly by *Torah* observant Jews who follow these laws. (For details see pp. 624-625)

Health and Medicinal Products: Organic health or vegetarian products may indeed be "all-natural", but so is arsenic! A *hechsher* will ensure a kosher product. Many vitamins have unlisted fillers or coatings such as oyster shells or glycerin from *treifah* animals. Flavorful medicines like cough drops, syrups, powders (to be mixed with liquids), chewable tablets, and chewable vitamins are ingested like food or drinks, and need a *hechsher*. A reliable *kashrut* agency will often have a list of acceptable products.

"Pure" Juices: All fruit or vegetable juices must be kosher certified even though they may be labeled "100 % pure". They can contain *treifah* derivatives such as gelatin or other items such as non-kosher colorings. Red coloring can be derived from the dried dead bodies of the coccus cacti insect (also called cochineal or carmine) which is used in many lipsticks and other cosmetics. Not only are the bugs *treifah*, just the idea alone is really disgusting! Needless to say, purchase pure juices with a reliable *hechsher*.

Disposables: What could be non-kosher about paper, plastic, and foam items? Glycerol monostearate, glycerol monooleate, Quilon (parchment coating) and calcium or zinc stearates, (chemicals derived from non-kosher beef fat) are used by manufacturers as acid neutralizers, lubricants and anti-static dissipaters. These chemicals remain in the finished product and leach out, especially when heated. Even cold, the molecular structure of fatty acids causes them to react with many foods, literally being drawn out. Not exactly a low-fat diet! A *hechsher* on disposable cutlery, plastic wrap, parchment or wax paper, storage or cooking bags, plates, bowls or cups ensures you'll have nothing to "beef" about. (See plastics on p. 602.)

ARE THERE ANY PROBLEM FOODS TO BE AWARE OF? Yes, there are some. Not only must the following items have a reliable *hechsher*, but it is helpful to know what makes them problematic. Read the ingredient labels on the potential troublemakers listed below:

Soy, Rice or Almond Milks: Watch out for a "D" next to the *hechsher*. These and other vegan "milks" can be processed on dairy equipment or use dairy ingredients.

Imitation Meat: These can contain dairy derivatives. Look for a "D" next to the *hechsher*, or buy *parve*.

Sherbet: Although it seems like sherbet is made only from fruit, it isn't. According to government regulations, all sherbets must contain milk (thus making them dairy). However, there is not always a "D" next to the *hechsher*. This can be very confusing! Therefore, it cannot be served with a meat meal.

Non-Dairy Creamer: As crazy it sounds, many powdered "non-dairy" creamers are really dairy! This is because they have dairy derivatives such as caseinates, whey, or lactose, which cannot be combined with meat products. Look for a "D" next to the *hechsher*. There are truly *parve* non-dairy creamers out there, but you may have to search for them. Usually they will display "parve" or "pareve" by the *hechsher*.

Non-Dairy Whipped Topping: Many "non-dairy" whipped toppings have dairy derivatives, with a "D" next to the *hechsher*. If you want a topping to serve with a meat meal, look for *parve* brands— they do exist. You can make your own from *parve* frozen liquid non-dairy whip topping. Thaw out, shake, and whip with a mixer in a cold bowl.

Margarine: Always look next to the *hechsher* for a "D". Often margarines contain dairy derivatives, so they're dairy like butter. Others contain animal fats or fish oils, further showing the need for a *hechsher*.

Imitation Cheese: Always look carefully next to the *hechsher* to make sure there is no "D". Some may contain casein- a dairy derivative, which cannot be eaten with meat. This totally defeats the purpose, unless one is lactose intolerant. Only buy *parve* brands with a reliable *hechsher*.

Creamed Herring: This contains dairy and fish. The "cream" part is made with sour cream. However, this is only is an issue for people who don't eat fish and dairy together (see "Fish Laws" for details).

Worcestershire Sauce: It's important to know that many name brand Worcestershire sauces are made from whole fish. This isn't a problem for fish or totally *parve* meals, but it shouldn't be used for recipes containing meat (or dairy, depending on a person's *minhag*). It may not always be labeled "fish" next to a *hechsher*, and may even be labeled "parve". The safest thing is to purchase Worcestershire sauce without anchovies in the ingredients. Read the label (or make *Fishless Worcestershire Sauce* on p. 92).

Omega-3 Fatty Acids: Talk about an item being "fishy", this one must top them all. Omega-3 fatty acids come almost exclusively from fish! This is often taken as a supplement, but most people are totally unaware that it is also an ingredient in many foods. Often, products listed as being "Omega-3 enriched", even though they are listed as kosher *parve* (and not "fish"), they present a serious problem if eaten with a meat meal. In this case, read the ingredient label.

Gelatin: Gelatin is often made from the skin and bones of animals or fish. Non-kosher or even "K" gelatin can be made from *treifah* animals, as well as improperly slaughtered animals. Therefore, most people use only kosher certified gelatins. (A rare view says gelatin is so far removed from the animal itself that it is not even considered meat anymore, but few people follow this.) There is still a question as to what can be served with meat or fish gelatin. By far the best and safest kosher certified gelatin is made of carrageenan. It is totally *parve*, and usable with anything. Read the ingredients and look for a *hechsher*.

Marshmallows: These contain gelatin (see above), and must have a *hechsher*. Read the ingredients to see whether it's made from fish gelatin (can't be eaten with meat) or carrageenan (which isn't a problem).

Grape Products: All products containing grapes or their flavorings must have a reliable *hechsher*. Also, wine and grape juice have a very special status, since they are used for *Kiddush* [a sanctification]. These should have reliable certification to ensure that they have been handled properly. For social events, wine or grape juice should be labeled "*mevushal*" [cooked].

Flavored Tea or Coffee: Flavorings are often non-kosher or even dairy. These must have a *hechsher*.

"Meat-Flavored" Items: All "meat-flavored" products must have a reliable *hechsher*, because the flavorings could be derived from non-kosher sources. Some "meat-flavored" products are actually *parve*, but others may contain meat without stating "meat" or "Glatt" next to the *hechsher*. Always read the labels, as a quick glance at the ingredient list may reveal that there is indeed a chicken in your soup!

WHAT IS MEAT OR DAIRY "EQUIPMENT"? A *parve* food prepared with or cooked in clean "meat items" is called "meat equipment". (However, if a roast were baking uncovered in the oven with it, the *parve* food gains the status of "actual meat".) The same concept applies to dairy. "DE" next to a *hechsher* means that the product was processed on equipment previously used for dairy, even if it doesn't contain any actual dairy ingredients. This affects how you eat the food. For example: You have just had a full-fledged meat meal, and you want to eat a dessert that is marked "DE". Could you eat it? Yes! It doesn't contain dairy ingredients, so it's not considered dairy. However, something *parve* must be eaten in between. Another stipulation is you can't serve it on a meat plate or use meat utensils. Since it's not a good idea to have a dairy plate on the table at a meat meal, it can easily be served on disposables.

WHAT ITEMS DO NOT NEED CERTIFICATION? Some 100% pure items (with no other additives whatsoever) don't need a *hechsher*. If in doubt ask a reliable rabbi or *kashrut* agency. Examples are:

- ✓ plain bottled water and unflavored seltzer

- ✓ fresh whole fruits, vegetables and herbs (excluding peeled, cut, processed, and produce from Israel)

- ✓ plain U.S. packaged frozen fruit with no coloring, syrup, or juices (excluding fruit grown in Israel)

- ✓ plain raw frozen veggies (no spinach, broccoli, cauliflower, Brussels sprouts, artichoke hearts, potato)

- ✓ plain dried mushrooms; sun-dried chili peppers or tomatoes; dried mushroom powder (domestic)

- ✓ unprocessed dry barley; plain dry legumes such as beans or split peas (without additional seasonings)

- ✓ plain non-enriched bulk rice (excluding parboiled or quick-cooking)

- ✓ plain bulk raw popping corn kernels (unprocessed and without additives)

- ✓ raw unprocessed unshelled or raw shelled nuts or seeds; blanched nuts (without oils or flavorings)

- ✓ fresh whole uncut fish complete from head to tail, including innards, scales and fins

- ✓ fresh unprocessed eggs in the shell (excluding "fertilized" eggs)

- ✓ plain unflavored tea bags or leaves including decaffeinated (excluding instant or herbal)

- ✓ plain salt (excluding sea salt); pure baking soda (not baking powder); plain granulated white sugar

- ✓ plain flours such as wheat, vital gluten, rye, corn flour or masa harina, soy, etc.

- ✓ plain unflavored TVP® or wheat gluten/seitan (no ingredients other than soy or wheat and water)

Kosher Food Details

HOW DO PETS FIT INTO KASHRUT? Although your pets may find kosher food to be the "cat's meow" or the "doggie's delight", they don't have to keep kosher (*Shemot* 22:3), or wait between eating meat and dairy. The only real stricture is that pet food cannot contain meat and dairy mixtures. Animals can have fish and meat mixtures. (See p. 649 for other pet feeding details on Passover.)

If you have a pet that is a non-kosher species, you should not let it lick your dishes. Even if your pet were to eat a diet of kosher food, the pet's saliva is not kosher. If such a pet did try to "do the dishes for you" while your back was turned, quickly wash the item with cool soapy water and it will be fine.

It is a *Halachah* (as said in Section 1) that you must feed your pets before yourself. This comes from the "*Shema*" ["Hear Israel..." recited twice daily], where Hashem [our Creator] states that "I will give food to your cattle, and (then) you will eat and become full" (*Devarim* 11:15). The aroma of food can cause a pet to become hungrier, and feeding them first is yet another kindness to animals. There was once a very famous rabbi named Rabbi Yisrael Meir Kagen (affectionately nicknamed the "Chafetz Chaim" after the book he wrote of that title), who absolutely refused to make *Kiddush* on *Shabbat* [the Sabbath] until the chickens were fed!

On the contrary, one may drink before their animals do, since water is not so tempting. We find the *Halachic* source for this from Rivka (Rebecca) first giving Avraham's (Abraham's) servant Eliezer the water first, and then watering the camels (*Bereshit* 24:18-19).

ARE THERE OTHER DETAILS CONCERNING FOOD? There are some:

Challah: Many women find it meaningful to take "*challah*" [A portion taken from dough], but even men take *challah* if they bake. About $^1/_{24}$ is removed from a large batch of dough or baked goods made of barley, rye, oats, wheat, or spelt. This represents the portion set aside in *Bamidbar* [Numbers] 15:19-21 intended for the *Kohanim* [priests] who served in the Temple. Since there is no Temple now, one cannot benefit from it, so we burn it and dispose of it. We call traditional *Shabbat* bread "*challah*" to signify that this has been done. (For complete details, see *The Mitzvah of Challah* in Section 7 on pp. 622-623.)

There is a *Halachah* that one should never throw out *challah* or bread, since it has a special status. It should either be used, or if it's no longer considered edible to humans, put it out during weekdays to feed the birds or squirrels. It should not be tossed around or left on the floor, out of respect.

Commercially Baked Goods: Although a non-Jewish individual cannot bake for a Jew (even if all the *kashrut* laws are observed), there is a leniency that allows them to commercially bake food for Jews. This is generally called *pat palter* [commercial baked goods made by a non-Jewish bakery, but supervised by a reliable *kashrut* agency]. The majority of bakeries with good *hechsherim* fall into this category. *Pat palter* bread with a "dairy" designation is *Halachically* incorrect and should not be eaten.

There is a stricter category called *pat Yisrael*, [goods baked by a Jew]. A Jew must have some part in the baking such as turning on an oven, and this only applies to foods fancy enough to serve at a wedding. "Pat Yisrael" will be clearly marked on the label. *Chassidim*, *Sefardim* and others usually eat only *pat Yisrael*, except minor snack foods. (If it is hard to get or too expensive, *pat palter* is permissible.)

Another issue for commercial bakeries is taking *challah*, although less is taken proportionally, it is still a substantial amount. The overseeing *kashrut* agency ensures that *challah* is taken from Jewish-owned bakeries that are *pat palter* or *pat Yisrael*. Non-Jewish-owned bakeries do not have to take *challah*.

Sometimes you see a label marked "yoshon". This has to do with a lesser-known *mitzvah* [law/good deed] in the *Torah*— to refrain (until the next year) from eating products containing barley, rye, oats, wheat and spelt that sprouted after the *Omer* [barley offering] was brought at Passover (*Vayikra* 23:14). *Yashan* [old] doesn't mean it's stale! It simply means that the product complies with this *mitzvah*. From fall to Passover, many look for labels marked "yoshon" or stash problematic products until after Passover of the next year. *Yashan* is covered in detail in Section 7, see "*New Grain*" on p. 621.

Commercially Cooked Foods: A Jew must cook (fry, boil, or broil) or assist in cooking any fancy foods that aren't eaten raw. For *Ashkenazim*, a Jew can merely turn on a pilot light or increase a flame. For *Sefardim*, a Jew must place food on the hot burner, or start the flame after a non-Jew places the uncooked food on it. See "*Commercial Baking, Cooking and Maids*" on p. 627 for more details.

Gifts: Many times, people will fix food to give as gifts. Is it *parve*, meat, meat equipment, dairy, or dairy equipment? When giving food, it's a good idea to write the status on jars, zipper bags or aluminum foil with a permanent marker. It's an easy way to be considerate, so others won't have to ask you later.

Keep Bread Parve: If *parve* bread were baked in a meat pan or in a meat oven, it would be considered meat equipment, and couldn't be used with dairy. Avoid making bread or rolls with meat fat, as it's *Halachically* like a hunk of steak! Neither should bread be made with dairy ingredients or using dairy equipment. (Small amounts made with dairy must have an unusual shape prompting others to this.)

Washing Hands: Before touching food or especially wet produce with one's hands, one should do a hand-washing. (The Sages taught this long before science identified germs!) Generally, one should wash after touching shoes or a normally covered body part, scratching one's scalp, and cutting nails or hair.

Sleeping Above Food: One should not store food or drink (even in an unopened can) underneath anything that a person sleeps on. This includes a snack kept beneath a sleeping child in a stroller, or food in a bag under an airline seat. Sleep is said to be $1/60$ of death, causing spiritual impurity (one reason why we wash our hands immediately after waking). This is based on *kabbalistic* principles, but as many people say, there are spiritual forces out there which we cannot see and don't necessarily understand.

Uncovered Beverages: Some never leave uncovered beverages (bee's honey, milk, water or anything containing them, beer and uncooked wine) unattended, especially overnight. The *Talmud* [Oral *Torah*] describes how a snake can drink from an open vessel, contaminating it with venom. Being less common now, not everyone finds it a problem. Dust or microorganisms fall in open drinks. Microscopic "snakes" (known as "bacteria") are often harmless, but their byproducts can be quite toxic (like venom).

Eggs: Always store eggs in the shell, as it acts as an airtight seal to keep out bacteria. When broken, eggs become especially susceptible to pathogenic bacteria. There is a *Halachah*, which states that one should never store eggs out of the shell overnight, even covered. This applies to all raw or cooked eggs. Peeled eggs can be stored coated (such as with mayonnaise in egg salad) or mixed in with a substantial amount of other foods (such as in soup), but never with raw onions, raw garlic, or plain water.

Onions and Garlic: Always store bulbs with their protective outer skin. When cut, these produce enzymes that create sulfur compounds. Most hold that (just like eggs above) one shouldn't store totally peeled raw onions or garlic overnight, even covered. The exception is the remaining portion having a root base and skin still attached. Chopped onions or garlic can be stored combined with a substantial amount of another ingredient (such as coating in oil). Cooked onions or garlic are not problematic.

WHAT FOODS NEED CHECKING BEFORE EATING? Most of the following foods do not need *hechsherim*, but should be checked for certain things. Here's what to look for:

Eggs: Eggs must be inspected for bloodspots, since the blood would render them *treifah*. Just crack it into a container and look, it's as simple as that. Any egg that has a red spot has to be thrown out. The container should be washed out with soap and cold water right away, without making the container *treifah*. Had the egg been added to other ingredients or a hot pan, it could be a major *kashrut* problem. Regular grocery store eggs do not need a *hechsher* because they are usually unfertilized, and you do the checking. However, some health food stores sell fertilized eggs, which are never kosher.

For hard-boiled eggs, cook a minimum of three. Cooking them in odd numbers helps *Halachically* nullify anything that could be questionable. Many people use a special pot only for hard-boiling eggs.

Packaged Salads: Bagged salads containing only vegetables (without sauces or other additives) do not need a *hechsher*. However, you may be getting more than you bargained for— bugs. Take out three handfuls and inspect them visually, if there are no bugs it can be presumed to be kosher. To avoid the pesky problem, buy salads with a *hechsher*, they have been checked and found to be bug-free.

Frozen or Fresh Vegetables: Frozen vegetables without a *hechsher*, and all fresh vegetables must be checked thoroughly for bugs (seen only with the naked eye, not a magnifying glass). Special attention should be paid to crevices. Generally, flowery or leafy vegetables having close-knit areas are susceptible to insects or caterpillars. Aphids (small oval green or black bugs) particularly love to hide in cabbage, lettuce, Brussels sprouts, asparagus, artichokes, broccoli, cauliflower and the like. Chives and green onions often have thrips (tiny gray or brown sliver-like bugs). An easy way to eliminate these non-kosher pests is to fill a large bowl with water, and swish in a drop or two of kosher dish soap. Submerge the vegetables, jostling them slightly to remove air bubbles, and let them soak about thirty minutes. Bugs will usually sink or float (looking like splinters or blobs). Rinse produce well to remove remaining bugs.

Frozen or Fresh Fruits: Frozen berries with no *hechsher*, and all fresh fruit must be checked for bugs. (Do the same procedure as for vegetables above.) Thrips are found on leafy strawberry tops, or hidden in crevices of berries. Some fruits such as figs, dates, or carob pods should be cut open and checked for worms or insects inside, prior to consumption. This is mandatory if fruit has any blemishes, especially if having been grown without pesticides. If you find a worm in your apple, cut it out with some of the fruit.

Dried Produce: Dried figs, dates and prunes are pest-prone, even with a *hechsher*. Cut open and remove any critters. Dried mushrooms from China, and kelp or seaweed must be checked for infestations.

Store-Bought Fresh Fruits & Vegetables: It helps to check for bugs under natural light. In addition to this, you may want to read shipping cartons. Produce is often coated to preserve and beautify. If coated, the box should state "coated with food-grade animal-based wax…" or "…vegetable, petroleum, beeswax and/or shellac-based wax or resin…" The word "Animal" can refer to non-kosher species or even dairy derivatives. "Shellac", or "lac-resin", is a secretion of the Lac bug. With this in mind, it's a good idea to scrub produce with detergent and water. Not only will this remove these coatings, but pesticides as well.

Dried Legumes and Rice: Legumes, rice and quinoa should be casually checked for bugs when dry. When the examined legumes are soaked, any bad ones that either contain worms or mold will float. Only "floaters" need to be discarded. Rice can be stored in airtight containers enabling it to stay bug-free.

Grain Products: Grain products such as barley and orzo pasta should be inspected for bugs, caterpillars, moths, cocoons or webs. If there is any evidence of them, you may not be able to eat it. Many people sift their flour to ensure there are no bugs. An easy way to avoid this problem is to store grains in an airtight container. Flour and creamed wheat cereals store well in a plastic zipper bag in the refrigerator.

Fresh Fish: Checking fish is not mandatory, but it can occasionally have parasites. Although generally harmless to humans, these parasites are not kosher. Fortunately, the parts where parasites are found are not usually eaten. Examine fish for worms or cysts on the scales and skin and remove any that are found. Wash unscaled fish with a little vinegar or salt water, and rinse all fresh fish (even fillets) before cooking.

HOW DO I HAVE FISH AT A MEAT MEAL? Simply eat the fish first on a totally separate plate with separate silverware. Some people use disposables for this. Others use smaller plates or saucers with smaller salad or dessert forks in order to keep them distinct. These can be "meat designated" as long as they are clean and the fish is never allowed to be eaten together with meat. After eating, the plates and forks are collected and removed from the table, and then the meat part of the meal is served. Between the courses, some people either take a swallow of drink, or eat a piece of *parve* bread or salad. There is no need to wait any length of time between eating fish and meat. All the dishes can be washed together (except for the minority of people who use *parve*-only items for fish).

Cooking fish and meat for the same meal is a little trickier. In addition to not mixing or touching, the steam from both items cannot mingle either. On the stovetop this is not quite as crucial since they are in their own pots (as long as they do not splatter into each other). When it comes to the oven, steam can penetrate even a covered casserole dish. Therefore, baking gefilte fish at the same time as chicken for *Shabbat*, is a no-no. Ideally cook them at different times, or cover them both tightly with foil.

(Those who don't mix fish and dairy should follow the guidelines above to serve fish at a dairy meal.)

WHAT CONDITIONS AFFECT KASHRUT? Certain specific circumstances cause foods or vessels to change or even lose their kosher status. The following can affect *kashrut*:

Temperature: Heat can facilitate the absorption of foods and their flavors affecting *kashrut* status instantly. For example, if a cold meat pot were accidentally set down on a cold piece of cheese, you only need to wash the pot and rinse off the cheese, both with cool water, then they are able to be used as normal. Suppose the same pot were filled with boiling hot chicken soup, and you mistook the cheese for a yellow trivet: Not only would the cheese and the outside of the pot be rendered *treifah*, but also the chicken soup inside the pot as well! The heat causes the metal to act as though it is semi-permeable. (See "*What is Involved in Keeping Kosher?*" on p. 7 for a scientific example of this principle.)

When something is so hot that it will affect *kashrut* status, it is called "*yad soledet bo*" [the hand recoiling back]. This temperature is anywhere between about 110° F to 160° F (or over), and applies with anything. The general rule is if you can easily touch it, it is not hot enough to affect *kashrut*.

Steam: Tiny particles of food flavor go up with the steam (which is where the aroma comes from), and will affect the *kashrut* status of whatever food that it contacts. Let's say you squeeze out some *parve* mayonnaise onto a hot steaming hamburger fresh from a grill. The steam coming up could give the whole bottle of mayonnaise the status of "meat". Even though the steam is cool enough to hold your hand over, it can still change *kashrut* status. Thereafter, the mayonnaise can never again be used on dairy foods.

Sharpness: Sharp foods can penetrate even when they are cold, instantly changing *kashrut* status at all times. They are considered the same as if they were boiling hot food. To illustrate sharpness, there are recipes which have raw fish marinated in chilled lemon or lime juice for 2 to 4 hours. Afterwards, the fish has turned white and tender—it is completely "cooked" and ready to eat. If you hypothetically dropped a cherry tomato into milk, washed it off with cold water then it rolled onto cold meat, all would be kosher. However, if you had dropped a *parve* pickle into milk, that pickle becomes just like boiling hot dairy. Even if you washed it off with cold water, if it then slipped onto cold meat, the sharpness of the pickle renders both itself and the meat *treifah* and a rabbi must be consulted to see if anything can be salvaged.

Salted Foods and Brine: Highly concentrated salt can affect *kashrut* status and is like heat because it has the ability to extract. (Two examples are salting meat to remove blood, and soaking vegetables in salt water before pickling or canning to remove moisture and impurities for better preservation.) If a cold dairy item were to touch a cold piece of salt-coated meat, one or both items may have to be discarded, or perhaps have a layer cut away and be rinsed in order to be eaten. Either way, a rabbi must be consulted. The principle is exactly the same for brine or salted water (depending on salt concentration).

Wetness: When a food is wet, it can affect *kashrut* status more readily than something that is dry. When something is liquid, it can mix with or soak into other foods making the two impossible to separate. For instance, if a spoonful of milk fell into a cold pot of beef stew sitting on the counter, a rabbi must be consulted immediately as to how to proceed. Whereas if a cold, dry piece of roast beef briefly came into contact with cold, dry cheese, one merely needs to rinse them off, then they would both be permitted.

Liquid and Time: Liquids can absorb into food or vessels over time, thus affecting *kashrut* status. When something is sitting in liquid for 24 hours or more, it is considered to have penetrated just as if it had been cooked. Suppose there was a piece of meat in the meat drawer that was sitting in a puddle of milk that had leaked out of the carton stored above. If it was only for a couple of hours, depending on the circumstances it may be permitted. However, if 24 hours had elapsed, it is considered *treifah*.

Time Period Since Last Usage: When a pot or utensil has been recently used, it can affect *kashrut* status far more readily than one that has not been used for over 24 hours. (The taste has spoiled.) For example, a clean and residue-free meat spoon that had not been used for two days was accidentally used to stir a glass of chocolate milk. Once the error was discovered, one only needs to wash the spoon and the glass in cold water. The spoon can be used with meat as normal, and the glass will be able to be used with dairy as normal. As long as it was unintentional, the milk may be salvageable, but a rabbi should be consulted. However, if that same meat spoon was used earlier in the day for eating chicken soup (even though washed and dried), and used in the milk, then a competent *Halachic* authority must be consulted. The spoon and perhaps even the glass might have to be *kashered*, and the milk may be considered *treifah*.

Volume: In certain cases involving non-sharp foods, the volume of food can affect *kashrut* status. Suppose a drop of milk accidentally dripped into a large pot of beef stew. If the milk was less than $1/60$th of the total volume of the stew, it may be salvageable, since the milk is too little to be detected. However, if the milk were more than $1/60$th, it is considered able to be tasted and the stew is *treifah*. Moreover, it's strictly forbidden to purposely add more stew to the pot to make the volume permissible. Also, the $1/60$th rule doesn't work with a whole bug if you know it's there, or tastes that can be detected in tiny volumes.

Flavor: A beneficial flavor can affect *kashrut* status more than a detrimental flavor. Extracts are so highly concentrated that they can be tasted regardless of how small an amount is used. For example, a drop of *treifah* extract (less than $1/60$th) falls into a huge batch of tea. The tea is *treifah* because the extract enhances the flavor. Now, let's say you find a fly in your soup. Eating a whole bug is a serious *Halachic* problem no matter how tiny! (It can be noted that only part of the bug like a wing, is not such a problem, but yuck!) However, since the fly does not impart a desirable flavor to the food, it can simply be removed. Both bowl and soup are still kosher. (It doesn't mean you have to eat the soup!)

Examples of Situations Which Do Not Affect Kashrut Status:

⇨ If a cool dairy plate that is clean on the bottom were put on a clean meat tablecloth, both would still be kosher. If there were dry crumbs on the tablecloth, the plate can be washed with cool water.

⇨ If a clean cold meat pot is set down on a clean dairy counter, both are still kosher.

⇨ If a dairy dish is being washed in a *treifah* sink with cool or not-quite-warm water, and it happened to touch the side of the sink for a second, as long as it had nothing sharp on it, the dish is still kosher.

⇨ If a meat pot were stored inside of a dairy pan in the cabinet, as long as they were clean, cold and dry, each would be kosher. Keeping them in separate cabinets basically avoids accidents and mix-ups.

⇨ If the sweating milk jug you are about to buy was placed in pork chop blood that leaked onto the grocery store conveyor belt, it can be washed off at home with cool soapy water and still be kosher!

⇨ Cold cottage cheese was eaten in a *parve* plastic bowl, it was then washed in cold water and dried, all before 24 hours had elapsed. If hot *parve* food were then put in the bowl, both would remain *parve*.

WHAT IF I DO SOMETHING WRONG? Accidents can and do happen to everyone, and there is no reason to be embarrassed. If you make a mistake, just call a competent *Halachic* authority that deals with *kashrut* issues. Many times, there will be a simple solution, and even if there is not, it is good to catch a problem early, or it could wind up affecting the rest of the kitchen. You may want to make a note of what you did, how it happened, and the conditions that surrounded whatever occurred. Here are examples of general things to make a note of:

For Foods: What types of foods were involved? How hot or cold was it when it occurred? Was steam, sharpness or salt involved? Were they wet or dry? How long did they touch? What was their volume?

For Utensils: What designation was it? What was it used in or on? What temperature did it become? How long ago was it last used? In what manner and temperature was it last used?

For Potential Change of Kashrut Status: What were the type of foods? What temperatures were involved? Were they sharp or salted? Wet or dry? Steamy? What type of utensils or cookware did they touch? When were the utensils last used? For how long did they touch? How much food was involved?

For Mix-ups or Mixtures: What type of foods? What temperature? Sharp or salted? Wet or dry? For how long? What cookware was involved? When was the cookware last used? What proportions of food?

As in any case, whatever the circumstance, it is always best to ask a *shelah* [*Halachic* question] to a rabbi. He can tell you what needs to be done to solve the problem.

WHY SHOULD I CONSULT A RABBI? Often, one might think they're doing the right thing, but it turns out a rabbi should have been consulted. For example: A woman has a medical condition and needs a certain medication that contains glycerin. Glycerin is not kosher, but she asked a *shelah* and was told that she could take the medicine. Her husband hears this and thinks it is perfectly fine to take a cheaper vitamin supplement that also contains glycerin, since it too is a pill that is swallowed as opposed to eaten. Wrong! A situation pertaining to one person could be totally different for another person because every case is decided individually. If the husband had consulted a rabbi, he would have found out why. His wife could not survive without the medication and no kosher substitute was available, whereas he does not necessarily need the supplement and could easily get a kosher equivalent. If you have a question, no matter how silly or insignificant it may seem, ask it!

Ask An Expert: I had a lot of questions when I started to study about *kashrut*, so I asked people who seemed to know what they were doing... and later found out that they were wrong! As a rabbi once told me, they may be wonderful, well-meaning people, but they're not experts. If you have a valuable car with a precision engine, you wouldn't take it to a backyard mechanic to be serviced. The same goes for *kashrut*. Your body and soul are priceless and one-of-a-kind! If you value them, you'll want the best. *Kashrut* is derived from precise *Torah* Laws and can't be compromised, and the certified *kashrut* agency or rabbi you consult must be knowledgeable in this field. *Kashrut* agencies have rabbis who meticulously inspect commercial processing plants, from ingredients to packaging. They are educated in *kashrut* laws, studying *Halachic* issues constantly. These rabbis have access to up-to-the-minute information on changes that constantly occur in the commercial food industry, which the average consumer couldn't possibly know. Concerning specific *kashrut* questions, only a practicing *posek* [a rabbi who is a *Halachic* expert] should be consulted. Orthodox Rabbis are expert in *Torah* Law, and will be more than happy to answer your questions without pay. Whether you are "Orthodox" or not makes no difference to them— we're all Jews!

Be Prepared to Accept the Answer: Once you've asked a *shelah* and gotten an answer, you must follow it! (It's not ethical to "shop around" for an answer you want, or go to a certain rabbi because he's more lenient.) If you feel your question wasn't understood properly or you received a wrong answer, it's possible to ask another rabbi— only if you inform him that you had asked the question to another rabbi.

Note: It is very important to choose a rabbi who you feel comfortable with and does not intimidate you. Normally, for personal *shelot* [*Halachic* questions], once you choose a rabbi you should stick with him, as he knows you well and can *pasken* [make a *Halachic* decision] correctly for you. However, for general *kashrut* questions, your established rabbi need not be consulted. In many cases, a rabbi knows his limitations and may even refer you to another rabbi who's an expert in the field of your question.

Actually Switching Over

HOW DO I SET UP A KOSHER KITCHEN? You don't really need space to set up a kosher kitchen! Factors to consider are how often you cook, what you cook the most, how much space you have in your kitchen, and your budget. Here is a list of different ideas to help you set up your kosher kitchen:

Determining What You Need: For those who cook a lot, it may be wise to have extra items, but for those who don't cook much, it may be advisable to keep things to a minimum. If you eat mostly dairy, you may want to have the gamut of dairy items, and maybe just a few meat items for special meals.

If you have limited space to work with you can make-do with very little. If you have plenty of room and/or a large budget to work with, you can have multiple cookware, dish sets, sinks, ovens, and even separate countertops and dishwashers for each type of food. However, one does not need to go wild remodeling to become kosher; most kitchens are able to be *kashered* and used as-is.

Sinks: If you have a single-bowl sink, you just have to be careful how you use it. If you have a stainless steel double-bowl sink, it is ideal because you can *kasher* it and have one side for meat and the other for dairy. A helpful tip is to get a piece of Plexiglas to cover the side you are not using. This prevents hot water from splashing onto dishes in the sink of the opposite food. The cover can be flipped over when using the other side. (Dirty dishes should not be covered for a long time. Leave a gap to keep them from smelling.) If you have the space and money to remodel it is helpful to have two sinks, but not mandatory.

Designating: Allocate which part of your countertops, drawers and cabinets will be meat or dairy. The largest or most convenient sections should be reserved for whatever type of food you cook the most. For drawers and cabinets, it is helpful at first to label them with sticky notes until you get used to what is stored where. If you have multiple utensils and/or cookware, choose which will become meat or dairy, and these must always be kept separate.

You don't necessarily need to have refrigerated foods in designated places, but it is a good idea—especially if you have *parve* imitation items that could get mixed up with their real counterparts.

Over-the-Stove Cabinets: If you have cabinets above a stove, it might be a good idea to store non-food items such as cleaning agents in them. Any items stored there can pick up the status of what you are cooking due to steam, thus rendering the contents of the cabinet *treifah*.

Conventional Stoves: Preferably, select which stovetop burners will be used for meat and which for dairy (and perhaps one for *parve*). However, check to see if the oven vents through a stove burner (usually an insert located under one of the rear burners). Ideally, that burner should be used for the same type of food you cook in the oven because of the heat and moisture coming out of the vent. For instance, if meat were cooking in the oven, it would cause a problem for a dairy pot sitting on the vent-burner. Consider designating the oven for the type of food baked most often or for the largest sized meals (such as a turkey dinner), and having a toaster-oven for less frequently eaten or smaller sized meals (like pizza). If you rarely bake, you can easily get by with only one oven using a method that is discussed on p. 41.

Surface-Mount Burners, and Double-Ovens: It is ideal to have separate burners in each separate area. You can get creative and accomplish the same thing by using your burners for one type of food, and having a hotplate for the lesser-used type of food. It all depends on your space, budget and needs. If you are really into cooking, you may want a double-oven, one for meat and one for dairy. Just be sure that one oven does not vent into the other one or this would defeat the purpose. If you already have one that vents in this manner, the one that vents into the other (usually the bottom oven) must be used for *parve*.

Glass Cooktops: Although very convenient for cleaning, glass cooktops are not easily *kashered* and therefore not practical in a kosher kitchen. You may want to consider getting a conventional stove.

Microwaves: Determining if you should have more than one microwave can depend on your individual needs. If you have little use for more appliances, or your kitchen or budget is too small, you can get by with a single (even *treifah*) microwave using a method that will be discussed later. Over-the-stove microwaves are not ideal because steam from food cooking below could make the microwave *treifah*.

New Appliances or Cookware: If you wish to purchase new appliances or cookware, see the section called *"Kitchen Items: Purchase & Use"* (pp. 605-619), for in-depth advice on what qualities to look for.

Tables: Since you do not generally have separate tables for eating dairy and meat, you should have separate tablecloths for each. They can be color-coded and quite decorative.

High Chairs: Since babies rarely eat hot food, just clean the high chair well, especially any crevices.

Things to Buy: You will need separate and easily identifiable gadgets for each specific type of food. Fortunately, these are readily available at dollar or discount stores. Some things you might not think of that should be bought in duplicate (or even triplicate) are salt and pepper shakers, food storage containers, can openers, knives, cutting boards, graters, pot holders, place mats, tablecloths, sponges, kitchen gloves, dish pans, and drying racks. Often starting anew gives you a psychological boost and keeps you from falling back into old habits. These items can be bought slowly or added as needed.

Other things that you might want to buy include additional utensils, plate sets and cookware. One mixer can be used if multiple beaters are purchased for each type of food. For those who don't measure their spices and seasonings, it is a good idea to have separate and distinguishable spices.

Kashering: Some items that involve heat or come into direct contact with food may be *kasherable*. If possible, find a rabbi who will go through the *kashering* process with you. He can help you determine which things to keep and what to sell or give away. The processes will be addressed in *"Kashering"* later.

Immersing: Old *kashered* utensils and cookware, as well as any new ones, must be immersed before use. This procedure will be discussed in *"Immersion"*.

Labeling: An easy method of labeling items is to use colored permanent markers, or even better, solid-colored nail polish. The standard for labeling is red for meat, blue for dairy, and green for *parve*.

Eventually you can label your cookware and cabinets with professional, permanent heat-proof stickers designed just for the purpose. However, since they are difficult to remove, it is advisable to label them after you have totally switched over and are ready to use them permanently. Some people use colored electrical tape for permanent use, but from my experiences, it is prone to getting very sticky (especially with heat), and even has a tendency to peel off over time, leaving a gummy residue. It is better to use electrical tape on disposable items, or colored paper stickers for dry items such as spice jars (which often have incorrectly-colored labels or lids that can conflict with your color-coding system.)

Color-coding helps immensely; you have an immediate visual aid to help you remember which item is what type of food. The creative individual can really get decorative and inspired. Nowadays, there is an unlimited supply of color-coded gadgets and cookware to help you become a *kashrut* pro.

HOW DO I MAINTAIN MY KOSHER KITCHEN? It's easy to maintain your kosher kitchen when you are familiar with the *kashrut* laws. Here is a list of helpful tips:

Working With a Non-Kosher Countertop: If your countertop is not *kasherable*, or is too small to have multiple food areas, it must be used very carefully. You must be especially cautious when it comes to the things that affect *kashrut* status.

⇨ Always put pot holders, trivets, or towels on the counter before setting any hot or sharp items down.

⇨ When cutting vegetables, you must use a cutting board. When cutting sharp foods, put a layer of foil or plastic underneath the cutting board to keep spilled juices from making the cutting board *treifah*.

⇨ Cold utensils, cookware and dishes can be put directly on a clean counter as long as no food is spilled on the outside. It is best to avoid putting meat and dairy items down on the counter at the same time.

💣 Any food that is hot, sharp or highly salted that comes in contact with the counter must be discarded.

Working With Designated Countertops: There isn't very much to worry about when you have designated kosher countertops, as long as you keep the proper foods on their specifically-designated countertop.

⇨ Cold containers or pots of food can be placed on an "opposite" designated counter (as long as there is no sharp food spilled on the outside), without compromising the *kashrut* of the countertop.

⇨ Never put hot, sharp, salted or wet foods down on an "opposite" designated counter. Setting a hot meat roasting pan on a dairy counter could render both the roaster and the counter *treifah*.

Using Tables: Since most people use only one table for multiple foods, here are some practical tips:

⇨ Use separate tablecloths and/or separate place mats designated for each type of food.

⇨ Separate place mats must be used if people are eating different "opposite" meals at the same table.

⇨ A new table could be kept kosher by using it uncovered for dairy, and always double-covering it for meat meals (which are often more fancy or formal anyway). Use trivets for very hot serving vessels.

⇨ Put clear plastic table protectors on top of fancy color-coded decorative tablecloths for easy clean up.

⇨ Have separate designated salt and pepper shakers and condiments for adding to hot foods.

Adding Seasonings to Cooking Foods: These methods not only keep the spices or ingredients kosher, but also keep moisture out of the containers which would make them cake-up or become stale.

⇨ Never shake or hold any items such as baking goods, garlic powder, salt & pepper or other herbs and spices over steaming foods. The steam coming up can turn them whatever type the hot food is.

⇨ Measuring spoons can be kept dry and *parve* by measuring the amount of seasoning into your hand (or an empty bowl of the same-type as the cooking food), before adding it to the steaming food.

💣 If designated seasonings were used over "opposite" types of steamy foods, they must be thrown out.

Cooking on Conventional Stovetops: There are a few details to keep in mind concerning cooking and use of a single conventional stovetop used for both meat and dairy.

⇨ The middle area of a conventional stovetop should always be considered *treifah* since both meat and dairy splatters on it when hot. Never put lids, pots or utensils on it directly. If you do use it, put down separate coverings for each food type (or line it with foil). If a pot was accidentally set in the center of the stove, and they were both cool and clean (free of any residue at all) the pot will still be kosher.

⇨ Although it is not forbidden to cook meat and dairy in separate pots on the same stove at the same time, it is very dangerous and should be avoided. Foods could splatter onto the "opposite" food and cause them to become *treifah*. Also, steam can cause problems with utensils if they are accidentally passed through the steam of an "opposite" food. It is advisable to keep any "opposite" utensils or cookware off the stovetop when cooking.

⇨ If your oven vents through one of the back burners, that burner should be used for the same type food that the oven is designated for. If the oven is *treifah*, don't use or set anything on that burner while the oven is in use, and after the oven cools off, remember to *kasher* the burner before using it (see p. 44).

Cooking on Non-Kosher Glass Cooktops: Glass cooktops can be temporarily used in the same manner as any conventional stove when using the following guidelines:

⇨ Two sheets of aluminum foil can be put on each burner and designated for one particular type of food. The whole cooktop should not be covered since it could cause the top to crack.

⇨ Always have a pot containing some food or water on the burner before turning it on. Never turn the burners on with foil only. The foil is just like an empty pan reflecting the heat back into the stovetop.

⇨ Avoid using the burners on high unless the pot or pan is the same size or bigger than the burner you are using (but never smaller), and is always centered over the burner (not off to one side) or you could cause a meltdown situation. Tipping up the edges of the square foil to the form of the pot is helpful.

⇨ If the foil is used repeatedly, be sure to check it for tiny holes before each use by holding it up to a light. Never put it back upside down, or swap the order of the foil—or you could risk making your pots *treifah*. If you see light coming through, discard it and get a new piece, replacing the bad one in its order. The bottom piece usually gets a wrinkly pattern, but this is normal.

Microwaving Without Affecting Kashrut: An easy method can be used if you must use only one microwave for various types of food, or even when working with *treifah* microwaves (such as at work).

⇨ Completely cover the container that the food is in with two layers of plastic wrap, or two zipper bags.

⇨ Food must be sealed so that no steam comes out. (Be careful of the steam when you open it.)

⇨ In dirty *treifah* microwaves, also use two paper plates or two paper towels under the wrapped food.

Baking Without Affecting Kashrut: There is an easy way to bake (or broil) if you have only one oven that must be used for multiple food types. It can be *kashered* and designated as one type of food.

⇨ Completely cover bakeware in two layers of foil. Double-wrapping keeps food kosher, even in *treifah* or opposite-food designated ovens. (Double-wrapped foods don't brown, but they taste just as good.)

⇨ Double-wrapped items must be completely sealed so that no steam comes out. Example: Put food in an aluminum baking pan, lid it with foil beyond the lip, insert it into a second pan, then lid it also.

⇨ You can eat totally kosher during the transitionary period or anytime by utilizing double-wrapping.

⇨ This method can be used in emergencies due to time constraints, if one absolutely has to bake meat and fish in the oven at the same time. However, do not make a habit of this.

⇨ If using the double-wrap method, allow a longer baking time or raise the oven temperature by 25° F.

Washing Dishes in General: If you have separate sinks, there is little to worry about other than keeping the same-type foods in each sink. Whether you have one sink or more, these apply to all:

⇨ Separate color-coded sponges, scrubber pads, brushes, dish rags, etc. must be used for each food type.

⇨ Use separate designated drying racks and towels color-coded for each food type.

⇨ If you have a kosher dishwasher, it should be used for one designated food type only.

⇨ If you have only one set of drinking glasses that you use for meat and dairy, you must wash them by hand. A dishwasher uses high heat, and could possibly compromise the *kashrut* status.

Washing Dishes in Single-Bowl Sinks: If you must use one single-bowl sink for different-type foods or a non-*kasherable* sink, here are various guidelines to follow:

⇨ Soak dishes in separate color-coded dishpans designated for each type of food. If you put the dishpan in the sink, raise it by using a wire rack or sink pad in the bottom of the sink. Though the rack or pad is designated for the dishes' food type, it should essentially be treated as *treifah*.

⇨ When using hot water, wash dishes in mid-air so that they do not touch the sink or the faucet.

⇨ When washing non-sharp food residues using only cold or cool water, the dishes can touch the sink or faucet, or even be set in the bottom of the sink temporarily, but this should be avoided.

⇨ Wash faucet handles with soapy cold water if food gets on them. Separate soap dispensers are helpful.

Proper Refrigerator Use: Refrigerators and freezers are cold, but there are a few things to remember:

⇨ In case of leakage, meat should be kept in a meat drawer, and milk should be in a containable area.

⇨ Wait for warm items to cool off before putting them in the fridge. Not only will it be safer *kashrut*-wise, but it also saves money on your energy bill since the fridge won't have to work as hard.

⇨ Some people designate different areas in their refrigerator to avoid mix-ups with imitation foods.

Kashering

WHAT IS "KASHERING"? Unless your husband is a pyromaniac, the process isn't as scary as it seems. *Kashering* [making items fit for use] is simply a way to remove any traces of food or absorbed flavor from certain used vessels, utensils, kitchen appurtenances, and food contact equipment making them *Halachically* fit for kosher use. The laws are mentioned in the *Torah* in *Bamidbar* 31:21-23.

The need for *kashering* can be illustrated by an event that happened to me when my water was to be turned off for repairs. I filled a new stainless steel pot full to the brim with water for later use. A day or so later, I opened the lid to use the water. Although the pot was only used once to make spaghetti and had been scrubbed totally clean, there was white goop seeping out and dropping from the submerged rivets inside! I always scrub my pots well (especially around rivets), and I know there was nothing there when I put the water in. Having just learned about *kashering*, I looked down at the ooze, realizing that it was starch from the first and only use, saying, "Wow, the sages really knew what they were talking about!"

When to *Kasher*:

➤ To make *kasherable* non-kosher items that come in direct contact with food, totally kosher.

➤ If an accident occurs or a mistake has been made with a *kasherable* item.

➤ If the history of a *kasherable* item is unknown or its designation is not remembered.

➤ To make a *kasherable* item kosher for Passover use.

➤ Some *kasher* when going from *Chalav Stam* to *Chalav Yisrael*.

➤ Many *kasher* new metal items due to non-kosher oils possibly being used in the polishing process.

(One should never *kasher* things constantly in order to switch them from one food type to another.)

WHAT MATERIALS ARE GENERALLY KASHERABLE? The *kasherability* of an item often depends on what it is made of. Questionable materials may or may not be *kasherable* and a *shelah* should be asked. Below is a list of *kasherability* of specific materials according to the majority of views:

Kasherable	Questionable	Non-kasherable
☑ Glass (used-cold-only)	☐ Glass (used-warm)	☒ Ceramics and China
☑ Crystal (used-cold-only)	☐ Glass (used-hot)	☒ Earthenware and Stoneware
☑ Stainless Steel and Iron	☐ Pyrex® and Duralex®	☒ Porcelain-Enamel
☑ Copper and Brass	☐ Corelle® and Arcorac®	☒ Coated or Painted Items
☑ Aluminum	☐ Corningware®	☒ Teflon® or Non-stick Items
☑ Silver and Gold	☐ High-Temp Plastic	☒ Plastics
☑ Chrome	☐ Formica®	☒ Melamine® and Melmac®
☑ Bone or Ivory	☐ Natural Rubber	☒ Synthetic Rubber
☑ Seashells	☐ Wood	☒ Composite Stone
☑ Smooth Marble or Stone	☐ Fiberglass and Corian®	☒ Rough Marble or Stone

WHAT ARE THE METHODS OF KASHERING? There are several methods of *kashering*:

Sanding Method: In rare cases, items are sanded until a thin layer is taken off. This method is used for smooth wood (and Corian® according to some). Absorbed flavor or particles are physically removed.

Cold-Kashering Method: ("Miluy V'Eruy".) Items are immersed in fresh cold water for 24-hours, three consecutive times. This method is done by *Ashkenazim* exclusively for used-cold-only glassware, such as drinking glasses or measuring cups. It draws out any absorbed flavor or food particles over time.

Boiling Method: ("Hagalah".) All areas of items must make contact with rapidly boiling water, then cold water immediately afterwards. This method is used for items having been used with boiling water or other non-oil liquids such as pots, utensils and silverware. Boiling purges the flavor or particles.

Pouring Method: ("Eruy Roschim".) Boiling water poured along entire surface of item to be *kashered*. This method is used primarily for sinks and countertops. The boiling water purges flavor or particles.

Baking Method: ("Libun Kal".) Items are heated in an oven at 550° F for 1-2 hours. This method is used to *kasher* conventional ovens, shredders, colanders and bakeware. High heat ruins flavor or particles.

Glowing Method: ("Libun Gamur".) The item or area is heated until "red-hot" (800-900° F). It is used on rivets, crevices, stovetops, frying pans, grills and broilers. Intense heat burns off flavor or particles.

HOW ARE KITCHENS KASHERED? When you're ready to switch over your whole kitchen, contact a rabbi who specializes in *kashrut* to guide you through the process. First have him come to determine what can be *kashered* and which method to use. Then prepare the items, and ask if he can help, or even *kasher* for you. These are the general procedures that may occur when your kitchen gets *kashered*:

Cleaning: Anything that is to be *kashered* should be scrubbed clean, and free of any residues, stickers, rust, corrosion or tarnish before *kashering*. Using a cleanser containing oxalic acid and a scrub pad makes it much easier to clean stubborn spots on pots and other metal items. There should be no separation between any part of the item and the water or heat, however, some stains may be permissible. Items with crevices, rivets, or lips that have food embedded there should be scrubbed extra well in these areas.

Clean sticky knobs, switches and areas where food and crumbs can be found such as cabinets, drawers, and floors. Refrigerators and freezers need only be cleaned well (no *kashering* is needed).

Preparation: This is perhaps the easiest part. After cleaning and rinsing, anything to be *kashered* must sit unused for at least 24 hours (except for burners). They are then ready for their specific procedures.

Electric Burners: Elements are extremely easy to *kasher* and are a rare exception to the 24-hour waiting period. Be sure the center and brace assembly are clean and turn each element on high for 3-5 minutes until it glows. It is now kosher! Since the reflector pans generally do not make contact with food or cookware, they only need to be cleaned. However, they can be replaced easily or covered inexpensively with aluminum foil, but be sure to leave the center open for proper air circulation.

Gas Burners: Clean the burner heads, and scour the grates well. The heads don't need *kashering*, and the grates are another exception to the 24-hour waiting rule. The easiest way to *kasher* the grates is to put them in the oven while you *kasher* it. Other methods invert the grates on the heads, and/or cover them with foil, then blast them in the flame 10-20 minutes (making sure not to melt the control panel or knobs).

Glass Cooktops: Most rabbis advise against *kashering* a glass cooktop stove. Some hold that the burners can be turned on until they glow, but this only *kashers* the area of the burner itself, not the remainder of the top. Being flat and smooth, cookware can easily slide off the *kashered* burner and onto the *treifah* area, rendering the cookware *treifah*. If a propane torch is used to *kasher* the *treifah* area, the glass could shatter or develop minute cracks that could ruin it, and will void the warranty. A person *kashering* it may be hesitant to get it hot enough to actually be effective, and therefore it would not be a valid *kashering*. Some *Sefardim kasher* the areas between the burners by the pouring method after being cleaned and waiting 24 hours. (See "*Stovetop Areas*" on the next page.) Ask your rabbi how he holds.

Stovetop Areas: The area underneath the stovetop should be cleaned thoroughly (most lift up for easy cleaning). Porcelain-enamel tops cannot be *kashered*; clean it well and consider it *treifah* when hot. For a stainless-steel top, scour all areas well and rinse, then don't use the burners for 24 hours. If electric, turn off the stove's circuit breaker at the service panel immediately before *kashering*. Boiling water from a *parve* kosher pot is poured on the entire top. (Some pour cold water immediately afterwards.)

Controls: Knobs, switches and input pads do not need *kashering*, but should be cleaned very well.

Stove Hoods: These must be cleaned thoroughly and the filter (if any) changed. Steam coming up can condense and end up dripping *treifah* residue on your kosher food. Grease-cutting sprays can be used.

Broiler Racks and Pans: Stainless steel can be *kashered* by glowing. Porcelain must be replaced.

Broiler Area in Gas Ovens: Take out the broiler pan and scour the broiler area, then let it sit unused for 24 hours. The broiler area is *kashered* as the oven is being *kashered*, with the broiler pan removed.

Ovens: Scour the oven and racks, using oven-cleaner up to two times for stubborn stains. An easy way to clean racks is spray them with oven cleaner and put them in a large plastic garbage bag. Seal it up tight overnight. Afterwards, they just need rinsing off and they are totally clean with little or no scrubbing! The oven and racks must sit unused for 24 hours. For non-self-cleaning ovens: Put only the racks in the oven, and turn it on the highest setting (usually broil, which reaches about 550° F) for 1 hour, keeping the door closed at all times. For self-cleaning ovens: Run it through a full cleaning cycle. (If any other items are to be *kashered* at the same time, see "*Glowing Method Tips for Self-Cleaning Ovens*" in this section.)

Faucets: Metal can be *kashered* with the pouring method, but plastic imitations and ceramic cannot.

Kasherable Sinks: Stainless steel, as well as pure smooth marble or granite that is free of cracks or chips can be *kashered*. The sink stopper must be discarded, and the sink, fixture, and appurtenances thoroughly cleaned and rinsed. Ideally, the sink should not be used for 24 hours, but if you must use it, turn off the hot water cut-off. No hot water or food may come into contact with the sink during this time. When the time has elapsed, boil water in a kosher *parve* pot, or several if possible. Most pour the boiling water top-to-bottom over all metal parts of the faucet and the entire surface of the sink so that every part has been touched by boiling water directly from the pot (not the residual water that has flowed down). Some *Sefardim* hold that it goes in the reverse, around in circles from bottom-to-top and then the faucet. As soon as every part of the sink has been done, immediately run the cold water (or have filled pots of ice water), making sure all surfaces and the faucet have been cooled off. The sink is now done.

Drains, Disposals, And Sink Stoppers in Kasherable Sinks: If the drain flange (which holds the stopper) or the disposal lip is metal, it will get *kashered* with the sink, but if it's made of plastic, it may be questionable. The old sink stopper will need to be replaced with a new one, as synthetic rubber seals cannot be *kashered*. You may want to bring the old one to a hardware store to make sure the new one fits. The slotted rubber insert on disposals (that keeps things from flying up while grinding) is below the seal of the stopper on most models, so it would not cause any problems if the sink were filled with hot water.

Porcelain Sinks: According to most opinions, porcelain cannot be *kashered*. Some *Sefardim kasher* porcelain sinks as follows: The sink is dry and not used for 24 hours. When the time is up, boil water in a kosher *parve* pot, or several if possible. Pour the boiling water in a circle around the drain, then gradually out further (still circling), spreading out until the entire sink has been touched by the water. Immediately dry the sink, boil more water and repeat this process two more times. (No rinsing is necessary.) Thereafter, use only cool to lightly warm water, especially if you put dishes or pots down in the sink.

Non-Kasherable Sinks: China, Corian®, composites, and either marble or granite that is rough, cracked or chipped cannot be *kashered*. These type sinks should be cleaned well, and considered *treifah*.

Kasherable Countertops: Stainless steel, crack-less smooth wood (rough wood can be sanded first), as well as pure smooth marble or granite that is free of cracks, chips or silicone sealer can be *kashered*. Clean the countertop, rinse it thoroughly, and let sit unused for 24-hours. Boil water in some kosher *parve* pots. Quickly pour the boiling water along the center of the countertop for the full length of the top, making sure that every inch has been touched by fully boiling water. Water spreads out— use this to your advantage. Then, take cold water and pour it along the counter following the same path. It is now kosher.

Corian Countertops: Corian® tops are possible, but not very practical, to *kasher*. This involves hiring a kitchen contractor to sand off a layer and buff it out. Most likely, with the amount of time, mess, and money spent on *kashering* the top, it may be better to just get a new one.

Questionably Kasherable Countertops: Formica® and other plastic-based laminates are a matter of debate. Some rabbis hold that these materials can be *kashered* by the pouring method, others hold they cannot be *kashered* at all. Either way you shouldn't put sharp or hot items directly on these countertops— always use a pot holder or trivet. Ask your rabbi how he holds.

Non-Kasherable Countertops: Composite stone or marble, rough marble or granite, plastic-based tops, tile, porcelain drainboards, and any material that is too rough or scratched cannot be *kashered* at all. These type countertops should be cleaned well and considered *treifah*, always using a pot holder or trivet.

Dishwashers: Ask your rabbi how he holds, as dishwashers are a matter of debate. If the sides are porcelain or the filter screen catching food particles is not removable, most likely it cannot be *kashered*. If it is *kasherable*, the screen should be removed and cleaned, and the racks should be discarded. It is then run empty through one cycle on its highest heat setting using a caustic substance like chlorine scouring cleanser in place of the dishwasher detergent (some *Sefardim* hold it only needs dishwasher detergent). New racks must be installed. Dishwashers have to be designated as dairy or meat, since they involve heat.

Microwaves: There are differing opinions on whether or not a microwave can be *kashered*. Most *Chassidim* hold that you cannot. A lot depends on whether the walls of the microwave get hot. Test this by heating a cup of water in the microwave until it has been boiling for a few minutes. If the sides of the microwave are hot immediately afterwards, it probably cannot be *kashered*. If the sides are cool, it is likely *kasherable*. As with anything, ask your rabbi how he holds, especially concerning microwaves with browning element or convection features. (For over-the-stove microwaves, see "*Stove Hoods*" for cleaning instructions. Once *kashered*, the door must always be kept closed when cooking on the stove below, because steam from the food could cause the microwave to become *treifah*.)

Those who hold you can *kasher* a microwave, do it in the following manner: Clean it thoroughly, so that there's no residue or food anywhere on the oven. If the oven has a removable splatter screen, or a rotating plate and rollers, all must be taken out, cleaned thoroughly as well, and put back in. When done, let the microwave sit unused for 24 hours. When it's time, there are two different methods to use.

Method 1: Fill a disposable bowl with water and heat it on high for 5-10 minutes or until the whole microwave is totally steamed up like fog. Discard the bowl and dry the microwave with paper towels.

Method 2: Fill a disposable bowl only halfway full with water mixing in a caustic solution (such as a drop or two of dish detergent). Run the microwave on high until all the solution boils away (10 minutes or so), then immediately turn it off and dry it out with paper towels. (Note: A microwave should not be run without any food or water in it for any length of time, so do not leave it unattended.) This method really does get the microwave clean!

Once *kashered*, some say the bottom of a tray-less microwave should be lined with a double-layer of paper towels for regular use. Many *Ashkenazim* say to replace the glass tray or cover it with either foam, cardboard, corrugated plastic, or glass. *Sefardim* hold a glass tray is *kashered* with a microwave, but if it's high-temperature plastic it must have boiling water poured over its entire surface after waiting 24 hours.

Sanding Method Tips: On small items, a high-speed rotary tool with a sanding bit will remove wood quickly and easily. The wood can then be smoothed by using a polishing bit. On large surface areas, use a hand-held orbital sander. Coarser grit paper removes more material. Finer grit paper smoothes, but clogs.

Cold-Kashering Method Tips: Some *Ashkenazim* hold that clean glassware used-cold-only (below 115° F) can be "cold-*kashered*". A clean five-gallon plastic bucket works great. Fill your bucket with cool water and totally submerge the glasses, being sure to get out any air that may be pocketing. Leave them there for at least 24 hours— no less. When the time is up, take out all the glasses, dump the water, refill the bucket with fresh water, and totally submerge the glasses again for another under 24-hour period. Drain and submerge once more for 24 hours. Afterward, dry your glasses or crystal and they are perfectly kosher. (*Sefardim* hold that glass does not absorb and needs only to be cleaned well.)

Boiling Method Tips: Buy an inexpensive new pot made from any material, or pick a kosher pot that has not been used in 24 hours. It must be large enough to fit whatever it is you're *kashering* inside. This will be your "*kashering* kettle". Keep in mind that the larger the pot, the longer it takes to boil water! Items to be *kashered* must be cleaned and sit unused for 24 hours. The *kashering* kettle is filled with water and brought to a rapid boil. Every part of each item to be *kashered* must have contact with the boiling water, and immediately rinsed or submerged in cold water. The item will then be kosher. Many use a *parve* kosher tongs to dunk each item, being sure to grab the item in a different spot when taking it out. Others use commercial-grade insulated rubber gloves, submerging the item with the right glove, and taking out with the left. When items are added to the *kashering* kettle, it tends to cool the water, so always let the water return to a rapid boil before dunking the next item. However, items that were used directly on a burner must touch rapidly boiling water at all times, so allow the water to return to a rapid boil before removing it. If the whole item can't fit in the *kashering* kettle all at once, it can be rotated so that the entire surface of the item has come in contact with the boiling water. The water will get dirty as it draws out the impurities; however, the dirt does not impart any flavor, so it is not considered a problem. If it gets really nasty, simply dump it down a bathtub or toilet, refill it, and re-boil the water, proceeding as normal. When finished, the *kashering* kettle can even be used for kosher cooking from then on.

Get Rockin': To *kasher* a large pot at home you'll need a 4-inch "pet rock" to help. Get a chemical-free rock, and give him a good bath. Clean the pot and let it sit unused for 24 hours. It's best to have a set of oven mitts that cover your whole hand for this process. Bake your rock at 500° F for about 10 minutes or so in a *parve* kosher oven. He must be over 212° F to be effective. (Some put the rock on a flame or burner, but this is very dangerous— water trapped inside could cause him to explode, sending fragments everywhere!) Fill the pot to the brim with water and bring it to a rapid boil. Using a *parve* kosher tongs, pick up your baked rock and drop him in the middle of the pot. (Beware of his heated temper— he will surely spit scalding hot water at you!) The water should overflow evenly. Fish out your rock, putting him on a *parve* kosher surface. Now quickly dump the water out of the pot and immediately rinse it under cold running water. This *kashers* the pot. (Keep your pet rock for future *kashering*, but let him cool off!)

Pouring Method Tips: Line the floor under any stove or counters to be *kashered* with lots of towels. Have several kosher pots ready for boiling water, and several kosher buckets for cold water. The item to be *kashered* must have been cleaned and sat unused for 24 hours. It might be a good idea to wear oven mitts and long-sleeve clothing, or put on a heavy raincoat to protect yourself from scalding hot splatters. Covered shoes or boots are a good idea as well.

In electric stoves, most of the wiring is run in areas that do not get wet, but it's still a good idea to have someone turn off the stove's circuit breaker at the service panel immediately before *kashering* the stove. Sop up any water around element connectors and underneath the top before restoring power.

Baking Method Tips: Items that need a more intense heat than boiling water get the baking method called *libun kal* [light heating] at 550° F. (This should not be confused with the higher temperature "glowing method" for self-cleaning ovens only.) The baking method will not warp or discolor racks and most items at this temperature. However, if items have any non-metal parts from such as handles or grips, it's a good idea to remove them unless they are designed specifically for oven use. The oven, racks, and items need to be cleaned well, and must sit unused for 24 hours. (See "*Ovens*" for details on cleaning racks.) Any items to be *kashered* should only be done in an already kosher oven. Bake them on the highest setting, broil or 550° F, for 1-2 hours with the door closed. Turn the oven off and keep the door shut an hour or more to let the items cool slowly. The oven (and items inside) are now kosher.

Glowing Method Tips for Self-Cleaning Ovens: Some hold that items put in a self-cleaning oven run on its cleaning cycle will get hot enough to fulfill *libun gamur* [absolute heating] 800-900° F, to a "glow". This temperature is so hot that the oven doesn't even have to be kosher in order to *kasher* other items. There is always a risk that warping could occur, ruining some items, and many suggest buying new ones instead. Clean the oven, racks, and items thoroughly, and let them sit unused for 24 hours. (Some rabbis allow *kashering* without waiting 24-hour for the glowing method only.) Any non-metal parts such as handles or grips must be removed. Usually this is as simple as unscrewing them, but if they can't be removed the item can't be *kashered*. After preparation, space the items evenly on the racks with any lids off, so that that air can circulate around the items evenly. Lighter items can be stacked on top of heavier items, being sure that they are supported. Don't be alarmed if there's a smell while being "toasted", this is normal. Never leave your oven unattended when there are things glowing inside. The metal will oxidize, leaving a nasty brown film and corroded spots on your formerly shiny items. This can be removed with a cleanser containing oxalic acid and a scrub pad, but polished surfaces will have a permanent dull appearance. The handles should be *kashered* by the boiling method. You can then reassemble everything after *kashering* and any removal of oxidation. Oven racks left in the self-cleaning cycle will also turn brown and could warp or come unwelded. If you buy a new pair, keep the old ones for future *kashering*.

Glowing Method Tips with a Propane Torch: The item should be clean, and each area of the item must be heated until it glows "red-hot". This method is ideal for smaller items that have been used with cooking oils, *treifah* foods, or high heat, or for isolated areas of pots with rivets, lips, grooves, or cracks. (If a pot also needs a lower-heat method of *kashering*, do that first before torching the isolated areas.)

It is best to do this method outside at night (or in a dimly lit room with a vent) because it is easier to see when the item is actually glowing. Protect your eyes with glasses or safety-goggles. Adjust the flame according to the area and thickness of the item to be heated (full-flame for large or thick areas, a small flame for small or thin areas). Items with insulated handles may be held by the handle, or grip it firmly with a rubber-handled pliers. Hold the propane torch in your dominant hand, and the item with your other hand with the area to be heated always kept upwards. Start at the bottom and work your way up or to the right. The flame has two parts, a dimmer outer blue area, and a bright inner blue area that is much hotter. Bring the inner flame to the item, but do not touch the torch nozzle to the area being heated. The flame will change to a yellowish color, or even shades of green as impurities burn off. Use a slight circular motion as you heat the item (this helps distribute the heat to minimize warping). Heat each area until it glows- it will literally emit a kind of eerie orange light, like coals in a fire. Move the flame on, keeping the outer flame pointed in the direction you will be going to next. This helps to preheat the next area. Systematically cover all areas that need *kashering*, overlapping a little to be safe. After the item is done, set it down on something kosher that can take intense heat (such as doubled aluminum-foil over concrete or *parve* oven racks). Rapid cooling increases the risk of warping or cracking. Weird colors will develop from oxidation as the item stops glowing, especially on the edge of the heated area.

Different metals, temperatures, and conditions produce different results. A chrome-plated pair of tongs turned a nice shade of blue after *kashering*, so I designated them as my "dairy" tongs. A stainless steel tongs turned pinkish, perfect for "meat". Be careful what you torch. I had an all-metal tin or aluminum dry-measure cup from my grandmother "*aleyha hashalom*" [may she rest in peace], which I knew I had put hot *treifah* broth in. It had a riveted metal handle that needed the glowing method. As it was being torched, the metal rivet joint where the handle met the cup started melting before the joint would glow. The process was stopped and the cup was saved, but I had to give it up.

Torching Tips: A small handheld plumber's propane tank and the nozzle that screws onto it, can be easily bought at any hardware store. (It can be used for burning *challah* portions too! See p. 623.)

⇨ It can be lit with a spark igniter as it tends to blow out a match (or a used empty grill lighter works great).

⇨ Keep hair and loose clothing tucked away from the flame, and don't work near flammable materials.

⇨ When finished, simply tighten down the valve and the flame will fizzle out.

⇨ Remove the nozzle after it cools so that the fuel doesn't leak out while being stored.

⇨ Keep the nozzle and tank indoors so they don't corrode. One tank will last many years.

General Tips on Kashering:

⇨ Always consult a rabbi before *kashering* anything.

⇨ If you are afraid an item could be ruined because of *kashering*, never attempt to *kasher* it.

⇨ If the history of a *kasherable* item is unknown, it should be treated as though *treifah*, and *kashered* with a more severe level than needed.

⇨ Any *kasherable* item that may have been washed in a dishwasher or by hand with hot water in a non-kosher dish pan is likely to need at least the boiling method.

⇨ Virtually any small electrical item that heats or deals with heat is problematic and cannot be *kashered*.

Unkasherable Kitchenware

Bag Sealers; Basting Brushes or Syringes; Breadmakers; Broiling Racks (porcelain); Canning Equipment; Ceramic Mugs; China; Crock Pots; Cutting Boards; Deep Fryers; Electric Knives; Griddles; Meat Grinders; Melamine®, Melmac®; Pasta Makers; Plastic Microwave Cookware; Porcelain/Stoneware Cups; Portable Electric/Stovetop Grills; Pressure Cookers; Rotisseries; Sandwich Makers; Sieves; Splatter Screens; Stoneware Crocks; Strainers; Toaster Ovens; Toasters; Waffle Irons; Warming Trays.

Questionable Kitchenware

Apple Slicers/Corers; Arcorac®; Bagel Cutters; Blenders; Canning Jars; Can Openers; Carafes; Carving Knives; Casserole Dishes; Cherry Pitters; Cleavers; Coffee Grinders; Coffee Pots w/ Plastic Parts; Colanders; Corelle®; Corningware®; Custard Cups; Decanters w/ Stoppers; Duralex®; Egg Beaters; Electric Juicers; Food Choppers; Food Processors; Glass Bakeware; Glass Plates; Graters; Gravy Boats/Servers; Kettle-Style Popcorn Poppers; Knives; Peelers; Pie Plates; Pizza Cutters; Pizza Stones; Pyrex®; Serving Dishes; Shredders; Sifters; Soufflé Dishes; Thermos®; Water Dispensers; Water Filters; Zesters.

Kasherable Kitchenware

Each item depends on specific details. The list below is in no way meant to replace rabbinical advice; it illustrates the method of *kashering* for items used in average situations:

Bakeware (Metal): Use the glowing method. Items may warp or get ruined, so if this is a concern, do not try to *kasher* them, buy new instead. (If Teflon® or non-stick-coated, porcelain-enameled, or painted, discard and buy new.)

Bone Items: (See "Ivory Items".)

Bowls: (See "Dishes".)

Cake Pans: (See "Bakeware".)

Candy Molds (Metal): Use the boiling method. (If non-stick-coated, porcelain-enameled, painted, or made of plastic or silicone, discard and buy new.)

Coffee Makers, Urns, and Percolators: Internal parts should be removed and all items can be *kashered* by the boiling method. *Ashkenazim* must replace any glass parts including the carafe.

Coffee Mugs (Glass): Some *Ashkenazim* allow the boiling method. Most *Sefardim* simply clean well.

Cookie Sheets: (See "Bakeware".)

Cooling Racks (Metal): Use the glowing method. Rack may warp or get ruined, so if this is a concern, do not try to *kasher* it, buy new instead. (If painted or coated, discard and buy new.)

Dessert Forks: (See "Silverware".)

Dishes (Glass): If glass, crystal, Corelle®, Arcorac® or Duralex®, many *Ashkenazim* allow *kashering*. If used cold-only, use the cold-*kasher*ing method. If used warm or the history is unknown, use the boiling method. Ask your rabbi. *Sefardim* clean well. (If plastic or china, discard and buy new.)

Drinking Glasses (Glass): Some *Ashkenazim* allow the cold-*kashering* method, others suggest the boiling method. Ask your rabbi. Most *Sefardim* clean well. (If plastic, discard and buy new.)

Egg Slicers (Metal): Use the boiling method. (If plastic or painted, discard and buy new.)

Fish Forks: (See "Silverware".)

Forks: (See "Silverware".)

Frying Pans (Metal): Many rabbis hold they can be *kashered* using the glowing method. Torch every inch of the entire pan including any lips, crevices and rivets, or put it in a self-cleaning oven cycle that reaches 800-900° F. This method could warp or ruin the pan. If this is a concern, do not try to *kasher* it. Some *Chassidim* hold that you can't *kasher* frying pans and the like. (If non-stick-coated, porcelain-enameled, or painted, discard and buy new.)

Funnels: If metal, use the boiling method. (If plastic, discard and buy new.)

Garlic Press (Metal): Use the boiling method.

Gelatin Molds (Metal): Use the boiling method. (If plastic or silicone, discard and buy new.)

Gravy Ladles (Metal): Use the glowing method. Ladle may warp or get ruined, so if this is a concern, do not try to *kasher* it, buy new instead. (If plastic or coated, discard and buy new.)

Grills (Outdoor) Gas or Charcoal: Grills can be cleaned and *kashered* in the same manner as a broiler. For gas grills, the lid should be closed, and the grill put on broil for about one hour. Charcoal grills should have charcoal both underneath the racks and on top of them, and then lit, closing the lid after it gets going. For areas touching the racks, use the glowing method with a torch. For racks that come into contact with food, use the glowing method. It may be easier to sell an old grill or racks and buy new.

Hot Plates (Coil-Burner): Can be *kashered* like a conventional electric burner, however, there may be areas of the element that do not glow. Turn on high until red and heat non-glowing element areas with a propane torch until glowing. Always use safety glasses. Remaining areas must be treated as *treifah*.

Hot Plates (Glass): Treat as you would a glass stovetop. (See "Glass Cooktops".)

Hot Water Urns: If used with anything other than water, boil water filled to the brim inside it.

Ice Cream Scoops (Metal): Use the boiling method. (If plastic, discard and buy new.)

Iron Skillets: (See "Frying Pans".)

Ivory Items: If never used with heat, scrub well and let dry for several days. They must be totally clean and completely dry. Once dry, use the boiling method. (If plastic imitation, discard and buy new.)

Juicers (Glass): Some *Ashkenazim* allow the cold-*kashering* method, others suggest the boiling method. Ask your rabbi. Most *Sefardim* clean well. (If plastic, discard and buy new.)

Juicers (Metal): Use the boiling method. (If plastic or painted, discard and buy new.)

Kettles: (See "Pots".)

Kitchen Scissors: If all metal, use the glowing method. This may warp the scissors, so it is probably better to buy new. (If it has plastic rivets, do not use it for food anymore.)

Knives: Including blades of all kinds. Ask your rabbi how he holds. Unfortunately, I've seen books that state knives can merely be plunged into dirt a certain number of times, but this is not really an acceptable method of *kashering*! (I chose to play it safe and just got all new knives- they're even color-coded.)

Ladles: (See "Gravy Ladles" or "Soup Ladles".)

Loaf Pans: (See "Bakeware".)

Marble Items (Pure): Use the boiling method. (If made of composite marble, discard.)

Measuring Cups: If metal, use the boiling method. If it has been used with hot oils, or there are any rivets, use the glowing method, although they may warp or get ruined. If this is a concern, do not try to *kasher* them, buy new instead. If glass, ask a rabbi. (If plastic, discard and buy new.)

Measuring Spoons (Metal): Use the boiling method. (If plastic, discard and buy new.)

Meat Tenderizers: If without crevices, use the boiling method. Otherwise, use the glowing method.

Mixers: Clean all parts thoroughly. The beaters can be replaced or torched until they glow.

Mixing Bowls: If metal and used cold only, use the boiling method. If metal and used in the oven or the history is unknown, use the glowing method, although they may warp or get ruined. If this is a concern, do not try to *kasher*, buy new instead. If glass, ask a rabbi. (If plastic, discard and buy new.)

Mortar & Pestle: If made from whole natural stone or marble without cracks, use the boiling method.

Mother of Pearl or Shell Items: If not used with heat, scrub well and let dry for many days. It must be totally clean and completely dry. Once dry, use the boiling method. (If plastic imitation, discard.)

Muffin Tins: (See "Bakeware".)

Omelet Pans: (See "Frying Pans".)

Pans: (See "Frying Pans".)

Pasta Pots: (See "Pots".)

Pie Pans: (See "Bakeware".)

Pie Servers: (See "Serving Utensils".)

Pitchers: If glass, some *Ashkenazim* allow the cold-*kashering* method, others suggest the boiling method. Ask your rabbi how he holds. Most *Sefardim* clean well. If metal, use the boiling method. (If china, ceramic, porcelain or plastic, discard and buy new.)

Pizza Pans: (See "Bakeware".)

Popcorn Poppers (Hot Air): If used only with popcorn alone, it may just be kosher, because all plain popcorn kernels are kosher and *parve*. However, models that have a butter melting area will be *treifah* if this area was used. If the butter melting area is made of metal it may just be *kasherable*. Ask your rabbi. (If plastic, it's probably better to sell the popper and buy new.)

Potato Mashers: If metal without grooves, use the boiling method. If metal with grooves or crevices, torch it until it glows. (If plastic, discard and buy new.)

Pots: If metal and used for boiling only, use the boiling method. If metal and used with oil at high temperatures, or the history is unknown, disassemble handles and use the glowing method, although items may warp or get ruined. If this is a concern, do not try to *kasher* it. (If non-stick-coated, porcelain-enameled, or painted, discard and buy new.)

Rice Cookers: If there is a removable metal bowl (used only for rice and water) use the boiling method.

Riveted Items: One must use the glowing method with a blow torch on and around any rivets.

Roasters: If made of stainless steel or other metal, use the glowing method. Roaster may warp or get ruined, so if this is a concern, do not try to *kasher* it, buy new instead. If it is made of heatproof glass, ask your rabbi. (If porcelain-enamel, discard and buy new.)

Rolling Pins: If metal or marble, use the boiling method. If smooth wood, use the sanding method followed by the boiling method. (If plastic, discard and buy new.)

Salt Shakers: If glass or metal, use the boiling method. (If plastic, discard and buy new.)

Scoops (Metal): Use the boiling method. (If plastic, discard and buy new.)

Seashells: If never used with heat, scrub well and let dry for several days. They must be totally clean and completely dry. Once dry, use the boiling method.

Serving Utensils (Metal): If without grooves or crevices, use the boiling method. If they do have grooves, rivets or crevices, use the glowing method, although items may warp or get ruined. If this is a concern, do not try to *kasher* it, buy new instead. (If plastic or painted, discard and buy new.)

Silverware (Metal): If they do not have grooves or crevices, use the boiling method. If they do, use the glowing method, although items may warp or get ruined. If this is a concern, do not try to *kasher* them, buy new instead. For wood or plastic handles, ask a rabbi. For knives, ask a rabbi.

Skewers: If metal and not used with high heat, use the boiling method. If metal and used in an oven or on a grill, use the glowing method. If wooden or bamboo and not used with high heat, clean well and use the boiling method. (If wooden or bamboo and used in an oven or on a grill, discard and buy new.)

Slotted Spoons: (See "Serving Utensils".)

Soup Ladles (Metal): Use the boiling method. (If plastic or painted, discard and buy new.)

Soup Spoons: (See "Silverware".)

Spatulas (Metal): Use the glowing method. Spatula may warp or get ruined, so if this is a concern, do not try to *kasher* it, buy new instead. (If plastic, discard and buy new.)

Spoons: (See "Silverware".)

Stew Pots: (See "Pots".)

Stock Pots: (See "Pots".)

Stone Items: If made of pure stone, use the boiling method. (If made of composite stone, discard.)

Tea Kettles: (See "Pots".)

Tongs: If metal and used for cold salads only, use the boiling method. If metal and used for frying or the history is unknown, use the glowing method. (If plastic, discard and buy new.)

Water Coolers (Cold): Clean well. Spigots should be cleaned thoroughly. *Kashering* is not needed.

Water Urns (Metal): Use the pouring or boiling method inside and outside.

Whisks: If solid metal, and not used with intense heat, use the boiling method. If the history is unknown, use the glowing method. If metal with a plastic handle, use the glowing method on metal parts.

Wooden Items: If it has no cracks and is smooth, use the boiling method. If it has no cracks but is not smooth, use the sanding method followed by the boiling method. For items used in an oven, ask a rabbi.

Once your items are *kashered*, they are ready for the last step of "Immersion"...

Immersion

WHAT IS IMMERSION? It's kind of a deep concept, but you don't have to go diving to do it. Although *kashering* will make items physically fit for use, they must undergo a final process in order to make them spiritually fit. *Tevilah* [immersion] in a *mikvah* [special purification pool] is the way to make susceptible materials spiritually pure and *Halachically* usable. This *Torah* law is mentioned in *Bamidbar* 31:23.

WHAT NEEDS IMMERSION? Any item containing metal or glass that contacts kosher food, and has been manufactured, altered, owned or sold by non-Jews must be immersed in a *mikvah*. Even if you have used the old *kashered* items for many years, they still must be brought to the *mikvah* for *tevilah*, but no *treifah* items can be immersed. Once an item has been immersed, it should not need immersion again.

The use of an item or its construction affects whether a *brachah* [blessing or acknowledgement] is said or not. If metal or glass comes into direct contact with kosher food in its edible finished form (such as cooked meat or a cake), one recites a *brachah* before immersing it. If metal or glass contacts unfinished food products (such as flour or dough), or is used exclusively for storage and never brought to the table, or is coated with a material that does not require *tevilah*, immerse the item without reciting a *brachah*.

Materials

Immersion w/ Brachah	**Immersion w/o Brachah**	**No Immersion**
☑ Brass	☐ Aluminum * **	☒ Bone and Ivory
☑ Cast Iron	☐ Porcelain China *	☒ Shell and Stone
☑ Copper	☐ Bone China *	☒ Cork
☑ Crystal	☐ China *	☒ Wood
☑ Glass	☐ Glazed Ceramic *	☒ Earthenware (unglazed)
☑ Gold	☐ Glazed Stoneware *	☒ Paper
☑ Silver	☐ Non-Stick/Teflon®,	☒ Plastic
☑ Stainless Steel	☐ Porcelain-Enamel,	☒ Rubber (natural)
☑ Steel	☐ Painted, or	☒ Silicone
☑ Tin	☐ Plastic Coated Items	☒ Foam (kosher)

* Ask your rabbi as to whether these items need immersion, and if so, with or without a *brachah*.

** Some allow disposable aluminum items to be used only once without immersion.

Examples of Items Requiring Immersion with a Brachah

(All Items of Metal or Glass) Apple Slicer/Corer; Arcorac®; Baking Dish; Baking Pan (uncoated metal); Blender Blades & Glass Jar; Broiler Rack (uncoated); Butter Dish; Cake Decorator Nozzle; Casserole Dish; Cheese Slicer; Coffee Maker; Coffee Pot; Colander; Cookie Sheet (uncoated); Corelle®; Corn-Cob Holder; Creamer; Crock Pot (metal inserts); Decanter (glass/crystal); Double Boiler; Drinking Glass; Duralex®; Egg Beater; Egg Slicer; Electric Knife; Electric Peeler; Food Chopper; Food Processor Blades; Fruit Basket (metal); Frying Pan (uncoated); Garlic Press; Grater; Gravy Ladle; Grill Grate; Honey Dish (glass or silver); Hot Water Urn; Ice Cream Scoop; Juicer (metal/glass); *Kiddush* Cup (metal/glass made by non-Jew); Knife; Ladle (metal); Loaf Pan (uncoated metal or glass); Measuring Cup (glass or metal); Measuring Spoon (metal); Meat Slicer; Melon-Baller; Mixer Beaters; Mixer Bowl (glass/metal); Mixing Bowls (glass/metal); Mixing Spoon (metal); Muffin Tin (uncoated); Mug (glass); Nutcracker (used at table); Peeler; Pepper Mill; Percolator; Pie Pan (uncoated metal or glass); Pie Server (metal); Pitcher (glass/metal); Pizza Cutter; Pizza Pan (uncoated); Plate (glass); Popcorn Popper (uncoated metal kettle-style); Pot Lid; Pots (uncoated metal or glass); Pyrex®; Roaster (uncoated metal or glass); Salt & Pepper Shakers (glass/metal); Serving Bowl (glass); Sieve; Silverware; Skewers (metal); Slotted Spoon (metal); Spatula (uncoated metal); Steamer or Steamer Basket (metal); Strainer; Sugar Bowl (glass); Tea Cup (glass); Tea Pot (metal); Thermos® (metal interior); Tongs; Waffle Iron (uncoated); Wok.

Examples of Items Requiring Immersion with No Brachah

Baking Pan (non-stick/coated); Bread Box (metal); Breadmaker Pan and Blade; Casserole Dish (Corningware®); Coffee Mill; Cookie Cutters (metal); Cookie Sheet (non-stick/coated); Corningware; Deep Fryer (coated); Dough Hook; Flour Canister (metal/glass); Frying Pan (non-stick/coated); Griddle (non-stick/coated); Kneading Hook; Loaf Pan (non-stick/coated); Meat Grinder; Meat Tenderizer; Muffin Tin (non-stick/coated); Pasta Machine; Popcorn Popper (nonstick coated metal kettle-style); Pot (painted/non-stick/coated); Roaster (painted/non-stick/coated); Sandwich Maker (non-stick/coated); Sifter (metal); Storage Canister (Metal); Sugar Canister (glass/metal); Waffle Iron (non-stick/coated).

Examples of Items Not Requiring Immersion

Any Item Made by a Jew; Baby Bottle; Bamboo Skewers; Basting Brush/Syringe; Blender Base; Bottle Warmer; Bowl Scraping Spatula (rubber/silicone); Breadmaker (metal body); Cake Decorator (plastic); Cake Plate Cover; Candy Mold (plastic); Canister Cover; Can Opener; Cork Screw; Cup (plastic/foam); Crock Pot (outer metal body); Cutting Board; Dish Rack (metal); Drinking Straws; Electric Mixer (stand & motor); Food Processor (body); Hand-Held Mixer (body); Hand-Washing Cup (metal); Hot Plate; Ice Cube Tray (plastic/silicone); *Kiddush* Cup (made by Jew); Knife Sharpener; Ladle (plastic); Melamine®; Melmac®; Microwave; Microwave Cookware (plastic); Oven Rack; Pastry Brush; Plate (plastic/foam); Pocket Knife (non-food); Rolling Pin (any type); Seder Plate (made by Jew); Serving Tray; *Shabbat Blech*; Sink Rack (metal); Spatula (plastic/nylon); Spoon Rest (metal); Stove Grate; Toaster Oven (body); Toothpicks; Tortilla Warmer (unglazed terra cotta); Tupperware®; Warming Tray; Wooden Spoon.

Examples of Questionable Items

All Glazed Ceramic or China Items; Aluminum; Cooling Rack; Crock Pot Insert (ceramic); Crock Pot Lid (glass); Cookie Cutters; Cookie Jar (glass); Disposable Aluminum Items; Electric Portable Grill; Hamburger Maker; Kitchen Scale; Meat Thermometer; Medicine Spoon (metal); Microwave (tray or turntable); Pot (porcelain-enameled); Roaster (porcelain-enameled); Toaster; Toaster Oven (rack or tray).

HOW DO I IMMERSE THE ITEMS? It's as easy as saying a *brachah* and dipping the items, but you can't just dunk the items in your bathtub or a swimming pool. Although you can immerse your items in a natural body of water that never dries out, don't "go jump in a lake"! Most Jewish communities have a *mikvah*. They are constructed to very precise specifications, and some are small and made especially for dunking your dishes! Areas with large Jewish populations even have stores with one conveniently built-in for new kitchen items. Before you immerse items, you need to prepare them for their "spiritual transformation".

Preparation: There can be no separation between any part of the item and the water.

Old items that have just been *kashered* often have a brown greasy residue from the *kashering* process, and should be washed again with dish detergent or oxalic acid cleaner. Rust and tarnish must be removed, but items having non-removable stains or blemishes can be immersed as long as they are clean.

New metal items usually have excess metal polish, a black gunk, especially under the lip or in crevices. Some *kasher* new metal items due to non-kosher oils used in polishing. Often glass, Corelle® and China dishware has an oil coating. One should wash any oily items in detergent and cool water first.

Adhesive Removal Tips: Items must be free of any stickers, labels, or their residues left behind.

Don't let stickers get wet if you want to remove them! Even after they dry, they can still resist peeling.

Start by lifting a corner, then flip it back over itself (upside down) pulling with your thumb pressed firmly on the sticky side as you slowly peel it along. The paper rolls along with your thumb stuck on the same spot where you started until the whole sticker rolls off. If the paper tears, try another corner. If the sticker separates leaving behind torn paper, pick it with your fingernail to get it rolling again.

A few spots of sticker glue can be removed by dabbing at it quickly with either packing tape or duct tape. Press the tape firmly on the residue, then yank it back quickly several times until it is gone.

Pine-cleaner (containing 10-20% pine oil) is water-soluble, and a quick, effective way to remove stubborn adhesives. Remove as much of the label as possible, leaving the glue, and pat dry. Cut two pieces of paper towel slightly larger than the glue. Wearing rubber gloves, soak the towels with pine cleaner straight out of the bottle, and place over the glue. Let sit for a few minutes. Next, rub with the saturated towel until the glue is dissolved, flip towel over, and wipe. Repeat if needed. When finished, wash with dish detergent and cool water, then rinse. Pine cleaner washes off without any residue!

WD-40® was *designed to leave a water-repelling residue*, and to not easily wash off. (Indeed, it can water-proof shoes!) "Water Displacement, 40th formula" is a type of penetrating oil consisting of 50% mineral spirits, distilled paraffin and mineral oil. Its chemicals are main ingredients in things such as gear lubricant, engine oil products, fuel injector cleaners, and furniture polish. Great for stopping squeaks, it was designed for machinery– not dishes! It may remove rust, but should not be used to remove stickers before immersion. It's poisonous, flammable, and creates an invisible waterproof barrier between the item and the *mikvah* water.

Nail-polish removers (often acetone) are highly flammable with toxic chemicals. (Some can contain *treifah* glycerin.) Paint thinner and mineral spirits can also dissolve adhesives, but when breathed or absorbed into skin, they can cause permanent reproductive, brain, and nervous system damage. They can possibly leave residues creating a separation between the item and the *mikvah* water.

60

Brachah: Once you get to the *mikvah*, the *brachah* to say will often be posted on the wall, or it can be found in a *siddur* [Jewish prayer book]. There are transliterations available if needed, or the *brachah* can even be said in English, but one must be an adult Jew to say it. (This is because the formula for a *brachah* states "...Who has commanded us to...", and only Jews were instructed to perform whatever action it is.)

⇨ Some have the *minhag* to wet their hands with the *mikvah* water before proceeding, others don't.

🚹 If it is a *mikvah* used for immersing people, some hold to say the *brachah* outside the *mikvah* room.

🍸 If it is a *mikvah* used only for *kelim* [kitchen items] (never people), the *brachah* can be said there.

⇨ Only one *brachah* is said when there are many items to immerse (but it is in the plural "*kelim*", not singular "*k'li*"). However, don't talk between the *brachah* and the immersion, until all items are done.

⇨ Questionable Items: After the *brachah*, always immerse at least two items that *definitely do need immersion with a brachah*, before any other items that are questionable or don't require a *brachah*.

Immersing: The water must contact the entire surface of the item all-at-once (unlike *kashering*) for at least a split-second. In fact, even holding the item will cause a separation between the water and the item.

<u>Large Items</u>: Slip the item into the water so that the dunking action doesn't create an excess of bubbles. The whole item must be totally submerged inside and out, having no air trapped inside. If tiny bubbles cling to it, tap the item while it is submerged. Keep a flat item horizontal, so that it will be somewhat "suspended" in the water. Heavy areas should be kept downwards. While holding the item underwater from underneath, gently toss it up and let it fall back into your hands so that you are not actually touching the item for a moment. It's wise to practice with something unbreakable first, until you get the hang of it.

<u>Small Items</u>: After the item is put in the water, let it drop to your other hand so that the water contacts the item without interruption. Watch for bubbles, swishing the item to free them before dropping. If there are many small items, drop each item one-at-time into a small basket (such as a plastic laundry basket, but make sure the holes aren't so big that your items would slide out).

<u>Many Items</u>: Need help? After an adult Jew says the *brachah* and immerses a few items, someone else (even a non-Jew or a Jewish child) could help while the adult Jew is there. Just remember not to talk.

Small Appliances: Check these with your rabbi. Hot water urns, portable indoor gills, sandwich makers, and the like can be problematic if there are non-removable parts that make direct contact with food. Many times, the entire appliance needs to be immersed. Afterwards, be sure to let it dry out for a minimum of a week before using it. Not only could moisture short out the appliance, but it could also be a fire hazard or shock risk. I've heard cases of some more intricate appliances (with number-pads and computer chips) not working perfectly afterwards, probably due to being used before they are completely dry. Placing the item in an attic or in front of a running dehumidifier can also help the item dry out.

Eating Away From Home

HOW DO I KEEP KOSHER WHEN I'M TRAVELING? Traveling kosher doesn't require going on a "wild goose chase". Technology has come a long way from lugging around a hot plate, pots and searching through stores for kosher canned goods. Today, one can purchase vacuum-packed, self-heating, kosher certified meals. A friend used these on a cruise to Alaska and she really liked them. An Internet search for "vacuum-packed kosher meals" yields quite a few web sites with reasonable prices. Some companies offer to express-mail meals in case one is stranded unexpectedly. If you choose to rough it the old-fashioned way, newly bought metal or glass cookware must be immersed before use. (See "Immersion".)

Traveling by Plane, Ship or Train: On shorter trips, any snack foods must have a good *hechsher*. If it is a longer trip that includes a meal, when making the reservation, one must specifically request a "*special kosher meal*" provided by a certified-kosher caterer (not just a "kosher meal"). The meals will have a *hechsher*, and are usually listed as "*glatt* kosher" (sometimes even when dairy). Hot foods will be double-wrapped for *treifah* ovens, and cool foods will be completely sealed. Only sealed foods are certified kosher— do not eat it if it has been opened! The meals usually come with a plastic cup inside the sealed package. Check with a reliable *kashrut* agency to see if coffee and tea will be kosher on your trip.

Staying At Hotels: If kosher meals are provided, the same rules above apply. If there's a microwave either double-wrap your meals in zipper bags, or *kasher* the microwave. (See "*Kashering*".) Many motels offer individually wrapped products bearing a reliable *hechsher* in their continental breakfasts.

Kosher Restaurants: If you're going to a big city with a Jewish population, you've got it made. Ask local *Torah*-observant people what restaurants are kosher, and make sure they're properly certified. A currently dated, signed *kashrut* certificate is usually displayed on the wall. For *Sefardim*, restaurants must comply with guidelines in "*Commercially Cooked Foods*" p. 28. (If in doubt they should contact a rabbi.) *Note:* If a restaurant or food is called "Kosher-Style" stay away, it is not actually kosher! Look for a real kosher restaurant that is under reliable *hashgacha*. A local *kashrut* agency will have a list of kosher places in the area.

Vegetarian Restaurants: Some people might think that any vegetarian restaurant is automatically kosher. Wrong! One can clearly see by reading this book that salads, dressings, condiments, baked goods, margarine, seafood, fertilized eggs, milk products, and cheese are not always kosher! Knives, plates, and cookware could have been used on *treifah* food, or washed in non-kosher dishwashers. If they bought or leased used equipment without *kashering* it, any residues would render the whole restaurant *treifah*.

Drinks in Non-Kosher Establishments: The problem with going into totally non-kosher restaurants is "*marit ayin*" [seemingly doing wrong] (as if eating *treifah*), thus one should not go in. When in transit, it is okay to buy drinks or coffee from non-kosher U.S. establishments that sell some kosher products.

<u>Soft Drinks</u>: If it is a well-known national chain that contracts with a kosher brand-name drink company, and they serve the beverage in a disposable cup, you should be fine. However, if it is a small independent operation, they may use a generic brand of syrup that is not kosher.

<u>Frozen Carbonated Drinks</u>: Some brand names have kosher flavors: Always ask to see the box of the flavor you want, to check for a *hechsher*. Be aware that diet flavors are often dairy. Switching flavors is not a problem as long as the one you're drinking is kosher. Most generic brands are not kosher.

<u>Coffee and Tea:</u> Stay away from places that sell non-kosher flavored coffees and teas. Since heat is involved, the equipment can make kosher coffees and teas *treifah*. Even vending machines are not safe. However, if an establishment sells strictly plain unflavored coffee and tea, or only hot water from an urn (where you add a packet of kosher coffee or tea), it's okay if served in a paper cup (preferably not foam).

Food In Israel: Don't think that all Israeli food is automatically kosher! It must be reliably certified just like anywhere else. Fortunately, many packaged foods have the reliable large, fancy *hechsher* known as "B'Datz" (see "*Kosher Certification*" on p. 22). You can also ask religious locals what other symbols to look for. Make sure all meat, or restaurant foods are "*Li'Mehadrin*" or "*Mehadrin*" [highest quality]. For *Sefardim*, some *Bet Yosef* kosher meat isn't the same strict standards as it is in the U.S., so it's advisable to ask a knowledgeable rabbi in Israel.

HOW CAN I EAT KOSHER IN A NON-KOSHER PLACE? Use disposable plates, cups and utensils, and follow the guidelines in the section "*How Do I Maintain My Kosher Kitchen?*". Non-kosher hosts can provide kosher-certified foods (such as a bag of potato chips or the like), but they must be unopened. As explained on p. 28, non-Jews can't cook for Jews (even if all the *kashrut* laws were observed) unless supervised, or a Jew turns on the flame.

Hospitals: Request kosher meals in advance if possible. They can usually give you double-wrapped meals. If kosher meals are not available, or there is no way to heat the food, bring your own. There are even self-heating kosher meals available for purchase, if you look online. It is a good idea to keep them on hand in case of emergencies.

If a baby must be fed formula, research and request a kosher-certified formula that meets your approval.

Now that you can keep kosher anywhere, we'll learn about— "*The Kingdom of Brachot*"…

Section 3
The Kingdom of Brachot
A Food Hierarchy

Bountiful Blessings

WHAT IS A "BRACHAH"? A *brachah* is an acknowledgement that there is a Creator, Who has given us the ability to choose to do spiritual actions. (When going through this section, it may be helpful to have the prayer book containing these *brachot* to refer to.) All *brachot* [*brachah* plural] start with a specific formula: "*Baruch…(through)…Melech ha-olam*" ["Blessed…(through)…King of the universe"], which can be found in *siddurim* [Jewish prayer books]. On a *kabbalistic* level, a *brachah* elevates an action to a higher level, transforming physical into spiritual, which is said to be a unique role of a Jew. Most of the time, a *brachah* is said just before an action. Eating is the only action where a *brachah* is said before and after.

Before Eating: A *brachah rishonah* [blessing before] is said before starting to eat or drink. When we say, "*Baruch atah…*" ["Blessed are You…"], "blessed" does not mean "bestowing goodness", for how could a mere human being give anything to the Creator of the universe? Rather, we are recognizing that everything in the world belongs to the One Who created it, therefore requesting the opportunity to utilize it to our advantage. Eating or drinking without acknowledgment is comparable to stealing from Hashem.

⇨ One *brachah* is said for each type of food, intending it to cover all like-kind foods eaten in the meal.

⇨ A *brachah* before is said only on kosher items— never say it on *treifah* or disgusting things.

⇨ Say a *brachah* before, even when taste-testing delicious food, unless intending to spit it out.

After Eating: A *brachah acharonah* [after-blessing] is said when one is finished eating or drinking. This was instituted by Avraham. The *Torah* states: "You will eat and be sated and [afterward] you shall bless Hashem…" (*Devarim* 8:10). Hashem has designed our need to eat, as well as food to fulfill this need, therefore we express our gratitude for giving us a means to satisfy our necessity in an enjoyable way.

⇨ Say an after-*brachah* on food the size of an olive (1 oz./28-29g or more), or on 3-4 oz. or more of drink.

⇨ Only one after-*brachah* is said for each type of food, and covers all foods of that type.

⇨ Say an after-*brachah* within 72 minutes of finishing a meal (possibly longer if still hungry).

⇨ Ideally, the after-*brachah* should be said in the place the food was eaten, even if one left and returned.

How To Say a Brachah:

⇨ Ideally, *brachot* should be said in Hebrew, but one can say them in another language if necessary.

⇨ When *brachot* are said, men and married women should have their heads covered out of respect.

⇨ For a *brachah* before eating, take the food item itself (or within a utensil if used) in the dominant hand.

⇨ Say the *brachah* before softly or aloud, and take a bite or sip without interruption until swallowing.

⇨ If one must eat in transit, say a *brachah* with the intent that the meal will be finished elsewhere.

⇨ One should not say a *brachah* when one has food or drink in their mouth.

When One Should Not Say a Brachah: (Read the following carefully.)

🖐 No *brachah* before needs to be stated if one must take a bad tasting medicine, drinks to swallow a pill, or to stop one from choking, as the objective is not to enjoy the drink. (However, if one likes the taste of a medicine, say a *brachah* before. If one plans to drink more, say *brachot* both before and after.)

🖐 No after-*brachah* is said if a food is less than the size of an olive (1 oz./28g), or if a drink is less than 3 oz.

🖐 If one can't remember making a *brachah*, another one should not be said. When in doubt, leave it out!

Errors: The following "fixes" should only be used out of necessity:

💣 If one said Hashem's name (but not the whole formula) for no reason, one should say "*Baruch Shem kavod Malchuto l'olam va-ed*" ["Blessed is the Name of His glorious Kingdom forever and ever"].

💣 If one accidentally said the whole formula in error, it is a *brachah l'vatalah* [a blessing said in vain], a very serious *Torah* prohibition. In such a case, one should immediately add "*Lamdeni Chukecha*" ["Who teaches me His laws"], which is a complete verse in Psalms (one is simply reciting *Torah*).

💣 If one realized they said a wrong *brachah* before within three seconds, the correct part is said.

A Brachah for a Group: Sometimes a group of people eating *challah*, *matzah*, or wine can be part of a *brachah* said by one person. The designated person must have everyone else in mind who is to be part of the *brachah* and listeners must hear it intending to be a part of it. After the *brachah* they must respond "*Amen*" meaning that they agree, and consume some of the item without interruption. (Daytime *Kiddush* is an exception, one can be included without drinking if answering "*Amen*" with the intent.)

Hearing a Brachah: In general, anyone hearing a *brachah* should always answer "*Amen*", even if not intending to be a part of it. This simply means that they agree with what was said, and one even gets spiritual merit for it!

WHICH BLESSING DO I SAY FOR EACH CLASS OF FOOD? *Brachot* for foods and drinks are grouped into six different categories following a certain order of priority. The highest-ranking *brachah* is generally said on its class first. A bit of personification can help one remember them with ease:

1. 🍞 **Bread Only: King "*HaMotzi*":** *HaMotzi* = "brings forth"; the second part "*lechem*" = "bread".
2. 🧁 **Non-Bread Grain: Queen "*Mezonot*",**
   and **The White Rice Diplomat: Ambassador "*Mezonot*"** = "food", as grain is a staple food.
3. 🍷 **Wine or Grape Juice: Prince "*Gefen*":** *Gefen* = "grape vine".
4. 🍒 **Special Five Israeli Tree-Fruits: Princess "*Etz*",**
   and **Any Other Tree-Fruits: The "*Etz*" Maid:** *Etz* = "tree".
5. 🌶 **Non-Tree Land Produce: The "*Adamah*" Gardener:** *Adamah* = "land".
6. 🥤 **Various Edibles: The "*Shehakol*" Citizens:** *Shehakol* = "all things that are existing.

1. Bread—King HaMotzi: The king of foods, bread or main-meals baked from any of five "royal" Israeli grains: Barley, Rye, Oats, Wheat and Spelt— "B.R.O.W.S.", demands an inclusive *brachah* exempting other foods and drinks from brachot in that meal (except wine or grape juice). It has a two-step process:

>   **a.** Washing with a *brachah*, and;

>   **b.** The *brachah* before eating the bread itself.

a. Washing: First we cleanse the hands, just as the *Kohanim* would do before handling the holy "showbread" in the Temple. This special hand washing purifies our hands both physically and spiritually, and is one of the few exceptions where the action comes before the *brachah*. Most wash as follows:

☞ Any rings or bandages must be taken off to eliminate any separation between the water and the hands.

☞ Fill a large two-handled cup with water, (some will pick up the cup with the right hand and pass it to the left hand) then pour some of the water on the right hand up to the wrist a certain number of times:
Ashkenazim: most pour twice, using about half of the water (some rotating the hand while pouring).
Chassidim and *Sefardim:* most pour three times, using about half of the water.

☞ (Some put the cup down and lift it with the right hand.) Pour the same way on the left hand.

☞ *Sefardim:* Rub the hands together three times after pouring.

☞ Pick up a towel and say the *brachah*, "...*al netilat yadayim*" ["...for uplifting of the hands"]:
Ashkenazim and *Chassidim:* pronounce it "*al netilas*" (some raise their hands slightly).
Sefardim: pronounce it "*al netilat*" (some hold their hands up with the palms down under the towel).

☞ Dry the hands (so that there is still something left to do after the *brachah* has been said).

If there is no water available (such as on a picnic), or one is unable to wash their hands (wearing a cast), the hand-washing and its *brachah* is skipped, reciting only the *brachah* for bread. (However, the bread should be held with a napkin or in a sandwich bag, never touching the bread with bare hands.)
Only a Jew can say this *brachah*, as it would be a *brachah l'vatalah* for a non-Jew to say it in the normal manner. If a non-Jew wants to say a blessing, they can say the formula through "universe" adding "... Who has sanctified Israel with His *mitzvot* [laws] and commanded them in the washing of the hands".

b. Brachah Before Bread: The *brachah* for the bread is referred to as "*HaMotzi*":

🍞 *Ashkenazim* and *Chassidim:* Don't talk between washing and *HaMotzi*, except to reply "*amen*".

🍞 *Sefardim:* Same as above, except to say "*Pote-ach et Yadecha...*" ["You open Your hand..."] with uplifted hands (and sometimes other praises from a *siddur*) without it being an interruption.

🍞 Say the *brachah* "...*hamotzi lechem min ha-aretz*" ["...brings forth bread from the earth"], and eat.

💣 If one talks between washing and *HaMotzi* (except for "*amen*") one must re-wash without a *brachah*.

Bread After-Brachah: Bread and baked B.R.O.W.S. main meals are a "kingly" class, and deserving of a majestic after-*brachah*. One must have had 1 oz. (28-29g), or the size of an olive. It is all-inclusive, exempting all foods and drinks (even wine or grape juice) from after-*brachot* in the meal. It also has a two-part process:

    c. Rinsing without a *brachah* (although some have a *minhag* to skip this step); and

    d. "*Birkat HaMazon*" ["Blessing of the Food"] (the after-*brachah* for the bread itself).

c. Rinsing: One should cleanse the fingers after eating a meal, known as *Mayim Acharonim* [waters afterwards]. Some prefer to do this in the sink, others have a special vessel to pass around for guests.

☞ A bit of water is poured over the fingertips of each hand, and the hands are dried ideally on a napkin.

☞ The basin is covered or the whole vessel is removed from the table.

☞ One should not talk afterwards between rinsing and *Birkat HaMazon*.

d. Birkat HaMazon: This is the longest after-*brachah*, which *Ashkenazim* refer to as "benching".

🍞 Many will leave a piece of leftover bread on the table as a sign of prosperity.

🍞 Any metal knives should be removed from the table.

🍞 The after-*brachah* is always said sitting, and should be read (as opposed to memorizing it) as this helps one have more *kavanah* [concentration and intention].

🍞 A *siddur*, or booklets of *brachot* called "birchonim" or "benchers" have easy, specific instructions.

🍞 If your host has a different *minhag*, it's acceptable to use their *siddurim* or *benchers* out of courtesy.

🍞 Usually on special days or occasions, a song is sung before the after-*brachah*. Both *Ashkenazim* and *Chassidim* sing "*Shir HaMa'alot*" ["A Song of Ascents"- Psalm 126] to various tunes, and *Sefardim* will chant or say *Avar'chah* ["I Will Bless"- a collection of verses from various Psalms].

🍞 Three or more men over age 13 eating bread form a special group called a *zimun* [invitation]. This honor is said with a cup of wine or grape juice, and is considered a more meritorious after-*brachah*. Ten or more men over age 13 eating bread adds Hashem's Presence to the *mezuman* [summoned].

🍞 Many will sing *Birkat HaMazon* to a special tune, which also helps one learn the Hebrew words.

🍞 Parts are added for *Shabbat*, *Chanukah*, *Purim*, holidays, and *Rosh Chodesh* [new Hebrew month].

🍞 Before the last paragraph, "*Magdil*" [tower] is inserted on weekdays. On *Shabbat* (and after it), *Rosh Chodesh*, major holidays ("in-between days"), *Purim* and a *Brit*, "*Migdol*" [magnifies] is inserted.

🍞 On special occasions such as a *Brit Milah* or wedding, additional *brachot* are said before or afterward. Reciting these is a great honor reserved for important guests. All present reply "*Amen*" as a group.

🍞 If you are eating at someone else's home, there is a special blessing you can include for your host. (*Ashkenazim* and *Chassidim* can also add a blessing for parents, others present, or even one's self.)

🍞 *Sefardic* women who are pressed for time can say a special shorter version listed in their *siddur*.

2. Non-Bread Grain- Queen Mezonot: The queen says, "Let them eat cake!" Any B.R.O.W.S. not under the king's rule is subject to the queen. These include baked snacks and fried or boiled items, and bits of bread soaked in liquid. The *brachah* before exempts like-kind products in the meal.

White Rice- The Ambassador: In absence of nobility, the ambassador is usually greeted with royal treatment, and when retired he is treated as a "citizen". (Brown rice can be a "Land Produce" imposter.)

Brachah Before Non-bread Grain or White Rice: This *brachah* is called "*Mezonot*" or "*Mezonos*".

🧁 If one has a choice between baked or cooked B.R.O.W.S., the *brachah* should be made on the baked.

🧁 If given a choice between wheat and other "royal" grains, a *brachah* should be made on the wheat.

🧁 If choosing between B.R.O.W.S. and white rice, the "royalty" takes precedence for the *brachah*.

🧁 Say the *brachah* "*…boreh minei mezonot*" ["…creates various foods"], and eat.

Non-bread Grain After-Brachah: When a "kingly" course isn't served, B.R.O.W.S. is part of a three-way after-*brachah* called *Me'ein Shalosh* [Three Condensed], which is said sitting. The three "royal" classes cover their specific food group, but the queen's only covers B.R.O.W.S. products.

🧁 Say the after-*brachah* adding "*…al hamichyah v'al hakalkalah…*" ["…for the nourishment and for the sustenance…"] both in the beginning and end (although some omit the last "*v'al hakalkalah*").

🧁 If other "royal" classes of food were eaten with the meal, only one *Me'ein Shalosh* is recited, but the proper section must be added for each class of food. Naturally, the queen's section is said first.

🧁 *Sefardim:* If the grain product was from Israel, there is a slightly different wording "*…al hamichyatah v'al hakalkalatah…*" ["…for its nourishment and its sustenance…"], found in a *Sefardi siddur*.

🧁 On special days (*Shabbat, Rosh Chodesh*, and main holidays), an extra sentence is inserted.

White Rice After-Brachah: Even if eaten with B.R.O.W.S., the ambassador gets a humble farewell.

🥛 Say the after-*brachah* "*…boreh nefashot…*" ["…creates souls…"].

3. Wine and Grape Juice- Prince Gefen: The prince is independent of the king's rule, having his own *brachah*, but is subject to the king's after-*brachah* when in his presence. This *brachah* is said for grape or raisin wine, and grape juice only regardless of the amount, but will exempt all other beverages consumed later in that meal. However, the prince is rather finicky, and won't cover any food items containing wine or grape juice, grapes or raisins themselves, nor other products derived from them (such as wine vinegar). Mixed juices must contain over $1/6$-grape juice to be worthy the prince's blessing.

Brachah Before Wine or Grape Juice (Even With Bread): "*P'ri HaGefen*" or "*HaGafen*".

🍾 Say the *brachah* "*…boreh p'ri hagefen*" ["…creates the fruit of the vine"], and immediately take a drink.
    Sefardim: Say "*L'Chaim*" [To life!] (those present answer "L'Chaim!") then say *P'ri HaGefen*. (See p. 633.)

Wine or Grape Juice After-Brachah (With Bread): The prince defers to the king of food.

🍞 *Birkat HaMazon* exempts the after-*brachah* for the wine or grape juice as well as all other drinks.

Wine or Grape Juice After-Brachah (Without Bread): When the king is away the prince will play!

🍾 Say *Me'ein Shalosh* adding "*...al hagefen v'al p'ri al hagefen...*" ["...for the vine and for fruit of the vine..."] in the beginning, and "*...al p'ri hagefen*" ["...for fruit of the vine"] twice at the end.

🍾 If other "royal" classes of food were eaten with your drink, only one *Me'ein Shalosh* is recited, but the proper section must be added for each class of food. The prince's section comes after the queen's.

🍾 If the grapes were grown in Israel, most will say the slightly different wording (which can usually be found in a *siddur*) "*...al p'ri hagafnah*" ["...for the fruit of <u>its</u> vine"] at the end.

🍾 On special days (*Shabbat*, *Rosh Chodesh*, and main holidays), an extra sentence is inserted.

🍾 No additional after-*brachah* is needed for other beverages consumed after the wine or grape juice.

Kiddush: Wine or grape juice is used for *Kiddush* on *Shabbat* and Holidays. Since sanctification of the day comes first, the crafty prince outfoxes the king's *brachah*. We cover inanimate *challah* so as not "embarrass" it by upstaging it. How much more so should we consider the feelings of our fellow humans!

Zimun: The prince likes the limelight and can steal the last act with a *zimun*, said on wine or grape juice. Afterward, the leader drinks, saying the after-*brachah*. (Section 6 has more on *Kiddush* and *Zimun*.)

4. Special Tree-fruit- Princess Etz: The princess has a nickname to help remember her class— the five "royal" Israeli fruits: (Puffdog) <u>P</u>omegranates, <u>F</u>igs, <u>D</u>ates, <u>O</u>lives and <u>G</u>rapes— "P.F.D.O.G.". Grape vines are woody enough for the little princess to call a "tree", and she covers raisins as well.

Other Tree-fruit- The Etz Maid: The maid's class covers all other tree-fruits, tree-nuts, and woody-stemmed perennial fruits (blueberry, raspberry, etc.). This includes avocados, carob, star fruit, lychees, and kumquats. Since she is always around the palace, she can usually slip in with the princess' *brachot*.

Brachah Before All Tree-fruit: Called "*HaEtz*" or "*HaEytz*", this *brachah* covers all tree-fruits eaten in that meal. The princess and the maid are both choosy, demanding that the fruit be discernable, regardless of whether fresh, dried, cooked, or baked. Their *brachah* will not cover juices or pureed items that look nothing like the original fruit (such as jellied cranberry sauce or commercial applesauce).

🍓 If choosing between P.F.D.O.G. and "common" fruit, "royalty" takes precedence for the *brachah*.

🍓 Of two fruits in the same class, one being whole and the other cut, say a *brachah* on the whole fruit.

🍓 If two same-class fruits are both whole or both cut, say a *brachah* on your favorite or the nicest.

🍓 Say the *brachah* "*...boreh p'ri ha-etz* " ["...creates the fruit of the tree "], and eat.

Special Tree-fruit After-Brachah: When the king is gone, princess P.F.D.O.G. is on.

🍇 Say the *Me'ein Shalosh* after-*brachah* adding "*...al ha-etz v'al p'ri ha-etz...*" ["...for the tree and fruit of the tree..."] in the beginning, and "*...al haperot (al hapeyros)*" ["...for the fruits"] twice at the end.

🍇 If other "royal" classes of food were eaten with the meal, only one *Me'ein Shalosh* is recited, but the proper section must be added for each class of food. The little princess' section always comes last.

🍇 If the fruit was actually grown in Israel, most will say the slightly different wording (which can usually be found in a *siddur*) "*...al perot<u>eh</u>ah (al peyros<u>ey</u>hah)*" ["...for <u>its</u> fruit"] at the end.

🍇 On special days (*Shabbat*, *Rosh Chodesh*, and main holidays), an extra sentence is inserted.

Other Tree-fruit After-Brachah (With P.F.D.O.G.): The maid is covered if she's with the princess.

🍇 Say the *Me'ein Shalosh* after-*brachah* for P.F.D.O.G. (see above).

🍇 No additional after-*brachah* is needed for other "common" tree-fruit eaten with P.F.D.O.G.

Other Tree-fruit After-Brachah (Without P.F.D.O.G.): Since the maid is not of "royal" blood, she gets the plain citizen's after-*brachah* when the princess isn't present.

🥛 Say the after-*brachah* "*...boreh nefashot...*" ["...creates souls..."].

5. Land Produce- The "Adamah" Gardener: The gardener's turf is soil-grown vegetables, seeds, peanuts, and non-woody-stemmed fruits (bananas, papaya, pineapple, strawberries, etc.). Brown rice with its kernel intact within the bran is considered a seed (*not* an Ambassador). Kasha ("buckwheat") is also in this class, as it is actually a pseudocereal. The gardener is picky about her produce, not covering juices, pureed and strained items, or foods that are ground-up before processing (such as corn meal). Being "down to earth", she does allow mashed potatoes, (even from mixes, as it is cooked before being ground) and popcorn (since it's a whole kernel). However, she doesn't "dig" mushrooms (grown on decaying organic matter) and hydroponic vegetables or fruits (water-grown), since neither get nourishment from soil. Raw onions, garlic, horseradish, and black radishes are too pungent for her taste, until they are tamed with cooking.

Brachah Before Land Produce: This *brachah* is referred to as "*HaAdamah*".

🥕 Say the *brachah* "*...boreh p'ri ha-adamah*" ["...creates fruit of the earth"], and eat.

🥕 If in doubt of what *brachah* to say for a fruit or vegetable, use this one, as trees also grow in soil.

🥕 If the gardener's *brachah* was accidentally said on a tree-fruit 🍇, no other *brachah* needs to be said.

Land Produce After-Brachah: The gardener gets the citizen's after-*brachah*.

🥛 Say the after-*brachah* "*...boreh nefashot...*" ["...creates souls..."].

🍇 If one had said the gardener's *brachah* on a P.F.D.O.G., the princess' after-*brachah* still must be said.

71

6. Various Edibles- The Shehakol Citizens: All other foods and drinks throughout the kingdom of *brachot* get a common *brachah*. Being the most general, it comes last after all other classes of foods. Common examples of the citizen status are: Dairy products, eggs, fish, poultry, meat, candies, fruit or vegetable juices, and all drinks (except wine or grape juice). It also includes items demoted from the other classes: Bran (the outer covering of the wheat that is not worthy of "royalty"), strained applesauce, jellied cranberry sauce, jelly, mushrooms and truffles, hydroponic vegetables, sea vegetables like seaweed nori sheets, soy protein, soy flour, corn meal, and Passover items made solely from potato flour or potato starch. Fruits with a "sour personality" (such as lemons and limes) are considered citizens in regions where they are only used as flavor (not eaten raw).

Brachah Before Various Edibles: This *brachah* is referred to as "*Shehakol*".

- If one will be eating any higher-class foods in the same meal, ideally say the *brachah* on them first.
- It is preferable to say this *brachah* on solid foods (rather than liquids) if there is a choice in the meal.
- Say the *brachah* "*...shehakol niyah bidvaro*" ["...all things became existent by His Word"], and eat.
- *Ashkenazim and Chassidim*- say "*niyeh*" [becoming].
- *Sefardim*- say "*niyah*" [became].
- If the citizen's *brachah* was erroneously said on a higher-class food, no new *brachah* need be said.

Various Edibles After-Brachah: The citizens get their common after-*brachah*. Also, other items eaten in the meal that were not covered by a "royal" after-*brachah* (specifically the ambassador, *Adamah* gardener, and *Etz* maid without P.F.D.O.G.) are covered as well. (Only one after-*brachah* is said for all).

- Say the after-*brachah* "*...boreh nefashot...*" ["...creates souls..."].
- *Ashkenazim and Chassidim*- pronounce it "*borey nefashos*".
- *Sefardim*- pronounce it "*boreh nefashot*".
- If a citizen's *brachah* was wrongly said on a higher-class food, the proper after-*brachah* must be said.
- If one intends to sip on a drink all day, say the after-*brachah* only when finished for the day.

Add-Ons: If one wants to add a higher-class food during a meal it's okay to say the *brachah* out of order. An exception is adding bread. End the old meal with the proper after-*brachah* and start a new bread meal. Some consider dessert in a formal meal as a separate meal, and may say additional *brachot* for it.

HOW DO I DETERMINE THE CLASS OF A FOOD? With so much diversification in the kingdom of food, it can be difficult to determine whose class a food will be in. Sometimes the king and queen battle over who will rule over a meal. Often different classes of food will get mixed together— should they treated royally or as commoners? The following details will help keep peace in the kingdom:

Bread Defined: The king likes hearty bread, which must be made with a specific regimen. It must be:

a. **Made from Proper Ingredients:** "Royal" B.R.O.W.S. grain must be the majority ingredient. It should preferably be made with at least some water. Furthermore, there are two customs:

    1. <u>*Ashkenazim and Chassidim*</u>: This king likes variety, allowing the dough to contain some quantities of egg, sugar, oil, and even fruit— "raisin bread", and "sweet" or "egg *challah*". He will cover all types of flavored bagels, *matzah* as well as egg *matzah* (but not *matzah* crackers).

    2. <u>*Sefardim*</u>: This king is precise. Dough must contain mostly flour, water, yeast and salt. It can't taste sweet, eggy or oily, or contain fruit or veggies. Egg or seed coatings are permitted. He covers plain bagels and handmade *shmurah matzah* [watched Passover *matzah*]. Square *matzah* is the queen's, except at Passover. The *Sefardi* king covers *Ashkenazi* "bread" only if 8 oz. is eaten.

b. **Made of a Firm Dough:** The dough must keep in shape, no saggy-baggy batters for the king!

c. **Baked:** Either baked in an oven, or dry-fried in a pan (like flour tortillas), using little or no oil.

d. **Satisfying:** It <u>could be</u> eaten as a main-meal— even if one is just nibbling. By virtue of its essence, it maintains the "royal" status. This means stuffing, bread crumbs, and croutons can still be "bread".

Portions Fit for a King: The king can take over the queen's class if her food meets certain conditions:

    1. It must be baked, and;

    2. A portion is eaten equal to what a person would normally have of bread, and;

    3. One or more of the following:

        a. It is eaten as a main meal (like bread is eaten).

        b. It is eaten with a main course (like bread is eaten).

        c. So much is eaten that it grossly exceeds the amount normally eaten as a snack.

Baked Non-bread Grains: The queen schemes ways to demote foods from the king's class, and get other classes under her control, utilizing her "royal" taste with three sneaky-snacky techniques:

a. **Crispy:** The queen thinks "hard" to trick the king. Crackers, hard pretzels, and tea biscuits are eaten as snacks, and thus unfit for the king. The queen can be in a crunch if many crackers are eaten with tuna, as they only substitute bread (like a tuna sandwich), so the king wins the *brachah*. (Melba toast is thin toasted bread and always under the king's rule, as are baked bagel chips made of leftover bagels.)

b. **Enriched:** The king yields to the queen when she pours on the sugar and spice. Various ingredients mixed into a dough sways it into her snackly class. Mix the dough with only fruit juice— it's cake. Turn dough into batter— it's under her reign. Is it any wonder that the king calls the queen "honey"?

c. **Filled:** When it comes to snacking, the queen is guilty of entrapment. "Royal" grain takes priority over common foods when combined. Be it cocktail franks made into hors d'oeuvres, or a fruit filling made into a pie, she closes in on her victim and takes away their blessing. Will she ever get her fill?

Boiled Non-bread Grains: Since the queen has a monopoly on B.R.O.W.S. cooked in oil or liquid, her deep-fried plot can steal bread crumbs or even croutons from the king's domain. As if this weren't enough, the tiny onion might cry because it too loses its *brachah* when the onion ring is fried.

The Majority Rules: The citizens can gang up on the queen and get their revenge by overriding her "royal" taste. If B.R.O.W.S. is used as a binder (as in meatloaf or gefilte fish), or is indiscernible (such as flour used to thicken a gravy or pudding), it becomes subordinate to the majority, and retains the citizen's *brachah*. Diet shakes, malted milk and beer are citizen's drinks, despite their queenly ingredients.

Masters and Servants: When non-B.R.O.W.S. foods of separate classes come together and form one entity, they can get a single *brachah*. Even though one can distinguish the individual classes, they are eaten together as a unit, so one food becomes the master and the other becomes the servant to enhance its master. They could be combined in a mixture (such as salad with dressing), or eaten together (such as celery sticks with cream cheese), but only one food wins the *brachah*. Because you came to visit the master, not the servants, the *brachah* goes to the master. How would one eat vegetable soup? The gardener will pick out the vegetables, whereas a citizen may favor the broth. The master is determined by:
1. The food most preferred.
2. If there is no preference, the food that is in the majority.
3. If nothing is preferred, and all foods are in equal amounts, the more inclusive *brachah* is said.

Royal Problems: Disputes arise with the king and queen over foods like meat pot pie— is the kingly crust a main-meal, or has the queen taken her fill to demote the dough? Sometimes it's better to appease the king by eating some bread or baked croutons first, thus making a "meal", and avoiding the problem.

General rules can conflict with the queen and citizens, such as with fried or breaded meats— is her "royal" taste taking preference, or is the coating so thin that the meat is in the majority? Many times the meat will win the *brachah*, but one could always keep the queen happy by saying her *brachah* on a different food first, and a citizen's *brachah* on the meat (or some other "citizenly" food).

Eating habits can dictate the *brachah*, as with sandwich cookies— does one bite the cookie or lick the crème? If you are the type that eats the crème first, you would have to snub the queen by saying the citizen's *brachah* before hers (you still say the queen's *brachah* on the cookie if you want to eat it).

WHAT IF I HAVE AN UNIDENTIFIED FOOD OBJECT? If one doesn't know what in the world the *brachah* is on an item, say a *brachah* on a food of a similar known class, having the "U.F.O." in mind. Nowadays, space-age cereal processing can mutate foods into unsuspected classes unidentifiable by ingredients. Fortunately, many *kashrut* agencies have a list of cereal *brachot*— just call and request it.

Brachah Chart			
Food Type	**Examples**	**Brachah Before**	**After-Brachah**
Bread, or grain products eaten as a main meal. * *Al Netilat* (washing) comes first.	*Challah*; Wraps; Flour Tortilla; Burrito; French Toast; Sandwich; Hamburger on Bun; Pizza (3+ slices); Calzones; Bagel; Pita; Cake (a whole or half).	* ***HaMotzi.*** (Inclusive except for wine & grape juice) King *HaMotzi*	***Birkat HaMazon.*** (All-inclusive)
Grain products eaten as a snack, side dish, or dessert. Foods containing any of the 5 "royal" Israeli grains. (B.R.O.W.S.)	Pancakes; Stuffing; Noodles; Fried Croutons; Cookies; Pie; Cake; Cornbread (if having a large amount of wheat flour). Barley, Rye, Oats, Wheat, Spelt, or foods containing them (except when used as thickeners).	***Mezonot.*** (Covers B.R.O.W.S. and Rice products.) Both Queen *Mezonot* and The Ambassador (B.R.O.W.S. is first. Rice outranks all fruit, but never outranks wine.)	***Me'ein Shalosh: Al HaEtz.*** (P.F.D.O.G. includes any tree-fruit eaten with it)
Rice or foods containing rice.	Boiled or Baked Rice; Rice Cakes; Rice Cereals.		***Boreh Nefashot.***
Grape Juice; Wine.	Grape Juice or Wine.	***HaGefen.*** Prince *Gefen* (Outranks rice.)	***Me'ein Shalosh: Al HaGefen.*** (includes all drinks)
Any of the 5 Israeli fruits. (P.F.D.O.G.)	Pomegranates, Figs, Dates, Olives, Grapes & Raisins, or foods containing them.	***HaEtz.*** (Covers all tree-fruits) Both Princess *Etz* and the *Etz* Maid (The *brachah* should be made on P.F.D.O.G. fruits when other fruits are present.)	***Me'ein Shalosh: Al HaEtz.*** (P.F.D.O.G. includes any tree-fruit eaten with it)
Fruits from trees or woody-stemmed perennials.	Blueberries; Raspberries; Cranberries; Apples; Pears; Pistachios; Mangos; Avocados; Almonds; Walnuts; Oranges.		***Boreh Nefashot.***
Fruit growing from the ground; Fruits without woody stems.	Bananas; Papayas; Peanuts; Eggplant; Strawberries; Beets; Lettuce; Tomatoes; Potatoes (whole or mashed); Pineapples; Corn (including popcorn).	***HaAdamah.*** (This can also cover ***HaEtz*** as well.) *Adamah* Gardener	***Boreh Nefashot.***
Any foods other than those mentioned in the above classes; Beverages other than wine or grape juice; Any hydroponically-grown produce; Fungi.	Meat; Fish; Eggs; Dairy Foods; Margarine; Applesauce (non-chunk); Processed Foods (far from original form). Fruit Juice; Milk; Soda; Beer; Passover Cookies & Cakes (from potato starch); Mushrooms; Truffles (fungi); Hydroponic Tomatoes.	***Shehakol.*** (Covers anything any other *brachah* doesn't. Generally said for unknown items as well.) The *Shehakol* Citizens	***Boreh Nefashot.***

Royal Priority Chart	
Class of Foods	**Preference for Saying the Bracha On, If Eaten in the Same Meal**
B.R.O.W.S.	1. Wheat 2. Barley 3. Spelt 4. Rye 5. Oats
P.F.D.O.G.	1. Olives 2. Dates 3. Grapes 4. Figs 5. Pomegranates

Brachah Priority Chart		
Sample Meal	**Say Brachah Before on:**	**Say After-Brachah (Which Covers):**
Bread & Wine (Sunday through Friday)	1. *HaMotzi* (Bread) 2. *HaGefen* (Wine)	1. *Birkat HaMazon* (*Challah*)
Challah & Wine on *Shabbat* with *Kiddush*	1. *HaGefen* (Wine) 2. *HaMotzi* (*Challah*)	1. *Birkat HaMazon* (*Challah*)
3 Pizza Slices and Salad. Drink: Lemonade.	1. *HaMotzi* (Pizza)	1. *Birkat HaMazon* (Pizza & everything else)
Lasagna and Salad. Drink: Milk.	1. *Mezonot* (Lasagna) 2. *HaAdamah* (Salad) 3. *Shehakol* (Milk)	1. *Me'ein Shalosh: Al HaMichyah* (Lasagna) 2. *Boreh Nefashot* (Salad & Milk)
Buttered Noodles, Peas, and Figs. Drink: Grape Juice.	1. *Mezonot* (Noodles) 2. *HaGefen* (Grape Juice) 3. *HaEtz* (Figs) 4. *HaAdamah* (Peas)	1. *Me'ein Shalosh: Al HaMichyah* (Noodles), *Me'ein Shalosh: V'al HaGefen* (Juice), **and** *Me'ein Shalosh: V'al P'ri HaEtz* (Figs) 2. *Boreh Nefashot* (Peas)
Rice Pilaf. Drink: Wine.	1. *HaGefen* (Wine) 2. *Mezonot* (Rice)	1. *Me'ein Shalosh: Al Gefen* (Wine) 2. *Boreh Nefashot* (Rice)
Spaghetti with Meatballs, Salad, and Grapes. Drink: Cola.	1. *Mezonot* (Spaghetti) 2. *HaEtz* (Grapes) 3. *HaAdamah* (Salad) 4. *Shehakol* (Meatballs)	1. *Me'ein Shalosh: Al HaMichyah* (Spaghetti), **and** *V'al P'ri HaEtz* (Grapes) 2. *Boreh Nefashot* (Salad, Meatballs & Cola)
Fish, Rice, Whole Grapes & Sliced Melon. Drink: Water.	1. *Mezonot* (Rice) 2. *HaEtz* (Grapes) 3. *HaAdamah* (Melon) 4. *Shehakol* (Fish)	1. *Me'ein Shalosh: Al P'ri HaEtz* (Grapes) 2. *Boreh Nefashot* (Rice, Fish, Melon and Water)
Cut Grapes and 1 Whole Peach.	1. *HaEtz* (Peach)	1. *Me'ein Shalosh: Al P'ri HaEtz* (Grapes and Peach)

An easy tip to figure out if you have had 1 ounce of food, (generally the size of an olive and enough to say an after-*brachah*), is to check a food package to see the nutritional panel that lists nutrients per serving. Most often, the serving size will be 1 oz., which is usually listed in grams. So, if you see that an item is 28-29g, or more, that means you should say the after-*brachah*.

Now that you know which *brachah* to say on the different foods— "*Let's Get Cooking*"…

Section 4
Let's Get Cooking
Fabulous Food Forgeries

The Uniquely Kosher Recipe System

Titles Are Often Food Forgeries

[*Brachah* Before symbol]

[After-*Brachah* symbol]

□ = *HaMotzi*	*Birkat HaMazon* =
= Preferably eat with a bread meal (or ask your rabbi)	*Birkat HaMazon* =
= *Mezonot*	*Me'ein Shalosh- Al HaMichyah* =
= *HaGefen*	*Me'ein Shalosh- Al HaGefen* =
= *HaEtz*	*Me'ein Shalosh- Al HaEtz* =
= *HaAdamah*	*Boreh Nefashot* =
= *Shehakol*	*Boreh Nefashot* =

Ingredients are always indented, bolded, and listed in the order used.

Italicized Capitalized Ingredients Indicate a "Uniquely Kosher" Recipe (with page #).

Substitute ingredients are separated by a capital "**OR**" when they differ in quantity.

And of course, featuring the *Uniquely Kosher* "Tri-Optional Ingredient System":

"Alternative Ingredients" = offers choices.
- **D-** Donning a delicious dairy dinner? Do delicacy designated "D".
- **P-** Planning plural portions? Produce plentiful *parve*- pick "P".
- **M-** Making a marvelous meat meal? Mix morsel marked "M".

⊛ Step Enumeration minimizes confusion for complex recipes. (Tips are parenthetical.)

Recipe comments are here, often *Other Recipes* that go with it, followed by serving quantities.

☺   ☺   ☺

"Variations" of Main Recipes are listed after the smiley faces. Make a whole new dish just by substituting, adding, or omitting ingredients! (If a variation's *brachah* is different, it is listed here.)

✡ ✡

Jewish Stars Separates Main Recipes When on the Same Page

🔔   🔔   🔔

Different Versions: (Such as Fillings) Are Listed After Dinner Bells

🏆   🏆   🏆

Add-Ons (Like Sauces) Are Listed After Prize-Winning Cups

Overview: For those who don't like to cook, or simply haven't the time, these recipes are made as simplistic as possible. Often, they are food forgeries, and (being kosher), not at all indicative of actual ingredients.

If a specific recipe category is needed, (such as microwave or Chinese), the "*Quick Specific Recipe Directory*" is there to help (pp. 671-678), a little bit before the "*Index*".

Converting Other Recipes: Let's say you have a famous lasagna recipe. If you wanted to make a meat version- see "*Dairy Substitutes (For Meat or Parve Recipes)*" on pp. 575-576 for non-dairy *parve* substitutes. For that lasagna in dairy- see "*Meat Substitutes (For Dairy or Parve Recipes)*" on pp. 577-578. Or, combine both substitutes to make a totally *parve* lasagna! To transform pork or seafood recipes into kosher dishes, see "*Treifah Substitutes That Are Kosher*" on pp. 579-580. Of course, there's the main "*Substitutions*" on pp. 557-573.

Ingredient Notes: Most substitutes can be successfully used. Exception: Bouillon is concentrated. Soup mixes vary in quantity per cup of water- some are 1 tsp. per cup and others 1 Tbs. To substitute soup mix for powdered bouillon, generally use twice the amount of soup mix. (Soup cubes and bouillon cubes are pretty interchangeable.)

For Alternative Diets: As stated earlier, vegetarians or the lactose intolerant should be particularly fond of this book, since *all* recipes can be fixed *parve* (except one- "*Learn to Churn*" homemade butter in "*Fun Kitchen Projects for Kids*"). People with health issues or special diets can use artificial sweeteners or salt substitutes to enjoy their old favorites. Oil is often used to duplicate authentic consistency for *parve* meats and can be omitted. Special kosher low-sodium soup mixes can be used instead of bouillon.

Recipe Sources: The vast majority are my own personal concoctions. If it is an exact recipe given from someone specifically, credit (even if anonymous) is given under that recipe or in the title. Some were recipes I changed or improved from unknown origins. Others are my own intentional duplications of *treifah* recipes adapted with kosher ingredients. A few came from happy "accidents" (namely Hashem)!

Duplicated Products: The original restaurant foods won't be eaten by those who are kosher, so this book isn't competing with these companies. Some grocery products may be kosher dairy, but if one doesn't need it *parve*, I encourage the purchase of the original. Also, recipes for kosher *parve* imitation ingredients should be used only if a commercial product isn't available. Due to commercial processes, the original is usually far superior. These recipes are not meant to take away business from kosher food-producing companies.

No recipe is based on any manufacturer or restaurant's formula or secret ingredient. They are strictly imitations, coming as close as possible to the taste of the actual product. To the best of my knowledge (or lack thereof), no proprietary secrets are revealed. Many of the recipes are from decades ago, collected over time. Some may no longer be available, so that makes this unique recipe collection even more special. All have been tested. Any recipes that did not come out properly and to my satisfaction were *not* included in this book.

Now that you're familiar with the *Uniquely Kosher Recipe System, Let's Get Cooking* with— "*The Recipes*"...

The Recipes

Various Ingredients

Brachot are listed only for ingredients that would likely be eaten alone. Although most of the ingredient recipes are best fixed in with other foods, some are delicious eaten alone.

Miscellaneous

Spreads and Fillings

Taco Bell® Style Taco Seasoning Mix

1½ Tbs. masa flour or masa harina

2 tsp. *Chili Powder* (p. 434)

2 tsp. dried minced onion flakes

¾ tsp. paprika

2¼ tsp. *parve* beef soup mix, OR ¾ tsp. *parve* beef bouillon powder

¼ tsp. onion powder

1¼ tsp. sugar

1 tsp. garlic salt

¼ tsp. black pepper

⅛ tsp. cayenne pepper

⅛ tsp. ground cumin

Put ingredients together in a small plastic zipper bag. Seal, and shake contents until thoroughly blended. It can now be stored until ready to use. Makes slightly over ¼ cup, or the equivalent of 1 envelope.

Use for *Taco Bell® Style Taco Meat* (p. 115), or use as a substitute for chili powder.

Masa flour is finely ground corn flour and can be easily found in the ethnic or Mexican section in supermarkets. Since it is a type of flour, it doesn't necessarily need a *hechsher*.

Kentucky Fried Chicken® Style Breading Mix

½ tsp. **crushed rosemary leaves** (or ground rosemary if at all possible)

½ tsp. **ground oregano**

1¼ tsp. **ground sage**

¼ tsp. **ground ginger**

¼ tsp. **ground marjoram**

⅜ tsp. **ground thyme**

1 Tbs. **parsley flakes**

¾ tsp. **paprika**

¾ tsp. **garlic powder**

⅜ tsp. **onion powder**

⅜ tsp. **salt**

1 Tbs. *parve* **chicken soup mix, OR 1½ tsp.** *parve* **chicken bouillon powder**

2 Tbs. *parve* **beef soup mix, OR 1 Tbs.** *parve* **beef bouillon powder**

1½ cups **flour**

3¼ tsp. **packed brown sugar**

⅜ tsp. **coarse ground black pepper**

Combine all ingredients except pepper, and put through a sieve. Add black pepper and blend well. Store in an airtight jar or bag. Coat and fry any items. Makes a little over 1¾ cups.

✡ ✡

Beer Batter Tempura

1 cup **flour**

2 **egg yolks**

1 tsp. **salt**

dash **black pepper**

¾ cup **flat beer**

avocado oil for frying (other vegetable oil can be used)

Combine ingredients and blend well. Coat vegetables or fish, and fry in oil. Makes 2 cups batter.

All-Purpose Breading Mix

1½ cups flour

4 tsp. *Poultry Seasoning* (p. 434)

1½ tsp. salt

1 tsp. paprika

1 tsp. coarse ground black pepper, OR ¾ tsp. finely ground black pepper

1 tsp. garlic powder

Combine ingredients, blending thoroughly, and store in airtight container. For frying vegetables, omit garlic and paprika. For "crumbier" texture such as with chicken or fish coating, substitute matzah meal, bread crumbs, or corn flake crumbs. Makes about 1⅔ cups.

✡ ✡

Parve Bisquick® Style Mix

4 cups flour

1½ tsp. salt

2 Tbs. baking powder

⅔ cup dry powdered *parve* non-dairy creamer

1 cup *parve* margarine or shortening

Combine dry ingredients in bowl, cut in margarine, blend well until it's a crumby consistency. Put in well-sealing container, store in refrigerated until ready to use. (When measuring for recipes, pack down in measuring cup for accurate and equivalent measurements.) Makes about 6 cups. For various amounts needed, use chart below. Recipe yields about or slightly more than listed.

Parve Bisquick® Mix	3 cups:	1½ cups:	¾ cup:	⅓ cup:	¼ cup:
Flour	2 cups	1 cup	½ cup	¼ cup	8 tsp.
Salt	¾ tsp.	⅜ tsp.	¼ tsp.	⅛ tsp.	3 dashes
Baking Powder	1 Tbs.	1½ tsp.	¾ tsp.	⅜ tsp.	¼ tsp.
Parve Dry Creamer	¼ cup + 1 Tbs.	2½ Tbs.	3¾ tsp.	3 tsp.	1¼ tsp.
Parve Margarine	½ cup	¼ cup	2 Tbs.	1 Tbs.	2 tsp.

Oven-Roasted Garlic

6-8 whole garlic bulbs (peeled, clove ends sliced off and sheathes removed)

½ cup olive oil

Step 1   Put whole garlic cloves in a greased baking dish and drizzle with oil.

Step 2   Bake in a preheated 350º F oven 15 minutes, or until garlic is soft. Let cool.

Step 3   Store refrigerated, or freeze oil-and-all in a jar. (Amounts vary greatly.)

✡ ✡

Parve Meat Drippings

1 cup *parve* margarine

4 tsp. *parve* beef or chicken soup mix, OR 2 tsp. *parve* bouillon powder

Put margarine in a pot or microwave bowl and heat until melted. As soon as melted, quickly stir in soup mix until blended and dissolved. Keep refrigerated. Makes 1 cup drippings.

✡ ✡

Parve Imitation Butter

Version 1	**Version 2**
½ cup warm *parve* margarine	**¼ cup *parve* margarine**
8 tsp. *parve* powdered creamer	**¼ cup *parve* imitation sour cream**
⅝ tsp. salt (optional for "salted" butter)	**¼ tsp. *parve* imitation butter extract**

Version 1: When margarine is creamy to the touch, sprinkle in creamer, stir to blend, and crush chunks. Refrigerate up to 2 weeks or freeze. (If speed is required, put margarine and salt in pot or microwave bowl. Melt, blend, then take off heat. Let sit until cool to touch. Timing is crucial- if too hot, creamer gets stringy, if too cold it won't blend.) Makes ½ cup, or 1 stick.

(½ cup liquid creamer can be substituted for dry. Use for sauce, not for spreads. Makes 1 cup.)

🔔   🔔   🔔

Version 2: Melt margarine and sour cream together. Add extract and mix until thoroughly blended and smooth. (Don't add salt.) Keep refrigerated. Makes ½ cup, or 1 stick "sweet butter".

Parve Cream/Milk

8 cups water (divided, plus extra for thinning to proper consistency if needed)

½ tsp. salt (or to taste)

8 tsp. white rice

¾ cup uncooked rolled oats ("old-fashioned oats")

5 tsp. sugar

⊛   Step 1   Bring 4 cups water to a rolling boil in a pot, then add salt, rice and oats.

⊛   Step 2   Reduce heat to very low, cover and barely simmer ½ hour, stirring occasionally.

⊛   Step 3   Take off heat and let cool slightly. Put contents of pot into blender and add sugar and 2 cups water. Puree until smooth about 1 minute.

⊛   Step 4   Scrape sides with rubber spatula and puree again to thoroughly blend.

⊛   Step 5   Put blender pitcher in refrigerator overnight. (It will thicken.)

⊛   Step 6   Take out of fridge. Add 2 cups water (for Cream), or 2½ cups (for Milk). Puree to blend.

⊛   Step 7   Take a clean new (washed and dried) nylon stocking and stretch it over the mouth of a regular drink pitcher.

⊛   Step 8   Pour blender contents through stocking into drink pitcher. Strain (gently kneading- but not tight squeezing. (Discard the fistful of mushy glob, eat as-is, or use it to thicken soups.) Add extra water for milk if necessary for desired consistency. (½ cup is good.)

⊛   Step 9   Store in refrigerator and shake before using. If it thickens after a few days, add extra water until desired consistency is achieved. Milk will last 1 week.

A delicious, simple, cheap recipe- great to drink, or use in any recipe whether sweet or salty. Being a blend, it has natural creaminess of oats with less oat flavor, but enough rice to make it white but not grainy. (The only drawback is when adding powdered flavorings, the consistency doesn't come out as well as commercial products, due to superior processing.) Makes 2 qt.

Use this method for full strength oat or rice milk. (Adjust sugar to taste.) The only deviation is in Step 1, use ½ cup rice and 2 cups water, or 1 cup oats and 4 cups water. (Rice tends to thicken over time. More water can be added for desired consistency without effecting flavor.) Rice milk is good in sweet recipes. Oat milk is deliciously creamy, versatile and can be used for anything. Rice makes about 8 cups. Oats make about 6 cups. Personal Suggestion: Don't drink when thick.

The consistency is so distasteful you won't want to drink it! (Cream doesn't freeze well.)

Imitation Coconut Milk

½ cup water

½ cup *Parve* Cream (p. 85)**, OR other *parve* milk alternative**

¼ tsp. coconut extract

Step 1   Combine water and Cream in a pot and heat until warm but not boiling.

Step 2   Take off heat add extract and blend well.

Step 3   Pour in an airtight container and refrigerate, or use immediately.

Used in Asian and Polynesian cooking. (If using in heated or boiling foods, add extract after cooking if possible, since heat boils off extract and it virtually disappears.) Makes 1 cup.

This is not to be confused with the fairly clear and somewhat tasteless liquid that comes straight from a coconut (coconut water), which comes from green or ripe coconuts. Real coconut milk and cream are produced via a long tedious process from hand grating the coconut meat or pureeing it, then soaking in water or milk, squeezing or pureeing again, and finally straining and/or skimming. This recipe is far much easier and tastes the same.

✿ ✿

Imitation Thai Coconut Cream

1 cup *Parve* Cream (p. 85)

1 tsp. coconut extract

Step 1   Put Cream in a pot and heat until warm but not boiling.

Step 2   Take off heat and add extract, stirring until well blended.

Step 3   Pour in an airtight container and refrigerate, or use immediately.

Used in Asian and Polynesian recipes as a cream substitute. (If using in hot foods, add extract after cooking if possible, as extracts tend to boil off- especially in heated liquids.) Makes 1 cup.

Far easier than making the real thing, in which oil that rises to the top is mixed with milk. Plus it's very fattening! (An alternative for D is to substitute real cream for creamer.) If you are using this for heated sauces, 1 Tbs. *parve* margarine can be added for authentic cooking properties.

Salad Dressings, Sauces & Gravies

Blueberry Vinaigrette

1 cup blueberries (drained of all liquid)

2½ minced garlic cloves

½ tsp. dried thyme leaves

⅓ cup olive oil

¼ tsp. salt (or more to taste)

⅛ tsp. black pepper (or more to taste)

1 Tbs. vinegar (or more to taste)

Combine first 6 ingredients in a blender. Puree, drain, and add vinegar. Pour into a tightly-sealing jar and store in the refrigerator. Shake before using. Use within 3 days. Makes ¾ cups.

☺   ☺   ☺

For **"Blueberry Steak Sauce"**, omit vinegar and thyme, substitute melted *parve* margarine for oil, and add 3 Tbs. sugar. Heat and put in crocks. Serve warm. Also great for use as a French fry dip. Makes slightly less than ¾ cups, or about 4 servings.

✡ ✡

Thousand Island Dressing

¾ cup *Restaurant Tartar Sauce* (p. 92)

1 mashed hard-boiled egg

1 Tbs. minced green bell pepper

½ cup *Chili Sauce* (p. 95)

2 Tbs. *Parve* Cream (p. 85)

Combine ingredients, blend well. Refrigerate in an airtight container. Makes a little under 2 cups.

☺   ☺   ☺

For **"Thousand Island Burger Sauce"**, omit lemon juice in tartar sauce, and omit *Parve* Cream, blend well and refrigerate in an airtight container. Makes about 1¾ cup.

Parve Ranch Dressing Mix

1 Tbs. garlic powder

1 Tbs. onion powder

1 tsp. sugar

1½ tsp. *Seasoned Salt* (p. 434)

1½ tsp. finely crushed parsley

1½ tsp. lemon pepper seasoning

½ tsp. ground thyme

Combine ingredients and blend well. Store in a zipper bag. Makes ¼ cup, or 1 envelope.

✡ ✡

Ranch Salad Dressing

2 Tbs. *Parve Ranch Dressing Mix* (above)

1 cup mayonnaise

"Milk" =
- **D-** 1 cup buttermilk.
- **P-** ¾ cup *parve* sour cream + 1 tsp. vinegar + ¼ cup *Parve Milk* (p.85).
- **M-** ¾ cup *parve* sour cream + 1 tsp. vinegar + ¼ cup *Parve Milk* (p. 85).

Combine ingredients and blend thoroughly. Makes a little over 1 cup.

✡ ✡

Ranch Dip

2 Tbs. *Parve Ranch Dressing Mix* (above)

"Sour Cream" =
- **D-** 1 cup real dairy sour cream.
- **P-** 1 cup *Parve Imitation Sour Cream* (p. 105).
- **M-** 1 cup *Parve Imitation Sour Cream* (p. 105).

Combine ingredients and blend thoroughly. Makes about 1 cup.

Parve Italian Dressing/Mix

Mix: (Store dry until ready to use.)   **Dressing:**

⅝ **tsp. fine bread crumbs**   ⅔ **cup olive oil**

½ **tsp.** *parve* **chicken soup mix**   **3-4 Tbs. vinegar** (or to taste)

½ **tsp. sugar**   **2 Tbs. water**

½ **tsp. garlic salt**

½ **tsp. onion powder**

¼ **tsp. ground oregano**

¼ **tsp. dried crushed basil leaves**

½ **tsp. parsley flakes**

dash ground thyme

¼ **tsp. black pepper**

¼ **tsp.** *parve* **dry powdered non-dairy creamer**

dash celery salt

1 tsp. *Seasoned Salt* (p. 434)

½ **tsp. dried grated lemon peel**

Blend Mix ingredients together and sieve or grind in a blender. Store in an airtight container or zipper bag until needed. Lasts 6 months. Makes about 2 Tbs., or the equivalent to 1 envelope.

To make dressing, combine Mix with Dressing ingredients in tightly sealing jar, and shake until well blended. Makes 1 cup.

✡ ✡

Parve Creamy Italian Dressing

1 cup prepared *Parve Italian Dressing* (above- omit oil and use 3 Tbs. vinegar)

3-4 Tbs. sugar (or to taste)

1 cup mayonnaise

2 Tbs. *Parve* **Cream** (p. 85)

Blend well and keep refrigerated. Makes 1½ cups.

Parve Creamy Parmesan Salad Dressing

6 Tbs. mayonnaise

6 Tbs. ground walnuts

6 Tbs. *Parve* Cream (p. 85)

1 Tbs. vinegar

2 Tbs. *Parve Imitation Sour Cream* (p. 105)

¼ tsp. garlic salt

⅛ tsp. black pepper

⅛ tsp. mustard powder

1½ Tbs. melted *Parve Imitation Cream Cheese* (p. 105)

Combine ingredients, blending until smooth. Pour in a bottle and refrigerate. Makes 1½ cups.

✿ ✿

Parve Blue Cheese Dressing

1 Tbs. flour

½ Tbs. sugar

¾ tsp. salt

¼ tsp. garlic powder

1 tsp. mustard powder

¾ cup *Parve* Cream (p. 85)

1 tsp. *Fishless Worcestershire Sauce* (p. 92)

¼-⅓ cup water

2 Tbs. vinegar

1 Tbs. melted *parve* margarine

¾ cup shredded *parve* imitation Mozzarella cheese

½ cup melted *Parve Imitation Cream Cheese* (p. 105)

Combine ingredients in pot (or microwave bowl). Heat on low (or in 1-minute increments). Stir to blend. Jar and refrigerate. Good dip for celery or *Easy Buffalo Wings* (p. 142). Makes 2¾ cups.

Hawaiian Burger Sauce

2 Tbs. ketchup

1 Tbs. prepared mustard

1 Tbs. mayonnaise

Blend together all ingredients and use as-is or refrigerate. Makes 4 Tbs., or 4 servings.

Obviously, this is not a typical "Hawaiian" food, but this is based on a sauce always available at a fast-food joint called the "Molokai Drive-In" back in 1993. It is indeed great on hamburgers.

✿ ✿

Hollandaise Sauce

1⅓ cup *parve* margarine

8 beaten egg yolks (½ cup)

3 Tbs. kosher sherry or lemon juice

1 tsp. salt

4 tsp. mustard powder

⅛ tsp. hot pepper sauce

❀ Step 1   Put margarine in a saucepan or baking dish and melt, then take off heat.

❀ Step 2   Combine remaining ingredients with margarine, blending thoroughly until smooth.

❀ Step 3   For Stove- Put saucepan on very low heat on stove. For Microwave- Loosely cover baking dish with plastic wrap and microwave in 1-minute increments.

❀ Step 4   Stir as cooking (or after every minute for microwave), until mixture has thickened and is smooth.

Serve hot over vegetables such as broccoli, or use in *Eggs Benedict* (p. 251). Makes 2 cups.

Fishless Worcestershire Sauce

3⅓ Tbs. molasses or honey

3½ Tbs. soy sauce

¾ cups apple cider vinegar

1½ Tbs. lemon juice

¾ tsp. mustard powder, OR 1 tsp. prepared mustard

½ tsp. cayenne pepper

¼ tsp. black pepper

⅛ tsp. garlic powder

½ tsp. onion powder

⅛ tsp. ground cinnamon

⅜ tsp. ground ginger

pinch ground cloves

1¼ tsp. ground cardamom, OR ⅜ tsp. ground nutmeg

✡ Step 1   Combine ingredients in a pot, blend thoroughly and bring to a boil, stirring. (I find it somewhat irritating to the eyes when cooking. Try not to breathe over top of it!)

✡ Step 2   Remove from heat and let cool completely, pour into an airtight container.

Keep refrigerated. Shake well before using. It lasts for months. Makes about 1⅓ cups.

✡ ✡

Restaurant Tartar Sauce

¾ cup mayonnaise

½ tsp. lemon juice

2½ Tbs. minced onion

2½ Tbs. minced dill pickles or dill relish

¼ tsp. hot pepper sauce

Combine ingredients and blend well. Refrigerate in an airtight container. Makes 1 cup.

Benihana® Style Ginger Sauce

2 Tbs. chopped onion

2 tsp. grated fresh ginger

¼ cup soy sauce

1 tsp. vinegar

Combine all ingredients in a blender, and blend at high speed 2 minutes until smooth. Use as-is, or store in an airtight container in the refrigerator. Makes about ¾ cup, or 4 servings.

This goes especially well in *Shrimp Benihana Style* (p. 359), but can be used in any Chinese dishes calling for ginger and soy sauce.

✿ ✿

Chinese Hoisin Sauce

¼ cup soy sauce

¼ cup mashed pinto beans or *Refried Beans* (p. 104)

2 tsp. sesame or peanut oil

1 tsp. minced cloves *Oven-Roasted Garlic* (p. 84)

1½ tsp. finely minced pickled jalapeño pepper (seeded)

1 Tbs. honey (more can be added for sweeter sauce)

1 Tbs. molasses

4 tsp. white vinegar (more can be added for sour sauce)

½ tsp. Chinese 5-spice powder (optional for spicy-sweet flavor)

Combine all ingredients in a blender and puree until smooth, or put ingredients through a sieve and blend thoroughly until smooth. (More honey and vinegar can be added for a pungent sauce.) Use right away or store refrigerated for up to 1 week.

Use in Chinese cooking, or as a condiment like soy sauce. Makes about ½ cup sauce.

Chinese 5-spice powder can be found in supermarkets with a larger selection of spices.

🥛 (🥕 if pineapple is eaten)   **Sweet & Sour Sauce**   🥛

⅔ cup vinegar

⅛ cup brown sugar

2 Tbs. ketchup

2 tsp. soy sauce

8 tsp. corn starch

8 tsp. water

⅔ cup small pineapple chunks (optional)

12 drops red food coloring (optional)

✿ Step 1   Blend together first 4 ingredients in a saucepan. Bring to boil, then reduce heat.

✿ Step 2   Mix corn starch with water, and add to other ingredients, stirring until thickened.

✿ Step 3   Add pineapple chunks and food coloring, if desired.

✿ Step 4   Put in an air tight container and refrigerate, or use warm.

Use for Chinese chicken or fish dishes, dipping sauce for chicken nuggets, etc. Makes 1 cup without pineapple, or 1½ cups with pineapple.

✿ ✿

Stir-Fry Cooking Sauce

⅛ cup soy sauce

1½ Tbs. *Fishless Worcestershire Sauce* (p. 92)

3 Tbs. corn starch

1½ Tbs. kosher cooking sherry

1½ tsp. curry powder

⅔ cup water

Combine all ingredients and blend well. Heat until thickened, or add directly to stir-fry. Use in either delicious *Beef Stir-Fry* (p. 279) or *Chicken Stir-Fry* (p. 283). Makes about 1 cup.

Chili Sauce

1 cup tomato sauce

2 Tbs. brown sugar

1 Tbs. vinegar

¼ tsp. *Spice Parisienne* (p. 434)

⅛ tsp. onion powder

1 tsp. *Chili Powder* (p. 434)

Blend all ingredients and store in an airtight container in the refrigerator. Makes about 1 cup.

✿ ✿

Outback Steakhouse® Style Creamy Chili Sauce

"Sour Cream" =
- **D-** 1½ cups real dairy sour cream.
- **P-** 1½ cups *Parve Imitation Sour Cream* (p. 105).
- **M-** 1½ cups *Parve Imitation Sour Cream* (p. 105).

1½ cups mayonnaise

1 Tbs. paprika

½ tsp. salt

¾ cup *Chili Sauce* (above)

rounded ⅛ tsp. cayenne pepper

Combine ingredients and blend well. Store up to 1 week in an airtight container in refrigerator until ready to use. Use as a dipping sauce for *Outback Steakhouse® Style Bloomin' Onion®* (p. 201). Makes about 3 cups.

(eaten alone)   **Super Salsa**   (eaten alone)

2 medium diced tomatoes (1 cup)

1 Tbs. finely minced pickled jalapeño peppers (double for spicy salsa)

1 Tbs. diced fresh green bell peppers (green chiles can be used as well)

2 Tbs. diced onion (frozen onion in oil works exceptionally well)

2 minced garlic cloves (1 tsp.)

3-4 Tbs. chopped fresh cilantro (Chinese parsley or fresh coriander)

1 tsp. salt

Combine ingredients and blend well. Serve in crocks with warm tortilla chips, or put in an airtight container in the refrigerator. (Can be stored a few days, but no longer unless it's cooked.) It goes great with *Grilled Meat Fajitas* (p. 277) or *Shredded Chicken Chimichangas* (p. 266). (For an unusual story about salsa, see "*The Salsa Solution*" p. 430.) Makes 1⅓ cup.

✡ ✡

Taco Bell® Style Enchirito® Sauce

1 small minced onion (¼ cup)

1 pressed or minced garlic clove (½ tsp.)

1 Tbs. avocado oil (other vegetable oil can be used)

1¾ cups tomato sauce, OR 2 (8 oz.) cans tomato sauce

2 Tbs. *Chili Powder* (p. 434)

⅛ tsp. ground oregano

½ tsp. salt

¼ tsp. ground cumin

1 cup water

Step 1   Cook onion and garlic in oil in pot on medium heat until onion turns transparent.

Step 2   Add remaining ingredients and simmer covered 30 minutes, stirring occasionally.

Use in *Taco Bell® Style Enchiritos®* (p. 269), *Neo-Classic Tamales* (p. 273) and *Pintos & Cheese* (p. 127). This freezes well in 1 cup containers to have on hand. Makes 2½ cups.

Taco Bell® Style Green Taco Sauce

2 cups water

4 tsp. *parve* **chicken soup mix, OR 2** *parve* **chicken bouillon cubes**

1 lb. fresh tomatillos (husked and halved)

3 Tbs. minced pickled jalapeño peppers

1 chopped medium onion (½ cup)

2 minced garlic cloves (1 tsp.)

1 Tbs. minced fresh cilantro (Chinese parsley or fresh coriander)

1 Tbs. avocado oil (other vegetable oil can be used)

❀   Step 1   Bring water to a boil in a saucepan, and add soup mix stirring until dissolved.

❀   Step 2   Add tomatillos and boil 10 minutes, remove from heat and let cool.

❀   Step 3   Pour through a strainer into a bowl and set liquid aside for later use.

❀   Step 4   Combine tomatillos and next 4 ingredients in blender, blend until fairly smooth.

❀   Step 5   Heat oil in pan until hot, add mixture and cook 4-5 minutes or until thickened.

❀   Step 6   Add reserved strained liquid to pan, and bring to a boil. Reduce heat, stirring occasionally, and cook for about 10-15 minutes or until sauce is thickened.

❀   Step 7   Remove from heat. Once sauce has cooled, refrigerate in sealed containers.

This is used as a dip for *McDonald's® Style International Chicken McNuggets* (p. 294). Makes 1⅓ cups.

☺   ☺   ☺

For **"Mild Green Taco Sauce"**, substitute green chiles for jalapeños, and add ¼ cup finely chopped almonds in Step 3. Makes a little over 1⅓ cups.

Taco Bell® Style Nacho Cheese Sauce

2 Tbs. room temperature *parve* margarine

2 Tbs. flour

"Milk" =
- **D-** ¼ cup half & half.
- **P-** ¼ cup *Parve* Cream (p. 85).
- **M-** ¼ cup *Parve* Cream (p. 85).

½ tsp. onion salt

1 tsp. finely minced pickled jalapeño peppers

2 Tbs. pickled jalapeño pepper juice (vinegar from jar of above peppers)

¼ cup water

"Cheese" =
- **D-** 8 minced slices processed American cheese.
- **P-** 1 cup shredded *parve* American cheese.
- **M-** 1 cup shredded *parve* imitation American cheese.

"Sour Cream" =
- **D-** ½ cup dairy sour cream.
- **P-** ½ cup *Parve Imitation Sour Cream* (p. 105).
- **M-** ½ cup *Parve Imitation Sour Cream* (p. 105).

Step 1 Combine ingredients, in a pot for stove, or bowl for microwave. Blend well.

Step 2 Heat until smooth, thickened and well blended. For Stove- Heat on low stirring constantly. For Microwave- Heat in 30-second intervals, stirring in-between. Keep warm.

Use on *Taco Bell® Style Nachos* (p. 128) or *Nachos Bell Grande®* (p. 275). Makes about 1 cup.

☺ ☺ ☺

For **"Tangy Restaurant Cheese Sauce"**, omit jalapeño peppers and substitute 2 Tbs. extra water for jalapeño juice. Fix as normal. Use on big salty soft pretzels, *Arby's® Style Beef & Cheddar Sandwiches* (p. 241), etc. Makes about 1 cup.

Kraft® Cheez Whiz® Style Sauce

"Cheese" = $\begin{cases}\end{cases}$
D- 8 minced processed kosher American cheese slices.

P- 1 cup shredded *parve* American cheese.

M- 1 cup shredded *parve* American cheese.

"Milk" = $\begin{cases}\end{cases}$
D- ½ cup evaporated milk (preferably regular, do not use no fat).

P- ½ cup *Parve* Cream (p. 85).

M- ½ cup *Parve* Cream (p. 85).

⅜ tsp. salt

⅜ tsp. mustard powder

1 tsp. *Fishless Worcestershire Sauce* (p. 92)

✾ Step 1   Combine ingredients in a pot (or large microwave bowl or even a large glass jar).

✾ Step 2   Heat until melted, thoroughly blended, and smooth. <u>For Stove</u>- Use low heat, stir constantly. <u>For Microwave</u>- Heat in 30-second intervals, stirring in-between.

✾ Step 3   Take off heat and pour quickly into a sealable container or glass jar. Cool completely and chill.

Store in refrigerator. (If using D, do not use regular shredded Cheddar cheese for this recipe, it does not melt as well.) This keeps for several weeks in the refrigerator. Serve over vegetables, spread on crackers or use as a chip dip. Makes 1 cup.

✡ ✡

Papa John's Pizza® Style Garlic Sauce

½ cup melted *parve* margarine

1 tsp. garlic powder

⅛ tsp. salt (more to taste if desired)

Combine ingredients in a microwavable bowl or crock, heat again slightly and serve.

Fix 2 pizzas, pour sauce over it, and serve with pepperoncini peppers on the side for authenticity. Can be put on other items needing garlic butter such as *Easy Artichokes* (p. 201). Makes ½ cup sauce (enough for 2 large pizzas).

Professional Pizzeria Sauce

1 (6 oz.) can tomato paste (add sugar to taste, if desired)

1 tsp. garlic salt, OR ½ tsp. garlic powder + ½ tsp. salt

½ tsp. crushed oregano leaves

½ tsp. *Italian Seasoning* (p. 434)

⅛ tsp. black pepper

2 Tbs. water (or more to desired thickness)

Blend ingredients until smooth and spreadable. Refrigerate or freeze. Makes ¾ cup.

✩ ✩

Nana's Classic Spaghetti Sauce

"Meat" =
- **D-** 1 pkg. (2 cups) imitation hamburger crumbles + 2 Tbs. avocado oil.
- **P-** 1 pkg. (2 cups) *parve* soy crumbles + 2 Tbs. avocado oil.
- **M-** 1 lb. kosher ground beef (browned and drained).

3 minced garlic cloves (1½ tsp.)

1 medium chopped onion (½ cup)

1 (15 oz.) can chopped tomatoes

1 (6 oz.) can tomato paste

1 (8 oz.) can tomato sauce

¼ cup kosher burgundy or other kosher red wine (optional)

2 Tbs. apple cider vinegar

¼ cup sugar (or to taste)

1 tsp. salt

dash hot pepper sauce

Sauté first 3 ingredients in pot until onion is limp. Add remaining ingredients, simmer 1 hour.
(Nana *aleyha hashalom* [may she rest in peace] made great sauce!) Makes 4 servings.

☺   ☺   ☺

For **"Spicy Spaghetti Sauce"**, add 1½ tsp. pepper flakes and ¾ tsp. *Italian Seasoning* (p. 434).

Tzatziki Sauce

½ cup cucumber (peeled and chopped)

"Sour Cream" = $\begin{cases}\end{cases}$ **D-** ½ cup real dairy sour cream (add more for thicker sauce).

P- ½-⅔ cup *Parve Imitation Sour Cream* (p. 105).

M- ½-⅔ cup *Parve Imitation Sour Cream* (p. 105).

⅛ tsp. salt (more can be added to taste)

4 minced garlic cloves (2 tsp.)

¾ tsp. finely minced dill weed (more can be added to taste)

Combine in blender and puree until smooth. A must for *Kosher Gyros* (p. 242). Makes 1 cup.

✡ ✡

White Sauce

¼ cup flour, OR 2 Tbs. potato starch

¼ tsp. salt, OR 2½ tsp. *parve* chicken soup mix, OR 1¼ tsp. *parve* bouillon

¼ tsp. onion powder

¼ tsp. ground nutmeg (optional)

dash black pepper (optional)

"Milk" = $\begin{cases}\end{cases}$ **D-** 1¼ cup milk.

P- ¾ cup *Parve Milk* (p. 85) + ½ cup water.

M- ¾ cup *Parve* Cream (p. 85) + ½ cup chicken broth or water.

¼ cup *parve* margarine (room temperature)

Blend first 5 ingredients in pot or microwave bowl, blend in a bit of "Milk". Add rest of "Milk" and margarine, cook stirring on low, (microwave 30-seconds, stir, repeat), until thick and smooth.

Add to spinach for quick creamed spinach. For *Banquet® Chicken Fried Beef Steak Meal* (p. 310), omit margarine, and blend ingredients together before adding. Makes 1½ cups.

☺ ☺ ☺

For **"Curry Sauce"**, use *parve* soup mix or bouillon (beef flavor for beef dishes, chicken flavor for chicken dishes), and add 1½ tsp. curry powder. (Use in *Peruvian Chicken Curry* on p. 296.)

Universal Gravy

"**Liquid**" =
- **D-** 1½ cups milk or water.
- **P-** ¾ cup *Parve* Cream (p. 85) + ¾ cup water.
- **M-** 1½ cups thin kosher meat broth or water.

¼ cup flour, OR 2 Tbs. potato starch

parve **flavor:** 3 Tbs. soup mix, OR 4 tsp. dry bouillon, OR 4 bouillon/soup cubes

"**Drippings**" =
- **D-** 2 Tbs. oil, OR 2-4 Tbs. melted margarine or butter.
- **P-** 2 Tbs. oil, OR 2-4 Tbs. melted *parve* margarine.
- **M-** 2-4 Tbs. hot kosher meat drippings (omit ½ of *parve* flavor).

⅛ tsp. garlic powder or onion powder

¼ tsp. *Poultry Seasoning* (p. 434)

⅛ tsp. coarse ground black pepper

✿ Step 1   Put some of "Liquid" with flour in a pot or microwave bowl, blend well.

✿ Step 2   Add remaining ingredients, blend well and heat until thick and smooth. <u>For Stove-</u> Use low heat, stir constantly. <u>For Microwave-</u> Heat in 30-second intervals, stirring in-between.

Universal Gravy is "out of this world"! It also freezes well. Makes about 1½ cups.

☺   ☺   ☺

For "**Chicken Gravy**" use chicken *parve* flavor and garlic powder.

☺   ☺   ☺

For "**Beef Gravy**" use beef *parve* flavor, onion powder, and add 1½-2 tsp. browning sauce.

☺   ☺   ☺

For "**Turkey Gravy**", for *parve* flavor use 2 Tbs. beef soup mix and 2 Tbs. chicken soup mix (or 1 Tbs. beef bouillon and 1 Tbs. chicken bouillon). Add an additional ⅛ tsp. black pepper and ¼ tsp. garlic powder. Also add ½ tsp. paprika, and 4 drops liquid smoke.

☺   ☺   ☺

For "**KFC® Style Gravy**", for *parve* flavor use ½ beef soup mix and ½ chicken soup mix, use garlic powder, twice the pepper, and add 1 tsp. microwave browning sauce.

☺   ☺   ☺

For "**Onion Gravy**" substitute ¼ cup onion soup mix for *parve* flavor. Use 1½ cups water as "Liquid", use garlic powder (not onion powder), and omit poultry seasoning.

☺   ☺   ☺

For "**Mushroom Gravy**" do like *Onion Gravy* above, substituting mushroom soup mix for onion.

Spreads, Fillings, Imitation Dairy & Meat Items

Refried Beans

3 cups cooked pinto beans (drained well)

1 tsp. onion salt

¼ cup melted *parve* margarine

❀ Step 1   Put beans in a blender, thoroughly puree and add remaining ingredients.

❀ Step 2   Blend well until a creamy consistency is achieved— it should be an easily spreadable paste. (If beans are too dry, add more margarine or add a bit of water if necessary.)

❀ Step 3   Heat through if serving. (If beans are too watery, cook until liquid evaporates.)

These freeze very well. For a spicier flavor, 1 tsp. *Chili Powder* (p. 434) can be added. Instead of dry beans, 2 (15 oz.) cans of kosher pinto beans can also be used- but must be thoroughly drained. Makes about 2 cups, or the equivalent of slightly over 1 (15 oz.) can.

✧ ✧

Mexican Restaurant Guacamole

2 large soft ripe avocados (peeled, any bad areas and seeds removed)

2 Tbs. white vinegar

½ tsp. garlic powder

½ tsp. salt

2 tsp. ground cumin

pinch cayenne pepper

❀ Step 1   Mash avocado until no large chunks remain and it is relatively smooth.

❀ Step 2   Add remaining ingredients, blending thoroughly.

❀ Step 3   Put in an airtight container and chill. Keep refrigerated up to 3 days, or freeze until ready to use. (Always keep in sealed container to keep it from turning brown.)

Flavors blend nicely if kept overnight. Goes great with *Shredded Chicken Chimichangas* (p. 266) and *Grilled Meat Fajitas* (p. 278). Makes enough for 4 sandwiches, or 8 servings tortilla chip dip.

Roasted Eggplant Spread

2 small eggplants (peeled & cut into 2-inch cubes)

1 chopped small-medium sweet Vidalia onion (1/2 cup)

8 large whole garlic cloves

1 red bell pepper (seeded & chopped in large pieces)

¼ cup olive oil

1½ tsp. ground cumin

¼ tsp. ground turmeric

¾ tsp. salt

2 Tbs. tomato paste

Coat vegetables well with oil and set on cookie sheet. Bake 45 minutes in 400° F oven until tender. Let cool. Put in blender and add last ingredients. Puree 1 minute. Makes 1-1½ cups.

✩ ✩

(🥛 if made of tahini) **Koogle™ Style Peanut Butter**

1 cup warm creamy peanut butter (tahini can also be used- add sugar to taste)

1 **Koogle™ Flavor**

Combine 1 Koogle™ Flavor (below) with peanut butter. Blend well and refrigerate.

Koogle™ Flavors:

Banana: 2½ tsp. banana extract

Chocolate: ⅓ cup *parve* chocolate syrup

Cinnamon: 1-3 Tbs. ground cinnamon (or to taste)

Vanilla: 4 tsp. vanilla extract

Based on a Kraft® product from the 1970s. Makes 1 cup.

☺ ☺ ☺

For **"Spicy Mexican Peanut Butter"**, omit Flavors, add ⅛ tsp. cayenne pepper, 1 tsp. *Chili Powder* (p. 434), and ½ tsp. garlic powder. Refrigerate. (Tahini doesn't work.) Makes 1 cup.

☺ ☺ ☺

For **"Spicy Bacon Peanut Butter"**, instead of above Flavors, add ¼ cup *parve* bacon bits, and ½ cup chili sauce. Refrigerate up to 1 week. (Tahini works well.) Makes about 1½ cups.

Imitation Dairy Items

Parve Imitation Sour Cream

1 cup finely chopped firm silken tofu (do not use extra-firm)

2 Tbs. avocado or other vegetable oil

2 Tbs. lemon juice

¼ tsp. salt (or to taste)

Step 1   Drain tofu completely. (If there is excess water, this recipe won't turn out well.)

Step 2   Add tofu to blender and puree, then add remaining ingredients.

Step 3   Set blender on liquefy until smooth, and flavors are well blended. Refrigerate.

This recipe is great for times when you have run out of *parve* sour cream or can't find it in stock. Great for making dips or to use in recipes. Use within 2 weeks. Keep refrigerated. Makes a little over 1 cup.

✡ ✡

Parve Imitation Cream Cheese

¾ cup (6 oz.) mashed firm silken tofu (do not use extra-firm)

3¼ tsp. sugar, OR 1 Tbs. honey

½ tsp. lime juice

1 tsp. salt

½ cup melted *parve* vegetable shortening (kept warm and in liquid form)

Step 1   Drain tofu of all excess water. Put in blender and puree until no chunks remain.

Step 2   Add sugar, lime juice and salt and puree until well blended and creamy.

Step 3   Add shortening, puree to blend. Pour into a container and refrigerate.

This is good for times when you have run out of *parve* cream cheese or can't find it in stock. Great for dips, spreads or sauces. (Do not use for items that need a firm consistency. Preferably don't use in baked desserts– they must bake much longer and turn brown, although they taste pretty much the same.) Use within 1-2 weeks. Keep refrigerated. Makes a little over 1 cup.

Mum's Pimiento Cheese Spread

"Cheese" =
- **D-** 1 (8 oz.) bar kosher sharp Cheddar cheese.
- **P-** 2 cups shredded *parve* Cheddar cheese + 2 tsp. mustard powder.
- **M-** 2 cups shredded *parve* Cheddar cheese + 2 tsp. mustard powder.

1 (4 oz.) jar chopped pimientos (¼ cup) (drained)

6 Tbs. finely minced onion

¼ cup mayonnaise

½ tsp. sugar (optional- do not add if sweet mayonnaise is used)

✺ Step 1   Have "Cheese" at room temperature, and put it into a bowl.
✺ Step 2   Add remaining ingredients, blend and mash together thoroughly until creamy.
✺ Step 3   Put in airtight container and keep refrigerated. Use within 1 week. Makes 2 cups.

✡ ✡

Port Wine Cheese Spread

"Cheese" =
- **D-** 1 (8 oz.) bar kosher sharp Cheddar cheese (grated).
- **P-** 2 cups shredded *parve* Cheddar cheese + ¾ tsp. mustard powder.
- **M-** 2 cups shredded *parve* Cheddar cheese + ¾ tsp. mustard powder.

2 Tbs. melted *parve* margarine

⅓ cup kosher port wine, or kosher cooking sherry

"Cream Cheese" =
- **D-** ½ (8 oz.) pkg. cream cheese (½ cup).
- **P-** ½ cup *parve* imitation cream cheese.
- **M-** ½ cup *parve* imitation cream cheese.

¼ tsp. onion salt

3-6 drops red food coloring

✺ Step 1   Set ingredients out at room temperature. Put "Cheese" into pot or micro bowl.
✺ Step 2   Add next 4 ingredients, heat on low or microwave until melted. Stir, blending well.
✺ Step 3   Put in a decorative crock or an airtight container and let cool slightly.
✺ Step 4   Add food coloring to mixture, swirling it around to make pinkish streaks, and chill
at least 1-2 days. (The longer it sits, the more the flavors blend.) Makes slightly under 2 cups.

Smoky Bacon Cheese Spread

1 cup *Kraft® Cheez Whiz® Style Sauce* (p. 99)

1 Tbs. *parve* **imitation bacon bits**

2 tsp. liquid smoke

Slightly heat sauce until easily stirred. Add bacon bits and liquid smoke to taste, blending well. Put in an airtight container and chill a day. Store in the refrigerator. Makes 1½ cups.

✩ ✩

Kraft® Velveeta® Style Cheese

"Swiss Cheese" =
- **D-** 2⅔ large slices kosher Swiss cheese + ⅛ tsp. salt.
- **P-** ⅔ cup shredded *parve* American cheese.
- **M-** ⅔ cup shredded *parve* American cheese.

"Cheddar" =
- **D-** 14 slices processed kosher Cheddar cheese slices.
- **P-** 1⅛ cup grated *parve* Cheddar + 2 tsp. mustard powder.
- **M-** 1⅛ cup grated *parve* Cheddar + 2 tsp. mustard powder.

"Mozzarella" =
- **D-** ⅔ cup grated kosher Mozzarella cheese.
- **P-** ¾ cup shredded *parve* Mozzarella.
- **M-** ¾ cup shredded *parve* Mozzarella.

5 Tbs. *Parve Cream* (p. 85)

- **Step 1**   Line a small loaf pan (form) with 12 x 12-inch aluminum foil, and set aside.
- **Step 2**   Cut D cheese slices in bits. Put ingredients in a pot for stove, or microwave bowl.
- **Step 3**   Cook on stove on low stirring constantly, (or microwave in 30-second intervals on 50% power stirring vigorously between times), until completely melted and thoroughly blended.
- **Step 4**   Immediately pour into foil-lined pan all at once, and refrigerate until hardened.
- **Step 5**   Remove pan, wrap tightly and refrigerate in zipper bag. Makes about a 1 lb. loaf.

☺   ☺   ☺

For **"Kraft® Mexican Mild Velveeta® Style Cheese"**, add 1 Tbs. minced jalapeño peppers in Step 1, and substitute kosher Monterey Jack cheese for Mozzarella for D. (P and M can either stay the same or use *parve* Monterey Jack instead of Mozzarella.) Makes about a 1 lb. loaf.

Kraft® Casino® Style Cheeses

"Cheese" = {
D- 16 minced slices or 1 (8 oz.) bar kosher Monterey Jack.
P- 2 cups grated *parve* Mozzarella or Jack cheese.
M- 2 cups grated *parve* Mozzarella or Jack cheese.
}

Flavoring (below)

❀ Step 1   Combine "Cheese" and 1 Flavoring in microwave bowl or pot.

❀ Step 2   Melt in microwave on 50% power, or on low on stove, stirring often.

❀ Step 3   For Bar- Pour into small foil-lined loaf pan. For Sandwich Slices- Take off heat and immediately pour into a metal cookie sheet. Chill until hardened, at least 2 hours.

❀ Step 4   For Bars- Remove from loaf pan and wrap with foil, or put it in a zipper bag.
For Slices- Slice into 4 (4-inch) squares and take a spatula, and slide it underneath one end of cheese as pushing in. Slide spatula evenly until cheese is free from pan. Put slices in a zipper bag separated with kosher wax paper or plastic wrap in-between. Store in the refrigerator.

Delicious on crackers, burgers, etc. Makes 1 (8-oz.) bar or 8 thick slices.

Flavorings:

Pepper Jack: 2 tsp. minced jalapeño peppers

Caraway: 2 tsp. caraway seeds

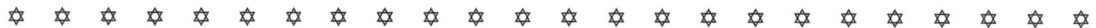

✡ ✡

Parve Parmesan Cheese

Version 1	Version 2
2 Tbs. *parve* powdered creamer	¼ cup *parve* kosher nutritional yeast
2 Tbs. ground walnuts (or almonds)	2 tsp. sugar
½ tsp. salt	¾ tsp. salt

Both Versions: Blend ingredients together thoroughly. Makes ¼ cup.

As with real Parmesan, Version 1 (far superior) is a bit oily due to nuts. It also looks more authentic sprinkled on foods. Version 2 is dry, best served in dishes containing oil or margarine to blend or stick to. Nutritional yeast can be found in health food stores. (Look for a *hechsher*.)

This recipe is good for emergencies. Vegan imitation Parmesan can also be found at health food stores.

Parve Cottage Cheese

¼ cup *Parve Imitation Sour Cream* (p. 105)

¼ cup *Parve* Cream (p. 85)

¾ tsp. salt

1 cup unsalted unflavored overcooked white rice (also see alternative below)

Step 1   Put first 3 ingredients in a bowl, add rice, and blend until smooth. Chill until cold.

Step 2   Keep refrigerated up to 2 weeks. (Add water if it dries out.) Makes 1¼–1⅔ cups.

One can use ½ cup rice + ¾ cup diced boiled egg white. Refrigerate. (Keeps only up to 3 days.)

✡ ✡

Parve Ricotta Cheese

¼ cup flour

½ cup *Parve Milk* (p. 85), OR other *parve* milk alternative

2 Tbs. *parve* margarine

¾ cup *parve* imitation cream cheese

¼ cup grated *parve* imitation Mozzarella cheese

Step 1   Blend flour and milk and set aside. Melt other ingredients on low heat.

Step 2   Add flour mixture to cheese. Heat on low, stir until thickened (lumps are fine).

Step 3   Chill and store refrigerated in a sealed container. Makes 1½ cups, (or 1 tub).

✡ ✡

Parve Feta Cheese

6 Tbs. *parve* imitation cream cheese

1 cup grated *parve* imitation Mozzarella cheese

1½ tsp. salt

Step 1   Combine ingredients in a pot or microwavable bowl, and heat to melt completely.

Step 2   Stir to blend thoroughly, take off heat and pour in small zipper bag or 3-inch square sealable container. Chill until firm, and store in refrigerator. Makes 1 (8 oz.) block Feta.

Imitation Meat Items

Parve Broth

5 cups water

2½ tsp. avocado oil (or other vegetable oil)

1 Parve Flavor

Bring water, oil and 1 Parve Flavor to boil in a large pot. Stir to dissolve until well-blended. Use warm as-is, or refrigerate in jars (shake before using). Makes 5 cups.

For 1 Cup: Use 1 cup water + ½ tsp. oil. For Beef or Chicken, use 2 tsp. soup mix, OR 1 soup/bouillon cube (+ 1 drop liquid smoke for Beef). For Turkey, use 1 tsp. chicken + 1 tsp. beef soup mixes + pinch garlic powder + 1 drop liquid smoke + dash pepper. Use in *Seitan* (p. 111).

Parve Flavors:

Beef: 5 drops liquid smoke + 3⅓ Tbs. beef soup mix, OR 5 beef bouillon or soup cubes.
   (For a little different flavor, use half beef + half onion or mushroom soup mixes.)

Chicken: 3⅓ Tbs. chicken soup mix, OR 5 chicken bouillon or soup cubes.

Turkey: 5 tsp. chicken soup mix + 5 tsp. beef soup mix + ¼ tsp. garlic powder + 5 drops liquid smoke + ⅛ tsp. black pepper.

✡ ✡

Parve Soy Crumbles

1 cup water

4 tsp. beef soup mix

1 tsp. browning sauce

1 tsp. avocado oil (or other vegetable oil)

¼ tsp. liquid smoke

1 cup + 1 Tbs. dry TVP®

Step 1   Put all but TVP® in pot or micro bowl. Bring to a boil, stir to dissolve soup mix.

Step 2   Turn off heat and stir in TVP®, let sit 5-10 minutes. Stir vigorously with a fork.

Step 3   Use as-is, refrigerate, or freeze. Makes 2 cups, or equivalent to 1 lb. meat.

Seitan (Imitation Meat)

Parve Broth (p. 110)**: 4-5 cups** (for boiling/crock pot only)

1 Parve Flavoring (below. Note: Only Chicken and Turkey are designed for stuffing)

1½ cups vital wheat gluten (wheat gluten flour or vital gluten)

❀ Step 1   <u>Boiling/Crock Pot</u>- Put 4 cups *Broth* in pot, 5 cups in crock. (Broth turns to gravy.)

❀ Step 2   In bowl, quickly blend gluten with *Parve Flavoring*. Knead and stretch 3 minutes.

❀ Step 3   Shape into desired form. ***Breasts:*** Divide into 4 patties, and stretch them out as thin as possible; ***Stuffed Breast*s:** Stretch from center out (don't tear), wrap around food, pinch shut, coat with olive oil; ***Loaves:*** Divide into 3 and place in mini loaf pans; ***Burgers/Cutlets*** ***(Patties):*** Divide into 8 thin patties; ***Nuggets:*** Roll into a log and cut into ½ inch slices; ***Meat Balls:*** Prepare and mix-in desired seasoning, roll into 1-inch balls. Cook Seitan right away (or wrap in plastic and freeze).

❀ Step 4   Boil or bake as desired. **<u>To Boil</u>**- Bring broth to boil. Add Seitan, simmer covered, flipping every 15 minutes: ***Loaves/Breasts:*** (*Unstuffed only*) 1 hour; ***Patties:*** 45 minutes; ***Nuggets:*** ½ hour.

<u>In Crock Pot</u>- All: (*Unstuffed only*) Cook on Low 4-5 hours, or High 2-3 hours. Flip after ½ hour.

<u>To Bake</u>- Put in well-greased pan (**seam-down if *Stuffed***). Coat well with oil, thick sauce or *Parve Meat Drippings* (p. 84), but no thin liquids. (Bread if desired, spray with oil.) Cover with foil. Bake at 350º F: ***Loaves/Stuffed Breasts***: 1 hour; ***Breasts/Meatballs/Patties***: 50 minutes; ***Nuggets***: 15-20 minutes. Don't overcook! Seitan keeps cooking after being removed from heat. (Note: Never microwave raw Seitan. Re-heat cooked Seitan only until warm.) Makes 1¼ lb.

Parve Flavorings (Blend dry ingredients in a bowl, wet in a separate bowl.)

Chicken: 1 cup chicken *Parve Broth* (+ 2 Tbs. if baking) + 2 Tbs. olive oil + 3 Tbs. instant mashed potato flakes + 2 Tbs. chicken soup mix + 1½ tsp. garlic powder.

Turkey: 1 cup turkey *Parve Broth* (+ 2 Tbs. if baking) + 2 Tbs. olive oil + 3 Tbs. potato flakes + 1 Tbs. chicken soup mix + 1 Tbs. beef soup mix + 1 tsp. garlic powder.

Beef: ¾ cup beef *Parve Broth* + ⅓ cup tomato sauce + 1¼ tsp. browning sauce + 1 tsp. liquid smoke + 1 tsp. *Fishless Worcestershire* (p. 93) + 1 tsp. shortening + 1 tsp. garlic powder + ½ tsp. onion powder + 2 Tbs. beef soup mix + 2 Tbs. raw quick tapioca.

For *Burgers* & *Meatballs* add 2 Tbs. *Broth*. (Grilled *Burgers* add 1 Tbs. liquid smoke).

Ham: ⅞ cup chicken *Parve Broth* + 1 tsp. melted shortening + ¼ cup tomato sauce + 1 Tbs. liquid smoke + 1 tsp. salt + 1½ tsp. garlic powder + 1 Tbs. sugar.

Classic Meatballs

"Meat" =
$\begin{cases} \textbf{D-} \text{ 1 pkg. soy burger + 2 tsp. avocado oil.} \\ \textbf{P-} \text{ 1 pkg. } \textit{parve} \text{ soy burger + 2 tsp. avocado oil.} \\ \textbf{M-} \text{ 1 lb. kosher ground beef or turkey burger.} \end{cases}$

¼ cup plain bread crumbs

1 beaten egg

salt (optional to taste)

black pepper (optional to taste)

Step 1   Knead together all ingredients. Roll into 1-1¼-inch balls. Preheat oven to 350º F.

Step 2   Bake on greased cookie sheet 20 minutes (preferable for D and P), or microwave in glass casserole 5-7 minutes. (For M, until juices run clear.) Makes 24-32.

✡ ✡

Italian Sausage

"Meat" =
$\begin{cases} \textbf{D-} \text{ 1 pkg. (2 cups) raw soy burger (or soy crumbles) + 1 Tbs. oil.} \\ \textbf{P-} \text{ 1 pkg. (2 cups) raw soy burger (or soy crumbles) + 1 Tbs. oil.} \\ \textbf{M-} \text{ 1 lb. kosher ground beef or turkey burger.} \end{cases}$

¼-½ tsp. red pepper flakes

¾ tsp. caraway seeds

¾ tsp. *Italian Seasoning* (p. 434)

1 tsp. garlic powder

½ tsp. salt

1 tsp. black pepper

⅛ tsp. cayenne pepper (optional- for spicier sausage)

Step 1   Knead ingredients together, and shape into 8 patties, balls, or links, or crumble.

Step 2   Brown in a frying pan, or microwave 2½ minutes in batches of 4, covered loosely with kosher wax paper. If using real meat, flip and cook 2½ more minutes until juices run clear.

Add to spaghetti sauce for a meatball sandwich, or crumble for pizza. Makes 1 lb.

Goetta Sausage

½ cup plain uncooked oatmeal

½ cup water

"Meat" =
- **D-** ½ pkg. soy burger, OR 1 cup soy crumbles + 3 Tbs. avocado oil.
- **P-** ½ pkg. soy burger, OR 1 cup soy crumbles + 3 Tbs. avocado oil.
- **M-** ½ lb. kosher ground beef or turkey burger + 2 Tbs. avocado oil.

⅛ tsp. onion powder

⅜ tsp. salt

½ tsp. minced onion or dried minced onion flakes

¼ tsp. ground sage

⅛ tsp. ground nutmeg

⅛ tsp. cayenne pepper

⅞ tsp. coarse ground black pepper

Step 1   Combine oatmeal and water and cook either on stove or microwave, 1½ minutes.

Step 2   Add last ingredients, knead well. Shape into 4-inch patties (¼ inch, no thicker).

Step 3   Ideally, fry in a well-greased frying pan until brown, crispy and firm. (Microwave in glass casserole in sets of 4 covered on high 2½ minutes. Flip. Cook 2½ more minutes, until starting to brown and crisp for D or P, or until juices run clear for M.) Makes 4 servings.

✡ ✡

Parve Chopped Beef Kidney

½ cup *Parve Chopped Liver* (p. 139- use browned onion)

1½ tsp. plain *Bread Crumbs* (p. 116)

1½ tsp. beaten egg

vegetable oil spray

Step 1   Blend first 3 ingredients into a paste, press evenly in a greased loaf pan.

Step 2   Spray with oil. Bake 10 minutes in preheated 425° F oven, take out and let cool.

Step 3   Turn oven to 350° F, slice into ½-inch cubes. Stir, then bake 10 minutes to firm.

Let cool. Cut or crumble into large irregular pieces. Use right away or refrigerate up to 1 week. (Being delicate, it doesn't freeze well.) Makes ½ cup.

(🥕 for P or D) (🥛 for M)   **Braunschweiger Sausage**   🥛

"Liver" = {
  D- 1 tsp. onion salt + 1¾ cups *Parve Chopped Liver* (p. 139).
  P- 1 tsp. onion salt + 1¾ cups *Parve Chopped Liver* (p. 139).
  M- 1 (12 oz.) (1¾ cups) tub real kosher chopped liver + ¼ tsp. salt.
}

1 tsp. liquid smoke (or more to taste)

dash ground nutmeg

dash ground cloves

⅛ tsp. ground allspice

⅛ tsp. black pepper

✡ Step 1   Combine all ingredients in a bowl, blend thoroughly, and shape into a loaf.

✡ Step 2   Wrap with foil and refrigerate 24 hours. Makes about a ¾ lb. sausage.

✡ ✡

🥛   **Country Sausage**   🥛

"Meat" = {
  D- ½ pkg. soy burger + 3 Tbs. avocado oil.
  P- ½ pkg. *parve* soy burger + 3 Tbs. avocado oil.
  M- ½ lb. kosher ground beef or turkey burger + 2 Tbs. avocado oil.
}

½ cup bread crumbs or matzah (matzo) meal

2 tsp. lemon juice

1 tsp. ground sage

⅛ tsp. ground marjoram

⅛ tsp. ground thyme

½ tsp. coarse ground black pepper

½ tsp. salt

⅛ tsp. ground nutmeg

✡ Step 1   Combine ingredients, knead well. Crumble, or shape into 8 patties or 8 links.

✡ Step 2   Brown in pan, or microwave covered loosely in batches of 4 patties or links 2½ minutes (for M, flip patties and cook 2½ minutes, until juices run clear). Makes 4 servings.

Mexican Chorizo Sausage

"Meat" =
- **D-** 1 pkg. (2 cups) imitation hamburger crumbles + 2 Tbs. avocado oil.
- **P-** 1 pkg. (2 cups) *parve* soy crumbles + 2 Tbs. avocado oil.
- **M-** 1 lb. kosher ground beef or turkey (browned and drained).

1 Tbs. avocado oil (other vegetable oil can be used)

¾ cup minced onion

1¾ tsp. *Chili Powder* (p. 434)

1¾ tsp. slightly crushed oregano leaves

½ tsp. ground cumin

¼ tsp. ground cinnamon

¼ tsp. black pepper, OR ⅛ tsp. cayenne pepper (for spicy sausage)

¼ tsp. salt

3⅓ Tbs. vinegar

1 cup *Taco Bell® Style Enchirito® Sauce* (p. 96)

Step 1   Combine all ingredients except sauce, heat in pan or microwave 5 minutes.

Step 2   Add sauce and boil uncovered until liquid is gone, stirring often. (Drain if desired.)

Use wherever chorizo filling is called for in Mexican recipes. For hotter sausage, add ¼ tsp. pepper sauce. Can freeze in small batches. Makes a little over 2 cups, or 1 lb.

✿ ✿

Taco Bell® Style Taco Meat

"Meat" =
- **D-** 1 pkg. (2 cups) imitation hamburger crumbles + 1 Tbs. avocado oil.
- **P-** 1 pkg. (2 cups) *parve* soy crumbles + 1 Tbs. avocado oil.
- **M-** 1 lb. kosher ground beef or turkey (browned and drained).

1 batch (slightly over ¼ cup) *Taco Bell® Style Taco Seasoning Mix* (p. 81)

¾ cup water if cooking on stove, OR ½ cup water if microwaving

Blend ingredients thoroughly. Cook 5 minutes, or until thickened, done and hot. Makes 1 lb.

Toppings, Wraps & Crusts

Salad Croutons

11 slices slightly stale or dry bread (cut into ¼-½ inch cubes)

vegetable oil cooking spray

optional seasonings: garlic powder, paprika, oregano, basil or other herbs

- Step 1   Preheat oven to 325º F, spray a cookie sheet with oil, evenly spread cubes on it.
- Step 2   Spray cubes with oil, (sprinkle on seasoning, if desired) stir and spray again.
- Step 3   Bake 15-20 minutes, stir occasionally, until lightly toasted (but not dark brown).

Let cool and store sealed in zipper bags. These are just as good as store-bought, and you can adjust the seasonings you like to taste. Makes 4 cups without crusts, 7 cups with crust.

Fresh **"Bread Crumbs"**, can be made by finely chopping unseasoned croutons (with crusts) in a food chopper or blender. Store in the same manner. For Italian style crumbs add ¼ tsp. garlic powder and 2 tsp. *Italian Seasoning* (p. 434). Makes about 2 cups coarse crumbs.

✿ ✿

Wonton Wrappers

1 lightly beaten egg

¾ tsp. salt

½ cup water (divided)

2 cups flour (plus extra for sprinkling)

- Step 1   Combine egg, salt, and ¼ cup water and blend well. Put flour in a separate bowl
- Step 2   Make a pit in flour and put in egg mixture. Add water as needed to form a dough.
- Step 3   Form dough into a ball and knead until smooth, cover bowl and let it rest ½ hour.
- Step 4   Roll dough out on lightly floured surface until thin, but uniform with no thin areas.
- Step 5   Lightly flour surface of dough and cut it into 3½-inch squares.
- Step 6   Use right away, or place layers of plastic wrap between wrappers and stack in a zipper bag. Refrigerate for a short time, or freeze until ready to use.

Extremely versatile, these can be used not only for Wontons, but for Egg Rolls and Pizza Rolls, Pierogies, Potstickers, Ravioli, Crab Rangoons, and even in Kreplach recipes. Makes 24 wrappers.

Quiche or Pot Pie Crusts

1¼ cup flour (if a top crust for a pot pie is desired, add ¾ cup flour)

slightly rounded ½ tsp. salt (for top crust, add ⅜ tsp. salt)

6 Tbs. room temperature *parve* margarine (for top crust, add ¼ cup extra)

1 large slightly beaten egg (for top crust, add another small slightly beaten egg)

✤ Step 1   Mix together flour and salt, cut in margarine until mixture forms coarse crumbs.

✤ Step 2   Add egg, stirring with a fork until it clings together, and shape into a smooth ball.

✤ Step 3   Roll out into a 12-inch circle (plus another 9-inch circle for top crust) on floured surface, ⅛ inch thick. Let "rest". (Can now freeze for future use.)

✤ Step 4   Put in a 9-inch pie plate, pressing lightly into pan, flute edges with fingers or fork.

✤ Step 6   Make tiny punctures in crust so steam can escape (especially if microwaving).

✤ Step 7   To prebake crust- Make pricks in bottom. Bake in preheated 450º F oven 10-12 minutes, or microwave on 70% power 4-6 minutes, until dry (don't let burn). Let cool.

(Store frozen or refrigerated until ready to use. Fill with desired fillings such as eggs blended with omelet fillings, or meat and gravy with vegetables (then top with top crust, if desired. Prick top crust before baking). This can also be made into several 3-inch single-sized mini pies, pastry can also be cut, filled, and used for crust-enclosed foods. Makes a 9-inch pie crust.

✡ ✡

Taco Salad Bowls

6 aluminum foil sheets, OR 6 (6-inch) microwave plastic or glass bowls

avocado oil (other vegetable oil can be used)

6 extra-large (12-inch) flour tortillas (preferably thin)

✤ Step 1   To Bake- Shape foil into 6-inch balls, put on cookie sheet. To Microwave- Set a bowl on a microwavable plate.

✤ Step 2   Coat tortillas thoroughly with oil and drape over foil balls or microwave bowls.

✤ Step 3   To Bake- Put in a 350º F oven 10-15 minutes or until no longer soft. (Don't let brown.) To Microwave- Heat each on high in 30 second increments until starting to harden.

In the original recipe, tortillas are placed between two strainers and deep-fried. Makes 6 bowls.

Dessert Ingredients

Dessert Taco Bowls

4 aluminum foil sheets, OR 4 (4-inch) microwave plastic or glass bowls

avocado oil or vegetable oil spray (preferably *parve* butter-flavored)

4 small-sized (7-9 inch) flour tortillas (preferably thin)

2 Tbs. *Cinnamon Sugar* (p. 434), **OR ¼ cup sifted powdered sugar**

✸ Step 1 To Bake- Shape foil into 4 4-inch balls and set in a 8 x 8 inch square baking pan. To Microwave- Set a microwave-safe bowl on a microwavable plate.

✸ Step 2 Coat tortilla sides well with oil, sprinkle both sides with sugar. Repeat for each.

✸ Step 3 After tortillas are sprinkled, drape over foil balls or microwave bowls.

✸ Step 4 To Bake- Put in a 350° F oven 10 minutes, or until no longer soft. (Don't let brown.) To Microwave- Heat each on high in 30 second increments until starting to harden.

These can be filled with ice cream, pudding, whipped cream, fruit or all of these. Makes 4 bowls.

✧ ✧

Graham Cracker Pie Crust

1 cup graham cracker crumbs

¾ tsp. ground cinnamon

⅓ cup melted *parve* margarine

✸ Step 1 Blend ingredients. Press into bottom and sides of a 9-inch glass pie pan (press an equal size pan on top to even out). For Cheesecakes- Press into an 8 x 8 pan (bottom only).

✸ Step 2 To pre-bake, put in 375° F oven 10 minutes, or microwave 2½ minutes. Makes 1.

☺   ☺   ☺

For **"Chocolate Graham Cracker Crust"**, add ¼ cup cocoa, 3⅓ Tbs. sugar and 1 Tbs. extra *parve* margarine in Step 1. For ice cream sandwiches- Press flat in 8 x 8 inch baking pan. Cut in rectangles and bake 20 minutes. Makes 1 (8 x 8 or 9 inch) crust, or 8 crusts for 4 sandwiches.

☺   ☺   ☺

For **"Mini Graham Cracker Crusts"**, double either of above recipes. Press mixture into liners in tins and bake. (For mini cheesecakes, do not double- press into bottom only.) Makes 12.

Flaky Pie Crusts

1¼ cup flour (if a top or lattice crust is desired, add ¾ cup flour)

dash salt (for top or lattice crust, add a dash salt)

7½ Tbs. warm *parve* margarine (for top or lattice crust, add 4½ Tbs. margarine)

3¾ tsp. cold water (for top or lattice crust, add 2¼ tsp. cold water)

❀ Step 1 Mix together flour and salt, cut in margarine, until mixture forms coarse crumbs, then add water to flour mixture. Stir with a fork until pastry begins to cling together.

❀ Step 2 Shape dough into a smooth ball and roll out on a floured surface into a 12-13 inch circle about ⅛ inch thick. Set a few minutes to "rest". (It can now be frozen if desired.)

❀ Step 3 Put dough in a 9-inch pie plate, press in to form, and flute edges with fingers (helps catch overflows) or press perimeter with a fork. Preferably, make tiny pricks in crust.

❀ Step 4 To pre-bake crust- Make pricks in bottom. Bake in preheated 450° F oven 10 minutes, or microwave on 70% power 4-6 minutes, until dry (don't let burn). Cool completely.

Makes 1 single 9-inch crust, (if desired use parenthesized amounts for extra top crust). For tarts or mini pies, cut dough in 6-inch circles and press into foil-lined muffin tins. Bake until firm.

✡ ✡

Nabisco® Style Famous Chocolate Wafers®

1 beaten egg

4½ tsp. vegetable oil

8 tsp. water

¼ tsp. baking soda

1½ cups flour

¾ cup sugar

1 tsp. baking powder

¼ cup cocoa

❀ Step 1 Heat oven to 350° F. Blend all ingredients. Roll out to ⅛-inch on floured surface.

❀ Step 2 Cut out with 3-inch round cutter or jar, and set on greased cookie sheet.

❀ Step 3 Bake 10 minutes until no longer mushy (do not let harden). Let cool.

Use for Ice Box Cake (p. 387), or eat plain as-is. Makes 20 large wafer cookies.

Parve Ready-To-Use Icing

½ cup *parve* **margarine**

1 tsp. vanilla (or other flavored extract)

1½ Tbs. corn syrup

1 Tbs. *Parve* **Cream** (p. 85)

3½ cups pre-sifted powdered sugar

food coloring (optional)

optional add-ins: 2 tsp. grated peel, OR 1½ cups coconut or tiny *parve* candies

Step 1   Beat first 4 ingredients together until fluffy, gradually blend in last ingredients.

Step 2   Use, or store refrigerated in airtight container. (Re-whip if needed. If it dries out after a few months, simply add a bit of water and stir.) Makes 1⅔ cups (or 1 can icing).

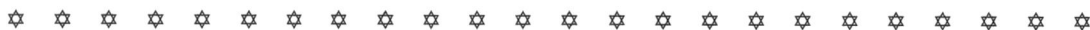

✿ ✿

Parve Chocolate Ready-To-Use Icing

½ cup *parve* **margarine**

1 tsp. vanilla (or other flavored extract)

1½ Tbs. corn syrup

2 Tbs. *Parve* **Cream** (p. 85– for darker chocolate add 1 tsp. more)

3½ cups pre-sifted powdered sugar

6 Tbs. cocoa (for darker chocolate add ¼ cup more)

Step 1   Beat together first 4 ingredients until fluffy, and gradually beat in last ingredients.

Step 2   Refrigerate in an airtight container to store, or until using. (Re-whip if needed. If it dries out after a few months, simply add a bit of water and stir.) Makes 1⅔ cups (or 1 can icing).

Parve Cream Cheese Ready-To-Use Icing

2 Tbs. *parve* **margarine**

½ cup *parve* **imitation cream cheese** (do not use homemade)

¾ tsp. *Parve* **Cream** (p. 85)

½ tsp. vanilla (or other flavored extract)

3¼ cups powdered sugar

Step 1   Melt first 2 ingredients in a pot on low stirring until smooth. Put in a mixing bowl.

Step 2   Add Creamand vanilla, gradually beat in sugar until smooth and well-blended.

Step 3   Use, or refrigerate in an airtight container to store. (Heat slightly, or leave out at room temperature and re-whip if necessary.) Makes 1½ cups (about 1 can icing).

✡ ✡

Parve Whipped Cream Icing

¼ cup cold water

1½ tsp. *parve* **plain kosher gelatin** (often billed "unsweetened clear diet jell")

½ pint (1 cup) shaken *parve* **liquid non-dairy whip topping** (thaw if frozen)

¼ cup powdered sugar

½ tsp. vanilla

food coloring (optional)

Step 1   Chill bowl and beaters. Blend water and gelatin well in a pot and let sit 5 minutes.

Step 2   Heat gelatin on very low heat until dissolved, then let stand warm 10 minutes.

Step 3   As gelatin stands, put whip, sugar, vanilla (and coloring, if desired) in chilled bowl, and beat slowly until it starts to get thick.

Step 4   Add gelatin while beating whip. Beat until stiff about 8 minutes on fast speed.

Step 5   Put in piping tube and decorate cake, then freeze a few hours as this will allow the icing to remain firm. (It is preferable to keep cake refrigerated afterwards.)

Similar to delicious bakery "professional type" decorating icing. Must be used immediately, as it doesn't store very well. Leftovers can be frozen and used as *parve* ice cream. Makes 2 cups.

Parve Coconut-Pecan Ready-To-Use Icing

½ cup chopped pecans

1½ cups grated coconut

¾ cups packed brown sugar

¼ cup corn starch

¼ cup room temperature *parve* margarine

½ cup *Parve* Cream (p. 85)

¼ cup corn syrup

½ tsp. vanilla extract

Step 1   Spread nuts and coconut on a cookie sheet, bake at 300° F about 20-25 minutes (stirring every 5-10 minutes) until lightly toasted. (Do not let them burn.) Set aside.

Step 2   Blend sugar and corn starch in a pot, add last 4 ingredients, nuts and coconut.

Step 3   Put on medium heat, stirring constantly until starting to thicken when dropped from a spoon (about 10 minutes), take off heat. (Don't overcook— it becomes a brick!) Thickens as normal once it cools. Use or store refrigerated in airtight container (warm slightly to spread).

Use on *Devil's Food Cake* (p. 389) for a German chocolate cake "to die for"! Makes 2 cups.

✿ ✿

Fruit Syrup/Flavored Syrup

½ cup fruit juice, OR ½ tsp. favorite extract (or more if needed)

¾ cup water

1 cup sugar

4 drops food coloring (optional)

Step 1   Put ingredients in a small pot, stir to dissolve sugar. (Good fruits: Lime with green coloring or lemon with yellow. Flavors: Peppermint with green or red.) Bring to boil and simmer 5 minutes stirring constantly. (Don't heat longer or hotter— it will become one giant, hard lollypop!)

Step 2   Quickly pour in airtight container. Refrigerate. (It thickens when cooled.)

Stir or shake before each use. Great in Phosphate Drinks (p. 372), or over Ice Cream. Makes ¾-1 cup.

Berry Syrup

1 cup berries (drain any liquid)

¼ cup corn syrup

3 tsp. sugar

⅓ cup water or drained berry juice

⊛ Step 1   Put berries and corn syrup in a blender and puree until it reaches a smooth consistency.

⊛ Step 2   Put mixture in a small pot, add sugar and water, then bring to a boil stirring.

⊛ Step 3   Cook about 5 minutes but no longer. (Any longer and it becomes too thick.)

⊛ Step 4   Pour in an airtight container and let cool completely. Store in the refrigerator.

Use hot or cold for desserts or pancakes. Makes ½ cup.

✿ ✿

Parve Chocolate Malt Syrup

½ cup cocoa

1 cup sugar

1 cup dried barley malt extract powder

1½ cup water

⊛ Step 1   Combine cocoa, sugar and barley malt in a bowl, and blend together thoroughly.

⊛ Step 2   Bring water to rolling boil in a saucepan, then take off heat.

⊛ Step 3   Gradually add cocoa mixture to boiling water and stir until smooth and well blended.

⊛ Step 4   Reduce heat to very low and simmer mixture 5 minutes, stirring constantly.

⊛ Step 5   Remove from heat, and let cool completely, stirring occasionally.

⊛ Step 6   When completely cool, pour into an airtight container and store refrigerated.

Use for milk shakes, malted soy milk, on ice cream sundaes, or whatever you like. Makes 1 cup.

Kosher certified barley malt extracts can be found and ordered on the Internet.

Imitation Cream of Coconut

½ cup water

2 cups sugar

1½ *Parve Cream* (p. 85)

2 tsp. coconut extract

Step 1   Combine water, sugar and Cream in a pot and blend until sugar is dissolved.

Step 2   Bring to a boil, reduce heat and simmer 5 minutes stirring constantly.

Step 3   Take off heat and let cool completely, stir in extract and blend well.

Step 4   Pour into an airtight container and store refrigerated. No re-heating is necessary.

Real cream of coconut (which isn't coconut cream) congeals and needs heating. This recipe tastes the same and can be added to cold drinks. Makes 2 cups, or equivalent to 1 (15 oz.) can.

✧ ✧

Parve Caramel

½ cup room temperature *parve* margarine

⅔ cup *Parve Cream* (p. 85)

¼ cup corn syrup

1 tsp. vanilla extract

1½ cups packed brown sugar

½ cup flour

Step 1   Grease 8 x 8 or 7 x 5 baking dish well with oil. Set aside. Melt margarine in a pot.

Step 2   Add next 3 ingredients to pot, then combine and add dry ingredients. Blend well.

Step 3   Cook (always stirring) on medium-low 10 minutes or until stringy if spoon is lifted.

Step 4   Spread mixture evenly into greased baking dish and refrigerate overnight.

Step 5   Use as-is or cut into cubes, freeze until firm and wrap in plastic wrap squares for individual candies. No matter how it's used, keep refrigerated, it remains sticky and oozes.

Normally made with condensed milk. Eat as-is, melt and dip apples in it, or make *Parve Samoas*® (p. 377) or *Parve Cracker Jack*® *Style Snacks* (p. 125). Makes 1½ cups.

Snacks and Appetizers

Snacks

Parve Cracker Jack® Style Snacks

¼ cup unsalted roasted peanuts

1 quart plain unsalted *parve* popped corn

½ cup *Parve Caramel* (previous page)

Step 1   Combine peanuts and popcorn in a bowl, blending well.

Step 2   Heat caramel in a pot or microwave safe bowl until completely melted.

Step 3   Pour mixture over peanuts and popcorn, and stir to coat completely.

Step 4   Bake 1 hour in a preheated 250° F oven, stirring and breaking up clumps every 15 minutes.

Step 5   Let cool completely, and crumble into 4 individual plastic zipper bags.

Great snack for *Shabbat* when almost everyone has had meat. The only thing that could make this more authentic is to buy 4 gumball machine prizes and hide them in the bags! Makes 4 servings.

For just plain caramel corn, omit the peanuts. If you don't care whether this is *parve* or not, just go out and buy the real thing- it's kosher, but dairy.

Stovetop-Popped Corn

2 tsp. avocado oil (other oil can be used- even olive oil, which is so delicious!)

2 Tbs. fresh popcorn kernels

⅛ tsp. salt (optional), **OR 1 favorite Popcorn Seasoning** (optional, listed below)

Step 1 — Blend oil and popcorn in 1½ qt. pot, coat pot well with oil, and put on lid.

Step 2 — Heat on high, and swirl pot occasionally. Cock lid at an angle to release steam.

Step 3 — When corn starts to pop, turn electric off, or set gas to medium. Shake as it pops.

Step 4 — As popping slows, remove from burner. Add salt and shake to blend. Makes 1 qt.

Serve hot with melted *Herb Butters* (p. 438) if desired. Use larger pot for larger amounts. For larger quantities: 2 qt. = ¼ cup corn + 4 tsp. oil + ¼ tsp. salt; 3 qt. = 6 Tbs. corn + 2 Tbs. oil + ⅜ tsp. salt; 1 gallon = ½ cup corn + 8 tsp. oil + ½ tsp. salt.

Popcorn Seasonings

Fix plain stovetop-popped corn, drizzle 1 Tbs. melted *parve* margarine over it and stir to coat well. Blend ingredients below, sprinkle over corn and stir well to coat. (For plain microwaved or air-popped corn, spray with vegetable oil spray and shake to coat before adding seasoning.)

Cajun: ½ tsp. paprika + ¼ tsp. lemon pepper + ½ tsp. onion powder + ½ tsp. garlic powder + ⅛ tsp. cayenne pepper.

Chili: ¼ tsp. ground oregano + ½ tsp. garlic powder + 1½ tsp. *Chili Powder* (p. 434)

Pesto: Combine ¾ tsp. crushed basil + ¼ tsp. parsley flakes + ¼ tsp. garlic powder, + 2 Tbs. kosher Parmesan Cheese for D, or 1-2 Tbs. *Parve Parmesan Cheese* (p. 108) for P or M.

For **"Movie Theater Type Popcorn"**, coat 1 qt. plain *Stovetop-Popped Corn* with:

"Butter" =
- **D-** 1-2 Tbs. melted real sweet butter + ⅛ tsp. salt (or to taste).
- **P-** 1 Tbs. melted *Parve Imitation Butter* (p. 84, preferably salted).
- **M-** 1 Tbs. melted *Parve Imitation Butter* (p. 84, preferably salted).

Hawaiian Coconut Chips

1 fresh coconut (shelled, peeled, and cut in half)

½ tsp. salt, OR 1 tsp. sugar

- Step 1   Slice coconut from meat into paper-thin chips using vegetable peeler.
- Step 2   Spread in a single layer on a cookie sheet, sprinkle with salt or sugar.
- Step 3   Bake in preheated 325° oven ½ hour or until crisp and brown. Let cool and store in airtight jar 2-3 weeks, (maybe longer if kept refrigerated. Makes 3 cups, 6-8 servings.

✫ ✫

Sweet Potato Chips

1 lb. sweet potatoes (peeled and sliced into paper-thin chips)

ice water

avocado oil for frying (other vegetable oil can be used)

1 tsp. garlic salt or salt, OR 2 tsp. powdered or *Cinnamon Sugar* (p. 434)

- Step 1   Put sweet potato chips in ice water and chill 45 minutes, then drain and pat dry.
- Step 2   Heat oil in frying pan or deep fryer, fry chips until browned, drain on paper towels.
- Step 3   Sprinkle with salt or sugar. Store refrigerated. Makes about 4 cups, 8-10 servings.

✫ ✫

Taco Bell® Style Pintos N' Cheese®

2 cups hot Refried Beans (p. 103)

½-1 cup *Taco Bell® Style Enchirito® Sauce* (p. 96)

"Cheese" =
- D- ½ cup finely grated kosher Cheddar cheese.
- P- ½ cup grated *parve* American or Cheddar cheese.
- M- ½ cup grated *parve* American or Cheddar cheese.

- Step 1   Put beans in 4 microwave safe bowls and spoon sauce over beans.
- Step 2   Top with "Cheese" and heat until "Cheese" melts. Makes 4 generous servings.

Taco Bell® Style Nachos

1 cup *Taco Bell® Style Nacho Cheese Sauce* (p. 98)

4 cups fresh small-sized tortilla chips

❀ Step 1   Put cheese sauce in a pot or microwave safe bowl.

❀ Step 2   Heat sauce stirring on low heat or 1-minute increments until smooth and hot.

❀ Step 3   Pour sauce into 4 crocks or small bowls, and microwave chips 30 seconds.

❀ Step 4   Divide chips into 4 servings and place next to crocks on a plate. Serve hot.

Cheese sauce can also be drizzled over chips instead put into crocks. Makes 4 generous servings.

✡ ✡

Parve Nabisco® Style Cheese Tid-Bits®

¼ cup *parve* **margarine** (melted)

1 cup grated *parve* **Cheddar or American soy cheese**

¼ tsp. mustard powder

⅛ tsp. cayenne pepper

½ tsp. baking powder

½ tsp. salt

¾ cup flour

❀ Step 1   Preheat oven to 450° F. Blend ingredients, knead into a smooth dough, and put in a pastry tube with a round ¼-inch nozzle (½ inch can be used, but will take longer to bake).

❀ Step 2   Squeeze dough out in rows (¼ inch apart) on a greased cookie sheet.

❀ Step 3   Cut rows with a plastic knife in 1 inch increments. (Pieces should be 1 x ¼ inch.)

❀ Step 4   Bake 10 minutes. Stir and bake 5 more minutes, or until hardened. (Do not burn!)

These small capsule-shaped crackers date back to the 60s, and are no longer being made. They also are an ingredient in the old snack on the next page, "Nabisco ® Style Doo Dads®". Makes 264 tiny crackers (2 cups).

(✎on peanuts only)   **Nabisco® Style Doo Dads®**   (▯ peanuts only)

8 tsp. melted *parve* margarine

1 Tbs. *Fishless Worcestershire Sauce* (p. 92)

½ tsp. onion salt

¾ tsp. garlic salt

½ tsp. ground rosemary

1½ tsp. sugar

¾ cups shredded wheat squares cereal

¾ cups shredded rice squares cereal

¼ cup unsalted dry roasted peanuts

¼ cup small pretzel sticks

¼ cup *Parve Nabisco® Style Cheese Tid-Bits*® crackers (previous page)

✼	Step 1	Preheat oven to 250°F. Blend first 6 ingredients thoroughly.
✼	Step 2	Add cereals, mix until well coated, and spread out evenly on a cookie sheet.
✼	Step 3	Bake 20 minutes. Take out of oven, stir, then bake 20 more minutes.
✼	Step 4	Take out, add last 3 ingredients, and stir until well mixed.
✼	Step 5	Spread mixture out evenly and bake 20 more minutes. (Do not let burn.)
✼	Step 6	Take out of oven and let cool, then put in an airtight container or zipper bag.

The original is no longer available. It was produced back in the 1960s for about 30 years. Makes 2¼ cups.

☺   ☺   ☺

For **"Spicy Nabisco® Style Doo Dads®"**, omit rosemary, halve the Worcestershire, and add 1½ tsp. *Chili Powder* (p. 434), 1 Tbs. hot pepper sauce, ¼ tsp. cayenne pepper and ⅛ tsp. ground oregano in Step 1.

Pepperidge Farm® Style Mixed Suits®

2 tsp. onion powder

1 tsp. garlic powder

1 tsp. baking powder

1 tsp. salt

1½ cups flour

¼ cup sesame seeds

½ cup *parve* margarine (room temperature)

¼ cup water

½ tsp. liquid smoke

Step 1   Combine and blend the first 5 ingredients thoroughly, then blend in margarine.

Step 2   Add water and liquid smoke and knead into a smooth dough.

Step 3   Refrigerate dough ½-hour until firm.

Step 4   Roll dough out onto a lightly floured flat surface to ¼ inch thick.

Step 5   Place sheet of dough in greased 10 x 8 inch baking pan, pressing dough evenly until it fits nicely.

Step 6   Cut into 1-inch squares with a plastic knife.

Step 7   Bake 10 minutes in a preheated 450° F oven. Take out of oven and stir.

Step 8   Put back in oven and bake 5-7 more minutes, or until edges are barely starting to brown. (Do not let burn!)

These were short-lived in the mid-70s, but so addictive. Makes 140 tiny crackers, or 3 cups.

In Step 6, tiny 1-inch candy cutters in the shapes of hearts, diamonds, clubs and spades can also be used, (which were the shapes of the crackers- hence the name). Remove excess dough, rolling and cutting out pieces until all dough is used. Set on a greased cookie sheet and do Steps 7-8 as normal.

(as a snack) (as a meal) **Egg Rolls** (snack) (meal)

½ tsp. ground ginger

1 tsp. soy sauce

1 Tbs. minced fresh cilantro (Chinese parsley or fresh coriander)

2 finely chopped green onions (¾ cup)

1 cup finely chopped shredded cabbage

1 cup finely chopped bean sprouts

1 batch (24) 3 x 3-inch *Wonton Wrappers* (p. 116)

water

cooking oil spray for baking

Step 1   Mix together first 6 ingredients in a bowl, and blend thoroughly.

Step 2   Put a bit of filling in the middle of each wonton, spreading it near the edges.

Step 3   Seal edge of each wrapper with a bit of water, and pinch closed tightly.

Step 4   Place egg rolls on a greased cookie sheet, and spray them with oil.

Step 5   Bake in a preheated 450° F oven 10 minutes on each side, until both sides are lightly browned.

Serve hot with dipping sauces such as *Hot Chinese Mustard* (p. 440) or *Sweet & Sour* Sauce (p. 94), if desired. Freeze raw for quick snacks, or for use in *Easy Wonton Soup* (p. 156). Makes 24 small-sized egg rolls.

An alternative is to microwave them. Lay them on a microwave safe plate, and microwave in 1-minute increments, until dough is firm and nearly getting hard. Do not let them burn.

☺   ☺   ☺

Alternative Fillings:

For **"Chicken" Egg Rolls"**, use half the amount of cabbage and bean sprouts, and add 1 cup finely chopped *parve* imitation chicken chunks for D or P, or for M 1 cup finely chopped cooked kosher chicken as filling.

For **"Pork Egg Rolls"**, use half the amount of cabbage and bean sprouts, and add 1 cup *parve* imitation sausage crumbles or minced *parve* imitation ham for D or P, or 1 cup finely chopped *Country Sausage* (p. 114) or minced kosher smoked turkey for M as filling.

131

(snack) (meal)   **Parve Combination Pizza Rolls**   (snack) (meal)

½ lb. (1 cup) crumbled *parve Italian Sausage* (p. 112)

1 cup chopped *parve* **imitation pepperoni**

¾ cup *Professional Pizzeria Sauce* (p. 100)

¼ cup grated *parve* **Mozzarella soy cheese**

1 batch (24) 3 x 3-inch *Wonton Wrappers* (p. 116)

water

cooking oil spray

✤ Step 1   Mix together first 4 ingredients in a bowl, and blend thoroughly.

✤ Step 2   Put a bit of filling in the middle of each wonton wrapper. Do not get filling near edge, it may not seal.

✤ Step 3   Seal edges of each wrapper with water, and pinch edges closed tightly.

✤ Step 4   Place pizza rolls on a greased cookie sheet, and spray them with oil.

✤ Step 5   Bake in a preheated 450° F oven 10 minutes on each side, until both sides are lightly browned.

A little larger than the real thing. Great by themselves or dipped in *Kraft® Cheez Whiz® Style Sauce* (p. 99). Makes 24 small-sized pizza rolls.

An alternative is to microwave them. Lay them on a microwave safe plate, and microwave in 1-minute increments, until dough is firm and nearly getting hard. Do not let them burn.

🔔   🔔   🔔

Alternative Fillings:

For **"Parve Sausage Pizza Rolls"**, omit pepperoni and double the sausage.

🔔   🔔   🔔

For **"Parve Pepperoni Pizza Rolls"**, omit sausage and double the pepperoni.

🔔   🔔   🔔

For **"Parve Cheese Pizza Rolls"**, omit pepperoni and sausage, and use 1 cup grated *parve* imitation cheese.

(🧁 as snack) (🧁 as a meal)   **Chili Cups**   (🧁 as snack) (🥣 as a meal)

1 batch raw *Simple Biscuits* dough (p. 217)

2 cups *Hormel® Style Chili* with or without beans (p. 171)

"Cheese" = {
D- 1 cup grated kosher Cheddar cheese.
P- 1 cup grated *parve* American or Cheddar.
M- 1 cup grated *parve* American or Cheddar.

garnish: 12 jalapeño slices, 6 halved green or black olives, sprinkles of chopped green onions or *parve* imitation bacon bits

⊛ Step 1   Grease muffin tin heavily with oil spray. Stretch dough out and put in each cup.

⊛ Step 2   Press spoonfuls of chili firmly into each biscuit. (Do not poke holes in dough!)

⊛ Step 3   Set foil or a cookie sheet on oven rack, and put muffin tin on top to catch drips.

⊛ Step 4   Bake 10 minutes in preheated 425° F oven. Top with "Cheese" and garnish.

⊛ Step 5   Bake 2-5 more minutes, or until lightly browned and "Cheese" starts to melt.

These can be messy but are so good. Serve hot, or reheat in microwave. Makes 12 cups, or 4-6 servings.

☺   ☺   ☺

For **"Scramble Cups"**, substitute raw scrambled eggs for chili. For the egg mixture: Blend together 4 eggs, 4 Tbs. *Parve* Milk (p. 85), ¼ tsp. salt, ⅛ tsp. pepper, and 2 Tbs. cooked crumbled *Country Sausage* (p. 114). Do Steps 1-5 exactly as above, but bake a bit longer until lightly browned and "Cheese" starts to melt. Makes 12 cups, or 4-6 servings.

(🧁 snack) (🍞 meal) **Parve Hot Pockets® Style Snacks** (🧁 snack) (🍞 meal)

flour for dusting

10 x 10-inch plastic zipper bag

1 raw *Pot Pie Crust* (p. 117- kept in a ball)

1 batch favorite Fillings and their "Cheeses" (see below)

✳ Step 1   Put a spoonful flour in zipper bag, and place pie crust ball in it, then zip it partially but not entirely closed. Roll crust out to the edges of bag and let rest a few minutes.

✳ Step 2   Carefully roll crust up onto itself, take it out of bag, and set it out on a flat surface.

✳ Step 3   Cut crust in half, then cut in half again to make 4 individual 5 x 5 inch squares.

✳ Step 4   Lightly roll edges on sides of squares to become 5 x 6 inches.

✳ Step 5   Place ¼ of filling on half of each square. Cut "Cheese" slices in half (each gets 1½). (Keep filling and "Cheese" ¼ inch away from edge.) Preheat oven to 425° F.

✳ Step 6   Take one edge of each crust and fold it in half over filling to meet its other side.

✳ Step 7   Pinch edges tightly and put on a greased cookie sheet or microwave-safe plate.

✳ Step 8   Bake 15 minutes or until brown, or microwave in 1-minute increments, (3½ minutes per 2 pockets, flipping halfway through) until crust hardens (they won't brown).

Makes 4 servings.

Fillings:

"Pepperoni Pizza": ¾ cup grated or 6 slices *parve* soy Mozzarella "Cheese" + ½ cup chopped *parve* soy pepperoni slices + ¼ cup *Professional Pizzeria Sauce* (p. 100).

🔔   🔔   🔔

"Ham & Cheese": 8 slices *parve* soy ham + 6 slices *parve* soy Mozzarella "Cheese".

🔔   🔔   🔔

"Broccoli & Cheese": ¾ cup grated or 6 slices *parve* American soy "Cheese" + ½ cup cooked chopped broccoli.

🔔   🔔   🔔

"Broccoli, Chicken & Cheese": ¾ cup grated or 6 slices *parve* American soy cheese + ¼ cup cooked chopped broccoli + ¼ cup *parve* imitation chicken cut in 1 inch pieces.

🔔   🔔   🔔

"Beef & Cheddar": ½ cup *parve* imitation steak slices or chunks (cut in 1-inch pieces) + 6 slices *parve* American soy "Cheese", OR ¼ cup *parve Kraft® Cheez Whiz® Style Sauce* (p. 99).

(🧁 as snack) (🍞 as meal)   **Doggies in a Blanket**   (🧁 snack) (🌭 as a meal)

½ pkg. puff pastry (thawed), **OR 1 raw *Pot Pie Crust*** (p. 118- kept in a ball)

"Cheese" = {
 D- 8 slices kosher Cheddar or American cheeses, (cut in half).
 P- 8 slices *parve* imitation American cheese, (cut in half).
 M- 8 slices *parve* imitation American cheese, (cut in half).
}

"Hot Dogs" = {
 D- 8 soy hot dogs, (cut in half).
 P- 8 *parve* soy hot dogs, (cut in half).
 M- 8 kosher beef or turkey hot dogs, (cut in half).
}

❀ Step 1   Shape dough exactly as for *Parve Hot Pockets* on previous page (Steps 1-4).

❀ Step 2   Heat oven to 375º F. Lay dough flat, cut in half. Top 1 half with ½ "Cheese" slice.

❀ Step 2   Put ½ "Hot Dog" in center, wrap with dough (curl edges over). Repeat for each.

❀ Step 3   Place on a greased cookie sheet seam-down, bake 25 minutes until light brown.

Another option is to use 8 pieces of bread (🌭 🍞). Fix as above, (pin together with toothpicks), and toast 10 minutes. (Good fixed whole with "Hot Dogs" placed diagonally.) Makes 16 snacks.

✩ ✩

(🧁 as a snack) (🍞 as a meal)   **Baked Corn Dogs**   (🧁 snack) (🌭 as a meal)

**4 (12 x 12 inch) foil squares + 4 (3 x 5) mini loaf pans + 8 optional skewers
vegetable oil spray**

"Hot Dogs" = {
 D- 1 (8 ct.) pkg. soy hot dogs.
 P- 1 (8 ct.) pkg. *parve* soy hot dogs.
 M- 1 (8 ct.) pkg. kosher beef or turkey hot dogs.
}

1 raw batch *Corn Bread* batter (p. 216)

❀ Step 1   To make special double pans- slightly stretch pans. Fold each sheet of foil in half and spread out edges (upside-down "T"). Place foil in pans- fold straight-up, and round edges.

❀ Step 2   Preheat oven to 400º F. Spray pans well with oil, pour ½ of batter evenly in each pan, top with a "Hot Dog" (leave gap around edges), and evenly pour rest of batter in each.

❀ Step 3   Bake 40 minutes until browned and separating from edges of pan.

❀ Step 4   Carefully remove from pans and insert skewers, if desired. Makes 8 corn dogs.

Appetizers

(with Melba) (eggs only)   **Little Penguins**   (with Melba) (eggs only)

(with snack bagel chips, not fried real bagels)   (snack bagel chips)

18 black olives (more can be used if needed)

8 small hard-boiled eggs

16 large pieces Melba toast or bagel chips (larger in diameter than eggs)

1 small carrot

salt or onion salt (optional)

✸	Step 1	Rinse olives and pat dry, and carefully halve eggs and olives and set aside.
✸	Step 2	Put 16 Melba toasts on a serving platter, and set eggs flat side down on each.
✸	Step 3	Shred carrot so pieces are somewhat sharp like toothpicks, and mince 2 olives.
✸	Step 4	Stick 2 pieces of olive into eggs at the top, towards the middle to make eyes.
✸	Step 5	Poke a piece of carrot into egg—just below and between "eyes" to make a beak.
✸	Step 6	Poke 2 flatter pieces of carrot into bottom of egg to make feet.

✸   Step 7   Gently take small carrot shards and insert 2 next to each other into eggs slightly toward the center, then hang half of an olive from shards, gently pressing in on them. Do the same for the other side of egg to make wings. (Shards act like pegs, much like you would hang up a coat. It works to help keep them stable, and are less fragile than just laying the olive halves on the eggs.)

✸   Step 8   Sprinkle eggs with a little salt if desired, and serve as soon as possible.

These are cute little appetizers based on someone's recipe way back when I was in 6th grade. The originals stood upright on the flat end of the egg, and used whole cloves and toothpicks, both of which had to be removed before eating. In this version, these little fellows are entirely edible. Makes 16 appetizers.

Mum's Deviled Eggs

6 large hard-boiled eggs

½ cup mayonnaise (add extra if too dry)

½ tsp. salt

½-1 tsp. sugar (or to taste)

1 tsp. olive oil

1 tsp. prepared mustard

1 tsp. *Parve* Cream (p. 85– optional)

paprika

Step 1   Halve eggs, scoop out yolks into a bowl, (set aside whites), and mash yolks well.

Step 2   Add next 6 ingredients, blending well. (Mixture should be a creamy consistency.)

Step 3   Put mixture in each egg white hole. Sprinkle with paprika and chill. Serve as soon as possible the same day. Makes 12, or 4-6 servings.

✡ ✡

Parve Fried Mozzarella Sticks

½-1 cup *Parve Milk* (p. 85), **OR other *parve* milk alternative**

1 cup flour

1-1½ cup matzah (matzo) meal or plain *Bread Crumbs* (p. 116)

avocado oil for frying or vegetable oil spray for baking

1 (10 oz.) bar *parve* Mozzarella (room temperature)

Step 1   Get three separate shallow bowls, put milk, flour and bread crumbs in each.

Step 2   Slice bar down center of side to make 2 pieces ½ inch thick. Cut in ½ inch strips lengthwise.

Step 3   Roll each in milk, coat with flour, set out to dry. Repeat using bread crumbs.

Step 4   Repeat process again to coat well.

Step 5   To Fry- put oil ¼ inch deep in pan and heat until very hot. Fry until browned on each side. Drain on paper towels. To Bake- spray with oil, put on well-greased cookie sheet and bake in preheated 450° F oven 7-10 minutes until crisp. Serve hot. Makes 24.

Jalapeño Poppers® Style Snacks

½-1 cup *Parve* Cream (p. 85), **OR other *parve* milk alternative**

1 cup flour

1-1½ cup matzah (matzo) meal or plain *Bread Crumbs* (p. 116)

12 whole large jalapeño peppers (tops cut off, halved lengthwise and seeded)

Cream Cheese* or *Cheddar Filling Flavors (below)

avocado oil for frying or vegetable oil spray for baking

Step 1   Put cream in one bowl, flour in another, and bread crumbs in the last bowl.

Step 2   Set "Cream Cheese" out to room temperature, or melt "Cheddar" on low heat.

Step 3   Fill half of jalapeños with 1-2 tsp. favorite filling, press into place, and mound it.

Step 4   Roll each piece in cream, coat with flour, and let dry (about 10 minutes).

Step 5   Roll each piece in cream, then coat with bread crumbs, and let dry.

Step 6   <u>To Fry</u>- heat a frying pan ¼ inch deep with oil and fry each jalapeño piece, turning until fully browned. Drain on paper towels.

<u>To Bake</u>- put on well-greased cookie sheet, spray with oil. Bake in preheated 450° F oven 7-10 minutes. Serve hot.

Those with sensitive skin may want to wear gloves for Steps 3-5 (it will catch up with you later—like sunburn). Never touch eyes, nose or sensitive areas when handling cut jalapeños. When done, wash hands with soap and cold water. (Jalapeño heat can be minimized by boiling halves in water 5-10 minutes. If boiled any longer, they lose their flavor and taste like regular green bell peppers.) Makes 24 snacks.

Filling Flavors:

"Cream Cheese" =
- D- 1 (8 oz.) bar cream cheese.
- P- 1 cup *Parve Imitation Cream Cheese* (p. 105).
- M- 1 cup *Parve Imitation Cream Cheese* (p. 105).

"Cheddar" =
- D- 1 cup grated kosher Cheddar cheese.
- P- 1 cup grated *parve* American or Cheddar.
- M- 1 cup grated *parve* American or Cheddar.

Parve Chopped Liver

2 cups very well cooked kidney or pinto beans (drained completely)

1 cup chopped sweet Vidalia onions

1 Tbs. olive oil, OR 1½ Tbs. *parve* margarine

2 hard-boiled eggs (peeled and finely chopped)

½ cup chopped walnut pieces, OR ⅓ cup ground walnuts

½ tsp. salt (plus more to taste if needed)

❈ Step 1   Mash beans in a bowl or blend in a food processor until it is a paste.

❈ Step 2   Sauté onions in oil or margarine until onions are limp and browned.

❈ Step 3   Add onions, eggs, walnuts and salt to beans, blend lightly. Keep slightly chunky.

Authentic! Based on a recipe from an anonymous friend. Ground walnuts and pinto beans yield a creamy texture (good for *Braunschweiger Sausage*- p. 114). Makes 1¾ cups or 4-6 servings.

✡ ✡

(P or D) (for M)   **KFC® Style Fried Chicken Livers**

"Chicken Liver" = { **D-** 1¾ cups *Parve Chopped Liver* (above).
  P- 1¾ cups *Parve Chopped Liver* (above).
  M- 1 (12 oz.) kosher chopped liver (1¾ cups).

1 small beaten egg

2 Tbs. melted *parve* margarine

1 cup *Kentucky Fried Chicken® Style Breading Mix* (p. 82)

3-4 Tbs. avocado oil (other vegetable oil can be used)

❈ Step 1   Put first 3 ingredients in a bowl, blending into a paste, roll into 1 x 1½ inch balls.

❈ Step 2   Dredge balls in breading, pressing it in and repeat to coat thoroughly.

❈ Step 3   Put oil in a skillet and heat it until hot, then carefully fry balls browning all around.

For M only, 1-2 pkg. real pre-broiled, pre-*kashered* whole chicken livers can be used. Skip Step 1 and omit egg. Coat livers in melted margarine and proceed with Steps 2-3. Makes 16-24 livers.

(P or D) (for M) **Liver Bacon Balls**

"Liver" =
- **D-** 1 small beaten egg + 1¾ cups *Parve Chopped Liver* (p. 140).
- **P-** 1 small beaten egg + 1¾ cups *Parve Chopped Liver* (p. 140).
- **M-** 1 (12 oz.) container real kosher chopped liver (1¾ cups).

2⅛ Tbs. *parve* imitation bacon bits

"Optional Cheese" =
- **D-** ½ cup grated kosher Cheddar cheese.
- **P-** ½ cup grated *parve* imitation American cheese.
- **M-** ½ cup grated *parve* imitation American cheese.

⅓ cup *All Purpose Breading* (p. 84)

4-6 Tbs. avocado oil (other vegetable oil can be used)

- Step 1   Combine "Liver", bacon bits and "Cheese" if desired, in a bowl and blend well.
- Step 2   Roll into 1-1½ inch balls, and double coat with breading, then heat oil in a pan.
- Step 3   Gently brown all sides. Drain on paper towels and serve hot. Makes 24-36 balls.

✿ ✿

Parve Steak Tartare (Raw Hamburger)

16 hard-boiled egg yolks

½ tsp. red food coloring

16 drops yellow food coloring

4 tsp. avocado oil (other vegetable oil can be used)

possible seasonings: salt & pepper, parsley flakes, hot pepper sauce, minced raw onion or capers, *Fishless Worcestershire Sauce* (p. 92)

- Step 1   Mash yolks into a paste, add food coloring and mix. Add oil and blend slightly.
- Step 2   Press mixture through a grinder or pastry bag with a plain non-fluted nozzle.
- Step 3   For a "meatier" texture, put in a baking dish and microwave 20 seconds just to "firm it up" a bit. Do not overcook! (Uncooked is softer texture.) Season as desired.

This is the *parve* alternative to raw hamburger. The leftover hard-boiled egg whites can be used for *Parve Cottage Cheese* (p. 109). Makes 1 cup, or 4-16 servings.

Kosher Escargot

1 (10 oz.) pkg. frozen spinach (thawed)**, OR 1 (15 oz.) can spinach**

1½ Tbs. olive oil

2 pressed or minced garlic cloves (1 tsp.)

½ cup *parve* **margarine**

1½ Tbs. dried minced onion flakes

1½ Tbs. parsley flakes

¼ tsp. garlic powder

Step 1   Squeezed spinach of all liquid, and put olive oil and garlic in a skillet. Sauté spinach in oil until liquid is reduced.

Step 2   Take fistfuls of spinach about 1½ inch chunks, and tightly squeeze each glob.

Step 3   Heat spinach globs in skillet until firm and rubbery.

Step 4   Combine margarine, parsley and garlic powder in saucepan, melt on low heat.

Step 5   Take a spinach glob and stuff in properly *kashered* seashells or small crocks.

Step 6   Drizzle garlic sauce over spinach globs and serve hot. Makes about 20.

✡ ✡

Totally Tubular Appetizers

"Salami" = {
D- 1½ pkg. (15 slices) imitation salami.
P- 1½ pkg. (15 slices) *parve* soy salami.
M- ½ lb. (15 slices) thin sliced kosher beef salami.
}

"Cream Cheese" = {
D- 1 (8 oz.) pkg. cream cheese (room temperature).
P- 1 cup warm *Parve Imitation Cream Cheese* (p. 105).
M- 1 cup warm *Parve Imitation Cream Cheese* (p. 105).
}

Step 1   Lay "Meat" slices flat on plate. Divide "Cream Cheese" into 15 oblong portions.

Step 2   Put 1 "Cream Cheese" piece in middle of 1 "Meat" slice.

Step 3   Roll "Meat" over "Cream Cheese", and secure each with decorative toothpick.

Wonderful for parties. Makes 15 appetizers.

 (on celery sticks)   **Easy Buffalo Wings**

⅓ cup melted *parve* margarine

⅓ cup hot pepper sauce

¼ tsp. coarse ground black pepper

¼ tsp. salt

½ tsp. cayenne pepper (add more if spicier chicken is desired)

4 tsp. paprika

2 Tbs. sugar

"Wings" = {
D- 18-20 pieces imitation chicken wings or strips.
P- 18-20 pieces *parve* soy or seitan chicken strips.
M- 1½ lb. (9-10) large kosher chicken wings (cut in half for 18-20).

"Optional Blue Cheese" = {
D- 1½ cups melted kosher blue cheese.
P- ½ batch *Parve Blue Cheese Dressing* (p. 90).
M- ½ batch *Parve Blue Cheese Dressing* (p. 90).

celery sticks (optional)

❀ Step 1   Blend first 6 ingredients in deep glass casserole. Set aside 2 Tbs. marinade.

❀ Step 2   Put "Wings" into casserole and coat well with marinade, cover casserole with lid or plastic wrap and refrigerate ½ hour or longer to marinate.

❀ Step 3   Turn oven on to broil, and broil "Wings" (or grill) 5 minutes on each side for P or D, or for M- broil 10 minutes on each side or until tender and inside is no longer pink.

❀ Step 4   Baste "Wings" with remaining marinade, coating well. Heat through.

❀ Step 5   Heat "Optional Blue Cheese" through and pour it into a crock or container.

❀ Step 6   Place "Wings" on a platter. Add celery sticks and crock of "Optional Blue Cheese", if desired. Serve hot or warm. Makes 18-20 wings, or 4-6 servings.

To microwave: In Steps 1-2, don't set aside marinade, (put thicker parts of "Wings" to outside to marinate). Microwave covered 3-5 minutes for D or P, or 10-12 minutes for M or until no longer pink and juices run clear. Flip pieces halfway through.

Breaded *parve* drummettes for D or P, or kosher breaded chicken wings for M, can all be used. Halve marinade, breading absorbs it. Skip Steps 3-4. Cook as package directs. Do Steps 5-6.

T.G.I. Friday's® Style Potstickers

"Meat" =
- **D-** 1⅓ cups imitation hamburger crumbles + 1 tsp. avocado oil.
- **P-** 1⅓ cups *parve* soy crumbles + 1 tsp. avocado oil.
- **M-** ⅔ lb. kosher ground beef, chicken or turkey (cooked & drained).

4 tsp. soy sauce

2 tsp. avocado oil (other vegetable oil can be used)

½ tsp. ground ginger

2 chopped green onions (½-¾ cup)

1 small beaten egg

2 tsp. corn starch

⅔ cup minced water chestnuts

2 minced garlic cloves (1 tsp.)

1 batch (24) *Wonton Wrappers* (p. 116)

boiling salted water

avocado oil for frying (other vegetable oil can be used)

optional dipping sauce (below)

Step 1	Combine first 9 ingredients together (for filling) in a bowl, blending thoroughly.
Step 2	Lay wrappers flat, put 2 tsp. filling in each center, then fold in half over filling.
Step 3	Squeeze out air, stand upright (pressing down slightly), and crimp closed tightly.
Step 4	Put 1-2 Tbs. oil in a frying pan and heat, then fry each one until slightly brown.
Step 5	Boil water. Gently add packets, boil 5 minutes, remove and drain well. Makes 24.

Potsticker Dipping Sauce

¼ cup soy sauce

2 Tbs. vinegar

⅛ tsp. cayenne pepper

½ tsp. avocado oil (other vegetable oil can be used)

⅛ tsp. onion powder

Combine ingredients in a bowl and blend well. put in a container or crock for dipping.

T.G.I. Friday's® Style Potato Skins

8 medium baked russet or Idaho potatoes

¼ cup melted *parve* **margarine**

Seasoned Salt (p. 434- to taste)

½ cup minced green onions

4 tsp. *parve* **imitation bacon bits**

"Cheese" =
- **D-** 1 cup grated kosher Cheddar cheese.
- **P-** 1 cup grated *parve* American cheese.
- **M-** 1 cup grated *parve* American cheese.

- Step 1   Cut potatoes in half, scoop most potato out of skins, leaving a border of potato.
- Step 2   Dot entire skins with margarine, sprinkle with salt and place on a cookie sheet.
- Step 3   Bake in preheated 425° F oven 15-20 minutes or until starting to crisp (but moist).
- Step 4   Evenly remaining ingredients on potato skins, and bake until "Cheese" melts.

Use extra potato for mashed potatoes. Serve with real or *parve* sour cream. Makes 4 servings.

✿ ✿

Tomatoes with Sour Cream

"Sour Cream" =
- **D-** ¾ cup real sour cream.
- **P-** ¾ cup *Parve Imitation Sour Cream* (p. 105).
- **M-** ¾ cup *Parve Imitation Sour Cream* (p. 105).

¼ tsp. salt

¾ tsp. *parve* **bacon bits**

3 small tomatoes (sliced in half widthwise)

2 Tbs. *parve* **margarine** (melted)

- Step 1   Combine "Sour Cream" with salt and *parve* bacon bits. Set aside.
- Step 2   Sauté or microwave tomatoes in margarine until they start to wrinkle.
- Step 3   Top each tomato with a spoonful of sour cream mixture, and lightly heat. Serve warm. Makes 6 servings.

Stuffed Mushroom Caps

1 lb. (preferably large) fresh mushrooms of equal size (wash & trim ends)

4 minced garlic cloves (2 tsp.)

1 Tbs. avocado oil (other vegetable oil can be used)

3 Tbs. *parve* onion soup mix

1 Tbs. parsley flakes

⅓ cup water

"Hamburger" =
- **D-** ½ cup imitation hamburger crumbles.
- **P-** ½ cup *Parve Soy Crumbles* (p. 110).
- **M-** ¼ lb. kosher ground beef or turkey.

"Sour Cream" =
- **D-** ¼ cup real sour cream.
- **P-** ¼ cup *Parve Imitation Sour Cream* (p. 105).
- **M-** ¼ cup *Parve Imitation Sour Cream* (p. 105).

3 Tbs. lemon juice

⊛ Step 1   Separate mushroom caps from stems: Grasp a mushroom cap tightly with one hand, and gently jiggle the stem end with the other hand until it pulls free. Repeat for each mushroom. (More stubborn ones may have to be carefully dug out with a knife, but do not cut into the cap.) Keep caps whole, and set aside in a small microwave bowl.

⊛ Step 2   Mince mushroom stems and put them in a large frying pan or microwave bowl.

⊛ Step 3   Add next 4 ingredients and "Hamburger".

⊛ Step 4   Cook until mushroom stems are tender. Remove mixture from pan or bowl (drain if necessary), and put mixture in a bowl.

⊛ Step 5   Add "Sour Cream" to "Hamburger" mixture for filling. Blend thoroughly and set aside.

⊛ Step 6   Pour lemon juice over mushroom caps, and coat outsides entirely with juice.

⊛ Step 7   Press filling into cavity of each mushroom cap, and heap extra filling on top.

⊛ Step 8   <u>For Stove</u>- Put water in pan just to cover bottom, and place caps in pan. <u>For Microwave</u>- Keep caps in bowl.

⊛ Step 9   Cook mushroom caps until soft and heated through.

Serve hot. Makes 1-2 dozen hors d'oeuvres, depending on mushroom sizes.

(⬜ with Melba) (🫒olives only) **Gourmet Goodies** (⬜ with Melba) (🫒 olives only)

16 pieces Melba toast or snack bagel chips

1 cup *Port Wine Cheese Spread* (p. 106)

"Liver Paté" = { **D-** ⅔ cup *Parve Chopped Liver* (p. 139).
P- ⅔ cup *Parve Chopped Liver* (p. 139).
M- ⅔ cup real kosher chopped liver.

Any or all these garnishes: sliced hard-boiled eggs, black or green olives

❀ Step 1 Lay toasts or bagel chips flat on a platter decoratively .

❀ Step 2 Spread on 1 Tbs. cheese to edge on each, then 1 rounded tsp. "Liver Paté" on top leaving a cheese border on edge.

❀ Step 3 Top with garnish. Makes 16 hors d'oeuvres.

✡ ✡

Chicken in Aspic

1 (.33 oz.) pkg. plain kosher gelatin (often billed as "unsweetened clear diet jell")

1¾ cups water

1 Tbs. *parve* chicken soup mix, OR 1½ tsp. *parve* chicken bouillon powder

2 Tbs. dry kosher cooking sherry

½ tsp. garlic salt

⅛ tsp. paprika

¼ tsp. ground thyme

"Chicken" = { **D-** 1½ cups chopped imitation chicken chunks.
P- 1½ cups chopped *parve* soy or seitan chicken chunks.
M- 1½ cups chopped cooked kosher chicken.

❀ Step 1 Put water in a pot or micro bowl. Crush gelatin lumps and add to water.

❀ Step 2 Add remaining ingredients, blending well. Bring to a boil, then remove from heat.

❀ Step 3 Stir in "Chicken", pour in small elegant molds or single bowls and chill until firm.

❀ Step 4 Unmold and serve on lettuce or in bowls. Never freeze.

Buy kosher gelatin at kosher groceries. (Do not follow gelatin package directions that state gelatin should be added after boiling.) Makes 4-6 servings.

Soups and Chilis
Cream Soups

Condensed Cream Soup

"**Butter**" =
- D- ¼ cup butter or margarine.
- P- ¼ cup *parve* margarine.
- M- ¼ cup *parve* margarine.

"**Milk**" =
- D- 1 cup whole milk.
- P- 1 cup *Parve Milk* (p. 85), OR 1 cup soy milk.
- M- ¾ cup *Parve Milk* (p. 85) + ¼ cup chicken broth.

⅓ cup flour, OR 3 Tbs. corn starch or potato starch

2 tsp. salt, OR 2½ tsp. *parve* chicken (or other flavor) soup mix

½ tsp. onion powder

dash ground nutmeg

pinch black pepper (optional)

✿ Step 1   Put "Butter" in a microwave container or pot, melt on low (keep warm if on stove).

✿ Step 2   Combine remaining ingredients in a jar and shake, or stir to blend thoroughly.

✿ Step 3   Slowly stir mixture into "Butter", raise heat and stir constantly, or microwave in 1-minute increments, stirring in-between.

✿ Step 4   Cook until thickened and smooth. This is now the base for any cream soup.

This recipe makes the equivalent of a 10 oz. can of condensed cream soup, or white sauce. Use in any recipe calling for cream-based soups. Makes about 1 cup.

☺   ☺   ☺

For "**Cream Soup**", add 1 cup water and heat through. Makes 2 cups soup, or 2 servings.

☺   ☺   ☺

For "**Cream of Potato Soup**", combine ½ -¾ cup cooked potatoes diced into ¼-inch pieces, ⅛ tsp. salt and ¼ cup extra water with *Cream Soup*. Blend gently and heat through. (For fancier soup, add ¼ cup cooked diced carrots, ½ tsp. paprika, ¼ cup more water, and ¼ cup instant mashed potato flakes. If raw veggies are used— cook in a bit of water 20 minutes or microwave 5 minutes, then add *Cream Soup*.) Makes 3-3¼ cups, or 3 servings. (🥤 soup) (✎ potatoes) 🥛

147

Condensed Cream of Mushroom Soup

½ (4 oz.) can mushrooms (drained- liquid can be used for soup water below)

½ tsp. parsley flakes (optional)

1 batch (1 cup) *Condensed Cream Soup* (previous) (w/ mushroom or chicken flavoring)

Mince mushrooms into ⅛ inch pieces. Combine with remaining ingredients, blend well and heat through.

(½ cup fresh diced mushrooms sautéed in 1 Tbs. parve margarine can also be used in place of canned.) This recipe can be used wherever 1 can of condensed mushroom soup is called for. This is perfect in recipes like *Morrison's® Eggplant Casserole* (p. 194), *Green Bean Casserole* (p. 196), and *Stouffer's® Style Turkey Tetrazzini* (p. 288). Makes about 1¼-1½ cups (equivalent to 1-10 oz. can).

☺   ☺   ☺

For **"Cream of Mushroom Soup"**, add 1¼ cups water and heat through. Makes 2½-3 cups soup (equivalent of a prepared 10 oz. can), or 2 large servings.

✡ ✡

Condensed Cream of Celery Soup

¼ cup chopped celery

1 Tbs. *parve* **margarine**

1 batch (1 cup) *Condensed Cream Soup* (previous) (w/ *parve* chicken soup mix)

�֍ Step 1   Sauté celery in margarine until tender, and add remaining ingredients.

✖ Step 2   Add soup and blend well. Heat through.

Add to any recipe requiring a 10 oz. can of cream of celery soup, such as Boston Chicken® Style Creamed Spinach (p. 197) or *Creamy Tuna Deluxe Casserole* (p. 363). Makes about 1¼ cups.

☺   ☺   ☺

For **"Cream of Celery Soup"**, add 1¼ cups water and heat through. Makes 2½ cups soup, or 2 servings.

Condensed Cream of Broccoli Soup

½ cup finely minced, well-cooked broccoli (divided)

1 batch (1 cup) *Condensed Cream Soup* (p. 147- w/ soup mix, omit nutmeg)

- Step 1   Take ¼ cup broccoli and puree it in a blender.
- Step 2   Combine with remaining ¼ cup broccoli and *Condensed Cream Soup*.
- Step 3   Blend well and heat through. Makes about 1¼ -1½ cups.

☺   ☺   ☺

For **"Cream of Broccoli Soup"**, add 1¼ cups water, and heat through. Makes 2¾ cups soup (a little over the equivalent of a prepared 10 oz. can), or 2 large servings.

✿ ✿

Condensed Cream of Chicken Soup

1 batch (1 cup) *Condensed Cream Soup* (p. 147- w/ chicken soup mix)

"Chicken" =
- **D-** ¼ cup finely diced imitation chicken.
- **P-** ¼ cup *parve* soy chicken, finely diced.
- **M-** ¼ cup finely diced cooked chicken.

- Step 1   Put *Condensed Cream Soup* in a microwave bowl or pot. Heat on low heat.
- Step 2   Add "Chicken" and heat through.

Eat plain or add to recipes needing a 10 oz. can of *Cream of Chicken Soup*. Makes 1¼ cups (the equivalent of a 10 oz. can).

☺   ☺   ☺

For **"Cream of Chicken Soup"**, add 1¼ cups water and heat through. Makes 2½ cups soup (a little over the equivalent of a prepared 10 oz. can), or 2 large servings.

☺   ☺   ☺

For **"Curried Chicken Soup"**, fix *Cream of Chicken Soup* (above), and add 1 tsp. ginger + 2 tsp. curry powder. Heat through. Serve hot, or chill and serve cold. Makes 2½ cups soup, or 2 large servings.

149

(soup) (asparagus)   **Cream of Asparagus Soup**

1 cup *Condensed Cream Soup* (p. 147- use chicken soup mix, omit nutmeg)

1¼ cups water

½ cup chopped, well-cooked asparagus (divided)

Step 1   For thicker more flavorful soup, take ¼ cup asparagus and puree in a blender.

Step 2   Put *Condensed Cream Soup* in a pot or microwavable bowl and add water.

Step 3   Stirring constantly, add remaining ¼ cup asparagus and heat through.

Makes 2½ cups soup (a little over the equivalent of a prepared 10 oz. can), or 2 large servings.

✡ ✡

Pumpkin Soup

2 Tbs. flour

"Milk" =
- **D-** 1½ cups milk (divided).
- **P-** 1½ cup *Parve Milk* (p. 85) (divided).
- **M-** 1½ cup *Parve Milk* (p. 85) (divided).

2 Tbs. *parve* chicken soup mix, OR 3 *parve* chicken bouillon cubes

½ cup tomato sauce

2 tsp. onion salt

¼ tsp. ground thyme

1 (15 oz.) can cooked pumpkin, OR 2 cups mashed pumpkin

¼ cup *parve* margarine

Step 1   Combine flour and ½ cup "Milk" in a pot or microwave bowl, blend until smooth.

Step 2   Add last 1 cup "Milk" and remaining ingredients, blending well.

Step 3   For Stove- Heat to a boil and simmer 10-15 minutes, until slightly thickened.

For Microwave- Heat in 1-minute increments stirring in-between until slightly thickened.

A delicious substitute for cheese soup, this can also be made with other types of cooked and mashed winter squash, such as Butternut Squash. Makes 3-4 servings.

Condensed Cheddar Cheese Soup

"Butter" = {
D- 2 Tbs. butter or margarine.
P- 2 Tbs. *parve* margarine + ½ tsp. salt.
M- 2 Tbs. *parve* margarine + ½ tsp. salt.

"Milk" = {
D- ¾ cup half & half or whole milk.
P- ¾ cup *Parve Cream* (p. 85).
M- ¾ cup *Parve Cream* (p. 85).

2 Tbs. flour

¼ tsp. onion powder

¼ tsp. salt

dash paprika

dash cayenne pepper

"Cheese" = {
D- 6 slices kosher Cheddar cheese.
P- ¾ cup grated *parve* American or Cheddar cheese.
M- ¾ cup grated *parve* American or Cheddar cheese.

✤ Step 1   Put "Butter" in a microwave container or pot, melt on low (keep warm if on stove).

✤ Step 2   Combine next 6 ingredients in a jar and shake, or stir to blend thoroughly.

✤ Step 3   Slowly pour into "Butter", stirring constantly and blending well until smooth.

✤ Step 4   Add "Cheese", still stirring until "Cheese" melts completely, and mixture is thickened and well blended.

Makes equivalent of a 10 oz. can condensed Cheddar cheese soup. Use on vegetables or as a dip. Makes 1-1¼ cups.

☺   ☺   ☺

For **"Cheddar Cheese Soup"**, add 1¼ cup milk for D, or for P or M add 1¼ cup water, OR ⅔ cup water + ⅔ cup *Parve* Cream (p. 85). Heat on medium to low heat or in the microwave until hot. Blend until smooth and heated through. Makes 2¼ cups soup, or about 2 servings.

151

Condensed Nacho Cheese Soup

1 Tbs. melted *parve* margarine

1½ Tbs. diced pickled jalapeño peppers

2 tsp. finely diced red bell pepper (previously frozen peppers cook quicker)

1 batch (1¼ cup) *Condensed Cheddar Cheese Soup* (previous page)

⊛ Step 1   Melt margarine in a microwave container or pot on low, then add jalapeños and red bell peppers and sauté until tender.

⊛ Step 2   Add cheese soup and heat on low. <u>For Stove</u>- Stir constantly. <u>For Microwave</u>- Heat in 1 minute increments stirring in-between. Blend thoroughly until smooth and heated through.

Instead of jalapeños, ¼ tsp. red pepper flakes can be substituted. For hotter soup, add 1 tsp. of jalapeño pepper juice. Makes the equivalent of a 10 oz. can, or 1¼ cups.

☺   ☺   ☺

For **"Nacho Cheese Soup"**, add 1¼ cup milk for D, or for P and M add 1¼ cup water (it will be hotter), OR ¾ cup *Parve* Cream (p. 85) + ¾ cup water. Heat on medium to low heat, and blend until smooth and heated through. Makes 2½ cups soup, or about 2 servings.

✿ ✿

Broccoli Cheese Soup

1 batch (2½ cups) *Cheddar Cheese Soup* (previous page)

½ cup cooked minced broccoli (drained if necessary)

1 tsp. garlic powder

⊛ Step 1   Put cheese soup in a microwave container or pot on low.

⊛ Step 2   Add broccoli and garlic powder, stirring to blend thoroughly.

⊛ Step 3   <u>For Stove</u>- Stir constantly. <u>For Microwave</u>- Heat in 1-minute increments stirring in-between. Blend thoroughly until smooth and heated through.

Makes 2¾ cups soup (a little over the equivalent of a prepared 10 oz. can), or 2 large servings.

Broth Soups

(soup) (asparagus)   **Delectable Asparagus Soup**

1 (8 oz.) pkg. frozen asparagus (thawed & drained), **OR ½ lb. fresh asparagus**

"Cream Cheese" =
- **D-** 1 (8 oz.) pkg. cream cheese (cut into ¼ inch cubes).
- **P-** 1 cup *parve* cream cheese (cut into ¼ inch cubes).
- **M-** 1 cup *parve* cream cheese (cut into ¼ inch cubes).

4 cups chicken *Parve Broth* (p. 110)

Step 1   Check asparagus for bugs. slowly bring water and soup mix to a boil.

Step 2   Cut asparagus into 1-inch pieces. Stir into "Broth". Boil 15 minutes or until tender.

Step 3   Take "Broth" off heat. Pour into bowls and float "Cream Cheese" cubes on top.

Real or imitation sour cream can also be used on top. (Don't add cream cheese or sour cream after Shabbat has started, as it melts rapidly and changes consistency.) Makes 4 servings.

☆ ☆

(on carrots) (on soup)   **Southern-Belle Soup**

5 cups water (more can be used for desired consistency)

2 Tbs. *parve* chicken soup mix, OR 3 *parve* chicken bouillon or soup cubes

¼ tsp. black pepper

1¼ cup chopped celery, OR ⅔ cup dried minced celery flakes

1¼ cups diced carrots

½ cup chopped onion

¾ cup creamy peanut butter or tahini (add 2½ cups extra water for tahini)

½ cup tomato sauce

optional garnish: ⅓ cup chopped peanuts, other nuts, or sesame seeds

Step 1   Combine all ingredients except garnish in a large pot, and bring to boil.

Step 2   Simmer 40 minutes or until vegetables are tender. Garnish and serve hot or cold.

Delicious with delicate flavor and wonderful aroma. Makes 4-6 servings.

(🍚 rice) (🥕 veggies) (🥛 the rest)   **Chicken Gumbo**

¼ cup chopped celery

¼ cup green bell peppers (seeded and chopped)

¼ cup chopped onion

¼ cup cut corn

1 cup chopped okra

2 minced garlic cloves (1 tsp.)

⅛ tsp. black pepper (use cayenne pepper instead if you like it spicy)

3 Tbs. avocado or other oil (stove) **or melted *parve* margarine** (microwave)

3 Tbs. flour, OR 1¼ Tbs. quick cooking tapioca

4 tsp. *parve* chicken soup mix, OR 2 parve chicken bouillon or soup cubes

2 cups water

½ (16 oz.) can chopped tomatoes (1 cup)

¼ tsp. ground thyme

¼ tsp. ground cumin

¼ tsp. basil leaves

¼ tsp. salt

½ tsp. hot pepper sauce (add double if you like it spicy)

1 Tbs. *Fishless Worcestershire Sauce* (p. 92)

"Chicken" = {
  D- 1 cup imitation chicken chunks.
  P- 1 cup *parve* imitation chicken chunks.
  M- 1 cup chopped cooked kosher chicken.
}

"Optional Hot Dogs" = {
  D- 2 chopped soy hot dogs.
  P- 2 chopped *parve* soy hot dogs.
  M- 2 kosher beef hot dogs cut into 1 inch pieces.
}

2 cups hot cooked white rice

❀	Step 1	Combine first 8 ingredients in a large pot, cooking until vegetables are tender.
❀	Step 2	Put next 9 ingredients in a large bowl, stirring mixture until thoroughly blended.
❀	Step 3	Add "Chicken", "Optional Hot Dogs" and mixture to vegetables, blending well.
❀	Step 4	B oil, reduce heat, cook until slightly thickened. Serve on rice. Makes 4 servings.

(🥕 spinach)   **Philippine Chicken Soup**

¼ cup olive oil (for stove) **or** *parve* **margarine** (for microwave)

1½ tsp. fresh grated ginger root, OR ¼ tsp. ground ginger

1 large thinly sliced onion (¾ cup)

"Chicken" =
- **D-** 1½ cups chopped imitation chicken chunks.
- **P-** 1½ cups chopped *parve* chicken chunks.
- **M-** 1½ cups chopped cooked kosher chicken.

6 cups water

4 Tbs. *parve* **chicken soup mix, OR 6** *parve* **chicken bouillon or soup cubes**

¼ tsp. garlic powder

¾ cup chopped fresh baby spinach leaves

✻ Step 1   Heat olive oil in a large skillet or put margarine in a microwave safe bowl, and add onion, ginger and "Chicken" and sauté or microwave until onion is tender.

✻ Step 2   Add water, bring to a boil, add soup mix and garlic powder stirring until dissolved.

✻ Step 3   Stir in spinach and take off heat. Serve hot. Makes 4-6 servings.

✡ ✡

Single-Serve Micro-Poached Egg Soup

1 cup water

2 tsp. *parve* **chicken soup mix, OR 1 tsp.** *parve* **chicken bouillon powder**

1 minced garlic clove (½ tsp.), OR ⅛ tsp. garlic powder

2 eggs

✻ Step 1   Combine all ingredients except eggs in a microwave safe bowl.

✻ Step 2   Carefully crack eggs into a separate bowl to check for bloodspots.

✻ Step 3   Gently poke center of yolks with your finger or fork, carefully pour into bowl.

✻ Step 4   Heat on high 2 minutes, rotate and repeat, take out and stir gently, egg whites should be cooked, heat 1 more minute, then let sit for a few minutes before eating.

Pepper, and chopped chives or cooked pasta can be added for heartiness. Makes 1 serving.

Easy Egg Drop Soup

6 cups water

4 Tbs. *parve* **chicken soup mix, OR 6** *parve* **chicken bouillon or soup cubes**

3 eggs (well beaten at room temperature)

¾ cup chopped green onions

Step 1   Bring water to a boil and add soup mix, stirring to dissolve.

Step 2   As water is boiling, pour eggs in a stream, stirring vigorously.

Step 3   As egg firms, add green onions, and turn off heat. Serve hot.

For heartier soup, add cooked noodles. Serve topped with *mandelin* (identical in flavor to Chinese restaurant chow mein noodles). Garlic or pepper flakes add a "nip". Makes 6 servings.

✿ ✿

(wontons) (broth)   **Easy Wonton Soup**   (wontons) (broth)

6 cups water

4 Tbs. *parve* **chicken soup mix, OR 6** *parve* **chicken bouillon or soup cubes**

24 raw plain *Egg Rolls* (p. 131)

¾ cup chopped green onions (optional)

Step 1   Bring water to a boil and add soup mix, stirring to dissolve.

Step 2   As water is boiling, gently add egg rolls. Do not stir at all.

Step 3   Soup is ready when egg roll wontons float to top of soup.

Step 4   Add green onions if desired, and turn off heat. Serve hot.

Can be served topped with *mandelin* (identical in flavor to Chinese restaurant chow mein noodles). Garlic or pepper flakes add a "nip". Makes 6 servings, 4 wontons per person.

(noodles) (soup) **Teriyaki Noodle Soup** (noodles) (soup)

4 cups water

8 tsp. *parve* **chicken soup mix, OR 4** *parve* **chicken bouillon or soup cubes**

2 Tbs. brown sugar

⅛ tsp. red pepper flakes

2 tsp. soy sauce

⅛ tsp. ground ginger (optional)

¼ cup chopped green onions

2 cups very fine uncooked noodles

Combine water and soup mix in a pot and bring to boil, then add remaining ingredients and boil 5 minutes, until noodles are done. Can microwave if using pre-cooked noodles. Makes 4 servings.

✪ ✪

(noodles) (soup) **Quick Curried Chicken Noodle Soup** (noodles) (soup)

4 cups water

8 tsp. *parve* **chicken soup mix, OR 4** *parve* **chicken bouillon or soup cubes**

4 tsp. curry powder

½ tsp. ground ginger

¼ tsp. garlic powder

½ cup couscous, OR 1 cup cooked egg noodles or thin spaghetti

Combine ingredients and bring to a boil, microwaving or cooking 5-7 minutes. Makes 4 servings.

For a single serving, use ¼ the recipe, (but add only a dash of ginger) and cook 1½ minutes, then let it sit 4 more minutes. Reheat, cooking 1½ more minutes.

For a spicier soup, add ¼ tsp. red pepper flakes.

(🧁 noodles) (🥤 soup) **Quick Spicy Chicken Noodle Soup** (🧁 noodles) (🥛 soup)

4 cups water

8 tsp. *parve* chicken soup mix, OR 4 *parve* chicken bouillon or soup cubes

¼ tsp. red pepper flakes

¼ tsp. garlic powder

⅛ tsp. ground cumin (optional)

½ cup couscous, OR 1 cup cooked egg noodles or cooked thin spaghetti

Combine ingredients and bring to a boil, microwaving or cooking 5-7 minutes. Makes 4 servings.

For a single serving, use ¼ of recipe, and microwave 1½ minutes, then let it sit 4 more minutes. Reheat 1½ more minutes. (I fix this soup to ward off colds.)

✡ ✡

🧁 **Fancy French Onion Soup** 🍞

1 envelope onion soup mix (¼ cup)

3½ cups water

½ cup kosher red wine

2 tsp. ground thyme

⅛ tsp. cayenne pepper

½ loaf prepared *parve Garlic Bread* (p. 213)

"Cheese" = {
D- 4-8 slices kosher Mozzarella or Muenster cheeses.
P- 4-8 slices *parve* imitation Mozzarella cheese.
M- 4-8 slices *parve* imitation Mozzarella cheese.

🌼 Step 1   Combine first 5 ingredients in a pot, bring to boil stirring, then simmer 10 minutes.

🌼 Step 2   Cut garlic bread into bite size pieces and divide it into 4 equal portions.

🌼 Step 3   Pour hot soup into 4 microwave bowls and put bread atop soup in each bowl, then top each with slices of "Cheese".

🌼 Step 4   Heat in microwave until "Cheese" is melted and soup is hot.

This makes a great and fancy lunch. Makes 4 servings.

Condensed Golden Mushroom Soup

1 cup mushrooms (divided), **OR 2 (4 oz.) cans mushrooms** (divided)

2 medium chopped fresh celery stalks (1 cup)

2 celery leaf tops (optional)

1 minced garlic clove (½ tsp.)

1 medium chopped onion (½ cup)

2 Tbs. avocado oil (other vegetable oil can be used)

2 cups water (add at least ⅔ cup more if there is no mushroom liquid)

8 tsp. *parve* **beef soup mix, OR 4 tsp.** *parve* **powdered beef bouillon**

4 tsp. tomato paste

⅛ tsp. black pepper

1 bay leaf

¾ cup kosher burgundy or other kosher red wine

1½ tsp. microwave browning sauce

½ cup *parve* **margarine**

3 Tbs. flour

✷ Step 1   Drain any liquid from mushrooms into a pot, and add ½ cup (or 1 can) mushrooms, celery and tops, garlic, onion, oil, water, soup mix, tomato paste, pepper, bay leaf, wine and browning sauce in a pot and simmer uncovered on low heat 45 minutes to 1 hour.

✷ Step 2   Take off heat and let cool, then remove bay leaf and set celery leaves aside.

✷ Step 3   Put pot contents in blender and puree until smooth. (Add extra water if needed.)

✷ Step 4   Dice ½ cup (or other can) mushrooms and put with margarine in pot, sautéing until tender.

✷ Step 5   Put blender contents into pot with mushrooms, add flour and heat until starting to thicken. Mince and add celery leaves if desired.

This is equivalent to 2 cans condensed golden mushroom soup. Use for sauces or other recipes, such as *Hardees® Style Mushroom & Swiss Burger* (p. 236). Makes about 2½-3 cups.

☺   ☺   ☺

For **"Golden Mushroom Soup"**, add 2½ cups water and heat through. Makes 4-5 servings.

(soup) (veggies) **Quick Home-Style Vegetable Soup**

5 cups water

1 (15 oz.) can beans, OR 2 cups cooked beans

2 Tbs. dried minced onion flakes, OR 1 chopped medium onion (½ cup)

1 tsp. dried minced garlic flakes, OR 2 minced garlic cloves (1 tsp.)

1 large diced potato, OR ¼ cup barley or rice + ½ cup extra water

1 (15 oz.) can (2 cups) diced tomatoes (undrained)

4 cups frozen mixed vegetables, OR 2 (15 oz.) cans (undrained)

½ tsp. black pepper

¼ tsp. ground cloves

⅛ tsp. cayenne pepper, OR dash hot pepper sauce

½ tsp. ground thyme

2 bay leaves

1 Tbs. dried minced celery flakes, OR ¼ cup diced celery

10 tsp. *parve* beef soup mix, OR 5 *parve* beef bouillon cubes

Combine ingredients in a large pot and simmer 30 minutes. (This rivals my mum's delicious homemade vegetable soup, that cooked many hours.) Makes 3½ quarts or about 6-8 servings.

✡ ✡

 soup) (veggies) **Quick Home-Style Vegetable Beef Soup**

1 batch Quick Homestyle Vegetable Soup (above) (omit beef soup mix for M)..

"Meat" = { **D-** 2 cups *parve* imitation beef chunks + 1 Tbs. olive oil.
P- 2 cups *parve* imitation beef chunks + 1 Tbs. olive oil..
M- 1 lb. kosher stew beef chunks.

Add "Meat" to soup, bring to boil, reduce heat and simmer ½ hour. To cook overnight- add 2-3 cups water. Makes 1 gal., or 8-10 servings. (soup or "Beef") (on veggies)

(🧁 pasta) (🫛 beans) (🥤 soup) **Simple Minestrone** 🧁 (🥛 if pasta is not eaten)

¾ cup cooked or canned kidney and/or navy beans

1 (15 oz.) can mixed vegetables (undrained)

1 cup raw small or medium shell macaroni

2 tsp. *parve* beef soup mix

4 cups beef *Parve Broth* (p. 110)

1 small chopped onion (¼ cup), OR 1 Tbs. dried minced onion flakes

1 minced garlic clove (½ tsp.), OR ½ tsp. dried minced garlic flakes

¼ cup chopped zucchini

½ cup chopped tomatoes

½ tsp. parsley flakes

Put ingredients in large pot, bring to boil, simmer until vegetables are tender. Makes 4 servings.

✡ ✡

(🧁 orzo) (🥤soup) **Quick Orzo Mushroom Soup** (🧁 orzo) (🥛 soup)

5½ cups beef *Parve Broth* (p. 110)

½ cup dry orzo pasta

1 cup store-bought or homemade *Parve Soy Crumbles* (p. 110)

1 (4 oz.) can mushrooms (finely chopped)

2 Tbs. lemon juice (or juice from a fresh medium-sized lemon)

"Sour Cream" = ⎰ D- ½ cup real dairy sour cream.
⎨ P- ½ cup *Parve Imitation Sour Cream* (p. 105).
⎱ M- ½ cup *Parve Imitation Sour Cream* (p. 105).

⬡ Step 1   Bring "Broth" to boil, add next 3 ingredients. Simmer 10 minutes stirring often.

⬡ Step 2   Pour into bowls and stir in "Sour Cream" or place on top. Makes 4 servings.

For dry mix: ½ cup orzo, ½ cup TVP, 6 Tbs. crushed dried mushrooms, 4 Tbs. *parve* beef soup mix, and 1 tsp. dried grated lemon peel. Boil 6¼ cups water, add mix and cook 10 minutes. (Don't add sour cream after Shabbat has started, it melts rapidly and changes consistency.)

161

(🧁 on barley) (🥤 soup or M "Lamb") **Scotch Broth** (🧁 barley) (🥛 soup or M "Lamb")

"Lamb" = {
D- 4 cups imitation steak chunks.
P- 4 cups 1-inch *parve* steak or *Seitan Beef Roast* (p. 319) chunks.
M- 2 lb. kosher stewing lamb or beef chunks (cut in 1-inch pieces).
}

"Broth" = {
D- 5½ cups water + 2 Tbs. avocado oil + 8 tsp. *parve* beef soup mix.
P- 5½ cups water + 2 Tbs. avocado oil + 8 tsp. parve *beef* soup mix.
M- 6 cups water
}

4 tsp. *parve* chicken soup mix, OR 2 *parve* chicken bouillon cubes

½ cup barley

1 cup chopped onion

1 cup diced celery, OR ½ cup dried minced celery flakes

1 cup diced peeled carrots

½ tsp. black pepper

¼ cup parsley flakes

1 tsp. minced garlic or *Oven-Roasted Garlic* cloves (p. 84)

Put ingredients in pot and bring to boil. Simmer 40 minutes for D or P, 1½ hours for M. (Crock pots, 4 hours on high, 8 hours on low. Overnight on low, add 4 cups water.) Makes 4-8 servings.

✡ ✡

Parve Oxtail Soup

2 cups very well-cooked navy beans (finely pureed)

2 Tbs. *parve* imitation bacon bits

1½ tsp. onion powder

4 cups water (can be from cooked beans if desired)

4 Tbs. *parve* beef soup mix, OR 6 *parve* beef bouillon or soup cubes

1 cup tomato sauce

1 Tbs. microwave browning sauce

Combine ingredients in a pot and blend well. Heat through and serve. (Based on a non-legume-based British classic. Bacon bits give texture like dry mix.) Makes 4-6 servings.

Jellied Beef Consommé

2 (.33 oz.) pkg. plain kosher gelatin (often billed as "unsweetened clear diet jell")

"Liquid" =
- **D-** 3¼ cups water + ½ tsp. microwave browning sauce.
- **P-** 3¼ cups water + ½ tsp. microwave browning sauce.
- **M-** 3¼ cups kosher beef broth.

⅛ cup vegetable juice

2 Tbs. kosher cooking sherry

"Soup Mix" =
- **D-** 10 tsp. *parve* beef soup mix.
- **P-** 10 tsp. *parve* beef soup mix.
- **M-** 1 tsp. beef soup mix + 2 tsp. sugar.

⊛ Step 1   Crush any lumps in gelatin packet so that it is a fine powder.

⊛ Step 2   Put "Liquid", juice, sherry, "Soup Mix" and gelatin in a pot.

⊛ Step 3   Stir ingredients vigorously with a fork until completely blended and no more gelatin chunks remain.

⊛ Step 3   Bring to a rolling boil (make sure that soup mix is dissolved).

⊛ Step 4   Remove from heat as soon as it gets to a boil and pour mixture either into 4 individual bowls or 1 large bowl.

⊛ Step 5   Refrigerate until gelled and firm. Serve cold.

This was a staple my Mum used to give me when I had the flu as a child. It was easy to digest, good on a sore throat, and gave at least some form of protein, (although the P and D versions are more for flavor than protein). Unlike most of the recipes in this book this recipe does not freeze well. Makes 4 servings, (3¾ cups) or the equivalent of about 3 (10¾ oz.) cans.

Parve kosher gelatin (also called "jell" or "gel") can be found at kosher groceries. Do not confuse "unflavored" with the sweetened type- look on the ingredients for sugar or artificial sweeteners. (Do not follow gelatin package directions that state gelatin should be added after boiling.)

Authentic jellied beef Consommé is made from a concentrated broth, and would normally be made of 6 cups beef broth slowly simmered down to 3¼ cups. This take awhile, and could likely be done. In lieu of this, soup mix is added to make it double-strength and speed things up.

Mock Turtle Soup

2 Tbs. avocado oil (other vegetable oil can be used)

1 large chopped onion (¾ cup)

2 minced garlic cloves (1 tsp.)

1 lemon (cut in half- ½ for juice, other ½ for slicing)

4½ cups water (divided)

4 Tbs. *parve* **beef soup mix, OR 6** *parve* **beef bouillon or soup cubes**

2 cups tomato sauce

1½ Tbs. microwave browning sauce

¼ tsp. ground thyme

¼ tsp. black pepper

¼ tsp. *Fishless Worcestershire Sauce* (p. 92)

¼ tsp. ground allspice

⅛ tsp. ground ginger

dash cayenne pepper

½ tsp. sugar

"Meat" = { **D-** 3 cups soy crumbles + 1 Tbs. avocado oil.
P- 3 cups *parve* soy crumbles + 1 Tbs. avocado oil.
M- 1½ lb. kosher ground beef (browned and drained).

½ cup flour

3 crushed hard-boiled eggs

1½ Tbs. kosher cooking sherry

	Step 1	Put oil, onion, and garlic in large pot, sauté until onion is transparent.
	Step 2	Add ½ lemon's juice (1 Tbs.), 4 cups water, next 11 ingredients, bring to a boil.
	Step 3	Turn down to simmer. Put last ½ cup water and flour in a cup, blend until smooth.
	Step 4	Stir flour mixture into soup and simmer 15 minutes, stirring often.
	Step 5	Add hard-boiled eggs, cook 5 more minutes, then stir in sherry and turn off heat.
	Step 6	Cut other lemon half in thin slices, put soup in bowls and garnish with lemon.

Soup should ideally be somewhat thick. Makes about 2½ qt. soup, or 8 servings.

(🧁 pasta) (🫒 olives) **Hearty Italian Sausage Soup** (🧁 pasta) (🫒 Olives)

(🥕 veggies) (🥤 the rest) (🥛 the rest)

"Sausage" =
- **D-** ½ lb. raw *Italian Sausage* (p. 112) or soy Italian sausages.
- **P-** ½ lb. raw *Italian Sausage* (p. 112) or soy Italian sausages.
- **M-** ½ lb. raw *Italian Sausage* or kosher Italian sausage links.

1 Tbs. olive oil (other vegetable oil can be used)

1 small chopped onion (¼ cup), OR 1 Tbs. dried minced onion flakes

2 minced garlic cloves (1 tsp.), OR ½ tsp. dried minced garlic flakes

4 cups water

2 Tbs. *parve* beef soup mix, OR 3 *parve* beef bouillon or soup cubes

1 cup chopped tomatoes, OR ½ (15 oz.) can chopped tomatoes

½ (8 oz.) can tomato sauce

1½ tsp. *Italian Seasoning* (p. 434)

1 cup raw shells or elbow macaroni

½ (15 oz.) can mixed vegetables

½ (15 oz.) can pinto or kidney beans

⅛ tsp. cayenne pepper or hot pepper sauce (optional)

½ cup sliced black olives

⊛ Step 1 Shape "Sausage" into 32 ½ inch balls, (for links, cut into 1-inch pieces).

⊛ Step 2 Sauté "Sausage" until browned, or microwave in a 2½ qt. glass casserole 5-7 minutes or until firm. (If using M, until juices run clear.)

⊛ Step 3 Put oil in a pot. Add fresh onion and garlic and sauté until tender (skip for dried).

⊛ Step 4 Add "Sausage", water, soup mix, tomatoes, tomato sauce, Italian seasoning, and macaroni to pot and boil 15 minutes.

⊛ Step 5 Add mixed vegetables, beans, black olives and cayenne or hot sauce if desired, and cook 5 more minutes until heated through and serve hot.

On non-*Shabbat* days, garnish with a dollop of *parve* sour cream or sprinkle with *parve* imitation Mozzarella for P or M. Garnish with a dollop of real sour cream or sprinkle with kosher Mozzarella cheese for D. For quicker soup, omit oil and substitute dried minced onion and garlic for fresh, and skip Step 4. It can be made in a crock pot, but don't cook overnight unless pasta is pre-cooked and added upon serving (it disintegrates). Makes over 2 qt. soup, or 4-8 servings.

(🫒 olives)(🥕 veggies) (🥤) **Hearty Mexican Meatball Soup** (🫒 Olives) (🥤 the rest)

"Meat" = {
D- 1 pkg. raw soy burger + 1 Tbs. avocado oil.
P- 1 pkg. raw *parve* soy burger + 1 Tbs. avocado oil.
M- 1 lb. kosher ground beef or turkey (browned and drained).
}

¼ cup taco seasoning or *Taco Bell® Style Taco Seasoning Mix* (p. 81)

½ cup plain *Bread Crumbs* (p. 116)

2 small beaten eggs

1 Tbs. olive oil (other oil can be used) **or melted *parve* margarine**

1 small chopped onion (¼ cup)

2 minced garlic cloves (1 tsp.)

4 cups water

8 tsp. *parve* beef soup mix, OR 4 *parve* beef bouillon or soup cubes

1-2 cups store-bought or *Super Salsa* (p. 96)

1 (15 oz.) can mixed vegetables

1 (15 oz.) can pinto or kidney beans

¼-½ cup sliced black olives (optional)

"Garnish" = {
D- ¾ cup sour cream or grated kosher Monterey jack cheese.
P- ¾ cup *parve* sour cream, OR grated *parve* Jack or Mozzarella.
M- ¾ cup *parve* sour cream, OR grated *parve* Jack or Mozzarella.
}

✡	Step 1	Blend first 4 ingredients in a bowl and knead. If baking, preheat oven to 350º F.
✡	Step 2	Shape "Taco Meat" into 64 ½-inch balls, and place on a greased glass casserole.
✡	Step 3	Bake 20 minutes, or microwave 5-7 minutes until firm (if M, until juices run clear).
✡	Step 4	Put oil in a pot for stove, or margarine in a 2½ qt. glass casserole for microwave.
✡	Step 5	Add onion and garlic and sauté or microwave until onion is tender.
✡	Step 6	Add "Taco Meat" balls, water, soup mix and salsa to pot, and boil 15 minutes.
✡	Step 7	Add vegetables, beans, black olives, and cook 5 minutes until heated through.
✡	Step 8	Put hot soup in bowls with preferred "Garnish" on top and serve hot.

Make entirely in microwave, or in crock pot from Steps 6-8. For quicker soup omit oil, substitute 1 Tbs. dried minced onion flakes and ½ tsp. dried minced garlic flakes for fresh and skip Step 4-5. Due to garnish, one shouldn't serve this on Shabbat. Makes about ½ gallon or 4-8 servings.

Legume Soups and Chilis

Legume Soups

Columbia Restaurant® Style Black Bean Soup

6 cups water

1 lb. black beans (rinsed)

1 tsp. baking soda

1½ Tbs. olive oil

6 (1 Tbs.) minced garlic cloves

3 Tbs. finely minced onion

2 Tbs. finely minced green pepper

1 Tbs. salt

1 tsp. ground cumin

¼ tsp. ground oregano

1¼ tsp. sugar

¼ tsp. black pepper

3-4 cups hot cooked white rice

1 additional small (½ cup) chopped onion (optional for serving on top)

Step 1   Put water in large pot or crock pot, add beans, and soak overnight (do not drain).

Step 2   Heat oil in a frying pan, add garlic and sauté until just starting to brown.

Step 3   Add minced onions and peppers to pan, sauté 5 minutes on low heat.

Step 4   Add contents of pan, salt, cumin, oregano, sugar and pepper to beans.

Step 5   Turn on crock pot, or heat beans on stove until starting to boil and reduce heat.

Step 6   Cook in crock pot 4 hours on high or 8 hours on low, or simmer 3 hours on stove.

Step 7   Serve hot in bowls on a bed of rice, topped with onions.

Garnish with dairy sour cream for D, or *Parve Imitation Sour Cream* (p. 105) for P or M. Goes great with *Columbia Restaurant® Style Cuban Sandwiches* (p. 244). Makes 6-8 servings.

For quick-soak method for beans, in Step 1, bring water to boil 10 minutes and let sit 1 hour.

Calico Bean Soup (13 Bean Soup)

1½ tsp. barley

2 Tbs. black beans

¼ cup black eyed peas

¼ cup garbanzo beans (chick peas)

¼ cup great Northern beans

⅔ cup red kidney beans (preferably ½ light red and ½ dark red)

¼ cup lentils (green, red, or a mixture of both)

⅓ cup baby lima beans

¼ cup large lima beans

¼ cup navy beans

¼ cup pinto beans

¼ cup split peas, OR 1½ Tbs. green split peas + 2½ tsp. yellow split peas

8 cups water

2 tsp. salt

⅛ tsp. baking soda

3 sliced *parve* soy hot dogs (optional)

dash cayenne pepper or hot pepper sauce

1 large chopped onion (¾ cup), OR ¼ cup dried minced onion flakes

1 (15 oz.) can chopped tomatoes, OR 1 (8 oz.) can tomato sauce

1 minced garlic clove (½ tsp.), OR ¼ tsp. dried minced garlic flakes

✹ Step 1　　Rinse all legumes and put in a large pot (or at least a 4 qt. crock), with water to cover for soaking overnight (or use the quick soak method found in Dry to Liquid Ratios).

✹ Step 2　　Drain legumes and add water, salt, and baking soda. (If using a crock pot, add an extra 5 cups water and 1 extra tsp. salt.) Bring to a boil, and simmer 2½-3 hours.

✹ Step 3　　Add onions, tomatoes or tomato sauce, garlic, cayenne or pepper sauce and hot dogs if desired, simmering another ½ hour. Serve hot.

If using a crock pot, cook on high 6-8 hours, or 10-12 hours on low. (For overnight cooking on low, add 2-3 cups extra water. No pre-soak is needed.) This recipe is about 20 oz. legumes. If cutting the recipe, it's about 2½ cups water for each 4 oz. legumes. Makes 12-14 servings.

Campbell's® Style Bean with Bacon Soup

1 cup great Northern beans (rinsed and presoaked)

4 cups water (or 3 cups water for thicker soup)

1 small minced onion (¼ cup), OR 1 Tbs. dried minced onion flakes

¾ tsp. garlic salt

dash cayenne pepper

⅛ tsp. black pepper

¼ tsp. baking soda

1 cup tomato sauce

2 Tbs. *parve* imitation bacon bits

Combine ingredients and bring to boil, simmering 2½-3 hours, or until beans are tender. (If using a crock pot cook 4 hours on high, or 8 hours on low.) Makes 4-6 servings.

☆ ☆

Campbell's® Style Split Pea with Ham Soup

2 cups split peas (rinsed and presoaked)

6 cups water

8 tsp. *parve* chicken soup mix, OR 4 *parve* chicken bouillon or soup cubes

dash cayenne pepper or hot pepper sauce

1 bay leaf

1-2 diced carrots (½ cup)

¼ cup diced celery, OR 2 Tbs. dried celery flakes

1 small minced onion (¼ cup), OR 1 Tbs. dried minced onion flakes

½ tsp. thyme leaves

½ tsp. parsley flakes

1-2 tsp. *parve* imitation bacon bits

Combine ingredients. Simmer 1 hour uncovered until peas are tender. (If using crock pot, cook 4 hours on high, 8 hours on low.) Strain 1 cup peas and put in soup. Makes 4-6 servings.

(🍿 rice) (🥤 all else)   **Indian Curried Bean & Lentil Soup**

1 cup cooked or canned black beans

½ cup raw lentils (rinsed)

½ cup raw white rice, OR 1 cup cooked white rice (reduce water by 1 cup)

3 Tbs. *parve* chicken soup mix

5 cups water (add more if needed— especially if wanting leftovers)

1 small chopped onion (¼ cup), OR 1 Tbs. dried minced onion flakes

2 minced garlic cloves, OR 1 tsp. dried minced garlic flakes

1 tsp. ground cumin

½ tsp. ground coriander

¼ tsp. ground ginger

1½ Tbs. curry powder

⅛ tsp. cayenne pepper (add more for spicier soup)

Bring all ingredients to boil in pot, simmer ½ hour or until lentils are tender. Makes 4-6 servings.

✡ ✡

(🥤 soup) (🥕 beans)   **Chili Bean Soup**

1 (8 oz.) can tomato sauce

2 tsp. *parve* beef soup mix, OR 1 *parve* beef bouillon or soup cube

1 (15 oz.) cans pinto or kidney beans, OR 2 cups cooked pinto beans

1 small chopped onion (¼ cup), OR 1 Tbs. dried minced onion flakes

1 cup water

¼ tsp. ground cumin

⅛ tsp. garlic powder

½ tsp. sugar

1½ tsp. *Chili Powder* (p. 434)

Combine all ingredients, bring to a boil and heat through. Serve hot. Makes 4 servings.

Instead of the last 4 ingredients, ½ packet (2 Tbs.) taco seasoning mix can be substituted.

170

Chilis

Ramen Noodle Chili

7 cups water (add 2 more cups if soup-style chili is desired)

4 (2.8 oz.) pkg. kosher chicken ramen soups (remove packets, break noodles)

2 whole packets from above kosher chicken ramen soups

½ cup *Taco Bell® Style Taco Seasoning* (p. 81), **OR 1 pkg. taco seasoning**

½ cup mild or medium store-bought salsa

¼ tsp. garlic powder

Bring water to boil. Add noodles, taco seasoning and salsa, blend well. Simmer 3 minutes, turn off heat and add only 2 (of the 4) seasoning packets. Serve immediately. Makes 4 servings.

✡ ✡

(if using beans) ## Hormel® Style Chili

3¼ cups water

½ cup corn starch

8 tsp. *parve* beef soup mix, OR 4 *parve* beef bouillon or soup cubes

2 tsp. dried minced onion flakes

2 tsp. dried minced garlic flakes, OR 2 minced garlic cloves (1 tsp.)

1 (8 oz.) can tomato sauce

1 tsp. sugar

2 Tbs. *Chili Powder* (p. 434)

¾ cup textured vegetable protein (TVP®)

"Hamburger" =
- **D-** 1 cup soy crumbles + 1 Tbs. avocado oil.
- **P-** 1 cup *parve* soy crumbles + 1 Tbs. avocado oil.
- **M-** ½ lb. kosher ground beef (browned and drained).

1 well-drained (15 oz.) can kidney beans (optional)

Blend first 2 ingredients in pot. Add last ingredients, bring to boil. Reduce heat, simmer stirring constantly, until thick. (Freeze in 2 cup increments to use like 16 oz. cans.) Makes 4-6 cups.

(✎with beans) (🧁 crackers) **Skyline® Style Chili** (🧁 for crackers)

"Meat" =
- **D-** 2 cups soy crumbles + 1 Tbs. *parve* beef soup mix + 1 Tbs. oil.
- **P-** 2 cups *Parve Soy Crumbles* (p. 110).
- **M-** 1 lb. raw kosher ground beef or turkey.

4 cups water

1 (8 oz.) can tomato sauce

1 tsp. dried minced onion flakes

2½ Tbs. *Chili Powder* (p. 434)

½ tsp. ground cinnamon

1½ tsp. garlic powder

1 tsp. salt

1 tsp. ground allspice

¾ tsp. ground cumin

¼ tsp. celery salt

½ tsp. ground marjoram

⅛ tsp. black pepper

⅛ tsp. ground cloves

¼ tsp. paprika

dash cayenne pepper

3 whole bay leaves

1 (15 oz.) can kidney beans (optional for "5-Way Chili")

✿ Step 1   Combine all ingredients except last in a pot. Blend with a fork and bring to a boil.

✿ Step 2   Reduce heat and simmer uncovered 1-1½ hours. (Do not use a crock pot.)

✿ Step 3   Add beans if desired within the last 5 minutes of cooking.

✿ Step 4   Strain out bay leaf, and serve hot in any of the ways listed below.

All dry ingredients can be combined and stored until ready to use. Just add the wet ingredients. This is an addictive favorite from Cincinnati, Ohio. The way it's cooked creates a special texture, and a slight wateriness blends to creates the flavor. Makes 1 quart chili, or 4-8 servings depending on how it is served). By itself is "1-Way Chili". All variations on opposite page (Ways 1-5) can be served with oyster crackers, to be authentic. Top with bottled hot pepper sauce if desired.

Other Skyline® Style Chili Variations

For **"2-Way Chili"**: Serve "1-Way" *Skyline Chili* on a plate of cooked spaghetti. 🧁　🧁

☺　　　　☺　　　　☺

For **"3-Way Chili"**: Serve "2-Way", top chili with grated kosher Cheddar cheese for D, or grated *parve* imitation American or Cheddar cheese for P or M. 🧁　🧁

☺　　　　☺　　　　☺

For **"4-Way Chili"**: Same as "3-Way", but additionally topped with chopped raw onions. 🧁　🧁

☺　　　　☺　　　　☺

For **"5-Way Chili"**: Serve as with "4-Way", adding optional beans to the recipe. 🧁　🧁

☺　　　　☺　　　　☺

For **"Coney Islands"**: Serve "1-Way" *Skyline Chili* over *parve* soy hot dogs in hot dog buns for D or P, or kosher beef hot dogs in hot dog buns for M. Serve hot. 🌭　🌭

☺　　　　☺　　　　☺

For **"Cheese Coneys"**: Top each D Coney Island with 2 Tbs. kosher grated Cheddar cheese or each P or M Coney with ½ slice *parve* imitation American cheese. Heat to melt. 🌭　🌭

✡ ✡

Quick No-Cook Chili

½ pkg. (1 cup) *parve* soy crumbles

1 (15 oz.) can kidney beans (undrained)

1 cup store-bought salsa

4 tsp. parve beef soup mix, OR 2 tsp. *parve* beef bouillon powder

½ (24-26 oz.) jar spaghetti sauce or marinara sauce (1½ cups)

1 Tbs. *Chili Powder* (p. 434)

½ tsp. garlic powder

Combine all ingredients together, blending well, and heat through on stove or in microwave. Makes 7 cups chili, or 4-6 servings.

Serve on 4 cups rice or spaghetti for a hearty meal. Top with kosher grated Cheddar or Parmesan cheeses or a dollop of sour cream for D, or top with grated imitation *parve* cheese, *Parve Parmesan Cheese* (p. 108), or a dollop of *Parve Imitation Sour Cream* (p. 105) for P or M. Use like canned chili. If desired, divide in 2 cup portions to freeze. It's as easy as opening a can.

(spaghetti or crackers) **Frisch's® Style Chili** (spaghetti)

1 Tbs. avocado oil (other vegetable oil can be used)

"Hamburger" =
- **D-** 1 pkg. (2 cups) imitation hamburger crumbles + ¼ cup oil.
- **P-** 2 cups *Parve Soy Crumbles* (p. 110) + ¼ cup oil.
- **M-** 1 lb. kosher ground beef or turkey.

½ cup chopped onion

2½ cups tomato sauce

2 Tbs. *Chili Powder* (p. 434)

1½ Tbs. ground cumin

¼ tsp. garlic powder

1¼ tsp. sugar

¾ tsp. salt

2 cups water

1 (15 oz.) can kidney beans (drained)

1 lb. cooked spaghetti (optional)

16-24 *parve* soda crackers (optional)

Step 1   Put vegetable oil in a large pot and heat until warm.

Step 2   Add "Hamburger" and onions and sauté until onions are tender (and "Hamburger" is browned if M). Do not drain.

Step 3   Add next 8 ingredients and blend thoroughly.

Step 4   Bring to a boil and simmer covered stirring occasionally until slightly thickened, 1-1½ hours for D or P, or 2 hours for M uncovering pot during last ½ hour of cooking.

Another Cincinnati favorite. Top with kosher Parmesan cheese for D, or *Parve Parmesan Cheese* (p. 108) for P or M. Serve on spaghetti with soda crackers on the side. (The D and P versions are actually more authentic tasting.) Makes 4 servings by itself, or 8 servings with spaghetti.

For quicker preparation, omit chopped onion and substitute 2 Tbs. dried minced onion flakes, adding them in Step 3 instead.

174

(✎ chili only) (🧁 on crackers)   **Wendy's® Style Chili**   (🥛 chili only) (🧁 on crackers)

2 tsp. avocado oil (other vegetable oil can be used)

"Hamburgers" = {
D- 4 soy burger patties.
P- 4 *parve* soy burger patties.
M- 4 kosher ground beef patties.
}

"Meat" = {
D- 1 pkg. (2 cups) imitation hamburger crumbles.
P- 2 cups *Parve Soy Crumbles* (p. 110).
M- 1 lb. cooked crumbled kosher ground beef or turkey.
}

1 (15 oz.) can tomato sauce

2 (15 oz.) cans kidney beans (undrained)

1 small chopped onion (¼ cup)

2½ Tbs. sugar

1 tsp. finely minced pickled jalapeño peppers

¼ cup minced celery, OR 2 Tbs. dried minced celery flakes

1 (15 oz.) can chopped tomatoes (undrained)

¾ tsp. ground cumin

½ tsp. garlic powder

1½ Tbs. *Chili Powder* (p. 434)

½ tsp. coarse ground black pepper

¾ tsp. salt

1¼ cups water

⚙	Step 1	Put oil in a large pot and fry "Hamburgers" until brown. (Drain if necessary.)
⚙	Step 2	Break "Hamburger" into chunks, add remaining ingredients and bring to a boil.
⚙	Step 3	Simmer 1½ hours, stirring occasionally. Serve hot.

Serve with soda crackers and hot pepper sauce if desired. Also can be served over *Super Stuffed Potatoes* (p. 191), just like the real thing. Goes well with a *Wendy's® Style Frosty* (p. 370). Makes 1½ quarts, 4-6 servings.

An alternative method is to make this with leftover hamburgers. For a complete meal, serve this over pasta or noodles. It makes a hearty dinner.

Texas-Style Chili

3½ cups water (divided)

7 Tbs. masa flour (divided)

"Meat" =
- **D-** 1 pkg. (2 cups) imitation burger crumbles + 1 Tbs. beef soup mix.
- **P-** 2 cups *Parve Soy Crumbles* (p. 110) + 1 Tbs. beef soup mix.
- **M-** 1 lb. kosher ground beef (browned and drained).

1 cup tomato sauce

4½ Tbs. *Chili Powder* (p. 434)

2 Tbs. ground cumin

1½ tsp. ground oregano

1½ tsp. dried minced onion flakes

1½ tsp. dried minced garlic flakes, OR 2 minced garlic cloves (1 tsp.)

1 tsp. salt

⅛ tsp. paprika

½ tsp. cayenne pepper (use more for super spicy)

1 (15 oz.) can pinto or kidney beans (optional)

1 (15 oz.) can diced tomatoes (optional)

Step 1   Put 3 cups water and 3 Tbs. masa flour in a pot, blending thoroughly.

Step 2   Add "Hamburger", tomato sauce, chili powder, cumin, oregano, onion, garlic, salt, paprika, and cayenne, bring to a boil and simmer covered 45 minutes.

Step 3   Combine remaining ¼ cup masa flour and ½ cup water in a bowl and blend mixture well.

Step 4   Add mixture to chili, mix well, and simmer 10 more minutes.

Step 5   Add beans and tomatoes if desired, for heartier chili and cook 5 more minutes.

A wonderfully spicy chili. Serve hot with oyster crackers. All dry ingredients can be combined to make a mix and stored until ready to use. Just add the wet ingredients according to the recipe. Makes ½-gallon chili, 6-8 servings.

Masa flour is finely ground corn flour and can be easily found in the ethnic or Mexican section in supermarkets. Since it is a type of flour, it doesn't necessarily need a *hechsher*.

Salads and Side Dishes
Salads & Potato Side Dishes
Salads

✎ (🍞 if eating bowls)   **Taco Bell® Style Taco Bowl Salad**   🥤 (🐄 bowls)

"Meat" = {
- **D-** 1 pkg. (2 cups) taco-flavored imitation hamburger crumbles.
- **P-** 1 pkg. (2 cups) *parve* taco-flavored soy crumbles.
- **M-** 1 batch (1 lb.) prepared *Taco Bell® Style Taco Meat* (p. 115).

6 cups shredded prepared tossed salad

2 large diced tomatoes (2 cups)

1 cup sliced black olives

2 (15 oz.) drained cans pinto or chili beans (optional)

6 pre-made *Taco Salad Bowls* (p. 117)

"Cheese" = {
- **D-** 1 cup grated kosher Cheddar cheese.
- **P-** 1 cup grated *parve* American or Cheddar.
- **M-** 1 cup grated *parve* American or Cheddar.

1 batch *Mexican Restaurant Guacamole* (optional- p. 103)

1½ cups taco sauce or favorite salad dressing, OR 2 cups favorite salsa

❀	Step 1	In a large bowl, toss together first 5 ingredients.
❀	Step 2	Divide mixture evenly in 6 portions and put into each taco bowl.
❀	Step 3	Top each salad with "Cheese" and guacamole if desired.
❀	Step 4	Drizzle on favorite salad dressing and serve.

A short-lived product from the 1980s . Makes 6 very generous servings.

An easy alternative to using the *Taco Salad Bowls* are to substitute a bag of corn tortilla chips. It isn't as authentic, but the taste is similar, although it isn't as fancy or tender. Line the finished salad with plenty of chips, standing upright, and it is still a nice effect.

177

(🥛 on "Meat") (🍞 croutons) **Classic Italian Antipasto Salad**   🥛 (🍞 croutons)

"Meat" =
- **D-** 1-2 pkg. soy imitation salami or pepperoni (chopped).
- **P-** 1-2 pkg. *parve* imitation salami or pepperoni (chopped).
- **M-** 1 lb. kosher beef salami or pepperoni (chopped).

1 pkg. (or 4 cups) pre-made mixed tossed salad

4 medium chopped tomatoes (2 cups)

3 large seeded and diced green or red bell peppers (about 2¼ cups)

2-3 chopped green onions (about 1 cup)

1 cup *Parve Italian Dressing* (p. 89)

"Cheese" =
- **D-** 1 cup grated kosher Mozzarella, OR ½ cup kosher Parmesan.
- **P-** ½ cup grated *parve* Mozzarella, or *Parve Parmesan* (p. 108).
- **M-** ½ cup grated *parve* Mozzarella, or *Parve Parmesan* (p. 108).

2 cups store-bought or homemade *Salad Croutons* (optional- p. 116)

✡ Step 1   Put first 6 ingredients in a large bowl, and mix thoroughly.

✡ Step 2   Put in bowls. Crumble "Cheese" and sprinkle on top of salads. Top with croutons.

Alter ingredients to taste. Makes 4 generous servings.

✡ ✡

Rainbow Pasta Salad

¾ cup *Parve Creamy Italian Dressing* (p. 89)

2 Tbs. *Parve Milk* (p. 85), OR other *parve* milk alternative

2 cups cooked rainbow rotini pasta (well-drained)

✡ Step 1   Combine dressing, water and milk in a large bowl, blending until smooth.

✡ Step 2   Add rotini and gently stir until completely coated.

✡ Step 3   Cover and refrigerate to sit a couple hours, then stir well. Keep refrigerated.

Based on a great product that came out in the early 1980s, but didn't last. Makes 4 servings.

(♻ if eating avocado) **Avocado Bean Salad**

1 medium chopped tomato (½ cup)

1 small ripe avocado (cut in chunks)

½ cup corn

1 cup cooked kidney beans

¼ cup chopped red onion

½ cup favorite chunky salsa

½ (4 oz.) can diced jalapeño peppers (2 Tbs.) (optional)

¼ cup chopped green onions

3 minced garlic cloves (1½ tsp.)

1½ Tbs. lime juice

1½ Tbs. olive oil

¼ cup chopped fresh cilantro (Chinese parsley) leaves (optional)

¼ tsp. sugar

dash garlic salt (or to taste)

Mix all ingredients together and chill. Another favorite from Hawaii. Makes 4-6 servings.

✩ ✩

Mum's Creamy Potato Salad

3-4 medium peeled and chopped Idaho potatoes (boiled and drained)

1 cup mayonnaise

½ tsp. sugar

½ tsp. salt

1 tsp. prepared mustard

1 tsp. olive oil

1 tsp. vinegar

Combine all ingredients together and blend thoroughly. Makes 3-4 servings.

Potato Side Dishes

McDonald's® Style French Fries

4 medium older potatoes, OR 1 bag frozen kosher shoestring cut potatoes

½ cup sugar

¼ cup corn syrup

3 cups hot water

1 cup avocado oil (other vegetable oil can be used)

2 tsp. salt

❀ Step 1   If using plain potatoes, peel and cut into 2-3 inches long by ⅜ inch thick strips. If using frozen potatoes, thaw them completely and drain any water.

❀ Step 2   Combine sugar, corn syrup and hot water in a bowl, and stir thoroughly until well blended and all sugar is dissolved.

❀ Step 3   Put potatoes in bowl of sugar water, then put bowl in refrigerator ½ hour.

❀ Step 4   Take potatoes out of water and drain, then pat dry with paper towels.

❀ Step 5   Heat oil until hot enough to fry a bread cube when dropped in.

❀ Step 6   Add potatoes in small batches to oil. (Be careful, they will splatter.)

❀ Step 7   Fry 1 minute, then remove from oil and let sit, repeat for each batch.

❀ Step 8   Put potatoes back in oil and fry until golden brown, then remove from pan and drain on paper towels if desired.

❀ Step 9   Sprinkle with salt and toss fries gently to mix salt evenly. Serve immediately.

An alternative is to bake these. Do Steps 1-4, and put them on a greased cookie sheet. Spray with oil, and bake 10-15 minutes at 400° F until browned. They may have to be stirred and flipped. They taste exactly the same and are healthier. Makes 4 medium sized servings.

Goes nicely with *McDonald's® Style Chicken McNuggets* (p. 294) or *McDonald's® Style Fillet O' Fish* (p. 352).

Chick-Fil-A® Style Waffle Fries

3 medium potatoes (washed, scrubbed & peeled)

wavy type cutting knife or slicer (for pickle slices, carrots, or crinkle fries)

2 cups peanut oil for frying, OR vegetable oil spray for baking

salt to taste

Step 1   Slice potatoes with "crinkle" or "wavy" cutter so that you have wavy-cut slices.

Step 2   Turn slices perpendicular and slice them again. You should now have raw waffle fries. (Use extra pieces that come out for hash browns or recipes calling for diced potatoes.)

Step 3   Pat slices dry if necessary. For frying- heat oil in a deep-frying pan or deep-fryer. For baking- spray a cookie sheet with oil, and preheat oven to 450° F.

Step 4   Put slices in oil for frying; or on cookie sheet, then spray with oil and put in oven.

Step 5   Fry or bake until light brown and barely crisp. Salt to taste. Makes 4 servings.

☆ ☆

Hot & Spicy Fries

1½ tsp. salt

½ tsp. cayenne pepper

¾ tsp. paprika

4½ tsp. sugar

¼ cup flour

3 medium potatoes (washed, peeled & cut into 3-inch long x ⅜-inch square strips)

olive oil spray or olive oil

Step 1   Put first 5 ingredients in a large zipper bag, and shake to blend thoroughly.

Step 2   Coat fries thoroughly with by spraying or dredging with oil.

Step 3   Place fries in spice bag and shake to coat evenly. Preheat oven to 400° F.

Step 4   Spread fries in a single layer on a well-greased cookie sheet. Spray with oil.

Step 5   Bake 15 minutes, stir and flip, then bake another 15 minutes.

Similar to Arby's® "curly fries", but a bit spicier and these have no curl. Makes 4 servings.

Savory Steak Fries

⅛ cup olive oil

¼ tsp. salt

⅛ tsp. black pepper

¼ tsp. basil leaves

¼ tsp. thyme leaves

¼ tsp. oregano leaves

⅛ tsp. paprika

2-3 medium potatoes (washed and scrubbed)

"Parmesan" = {
D- ¼ cup real grated kosher Parmesan cheese.
P- ¼ cup *Parve Parmesan Cheese* (p. 108)
M- ¼ cup *Parve Parmesan Cheese* (p. 108)
}

✾ Step 1   Combine olive oil and next 6 ingredients in a bowl, blend thoroughly and set aside.

✾ Step 2   Cut each potato in half lengthwise, then into thirds lengthwise.

✾ Step 3   Coat each slice of potato thoroughly in seasoned oil.

✾ Step 4   Spread on a cookie sheet in a single layer, and bake in a preheated 450° F oven 15 minutes.

✾ Step 5   Take out of oven, sprinkle with "Parmesan", and then bake 15 more minutes until crispy.

These are better than French fries, (although fried in oil they're very good too). Makes 4 servings.

Home-Style Hash Browns with Onions

3 thinly sliced or diced older medium potatoes (peeled)

1 small chopped sweet Vidalia onion (¼ cup)

½ tsp. salt

¼ tsp. coarse ground black pepper

¼ cup avocado oil (other vegetable oil can be used) **or *parve* margarine**

⊛ Step 1   Spread potatoes on paper towel, pat dry with another one to remove moisture.

⊛ Step 2   Combine potatoes, onions, salt and pepper in a bowl, mixing until well blended.

⊛ Step 3   Heat oil in large frying pan. Put mixture in oil and flatten with spatula.

⊛ Step 4   Flip when slightly browned, and fry until other side is lightly browned. Serve hot.

Old potatoes and sweet onions has such flavor! Bake like *Potatoes O'Brien*. Makes 4 servings.

✡ ✡

Potatoes O'Brien

3 diced or shredded older medium potatoes (peeled)

1 small chopped sweet Vidalia onion (¼ cup)

1 small seeded and diced green bell pepper (¼ cup)

½ tsp. salt (more to taste if needed)

2 tsp. parsley flakes

dash cayenne pepper

¼ tsp. coarse ground black pepper

¼ cup avocado oil (other vegetable oil can be used) **or *parve* margarine**

⊛ Step 1   Spread potatoes on a paper towel then cover them with a second and pat dry.

⊛ Step 2   Combine potatoes and next 6 ingredients in a bowl, mixing until well blended.

⊛ Step 3   Heat oil in a large frying pan until hot, put mixture in oil, and flatten with a spatula.

⊛ Step 4   Flip when slightly browned, and fry until other side is lightly browned. Serve hot.

To bake: Skip Step 1, do Step 2, skip Steps 3-4. Coat well with oil and put in baking pan. Bake 25 minutes in 400° F oven until browned. Flip and bake 20 more minutes. Makes 4 servings.

Simple Potato Pierogies

24 *Wonton Wrappers* (p. 116- shape into half circles if home-made)

1 batch pierogi filling (opposite p. Do not use *Deluxe Whipped Potatoes* on p. 192.)

salt water (for boiling)

optional sauce (heated- below)

✣	Step 1	Lay wrappers on a flat surface, put 2 Tbs. filling in the center of 12 wrappers.
✣	Step 2	Bring salt water to boil. Wet wrapper edges, place another wrapper atop mixture.
✣	Step 3	Seal edges together. (Freeze, if desired.) Gently put in water, and lower heat.
✣	Step 4	Simmer 5 minutes. Remove with slotted spoon. Serve with sauce. Makes 12.

Pierogi Sauces

Sour Cream Sauce

½ cup *Parve Imitation Sour Cream* (p. 105)

2 Tbs. *parve* margarine or *Parve Imitation Butter* (p. 84)

Heat on low heat, and blend together until smooth. Keep warm until serving.

Butter Sauce

½ cup *parve* margarine or *Parve Imitation Butter* (p. 84)

2 Tbs. *Parve* Cream (p. 85)

Heat together and blend until smooth. Keep warm until serving.

Butter & Onion Sauce

½ cup *parve* margarine or *Parve Imitation Butter* (p. 84)

¼ cup diced onion

Sauté onions in margarine in a pan until lightly brown. Keep warm until serving.

Pierogi Fillings

Blend ingredients together well, and continue from Step 1 on previous page. Leftovers can be used for *Superb Potato Patties* (p. 186).

Plain (Potato)

3 cups very stiff mashed potatoes

3 small beaten eggs

⅛ tsp. ground nutmeg

⅛ tsp. black pepper (optional)

Garlic Flavored

1½ tsp. garlic powder

2½ cups *Plain Pierogi Filling* (above)

Cheese Flavored

2½ cups *Plain Pierogi Filling* (above)

"Cheese" =
- D- ¼ cup real grated kosher American or Cheddar cheese (melted).
- P- ¼ cup grated *parve* American or Cheddar cheese (melted).
- M- ¼ cup grated *parve* American or Cheddar cheese (melted).

Onion Flavored

⅓ cup *parve* margarine

¾ cups chopped onions, OR 3 Tbs. snipped chives

2½ cups *Plain Pierogi Filling* (above)

Melt margarine in a pan and sauté onions or chives until limp. Add to filling and blend thoroughly.

185

Fried Potato Cakes

3 grated older medium potatoes (peeled)

¼ cup *parve* margarine or avocado oil (other vegetable oil can be used)

4 eggs

2¼ Tbs. flour

1 small chopped sweet Vidalia onion (¼-½ cup)

¾ tsp. salt

¼ tsp. coarse ground black pepper

❀ Step 1   Spread potatoes on paper towels, and cover with another one, patting them to remove excess moisture.

❀ Step 2   Put ¼ inch oil in a large frying pan and heat until hot.

❀ Step 3   Combine potatoes and remaining ingredients in a bowl and mix until blended.

❀ Step 4   Shape firmly into 18 cakes, and fry until browned. Flip and brown other side.

Put on paper towel lined plates to drain. Serve hot. Makes 12 cakes, or 4-6 servings.

✡ ✡

Superb Potato Patties

1 batch favorite pierogi filling (p. 185)

⅔ cup *All-Purpose Breading Mix* (p. 83)

olive oil for frying (other oil can be used)

❀ Step 1   Combine first 2 ingredients and blend together well.

❀ Step 2   Shape into 3-inch patties, and then coat each patty with breading.

❀ Step 3   Heat ¼ inch olive oil in a frying pan until hot, and gently place each patty in oil.

❀ Step 4   Fry patties until golden brown on each side, drain on a paper towel lined plate.

Serve hot. Makes 12 patties, or 4-6 servings.

Potatoes Au Gratin

¼ cup *parve* margarine

1 tsp. snipped chives (optional)

¾ tsp. salt

¼ tsp. paprika

½ tsp. mustard powder

dash cayenne pepper

1 batch (1 cup) *Tangy Restaurant Cheese Sauce* (p. 98)

"Cream" =
- **D-** ¼ cup half & half or real cream.
- **P-** ¼ cup *Parve* Cream (p. 85).
- **M-** ¼ cup *Parve* Cream (p. 85).

6 medium potatoes (peel, slice & boil), **OR 3 (15 oz.) cans sliced potatoes**

Step 1   Combine first 8 ingredients in a pot and heat through.

Step 2   Stir until sauce is thickened.

Step 3   Drain potatoes and stir into sauce, heat through and serve hot.

Tangy and delicious. Makes about 4-6 servings.

☺   ☺   ☺

For **"Ham Flavored Potatoes Au Gratin"**, add 4 tsp. *parve* imitation bacon bits in Step 1. Do the rest as normal.

Scalloped Potatoes

"Milk" =
- **D-** 1¼ cups whole milk.
- **P-** 1¼ cups *Parve Milk* (p. 85), OR *parve* milk alternative.
- **M-** 1¼ cup *Parve Milk* (p. 85), OR *parve* milk alternative.

½ cup *parve* margarine

¼ cup flour

¾ tsp. salt

dash black pepper

⅛ tsp. paprika

dash cayenne pepper

½ tsp. onion powder

"Cheese" =
- **D-** ¼ cup grated kosher American or Cheddar cheese.
- **P-** ¼ cup grated *parve* American or Cheddar cheese.
- **M-** ¼ cup grated *parve* American or Cheddar cheese.

4 medium potatoes (peel, slice & boil), **OR 2 (15 oz.) cans sliced potatoes**

Step 1	Stir together first 8 ingredients in a pot until smooth.
Step 2	Heat on low stirring constantly until starting to thicken, then add "Cheese".
Step 3	Keep stirring (keeping on low) until "Cheese" is melted and well blended.
Step 4	Drain potatoes if needed, and add sliced potatoes to pot and heat through.

It may not be quite as easy as a packaged mix, but still fairly simple and delicious. For oven method, Do Steps 1-3, then put potatoes in a greased 1½ qt. baking dish. Pour mixture over potatoes and bake in a preheated 350°F oven until top is starting to brown. Makes 4 servings.

☺   ☺   ☺

For **"Sour Cream & Chive Scalloped Potatoes"**, omit "Cheese". Add 2 Tbs. snipped chives or green onions and 1 tsp. flour, and substitute ⅓ cup real sour cream for D, or *Parve Imitation Sour Cream* (p. 106) for P or M for "Cheese" in Step 3.

Stouffer's® Style Potato Bake

7 older medium potatoes (peeled and diced into ½-inch cubes)

1 Tbs. *parve* margarine

"Cream Cheese" =
- **D-** 1 (8 oz.) pkg. real cream cheese, cut in chunks.
- **P-** 1½ cups *Parve Imitation Cream Cheese* (p. 105).
- **M-** 1½ cups *Parve Imitation Cream Cheese* (p. 105).

"Milk" =
- **D-** ¼ cup milk.
- **P-** ¼ cup *Parve Milk* (p. 85), OR *parve* milk alternative.
- **M-** ¼ cup *Parve Milk* (p. 85), OR *parve* milk alternative.

2 tsp. onion powder

1½ tsp. salt

¾ tsp. paprika (plus extra for sprinkling on top)

⊛ Step 1   Cook potatoes 15 minutes until slightly soft, but not crumbly. Drain and set aside.

⊛ Step 2   In a large pot or large microwave safe bowl, combine margarine, "Cream Cheese", "Milk", salt, onion powder and paprika. and heat on low until all cheeses start melting.

⊛ Step 3   Stir until well blended and smooth, add potatoes and stir gently until coated.

⊛ Step 4   <u>To Bake</u>- Put in a greased baking dish and sprinkle decoratively with paprika, bake 15 minutes in a preheated 350º F oven until heated through. <u>To Microwave</u>- Keep in bowl and sprinkle with paprika, cook about 4 minutes on high until heated through.

This was the addictive original potato bake that came out in the 1980s. (It gets better the longer it sits, as the flavors blend.)

For extra speed, the potatoes can be cooked in larger chunks and made like mashed potatoes. For more "bite", 1 small minced onion (¼ cup) can be sautéed in melted margarine until transparent, and added in Step 2. Makes 4-6 servings.

Stuffed Baked Potatoes

3 large baking potatoes

vegetable oil spray

"Milk" =
- **D-** ¼ cup milk.
- **P-** ¼ cup *Parve Milk* (p. 85), OR *parve* milk alternative.
- **M-** ¼ cup *Parve Milk* (p. 85), OR *parve* milk alternative.

5 Tbs. parve margarine

¾ tsp. salt

"Sour Cream" =
- **D-** ½ cup real sour cream.
- **P-** ½ cup *Parve Imitation Sour Cream* (p. 105).
- **M-** ½ cup *Parve Imitation Sour Cream* (p. 105).

favorite topping (optional- see below and opposite page)

Step 1   Preheat oven to 400º F. Prick potato skins, spray with oil, and wrap in foil.

Step 2   Bake 1-1½ hours or until potato is thoroughly cooked all the way through.

Step 3   Let cool slightly when done, and slice in half lengthwise.

Step 4   Carefully scoop out potato leaving skins intact, and put in a large bowl.

Step 5   Add next 4 ingredients to potatoes and mash together until well blended.

Step 6   Put mixture in skins and top with desired topping. Put back in oven to warm.

Serve hot. Eat as-is plain, or top with one or more of the various toppings listed below and on the opposite page. Makes 6 servings, ½ potato per person. (1 whole potato could even be eaten as a main meal, and would yield 3 servings.) Use toppings on regular baked potatoes to make like Wendy's® Style Super-Stuffed Potatoes.

These can also be done in the microwave- poke skins, place on a paper towel and cook 10-14 minutes. (However, it's not quite as good a flavor as baked.)

The Works: Combine all toppings or any combination (below and next page). Cut amounts of various vegetables in half. (See individual listings for *brachot* on specific toppings.)

☺   ☺   ☺

Chili: Top with 1½ cups hot *Wendy's® Style Chili* (p. 175). (Grated Cheddar cheese can be put on top of chili for D, or grated *parve* American or Cheddar cheese for P or M.) 🍴 (✎ beans) 🥛

Other Stuffed Baked Potato Toppings

Sour Cream & Chives Topping

"Sour Cream" = {
D- 1½ cup real sour cream (spread over potato).
P- 1½ cup *Parve Imitation Sour Cream* (p. 105- on top).
M- 1½ cup *Parve Imitation Sour Cream* (p. 105- on top).
}

6 Tbs. snipped chives (sprinkle on top of "Sour Cream")

Broccoli Cheese Topping

"Cheese" = {
D- 6 slices kosher Cheddar cheese (place onto potato).
P- 6 slices *parve* American or Cheddar (place onto potato).
M- 6 slices *parve* American or Cheddar (place onto potato).
}

1½ cups cooked minced broccoli (sprinkle on top of "Cheese")

Bacon Cheese Topping

"Cheese" = {
D- 6 slices kosher Cheddar cheese (place onto potato).
P- 6 slices *parve* American or Cheddar (place onto potato).
M- 6 slices *parve* American or Cheddar (place onto potato).
}

2 Tbs. *parve* imitation bacon bits (sprinkle on top of "Cheese")

Mushroom Swiss Topping

2 Tbs. *parve* margarine

1½ cups sliced mushrooms

"Swiss Cheese" = {
D- 6 slices kosher Swiss cheese
P- 6 slices *parve* imitation Mozzarella cheese.
M- 6 slices *parve* imitation Mozzarella cheese.
}

"Parmesan" = {
D- 6 Tbs. grated kosher Parmesan cheese.
P- 6 Tbs. *Parve Parmesan Cheese* (p. 108).
M- 6 Tbs. *Parve Parmesan Cheese* (p. 108).
}

Melt margarine in a pan, add mushrooms and sauté until tender. Top potato with mushrooms, then cover with "Swiss Cheese", and last sprinkle "Parmesan" over top of potato.

Deluxe Whipped Potatoes

6 medium potatoes (peeled & chopped)

salted water

"Butter" =
{
D- ⅓ cup butter or margarine.
P- ⅓ cup *parve* margarine.
M- ⅓ cup *parve* margarine.

2 tsp. salt

¼ tsp. fine ground black pepper

"Milk" =
{
D- 1 cup whole milk (divided).
P- 1 cup *Parve Milk* (p. 85), OR *parve* milk alternative.(divided).
M- 1 cup *Parve Milk* (p. 85), OR *parve* milk alternative.(divided).

❀ Step 1   Boil potatoes in salted water 20 minutes, or until tender.

❀ Step 2   Drain water (reserving ½ cup if using P or M, or use for soups), and put potatoes in a bowl.

❀ Step 3   Add "Butter", salt and pepper in bowl with potatoes, and mash together, adding ¼ cup "Milk".

❀ Step 4   Using a mixer (or a potato masher if extra tender), whip together potatoes with remaining ¾ cup "Milk", until smooth and creamy, (reheat if necessary). Serve hot.

Serve with gravy and real or *parve* imitation meat. Sprinkle with some extra coarse ground black pepper if desired for a garnish. This is one of the very few recipes that does not freeze well. Makes about 3½ cups or 4-6 servings.

☺   ☺   ☺

For **"Cheesy Whipped Potatoes"**, just after draining potatoes while still hot, in Step 3 mix in 1 cup warm kosher grated Cheddar cheese for D, or 1 cup warm grated *parve* imitation American or Cheddar cheese for P or M. Proceed with Step 4 as normal. These potatoes are extra creamy and so good. You won't believe your mouth that the P and M versions are not dairy! (Unlike some foods, this recipe is better fresh as opposed to sitting to let flavors blend.) Makes 4-6 servings.

(topping alone) **Crunchy-Cream Baked Potatoes**

2 small baked potatoes (split in half)

2 Tbs. *Parve* **Cream** (p. 85)

2 Tbs. *parve* **margarine**

¼ tsp. salt

"Sour Cream" = {
D- ¼ cup real sour cream.
P- ¼ cup *Parve Imitation Sour Cream* (p. 105).
M- ¼ cup *Parve Imitation Sour Cream* (p. 105).

2 Tbs. snipped chives (optional)

"Crumbs" = {
D- ¼ cup crushed dairy cheese crackers.
P- ¼ cup crushed *Parve Nabisco® Style Tid-Bits®* (p. 128)
M- ¼ cup crushed *Parve Nabisco® Style Tid-Bits®* (p. 128)

Step 1   Carefully scoop potato out of skin. Combine with next 5 ingredients, blend well.

Step 2   Put mixture back in skins, sprinkle crushed "Crumbs" over top of each potato.

Step 3   Bake 20 minutes in 400° F oven, until topping is crunchy. Makes 4 servings.

✩ ✩

(raisins alone) **Yummy Yams**

4 medium cooked sweet potatoes or yams, OR 1 (26 oz.) can yams (drained)

¼-½ cup *parve* **margarine**

½-¾ cup raisins (preferably soaked until starting to expand for tenderness)

2 tsp. ground cinnamon

Step 1   Mash sweet potatoes or yams. Add remaining ingredients and blend well.

Step 2   Heat in microwave or oven until hot. Serve hot.

A wonderfully easy and naturally-sweet recipe from Ayelet. The flavors blend nicely when refrigerated overnight. Freshly baked sweet potatoes can be used—cut each open and add 1-2 Tbs. margarine, 2-3 Tbs. raisins, and ½ tsp. ground cinnamon or to taste for each potato. Makes 4-6 servings.

Vegetable Side Dishes

Eggplant Patties

⅔ cup All-Purpose Breading Mix (p. 83)

1 large well beaten egg

1 large eggplant (peeled & sliced into ½-inch thick slices)

avocado oil for frying (other vegetable oil can be used)

Step 1   Put breading mix in one shallow bowl, and put egg in another shallow bowl.

Step 2   Dip eggplant slices lightly in egg, then dredge in breading mix to coat well.

Step 3   Put ¼ inch of oil in the bottom of a large frying pan and heat until very hot.

Step 4   Fry eggplant until brown on either side. Drain on paper towels and serve hot.

To Bake: As Step 3-4, put on a well-greased cookie sheet, spray well with oil. Bake at 400° F 10-15 minutes. Flip and bake 10 more minutes or until lightly browned. Makes 4 servings.

✿ ✿

(topping)   **Morrison's Cafeteria® Style Eggplant Casserole**   (topping)

1 medium eggplant (peeled, chopped and boiled 20 minutes until tender)

"Crackers" =
- D- 1¼ cup real kosher cheese crackers.
- P- 1¼ cup Parve Nabisco® Style Cheese Tid-Bits® (p. 128)
- M- 1¼ cup Parve Nabisco® Style Cheese-Tid-Bits® (p. 128).

¼ tsp. salt

1 tsp. dried minced onion flakes

1¼ cup Condensed Cream of Mushroom Soup (p. 148)

1 (4 oz.) can sliced mushrooms (drained)

Step 1   Drain and mash eggplant well. Crush "Crackers" to make ¾ cup, set aside.

Step 2   Add salt, onion, soup, mushrooms and ½ cup "Crackers" to eggplant, blend well.

Step 3   Put in greased casserole, sprinkle with last ¼ cup "Crackers".

Step 4   Bake 20 minutes in preheated 420° F oven (baking gives it the authentic crunchy topping). It can also be microwaved 4 minutes until heated through). Makes 5-6 servings.

Savory Stuffed Eggplant

½ cup water

1 medium eggplant (cut in half lengthwise)

1 Tbs. olive oil or melted *parve* margarine

¼ tsp. salt (optional or to taste)

1½ cups taco soy crumbles or *parve Taco Bell® Style Taco Meat* (p. 115)

Step 1   Set eggplant skin-side-down in a baking dish, coat cut parts with oil or margarine.

Step 2   Bake 25 minutes at 350º F or until inside is soft. Take out, but leave oven on.

Step 3   Carefully scoop meat out of skin. Put in a bowl, mash slightly and add taco meat.

Step 4   Blend well, put mixture in skins and bake 10 more minutes. Cut in half and serve.

Dramatic dish with a wonderful flavor- nothing like tacos! Makes 4 servings.

✫ ✫

Oven Roasted Vegetables

1 (4 oz.) pkg. fresh mushrooms, OR 4 portobella mushrooms

1 small eggplant (preferably peeled)

2 medium red or orange bell peppers (seeded)

2 small-medium zucchini squashes

1-2 cups cubed butternut or acorn squashes (optional- peeled & seeded)

1 small-medium sweet Vidalia onion (quartered & sliced)

8 large garlic cloves (sliced and/or minced)

¼ cup olive oil

¼ tsp. crushed basil leaves

¾ tsp. salt

¼ tsp. ground black pepper

Step 1   Chop veggies into 1-2 inch cubes/slices. Combine last 4 ingredients in big bowl.

Step 2   Put all vegetables in bowl. Stir to coat and spread on well-greased cookie sheets.

Step 3   Bake 45 minutes in preheated 400º F oven until tender. Makes 4-6 servings.

Broccoli with Cheese Sauce

2 (10 oz.) pkg. frozen cut broccoli (thawed)

1 tsp. salt (or to taste)

2 batches (2½ cups) *Condensed Cheddar Cheese Soup* (p. 151)

Cook broccoli according to package and heat condensed soup. Drain broccoli, add salt, stir and put in individual bowls. Pour soup over broccoli. Serve immediately. Makes 4-6 servings.

✡ ✡

Deluxe Green Beans

2 (15 oz.) cans green beans (drained), **OR 2 (10 oz.) pkgs. frozen** (thawed)

1 cup water

2 tsp. *parve* **chicken soup mix, OR 1** *parve* **chicken bouillon or soup cube**

1 Tbs. dried minced onion flakes

Combine ingredients. Simmer 15 minutes, stirring occasionally. Makes 4-6 servings.

☺   ☺   ☺

For **"Deluxe Almond Green Beans"**, add ¼ cup sliced almonds. (on almonds only)

☺   ☺   ☺

For **"Green Beans with Ham"**, add 1 Tbs. *parve* bacon bits.

✡ ✡

(topping)   ## Classic French Green Bean Casserole   (topping)

1 batch (1¼ cups) *Condensed Cream of Mushroom Soup* (p. 148- or canned)

1 (15 oz.) can French cut green beans

½ (4 oz.) can chopped mushrooms (¼ cup)

1 cup French fried onions (divided)

Step 1   Blend first 3 ingredients and ½ cup onions in glass loaf pan. Top with last onions.

Step 2   Bake 12 minutes at 350º F, or microwave 5 minutes until hot. Makes 4 servings.

Boston Chicken® Style Creamed Spinach

1 batch (1¼ cups) *Condensed Cream of Celery Soup* (p. 148- made with salt)

1 Tbs. flour

¼ cup avocado oil (other vegetable oil can be used)

½ tsp. garlic salt

2 (10 oz.) pkg. chopped spinach (cooked and drained)

1 small minced onion (¼ cup)

Step 1   Combine first 4 ingredients in a small pot on medium heat, stirring until smooth.

Step 2   Add spinach and onion and heat through. <u>For Microwave</u>- do as above, heating in 30-second intervals, stirring until thick and smooth. Serve hot. Makes about 4-6 servings.

✿ ✿

(on filling)   ## Pepper Surprises

4 green or red bell peppers (with even bottoms so peppers can stand upright)

"Cottage Cheese" = {
D- 4 cups real cottage cheese.
P- 4 cups *Parve Cottage Cheese* (p. 109).
M- 4 cups *Parve Cottage Cheese* (p. 109).

1 cup (any or all) garnish: black pepper, green onions, chopped olives, hot peppers, mushrooms, sunflower seeds, *mandelin* soup croutons or chow mein noodles.

Step 1   Carefully cut upper quarter of each pepper all the way around the top to make replaceable "hats". (Peppers should be self-supporting when put back into place.)

Step 2   Scrape at white pith. Scoop out all seeds and pith, leaving clean inner shells.

Step 3   Mix together "Cottage Cheese" and half of garnishes.

Step 4   Take mixtures and fill peppers, then sprinkle on remaining garnishes.

Step 5   Take top "hats" and put them back into place, so that peppers appear whole.

Salad with dressing or coleslaw can be used instead of cottage cheese.

These can also be cooked until tender: Fix with a cooked stuffing like burger and rice or *Mary Kitchen® Style Roast Beef Hash* (p. 328). After Step 5, put peppers in a greased baking pan at 350º F and bake 30-45 minutes, or microwave 2 peppers 10 minutes (rotate after 5 minutes). Makes 4 servings.

Whipped Squash

1 large (3 lb.) butternut squash (cut in half and seeded)

2 Tbs. *parve* **margarine** (plus extra to top if desired)

1 tsp. salt (or to taste)

paprika (optional)

- Step 1   Place halves skin side up in a glass baking dish filled with 1 inch water.
- Step 2   Bake at 350° F 1 hour or microwave 10 minutes until soft. Take out and let cool.
- Step 3   Take one squash half and scoop meat out with a spoon, (discard strings or skin).
- Step 4   Put in blender while still warm and puree until smooth. (Repeat with other half.)
- Step 5   Add margarine and salt, blend well. Remove from blender and heat through.
- Step 6   Put in bowls sprinkled with paprika and a dollop of margarine if desired.

Just like the frozen 10 oz. boxes of cooked squash, but kosher! After doing Step 6, it can be frozen in small zipper bags. This can be made into squash soup by adding an equal ratio of squash to water. Makes about 4 cups, or 4-8 servings (equivalent to 2½ frozen pkg.).

✿ ✿

Spaghetti Squash

1 large spaghetti squash (halved and seeded)

2 tsp. *parve* **margarine** (plus extra if desired, to top)

dash black pepper (optional)

1 (16 oz.) can or jar spaghetti sauce

"Parmesan Cheese" = {
D- ½ cup real kosher Parmesan cheese.
P- ½ cup *Parve Parmesan Cheese* (p. 108).
M- ½ cup *Parve Parmesan Cheese* (p. 108).
}

- Step 1   Place squash halves in a glass baking dish filled with 1 inch water.
- Step 2   Bake 45 minutes at 350° F, or microwave about 8 minutes until tender.
- Step 3   Scoop strings away from sides, add margarine, pepper and sauce, blending well.
- Step 4   Sprinkle with "Parmesan Cheese", heat through and serve. Makes 4-6 servings.

198

Egg-Zucchini Squares

1 medium-large minced onion (¾ cup)

3 minced garlic cloves (1½ tsp.)

2½ Tbs. avocado oil (other vegetable oil can be used)

1 medium-large or 3 small thinly sliced zucchini (2½-3 cups)

½ tsp. hot pepper sauce, OR ⅛ tsp. cayenne pepper

¼ tsp. crushed basil leaves

⅜ tsp. crushed oregano leaves

1 Tbs. parsley flakes

⅝ tsp. salt

"Cheese" =
  D- 1 (4 oz.) pkg. (1 cup) grated kosher Cheddar cheese.
  P- 1 cup grated *parve* American or Cheddar.
  M- 1 cup grated *parve* American or Cheddar.

⅓ cup plain matzah (matzo) meal or *Bread Crumbs* (p. 116)

5 small-medium beaten eggs

½ tsp. paprika

Step 1   Sauté veggies in oil until tender. Blend in all other ingredients except paprika.

Step 2   Spread mixture evenly in a well-greased 7 x 11-inch baking pan.

Step 3   Sprinkle on paprika and bake 40 minutes at 350º F until firm. Makes 4 servings.

☆ ☆

Oregano-Basil Veggies

2 minced or pressed garlic cloves (1 tsp.), OR 2 tsp. minced garlic flakes

1 medium eggplant (peeled and diced), **OR 2 medium zucchinis** (sliced)

2 (15 oz.) cans chopped tomatoes, OR 4 large diced tomatoes + 1 cup water

6 chopped Mexican oregano leaves, OR 3 tsp. dried crushed oregano

4 large fresh chopped basil leaves (2 tsp. dried can be used but isn't tender)

½ tsp. salt (or to taste)

Combine and cook all ingredients until tender. (Good sprinkled with cheese.) Makes 4 servings.

Savory Roasted Corn

4 large fresh ears sweet corn (carefully husked and silks removed)

4 sheets aluminum foil (cut in at least 6-inch lengths)

6 Tbs. room temperature *parve* margarine (divided)

1½ tsp. onion salt (divided- garlic salt can be used as well)

1½ tsp. dried thyme leaves (divided)

Step 1   Put an ear of corn on foil and coat each evenly with 1½ Tbs. margarine.

Step 2   Sprinkle ⅜ tsp. onion salt over each ear rotating and spreading to distribute evenly, then do the same with ⅜ tsp. thyme leaves each. Preheat oven to 475° F.

Step 3   Wrap each ear completely in its foil. To bake, set seam-side up in baking pan.

Step 4   Bake or put foil-wrapped corn on hot grill coals ½ hour. Serve as-is or cut off cob.

Delicate seasoning. Keep husks and silks for kid's "*Corny Cuties*" (p. 423). Makes 4-8 servings.

✡ ✡

Burger King® Style Onion Rings

½ cup *Parve Milk* (p. 85)**, OR other *parve* milk alternative**

½ cup water

1 cup flour

1 cup *Bread Crumbs* (p. 116)

avocado oil for frying (other vegetable oil can be used)

2 medium sweet Vidalia onions (sliced into rings and separated)

Step 1   Get 3 shallow bowls. Combine milk and water in first bowl.

Step 2   Put flour in a second bowl, and put bread crumbs in last bowl.

Step 3   Heat oil in until hot, and dip each onion ring into milk mixture, then into flour.

Step 4   Dip each coated onion ring into milk and then into bread crumbs.

Step 5   In small batches, deep fry onion rings until brown. Drain on paper towels.

These can also be baked: For Step 5, put on a greased cookie sheet sprayed well with oil, and bake 10-15 minutes at 400º F. They come out just as good. Serve hot. Makes 4 servings.

Outback Steakhouse® Style Bloomin' Onion®

Coating:	**Batter:**
1 cup *Bread Crumbs* (p. 116)	**1 cup flour**
1 tsp. paprika (divided)	**½ tsp. paprika** (divided)
¼ tsp. black pepper (divided)	**½ tsp. black pepper** (divided)
1 tsp. garlic salt (divided)	**1 tsp. garlic salt** (divided)
⅛ tsp. cayenne (divided)	**dash cayenne** (divided)
	1 (12 oz.) can beer

Onions:

vegetable oil spray

4 large sweet Vidalia onions (peeled, roots cut off, and 1 inch of top removed)

1 batch *Outback Steakhouse® Style Creamy Chili Sauce* (p. 95)

Step 1   Blend coating ingredients in one bowl, and blend batter ingredients in another.

Step 2   Cut each onion about ¾ of the way through, (being careful not to cut all the way to the bottom), slicing from top down every ½ inch (about 12 to 16 vertical cuts).

Step 3   Cut onion bottoms flat to stand upright, and remove an inch of "petals" from center of onions. Separate "petals" somewhat to be coated fully. Preheat oven to 450º F.

Step 4   Gently place an onion in batter, let dry. Dip in coating to cover in and out, let dry.

Step 5   Place onions upright on a well-greased cookie sheet. Spray with oil, and bake 30-40 minutes until done. Put sauce in crocks in center of onions. Makes 4 onions, or 4-8 servings.

✿ ✿

Easy Artichokes

1 huge artichoke (lower leaves removed and checked thoroughly for bugs)

1 batch (½ cup) hot *Papa John's Pizza® Style Garlic Sauce* (p. 99)

Step 1   Soak artichoke in soapy water ½ hour, rinse well, and check for bugs once more.

Step 2   Put ¼ inch water in glass baking dish or pot, set artichoke in water and cover.

Step 3   Boil 45 minutes or microwave 15 minutes (rotating every 5 minutes) until tender.

Step 4   Put hot garlic sauce in individual crocks for dipping. Makes 2-4 servings.

🍿 (🥕okra only)   **Church's Chicken™ Style Fried Okra**   🍿 (🥤 okra only)

½ -1 lb. fresh okra, OR 1 (10 oz.) pkg. frozen okra (thawed)

½ cup *Parve Milk* (p. 85), OR ½ cup avocado or other oil

½ cup flour

½ cup *Bread Crumbs* (p. 116)

corn oil for frying (other vegetable oil can be used)**, OR spray oil for baking**

✡ Step 1   (Wash fresh okra, check for bugs.) Remove stems, cut in 1-inch slices, set aside.

✡ Step 2   Put water or oil in a bowl. Set aside.

✡ Step 3   In a separate bowl combine flour and bread crumbs, blending well.

✡ Step 4   Dip okra in *Parve Milk* or oil, then roll in flour mixture, let okra dry a bit. Repeat.

✡ Step 5   Put oil in frying pan ¼ inch deep and heat until very hot.

✡ Step 6   Put okra in oil and fry until golden brown, and drain on paper towel lined plates.

Serve hot. Makes about 4 servings.

An alternative is to bake them. Do Steps 1-4 using oil to dip. For Steps 5-6, set okra on greased cookie sheet. Spray with oil and bake 10-15 minutes at 400° F until browned. Drain if needed and serve hot.

✡ ✡

🥤 (🍿 breading only)   **KFC® Style Fried Mushrooms**   🥤 (🍿 breading only)

½ lb. fresh mushrooms of about equal size (wash, trim stem ends & pat dry)

2 Tbs. melted *parve* margarine, OR ¼ cup avocado or other oil

⅓ cup *Kentucky Fried Chicken® Style Breading Mix* (p. 82)

avocado oil for frying (other oil can be used)**, OR spray oil for baking**

✡ Step 1   Coat mushrooms with margarine or oil, then roll in breading, coating very well.

✡ Step 2   Heat some oil in skillet, then gently add mushrooms, browning all around. Gently remove, drain on paper towels and serve hot. Makes 12-24 mushrooms (depending on sizes).

An alternative is baking. Do Step 1 with oil— let coating dry a bit. For Step 2, set on a greased cookie sheet, spray with oil, and bake 25 minutes at 400° F until browned. Drain if needed.

Cool Carrots

2 (15 oz.) cans carrots (drained)**, OR 4 cups cooked sliced carrots**

1½ tsp. lemon juice

¼ cup melted *parve* margarine

¼ cup fresh chopped mint

Combine ingredients, heat and serve. (Leaves mouths cool and fresh!) Makes 4-8 servings.

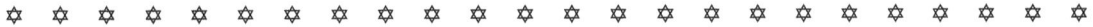

✿ ✿

Mum's Baked Beans

1 (28 oz.) can vegetarian baked beans (preferably half of liquid drained)

¾ cup brown sugar

½ tsp. onion powder, OR 2 tsp. dried minced onion flakes

2 tsp. *parve* imitation bacon bits (optional)

⅓ cup ketchup

2 tsp. prepared mustard

pinch pepper

pinch salt

Blend ingredients in a pot or microwave bowl. Heat through or serve cold. Makes 4-8 servings.

✿ ✿

Smoky BBQ Baked Beans

1 small chopped onion (¼ cup)

1 Tbs. avocado oil (other vegetable oil can be used) **or *parve* margarine**

2 (15 oz.) cans great Northern beans (drained)**, OR 4 cups cooked beans**

⅔ cups highly hickory smoke-flavored barbecue sauce

½ cup brown sugar

Sauté onions in oil or margarine until transparent Add remaining ingredients blending well. Simmer 15 minutes or microwave 5 minutes until heated. Serve hot or cold. Makes 8 servings.

Rice, Pasta and Grain Side Dishes

(on beans only)   **Red Beans & Rice**

½ cup dry pre-soaked small red beans (rinsed and drained)

4 cups water (more can be added if needed later on in cooking)

1½ tsp. avocado oil (other vegetable oil can be used)

1 small chopped onion (¼ cup)

¼ cup diced celery

1 bay leaf

¼ cup diced green bell pepper (seeded)

2 minced garlic cloves (1 tsp.)

1½ tsp. parsley flakes

½ tsp. ground thyme

4 tsp. *parve* chicken soup mix, OR 2 *parve* chicken bouillon or soup cubes

⅛ tsp. black pepper

⅛ tsp. cayenne pepper

⅔ cups raw white rice

2 *parve* soy hot dogs (chopped in ¼ inch pieces)

optional ½ cup cooked soy sausage or *parve* Country Sausage (p. 114)

bottled hot pepper sauce (optional for condiment)

Step 1   Put beans in a large pot and add water, oil, onion, celery and bay leaf.

Step 2   Bring to boil, reduce heat and simmer 1½ hours or until beans are tender, stirring occasionally. (If needed, add more water from now on.)

Step 3   Add green pepper, garlic, parsley, thyme, soup mix, black pepper, cayenne, rice, and hot dogs. Crumble sausage and add if desired. Cook 30 more minutes, stirring often.

Step 4   Strain out bay leaf and serve along with hot pepper sauce if desired.

For quicker preparation, use 1 (15 oz.) can undrained beans with only 2¼ cups water and half amount of soup mix or bouillon. (All remaining ingredients stay the same.) Combine ingredients and cook 40 minutes. Classic Cajun dish that can be eaten as a main dish as well as a side dish. Delicious with or without sausage. Makes 4 large servings.

Perfect Rice

2 Tbs. olive oil (other oil can be used)

1-2 (½-1 tsp.) minced garlic cloves (optional)

1 cup rinsed rice (basmati; jasmine; pearl/short-grain white; long-grain white; all brown)

¾-1 tsp. salt

water (jasmine and basmati: 1½ cups; all white and all brown: 2 cups)

Step 1   Combine first 3 ingredients in pot, sauté until rice is opaque. Add salt and water.

Step 2   Bring to boil, reduce heat and cover. Do not stir!. Simmer very gently:
White Basmati and *Jasmine*: 12-15 minutes.
Pearl/Short Grain and *Long Grain White Rice*: 25-30 minutes.
Brown Rice: 45-55 minutes.

Step 3   Cook until tender and liquid is absorbed, then take off heat.

Step 4   Let sit uncovered 5 minutes, then fluff with a fork and serve.

Tips: Stirring causes rice to break and get soggy. Rinsing omits excess starch that makes rice sticky. Sautéing keeps grains separate and fluffy. For "rice cooker-convenience", add all ingredients to a heavy pot with a steam hole. Do as above, and just leave it! No stirring needed. Makes 4-6 servings.

✡ ✡

Yellow Saffron Rice

2 cups water (1½ cups if using basmati)

¾ tsp. crushed saffron threads OR ¼ tsp. ground turmeric (imitation saffron)

2 Tbs. *parve* margarine or olive oil

2 minced garlic cloves (1 tsp.)

1 cup raw long grain white rice or white basmati rice (rinsed)

1 tsp. salt

Step 1   In a large sauce pan, bring water to a boil, then turn heat down to medium-low.

Step 2   Add saffron or turmeric, simmer uncovered 5-10 minutes, add remaining ingredients.

Step 3   Add margarine to water, then add garlic, rice and salt and bring to boil.

Step 4   Put on low, simmer covered (white rice- ½ hour, white basmati- 12 minutes).

Step 5   Take off heat, let sit 5 minutes uncovered. Fluff with fork. Makes 4 servings.

Simple Spanish Rice

2½ cups water

1 Tbs. *parve* margarine or avocado oil (other vegetable oil can be used)

1 cup raw white rice (rinsed)

1-1½ cups store-bought salsa (do not use homemade)

½ tsp. salt (or to taste)

"Optional Cheese" =
- **D-** 1 cup grated Cheddar cheese.
- **P-** 1 cup grated *parve* Cheddar cheese.
- **M-** 1 cup grated *parve* Cheddar cheese.

Step 1   Combine first 5 ingredients and bring to boil, reduce heat and simmer ½ hour.

Step 2   Top with "Optional Cheese" if desired, and heat through. Makes 4-6 servings.

✡ ✡

Vegetable Rice

2 Tbs. avocado oil (other vegetable oil can be used)

1 medium chopped onion (½ cup)

2 pressed or minced garlic cloves (1 tsp.)

1 cup raw white rice (rinsed)

¼ tsp. salt

dash cayenne pepper (optional)

4 tsp. *parve* chicken soup mix, OR 2 *parve* chicken bouillon or soup cubes

3 cups water

1 (16 oz.) can mixed vegetables, OR 1 (10 oz.) pkg. frozen vegetables (thaw)

Step 1   Put oil in large pot and heat until warm, then add onion, garlic and rice.

Step 2   Sauté until rice is opaque, stir in salt, cayenne, bouillon and water. Bring to boil.

Step 3   Stir to dissolve soup mix. Lower heat and simmer 25 minutes or until rice is tender and liquid is absorbed.

Step 4   Add mixed vegetables and cook 5 more minutes.

A colorful dish for guests, which keeps a long time in the refrigerator. Makes 4-6 large servings.

Luscious Long Grain & Wild Rice

⅓ cup rinsed raw wild rice (plus 2 cups boiling water if using non-par-boiled)

2 tsp. *parve* chicken soup mix, OR 1 *parve* chicken bouillon or soup cube

½ tsp. celery salt

¼ tsp. garlic powder

3 Tbs. dry onion soup mix

1 tsp. sugar

½ tsp. ground cumin

¼ tsp. ground ginger

1½ Tbs. parsley flakes

1 cup raw white rice (rinsed)

3 cups water

2 Tbs. *parve* margarine

⊛ Step 1   For non-par-boiled wild rice: Add to boiling water, simmer 50 minutes, drain and add other ingredients. For quick-cooking wild rice: Combine ingredients in pot and bring to boil.

⊛ Step 2   Simmer covered ½ hour (stir occasionally), until liquid is absorbed and rice is tender. (Dry ingredients can be stored until ready to use.) Makes 2 cups, or 6-8 servings.

✫ ✫

Country Grits

3 cups *Parve Milk* (p. 85) or other *parve* milk alternative

1½ tsp. salt

pinch black pepper

4½ tsp. *parve* margarine (plus extra to serve on top after cooking)

¾ cup quick grits (made from white hominy corn)

⊛ Step 1   Put first 5 ingredients in a pot, bring to a boil, add grits and reduce heat.

⊛ Step 2   Simmer covered 5-8 minutes. Serve hot, with margarine.

Delicious as-is, or an essential for *Country Ham with Grits and Red-Eye Gravy* (p. 325). Makes 4 servings.

Perfect Pasta

2 qt. salted water

1 tsp. olive oil (other vegetable oil can be used)

1 lb. dry noodles or pasta (for cooking Couscous see p. 499, Orzo p. 500.)

1 Tbs. *parve* margarine

Step 1   Combine water, oil and salt if desired, in a large pot and bring to a boil.

Step 2   Boiling times for specific pasta types– Angel Hair: about 4 minutes.

          Small Macaroni, Vermicelli or *Thin Egg Noodles*: 5 minutes.

          Manicotti, Thin Spaghetti, and *Medium or Wide Egg Noodles*: 7 minutes.

          Regular *Spaghetti* or *Large Macaroni*: 8 minutes.

          Linguini, Fettuccine, Lasagna or *Manicotti*: 10-11 minutes. (For baked recipes, like Lasagna or stuffed shells like Manicotti, "parboil" or boil half of normal cooking time.)

Step 3   Dump when it cuts easily, but do not overcook. Rinse with cold water.

Step 4   Add margarine and additional salt, stir to coat.

Pasta is always best "al dente" or "to the tooth"- somewhat soft, but firm with still a little "bite" to it. There's nothing worse than soggy overcooked pasta! Makes 6½ cups, or 4-8 servings.

✡ ✡

Creamy Mushroom-Garlic Pilaf

1 pkg. (4 oz.) fresh shiitake mushrooms (8 oz. drained can okay- not as good)

8 minced garlic cloves (4 tsp.)

1½ Tbs. olive oil (other vegetable oil can be used)

2 cups water (add more if too dry in Step 4)

1½ tsp. salt

1 tsp. dried thyme leaves

1½ tsp. dried crushed basil

1 cup (½ lb.) dry orzo pasta

1 cup *parve Condensed Cream Soup* (p. 147- use mushroom soup mix)

Step 1   Cut off root end of mushrooms, dice stems and chop caps into 1-inch pieces.

Step 2   Put mushrooms in pot, add oil and garlic, sauté on low until garlic is transparent.

Step 3   Add water, salt, thyme and basil, bring to rapid boil. Add orzo. Cook 8 minutes.

Step 4   Blend condensed soup into pot and heat through. Makes 4-6 servings.

Kraft® Style Macaroni and Cheese

"Cheese" = {
D- 5 slices kosher Cheddar or American cheese + ⅛ tsp. sugar.
P- 5 slices *parve* imitation Cheddar or American cheese.
M- 5 slices *parve* imitation Cheddar or American cheese.

4½ Tbs. *Parve Cream* (p. 85)

1 Tbs. *parve* margarine

1½ Tbs. water

¼ tsp. mustard powder

pinch cayenne pepper

⅜ tsp. salt

½ lb. (2 cups) hot cooked extra-small elbow macaroni (*Perfect Pasta* p. 208)

⚙ Step 1   Shred "Cheese" into bits and combine with all remaining ingredients except macaroni in a saucepan, or microwave safe bowl.

⚙ Step 2   Heat, stirring (in 30 second increments in microwave) until melted and blended.

⚙ Step 3   Immediately without delay, pour warm sauce over hot macaroni, stirring to coat.

Very close to the original. Oddly enough, the *parve* tastes a bit more authentic than the dairy!

For D- don't use real cheese, only processed slices. It does not work at all. Makes 2-4 servings.

✿ ✿

Lipton® Style Chicken Noodles & Sauce®

2 Tbs. *parve* margarine

½ cup *Chicken Gravy* (p. 102)

½ tsp. *parve* chicken soup mix, OR ¼ tsp. *parve* chicken bouillon powder

½ tsp. parsley flakes

¼ tsp. salt

2¾ cups (2 cups dry) hot cooked thin or medium egg noodles (see p. 208)

⚙ Step 1   Combine and warm first 5 ingredients. Blend thoroughly.

⚙ Step 2   Add hot cooked noodles. Blend well and heat through.

Noodles with a creamy chicken flavored sauce. Makes 4 servings.

Lipton® Style Sour Cream and Chive Noodles & Sauce®

2 Tbs. melted *parve* margarine

"Sour Cream" =
- **D-** ½ cup real sour cream + 1 Tbs. milk.
- **P-** ½ cup *parve* sour cream + 1 Tbs. *Parve Milk* (p. 85).
- **M-** ½ cup *parve* sour cream + 1 Tbs. *Parve Milk* (p. 85).

½ tsp. salt

2 tsp. snipped chives or green onions

2 cups (1½ cups dry) cooked thin or medium egg noodles (see p. 208)

Heat first 4 ingredients, blending well. Add noodles, mix and heat through. Makes 4 servings.

✡ ✡

Fettuccine Alfredo

"Cream Cheese" =
- **D-** 1 (8 oz.) pkg. real cream cheese, (softened).
- **P-** 1 cup warm *Parve Imitation Cream Cheese* (p. 105).
- **M-** 1 cup warm *Parve Imitation Cream Cheese* (p. 105).

"Parmesan" =
- **D-** ⅓ cup grated kosher Parmesan or Romano cheese.
- **P-** ⅓ cup shredded room temperature *parve* Mozzarella.
- **M-** ⅓ cup shredded room temperature *parve* Mozzarella.

"Milk" =
- **D-** ¾ cup half & half or liquid creamer.
- **P-** ¾ cup *Parve Cream* (p. 85).
- **M-** ¾ cup *Parve Cream* (p. 85).

2 Tbs. *parve* margarine

¼ tsp. garlic powder

¼ tsp. salt

3 packed cups (½ lb. raw) hot cooked fettuccine (see *Perfect Pasta* p. 208)

Step 1   Combine first 6 ingredients in a saucepan or a microwave bowl.

Step 2   Put on medium-low heat, stir constantly or in 1-minute increments, until smooth.

Step 3   Pour sauce onto warm fettuccine noodles and coat well. Makes 4 servings.

Quesadilla Spaghetti

3 cups (½ lb. raw) hot cooked spaghetti (see *Perfect Pasta* p. 208)

2 Tbs. *parve* **margarine**

"Cheese" =
- **D-** ½ cup grated kosher Cheddar cheese.
- **P-** ½ cup shredded *parve* American or Cheddar.
- **M-** ½ cup shredded *parve* American or Cheddar.

¼ tsp. red pepper flakes

¼ tsp. onion powder

Combine ingredients, and heat through. A delicious change of pace. Makes 2-4 servings.

✿ ✿

Tunisian Kukla (Sefardi Shabbat Stuffing)

¾ cup non-instant creamy wheat cereal (add extra *only* if too moist)

2 eggs (beaten)

1½ tsp. paprika

¼ tsp. turmeric

½ tsp. garlic powder

½ tsp. onion powder

1 tsp. salt

1 tsp. ground coriander

⅛ tsp. black pepper

dash cayenne

⅓ cup olive oil (add extra if too dry)

4 cups *Parve Beef Broth* (p. 110) **or water**

Step 1   Combine ingredients in a bowl and knead together until slightly firm but *not hard*.

Step 2   Let rest 5 minutes to see final consistency. It should hold together but not ooze flat.

Step 3   Shape into 2-inch-thick log, and wrap up in parchment. Set in broth, simmer 20 minutes.

The *Sefardi* equivalent to *Ashkenazi kishke*, this is ideally simmered for hours in *Chamin* (p. 321), Slice and serve warm. Based on a recipe from Chagit Hagage. Makes 8-12 servings.

Stove Top® Style Stuffing

2 cups water (add 2-3 Tbs. extra for moister dressing)

¼ cup *parve* margarine

1 Tbs. *parve* chicken or beef soup mix, OR 1½ tsp. *parve* bouillon powder

2 tsp. parsley flakes

¼ tsp. ground sage

½ tsp. ground thyme

3 Tbs. dried minced onion flakes

¼ cup dried minced celery flakes

¼ tsp. black pepper

6 packed cups chopped stale bread, OR 4 cups *Salad Croutons* (p. 116)

Step 1   Put all ingredients except bread in pot, bring to boil and simmer 15 minutes.

Step 2   Add bread, stir to moisten and let sit 5 minutes. Fluff with fork. Serve hot or cold.

2 cups *Bread Crumbs* (p. 117) can be substituted for croutons. Don't use store-bought. (If homemade croutons are brown, much more water is needed.) For flavor like it was baked in the bird, double margarine for D or P, or add ¼ cup meat drippings for M. For crusty texture, bake at 350° F 15-20 minutes. Variations can be made by adding chopped apples, raisins, nuts etc. For a different flavor, add ⅛ tsp. crushed rosemary leaves. Makes 2 cups, or 4-6 servings.

✡ ✡

Parve French Toast

4 eggs

¾ tsp. salt

1 cup *Parve Milk* (p. 85) or other *parve* milk alternative

8 bread slices

¼ cup melted *parve* margarine

Step 1   Beat first 3 ingredients in a bowl. Dip each bread slice in mixture, coating well.

Step 2   Put margarine in frying pan. Add each bread slice. Fry until brown, then flip and fry other side until browned. Makes 4 servings.

Texas Toast

¼ cup *parve* margarine

1½ tsp. garlic powder

⅛ tsp. salt

½ tsp. parsley flakes

½ tsp. paprika

8 thick bread slices, OR ½ baked loaf *French Bread* (p. 223)

Step 1   Melt margarine in a small pot or microwave bowl on low heat.

Step 2   Blend in garlic powder and salt to make garlic butter.

Step 3   Cut bread into 1-inch slices and put it on a cookie sheet.

Step 4   Spread bread evenly with garlic butter. Preheat oven to 350° F.

Step 5   Sprinkle bread with paprika and parsley flakes. (Spread evenly with a knife.)

Step 6   Bake 8-10 minutes or until bread gets toasted. Serve hot.

For quicker toast, use pre-made *parve* garlic bread, omitting garlic and margarine. Makes 4-8 servings.

✡ ✡

Garlic Bread

1 batch *Papa John® Style Garlic Sauce* (p. 99)

1 baked loaf *French Bread* (p. 223)

Step 1   Heat garlic sauce and keep warm. Preheat oven to 350° F.

Step 2   Cut bread down the side lengthwise in half.

Step 3   Spread bread evenly with the garlic sauce.

Step 4   Put bread on a greased cookie sheet.

Step 5   Bake 8-10 minutes or until bread gets toasted. Serve hot.

If you can't find kosher garlic bread frozen in the store, make your own, it's worth it! Works great for *Stouffer's® Style French Bread Pizzas* (p. 261) and *Fiesta Pizza* (p. 262). Makes 4-8 servings.

Parve Yorkshire Pudding

1¾ cup flour

1 tsp. salt

½ cup *Parve Milk* (p. 85), OR other *parve* milk alternative

1½ cups water

4 eggs

½ cup *parve* margarine

2 tsp. *parve* beef soup mix, OR 1 tsp. *parve* powdered beef bouillon

Step 1   Set all ingredients out and let stand until room temperature.

Step 2   Combine salt and flour in a mixing bowl, and make a pit in the center.

Step 3   Pour *parve* milk and water into pit, stir together and beat until fluffy.

Step 4   Add eggs and beat until bubbly, then cover and refrigerate 1 hour.

Step 5   Take batter out of fridge and let it become room temperature, then beat it again.

Step 6   Melt margarine on stove or in microwave and add soup mix, blending thoroughly.

Step 7   Divide soup mix mixture evenly into a warmed muffin tin for baking, or into a plastic microwave muffin pan or glass custard cups for microwaving.

Step 8   Spoon batter evenly into muffin pans or custard cups.

Step 9   For baking- Bake 20 minutes in a preheated 400° F oven, then reduce heat to 350° F, and bake 10 or 15 more minutes until firm. For microwaving- Heat on high in 1-minute increments until firm. Serve hot as soon as possible.

Normally, pudding has a connotation of being a sweet, smooth dessert. However, Yorkshire pudding has more the quality of a salty, savory biscuit or dinner roll. It is an elegant side dish that is not very common these days. My Mum used to serve it with prime rib for a special New Year's treat. Serve with imitation *parve* beef for D or P, or real kosher beef for M. (To the best of my knowledge, nobody else has ever had a recipe for Yorkshire pudding that was *parve* or could be done in the microwave prior to this.) Makes 12 servings.

Pre-made melted *Parve Meat Drippings* (p. 84) can be used. Skip Step 6, and use in Step 7.

Parve Home-Style Pancakes

1¼ cups flour

½ tsp. salt

1¼ tsp. baking powder

4 tsp. sugar (more can be added if desired)

3 beaten eggs

2 Tbs. melted *parve* margarine

1 cup *Parve Milk* (p. 85)

water (optional- add for thinner pancakes)

avocado oil, *parve* vegetable shortening, or *parve* margarine for frying

✿ Step 1   Blend dry ingredients in one bowl, and blend liquid ingredients in another bowl. (This recipe could possibly be used for *parve* waffles if margarine is doubled.)

✿ Step 2   Pour liquid mixture in center of dry, and blend quickly. (Do not over-beat batter.)

✿ Step 3   Grease a skillet with oil, and heat until a drop of water sizzles when dripped.

✿ Step 4   Pour batter in desired amounts in skillet. Turn once when starting to bubble and brown on bottom. (Repeat with remaining batter.) Freeze or serve hot. Makes 4-6 servings.

✡ ✡

Mandarin Chinese Pancakes

3 cups flour (plus extra for rolling out on)

1⅓ cup rapidly boiling water

3 Tbs. sesame or peanut oil (plus extra for frying)

¼ tsp. salt (optional)

✿ Step 1   Quickly blend ingredients well in mixing bowl and let dough rest a few minutes.

✿ Step 2   With floured or oiled hands, roll into 16 balls. Flour a surface and rolling pin.

✿ Step 2   Roll balls out into 6-inch circles. (They should look like flour tortillas).

✿ Step 3   Put a bit of oil in a small frying pan. Heat on medium-low heat until very warm.

✿ Step 4   Put one pancake at a time in pan and fry until starting to blister. Flip and repeat. (They can brown, but do not let them burn!) Add oil to pan if needed for remaining batches. Makes 16 pancakes.

(🧁 with food) (🍞 lots eaten alone) **Corn Bread** (🧁 with food) (🐑 alone)

1 cup flour

1 Tbs. baking powder

¼ cup sugar

1 tsp. salt

1¼ cup yellow corn meal or stone-ground corn meal

1 beaten egg

⅓ cup melted *parve* margarine

1 cup *Parve Milk* (p. 85) or other *parve* alternative milk

✤ Step 1   Blend dry ingredients together. (If desired, store in a zipper bag until ready to use, just like the packaged mixes.)

✤ Step 2   Put mixture and remaining ingredients in mixing bowl and blend lightly by hand.

✤ Step 3   Pour into a well-greased 8 x 8-inch pan, and bake in a preheated 425º F oven 20-25 minutes, or until starting to turn golden brown, and an inserted toothpick comes out clean.

Cut and serve hot. Great as-is, or put in muffin tins and bake 15-20 minutes. This recipe is also used with *Baked Corn Dogs* (p. 135). Makes 8-12 servings.

✡ ✡

(🧁 with food) (🍞 lots eaten alone) **Savory Corn Muffins** (🧁 with food) (🐑 alone)

1 batch raw *Corn Bread* dough (above)

1 tsp. ground savory

½ tsp. ground sage

¼ tsp. salt

1 Tbs. thyme leaves

4 drops red food coloring

✤ Step 1   Preheat oven to 425º F, blend ingredients. Pour into greased or lined muffin tins.

✤ Step 2   Bake 15-20 minutes until golden brown. Makes 12 muffins, or 8-12 servings.

Simple Biscuits

2 cups flour (plus extra for flouring)

⅜ tsp. salt

2½ tsp. baking powder

1½ tsp. sugar

½ cup softened *parve* margarine (plus extra for spreading)

¼ cup *Parve Milk* (p. 85)**, OR other *parve* milk alternative**

4½ tsp. water

Step 1   Preheat oven to 450° F. Sift together first 4 ingredients in a mixing bowl.

Step 2   Stir in margarine and blend until mixture has a "crumby" texture.

Step 3   Add water and milk blending lightly, then knead dough for a minute to basically mix together.

Step 4   Lightly flour a flat surface, and roll dough out to ½-inch thick.

Step 5   Cut out biscuits with 2½-inch-wide cutter. (A 4 oz. can also works beautifully, just twist as you cut.)

Step 6   Set biscuits 1 inch apart on a greased cookie sheet, and let dough rest ½ hour.

Step 7   Spread biscuit tops generously with margarine and bake 12-15 minutes until lightly browned.

Serve hot with dairy butter or *parve* margarine. Makes 12 biscuits.

After Step 5, biscuits can be wrapped up and refrigerated in zipper bags up to 1 week or frozen for future baking. Scrap dough can be used for dumplings in *Country Chicken Stew with Dumplings* (p. 299).

A quick and clean method is this: Do Steps 1-3. Get 2 large pieces of plastic wrap, spread one out on a flat surface, put half the dough on it and set the other wrap on top. Roll out dough to ½-inch thick, then peel off top wrap. Do Steps 5-7. This eliminates a floured surface and getting flour all over.

☺   ☺   ☺

For **"Garlic Cheese Biscuits"**, in Step 2, add ¼ tsp. garlic powder and ½ cup shredded *parve* American or Cheddar. Makes 1-1½ dozen biscuits.

Homemade Yeast Breads and Rolls

Breadmakers: Making bread sounded so intimidating, but my fear of the unknown was relieved when I tried it and found out how easy it is! These recipes for "no-frills" machines are quick, easy, tidy, and yield great results. Follow all breadmaker's manual instructions— machines vary in order of adding ingredients.

Ingredients: Keep at room temperature (about 70° F) before starting. Measure dry ingredients with dry measuring cups, leveling off the top with a knife. Flour should be high in gluten, (bread or all-purpose) for better rising and fluffier baked goods. For low-gluten flours (coarse or whole-grain) add 4-8 tsp. vital gluten (not the same as "high gluten flour"). Most flour is pre-sifted. Yeast is usually sold in packets, or jars if one bakes a lot. Active dry yeast is best for breadmakers, but rapid rise does just that- watch it closely or cut rise time short. Refrigerate after opening. Yeast and flour can be frozen up to 2 years.

Dough: The recipes are very stable, but atmospheric conditions can still affect them. Here are some tips:

⇨ **Humid Days:** In many places during a humid summer, or locations near water, usually you need to *add less water*. If dough looks more like batter, gradually add extra flour in 1 Tbs. increments. Moist dough can cause bread to fall during baking or stay raw inside.

⇨ **Cold Dry Days or Hot Locations:** In northern winters, or southwestern desert climates, generally you need to *add less flour*. If dough is too dry, add water in ½-1 tsp. increments. Dry dough yields cracked bread or can cause machines to stop, knock, or go off-balance.

⇨ **At High Altitudes:** Add less yeast and sugar. Also, treat as above for cold dry days.

Rising: Dough must be shaped and undisturbed before final rising. When rising, cover with greased plastic wrap and put it in a warm (not hot) area. (For good results, heat oven to 200° F then turn it off. After 5 minutes, set dough in oven.) If covering with plastic for final rise, be sure it's loose with room to rise, and don't forget to remove it before baking. Too much rising yields crumby bread, or it falls before or during baking.

Storing: After baking, put bread on racks and let cool completely. Seal in zipper bags. It can be room temperature 1-2 days, but being perishable, ideally refrigerate or freeze. Hold bread with its bag to cut it.

Freezing Dough: Take dough out after first rise and punch down. Put wax paper or greased plastic wrap in a loaf pan smaller than the size of pan to be baked in. Set loaf in lined pan and freeze. (Never braid prior to freezing.) Once frozen, wrap dough in plastic, put in zipper bag and freeze. (*Challah* can be taken before or after freezing or baking. See "*The Mitzvah of Taking Challah*" on pp. 622-623 for details.)

Using Frozen Dough: Unwrap dough and put in greased pan or bowl, cover, thaw in fridge overnight, divide, shape or braid, cover and set in a warm area 2-3 hours until doubled. Bake as for after final rise.

Pumpernickel Bread

1 cup hot water

1 tsp. instant coffee

5 tsp. molasses

¼ cup room temperature *parve* **margarine**

1½ tsp. salt

¼ cup sugar

2 Tbs. cocoa

1½ cups unbleached all-purpose or bread flour

1½ cups rye flour

4 tsp. vital gluten

2 tsp. caraway seeds

1 cake or pkg. active dry yeast (2¼ tsp.)

avocado oil for greasing (other vegetable oil can be used)

corn meal for dusting

1 egg white (optional)

Step 1   Blend together hot water, molasses and coffee, and let cool until slightly warm.

Step 2   Add coffee mixture and the next 9 ingredients (except corn meal) to bread pan in order according to machine instructions.

Step 3   Let breadmaker go through its kneading cycle, first rise and punch down. (Dough should be smooth, but will be sticky.)

Step 4   Grease hands very well with oil. Take dough out of breadmaker and divide it into 2 oval loaves.

Step 5   Dust a greased cookie sheet with corn meal. Grease loaves with oil, and gently set (spaced far apart) on cornmeal.

Step 6   Cover with greased plastic wrap, and let rise 1½ hours in a warm area until doubled.

Step 7   Remove plastic wrap. Brush tops with egg white if a shiny crust is desired.

Step 8   Bake in a preheated 350°F oven 20-25 minutes. Cool on racks.

European-style bread, made easy. Instead of the first 2 ingredients, 1 cup of leftover plain unflavored (or very lightly sweetened) black coffee can be used. Makes 2 small loaves.

Rye Rolls

1 cup water

¼ cup room temperature *parve* margarine

1 tsp. salt

4 tsp. vital gluten

1 cup rye flour

2 tsp. caraway seeds

1¾ cups unbleached all-purpose or bread flour

1½ tsp. active dry yeast

corn meal for dusting (optional)

optional egg wash: 1 egg + 1 Tbs. water beaten together

optional toppings: extra caraway seeds, or anise seeds

- Step 1   Add first 7 ingredients to breadmaker pan according to machine instructions.
- Step 2   Let breadmaker go through kneading, first rise and punch down cycles.
- Step 3   Take dough out of breadmaker before final rise begins.
- Step 4   Shape into 9 ovals and place on a greased cookie sheet (sheet can be dusted with corn meal if desired).
- Step 5   Put rolls in a warm area, cover with plastic wrap and let rise ½ hour.
- Step 6   Remove plastic. If desired, coat tops thoroughly with egg wash before baking and sprinkled with caraway or anise seeds.
- Step 7   Bake in a preheated 350° F oven 30-35 minutes or until barely starting to brown.

So delicious spread with butter! For a crisper crust, do not cover with plastic in Step 5. (Rye rolls are best eaten fresh, and do not last long. If they are not going to be used right away, it is a good idea to freeze them.) Makes 9 rolls.

Vital gluten is a protein derived from wheat. It is available in supermarkets with specialty flours.

☺   ☺   ☺

One can easily make a nice loaf of **"Rye Bread"**. Do Step 1-3. In Step 4, place entire loaf in a well-greased loaf pan dusted with corn meal, then do Steps 5-6. For Step 7, bake 45 minutes. Remove from pan and cool on rack. (Rye bread is best fresh, and doesn't last very long. Freeze if not to be used right away.) Makes 1 loaf.

Pita Bread (Pocket Bread)

1 cup + 2 Tbs. warm water

1 tsp. salt

¾ tsp. sugar

3 cups unbleached all-purpose or bread flour (plus lots extra for dusting)

1 cake or pkg. (2¼ tsp.) active dry yeast (do not use rapid-rise!)

olive oil for greasing bowl

Step 1   Add first 5 ingredients to breadmaker pan according to machine instructions.

Step 2   Let breadmaker go through its kneading cycle. (Dough should be smooth and stretchy, but not sticky.)

Step 3   Take dough out of breadmaker and put in a bowl greased very well with olive oil.

Step 4   Lightly grease dough ball with oil, cover and let rise in a warm area 1½ hours.

Step 5   Shape dough into an 18-inch-long log, cut it into 8 pieces, and shape each piece into a smooth ball.

Step 6   Roll each ball out on a very well-floured flat surface to ¼ inch thick and 7 inches in diameter. (Keep dough smooth- do not let it crease or double over, it may not puff properly.)

Step 7   Grease 4 small cookie sheets very well, and place pitas on them. Let rise ½ hour covered in warm area until doubled in thickness.

Step 8   Bake pitas individually or 2 at a time in a preheated 500° F oven 3 minutes on lowest oven rack. They should puff up, which makes a pocket. Little or no puff yields no pocket.

Step 9   Flip pitas with a spatula and bake 2 more minutes, but do not over-bake or let it get brown or burn- it will get too crisp and crack (although they are delicious toasted).

Step 10   Flatten pitas with a spatula, cover loosely and let cool, then store in plastic freezer zipper bags. Refrigerate or freeze. (If a pocket didn't form, slice one after cutting in half.)

These are so good they can be eaten alone! Once cut in half, the pocket easily tears open to stuff with meat or vegetables. Use for *Kosher Gyros* (p. 242), or any sandwich. Makes 8 pitas.

☺   ☺   ☺

For **"Parve English Muffins"**, Do Steps 1-5. In Step 6, do as above, but roll balls out to only 3 inches in diameter and ¾-inch thick. Creasing is not problematic. In Step 7, dust greased cookie sheets with corn meal before setting muffins down. Do Step 8, and for Step 9, bake 1-2 minutes more or until lightly brown. Do Step 10 as normal. (English muffins are usually dairy.) Makes 8.

Water Challah

1 cup water

1 tsp. salt

optional dough enhancer: 1¼ tsp. olive oil (or other oil)

flour: 2⅔ cups bread flour, OR 1 cup whole wheat + 1⅔ cups all-purpose

4 tsp. vital gluten (double if using bleached flour)

1½ tsp. active dry yeast

optional egg wash: 1 egg white or yolk + 1 Tbs. water (beaten together)

optional toppings: sesame seeds, poppy seeds

⚅ Step 1   Add all but last 2 ingredients to pan according to breadmaker instructions.

⚅ Step 2   Let breadmaker go through kneading, first rise and, punch down cycles.

⚅ Step 3   Separate dough into 6, 9 or 12 pieces, or 2 normal-sized loaves. For 1 huge loaf, don't separate (unless braiding). Keep dough covered when not in use. To Braid- One-at-a-time, separate into 3 snake-like strands. Stick all ends together at one point, and stretch strands out like a fan on unfloured surface. Braid like rope, tucking loose ends underneath to keep it pretty. (Do not freeze after braiding or dough may not rise well. Defrost frozen dough and then braid.)

⚅ Step 4   Set pieces or loaves on a greased cookie sheet, cover loosely with greased plastic wrap. Let rise in a warm area 1-2 hours (or longer for fluffier bread) until doubled.

⚅ Step 5   Remove plastic. Coat tops generously with egg wash for darker crust (yolk) or shiny crust (white).

⚅ Step 6   Sprinkle rolls with sesame or poppy seeds, or alternate between them if desired.

⚅ Step 7   Preheat oven to 350° F. Bake 6, 9, or 12 *challah* rolls 15-20 minutes, bake 2 loaves 25-30 minutes, or 1 loaf 30-35 minutes, all until barely starting to brown. Cool on racks.

Use dough for *Easy Calzones* or *Crisp-Crust Pizza* (p. 260). It's convenient to split a loaf and freeze after Step 2—perfect for 1 pizza or 6-7 fresh *challah* rolls. (In "*Using Frozen Dough*" on p. 218- let rise 3 hours.) Makes 6-12 rolls, or 1 huge, or 2 smaller loaves.

Sefardim can only use bread that doesn't taste eggy, oily or sweet. To be "*challah*", 4 batches are combined to take *challah* with no *brachah*, or 5-7 batches (depending on custom) with a *brachah*. Details are in "*The Mitzvah of Challah*" (pp. 622-623). Some *Sefardim* use 12 loaves on *Shabbat*, so a batch of 12 rolls is perfect— each roll is at least 1 oz.

French Bread

½ cup slightly warm water (plus extra in a loaf pan for steaming)

2 Tbs. room temperature *Parve Cream* (p. 85)

1 tsp. salt

2¼ tsp. room temperature *parve* margarine

1½ tsp. sugar

2 cups unbleached flour, OR 2 cups bleached flour + 4 tsp. vital gluten

1 pkg. active dry yeast (2¼ tsp.)

2-ft. long piece aluminum foil

olive oil (for greasing)

egg wash: 1 egg beaten with 1 Tbs. water

⊛ Step 1   Add first 7 ingredients to breadmaker pan according to machine instructions.

⊛ Step 2   Let breadmaker do its kneading, first rise and punch down, then take dough out.

⊛ Step 3   Roll out evenly on a floured surface to a ¼-inch thick, 21-inch-long rectangle.

⊛ Step 4   Roll long side of dough tightly "jelly-roll-style" up to middle. Do other side same way to meet. Pinch and round ends. (Loaf should be about 21-inches long by 2½-inches wide.)

⊛ Step 5   Grease foil well with olive oil. Gently set dough on foil seam-side-down.

⊛ Step 6   Lightly stretch or compress dough so that it is perfectly even and straight, then make several diagonal slits in top with a very sharp knife.

⊛ Step 7   Carefully bring sides of foil together and hold from the middle. (Transport loaf by using this "sling" method or prop it on an outstretched arm, being very careful not to let it bend.)

⊛ Step 8   Cover loosely with plastic wrap and let rise 45 minutes in a warm area until almost doubled.

⊛ Step 9   Preheat oven to 375º F. Put a pan of water on bottom oven rack and place loaf on center rack above, making sure it is perfectly straight. Remove plastic from bread.

⊛ Step 10   Bake ½ hour, pull rack halfway out of oven to coat entire loaf with egg wash, then push rack back in and bake 5 more minutes until lightly golden. (If bread starts to get too brown, put foil over top of loaf to reflect heat. It is a good idea to check the progress halfway through.)

⊛ Step 11   Remove from foil and let cool on 2 or more racks.

Delicious by itself, this is great for *Fancy French Onion Soup* (p. 158), *Fiesta* or *Stouffer's® Style French Bread Pizzas* (p. 262, 261), *Texas Toast* or *Garlic Bread* (p. 213). Makes 1 loaf.

Tender White Bread

¼ cup avocado oil (other vegetable oil can be used)

½ cup *parve* liquid non-dairy creamer + ¼ cup water, OR 1 cup *Parve Milk* (p. 85)

2 small egg whites (1 large beaten egg works, but turns bread slightly yellow)

1 tsp. salt

1 Tbs. sugar

3 cups bleached all-purpose flour

1 cake or pkg. active dry yeast (2¼ tsp.)

Step 1   Add ingredients to breadmaker pan according to machine instructions.

Step 2   Let breadmaker do kneading, first rise and punch down cycles, then remove loaf.

Step 3   Oil a piece plastic wrap. Divide dough in half and put in highly-greased loaf pans.

Step 4   Loosely cover with oiled plastic wrap. Put in a warm area ½ hour or more until doubled.

Step 5   Remove plastic. Bake in preheated 350º F oven 25-30 minutes, or until lightly golden brown. (Raise heat slightly if not getting browned. Overbaking dries it out and it won't be fluffy.)

Step 6   Cool completely on racks. When completely cool, put in zipper bags.

(Bread is best fresh and doesn't last very long. Freeze if not using right away.) Makes 2 loaves.

☺   ☺   ☺

For **"Homemade White Buns"**, do Steps 1-2. For Step 3: For hot dog buns- Form into 8 oblong buns and put in heavily greased 8 mini (3 x 5 inch) loaf pans. For hamburger buns- Form into 8 round buns, set buns on well-greased cookie sheet. In Step 4, let rise ½ hour, or longer if you like super fluffy. For plain buns simply bake. For topped or darker crusts, gently brush with 1 egg yolk mixed with 1 Tbs. water, top with poppy or sesame seeds, or top generously with finely minced raw onion. For Step 5, bake 15-20 minutes or until lightly golden (raising heat if needed). Makes 8 large buns.

☺   ☺   ☺

For **"Raisin Bread"**, add 1 tsp. cinnamon and 3 Tbs. extra sugar in Step 1. In Step 3, put ¾ cup raisins and dough in a bowl. (If raisins are added in with other ingredients, they will disintegrate- an interesting dark effect, but it still is delicious.) To keep raisins whole, knead them into dough in small batches until evenly distributed. Halve dough and press it into 2 highly greased loaf pans. Do Steps 4-5 as normal. Optional Glaze: Blend 8-8¼ tsp. warm water, ¾ tsp. vanilla extract and 1½ cups powdered sugar until smooth. Drizzle glaze over tops and let it harden before bagging. Makes 2 loaves. ⌂ for *Ashkenazim* and *Chassidim* ⌂ (🍿 *Sefardim* only 🍿)

Italian Rolls

⅞ cup slightly warm water

3 Tbs. olive oil (plus extra for brushing dough)

1 tsp. salt

1½ tsp. room temperature *parve* **margarine**

1½ tsp. sugar

2¾ cups unbleached all-purpose or bread flour (plus extra to flour flat surface)

1 cake or pkg. active dry yeast (2¼ tsp.)

2 tsp. corn meal

egg wash: 1 egg white beaten with 1 Tbs. cold water

✽	Step 1	Add first 7 ingredients to breadmaker pan according to machine instructions.
✽	Step 2	Let breadmaker do its kneading cycle. Dough should be smooth and stretchy.
✽	Step 3	Let breadmaker go through first rise and punch down, then take dough out.
✽	Step 4	Divide into 4 balls, and roll each out on floured surface into 8 x 5-inch rectangles.
✽	Step 5	Roll longer side up jelly-roll-style to make oblong loaf. Pinch and taper ends
✽	Step 6	Dust a well-greased cookie sheet with corn meal, set dough seam-side-down.
✽	Step 7	Brush with oil and make diagonal slits with a sharp knife. Grease plastic wrap.
✽	Step 8	Cover loosely with plastic wrap, let rise 45 minutes in warm area. Remove wrap.
✽	Step 9	Put a pan of water on bottom oven rack, and place bread on center rack above.
✽	Step 10	Bake buns in a preheated 400° F oven 15-20 minutes. Remove from oven.
✽	Step 11	Brush rolls with egg wash, coating thoroughly.
✽	Step 12	Bake 5-10 minutes more. Remove from sheet and let cool on racks.

These long, delicious rolls look like they came from an Italian grocery. Makes 4 large rolls.

☺   ☺   ☺

For **"Italian Bread"**, Do Steps 1-3. In Step 4, don't divide, roll dough out into 1 large 16 x 8-inch rectangle. In Step 5- For a long traditional-style loaf, roll dough up starting from long end. For a standard commercial-style loaf, roll up dough starting from smaller end. In Steps 6-7- For long loaf, do as normal. For a standard grocery store-style loaf, grease a large loaf pan thoroughly, omit corn meal, and skip Step 7. Do Steps 8-10. In Step 11, sprinkle on 1 tsp. sesame seeds after coating with egg wash. Do Step 12 as normal (bake a standard loaf 10 minutes longer). Makes 1 loaf.

🍞 (🧁 *Sefardim* if tomato is used) **Herbed Italian Rolls** 🍞 (🧁 *Sefardim* if tomato is used)

⅞ cup slightly warm water

3 Tbs. olive oil (plus extra for oiling hands, greasing pan and brushing dough)

1 tsp. salt

1½ tsp. room temperature *parve* margarine

1½ tsp. sugar

1 tsp. dried crushed oregano leaves (do not use ground)

½ tsp. garlic powder (more can be used)

2 Tbs. diced sun-dried tomatoes (optional)

2¾ cups unbleached all-purpose or bread flour (plus extra to flour flat surface)

1 cake or pkg. active dry yeast (2¼ tsp.)

2 tsp. corn meal

❀	Step 1	Put first 7 ingredients (and sun-dried tomatoes if desired) in breadmaker pan.
❀	Step 2	Add flour, make a pit in it and add yeast.
❀	Step 3	Let breadmaker do its kneading cycle. Dough should be smooth and stretchy.
❀	Step 4	Let breadmaker go through first rise and punch down, then take dough out.
❀	Step 5	Divide into 4 balls, and roll each out on floured surface into 8 x 5-inch rectangles.
❀	Step 6	Roll longer side up jelly-roll-style to make oblong loaf. Pinch and taper ends
❀	Step 7	Dust a well-greased cookie sheet with corn meal, set dough seam-side-down.
❀	Step 8	Brush dough with oil and make diagonal slits with a sharp knife.
❀	Step 9	Cover loosely with greased plastic wrap, let rise 45 minutes in warm area.
❀	Step 10	Remove wrap. Put a pan of water on bottom rack. Set bread on center rack.
❀	Step 11	Bake buns in a preheated 400º F oven 20 minutes or until lightly golden.
❀	Step 12	Remove from cookie sheet and cool on racks.

Savory and dramatic in appearance with or without the tomatoes. Makes 4 large rolls.

☺   ☺   ☺

This makes excellent **"Herbed Italian Bread"**, Do Steps 1-5 but divide in half, and roll dough into 2 big 12 x 7-inch rectangles. In Step 6- Roll up dough starting from smaller end. In Step 7- Grease 2 smaller loaf pans thoroughly, and omit corn meal if desired. In Step 8- Do not make diagonal slits. Do Steps 9-12 as normal but bake 5-10 minutes longer. Makes 2 smaller bakery-style loaves.

Subway® Style Italian Buns

⅞ cup slightly warm water (plus extra in a loaf pan for steaming)

3 Tbs. olive oil (plus extra for greasing and brushing dough)

1 tsp. salt

1½ tsp. room temperature *parve* **margarine**

1½ tsp. sugar

2¾ cups unbleached flour (plus extra for flouring flat surface)

1 cake or pkg. active dry yeast (2¼ tsp.)

4 disposable 8 x 5-inch aluminum loaf pans

2 tsp. corn meal

Step 1   Add first 7 ingredients to breadmaker pan according to machine instructions.

Step 2   Let breadmaker do its kneading cycle. Dough should be smooth and stretchy.

Step 3   Let go through first rise and punch down, take dough out. Divide into 4 balls.

Step 4   Roll each dough ball out onto a floured surface, into 8 x 5-inch rounded rectangles.

Step 5   Roll longer side up "jelly-roll"-style making an oblong loaf. Pinch and taper ends.

Step 6   Get 4 disposable 8 x 5-inch aluminum loaf pans and stretch each one out to make 4 round-ended elongated pans about 10 x 3 x 3 inches.

Step 7   Grease the special pans very well, and dust pan bottoms with corn meal, set dough seam-side-down.

Step 8   Brush dough with oil. Cover loosely with plastic wrap and let rise 45 minutes in a warm area until doubled. Preheat oven to 400° F. Remove plastic wrap.

Step 9   Put a pan of water on bottom oven rack, and place buns on center rack above.

Step 10   Bake buns 15-20 minutes, or until lightly golden brown.

Step 11   Remove from pans and let cool on racks.

Very authentic! (The special pans can be immersed in a *mikvah* for continual re-use.) Makes 4 buns.

Use for *Subway® Style Italian BMT® Sandwiches* (p. 243), or create your own submarine sandwich.

(🍿 Sefardim only)   **Subway® Style Honey Oat Buns**   (*Sefardim* only 🍿)

1 small beaten egg

1 Tbs. honey

¼ cup water (plus extra in a loaf pan for steaming)

3 Tbs. avocado oil (other vegetable oil can be used) **or *parve* margarine**

½ cup *Parve Milk* (p. 85)

2¼ tsp. lemon juice

4 tsp. sugar

1 tsp. salt

¼ tsp. baking soda

1 cup unbleached all-purpose or bread flour

1 cup whole wheat flour

2 tsp. active dry yeast

½ cup plain uncooked oatmeal (divided)

4 disposable 8 x 5-inch aluminum loaf pans

egg wash: 1 egg beaten with 1 Tbs. water

✿ Step 1	Add first 11 ingredients and ⅓-cup oats to bread pan according to instructions.
✿ Step 2	Let breadmaker go through kneading, first rise, punch down and final rise cycles.
✿ Step 3	Take out before baking cycle, divide into 4 balls, and shape into oblong loaves.

✿ Step 4   Get 4 disposable 8 x 5-inch foil loaf pans and stretch them to make 4 rounded elongated pans 10 x 3 x 3 inches. (*Tovel* for re-use). Grease pans well and put a loaf in each.

✿ Step 5   Cover loosely with plastic. Let rise in warm area 45 minutes until doubled. Remove wrap.

✿ Step 6   Coat tops of loaves well with egg wash and sprinkle with remaining 2⅔ Tbs. oats.

✿ Step 7   Put a pan of water on bottom oven rack, and place buns on center rack above.

✿ Step 8   Bake 20 minutes at 375º F until starting to brown. Cool on racks. Makes 4 buns.

☺   ☺   ☺

Use for **"Honey Oat Bread"**. Do Steps 1-2, remove after punch down. Put in greased loaf pan. Skip 3-4, do 5 (6 is optional), skip 7. Step 8- bake 35-45 minutes at 350º F. Cool. Makes 1 loaf.

☺   ☺   ☺

For **"Honey Whole Wheat Bread"**, do exactly as for *Honey Oat Bread* above, omitting oats. In Step 1 add ¼ cup water, ¾ cup whole wheat flour and 4 tsp. vital gluten. Makes 1 loaf.

Cuban Buns

¾ cup very cold water

1 tsp. salt

1 tsp. sugar

¼ tsp. olive oil (other vegetable oil can be used)

2 tsp. room temperature *parve* margarine

2¼ cups unbleached all-purpose or bread flour (more if needed)

1 Tbs. active dry yeast

⊛ Step 1   Add ingredients to breadmaker pan according to machine instructions.

⊛ Step 2   Let breadmaker go through kneading, first rise, punch down and final rise cycles.

⊛ Step 3   Take dough out just before baking cycle. The dough should be smooth and silky.

⊛ Step 4   With oiled hands, shape into 4 oblong loaves and set on a greased cookie sheet.

⊛ Step 5   Let rise ½-hour in a warm area. Slice loaves down the centers ½ inch in with a very sharp knife.

⊛ Step 6   Bake in a preheated 400º F oven 20-30 minutes or until nicely browned.

⊛ Step 7   Remove from cookie sheet and let cool on racks.

The original is made by inserting palm tree fronds down the center, which would be perfect for around the time of the holiday of *Sukkot* when palm leaves are used. Makes 4 buns.

Delicious flavor eaten as-is, or make *Columbia Restaurant® Style Cuban Sandwiches* (p. 244).

Olive Garden® Style Breadsticks

⅞ cup slightly warm water

2 Tbs. olive oil

1 tsp. salt

2 Tbs. room temperature *parve* margarine

1½ tsp. sugar

1½ tsp. garlic powder (more can be used)

2¾ cups all-purpose flour

1 cake or pkg. active dry yeast (2¼ tsp.)

egg wash: 1 egg beaten with 1 Tbs. water

- Step 1   Grease a cookie sheet well with oil and set aside.
- Step 2   Add first 8 ingredients to breadmaker pan according to machine instructions.
- Step 3   Let breadmaker go through kneading cycle, first rise and punch down. (Dough should be smooth but stretchy.)
- Step 4   Divide dough into 12 equal portions and shape into 6-inch oblong mini loaves.
- Step 5   Put mini loaves on cookie sheet and cover loosely with greased plastic wrap.
- Step 6   Put cookie sheet in a warm area and let mini loaves rise 15 minutes or until doubled in size. Remove plastic wrap.
- Step 7   Gently coat breadsticks thoroughly with egg wash.
- Step 8   Bake 10-15 minutes in a preheated 400º F oven, or until lightly golden brown.
- Step 9   Place cookie sheet directly on racks to cool.

Goes great with *Creamy Fettuccine Alfredo* (p. 210). Makes 12 breadsticks.

Fancy Hard Dinner Rolls

1 cup water

1 tsp. salt

2⅔ cups unbleached all-purpose or bread flour

1½ tsp. active dry yeast

1 tsp. caraway seeds (optional)

optional egg wash: 1 egg + 1 Tbs. water beaten together

optional toppings: sesame seeds, poppy seeds

✸ Step 1   Add first 4 ingredients to breadmaker pan according to machine instructions.

✸ Step 2   Let breadmaker go through kneading, first rise, punch down and final rise cycles.

✸ Step 3   Take dough out of breadmaker before the bake cycle begins.

✸ Step 4   Shape into 9 ovals and set on a greased cookie sheet, (uncovered) in a warm area for ½ hour.

✸ Step 5   If desired, coat tops with egg wash before baking and sprinkled with sesame or poppy seeds, if desired. (For better adhesion, mix a bit of egg wash with seeds and coat tops.)

✸ Step 6   Bake in a preheated 350° F oven 30-35 minutes or until barely starting to brown.

These are just like the fancy rolls served at weddings in a decorative basket. Delicious with *parve* margarine or butter. Makes 9 rolls.

Parker House Rolls

(🍞) (🧁 Sefardim only)   (Sefardim only 🧁) 🍞

¼ cup water

¼ cup *parve* margarine

¾ cup *Parve Milk* (p. 85), OR other *parve* milk alternative

¾ tsp. salt

2 Tbs. sugar

1 small well-beaten egg

2¾ cups unbleached all-purpose or bread flour

1 cake or pkg. active dry yeast (2¼ tsp.)

❀ Step 1   Combine water, margarine, *parve* milk, salt and sugar in a small pot.

❀ Step 2   Heat stirring on low until margarine melts, take off heat, set aside and let cool.

❀ Step 3   Add cooled margarine mixture, egg, flour and yeast to breadmaker pan according to machine instructions.

❀ Step 4   Let breadmaker go through kneading, first rise and punch down cycles, then take out dough.

❀ Step 5   With greased hands, form dough into 18 individual 2 x 2 inch square rolls and put on greased cookie sheet or in a 6 x 12 inch greased baking pan.

❀ Step 6   Cover rolls loosely with plastic wrap and let rise in a warm area another ½ hour. Remove plastic wrap.

❀ Step 7   Bake in a preheated 425°F oven 15 minutes or until lightly browned.

Once they are finished, they can be eaten as-is, or the middle sliced in half to make buns for *White Castle® Style Hamburgers* (p. 233). Makes 18 rolls.

Burgers and Sandwiches

Burgers

🍞(🍿 *Sefardim* on Rolls)　　**White Castle® Style Hamburgers** (🍿 Sefardim on rolls) 🐑

"Meat" = {
D- 1 pkg. soy burger + ½ tsp. salt.
P- 1 pkg. *parve* soy burger + ½ tsp. salt.
M- 1 lb. finely ground kosher beef or turkey.

½ tsp. salt

1 cup water (divided, plus extra for sautéing)

¾ cup finely diced onions

2 tsp. *parve* beef soup mix, OR 1 *parve* beef bouillon or soup cube

12 pre-baked *Parker House Rolls* (p. 232- sides sliced in half down the center)

12-24 dill pickle slices

"Optional Cheese" = {
D- 4-8 slices kosher American cheese.
P- 4-8 slices *parve* imitation American cheese.
M- 4-8 slices *parve* imitation American cheese.

✿　Step 1　　Combine "Meat", salt and ½ cup water and knead together thoroughly.

✿　Step 2　　Put a plastic wrap sheet on a table, set "Meat" on it and top it with another sheet.

✿　Step 3　　Roll "Meat" out ½ inch thick for D and P or ¼ inch thick for M, remove top plastic.

✿　Step 4　　Cut "Meat" into 12 squares, 3-inches wide for D or P, or 4-inches wide for M.

✿　Step 5　　Re-cover with plastic and freeze until frozen stiff about ½ hour.

✿　Step 6　　Put onions, soup mix and ½ cup water in a skillet and sauté until onion is tender.

✿　Step 7　　Add extra water to onions until pan bottom is barely covered, put patties in pan.

✿　Step 8　　Cook covered a few minutes until firm but not dried out, flip and cook a bit longer.

✿　Step 9　　Put a pickle or two on top part of each roll slice, and a patty on a bottom slice.

✿　Step 10　　Cut "Optional Cheese" slices in quarters and put ¼ slice on top of each burger to make cheese *White Castles®*.

✿　Step 11　　Top with other bun, and cook covered in microwave 1-2 minutes. Freeze for later use, or serve hot. Makes 12 hamburgers (now called "Slyders®"), or 3-4 servings.

Big Fast Food Burgers

"Burger" =
- **D-** 2 pkg. soy burger, OR 2 (4 ct.) pkg. imitation hamburger patties.
- **P-** 2 pkg. *parve* soy burger, OR 2 (4 ct.) pkg. soy burger patties.
- **M-** 2 lb. kosher ground beef or turkey, OR 8 kosher beef patties.

1 tsp. liquid smoke (optional- for grilled style burgers only)

"Cheese" =
- **D-** 4-8 slices kosher American cheese.
- **P-** 4-8 slices *parve* imitation American cheese.
- **M-** 4-8 slices *parve* imitation American cheese.

6 *Homemade White Buns* (p. 224) **or sesame seed hamburger buns** (toasted)

spreads: ketchup, prepared mustard, mayonnaise, *Thousand Island Dressing or Burger Sauce* (p. 87), *Restaurant Tartar Sauce* (p. 92), *Hawaiian Burger Sauce* (p. 91).

toppings: shredded lettuce, sliced tomato, thinly sliced onions, dill pickle slices.

Step 1   If using pre-made "Burger" patties, skip to Step 2. If using plain "Burger", add liquid smoke if desired (for grilled flavor only), and shape into 8 patties .

Step 2   Grill, fry or microwave until desired doneness.

Step 3   Assemble burgers: Bun bottom, next a "Burger" patty, then a "Cheese" slice.

Step 4   Put on a second or middle bun and spread it with favorite spread.

Step 5   Top this with a "Burger" patty, then preferred toppings, then a "Cheese" slice.

Step 6   Separately, put some spread on top bun, and put top bun on assembled burgers.

Step 7   Heat until hot in oven or microwave and serve.

To make the common restaurant-style burgers, they are as follows: **Wendy's Big Classic® Style** (square and fried, with ketchup); **Hardee's® Monster Thickburger Style** (fried, with double portion mayonnaise); **Rally's® Big Buford® Style** (fried, with ketchup); McDonald's® Big Mac® Style (fried, with *Thousand Island Burger Sauce*); **Frisch's® Big Boy® Style** (fried, sauce depends on locale- east coast has *Restaurant Tartar Sauce*, west coast has *Thousand Island Dressing*); **Burger King® Whopper® Style** (grilled, with mayonnaise). Makes 4 double-burgers.

For specialty burgers, add any of the following: Spreads– salsa or barbecue sauce; Toppings– cooked imitation bacon slices, *parve* or real Mozzarella or *Pepper-Jack* (p. 108) cheese slices, *Burger King® Style Onion Rings* (p. 200), sliced jalapeño peppers, or sautéed mushrooms or onions.

234

Hardee's® Style Mushroom & Swiss Burger

¾ cup *Condensed Golden Mushroom Soup* (p. 159)

1 (4 oz.) can sliced mushrooms (drained)

1 tsp. *Fishless Worcestershire Sauce* (p. 92)

½ tsp. *Seasoned Salt* (p. 434)

¼ tsp. black pepper

"Burger" =
- **D-** 4 imitation hamburger patties.
- **P-** 4 *parve* soy burger patties.
- **M-** 4 kosher ground beef burger patties.

"Cheese" =
- **D-** 4 kosher Swiss cheese sandwich-size slices.
- **P-** 4 slices *parve* imitation Mozzarella cheese.
- **M-** 4 slices *parve* imitation Mozzarella cheese.

4 hamburger buns or *Homemade White Buns* (p. 224)

Step 1   Combine soup, mushrooms and Worcestershire in a pot or microwave bowl. Heat through and keep warm.

Step 2   Sprinkle salt and pepper on each "Burger".

Step 3   Gently fry each "Burger" until done, and do not drain.

Step 4   Heat or toast buns and put bun bottoms on a platter.

Step 5   Place a "Burger" on each bun bottom, and top each one with a "Cheese" slice.

Step 6   Spoon warm mushroom sauce over "Burgers" and top with upper bun. Serve hot.

Very messy but really good. An alternative to frying is to grill or microwave the burgers, but they won't be as authentic. Makes 4 burgers.

Italian Seasoned Bacon Burgers

"Hamburger" =
{ **D-** 1 pkg. soy burger + 1 Tbs. avocado oil.
P- 1 pkg. *parve* soy burger + 1 Tbs. avocado oil.
M- 1 lb. kosher ground beef or turkey burger.

1 Tbs. *Italian Seasoning* (p. 434)

½ tsp. garlic powder

"Bacon" =
{ **D-** 12 slices soy imitation bacon.
P- 12 slices *parve* imitation bacon.
M- 12 slices kosher turkey bacon or *parve* imitation bacon.

4 *Homemade White Buns* (p. 224) **or large hamburger buns** (toasted)

"Cheese" =
{ **D-** 4 slices kosher Cheddar or American cheese.
P- 4 slices *parve* imitation American cheese.
M- 4 slices *parve* imitation American cheese.

dill pickle slices

✤ Step 1   Combine "Hamburger", Italian seasoning and garlic powder in a mixing bowl, and blend or knead until thoroughly mixed.

✤ Step 2   Shape into 4 patties, and fry in a frying pan or cook in microwave until somewhat browned. (M is done when juices run clear.)

✤ Step 3   Cook "Bacon" according to package directions.

✤ Step 4   Using a spatula, take out burgers and put on bun bottoms, then top each with 1 piece "Cheese".

✤ Step 5   Set 3 slices "Bacon" on top of each cheese-topped burger, and heat in microwave or pan, until cheese starts to melt.

✤ Step 6   Spread favorite condiment on bun tops, and put on pickles if desired. Put bun tops on burgers and heat once more until hot.

This was an invention of my Mum's many years ago. These were a favorite of mine, and Mum would fry French fries in oil to accompany it. That was so good! Makes 4 servings.

Spicy Onion-Burgers

"Hamburger" = {
D- 1 pkg. ground soy burger + 1 Tbs. avocado oil.
P- 1 pkg. *parve* ground soy burger + 1 Tbs. avocado oil.
M- 1 lb. kosher ground beef or turkey burger.

½ envelope onion soup mix (¼ cup)

4 small minced pickled jalapeño peppers

¼ cup water

8-12 pieces cooked *parve* imitation bacon

4 *Homemade White Buns* (p. 224) or large hamburger buns (toasted)

dill pickle slices

⊛ Step 1   Combine "Hamburger", onion soup mix, peppers and water in a bowl, and blend or knead until thoroughly mixed.

⊛ Step 2   Shape into 4 patties, and fry in a frying pan or cook in microwave until somewhat browned. (M is done when juices run clear.)

⊛ Step 3   Using a spatula, take out burgers and put on bun bottoms.

⊛ Step 4   Top burgers with 3 pieces bacon each.

⊛ Step 5   Spread favorite condiment on bun tops, and put pickles and jalapeños atop bacon.

⊛ Step 6   Put bun tops on burgers and heat until hot.

This is based on the original "Lipton®-Burger" recipe found on the package, but with a spicy twist. Lipton® does actually make a kosher version of their onion soup mix, (as well as other soup/dips) and it can be found in kosher groceries or larger supermarkets. (If there are people who don't like spicy foods, omit jalapeños and leave theirs plain. Don't torture them!) Makes 4 burgers.

Denny's® Style Patty Melt®

2 Tbs. avocado oil (other vegetable oil can be used)

"Patties" =
$\left\{ \begin{array}{l} \textbf{D-} \text{ 4 imitation hamburger patties.} \\ \textbf{P-} \text{ 4 } \textit{parve} \text{ soy burger patties.} \\ \textbf{M-} \text{ 4 large kosher hamburger patties.} \end{array} \right.$

1 small sliced sweet Vidalia onion

6 Tbs. room temperature *parve* margarine

8 slices *Rye Bread* (p. 220) **or light rye bread** (divided)

"Cheese" =
$\left\{ \begin{array}{l} \textbf{D-} \text{ 4 slices kosher Swiss cheese sandwich-size slices.} \\ \textbf{P-} \text{ 4 slices } \textit{parve} \text{ imitation Mozzarella cheese.} \\ \textbf{M-} \text{ 4 slices } \textit{parve} \text{ imitation Mozzarella cheese.} \end{array} \right.$

❀ Step 1   Put oil in a skillet and heat until hot.

❀ Step 2   Add "Patties" one or two at a time and fry on each side until brown. Remove from pan and set aside.

❀ Step 3   Add onion slices to pan, sauté until onion is browned.

❀ Step 4   Spread margarine generously on both sides of bread, and until lightly toasted on both sides but not dry.

❀ Step 5   Place each of the "Patties" on a slice of toast and top with a slice of "Cheese" and a portion of onions.

❀ Step 6   Heat items in a hot oven until heated through and "Cheese" is melted.

❀ Step 7   Serve with a patty-topped piece of toast on each plate and a piece of toast next to it on the side.

Delicious served with French fries. From what I've heard, Denny's® no longer offers their delicious Patty Melt®, but you can make an authentic one right here and make it kosher to boot! Makes 4 servings.

Sandwiches

Kosher Reuben Sandwich

1 cup sauerkraut (thoroughly drained)

8 slices *Rye Bread* (p. 220)**, OR 4 large *Rye Buns*** (p. 220)

"Corned Beef" =
- **D-** 8 imitation deli roast beef slices.
- **P-** 8 *parve* soy deli roast beef slices.
- **M-** ¾ lb. thinly sliced kosher corned beef.

"Cheese" =
- **D-** 4 large slices kosher Swiss cheese.
- **P-** 4 slices *parve* imitation Mozzarella cheese.
- **M-** 4 slices *parve* imitation Mozzarella cheese.

creamy style horseradish sauce (optional)

⊛ Step 1   Heat sauerkraut and set aside. Toast rye bread or buns lightly.

⊛ Step 2   Evenly distribute "Corned Beef" on bun bottoms or 4 slices of bread.

⊛ Step 3   Put sauerkraut evenly on top of "Corned Beef".

⊛ Step 4   Spread horseradish sauce on bun tops or top pieces of bread, and then put "Cheese" on top.

⊛ Step 5   Place upper buns or bread on lower ones to complete sandwiches. Heat and serve.

It is very ironic that most people think Reuben sandwiches are a Jewish food, when in fact they aren't even kosher, having cheese and meat! Well, this one is, and it's just as good. Makes 4 servings.

Kosher BLT Sandwich

8 slices *Tender White Bread* (p. 224)**, OR 4 *Homemade White Buns*** (p. 224)

"Bacon" =
- **D-** 16 pieces soy imitation bacon slices.
- **P-** 16 pieces *parve* imitation bacon slices.
- **M-** 16 pieces kosher turkey bacon.

spreads: prepared mustard, mayonnaise, ketchup, or horseradish cream sauce

4 to 8 iceberg lettuce leaves

2 small sliced tomatoes

trimmings: sliced onions, tomatoes, dill pickles, chopped lettuce.

Step 1   Toast buns or bread. Cook "Bacon" until crispy according to package directions.

Step 2   Spread favorite spread on buns or toast slices.

Step 3   Place 3 slices "Bacon" on bun bottoms or on 4 slices of bread.

Step 4   Add any other desired trimmings, and put lettuce evenly on top of "Bacon".

Step 5   Put tomato on lettuce and place upper bun on to complete sandwich.

Either serve as-is, or heat and serve. Can be spread with mayonnaise or other favorite sandwich spread. Makes 4 servings.

✿ ✿

Taco Bell® Style Bell Beefer®

1 batch (1 lb.) prepared *Taco Bell® Style Taco Meat* (p. 115)

4 *Homemade White Buns* (p. 224) **or large hamburger buns** (toasted)

Put meat evenly on each bun, and heat in microwave if needed. Serve hot. Makes 4 servings.

☺   ☺   ☺

For a **"Taco Bell® Style Bell Beefer® with Cheese"**, put 1 slice *parve* imitation American cheese over the meat on each *Taco Bell® Style Bell Beefer* sandwich. Heat and serve hot. Makes 4 servings.

Arby's® Style Original Roast Beef Sandwich

4 large onion *Homemade White Buns* (p. 224- spread with margarine)

"Beef" = {
D- 2 pkg. imitation deli roast beef slices.
P- 2 pkg. imitation deli roast beef slices.
M- ¾ lb. sliced kosher roast beef.

trimmings: sliced onions, tomatoes, dill pickles, chopped lettuce.

spreads: prepared mustard, mayonnaise, ketchup, or horseradish cream sauce.

Toast buns, assemble sandwiches as desired and heat through. Serve hot. Makes 4.

☺   ☺   ☺

For **"Arby's® Style Beef & Cheddar Sandwich"**, spread 2-3 Tbs. hot *Tangy Restaurant Cheese Sauce* (p. 99) on each bun top, assemble sandwiches and heat through. Makes 4.

✡ ✡

Arby's® Style Philly Beef & Swiss Sub

2 small green bell peppers (cut in large pieces)

2 medium onions (cut in large pieces)

2-3 Tbs. *parve* margarine (plus extra for buttering buns)

4 oblong sesame seed *Homemade White Buns* (p. 224)

"Beef" = {
D- 2 pkg. 2 pkg. imitation deli roast beef slices.
P- 2 pkg. 2 pkg. imitation deli roast beef slices.
M- ¾ lb. thinly sliced kosher roast beef.

"Cheese" = {
D- 4 slices kosher Swiss cheese.
P- 8 slices *parve* imitation Mozzarella cheese.
M- 8 slices *parve* imitation Mozzarella cheese.

✪	Step 1	Sauté peppers and onion in margarine until tender and nearly brown. Set aside.
✪	Step 2	Butter buns and toast, put "Beef" on bun bottoms, top with peppers and onions.
✪	Step 3	Top with "Cheese", then put on top bun. Heat until hot and "Cheese" melts.

Great with creamy horseradish sauce, and *Arby's® Style Jamocha® Shake* (p. 370). Makes 4.

Kosher Gyros

"Meat" =
- **D-** 1 pkg. soy burger + 2 Tbs. avocado oil.
- **P-** 1 pkg. *parve* soy burger + 2 Tbs. avocado oil.
- **M-** 1 lb. kosher ground lamb or turkey (if using turkey, add 1 Tbs. oil).

2 tsp. garlic powder

1 tsp. salt (cut in half or omit for D or P alternative below)

1½ tsp. crushed rosemary leaves (or ground rosemary if possible)

¾ tsp. ground oregano

1½ tsp. ground marjoram

1 tsp. ground cumin

¼ tsp. ground cinnamon

⅛ tsp. cayenne pepper

½ tsp. coarse ground black pepper

½ tsp. onion powder

4 individual *Pita Bread* (p. 221- halved) **or store-bought** (cut in half)

2 medium chopped tomatoes (1-1½ cups)

1 cup shredded lettuce

1 small thinly sliced onion

"Feta" =
- **D-** 1 (8 oz.) pkg. real Feta cheese (crumbled).
- **P-** 1 batch *Parve Feta Cheese* (p. 109- crumbled).
- **M-** 1 batch *Parve Feta Cheese* (p. 109- crumbled).

1 batch (1 cup) *Tzatziki Sauce* (p. 101)

❀ Step 1   Preheat oven to 350° F. Combine first 11 ingredients in a bowl and knead well.

❀ Step 2   Press "Meat" mixture firmly into a loaf pan. Bake 1 hour. (For D and P, cut in quarters after ½ hour, continue baking.) <u>For Microwave</u>- Cook 12-20 minutes on 30% power (or until juices run clear for M). Drain, let cool and slice into strips. (Chill overnight to blend flavors.)

❀ Step 3   Open pitas. Put in "Meat", tomatoes, lettuce, onion, "Feta" and Tzatziki sauce.

Classic Greek sandwich named for rotisserie meat. An alternative for D or P (but not nearly as good), is to use 2 pkg. *parve* imitation steak strips as soy burger in "Meat" (use oil if needed). Put with seasonings in a bag, and shake to coat. Skip Steps 1-2. Do Step 3. Makes 4 servings.

Subway® Style Italian BMT® Sandwich

4 *Subway® Style Italian* (p. 227) **or *Honey Oat Buns*** (p. 228)

spreads: prepared mustard, mayonnaise, ketchup, vinegar and oil with pepper.

"Salami" =
- **D-** 2-4 pkg. imitation salami slices.
- **P-** 2-4 pkg. *parve* soy salami slices.
- **M-** 2-3 (4 oz.) pkg. sliced kosher beef or turkey salami.

"Ham" =
- **D-** 2-4 pkg. imitation deli ham slices.
- **P-** 2-4 pkg. *parve* soy deli ham slices.
- **M-** 3-4 (4 oz.) pkg. sliced kosher smoked turkey.

"Pepperoni" =
- **D-** 2-3 pkg. imitation pepperoni slices.
- **P-** 2-3 pkg. *parve* soy pepperoni slices.
- **M-** 2-3 (4 oz.) pkg. sliced kosher beef pepperoni or spicy salami.

"Cheese" =
- **D-** 4-8 large slices kosher American, Cheddar or Swiss cheese.
- **P-** 8 slices *parve* imitation American or Mozzarella cheese.
- **M-** 8 slices *parve* imitation American or Mozzarella cheese.

trimmings: sliced onions, green bell peppers, tomatoes, black olives, dill pickles or hot peppers, chopped lettuce, or extra "Cheese" slices. (optional)

Step 1   Cut each bun lengthwise with a "V" notch and put on desired optional spread.

Step 2   Put 2 doubled layers each of "Salami" and "Ham" on top of spread.

Step 3   Place "Pepperoni" evenly on top of "Salami" and "Ham", then place "Cheese" on top of "Pepperoni".

Step 4   Place desired trimmings on top of "Cheese", if desired.

Step 5   Put bun tops on, cut in half at a slight diagonal and serve cold.

As titled, "BMT" for "Biggest, Meatiest, Tastiest", it's hearty. Makes 4 servings.

Cuban Buns (p. 229) can also be used, although they aren't as tender as Subway® Style buns.

Columbia Restaurant® Style Cuban Sandwich

4 *Cuban Buns* (p. 229)

"Smoked Ham Slices" =
- **D-** 16 slices imitation baked ham.
- **P-** 16 slices *parve* soy baked ham.
- **M-** 16 slices kosher smoked turkey cold cuts.

"Pork Slices" =
- **D-** 16 slices imitation ham.
- **P-** 16 slices *parve* soy ham.
- **M-** 16 slices kosher bologna.

"Salami Slices" =
- **D-** 16 slices imitation salami.
- **P-** 16 slices *parve* soy salami.
- **M-** 16 slices kosher beef or turkey salami.

"Cheese Slices" =
- **D-** 8 slices kosher Swiss cheese.
- **P-** 8 slices *parve* imitation Mozzarella cheese.
- **M-** 8 slices *parve* imitation Mozzarella cheese.

16 pickle slices

prepared mustard

❀ Step 1   Slice Cuban buns in half down the middle sides.

❀ Step 2   On each lower Cuban bun, evenly disperse a layer of "Smoked Ham Slices", "Pork Slices", "Salami Slices", "Cheese Slices", and top with 4 pickles each.

❀ Step 3   Spread mustard evenly on bun tops and assemble each sandwich.

❀ Step 4   Slice sandwiches in half with a diagonal cut, and wrap each one with foil. (Can do the same with kosher certified wax paper for microwave.)

❀ Step 5   Heat in a warm oven (or microwave) and serve warm, or serve cold if taking it to go or brown bagging lunch.

Especially good when served with the traditional *Columbia® Style Black Bean Soup* (p. 167). Makes 4 sandwiches.

Subway® Style Italian Buns (p. 227) can be used instead of *Cuban Buns*, but they aren't quite as authentic.

Breakfast Sandwiches

"Sausage" =
- **D-** 8 *parve Country Sausage* (p. 114) or imitation sausage links.
- **P-** 8 *parve Country Sausage* (p. 114) or soy sausage links.
- **M-** 8 *Country Sausage* links (p. 114) or kosher meat sausages.

"Bread" =
- **D-** 8 frozen store-bought waffles or pancakes.
- **P-** 8 precooked *Parve Pancakes* (p. 215) or *parve* waffles.
- **M-** 8 precooked *Parve Pancakes* (p. 215) or *parve* waffles.

"Cheese" =
- **D-** 4 slices kosher Swiss cheese sandwich-size slices.
- **P-** 4 slices *parve* imitation Mozzarella cheese.
- **M-** 4 slices *parve* imitation Mozzarella cheese.

☞ **Step 1** Cook "Sausage" in microwave or fry in a pan, and slice each one lengthwise down the middle in half.

☞ **Step 2** Heat 4 "Bread" slices until toasted or hot, and place on microwave safe plates.

☞ **Step 3** Place 2 sausages (4 halves) in a single layer on each piece of "Bread".

☞ **Step 4** Top "Sausage" with a piece of "Cheese", then place remaining 4 "Bread" slices on top of "Cheese".

☞ **Step 5** Heat sandwiches in microwave until "Cheese" is melted and sandwiches are hot.

Large *Simple Biscuits* can be substituted for "Bread". These are great quick meals. Mum and I actually had them for dinner when in a hurry. Makes 4 sandwiches.

✡ ✡

Sausage & Biscuit Sandwiches

8 prepared *Simple Biscuits* (p. 217)

8 prepared *Country Sausage* patties (p. 114)

Slit biscuits in the middle hamburger bun style, insert a sausage patty and heat in the microwave until hot. Eat as-is, or put in pairs in zipper bags to freeze or brown-bag it. Makes 8 little sandwiches, or 4 servings.

Main Dishes
Vegetable, Egg, Rice & Pasta Main Dishes
Vegetable Main Dishes
Vegetable Pot Pie

1¼ cup *parve Condensed Cheddar Cheese Soup* (p. 151)

¼ tsp. cayenne pepper (add more to taste, if desired)

2 pkg. (10 oz.) frozen mixed vegetables (thawed)

1 pre-baked *Pot Pie Crust* (p. 117)

1 raw *Pot Pie Crust* **top** (p. 117- optional)

Step 1   Mix together cheese soup, cayenne and vegetables until well blended.

Step 2   Heat until warm, and pour into partially baked crust. Preheat oven to 450º F.

Step 3   Moisten edges of bottom crust with some water, and take raw crust and put it on top of filling, tucking edges of upper crust under pre-baked crust to seal.

Step 4   Poke holes in top for steam to escape. Bake in 10 minutes.

Step 5   Reduce heat to 350º F and bake 20 more minutes until top is golden brown.

This stays very hot for a long time. Great with soup and salad in winter. Makes 6-8 servings.

An alternative is to microwave this. Put pie crust in glass pie plate, then do Steps 1-4. For Step 5-6, cook 11-13 minutes, or until top crust is cooked. Let sit to cool a few minutes before slicing.

✡ ✡

(seitan) (veggies)   **Seitan Stew**   (veggies)

1 cup chopped beef *Seitan* (p. 111) **or** *Seitan Beef Roast* (p. 319)

1 batch (1½ cups) *Beef Gravy* (p. 102)

2 Tbs. tomato sauce

¼ tsp. garlic powder

1 (15 oz.) can mixed vegetables (undrained)

Blend all ingredients gently, heat through and serve hot over bread pieces, noodles or rice. (Flavor is similar to delicious but non-kosher, canned Castleberry® Beef Stew.) Makes 4 servings.

Hearty Vegetarian Stew

1 smaller butternut squash (1 large acorn squash can be used- but less tasty)

2 medium chopped onions (1 cup)

4 minced garlic cloves (2 tsp.)

1 Tbs. paprika

2 Tbs. avocado or olive oil (other vegetable oil can be used)

1 cup store-bought salsa

1 cup diced tomatoes

¼ tsp. crushed oregano leaves

⅛ tsp. cayenne pepper

½ tsp. salt

2 cups cooked great Northern beans

- Step 1   Halve, seed, peel, and chop squash into 1-inch chunks and set aside.
- Step 2   Sauté onion, garlic and paprika in oil in a large pot, until onion is transparent.
- Step 3   Add salsa, tomatoes, oregano, cayenne and salt, blend well.
- Step 4   Add beans and squash to pot mixing together thoroughly.
- Step 5   Simmer uncovered stirring occasionally, about 1-2 hours or until squash starts to disintegrate and thickens stew. Serve hot.

Great on a cold winter night. For quicker preparation, skip Step 2 and 3, putting all ingredients except oil in a large pot and continue with Step 5. It is a bit less flavorful. Makes 4-6 servings.

Technically, this can be done in a crock pot on High for several hours, but it must be checked on and stirred periodically. It does not cook well overnight for Shabbat, as it tends to scorch on top.

Spicy Vegetable Curry

3 Tbs. olive oil (other vegetable oil can be used)

½ cup sliced almonds (optional)

1 medium large chopped onion (¾ cup)

4 minced garlic cloves (2 tsp.)

2 tsp.-1 Tbs. minced fresh ginger root (more ginger makes it spicier)

1 medium-large zucchini squash (cut into ½-inch cubes)

1 medium-large yellow squash (cut into ½-inch cubes)

1 medium red bell pepper (seeded and cut into ½-inch pieces)

2 large very green bananas (peeled and cut into ½-inch chunks)

½ tsp. ground cumin

4 tsp. curry powder

pinch ground cloves

¼ tsp. ground cinnamon

⅛ tsp. red pepper flakes (optional)

¼ cup minced fresh cilantro (Chinese parsley or fresh coriander)

4 tsp. *parve* chicken soup mix, OR 2 *parve* chicken bouillon or soup cubes

1 cup water

1 Tbs. lime juice

1 cup *Imitation Coconut Milk* (p. 86)

½-1 lb. extra firm tofu (cut into ½-inch cubes)

2 Tbs. chopped green onions

2 cups warm cooked *Perfect Rice* (p. 205)

Step 1   Combine oil and next 8 ingredients, sautéing until onion is transparent.

Step 2   Add cumin and next 9 ingredients, blend well and bring to a boil on medium until squash are tender about 20 minutes. (Bananas should disintegrate and slightly thicken sauce.)

Step 3   Reduce heat, add tofu and green onions, simmer 5 more minutes.

Step 4   Take off heat and serve over rice.

If bananas are even slightly yellow, the delicate flavored sauce gets sweeter. Makes 4 servings.

Egg Main Dishes

Spinach Quiche

2 Tbs. chopped green onions

2 Tbs. melted *parve* margarine

1 (10 oz.) pkg. spinach (cooked and drained)

½ tsp. salt

dash ground nutmeg

dash black pepper

"Filling" = {
D- 1 cup real dairy cottage cheese or Ricotta cheese.
P- 1 cup *Parve Cottage Cheese* (p. 109) + 1 Tbs. *Dijon* (p. 440).
M- 1 cup *Parve Cottage Cheese* (p. 109) + 1 Tbs. *Dijon* (p. 440).
}

3 well-beaten eggs

"Cream" = {
D- ½ cup heavy whipping cream.
P- ⅓ cup *Parve Cream* (p. 85) + 3 Tbs. *parve* margarine.
M- ⅓ cup *Parve Cream* (p. 85) + 3 Tbs. *parve* margarine.
}

1 Tbs. *French Dijon Mustard* (p. 440)

1 partially baked *Quiche Crust* (p. 117)

"Cheese" = {
D- 2 large slices kosher Muenster or Swiss cheese.
P- 4 slices *parve* imitation Mozzarella cheese.
M- 4 slices *parve* imitation Mozzarella cheese.
}

Step 1   Sauté onions in 2 Tbs. melted margarine, add spinach and stir over medium heat to reduce liquid.

Step 2   Stir in salt, pepper, nutmeg, "Filling", eggs and "Cream".

Step 3   Brush Dijon mustard on surface of crust, then pour mixture evenly into crust.

Step 4   Top with a single layer of "Cheese", and bake 25-30 minutes in preheated 375º F oven, or until set.

Slightly tangy and delicious. Can be done in the microwave if crust is put in a glass pie plate. For Step 4, microwave 5 minutes, take out and stir "Filling", smoothing it evenly, and cook 5 more minutes. Top with "Cheese" and cook 5 minutes until "Cheese" is melted. Makes 4-6 servings.

249

Pizza Quiche

2 Tbs. diced onions

2 Tbs. sliced black olives

2 Tbs. sliced mushrooms

2 Tbs. diced green peppers

1½ Tbs. *parve* **margarine**

"Pepperoni" =
- **D-** 2 Tbs. imitation pepperoni or salami.
- **P-** 2 Tbs. *parve* soy pepperoni or salami.
- **M-** 2 Tbs. kosher beef pepperoni or salami.

½ tsp. *Italian Seasoning* (p. 434)

½ tsp. salt

½ cup *Parve Milk* (p. 85)**, OR other** *parve* **milk alternative**

3 well-beaten eggs

¾ cup chopped tomatoes

1 Tbs. flour

1 pre-baked *Quiche Crust* (p. 117- if microwaving, use a glass pie plate)

"Cheese" =
- **D-** ¼ cup grated kosher Mozzarella cheese.
- **P-** ¼ cup shredded *parve* Mozzarella cheese.
- **M-** ¼ cup shredded *parve* Mozzarella cheese.

❀ Step 1   Sauté vegetables in margarine until onion is limp and transparent.

❀ Step 2   Add next 8 ingredients and blend thoroughly, then pour into crust.

❀ Step 3   Bake in preheated 350º F oven 20-25 minutes. <u>For Microwave</u>- Cook 5 minutes, then take out and stir filling, smoothing it evenly and cook 5 more minutes.

❀ Step 4   Top with "Cheese" and bake or cook 5 more minutes or until "Cheese" is melted.

Delicious quiche that should even appeal to kids. Makes 4-6 servings.

Eggs Benedict

2 cups *Hollandaise Sauce* (p. 91)

2⅔ Tbs. *parve* imitation bacon bits

3 cups water

1-2 Tbs. vinegar

8 eggs

4 halved store-bought or *Parve English Muffins* (p. 221), OR 8 slices bread

Step 1   Combine hollandaise sauce and bacon bits, stir until well blended, keep warm.

Step 2   Combine water and vinegar in a pot and bring to boil.

Step 3   Gently break eggs one by one into a bowl to check for blood spots. After each egg is checked, slide it gently into boiling water.

Step 4   Toast muffin halves or bread in a toaster, or place them on a cookie sheet in a preheated 350º F oven and bake 8-10 minutes, turning occasionally for even toasting. (Keep warm until ready to serve.)

Step 5   Boil each egg 5 minutes until egg white is firm. Remove each egg gently with a slotted spoon.

Step 6   Put 2 muffin halves or toasts on each plate, and place an egg on top of each one.

Step 7   Pour warm hollandaise sauce over eggs and muffins or toasts. Serve hot.

Pre-poached eggs, or lightly fried eggs can be used as well, as long as everything else is hot. Makes 4-8 servings.

Rice and Pasta Main Dishes

Popeye's® Style Dirty Rice

1 lb. (2 batches) raw *Country Sausage* (p. 114), OR 1 pkg. soy sausage

2 Tbs. avocado oil (other vegetable oil can be used)

2 Tbs. finely chopped onion, OR 1 tsp. dried minced onion flakes

4 tsp. *parve* chicken soup mix, OR 2 *parve* chicken bouillon or soup cubes

⅛ tsp. cayenne pepper (optional)

3 cups water

1¼ cups raw white rice

❈ Step 1   Crumble sausage into a frying pan and add oil and chopped onion. (If using onion flakes, add these in Step 3 with soup mix.)

❈ Step 2   Heat pan and sauté until onion is transparent and sausage is browned.

❈ Step 3   Add soup mix, cayenne, water and rice. Bring to a boil and simmer covered 30 minutes, stirring occasionally until rice is tender and most liquid is absorbed. Serve hot.

Oddly named Cajun dish. Goes with *Popeye's® Style Chicken* (p. 294). Makes 4-8 servings.

✡ ✡

Hearty Chili & Rice

2 cups hot cooked white *Perfect Rice* (p. 205)

2 cups favorite chili with beans (heated)

"Sour Cream" =
- **D-** ½ (8 oz.) container real sour cream.
- **P-** ½ cup *Parve Imitation Sour Cream* (p. 105).
- **M-** ½ cup *Parve Imitation Sour Cream* (p. 105).

Optional garnishes: sliced black olives, minced green onions or hot peppers

❈ Step 1   Heat rice and chili until warm in microwave or on stove.

❈ Step 2   In 4 individual bowls, put ½ cup rice, then ½ cup chili, and heat if needed.

❈ Step 3   Top each bowl with a large dollop "Sour Cream" and garnish. Makes 4 servings.

Chili Mac

"Cheese" = {
D- ½ cup grated kosher Cheddar cheese.
P- ½ cup shredded *parve* Cheddar or American.
M- ½ cup shredded *parve* Cheddar or American.

3 cups favorite chili with beans

2 large chopped tomatoes, OR 1 (15 oz. can) chopped tomatoes (undrained)

3 cups (1½ cups raw) cooked macaroni (see *Perfect Pasta* p. 208)

1 tsp. *Italian Seasoning* (optional- p. 434)

¼ tsp. crushed oregano leaves (optional)

½ tsp. ground cumin (optional)

¼ tsp. hot pepper sauce (optional)

"Optional Parmesan" = {
D- ½ cup grated kosher Parmesan cheese.
P- ½ cup *Parve Parmesan Cheese* (p. 108).
M- ½ cup *Parve Parmesan Cheese* (p. 108).

Optional garnishes: chopped green onions, minced or sliced jalapeño peppers, or sliced black olives.

⊛ Step 1   Set "Cheese" out to become room temperature.

⊛ Step 2   Combine all ingredients except for "Cheese" in a bowl or pot, and blend together thoroughly.

⊛ Step 3   For Stove- Put contents in a pot and bring to a boil. For Microwave- Put contents in individual microwave safe bowls, top with "Cheese" and heat through until it melts.

⊛ Step 4   For Stove- Put in individual bowls and top with "Cheese", allowing it to melt.

⊛ Step 5   Sprinkle "Optional Parmesan" on top if desired, and then top with optional garnishes. Serve hot.

Flavorful version of an old classic. Oregano and Italian seasoning gives an Italian twist, cumin and hot pepper sauce gives a Mexican flair. Makes 4 servings.

Middle Eastern Spaghetti

2 Tbs. olive oil

1 large chopped onion (1 cup)

4 minced garlic cloves (2 tsp.)

"Meat" =
- **D-** 1 pkg. (2 cups) imitation hamburger crumbles.
- **P-** 2 cups *Parve Soy Crumbles* (p. 110).
- **M-** 1 lb. kosher ground beef (browned and drained).

1 Tbs. ground cumin

1 Tbs. coriander

⅛ tsp. cayenne pepper

⅜ tsp. ground turmeric

¾ tsp. curry powder

6 cups chopped tomatoes, OR 2 (28 oz.) cans diced tomatoes (undrained)

1 tsp. salt

4 cups (1 lb. dry) cooked thin spaghetti (see *Perfect Pasta* p. 208)

Step 1 Combine oil, onion and garlic in a pot and sauté until onions are tender.

Step 2 Turn heat down to low, stir in "Meat", cumin, turmeric, curry powder and cayenne. Cook 3 minutes.

Step 3 Add tomatoes and salt, bring to a boil then reduce heat and simmer on low 1 hour stirring occasionally.

Step 4 Add spaghetti to pot and heat through.

Serve hot. Sumptuously flavored spaghetti inspired by sampling a dish made by Rabbanit Zevichi in Israel. Makes 4-6 servings.

Creamy Lasagna

1 Tbs. avocado oil (other vegetable oil can be used)

1 small-medium chopped onion (⅓ cup)

1¼ cups diced tomatoes (drained)

"Meat" =
- **D-** 1 pkg. (2 cups) imitation hamburger crumbles.
- **P-** 2 cups *Parve Soy Crumbles* (p. 110).
- **M-** 1 lb. kosher ground beef or turkey.

½ lb. (6 pieces) cooked lasagna (see *Perfect Pasta* on p. 208)

1½ cups *White Sauce* (p. 101- use soup mix or bouillon)

"Optional Cheese" =
- **D-** ½ cup grated kosher Mozzarella cheese.
- **P-** ½ cup shredded *parve* Mozzarella cheese.
- **M-** ½ cup shredded *parve* Mozzarella cheese.

⊛ Step 1   Put oil in a frying pan and add onion, sauté until onions are transparent.

⊛ Step 2   Add tomatoes (and "Meat" for M) to frying pan and sauté 5 minutes (or until "Meat" is done and juices run clear if using M). (Blend in "Meat" for D or P.) Set aside.

⊛ Step 3   Spread a layer of white sauce on the bottom of a greased 8 x 8 inch baking dish.

⊛ Step 4   Put a layer of "Meat" tomato mixture in dish, then lasagna noodles.

⊛ Step 5   Repeat Step 4, then top with "Cheese" if desired. Put in a 350° F oven 20 minutes, or microwave 5 minutes, until heated through. Serve hot.

Delicious dish based on a recipe from a friend. The flavors blend nicely after sitting in the fridge for a day. Makes 4 servings.

Perfect for *Shavu'ot*. A few more pieces of lasagna can be used with an 8 x 11½ inch baking pan, spread out a little thinner. The same amount of other ingredients can still be used, and it goes a bit farther.

Ethnic Main Dishes
Italian

Stuffed Manicotti Shells

1 (24-26 oz.) jar plain spaghetti sauce or marinara sauce (without chunks)

2 (8 oz.) pkg. parboiled manicotti shells (do not overcook!)

Cheese* or *Meat Pasta Filling (opposite page)

"Parmesan" = {
- **D-** 1 Tbs. grated kosher Parmesan cheese.
- **P-** 1 Tbs. finely *Parve Parmesan Cheese* (p. 108).
- **M-** 1 Tbs. finely *Parve Parmesan Cheese* (p. 108).

✽ **Step 1** Make either Filling recipe on opposite page by blending ingredients thoroughly in a bowl.

✽ **Step 2** Put some spaghetti sauce in a deep 7 x 11-inch baking dish, covering the bottom of baking dish.

✽ **Step 3** Carefully take manicotti shells and fill them with Filling mixture, then place them in the baking dish in a single layer.

✽ **Step 4** Pour spaghetti sauce over shells, smoothing it out evenly, and cover with foil for oven, or cover loosely with plastic wrap for microwave.

✽ **Step 5** Bake in a preheated 350° F oven 20 minutes, or microwave 10 minutes.

✽ **Step 6** Remove covering and sprinkle "Parmesan" over top of shells.

✽ **Step 7** Bake 10 more minutes (bake P or M covered), or microwave 5 more minutes and serve.

Delicious using either Filling recipe on the opposite page. Makes 4-8 servings.

Manicotti should be eaten fresh, unlike many foods that improve with age and marinating. The *parve* version made with *Parve* Meat Filling tends to turn dark and not look too pretty, especially if the manicotti shells are overly cooked. Pay special attention to the package directions as to how long to cook them, and cook about half as long as directed for partially boiled manicotti.

☺   ☺   ☺

For **"Combination Manicotti Shells"**, halve *Meat Filling* and halve *Cheese Filling* on next page, and fix both Fillings as *parve*. Stuff half the shells with *Cheese Filling* and the other half with *Meat Filling*. Makes 4-8 servings.

Pasta Fillings

Blend ingredients thoroughly and use to stuff ravioli, jumbo shells, or manicotti.

Cheese Filling

"Cheese" = {
- **D-** 3 cups real Ricotta cheese.
- **P-** 3 cups *Parve Ricotta Cheese* (p. 109).
- **M-** 3 cups *Parve Ricotta Cheese* (p. 109).

"Mozzarella" = {
- **D-** 1 cup grated kosher Mozzarella cheese.
- **P-** 1 cup shredded *parve* Mozzarella.
- **M-** 1 cup shredded *parve* Mozzarella.

2 eggs

1 Tbs. parsley flakes

dash salt & pepper and ground nutmeg

"Parmesan" = {
- **D-** 1 Tbs. grated kosher Parmesan cheese.
- **P-** 1 Tbs. *Parve Parmesan Cheese* (p. 108).
- **M-** 1 Tbs. *Parve Parmesan Cheese* (p. 108).

✡ ✡

Meat Filling

"Meat" = {
- **D-** 4 cups imitation burger crumbles, (sautéed in 1 Tbs. olive oil).
- **P-** 4 cups *parve* soy crumbles, (sautéed in 1 Tbs. olive oil).
- **M-** 2 lb. kosher ground beef or turkey, (browned in 1 tsp. olive oil).

"Mozzarella" = {
- **D-** 2 cups grated kosher Mozzarella cheese.
- **P-** 2 cups shredded *parve* Mozzarella.
- **M-** 2 cups shredded *parve* Mozzarella.

1 egg

3 slices bread (diced)**, OR ¾-cup bread crumbs or matzah (matzo) meal**

1 cup *Parve Cream* (p. 85)

1 Tbs. parsley flakes

dash salt & pepper

257

Three-Cheese Lasagna

¼ tsp. salt

1 beaten egg

1 Tbs. parsley flakes

"Ricotta" =
- D- 1½ cups real cottage cheese or real Ricotta cheese.
- P- 1½ cups *Parve Cottage* or *Parve Ricotta Cheese* (p. 109).
- M- 1½ cups *Parve Cottage* or *Parve Ricotta Cheese* (p. 109).

"Parmesan" =
- D- ¼ cup grated kosher Parmesan cheese.
- P- ¼ cup *Parve Parmesan Cheese* (p. 108).
- M- ¼ cup *Parve Parmesan Cheese* (p. 108).

1 (24-26 oz.) jar non-chunky plain spaghetti or marinara sauce (divided)

½ lb. (6-9 pieces) cooked lasagna noodles (divided).

"Meat" =
- D- 1 pkg. (2 cups) imitation hamburger crumbles (divided).
- P- 2 cups *Parve Soy Crumbles* (p. 110- divided).
- M- 1 lb. browned, cooked and drained kosher ground beef (divided).

"Mozzarella" =
- D- 1 cup grated kosher Mozzarella cheese.
- P- 1 cup shredded *parve* imitation Mozzarella.
- M- 1 cup shredded *parve* imitation Mozzarella.

⊛ Step 1   Blend together salt, egg, parsley, "Ricotta" and "Parmesan" to make "Cheese".

⊛ Step 2   Preheat oven to 375º F. Grease 7 x 11-inch baking dish, then coat it with sauce.

⊛ Step 3   Place ingredients in dish in the following order: Layer of noodles, half of "Cheese", half of "Meat", layer of sauce. Repeat using remainder of "Cheese" and "Meat".

⊛ Step 4   Top with a layer of noodles, remaining sauce, and cover with "Mozzarella".

⊛ Step 5   Bake ½ hour, or microwave until heated through.

A delicious classic the way it is supposed to taste! No omitting meat or cheese to make it kosher. Makes 4-8 servings.

Classic Ravioli

2 batches (48) *Wonton Wrappers* (p. 116)

"Meat" = {
D- 1 pkg. (2 cups) imitation hamburger crumbles.
P- 2 cups *Parve Soy Crumbles* (p. 110).
M- 1 lb. cooked kosher ground beef (drained and crumbled).

water

salted water for boiling

1 (24-26 oz.) jar plain spaghetti sauce or marinara sauce (no chunks)

Step 1   Place 24 wrappers on a flat surface, and put 2 Tbs. "Meat" in center of each.

Step 2   Put water along edges of wrappers, and place another wrapper on top.

Step 3   Pinch edges closed to seal, bring water to a boil, and put raviolis gently in water.

Step 4   Boil 5 minutes. Heat sauce and keep warm.

Step 5   Gently remove raviolis with slotted spoon and add to hot pasta sauce.

Not like the old canned stuff, these are delicious! Makes 24 large raviolis, or 4-6 servings.

✡ ✡

Cheese Ravioli

½ batch *Cheese Pasta Filling* (p. 257)

2 batches (48) *Wonton Wrappers* (p. 118)

water

salted water for boiling

1 (24-26 oz.) jar plain spaghetti sauce or marinara sauce (no chunks)

Step 1   Place 24 wrappers on a flat surface and put 2 Tbs. Filling in center of each.

Step 2   Put water along edges of wrappers, then place another wrapper on top.

Step 3   Pinch edges closed to seal, bring water to a boil, and put raviolis gently in water.

Step 4   Boil 5 minutes. Heat sauce and keep warm.

Step 5   Gently remove raviolis with slotted spoon and add to hot pasta sauce.

Serve hot with garlic bread for a great Italian meal. Makes 24 large raviolis, or 4-6 servings.

Easy Calzones

1 batch raw *Water Challah* dough (p. 222- no optionals, Steps 1-2 only)

8 tsp. olive oil

1 cup *Professional Pizzeria Sauce* (p. 100)

"Optional Cheese" =
- **D-** ¼ cup grated kosher Parmesan cheese.
- **P-** ¼ cup *Parve Parmesan Cheese* (p. 108).
- **M-** ¼ cup *Parve Parmesan Cheese* (p. 108).

additions: ¼-½ cup capers, sliced black olives, seeded & chopped green or red bell peppers, chopped onions, chopped tomatoes, sliced jalapeño peppers, or sliced mushrooms, crumbled *Italian Sausage* (p. 112).

"Meat" =
- **D-** 1-2 pkg. imitation pepperoni or chopped imitation ham.
- **P-** 1-2 pkg. *parve* soy pepperoni or chopped *parve* soy ham.
- **M-** ½ lb. kosher pepperoni, or chopped salami or smoked turkey.

"Mozzarella" =
- **D-** 1 cup grated kosher Mozzarella cheese (can use more).
- **P-** 1 cup shredded *parve* Mozzarella (can use more).
- **M-** 1 cup shredded *parve* Mozzarella (can use more).

❀ Step 1   Put dough in a bowl, cover and let rise in a warm area 1 hour. Divide into 4 balls.

❀ Step 2   Roll out on a floured flat surface, constantly flipping and rolling into circles, until dough is ¼-inch thick (stretch dough as working it if needed, but don't let any holes form).

❀ Step 3   Coat with oil, then sauce ½-inch from edges. Sprinkle on "Optional Cheese".

❀ Step 4   Put on any additions and "Meat", then top with "Mozzarella". Preheat oven to 400° F.

❀ Step 5   Wet edges, fold over making a half-moon, pinch edges shut pressing with a fork.

❀ Step 6   Place on well-greased cookie sheets and bake 25-30 minutes or until light brown.

Caution: Filling stays hot! Frozen dough can be used after thawing. Similar to "stromboli", made of sauce and cheese, rolled like burritos and served with marinara sauce. Makes 4-8 servings.

☺   ☺   ☺

For **"Crisp-Crust Pizza"**, grease 2 pizza pans or cookie sheets and dust lightly with cornmeal. For Step 1 divide in half, then do Steps 2-4, placing dough on pans after rolling. Double outer dough to form a ridge along edges to keep toppings from oozing out. (Anchovies can be added for P.) Skip Step 5. Do Step 6 as normal. Makes 2 (10-12-inch) pizzas, or 4 servings.

Stouffer's® Style French Bread Pizza

"Sausage" = {
D- 1 pkg. imitation sausage or *Italian Sausage* (p. 112).
P- 1 pkg. *parve* soy sausage or *Italian Sausage* (p. 112).
M- ½ batch (½ lb.) *Italian Sausage* (p. 112).
}

optional veggies: chopped green bell pepper, mushrooms, or sliced black olives

1 large chopped onion (¾ cup)

2 Tbs. parve margarine

2 (1 lb.) loaves *parve* garlic bread, OR 1 loaf *Garlic Bread* (p. 213)

½ cup *Professional Pizzeria Sauce* (p. 100)

"Pepperoni" = {
D- 2 pkg. *parve* imitation pepperoni.
P- 2 pkg. *parve* soy pepperoni.
M- 1 lb. kosher beef pepperoni or salami.
}

"Cheese" = {
D- 2 cups grated kosher Mozzarella cheese.
P- 2 cups grated *parve* Mozzarella.
M- 2 cups grated *parve* Mozzarella.
}

⚙ Step 1   Cook "Sausage" if necessary, and crumble into a bowl. Set aside.

⚙ Step 2   Sauté vegetables in margarine until onion gets limp, and set aside.

⚙ Step 3   Separate tops and bottoms of bread, (spreading garlic out if necessary), and cut in halves widthwise. You should now have 8 individual pieces.

⚙ Step 4   Place pieces on a cookie sheet, and bake in preheated 350º F oven 15 minutes.

⚙ Step 5   When done, spread some sauce on each piece to coat evenly.

⚙ Step 6   Chop "Pepperoni" in pieces, or keep whole, distribute evenly on pieces.

⚙ Step 7   Distribute vegetables and "Sausage" evenly on each piece, then do the same with "Cheese".

⚙ Step 8   Put back in oven 5-10 more minutes on rack closest to heat, or until cheese is melted. Serve hot.

Serve with soup for a hearty meal. Makes 8 pizzas, or 4-8 servings.

Mexican Main Dishes

Fiesta Pizza

½ cup sliced black olives (optional)

1 large chopped onion (¾ cup)

2 Tbs. *parve* **margarine**

2 (1 lb.) loaves *parve* **garlic bread, OR 1 loaf** *Garlic Bread* (p. 213)

2 cups store-bought salsa or *Super Salsa* (p. 96)

"Taco Meat" =
- D- 1 pkg. (2 cups) taco-flavored imitation hamburger crumbles.
- P- 1 pkg. (2 cups) *parve* taco-flavored soy crumbles.
- M- 1 batch (1 lb.) cooked *Taco Bell® Style Taco Meat* (p. 115).

"Cheese" =
- D- 2 cups grated kosher Monterey Jack cheese.
- P- 2 cups grated *parve* Jack or Mozzarella.
- M- 2 cups grated *parve* Jack or Mozzarella.

¼ cup chopped pickled jalapeño peppers (optional)

Step 1 Sauté onion and olives if desired, in margarine until gets limp, and set aside.

Step 2 Separate tops and bottoms of garlic bread, (spreading garlic out if necessary), and cut in halves widthwise. You should now have 8 individual pieces.

Step 3 Place pieces on a cookie sheet, and bake in preheated 350º F oven 15 minutes.

Step 4 When done, spread some salsa on each piece to coat evenly.

Step 5 Distribute "Taco Meat" evenly on pieces, then distribute jalapeño peppers evenly (if desired).

Step 6 Distribute "Cheese" evenly on each piece atop "Meat".

Step 7 Put back in oven 5-10 more minutes, or until cheese is melted. Serve hot.

Serve with soup for a hearty meal. Makes 8 pizzas, or 4-8 servings.

(🧁 fried) (🍞 baked)   **Taco Bell® Style Mexican Pizza**   🍞

8 large flour tortillas

avocado oil for frying (other vegetable oil can be used)

1 cup warmed *Refried Beans* (p. 103)

"Meat" = {
D- 1 pkg. (2 cups) taco-flavored imitation hamburger crumbles.
P- 1 pkg. (2 cups) *parve* taco-flavored soy crumbles.
M- 1 batch (1 lb.) prepared *Taco Bell® Style Taco Meat* (p. 115).
}

1 large chopped tomato (1 cup)

"Cheese" = {
D- 1 cup grated kosher Monterey Jack cheese.
P- 1 cup grated *parve* Jack or Mozzarella.
M- 1 cup grated *parve* Jack or Mozzarella.
}

½ cup chopped green onions

1 tsp. red pepper flakes (optional)

16-24 black olives (sliced)

⊛   Step 1   Put some oil in a large frying pan and heat until hot, then 1 at a time, place a flour tortilla in oil until stiff, (flip with a tongs if necessary). Drain on a paper towel-lined plate.

⊛   Step 2   After tortillas are fried, take 4 of them and put them on a cookie sheet.

⊛   Step 3   Spread refried beans evenly on 4 tortillas, then sprinkle "Meat" on each piece.

⊛   Step 4   Place 4 reserved tortillas on top of coated tortillas on cookie sheet, and place tomatoes evenly on these pieces.

⊛   Step 5   Evenly sprinkle "Cheese" on top, then green onions, pepper flakes, and place olives evenly on top.

⊛   Step 6   Bake in a 400° F oven until "Cheese" melts and pizzas are hot. (Heating in the microwave can be done, but tends to make them soggy.)

⊛   Step 7   Cut pizzas into quarters with a sharp knife or pizza cutter. Serve hot immediately.

Addictive and different, these are filling. Pizzas can be cut before frying. An alternative to frying, is coat both sides of tortillas with oil, margarine or shortening, place on cookie sheets, and bake in a 350° F oven 5 minutes until no longer soft, but not brown. If bubbles develop (within a minute or two), pop with a knife. They can't be used for pizzas if they have large bubbles- they must be very flat. (Use fried flour tortilla chips or pita chips for mini-pizzas.) Makes 4 servings.

Microwave Huevos Rancheros

12 eggs

1 tsp. salt

1 cup favorite salsa

¼ cup *parve* margarine

"Cheese" = {
D- 4 kosher American or Cheddar cheese slices.
P- 4 *parve* American or Cheddar slices.
M- 4 *parve* American or Cheddar slices.

Step 1   Break eggs into a bowl, checking for bloodspots.

Step 2   Add salt and beat well, then add salsa, blending thoroughly.

Step 3   Generously grease a glass loaf pan or small baking dish with margarine.

Step 4   Put egg mixture in baking dish, and microwave on 50% power, 5 minutes.

Step 5   Stir eggs, put in again on 50% power and cook in several 2-minute increments, stirring each time (chopping egg up if needed), until most egg is cooked.

Step 6   Place "Cheese" evenly on top, and cook 2 more minutes until cheese is melted. Serve hot.

This is actually a very quick and tasty Mexican dish ("Ranch Eggs".). It's great for Passover. Makes 4 servings.

Cut recipe in ¼ for a single serving, it makes a quick supper for one.

(🧁 (🥑 avocado) (🥛 egg)　　　**Chorizo & Rice**　　　🥛

1 Tbs. avocado oil (other vegetable oil can be used)

2 cups raw white rice

1 small minced onion (¼ cup)

1 batch (1 lb.) *Mexican Chorizo Sausage* (p. 115), **OR 1 pkg. vegan chorizo**

¾ cup tomato sauce

¼ tsp. black pepper, OR ⅛ tsp. cayenne pepper (for spicier)

4¾ cups water

8 tsp. *parve* chicken soup mix, OR 4 *parve* chicken bouillon or soup cubes

2 hard-boiled eggs (peeled)

1 large avocado (peeled and seeded)

1 (15 oz.) can peas (drained)

✤　Step 1　　Combine oil, rice and onion in a large frying pan and sauté until rice and onion are starting to brown.

✤　Step 2　　Add chorizo, tomato sauce, water and soup mix and bring to a boil, blending well and making sure soup mix is dissolved.

✤　Step 3　　Reduce heat and simmer covered 25 minutes, stirring occasionally.

✤　Step 4　　Slice eggs and avocados and set aside.

✤　Step 5　　Add peas and simmer 5 more minutes or until rice is tender.

✤　Step 6　　Put chorizo and rice on plates and garnish with egg and avocado slices on top. Serve hot.

A classic Mexican dish. Serve with hot pepper sauce on the side, if desired. Frozen peas can be substituted for canned, but should be added after 15 minutes of cooking, and cooked 15 minutes in Step 5. Makes 4-8 servings.

As an alternative for Steps 3-4, the contents of the frying pan can be transferred to a large covered casserole dish and baked in a 350° F oven 50 minutes or until rice is tender. Add peas and bake 5 more minutes. Proceed with Step 6 as normal.

(fried) (baked)   **Shredded Chicken Chimichangas**

2 minced garlic cloves (1 tsp.)

2 medium diced onions (1 cup)

2 medium diced tomatoes (1 cup)

1 tsp. ground cumin

avocado oil (other vegetable oil can be used)

"Chicken" =
- **D-** 2 cups imitation chicken strips (minced).
- **P-** 2 cups *parve* soy or seitan chicken strips (minced).
- **M-** 2 cups shredded cooked kosher chicken.

1 (4 oz.) can green chilies (chopped)

1 tsp. salt

"Cheese" =
- **D-** 1½ cups grated kosher Cheddar cheese.
- **P-** 1½ cups grated *parve* American or Cheddar.
- **M-** 1½ cups grated *parve* American or Cheddar.

10 pkg. large fresh flour tortillas

Step 1   Blend first 4 ingredients. Put 1 Tbs. oil in a pan and sauté mixture 3 minutes.

Step 2   Reduce heat and simmer uncovered 7 more minutes.

Step 3   Drain if necessary, and add "Chicken", chilies and salt, mixing together well.

Step 4   Put 2 Tbs. mixture and 1 Tbs. "Cheese" in the center of each tortilla.

Step 5   Fold one side of tortilla over filling, then the other, burrito-style, then fold one end in over the middle, then other end. If ends don't stay put, secure it with a toothpick or two. You should now have a square "packet" which is a chimichanga.

Step 6   Heat oil in a frying pan ½ inch deep until hot, and put a "chimmy" seam-side down in oil and fry until golden brown, then flip and fry until other side is brown.

Step 7   Drain on paper towel lined plate and put in heated oven to keep warm.

Garnish with *Mexican Restaurant Guacamole* (p. 103), *Super Salsa* (p. 96), *Chili Sauce* (p. 95), and real or *Parve Imitation Sour Cream* (p. 105). Makes 10 "chimmies", or 4-6 servings.

Alternative: After Step 3, coat tortillas with ¼ cup *parve* margarine, then fill and fold. Bake in a 350º F oven 15-20 minutes, flip and bake 15 more or until both sides are light brown and crisp.

266

Tio Sancho® Style Enchilada Dinner

avocado oil (other vegetable oil can be used)

12 small corn tortillas

1½ cup *Taco Bell® Style Enchirito® Sauce* (p. 96)

¼ cup water

"Meat" =
- D- 1 pkg. (2 cups) imitation hamburger crumbles.
- P- 2 cups *Parve Soy Crumbles* (p. 110).
- M- 1 lb. kosher ground beef or turkey (browned and drained).

"Cheese" =
- D- 1 cup grated kosher Cheddar cheese.
- P- 1 cup grated *parve* American or Cheddar.
- M- 1 cup grated *parve* American or Cheddar.

Step 1   Put oil in a frying pan about ¼ inch deep, and heat until hot.

Step 2   Place tortillas in oil and fry 1 minute, but do not let them get crisp.

Step 3   Take tortillas out of oil and place them flat in a greased deep baking dish.

Step 4   Combine sauce with water, mix well and set aside.

Step 5   Combine "Meat" and ¼ cup sauce, and blend together.

Step 6   Take a few spoonfuls of "Meat" mixture and distribute it evenly between tortillas, then fold each side over filling and roll them over so that seam side is down.

Step 7   Spoon sauce evenly over each tortilla, covering all edges in sauce.

Step 8   Top each tortilla evenly with "Cheese".

Step 9   Put baking dish in microwave 10 minutes covered loosely with plastic wrap until heated through, or bake in a preheated 375° F oven 15-20 minutes until "Cheese" melts. Serve hot.

Steps 1-2 can be omitted, but the results aren't quite as good. For variety, some refried beans can be mixed in with "Meat". Mexican *Chorizo Sausage* (p. 115) can be substituted for "Meat". Delicious with a cheese-flavored *Simple Spanish Rice* (p. 206) and *Refried Beans* (p. 103). Makes 12 enchiladas, or 3-6 servings.

Cheese Enchiladas

"Soft Cheese" =
- **D-** 3 cups real cottage cheese or Ricotta cheese.
- **P-** 3 cups *Parve Cottage* or *Parve Ricotta Cheese* (p. 109).
- **M-** 3 cups *Parve Cottage* or *Parve Ricotta Cheese* (p. 109).

"Cheddar" =
- **D-** 1¼ cup grated kosher Cheddar cheese.
- **P-** 1¼ cups grated *parve* imitation American or Cheddar.
- **M-** 1¼ cups grated *parve* imitation American or Cheddar.

1½ cup chopped green onions

¼ tsp. slightly crushed oregano leaves

avocado oil (other vegetable oil can be used)

12 corn tortillas

1½ cups *Taco Bell® Style Enchirito® Sauce* (p. 96)

¼ cup water

"Cheese" =
- **D-** 1 cup grated kosher Cheddar cheese.
- **P-** 1 cup grated *parve* imitation Cheddar.
- **M-** 1 cup grated *parve* imitation Cheddar.

✺ Step 1 Combine "Soft Cheese", crumbled "Cheddar", green onions and oregano, and blend together thoroughly. Set aside.

✺ Step 2 Put oil in a frying pan about ¼ inch deep, and heat until hot.

✺ Step 3 Place tortillas in oil and fry 1 minute, but do not let them get crisp.

✺ Step 4 Take tortillas out of oil and place them flat in a greased deep baking dish.

✺ Step 5 Take a few spoonfuls of cheese mixture and distribute it evenly between tortillas, then fold each side over filling and roll them over so that seam side is down.

✺ Step 6 Combine sauce with water. Spoon evenly over tortillas, covering edges in sauce.

✺ Step 7 Top each tortilla evenly with "Cheese".

✺ Step 8 Put baking dish in microwave 10 minutes covered loosely with plastic wrap until heated through, or bake in a preheated 375° F oven 15-20 minutes until "Cheese" melts.

Steps 1-2 can be omitted, but the results aren't quite as good. For variety enchiladas if desired, fix half this recipe and half of *Tio Sancho® Style Enchiladas* (previous page), baking together. Makes 12 enchiladas, or 3-6 servings.

Taco Bell® Style Enchiritos®

6 flour tortillas

2½-3 cups *Refried Beans* (p. 103)

"Meat" = {
D- 1 pkg. taco-flavored imitation hamburger crumbles.
P- 1 pkg. *parve* taco-flavored soy crumbles.
M- 1 batch (1 lb.) prepared *Taco Bell® Style Taco Meat* (p. 115).
}

½ cup chopped raw onions (optional)

1½ cups *Taco Bell® Style Enchirito® Sauce* (p. 96)

"Cheese" = {
D- 1 cup grated kosher Cheddar cheese.
P- 1 cup grated *parve* American or Cheddar.
M- 1 cup grated *parve* American or Cheddar.
}

18 black olives (halved)

� Step 1   Put 1 or 2 tortillas on microwave safe plates and spread a couple spoonfuls refried beans down the middle of each tortilla.

✿ Step 2   Take a few spoonfuls "Meat" and distribute it evenly, pressing it into beans.

✿ Step 3   Do this with onions as well, then fold each side over filling, and roll them over so that seam side is down.

✿ Step 4   Spoon sauce over each tortilla, covering all edges in sauce.

✿ Step 5   Top with "Cheese" evenly, then place 6 olives on each tortilla.

✿ Step 6   Put each plate in microwave and heat until "Cheese" melts, about 2-3 minutes each plate, and serve hot.

This is probably my most favorite of all recipes. Makes 6, or 3-6 servings.

Beef & Cheese Burritos

6 large flour tortillas

1½ cups *Refried Beans* (p. 103)

"Meat" =
- **D-** 2 cups taco-flavored imitation hamburger crumbles.
- **P-** 2 cups *parve* taco-flavored soy crumbles.
- **M-** 1 batch (1 lb.) prepared *Taco Bell® Style Taco Meat* (p. 115).

"Cheese" =
- **D-** 1 cup grated kosher Cheddar cheese.
- **P-** 1 cup grated *parve* American or Cheddar.
- **M-** 1 cup grated *parve* American or Cheddar.

❀ Step 1   Wrap tortillas in damp paper towels and warm in microwave.

❀ Step 2   Put 1-2 tortillas on microwave safe plates and spread refried beans down middle of each tortilla, then take "Meat" and distributing it evenly, pressing it into beans.

❀ Step 3   Fold one end over filling about a third of the way, and repeat with other end.

❀ Step 4   Fold one side over filling, then other, to make an enclosed rectangular packet.

❀ Step 5   Wrap in plastic and freeze in zipper bags for future use, or microwave 1-2 minutes until hot. These can be served cold as well. (For reheating, remove from plastic. If fresh- microwave 30 seconds. If frozen- microwave 1 minute, flip and cook 1 more minute.)

Mexican Chorizo Sausage (p. 115) can be used for "Meat". Makes 6 burritos, or 3-6 servings.

☺   ☺   ☺

For **"Beef & Bean Burritos"**, substitute 1 cup *Refried Beans* for "Cheese". An alternative to beans is use 3 cups *Hormel® Style Chili* (p. 171) as filling. Fix Steps 3-5 as normal.

☺   ☺   ☺

For **"Bean & Cheese Burritos"**, Omit "Meat", add 1 cup *Refried Beans*, and double amount of "Cheese". Fix Steps 3-5 as normal.

☺   ☺   ☺

For **"Bean Burritos"**, Omit "Cheese" and "Meat", and double amount of *Refried Beans* in their place. Fix Steps 3-5 as normal.

☺   ☺   ☺

For **"Spicy Bean Burritos"**, make as *Bean Burritos* above, but add ½ tsp. cayenne pepper, 1 Tbs. *Chili Powder* (p. 434), and 1 Tbs. minced pickled jalapeño peppers to beans (mixing thoroughly) before filling burritos. Fix Steps 3-5 as normal.

Microwave Tacos

12 taco shells

"Meat" =
- **D-** 1 pkg. taco-flavored imitation hamburger crumbles.
- **P-** 1 pkg. *parve* taco-flavored soy crumbles.
- **M-** 1 batch (1 lb.) prepared *Taco Bell® Style Taco Meat* (p. 115).

2 medium chopped tomatoes (1 cup)

2 cups shredded lettuce

"Cheese" =
- **D-** 2 cups grated kosher Cheddar cheese.
- **P-** 2 cups grated *parve* American or Cheddar.
- **M-** 2 cups grated *parve* American or Cheddar.

favorite taco sauce (optional)

⊛ Step 1   Place 3 taco shells on each plate butting together so that one shell opening faces left, another face right, and middle one is straight up.

⊛ Step 2   Put "Meat" evenly into each taco shell, then distribute tomatoes, lettuce and "Cheese" evenly as well.

⊛ Step 3   Drizzle a spoonful of taco sauce over each taco if desired, and carefully put each plate in microwave, heating 1-2 minutes until "Cheese" is just about to melt and tacos are hot.

Served with a bowl of *Nacho Cheese Soup* (p. 152), this is a real staple meal. *Mexican Chorizo Sausage* (p. 115) can be substituted for "Meat". Makes 12 tacos, or 4 servings (3 per person).

Jack in the Box® Style Tacos

"Meat" =
- **D-** 1 pkg. (2 cups) imitation hamburger crumbles + 1 Tbs. avocado oil.
- **P-** 1 pkg. (2 cups) *parve* soy crumbles + 1 Tbs. avocado oil.
- **M-** 1 lb. ground beef, (browned, drained slightly and finely chopped).

½ cup *Refried Beans* (p. 103)

3 Tbs. smooth mild taco sauce

⅛ tsp. salt

2 Tbs. *Chili Powder* (p. 434)

2 tsp. ground cumin

avocado oil for frying (other vegetable oil can be used)

16 fresh corn tortillas

"Cheese Slice" =
- **D-** 8 slices kosher American cheese.
- **P-** 8 slices *parve* imitation American cheese.
- **M-** 8 slices *parve* imitation American cheese.

2 cups shredded lettuce

❋ **Step 1** Combine first 6 ingredients in a mixing bowl and blend thoroughly. (This can be made ahead and gets better as it sits as the flavors blend.)

❋ **Step 2** Put oil in a large frying pan about ¼-inch inch deep and heat on low until hot.

❋ **Step 3** Place tortillas one at a time in oil, fry 1 minute or until it starts to blister. Set aside.

❋ **Step 4** Place limp tortillas out flat and put about 2 Tbs. "Meat" down the center of each.

❋ **Step 5** Fold tortillas in half and over filling. Press firmly so they cling together and stay.

❋ **Step 6** Turn up heat to medium-low, gently put a few tacos at a time in hot oil with a slotted spatula and fry 5 minutes on each side or until just starting to get crisp and change color.

❋ **Step 7** Remove tacos from oil and drain on paper towel-lined plate. Let cool slightly.

❋ **Step 8** Unwrap each "Cheese Slice" and cut it in half diagonally.

❋ **Step 9** Carefully open each taco and insert a halved "Cheese Slice" and pinch of lettuce.

❋ **Step 10** Press back together again and put in a microwave or a very warm oven just until heated through. (Any longer and they will become overly crisp, like any other old taco.)

Serve hot with taco sauce, if desired. I ate these in Hawaii and they had a delectably addictive flavor and texture. Makes 16 tacos, 4 servings (4 per person).

Neo-Classic Tamales

⅔ cup avocado oil (other vegetable oil can be used)

2 cups masa flour or masa harina

"Broth" = {
  D- 1¼ cups chicken *Parve Broth* (p. 110).
  P- 1¼ cups chicken *Parve Broth* (p. 110).
  M- 1¼ cup kosher chicken broth.
}

1½ tsp. salt

12 square wrappers: <u>Stove</u>- (6 x 6") foil. <u>Microwave</u>- (8 x 8 in) parchment paper**.**

"Meat" = {
  D- 1 pkg. taco-flavored imitation burger crumbles.
  P- 1 pkg. *parve* taco-flavored soy crumbles.
  M- 1 batch (1 lb.) prepared *Taco Bell® Style Taco Meat* (p. 115).
}

2 cups warm *Taco Bell® Style Enchirito® Sauce* (p. 96)

⊛ Step 1   Blend together oil, masa flour and salt to make a dough.

⊛ Step 2   Add 1 cup "Broth" if microwaving, or 1¼ cup if steaming. Knead until blended.

⊛ Step 3   Take 3 Tbs. dough, and place it in the middle of each square, flattening it out into a rectangle so the two long ends are 1-inch from edge of foil or 1½-inch from edge of paper.

⊛ Step 4   Put a couple spoonfuls of "Meat" along the center of dough.

⊛ Step 5   Gently pull one side of foil or paper toward the other so that dough meets. Let one side fall onto the other, and press slightly so that dough merges to become like a tube.

⊛ Step 6   Roll foil or paper tucking one side under dough, fold ends twice and crease ends.

⊛ Step 7   <u>For Stove</u>- Take a wire cake rack and put it atop a large pot of water to make a steamer, and fill bottom of pot with water. Spread tamales on rack so that steam can circulate, bring water to a boil, turn down to a simmer. <u>For Microwave</u>- Pile tamales in a glass baking dish.

⊛ Step 8   <u>For Stove</u>- Steam tamales 45 minutes until dough is firm. <u>For Microwave</u>- Cook 5 minutes on 70% power, then take them out and shift their positions, and cook 5 more minutes on 70% power, or until masa dough is firm.

⊛ Step 9   Take tamales out of wrappers, put on plates and cover with sauce. Serve hot.

Authentic tamales are wrapped in dried corn husks and steamed. Husks can be microwaved. Corn husks and masa flour can be found in the ethnic section in supermarkets. (Corn husks must be soaked in water until flexible before using.) Makes 12 tamales, 3-4 servings.

Tamale Casserole

"Meat" =
- **D-** 1 pkg. taco-flavored imitation hamburger crumbles.
- **P-** 1 pkg. *parve* taco-flavored soy crumbles.
- **M-** 1 batch (1 lb.) prepared *Taco Bell® Style Taco Meat* (p. 115).

1½ cups store-bought thick & chunky style salsa

½ raw batch *Corn Bread* (p. 216)

"Cheese" =
- **D-** ½ cup grated kosher Cheddar cheese.
- **P-** ½ cup grated *parve* American or Cheddar.
- **M-** ½ cup grated *parve* American or Cheddar.

optional garnishes: sliced black olives, chopped green onions or hot peppers

Step 1   Combine "Meat" and salsa, blend thoroughly and drain any excess liquid.

Step 2   Put corn bread batter in a greased 9 x 9-inch baking dish and spread out evenly.

Step 3   Spoon "Meat" mixture into center of batter, leaving a 1-inch border of cornbread batter around the edges). Preheat oven to 400º F.

Step 4   Bake 20 minutes, take out and top with "Cheese" and desired garnish.

Step 5   Bake until "Cheese" is melted. Cool slightly, cut and serve. Makes 6-9 servings.

✿ ✿

Chilaquiles Casserole

1½ cups small corn chips or slightly crushed tortilla chips

3 cups *Hormel® Style Chili with Beans* (p. 171)

"Cheese" =
- **D-** ½ cup grated kosher Cheddar cheese.
- **P-** ½ cup grated *parve* American or Cheddar.
- **M-** ½ cup grated *parve* American or Cheddar.

optional garnishes: sliced black olives, chopped green onions or hot peppers

Step 1   Cover a greased 9 x 9-inch baking dish with tortilla chips, and spread chili on top.

Step 2   Bake in preheated 350º F oven 20 minutes, or microwave until heated through.

Step 3   Top with "Cheese" and preferred garnishes, put back in oven or microwave, and heat until "Cheese" is melted. Serve hot. Makes 6-8 servings.

(🫒 olives) **Taco Bell® Style Nachos Bell Grande®** (🫒 olives)

1 large pkg. tortilla chips or corn chips

2½-3 cups warm *Refried Beans* (p. 103)

"Meat" = {
D- 1 pkg. taco-flavored imitation hamburger crumbles.
P- 1 pkg. *parve* taco-flavored soy crumbles.
M- 1 batch (1 lb.) prepared *Taco Bell® Style Taco Meat* (p. 115).
}

1¼ cups *Taco Bell® Style Nacho Cheese Sauce* (p. 98)

"Sour Cream" = {
D- 1 cup real sour cream.
P- 1 cup *Parve Imitation Sour Cream* (p. 105).
M- 1 cup *Parve Imitation Sour Cream* (p. 105).
}

1 large chopped tomato (1 cup)

1 cup chopped green onions

1 cup sliced black olives

1 cup *Mexican Restaurant Guacamole* (p.103- optional)

⊛ Step 1   Put tortilla chips on 4 microwave plates and warm them slightly.

⊛ Step 2   Take spoonfuls of beans and "Meat", cheese sauce and "Sour Cream", and plop them evenly throughout all 4 plates of chips.

⊛ Step 3   Sprinkle tomatoes, green onions, olives, and guacamole on chips as well.

⊛ Step 4   Gently mix chips, so that ingredients are interspersed, but do not blend together. There should still be pockets of various ingredients.

⊛ Step 5   Warm each plate in microwave until hot, and serve.

This is so delicious, and you get a different flavor with every bite! Periodically, Taco Bell® would offer guacamole for *Nachos Bell Grande®* when they had it in the 80s. Makes 4 servings.

Quick Quesadillas

6 large flour tortillas

parve **margarine**

"Cheddar" =
- **D-** ¾ cup grated kosher Cheddar cheese.
- **P-** ¾ cup grated *parve* American or Cheddar.
- **M-** ¾ cup grated *parve* American or Cheddar.

"Jack Cheese" =
- **D-** ¾ cup grated kosher Monterey jack cheese.
- **P-** ¾ cup grated *parve* Jack or Mozzarella.
- **M-** ¾ cup grated *parve* Jack or Mozzarella.

1 medium chopped onion (½ cup)

1-2 Tbs. minced pickled jalapeño peppers (optional)

2 Tbs. favorite taco sauce (optional)

❀ Step 1   Coat each tortilla with margarine on either side, then lay on a cookie sheet or foil.

❀ Step 2   Distribute "Cheddar", "Jack Cheese" and remaining ingredients evenly in the middle of each tortilla.

❀ Step 3   Fold one side of tortilla over the other, like folding a paper in half.

❀ Step 4   Broil in oven until starting to brown, 1-2 minutes, flip and broil another 1-2 minutes until starting to brown. (Do not let it burn, they heat fast!)

Literally, this is a Mexican toasted cheese sandwich. It is quick and easy to throw together, and makes a great meal when accompanied with soup. Makes 2-4 servings, or 4 quesadillas.

This can also be done in the microwave by heating until cheese starts to melt, but it won't get crisp.

Grilled Meat Fajitas

¾ tsp. liquid smoke (for lightly grilled flavor)**, OR 1¼ tsp.** (for well-done flavor)

¾ cup *Parve Italian Dressing* (p. 89)

8 tsp. lime juice

"Meat" =
- **D-** 3 cups imitation steak or chicken chunks.
- **P-** 3 cups *parve* soy steak or chicken chunks.
- **M-** 1½ lb. sliced kosher flank or skirt steaks, or chicken strips.

2-3 large onions (cut crosswise in ½-inch slices)

3 large green or red bell peppers (seeded and cut into strips)

2 Tbs. *parve* margarine or avocado oil (other vegetable oil can be used)

8 large flour tortillas

2 cups store-bought salsa or *Super Salsa* (p. 96)

"Optional Sour Cream" =
- **D-** ½ cup real sour cream.
- **P-** ½ cup *Parve Imitation Sour Cream* (p. 105).
- **M-** ½ cup *Parve Imitation Sour Cream* (p. 105).

½ cup *Mexican Restaurant Guacamole* (p. 104- optional)

✾ Step 1   Combine first 3 ingredients, and put "Meat", onions, and bell peppers in mixture.

✾ Step 2   Marinate 1 hour at room temperature.

✾ Step 3   Take "Steak", onions, and peppers out of marinade. Put oil in a pan or margarine in microwave bowl and sauté them until tender for D or P, or for M until juices run clear.

✾ Step 4   Warm tortillas and put "Meat" and vegetables in each flour tortilla and roll up or fold over.

✾ Step 5   Garnish with salsa, "Optional Sour Cream" and guacamole if desired. Serve hot.

Less trouble than grilling out, and really delicious. The leftover marinade can be used for pasta or salad dressings. Makes 6-8 servings.

Chinese Main Dishes

🥛 (🥕 on broccoli)   **Ginger Beef**   🥛

¼ cup corn starch

⅓ cup soy sauce

2 Tbs. kosher cooking sherry

1¾ cups water

¾ cup brown sugar

½ cup flour

½ tsp. ground ginger

"Beef" = {
  D- 2 cups large imitation beef or steak chunks.
  P- 2 cups *parve* soy beef or baked *Beef Seitan* chunks (p.111).
  M- 1-2 lb. 1-inch kosher steak chunks, (with slashes cut in them).

½ cup sesame or peanut oil

2 Tbs. fresh minced ginger

4 minced garlic cloves (2 tsp.)

1 (10 oz.) pkg. frozen broccoli florets (thawed and cut in 1-inch pieces)

½ lb. sliced mushrooms (½ cup), OR 2 (4 oz.) cans mushrooms (drained)

¾ cup green onions (cut in 2-inch pieces)

1-2 tsp. sesame seeds (optional)

¼ tsp. red pepper flakes (optional)

✾	Step 1	Blend together first 5 ingredients in a bowl, and set aside.
✾	Step 2	Combine flour and ground ginger In a small bowl, blending well.
✾	Step 3	Take "Beef" chunks, and dredge them in flour, coating them well.
✾	Step 4	Heat oil slightly in a large frying pan and add "Beef", fry and brown it all around.
✾	Step 5	Add fresh ginger, garlic, broccoli and mushrooms, stir fry 4 minutes.
✾	Step 6	Lower heat, stir and add corn starch mixture. Cook uncovered stirring constantly.
✾	Step 7	When sauce starts to thicken, stir in last 3 ingredients, and take off heat.

Serve hot on chow mein noodles or rice if desired. Makes 4-6 servings.

(rice)("Beef")(veggies) **Beef Stir-Fry**

¼ cup sesame or peanut oil

1½ tsp. minced fresh ginger

2 minced garlic cloves (1 tsp.)

1 large chopped onion (¾ cup)

"Beef" = { **D-** 2¼ cups *parve* imitation beef chunks, (cut in 1-inch pieces).
P- 2¼ cups *parve* soy beef or steak chunks, (cut in 1-inch pieces).
M- 1½ lb. kosher steak, (cut into thin strips).

1½ cups broccoli florets, OR 1 (10 oz.) pkg. frozen broccoli (thawed)

1½ medium yellow bell peppers (seeded and cut into thin strips)

1 (15 oz.) can sliced water chestnuts

1 batch (about 1 cup) *Stir-Fry Cooking Sauce* (p. 94)

2 cups hot cooked white *Perfect Rice* (p. 205)

	Step 1	Heat oil in a wok or very large frying pan, and add ginger, garlic, onions and "Beef".
	Step 2	Stir-fry until "Beef" is warm if D or P, or browned if M (about 4-6 minutes).
	Step 3	Add broccoli and bell peppers to wok or frying pan, and stir-fry 1 minute.
	Step 4	Add water chestnuts and stir fry sauce, and cook until sauce is thickened.
	Step 5	Put hot rice on plates, and dish stir-fry on top. Serve hot.

Mushrooms can be substituted for water chestnuts, and for additional crunch, top with *mandelin*, (soup croutons), they taste just like Chinese restaurant chow mein noodles. Makes 4-8 servings.

Egg Fu Yung

1½ cup water

2 Tbs. *parve* chicken soup mix, OR 3 *parve* chicken bouillon or soup cubes

2⅓ Tbs. soy sauce

3⅓ Tbs. corn starch or potato starch

½ cup *parve* margarine

1 medium chopped onion (½ cup)

1 (15 oz.) can bean sprouts (drained)

1 red bell pepper (seeded and cut into strips)

1 (4 oz.) can chopped mushrooms (liquid reserved)

1 cup chopped green onions

1 cup chopped water chestnuts (optional)

1 Tbs. kosher cooking sherry

¼ tsp. ground ginger

"Chicken" =
- D- 1½ cups chopped imitation chicken chunks.
- P- 1½ cups chopped *parve* soy or seitan chicken chunks.
- M- 1½ cups chopped cooked kosher chicken.

8 room temperature eggs

***parve* margarine or avocado oil** (other vegetable oil can be used)

⊛	Step 1	Combine water, soup mix, soy sauce and starch in a saucepan, blending well.
⊛	Step 2	Bring to boil and stir until thickened. Keep warm— you now have sauce.
⊛	Step 3	Melt margarine in a large skillet, coat entire pan bottom and sides with it.
⊛	Step 4	Add vegetables, sherry, ginger and "Chicken", sauté until vegetables are tender.
⊛	Step 5	Remove mixture from pan, put in a large mixing bowl.
⊛	Step 6	Beat eggs, add to mixture in bowl, stirring to blend well.
⊛	Step 7	Put oil in pan ¼ inch deep, and add egg mixture in one-quarter batches.
⊛	Step 8	Fry each batch until egg is brown on one side, flip and cook until brown on other

side. (Repeat Steps 7 and 8 until all batches are done.) Put on plates and pour on sauce.

Serve hot immediately, or freeze for later use. Makes 4-6 servings.

Fried Rice

2½ Tbs. *parve* margarine

8 large beaten eggs

1 tsp. salt

dash black pepper

½ cup sesame or peanut oil (other vegetable oil can be used)

2 medium chopped onions (1 cup)

6 minced garlic cloves (3 tsp.)

1½ cups frozen peas

5 cups cooked white *Perfect Rice* (p. 205)

1½ Tbs. soy sauce

2½ chopped green onions (2 cups)

Step 1   Put margarine in a large frying pan or wok and melt, coating pan bottom and sides.

Step 2   Lightly beat together eggs, salt and pepper and add to margarine, cooking until lightly scrambled but moist.

Step 3   Remove eggs from pan and set aside, then put in oil, onion, garlic and peas, cooking until onion is transparent.

Step 4   Add rice to pan and stir fry rice, breaking up any clumps, and add soy sauce.

Step 5   When heated through, stir in eggs and green onions, until well blended and heated through.

Serve hot with extra soy sauce if desired. This is a basic recipe and other items can be added as well, such as for *Pork Fried Rice* (p. 324). Instead of the first 4 ingredients, 1½ cups of leftover scrambled eggs can be used. Makes 4-8 servings.

Chicken Fried Rice

2 Tbs. *parve* margarine

6 large beaten eggs

1 tsp. salt

dash black pepper

⅓ cup sesame or peanut oil (other vegetable oil can be used)

1 large chopped onion (¾ cup)

4 minced garlic cloves (2 tsp.)

1 cup frozen peas (optional)

4 cups cooked white *Perfect Rice* (p. 205)

1 Tbs. soy sauce

"Chicken" =
- **D-** 2 cups imitation chicken chunks.
- **P-** 2 cups *parve* soy or seitan chicken chunks.
- **M-** 2 cups cooked kosher chicken chunks.

2 chopped green onions (1½ cups)

Step 1   Put margarine in a large frying pan or wok and melt, coating pan bottom and sides.

Step 2   Lightly beat together eggs, salt and pepper and add to margarine, cooking until lightly scrambled but moist.

Step 3   Remove eggs from pan and set aside, then put in oil, onion, garlic and peas if desired, cooking until onion is transparent.

Step 4   Add rice to pan and stir fry rice, breaking up any clumps, and add soy sauce.

Step 5   When heated through, stir in "Chicken", scrambled eggs and green onions, until well blended and heated through.

Serve hot with extra soy sauce if desired. This makes an excellent meal, or even can be served as a side dish. Instead of the first 4 ingredients, 1½ cups leftover scrambled eggs can be used. Makes 4-8 servings.

(rice)("Chicken")(veggies) **Chicken Stir-Fry**

¼ cup sesame or peanut oil

1 large chopped onion (¾ cup)

1 tsp. minced fresh ginger

4 minced garlic cloves (2 tsp.)

"Chicken" =
- **D-** 2¼ cups imitation chicken strips or chunks.
- **P-** 2¼ cups *parve* soy chicken strips or chunks.
- **M-** 2¼ cups kosher chicken strips or chunks.

1½ cups broccoli florets, OR 1 (10 oz.) pkg. frozen broccoli (thawed)

1½ medium yellow bell peppers (seeded and cut into thin strips)

1¾ cup sliced mushrooms, OR 1 (15 oz.) can sliced mushrooms

1 batch (about 1 cup) *Stir-Fry Cooking Sauce* (p. 94)

2 cups hot cooked white *Perfect Rice* (p. 205)

❀ Step 1   Heat oil in a wok or very large frying pan, and add onions, ginger, garlic, and "Chicken".

❀ Step 2   Stir-fry until "Chicken" is warm if D or P, or browned if M (about 2-3 minutes).

❀ Step 3   Add broccoli and bell peppers to wok or frying pan and stir-fry 1 minute or until slightly tender.

❀ Step 4   Add stir fry sauce, and cook stirring until sauce is thickened.

❀ Step 5   Put hot rice on plates and dish stir-fry on top. Serve hot.

Water chestnuts can be substituted for mushrooms. Can be served atop chow mein noodles instead of rice if desired. Makes 4-8 servings.

(🍗"Chicken")(🥜 cashews)(🥕veggies) **Cashew Chicken**   🥛

¼ cup corn starch

½ cup soy sauce

1 tsp. salt

1 tsp. sugar

⅓ cup sesame or peanut oil

"Chicken" = {
D- 2 cups imitation chicken chunks.
P- 2 cups *parve* soy or seitan chicken chunks.
M- 1 lb. boneless kosher chicken breasts, (cut into chunks).
}

4 tsp. minced fresh ginger, OR 1 tsp. ground ginger

4 minced garlic cloves (2 tsp.)

1 cup boiling water

2 tsp. *parve* chicken soup mix, OR 1 *parve* chicken bouillon or soup cube

1 medium red bell pepper (seeded and cut into strips)

½ lb. (2¼ cups) small sugar snap peas or snow peas (strings removed)

½ lb. sliced mushrooms (½ cup), OR 1 (8 oz.) can mushrooms (drained)

1 (16 oz.) can bamboo shoots (drained)

1½ cups roasted cashew halves (unsalted or rinsed in strainer if salted)

½ cup minced green onions

¼ tsp. red pepper flakes (optional)

❀ Step 1   Blend together corn starch, soy sauce, salt and sugar, and set aside.

❀ Step 2   Put oil in a frying pan or wok and heat until warm, add "Chicken", ginger and garlic. Stir fry 2 minutes, then lower heat.

❀ Step 3   Add water, soup mix, bell pepper, snow peas, mushrooms, and bamboo shoots to "Chicken" and simmer covered 2 minutes.

❀ Step 4   Add corn starch mixture, cook uncovered stirring constantly until sauce thickens.

❀ Step 5   Stir in cashews, green onions, and red pepper flakes, then take off heat.

Serve hot over rice or chow mein noodles sprinkled with 2 Tbs. minced fresh cilantro leaves, if desired. Makes 4-8 servings.

(🧁rice)(🥤"Chicken")   **Hong Kong Chicken**   🥤

2 cups hot cooked white *Perfect Rice* (p. 205)

"Chicken" = ⎰ **D-** 24 pre-baked imitation breaded chicken nuggets.
⎱ **P-** 24 pre-baked *parve* breaded soy chicken nuggets.
⎰ **M-** 24 pre-baked breaded kosher chicken nuggets.

1½ cups *Chicken Gravy* (p. 102)

1 cup chopped green onions

Chinese Hot Pepper Oil (p. 437- optional)

✤ Step 1   Heat first 4 ingredients, and divide rice and "Chicken" into 4 portions.

✤ Step 2   Put rice on plates, and place "Chicken" atop rice.

✤ Step 3   Put equal portions of gravy on "Chicken" and rice. Sprinkle onions on top.

✤ Step 4   Put little crocks of pepper oil with each portion, if desired.

Serve with *Crab Rangoons* (p. 334) as an appetizer first if having M (or D depending on *minhag*), and eat or drink something *parve* in between. This was based on a favorite lunch special at a local Chinese restaurant. Makes 4 servings.

Practical Peking Duck

7 tsp. kosher white wine or kosher cooking sherry

5 tsp. soy sauce

pinch ground ginger

5 ⅝ tsp. honey

3¾ tsp. white vinegar

2 tsp. corn starch

¼ cup + 1½ tsp. water (divided)

16 green onions (4-inches of green tops, white bulbs with roots cut off)

"Duck" =
- **D-** 4 pkg. imitation turkey slices (slices should be 5 pieces thick).
- **P-** 4 pkg. *parve* soy turkey slices (slices should be 5 pieces thick).
- **M-** 1 big well-baked kosher duck, OR 2 lb. kosher dark turkey slices.

1 Tbs. sesame, peanut, olive or avocado oil (other vegetable oil can be used)

¼ cup *Chinese Hoisin Sauce* (p. 93)

16 hot *Mandarin Chinese Pancakes* (p. 215)

Step 1   Preheat oven to 350º F if baking. Combine first 6 ingredients and ¼ cup water in a small saucepan, and simmer stirring until thickened to make basting sauce. Set aside.

Step 2   Slice onion leaves lengthwise 1-inch down. One can put them inside pancakes, or place on top as a fancy garnish. (For garnish, set onion tops in ice water until curled.)

Step 3   (For M made with real duck, slice into ¼ inch thick slices- preferably with brown skin.) Cut "Duck" slices into 16 squares 2 x 2-inches. Spread out slices in a glass baking pan.

Step 4   Baste or spread "Duck" with warm basting sauce. Bake "Duck" 10 minutes or microwave 3 minutes, or until heated through.

Step 5   Combine last 1½-tsp. water and oil with hoisin sauce. Set pancakes on plates.

Step 6   Spoon hoisin sauce mixture on pancakes, and spread it slightly.

Step 7   Place a hot "Duck" slice on each pancake. Repeat for each.

Step 8   Place an onion with "Duck" if having it inside. Roll pancakes around "Duck" and onion. Heat if needed. If onions are left out as garnish, place one onion atop each pancake.

For real Peking duck, one must blanch the duck, stuff, sew and hang it to dry in the wind 6 hours—all for crispy brown skin. This has the same flavor but is practical! Makes 4-8 servings.

Poultry and Meat Main Dishes

Poultry

(M "Duck") (rice)   **Duck À L'Orange**

2¼ tsp. *parve* **margarine**

6 Tbs. orange marmalade

4½ tsp. kosher white wine or kosher cooking sherry

1¾ tsp. white vinegar

2¼ tsp. soy sauce

⅜ tsp. ground thyme

> **"Duck" =** { **D-** 4 baked turkey *Seitan Breasts*, OR 2 pkg. soy turkey slices.
> **P-** 4 baked turkey *Seitan Breasts*, OR 2 pkg. *parve* turkey slices.
> **M-** 1 kosher roasted duck, OR 4 pieces cooked kosher dark turkey.

1 (11 oz.) can Mandarin oranges (drained)

Optional Orange Rice

¾ cup *Turkey Gravy* (p. 102)

½ cup orange juice

1½ Tbs. corn starch

2 cups hot cooked white basmati *Perfect Rice* (p. 205)

⊛ Step 1   Combine first 6 ingredients in a pot, blend and heat through to make duck sauce. Set aside; keep warm.

⊛ Step 2   Place "Duck" on plates (if using sliced, keep 5 slices stacked together). Pour duck sauce over "Duck".

⊛ Step 3   Decoratively top "Duck" with orange sections. Put plates in a warm oven or microwave (if microwavable). Serve as is, or continue with Steps 4-5 for optional orange rice.

⊛ Step 4   To make orange rice, combine turkey gravy, orange juice and corn starch in a larger pot. Blend well. Stir constantly on medium heat until slightly thickened.

⊛ Step 5   Stir rice into sauce. Serve hot with "Duck" on top or separately as a side dish.

Luscious orange rice compliments a fancy classic dish. Makes 4 servings.

Stouffer's® Style Turkey Tetrazzini

⅓ cup parve margarine

2 (4 oz.) cans chopped mushrooms (drained)

2½ cups *Parve Milk* (p. 85), OR other *parve* milk alternative (divided)

5 tsp. *parve* chicken soup mix, OR 2½ tsp. *parve* chicken bouillon powder

¼ cup flour

¾ tsp. dried crushed basil

¼ tsp. black pepper

"Turkey" =
- D- 1¼ cups chopped imitation turkey slices.
- P- 1¼ cups chopped *parve* soy or seitan turkey slices.
- M-1¼ cups chopped cooked kosher turkey.

3 cups hot cooked spaghetti or linguini (½ lb. raw)

"Parmesan" =
- D- ½ cup grated kosher Parmesan cheese.
- P- ½ cup *Parve Parmesan Cheese* (p. 108).
- M- ½ cup *Parve Parmesan Cheese* (p. 108).

✿ Step 1   Put margarine and mushrooms in a saucepan and sauté until tender.

✿ Step 2   Add 1 cup *Parve Milk*, bring to a boil, then add soup mix and stir to dissolve.

✿ Step 3   Put ½ cup *Parve Milk*, flour, basil and pepper in a tight sealing jar and shake together until well blended.

✿ Step 4   Gradually add flour mixture to boiling water, stir until thickened.

✿ Step 5   Add "Turkey" and pasta to creamy mixture, blending well.

✿ Step 6   Pour into a greased casserole dish and sprinkle "Parmesan" over top.

✿ Step 7   Bake in preheated 375º F oven 20 minutes until slightly browned, or microwave 8-10 minutes, until heated through.

This can be made in large batches and frozen for a quick and delicious meal, just like the real thing. Instead of the creamy mixture, 2 batches of *Condensed Cream of Mushroom Soup* (p. 148) can be used, omitting the first 7 ingredients, and Steps 1-4 skipped as well. Makes 4-6 servings.

Stuffed Turkey & Trimmings

1 batch *Stove Top® Style Stuffing* (p. 212- chicken flavor & double margarine)

3½ cups *Deluxe Whipped Potatoes* (p. 192)

1 batch *Classic French Green Bean Casserole* (p. 196)

"Turkey" = {
D- 2 pkg. imitation roasted turkey slices (double slices).
P- 2 pkg. *parve* soy or seitan roasted turkey slices (double slices).
M- 2 lb. kosher turkey slices, OR 1 baked whole kosher turkey.

1½ cups *Turkey Gravy* (p. 102)

½ cup finely minced *parve* chicken or soy crumbles (optional for giblets)

1 (15 oz.) can kosher jellied cranberry sauce (refrigerated)

1 prepared *Parve Pumpkin Pie* (p. 397- heated)

optional: 1 cup *parve* whipped cream, or *Parve Vanilla Ice Cream* (p. 411)

⊛ Step 1   Heat and/or make stuffing, potatoes and green bean casserole and keep warm.

⊛ Step 2   Put stuffing in 4 mounds (about ½ cup each) on a greased cookie sheet, or a microwave safe casserole dish for D and P, or if using turkey slices for M.

⊛ Step 3   Wrap 4 doubled "Turkey" slices around each mound tucking edges in at bottom, and place one on top. (For M, if using a whole baked turkey, it can be filled with stuffing.)

⊛ Step 4   Bake at 350º F 10-15 minutes (or microwave 5 minutes) or until heated through.

⊛ Step 5   Heat gravy in a saucepan and add minced imitation chicken if desired.

⊛ Step 6   Take out cranberry sauce, open both can ends, slide onto a plate and slice it.

⊛ Step 7   Put green beans and mashed potatoes on plates. (Make a "well" in potatoes.)

⊛ Step 8   Take out "Turkey" with spatula (or M- slice whole turkey) and put it on each plate.

⊛ Step 9   Pour gravy on potatoes and turkey. Serve hot, and serve pie for dessert.

Oyster Dressing (p. 349) can be substituted for stuffing. (Serve separately as appetizer for M).

For D or P, raw *Turkey Seitan* can be used as 4 individual portions as *Stuffed Breasts* (see p. 111). Wrap each piece around 2 Tbs. of stuffing. Set seam-down in pan, coat well with olive oil. Cover. Bake 1 hour. (Do not overcook, it keeps cooking even after it's taken out of the oven. Never cook seitan in microwave, only re-heat.) Makes 4 servings.

("Chicken")(rice) **Stuffed Chicken with Wild Rice**

1 large chopped onion (1 cup)

1 cup sliced mushrooms (divided)

¼ cup *parve* margarine (divided)

2 cups coarse *Bread Crumbs* (p. 116)**, OR 1 cup store-bought bread crumbs**

"Sour Cream" =
- **D-** ¼ cup sour cream.
- **P-** ¼ cup *Parve Imitation Sour Cream* (p. 105).
- **M-** ¼ cup *Parve Imitation Sour Cream* (p. 105).

⅛ tsp. garlic powder

⅛ tsp. salt

"Chicken" =
- **D-** 2-4 pkg. *parve* soy chicken slices (double slices).
- **P-** 2-4 pkg. *parve* soy chicken slices (double slices).
- **M-** 2 lb. kosher chicken slices, OR 4 baked kosher Cornish hens.

1½ cups *Chicken Gravy* (p. 102)

¼ cup chopped green onions

⅛ tsp. ground nutmeg

2 cups hot cooked *Luscious Long Grain & Wild Rice* (p. 207)

Step 1   Sauté onion and ½ cup mushrooms in 2 Tbs. margarine until tender.

Step 2   Combine bread crumbs, "Sour Cream", garlic powder, and salt with onion and mushrooms, kneading well to make stuffing. (If it's too dry and falls apart, add a little water.)

Step 3   Put stuffing in 4 (½ cup) mounds on greased cookie sheet or casserole dish.

Step 4   Wrap 5 "Chicken" slices around each mound of stuffing to cover it. (For M if using pre-baked Cornish hens, stuff each hen with stuffing.) Set aside.

Step 5   Sauté green onions and remaining ½ cup mushrooms in last 2 Tbs. margarine.

Step 6   Heat gravy in a saucepan, then stir in nutmeg, sautéed onions and mushrooms.

Step 7   Bake "Chicken" at 350º F 15 minutes, or microwave about 8 minutes until heated.

Step 8   Spatula out "Chicken" onto plates and pour gravy over each. Makes 4 servings.

For D or P, raw chicken *Seitan Breasts* (p. 111) can be used: In Step 3, wrap each piece around 2 Tbs. stuffing, set in greased pan seam-down, coat with olive oil. Cover. Bake 1 hour. Do Steps 6-8. (Don't overcook, it continues baking after it comes out of the oven.)

Chicken Cordon Bleu

"Cheese" =
- **D-** 8 slices kosher Swiss or Mozzarella cheese.
- **P-** 8 slices *parve* imitation Mozzarella cheese.
- **M-** 8 slices *parve* imitation Mozzarella cheese.

"Canadian Bacon" =
- **D-** 4 slices imitation ham or Canadian bacon.
- **P-** 4 slices *parve* soy ham or Canadian bacon.
- **M-** 4 slices kosher smoked turkey breast.

"Chicken" =
- **D-** 1 batch raw chicken *Seitan* ingredients (see p. 111).
- **P-** 1 batch raw chicken *Seitan* ingredients (see p. 111).
- **M-** 4 boneless skinless kosher chicken breasts (beaten until flat).

2 Tbs. melted *parve* margarine

½ cup crushed corn flake crumbs

1 tsp. paprika

⅛ tsp. black pepper

vegetable oil spray

⊛ Step 1   Preheat oven to 350º F. Cut "Canadian Bacon" and "Cheese" slices in quarters. Divide into 4 sets and sandwich "Cheese" between "Canadian Bacon" slices.

⊛ Step 2   (For D or P, do Steps 1-3 for *Chicken Seitan Breasts*.) Carefully stretch one "Chicken" piece, wrapping "Chicken" entirely around them to cover. (Try not to let edges touch filling for D or P, or it prevents a tight seal.)

⊛ Step 3   For D or P, pinch "Chicken" edges tightly closed. For M, secure "Chicken" closed with toothpicks.

⊛ Step 4   Blend together corn flake crumbs, paprika and pepper in a shallow, flat container.

⊛ Step 5   Coat "Chicken" with 2 Tbs. melted *parve* margarine, and then roll in crumbs.

⊛ Step 6   Set "Chicken" seam-side-down in a greased loaf pan, spray with oil, and cover.

⊛ Step 7   Bake 40 minutes (or until tender and juices run clear for M). (Do not overcook D or P, it keeps cooking even after it is taken out of the oven.) Makes 4 servings.

A quick alternative is to use 2 breaded (vegan for D or P, or real for M) chicken patties. Sandwich "Canadian Bacon" and "Cheese" between patties. <u>To Bake</u>- Put in preheated 400º F oven- 10 minutes D or P, or M 20 minutes. <u>To Microwave</u>- Cook in covered glass casserole 4 minutes for D or P until heated through, or 5-8 minutes for M until no longer pink and juices run clear.

Chicken Kiev

"Butter" =
- **D-** ¼ cup real dairy butter.
- **P-** ¼ cup *Parve Imitation Butter* (p. 84- use salt), or margarine.
- **M-** ¼ cup *Parve Imitation Butter* (p. 84- use salt), or margarine.

1½ Tbs. snipped fresh chives

⅛ tsp. garlic powder

¼ tsp. black pepper (divided)

"Chicken" =
- **D-** 1 batch raw chicken *Seitan* ingredients (see p. 111).
- **P-** 1 batch raw chicken *Seitan* ingredients (see p. 111).
- **M-** 4 boneless skinless kosher chicken breasts (beaten until flat).

2 Tbs. melted *parve* margarine

½ cup crushed corn flake crumbs

1 tsp. paprika

vegetable oil spray

⊛ Step 1   Warm "Butter" slightly to soften, and stir in chives, garlic and ⅛ tsp. pepper.

⊛ Step 2   Shape "Butter" mixture into 4 rectangular 1½ x 1 inch cubes, place on a small piece of plastic wrap. Freeze until firm. (For D or P, do Steps 1-3 for *Chicken Seitan Breasts*.)

⊛ Step 3   Place "Butter" mixture in the center of a "Chicken" piece. Carefully stretch piece around "Butter" mixture, wrapping "Chicken" entirely around it to enclose "Butter" completely. (Try not to let the edges touch the filling for D or P, or it prevents a tight seal.)

⊛ Step 4   For D or P, pinch "Chicken" edges tightly. For M, secure it with toothpicks.

⊛ Step 5   Blend together corn flake crumbs, paprika and remaining ⅛ tsp. pepper in a shallow, flat container. Preheat oven to 350º F.

⊛ Step 6   Coat "Chicken" with 2 Tbs. melted *parve* margarine, and then roll in crumbs.

⊛ Step 7   Set "Chicken" seam-side-down in a greased loaf pan, spray with oil, and cover.

⊛ Step 8   Bake 40 minutes (or until tender and juices run clear for M). (Do not overcook D or P, it keeps cooking even after it is taken out of the oven.) Makes 4 servings.

A quick alternative is to use 2 breaded (vegan for D or P, or real for M) chicken patties, sandwiching "Butter" mixture in between. To Bake- Put in preheated 400º F oven- D or 10 minutes for P, or M 20 minutes. To Microwave- Put in covered glass casserole 4 minutes for D or P just until heated through, or cook 5-8 minutes for M until no longer pink and juices run clear.

Popeye's® Style Chicken

½ cup flour

1 tsp. salt

1 tsp. white pepper (black pepper can also be used)

1 tsp. cayenne pepper (add ½ tsp. extra for spicier chicken)

¾ tsp. paprika

peanut oil for frying (other vegetable oil can be used)

1 large well beaten egg, OR 2 small well beaten eggs

"Chicken" =
- **D-** 4 imitation chicken cutlets or baked *Seitan Breasts* (p. 111).
- **P-** 4 *parve* soy chicken cutlets or baked *Seitan Breasts* (p. 111).
- **M-** 4 cooked boneless skinless kosher chicken breasts.

Step 1 Combine and blend first 5 ingredients in a plastic bag, and put egg in a bowl.

Step 2 Coat "Chicken" in egg, then put "Chicken" in bag, shaking to coat thoroughly.

Step 3 Heat ¼ inch deep oil in large skillet until hot, and drop in "Chicken" pieces.

Step 4 For D or P- Fry covered, brown on each side 2 minutes. For M- Reduce heat, fry uncovered 25-40 minutes until golden brown and done. Drain on paper towel-lined plates.

Serve hot. Goes well with *Popeye's® Style Dirty Rice* (p. 252). Makes 4 servings.

✡ ✡

KFC® Style Fried Chicken

"Chicken" =
- **D-** 4 baked *Seitan Breasts*, OR 2 cups imitation chicken chunks.
- **P-** 4 baked *Seitan Breasts*, OR 2 cups *parve* chicken chunks.
- **M-** 4 pieces kosher chicken, OR 2 cups kosher chicken strips.

¼ cup melted *parve* margarine

⅓ cup *Kentucky Fried Chicken® Style Breading Mix* (p. 82)

peanut oil for frying (other vegetable oil can be used)

Step 1 Coat "Chicken" well with margarine, then dredge in breading one time. Let dry.

Step 2 Heat oil in large skillet until hot. For D or P- Fry covered, brown on each side 2 minutes. For M- Fry uncovered 25-40 minutes until golden brown and done. Makes 4 servings.

🥛(🧁 breading) **McDonald's® Style Chicken McNuggets®** 🥛(🧁 breading)

1¼ cup flour

⅜ tsp. black pepper

¼ tsp. garlic powder

2½ tsp. salt

1¼ tsp. onion powder

1 egg

1 cup water

"Chicken" = {
D- 24 imitation chicken chunks.
P- 24 *parve* soy chicken chunks or cut up chicken *Seitan* (p. 111).
M- 4 kosher chicken breasts, (pounded and cut in chunks).

avocado oil for frying (other vegetable oil can be used)

✹ Step 1   Combine dry ingredients in a zipper bag shake it to blend, then put egg and water in a bowl beat them together and set them both aside.

✹ Step 2   Take "Chicken" and put it in zipper bag of flour and shake bag to coat it, (do this for each nugget).

✹ Step 3   Dredge each nugget in egg mixture and then put nuggets back in flour, and shake them to coat them again.

✹ Step 4   Immediately put (bag and all) in freezer 1 hour (refrigerate egg mixture).

✹ Step 5   When hour is up, take egg mixture out of fridge and nuggets out of freezer.

✹ Step 6   Dredge nuggets in egg mixture and put back in flour shaking to coat again.

✹ Step 7   Heat oil ¼ inch deep in frying pan until hot, fry each nugget until golden brown.

✹ Step 8   Drain on a paper towel lined plate, and serve hot.

Goes great with *McDonald's® Style French Fries* (p. 180), and *McDonald's® Style Pies* (p. 400) for dessert. Makes 4-6 servings.

In 1984, McDonald's had a promotion connected to the Olympics, in which they had "International Chicken McNuggets®" with a choice of 4 different sauces: Chinese sweet & sour, American barbecue, French Dijon, or Mexican green taco. To duplicate these, use *Sweet & Sour Sauce* (p. 94), any barbecue sauce, any honey-Dijon salad dressing, and *Taco Bell® Style Green Taco Sauce* (p. 97). Put a bit of each in a crock and serve, or choose your favorite.

(🧁 rice) **Easy Chicken & Rice Dinner**

2 cups raw white rice

4 cups water

1 envelope (3-4 Tbs.) onion soup mix (divided)

"Chicken" =
- **D-** 8 imitation chicken cutlets or cooked *Seitan Breasts* (p. 111).
- **P-** 8 *parve* soy chicken cutlets or cooked *Seitan Breasts* (p. 111).
- **M-** 1 whole kosher chicken (cut into 8 pieces).

Step 1   Blend rice, water and ½ soup envelope in a large baking pan or roaster.

Step 2   Put "Chicken" on rice mixture, then sprinkle last ½ soup mix over top.

Step 3   Seal pan completely with foil or lid it. Bake in a preheated 350° F oven 1½ hours.

This delicious recipe (M version) is from Mrs. Naomi Homnick. Chicken can be breaded or un-breaded, and either frozen or thawed. Even nuggets can be used. (If breaded, add 3 cup parve margarine.) Very versatile and quick. Makes 4-8 servings.

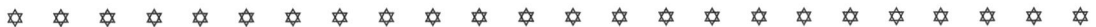

✿ ✿

Quickie Chickie Rice

2 tsp. *parve* chicken soup mix, OR 1 tsp. *parve* chicken bouillon powder

½ cup melted *parve* margarine

2 cups hot cooked white *Perfect Rice* (p. 205)

"Chicken" =
- **D-** ½ cup chopped imitation chicken chunks.
- **P-** ½ cup chopped *parve* soy or chicken *Seitan* chunks (p. 111).
- **M-** ½ cup chopped cooked kosher chicken.

½ tsp. salt

⅛ tsp. black pepper

¼ tsp. ground thyme

¼ tsp. paprika

dash cayenne pepper

Blend soup mix into margarine, add to rice and stir in last ingredients. Heat. Makes 3-4 servings.

🥛 (🧁 rice) **Peruvian Chicken Curry** 🥤

2 cups cooked white *Perfect Rice* (p. 205)

1½ cups *Curry Sauce* (p. 101)

"Chicken" = {
D- 4 veggie cutlets or cooked chicken *Seitan Breasts* (p. 111).
P- 4 veggie cutlets or cooked chicken *Seitan Breasts* (p. 111).
M- 4 cooked boneless skinless kosher chicken breasts.
}

2 hard-boiled eggs

4 small-medium whole boiled potatoes (for speed, microwaved can be used)

✳ Step 1   Heat rice, curry sauce and "Chicken", and halve eggs.

✳ Step 2   Divide up rice and spread out on each plate, and put "Chicken" on top of rice.

✳ Step 3   Put a potato next to rice, place eggs on top of "Chicken".

✳ Step 4   Pour curry sauce over chicken and serve hot.

This different dish is based on an authentic dinner fixed by a Peruvian friend. Makes 4 servings.

✡ ✡

(🧁 pasta) **Kraft® Chicken Applause® Style Dinner** (🧁 pasta)

(🥛 "Chicken") (🥤 "Chicken")

½ lb. medium shells or other small macaroni (2 cups raw)

"Chicken" = {
D- 4 veggie cutlets or cooked chicken *Seitan Breasts* (p. 111).
P- 4 veggie cutlets or cooked chicken *Seitan Breasts* (p. 111).
M- 4 cooked boneless skinless kosher chicken breasts.
}

3 cups boiling water

¾ cup *Smoky Bacon Cheese Spread* (p. 107)

¼ cup crushed *Parve Nabisco® Style Cheese Tid-Bits®* (p. 128)

✳ Step 1   Preheat oven to 350° F. Put pasta and "Chicken" in greased casserole dish.

✳ Step 2   Pour in boiling water, drop spoonfuls of sauce over top, sprinkle with bacon bits.

✳ Step 3   Bake 40 minutes then sprinkle crushed Tid-Bits® on top. Bake 15 more minutes.

✳ Step 4   Remove "Chicken", and stir pasta to blend. Makes 4-6 servings.

296

(peas)   **Malaysian Chicken and Peas**

3 small minced pickled jalapeños (3 Tbs.), OR ¾ tsp. cayenne pepper

1 large chopped onion (¾ cup), OR 2 tsp. onion powder

1 Tbs. grated fresh ginger, OR ¼ tsp. ground ginger

1½ cups *Imitation Thai Coconut Cream* (p. 86)

1 tsp. salt

4 tsp. *parve* chicken soup mix, OR 2 *parve* chicken bouillon or soup cubes

"Chicken" =
{
D- 2 cups imitation chicken chunks.

P- 2 cups *parve* soy or chicken *Seitan* chunks (p. 111).

M- 2 cups diced cooked kosher chicken.

1 (10 oz.) pkg. frozen peas (thawed)**, OR 1 (15 oz.) can peas** (drained)

1 tsp. lime juice

2 cups chopped green onions (optional)

※ Step 1   Combine jalapeño peppers or cayenne, onion, and ginger in a blender or food processor and process until well ground. (If using alternatives, skip this process.)

※ Step 2   Put mixture in a pot, add coconut cream, salt and soup mix, and heat on medium until hot, but not boiling.

※ Step 3   Reduce heat to low, simmer 10 minutes, stirring occasionally.

※ Step 4   Add "Chicken", peas, and lime juice to pot, simmering uncovered 10 minutes.

※ Step 5   Serve hot with chopped green onions sprinkled on top, if desired.

A little different chicken dish. This has been made accidentally with cream of coconut, and it was still very good— spicy yet sweet. Makes 4 servings

(✎ broccoli) (🧁 topping)   **Chicken Divan**   (🧁 topping)

2 (10 oz.) pkg. frozen florets or chopped broccoli (partly cooked and drained)

"Chicken" =
  D- 2 cups imitation chicken chunks.
  P- 2 cups *parve* soy or chicken *Seitan* chunks (p. 111).
  M- 2 cups chopped cooked kosher chicken.

1¼ cups *Condensed Cream of Mushroom* or *Chicken Soup* (p. 148-149)

¼ cup mayonnaise

1 tsp. lemon juice

"Crackers" =
  D- 1 cup real kosher cheese crackers.
  P- 1 cup *Parve Nabisco® Style Cheese Tid-Bits®* (p. 128)
  M- 1 cup *Parve Nabisco® Style Cheese-Tid-Bits®* (p. 128).

✾ Step 1   Grease a large rectangular baking dish, and line two sides of it with broccoli.

✾ Step 2   Combine soup, mayonnaise, lemon juice and "Chicken" in a bowl and mix well.

✾ Step 3   Pour "Chicken" mixture in the center of baking dish in between broccoli.

✾ Step 4   Crush "Crackers", and sprinkle over top of "Chicken" mixture.

✾ Step 5   Bake uncovered in 350° F oven 15-20 minutes, or microwave 10 minutes.

So pretty and delicious, yet so simple! Makes 4 servings.

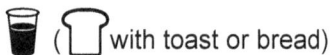

✡ ✡

(with toast or bread)   **Chicken à la King**   (with toast or bread)

"Chicken" =
  D- 3 cups imitation chicken chunks.
  P- 3 cups *parve* soy or chicken *Seitan* chunks (p. 111).
  M- 3 cups chopped cooked kosher chicken.

2½ cups *Condensed Cream Soup* (p. 147)

2 (15 oz.) cans peas (drained)**, OR 3 cups cooked frozen peas**

4-6 pieces toast or bread (optional)

✾ Step 1   Combine "Chicken, cream soup and peas in a pot or microwave bowl.

✾ Step 2   Heat through and serve over toast, if desired. Makes 4-6 servings.

🥛🧁 dumplings)   **Country Chicken Stew with Dumplings**   (🧁 dumplings)🥛

¼ cup *parve* margarine

1 sliced medium onion (½ cup)

4½ cup water (divided)

¼ cup flour

2 Tbs. *parve* imitation bacon bits

1 tsp. crushed oregano leaves

2 medium potatoes (2 cups) (peeled and diced)

2 chopped carrots (1 cup)

⅛ tsp. black pepper (optional)

2 Tbs. *parve* chicken soup mix, OR 3 *parve* chicken bouillon or soup cubes

1 Tbs. parsley flakes

"Chicken" = {
D- 1½ cups imitation chicken chunks + 2 Tbs. oil.
P- 1½ cups *parve* soy or chicken *Seitan* chunks + 2 Tbs. oil.
M- 1½ cups cooked kosher chicken chunks.

1 cup canned sweet peas

½ batch raw *Simple Biscuits* (p. 217)

⚙ Step 1   Heat margarine in a pot and add onion, sautéing until transparent.

⚙ Step 2   Combine 1 cup water and flour in a bowl, blend well and then add to pot.

⚙ Step 3   Stir in remaining 3½ cups water, imitation bacon bits, oregano, potatoes, carrots, pepper, soup mix, parsley and "Chicken", and bring to a boil.

⚙ Step 4   Reduce heat to medium-low, cover and simmer 15 minutes.

⚙ Step 5   Form biscuit dough into 24 1-inch balls and gently drop one at a time into liquid.

⚙ Step 6   Cover and simmer 15 more minutes (without stirring), then add peas.

⚙ Step 7   Heat through or cook until biscuit dough is firm and cooked through.

This can be done in the crock pot (even with raw "Chicken" for M), put all ingredients in crock and blend well. Cook on Low 6 hours or High 3 hours and add dumplings and cook 20 minutes more until biscuit dough is firm and cooked through. Do not cook overnight for *Shabbat*, as the biscuits will disintegrate into a mushy mess. Makes 4 servings.

Smoked Chicken Ravioli in Creamy Cheese Sauce

4½ tsp. liquid smoke

2 Tbs. water

"Chicken" =
- **D-** 2 cups minced imitation chicken chunks.
- **P-** 2 cups minced *parve* soy chicken chunks + ¼ tsp. salt.
- **M-** 2 cups cooked minced kosher chicken.

"Cream Cheese" =
- **D-** 1½ (8 oz). pkg. real dairy cream cheese.
- **P-** 1½ cups *Parve Imitation Cream Cheese* (p. 105).
- **M-** 1½ cups *Parve Imitation Cream Cheese* (p. 105).

"Parmesan" =
- **D-** 1 cup grated kosher Parmesan cheese.
- **P-** ½ cup ground walnuts + 4 slices *parve* imitation Mozzarella.
- **M-** ½ cup ground walnuts + 4 slices *parve* imitation Mozzarella.

"Milk" =
- **D-** 1 cup half & half or whole milk.
- **P-** 1 cup *Parve Cream* (p. 84).
- **M-** 1 cup *Parve Cream* (p. 84).

2 batches (48) *Wonton Wrappers* (p. 116)

salted water for boiling

Step 1　Combine liquid smoke, water and "Chicken" in a bowl, blend and let sit ½ hour.

Step 2　Put "Cream Cheese", "Parmesan" and "Milk" in a saucepan or microwave bowl.

Step 3　Heat on low heat, stir until smooth and well blended. Keep warm or reheat later.

Step 4　Place 24 wrappers on a flat surface, and put 4 tsp. "Chicken" in center of each.

Step 5　Put water on wrapper edges if too dry. Place another wrapper on top and pinch wrapper edges closed to seal.

Step 6　Bring salted water to a boil in a large pot, then gently place raviolis in water.

Step 7　Boil 5 minutes, gently remove with a slotted spoon, put in warm sauce and serve.

Serve hot with garlic bread for a gourmet Italian meal. For M only- Minced smoked turkey can be substituted for "Chicken", water and liquid smoke. Makes 24 large raviolis, or 4-6 servings.

Invention inspired by a 1990s radio commercial of Scarole's Village Pizzeria from Lahaina in Maui, Hawaii. The dish "Smoked Chicken Raviolis in a Gorgonzola Cream Sauce" sounded intriguing.

(🍷 "Chicken") (🧁 rice)   **Red Pepper Chicken**   🥛

1 batch (1 lb.) *Italian Sausage* (p. 112- crumbled)

2 Tbs. avocado oil (other vegetable oil can be used)

3 sliced medium red bell peppers (seeded)

1 medium chopped onion (½ cup)

"Chicken" = {
D- 1½ cups imitation chicken chunks.
P- 1½ cups *parve* soy chunks or cut-up chicken *Seitan* (p. 111).
M- 1½ cups cooked kosher chicken chunks.
}

5 cups hot cooked white *Perfect Rice* (p. 205)

Combine first 6 ingredients in pan and sauté until tender. Serve on rice. Makes 4-6 servings.

✡ ✡

🍷   **Chicken Cacciatori**   🥛

2 Tbs. olive oil or melted *parve* **margarine**

1 medium chopped onion (½ cup)

2 minced garlic cloves (1 tsp.)

1 small seeded and chopped green bell pepper (⅛ cup)

"Chicken" = {
D- 1½ cups imitation chicken chunks.
P- 1½ cups *parve* soy or chicken *Seitan* chunks (p. 111).
M- 1½ cups chopped cooked kosher chicken.
}

1 (15 oz.) can chopped tomatoes (drained for microwaving only)

¼ tsp. crushed basil leaves

¼ tsp. ground oregano

¼ cup kosher white wine

1¼ tsp. vinegar

1 tsp. *parve* **chicken soup mix, OR ½ tsp.** *parve* **chicken bouillon powder**

1 (4 oz.) can chopped mushrooms (drained for microwaving only)

✿ Step 1   Put oil in pot or casserole. Add first 4 ingredients, sauté until peppers are tender.

✿ Step 2   Add last ingredients. Simmer ½ hour on stove, or heat through for microwave.

(Cook longer for thicker sauce.) Serve over cooked pasta or rice (or as-is). Makes 4 servings.

301

Chicken Parmigiana

"Chicken" =
- D- 4 large imitation breaded chicken patties.
- P- 4 large *parve* breaded soy or seitan chicken patties.
- M- 4 large breaded kosher chicken patties.

"Cheese" =
- D- 4-8 slices kosher Swiss or Mozzarella cheese.
- P- 4-8 slices *parve* Mozzarella.
- M- 4-8 slices *parve* Mozzarella.

1 (26 oz.) jar spaghetti sauce

✡ Step 1   Spread spaghetti sauce evenly on bottom of greased glass baking dish.

✡ Step 2   Put "Chicken" in baking dish, and place 1 or 2 "Cheese" pieces on top.

✡ Step 3   Bake 20 minutes in preheated 400° F oven, or microwave 5-6 minutes until hot.

Serve patties with sauce. *Eggplant Patties* (p. 194) can replace "Chicken". Makes 4 servings.

✡ ✡

Chicken Pot Pie

1 cup *Chicken Gravy* (p. 102)

⅛ tsp. garlic powder

1 pkg. (10 oz.) frozen mixed vegetables (thawed)

"Chicken" =
- D- 1 cup imitation chicken chunks.
- P- 1 cup *parve* soy chunks or cut up chicken *Seitan* (p. 111).
- M- 1 cup cooked kosher chicken chunks.

1 pre-baked *Pot Pie Crust* (p. 117)

1 raw *Pot Pie Crust* top (p. 117- optional)

✡ Step 1   If baking, preheat oven to 450° F. Blend first 4 ingredients thoroughly.

✡ Step 2   Heat until warm and pour into baked crust, and place raw crust on top of filling.

✡ Step 3   Tuck edges underneath, and poke holes in top. Bake 10 minutes, reduce heat to 350° F and bake 20 more minutes until top is golden brown, or microwave in a glass pie plate 11-13 minutes until top crust is cooked.

✡ Step 4   Let sit to cool awhile as it stays very hot. Makes 6-8 servings.

Meat Main Dishes

Beef Pot Pie

1 cup *Beef Gravy* (p. 102)

⅛ tsp. onion powder

1 pkg. (10 oz.) frozen mixed vegetables (thawed)

"Beef" = {
D- 1 cup imitation beef or steak chunks, (chopped into 1-inch cubes).
P- 1 cup *parve* soy beef chunks, (chopped into 1-inch cubes).
M- 1 cup kosher steak or stew meat, (cut in 1-inch cubes & cooked).
}

1 pre-baked *Pot Pie Crust* (p. 117)

1 raw *Pot Pie Crust* top (p. 117- optional)

⊛ Step 1   If baking, preheat oven to 450° F. Mix together gravy, onion powder, vegetables and "Beef" until well blended.

⊛ Step 2   Heat until warm and pour into baked crust, and place raw crust on top of filling.

⊛ Step 3   Tuck edges underneath, and poke holes in top. Bake 10 minutes, reduce heat to 350° F and bake 20 more minutes until top is golden brown, or microwave in a glass pie plate 11-13 minutes until top crust is cooked.

⊛ Step 4   Let sit to cool several minutes before slicing. It stays very hot for a long time.

Great with soup and salad in winter. Makes 6-8 servings.

Steak & Kidney Pie

1½ Tbs. *parve* **margarine**

"Steak" =
- **D-** 1 cup imitation beef or steak chunks, (cut into 1-inch pieces).
- **P-** 1 cup *parve* soy beef or steak chunks, (cut into 1-inch pieces).
- **M-** ½ lb. kosher stew meat or steaks, (cut into 1-inch pieces).

1 small chopped onion (¼ cup)

¾ cup (½ batch) uncooked *Beef Gravy* (p. 102- put in a jar and shaken)

¼ cup kosher red wine or kosher cooking sherry

½ (4 oz.) can sliced mushrooms (undrained)

1 small diced peeled potato (½ cup)

"Kidney" =
- **D-** 1 batch *Parve Chopped Beef Kidney* (p. 113).
- **P-** 1 batch *Parve Chopped Beef Kidney* (p. 113).
- **M-** ½ cup real pre-cooked kosher liver (cut into ½-inch pieces).

1 raw *Pot Pie Crust* **top** (p. 117- use for top only, pie has no sides or bottom)

Step 1   Put margarine in a skillet to melt, add "Steak" and onions, sautéing until brown.

Step 2   Add gravy, wine, mushrooms and potatoes, and cook until gravy starts to thicken.

Step 3   Put gravy and "Kidney" in deep pie pan. (If only a regular pie pan is available, put it on top a cookie sheet in case of boiling over.)

Step 4   Blend gravy and "Kidney" very gently. Bake ½ hour in a preheated 350º F oven.

Step 5   Take pie out and turn heat up to 425º F. Put pie crust atop mixture, (as for a pot pie top crust). Make slits in crust to vent, and bake 20 minutes or until just starting to brown.

Based on the British specialty. This recipe mimics tender lamb or veal kidney, but is altered just a wee bit due to the fact that kidneys aren't exactly kosher. One would not believe that the *parve* version contains no meat, because it is so savory! Makes 1 pie, or about 4-6 servings.

Bite-Size Beef Wellington

"Liver" =
- **D-** ⅔ cup *Parve Chopped Liver* (p. 139).
- **P-** ⅔ cup *Parve Chopped Liver* (p. 139).
- **M-** ⅔ cup real kosher chopped liver.

1¾ cup *Condensed Golden Mushroom Soup* (p. 154- divided)

"Beef" =
- **D-** 1 pkg. large imitation beef or steak chunks.
- **P-** 2 cups chopped *Seitan Beef Roast* (p. 319).
- **M-** 1 lb. boiled or slow-cooked kosher beef roast (must be tender).

1 pkg. puff pastry sheets (thawed 25 minutes)

1 egg (separated into 2 containers)

1 Tbs. water

Step 1   Put "Liver" in a bowl, add ¼ cup mushroom soup and blend thoroughly.

Step 2   Cut pastry sheets into 4½ x 2¼-inch pieces, (cut a 4½-inch square in half).

Step 3   Spread 1 tsp. "Liver" mixture on each pastry piece ¼ inch away from edges.

Step 4   Cut "Beef" into 1-inch chunks and place each piece in the center of a pastry.

Step 5   Spread egg white along pastry edges, wrap up "Beef" and seal to meet in center.

Step 6   Pinch dough together to enclose "Beef" and set on a well-greased cookie sheet.

Step 7   Blend together egg yolk and water, then brush it on top of dough.

Step 8   Bake 25 minutes in a preheated 400° F or until crusts are nicely browned.

Step 9   Put remaining 1½ cups mushroom soup and ¼ cup water in a pot to make sauce, blend well and heat through.

Step 10   Pour warm sauce into individual crocks for dipping if desired, or serve over hot pastries. (Decorative toothpicks can be put in pastries for more convenient dipping.)

Unique way to serve a gourmet classic. Makes 4-8 servings, 2-4 pastries per person.

Beef En Croûte

1¾ tsp. salt (divided)

2 cups flour

½ cup melted *parve* **margarine**

"Liquid" =
- **D-** ¼ cup warm milk, OR ¼ cup hot water.
- **P-** ¼ cup *Parve Milk* (p. 85), or other *parve* alternative milk.
- **M-** ¼ cup kosher beef broth or water.

"Beef" =
- **D-** 1 pkg. soy burger + 2 tsp. *parve* beef soup mix + 1 Tbs. oil.
- **P-** 1 pkg. *parve* soy burger + 2 tsp. *parve* beef soup mix + 1 Tbs. oil.
- **M-** 1 lb. kosher ground beef or turkey.

1 beaten egg

⅓ cup plain *Bread Crumbs* (p. 116)

½ tsp. garlic powder

½ tsp. coarse ground black pepper

1 Tbs. ketchup

1 Tbs. microwave browning sauce

1 Tbs. *Fishless Worcestershire Sauce* (p. 92)

❀ Step 1   Combine 1½ tsp. salt and flour in a bowl, then add margarine and "Liquid", mixing and kneading until well blended.

❀ Step 2   Divide dough into 4 equal balls, roll each one out into 7-8-inch ovals.

❀ Step 3   Set aside and refrigerate crusts in a zipper bag.

❀ Step 4   Combine "Beef", ¼ tsp. salt and remaining ingredients and knead together until well blended.

❀ Step 5   Divide mixture into 4 rounded oval loaves, and put in a greased baking dish.

❀ Step 6   Take out crusts, and put a crust on top of each loaf to cover it, tucking crusts in at the bottom.

❀ Step 7   Bake in a preheated 425º F oven 20 minutes, (or microwave 8 minutes, rotating each loaf with a spatula for even cooking, and cook 8 more minutes), for D and P- until crust is done, or for M- until juices run clear and crust is done.

This French dish is one of the fancier ones, but still fairly easy. Makes 4 servings.

Ground Steak with Dijon Sauce

"Ground Beef" =
- **D-** 1 pkg. soy burger + 1 Tbs. avocado oil.
- **P-** 1 pkg. *parve* soy burger + 1 Tbs. avocado oil.
- **M-** 1½ lb. kosher ground beef.

"Cream" =
- **D-** 5 Tbs. heavy cream or whipping cream (divided).
- **P-** 5 Tbs. *Parve Cream* (p. 85- divided).
- **M-** 5 Tbs. *Parve Cream* (p. 85- divided).

2⅓ Tbs. *French Dijon Mustard* (p. 440- divided)

¼ tsp. black pepper

⅛ tsp. garlic powder

¼ tsp. salt

1 Tbs. avocado or other oil (optional and only for frying)

½ cup sliced mushrooms

3 Tbs. chopped green onions

2 Tbs. *parve* margarine

1 Tbs. kosher white wine

Step 1   Combine "Ground Beef", 2 Tbs. "Cream", 1 tsp. Dijon mustard, pepper and salt, kneading until thoroughly blended.

Step 2   Shape into 4 patties and grill, broil, or fry in oil until done and set aside, but keep warm.

Step 3   Sauté mushrooms and in margarine until tender, then add wine, green onions and remaining 3 Tbs. "Cream" and 2 Tbs. Dijon mustard.

Step 4   Simmer on low until sauce is somewhat thickened, and spoon over "Ground Beef" patties.

This is an elegant main dish. This can be microwaved, but may have a bit less flavor. Makes 4 servings.

Sumatran Shish Kebabs

3 Tbs. minced jalapeño peppers

2 tsp. grated ginger, OR ¼ tsp. ground ginger

2 cups chopped onion

4 tsp. minced garlic

⅔ cup water

½ cup avocado oil (other vegetable oil can be used)

1½ Tbs. ground turmeric

¾ tsp. ground cumin

2 Tbs. ground coriander

1½ tsp. salt

2 cups *Imitation Coconut Milk* (p. 86)

12 (6-inch) metal skewers

"Beef" = { D- 2 cups imitation beef or steak chunks, (cut in 1-inch pieces).

P- 2 cups *parve* soy beef or steak chunks, (cut in 1-inch pieces).

M- 1 lb. kosher steak, (cut in 1-inch cubes, boiled in water ½ hour.

Step 1   Combine first 10 ingredients in a blender and puree until smooth.

Step 2   Heat oil in a saucepan until warm, add mixture and cook until liquid evaporates.

Step 3   Reduce heat to low and stir in coconut milk, when warm remove from heat.

Step 4   Carefully place pieces of "Beef" on each skewer.

Step 5   Coat "Beef" with some of coconut sauce, and broil or grill them about 3 minutes or until browned and slightly crisp.

Step 6   Heat sauce until warm, put "Beef" on a warm serving tray and coat with sauce.

Step 7   Pour remaining sauce in small crocks for dipping or pouring and serve hot with "Beef".

A spicy shish kebab with a unique flavor somewhat similar to curry but without that certain "curry smell". (For D or P, 3 pkg. *parve* vegetarian shish kebabs on skewers can be used quite easily and successfully. Omit Step 4.) Makes 8-12 Shish Kebabs, or 4-6 servings.

(vegetables)   **Banquet® Style Western Meal**

"Meat" =
- **D-** 1 pkg. soy burger + 1 tsp. oil.
- **P-** 1 pkg. *parve* soy burger + 1 tsp. oil.
- **M-** 1 lb. kosher ground beef or turkey.

½ tsp. liquid smoke (or to taste, depending on concentration of brand)

1 Tbs. minced onion

1 Tbs. water

1 batch (1½ cups) *Beef Gravy* (p. 102)

1 batch cooked *Home-Style Hash Browns with Onions* (p. 183- use diced)

2 (15 oz.) cans pinto beans (drained), **OR 4 cups cooked pinto beans**

1 cup *Taco Bell® Style Enchirito Sauce* (p. 96)

  Step 1   Combine first 3 ingredients and knead together thoroughly, then shape into 4 patties.

  Step 2   Grill, fry, broil or microwave until very well done. If using D or P", be sure "Meat " is well done and browned, otherwise when refrigerating any leftovers, "Meat" sitting in gravy becomes very soft and soggy. If using M, it must be cooked until juices run clear.

  Step 3   Separately heat gravy and hash browns.

  Step 4   Combine beans and Enchirito sauce to make chili beans. Heat through.

  Step 5   Arrange portions of beans and hash browns on plates, put burger patties on plates, and spoon gravy over burgers (and potatoes too if desired). Serve hot.

Freeze in trays to have them just like old times. A wonderful treat because it's kosher! I dearly loved the gravy spooned over the potatoes, with lots of pepper. Makes 4 generous servings.

☺   ☺   ☺

For **"Banquet® Style Salisbury Steak Meal"**, omit liquid smoke, in Step 1. Substitute mashed potatoes for hash browns, omit *Enchirito Sauce* and substitute 2 cans of another vegetable for chili beans.

Freeze in trays to have just like old times, but be sure to use instant potatoes for better freezing quality.

(veggies) **Banquet® Style Chicken Fried Beef Steak Meal**

2 eggs

1 cup *All-Purpose Breading Mix* (p. 83)

"Steak" =
- **D-** 4 imitation hamburger patties.
- **P-** 4 *parve* soy or seitan hamburger patties.
- **M-** 4 small kosher flank or cubed steaks, (pounded very flat).

¼ cup avocado oil (other vegetable oil can be used)

1 uncooked batch (1½ cups) *White Sauce* (p. 101- soup mix & no margarine)

⅛ tsp. coarse ground black pepper

¾ batch *Deluxe Whipped Potatoes* (p. 192)

2 (16 oz.) cans corn (drained), **OR 2 (10 oz.) pkg. frozen corn** (thawed)

¼ cup *parve* margarine

dash white pepper (optional)

❀ Step 1   Put eggs in a bowl and lightly beat them, and put breading mix in another bowl.

❀ Step 2   Take each "Steak" and dip it in egg, then take each "Steak" and dredge it in breading.

❀ Step 3   Put oil in a frying pan and heat it hot, then place each "Steak" in hot oil and fry each side until golden brown.

❀ Step 4   When browned, set steaks on a plate (for less fat put on paper towels first) and keep warm in a hot oven.

❀ Step 5   Add white sauce and black pepper to pan of fried oil, heat on low stirring constantly until thickened.

❀ Step 6   Heat corn and add margarine and white pepper, then put even amounts on each plate.

❀ Step 7   Heat potatoes, and divide up evenly on 4 plates, put "Steak" on each plate.

❀ Step 8   Pour equal amounts of white sauce over each steak and serve hot.

This is so good, and a little touch of country. Makes 4 servings.

Mum's Cube Steaks

¼ cup flour

1 tsp. salt

1 tsp. black pepper

1 tsp. garlic powder

1 tsp. ground thyme

"Steak" = {
D- 4-8 imitation hamburger patties, (coated with 1 Tbs. oil).

P- 4-8 *parve* soy or seitan burger patties, (coated with 1 Tbs. oil).

M- 4 small kosher flank or cubed steaks, (pounded very flat).
}

1 large chopped onion (1 cup)

2 Tbs. avocado oil (other vegetable oil can be used)

2 batches (3 cups) *Beef Gravy* (p. 102- heated)

⊛ Step 1   Combine flour, salt, pepper, garlic powder and thyme in a zipper bag and shake it well to blend.

⊛ Step 2   Add "Steak" to bag and shake to coat both sides evenly, or sprinkle mixture evenly on both sides of each "Steak".

⊛ Step 3   Sauté "Steak" in oil on both sides in a skillet until browned, then add onions, sautéing until tender. (For Microwave- put contents of skillet in a glass casserole.)

⊛ Step 4   Put gravy on top and cook covered until heated through for D or P, or 35 minutes either in microwave (on 30% power) or in a covered skillet on stove for M.

Serve hot. Whether D, P or M, this tastes exactly how Mum made it. Delicious served with mashed potatoes. Freezes well. Makes 4 servings.

Mum's Swiss Steak

2 medium chopped onions (1 cup)

2 medium seeded and diced green bell peppers (1½ cups)

4 minced garlic cloves (2 tsp.)

4 Tbs. avocado or other vegetable oil (divided)

¼ cup flour

1 tsp. salt

1 tsp. black pepper

1 tsp. garlic powder

1¼ tsp. ground thyme (divided)

"Steak" =
{
D- 4-8 imitation hamburger patties.
P- 4-8 *parve* soy or seitan hamburger patties.
M- 4 small kosher flank or cubed steaks, (pounded very flat).

2 (15 oz.) cans diced tomatoes (undrained)

✽ Step 1   Sauté onions, bell peppers and garlic in 2 Tbs. oil about 5 minutes or until vegetables are tender, then set aside.

✽ Step 2   Combine flour, salt, pepper, garlic powder and 1 tsp. thyme in a zipper bag and shake well.

✽ Step 3   Add "Steak" to bag and shake to coat both sides evenly, or sprinkle mixture evenly on both sides of each "Steak".

✽ Step 4   Sauté "Steak" in remaining 2 Tbs. oil on both sides in a skillet until browned.

✽ Step 5   Combine tomatoes and ¼ tsp. thyme with sautéed vegetables, and add to "Steak", lifting each one up with a fork to get tomatoes underneath "Steak", to help keep from sticking. (For Microwave- put contents of skillet in a glass casserole dish.)

✽ Step 6   Cook covered on microwave or stove 15 minutes for D or P, or 35 minutes on either microwave (cook on 30% power) or in a covered skillet on stove for M. Serve hot.

Delicious served with mashed potatoes, the tomatoes and bell peppers become a wonderfully unique, slightly tangy gravy. Freezes so-so, it tends to separate leaving behind water and vegetable pieces. Makes 4 servings.

Home-Style Meat Loaf

1 (10 oz.) can *parve* tomato soup (divided)**, OR 1 cup tomato juice** (divided)

¾ cup plain uncooked oatmeal

1 beaten egg

1 very small chopped onion (2-3 Tbs.)

½ tsp. salt

¼ tsp. ground black pepper

"Hamburger" =
- **D-** 1 pkg. soy burger + 2 Tbs. avocado oil.
- **P-** 1 pkg. *parve* soy burger + 2 Tbs. avocado oil.
- **M-** 1 lb. kosher ground beef or turkey.

✽ Step 1   Combine half a can tomato soup or ½ cup tomato juice, oatmeal, egg, onion, salt, and pepper in a mixing bowl.

✽ Step 2   Add "Hamburger", blend well and press into a greased glass loaf pan.

✽ Step 3   Bake in a preheated 350º F oven 1 hour. (For D and P, cut in quarters after ½ hour and continue baking.) For Microwave- cook 12-20 minutes on 30% power (or until done and juices run clear for M).

✽ Step 4   Top with remaining half can tomato soup or ½ cup tomato juice, and cook 5 more minutes. Slice and serve.

Based on a recipe that was Mrs. Ruth Henn's specialty. Makes 6-8 servings.

(filling) (pepper) **Pepper Petals** (filling) (pepper)

2 cups beef *Parve Broth* (p. 110)

2 Tbs. *parve* beef or mushroom soup mix

⅛ tsp. ground black pepper

1 large bay leaf

1 Tbs. avocado oil

1 cup dry orzo

"Beef" =
- **D-** 1 pkg. (2 cups) soy crumbles + 1 Tbs. avocado oil.
- **P-** 1 pkg. (2 cups) *parve* soy crumbles + 1 Tbs. avocado oil.
- **M-** 1 lb. (2 cups) kosher ground beef (browned & drained).

4 uniformly-sized, flat-bottomed bell peppers (red, yellow, orange or green)

2 round vegetables (large mushrooms, mini peppers or zucchini slices)

Step 1 — Put broth, soup mix, black pepper, bay leaf, and oil in a pot and bring to a boil.

Step 2 — Add orzo. Simmer 10 minutes stirring constantly. (It thickens and absorbs liquid.)

Step 3 — Remove bay leaf, add "Beef" and blend well. Set this stuffing mixture aside.

Step 4 — Cut peppers exactly in half across the middle to make them uniform in size and appearance. Place tops upside-down, cut around stems to make a hole. Slice a portion under the stem for a hole plug. De-seed, scrape off most white. Each pepper should look like a "cup".

Step 5 — <u>To Bake</u>: Set raw cups on a greased cookie sheet. Preheat oven to 350° F. <u>To Microwave</u>: (Far superior!) Place 4 "cups" at a time in covered glass dish. For very large peppers or all green peppers, cook on high 3 minutes. Peppers should still retain original shape.

Step 6 — Pack cups tightly with stuffing. (Round veggie can be cooked too.) <u>To Bake</u>: Lay a sheet of foil loosely over top to keep stuffing from drying out. Bake small peppers 25-30 minutes, medium-large up to 45-50 minutes, or until tender. (Add at least 20 more minutes for green peppers, which are thicker, until tender.) <u>To Microwave</u>: Cook 7-10 minutes until tender.

Step 7 — Carefully remove cups with a solid spatula, so as not to disrupt stuffing in tops.

Step 8 — Set 4 cups tightly together to make a flower pattern on decorative platters.

Step 9 — Place a round veggie in the center of each of both flowers. Serve hot.

A beautiful way to serve stuffed peppers, combining elegance with a delicate flavor. Mix colors or keep each flower the same. (Stuffing can be made a few days before. There's enough for the largest peppers.) It's good cold too! Makes 2 flowers or 4 servings. (2 "petals" is 1 portion.)

(on noodles) (on "Beef")   **Beef Stroganoff**   (noodles) ("Beef")

1 Tbs. avocado oil for stove, OR 2 Tbs. *parve* margarine for microwave

"Beef" =
- **D-** 2½ cups imitation beef or steak slices or chunks.
- **P-** 2½ cups *parve* soy beef or steak slices or chunks.
- **M-** 1½ lb. kosher steak, (cut in 1-inch slices).

1 small chopped onion (¼ cup)

1 cup water

4 tsp. *parve* beef soup mix, OR 2 *parve* beef bouillon or soup cubes

¼ cup flour

1 tsp. salt

¼ tsp. garlic powder

2 Tbs. ketchup

¼ cup kosher red wine or kosher cooking sherry

1½ (4 oz.) cans mushroom pieces and stems (1 cup)

"Sour Cream" =
- **D-** ½ cup real dairy sour cream.
- **P-** ½ cup *Parve Imitation Sour Cream* (p. 105).
- **M-** ½ cup *Parve Imitation Sour Cream* (p. 105).

2 cups hot cooked fettuccine, linguini or long egg noodles (⅓ lb. raw)

Step 1   Put oil in a pan for stovetop, or margarine in a glass casserole for microwave.

Step 2   Add "Beef" and onion and sauté until onion is tender (and for M, until meat is done with juices running clear). Drain if necessary and set aside.

Step 3   Heat water and dissolve soup mix, bouillon or soup cube in it, then add flour, salt, garlic powder, ketchup, wine and mushrooms to "Beef".

Step 4   Cook covered, simmering 8 minutes or until starting to thicken.

Step 5   Reduce heat and stir in "Sour Cream" and heat through.

Step 6   Arrange hot noodles on plates and serve hot stroganoff over it.

This is a classic delicious recipe made even better by making it kosher. Makes 4 servings.

Swedish Meatballs

¼ cup minced onion

2 Tbs. avocado oil (other vegetable oil can be used)

"Meat" = {
D- 1 pkg. soy burger (+ 2 Tbs. *parve* beef soup mix in Step 5).
P- 1 pkg. *parve* soy burger (+ 2 Tbs. *parve* beef soup mix in Step 5).
M- 1 lb. kosher ground beef or turkey.
}

½ cup matzah (matzo) meal or plain *Bread Crumbs* (p. 116)

1 beaten egg

1¼ tsp. salt (divided)

⅛ tsp. ground mace

10 Tbs. *Parve Cream* (p. 85- divided)

2 Tbs. melted *parve* margarine

2 Tbs. flour

½ cup water

¼ tsp. black pepper

❀ Step 1   Put oil and onion in a pan, sautéing until tender and starting to brown.

❀ Step 2   Take onions out of pan and put in a mixing bowl, then add "Meat", bread crumbs, egg, ½ tsp. salt, mace, and 2 Tbs. *Parve Cream*.

❀ Step 3   Blend thoroughly and shape into 20-25 balls about 1½ inches in diameter.

❀ Step 4   Put balls in frying pan and cook 5-7 minutes until done and balls are browned (for M- when juices run clear). Set balls aside.

❀ Step 5   Drain off juices (if any) into a measuring cup, or add margarine to make equivalent of 2 Tbs. (half of ¼ cup), add soup mix for D or P, and pour into a pot.

❀ Step 6   Stir in flour, water, pepper, and remaining ½ tsp. salt and ½ cup *Parve Cream* into juices or margarine. Blend well.

❀ Step 7   Cook on low heat, stirring until mixture is bubbling and thickened.

❀ Step 8   Add balls to mixture and heat through. Serve hot immediately.

Delicately flavored dish. Can be served with hot buttered linguini. Makes 4-6 servings.

Seitan Burger Meatballs (p. 111) could be used, but they must bake 55 minutes.

(on vegetables) **Ratatouille with Meatballs**

¼ cup olive oil for stove, OR 2 Tbs. *parve* margarine for microwave

4 minced garlic cloves (2 tsp.)

1 medium chopped onion (½ cup)

1 (2 cups) small eggplant (peeled and cubed in 1-inch pieces)

1 large seeded and chopped green bell pepper (1 cup)

2 small (2 cups) zucchini (sliced and chopped in 1-inch pieces)

1½ tsp. *Italian Seasoning* (p. 434)

⅛ tsp. black pepper

1 (15 oz.) can chopped tomatoes (undrained)

½ cup water

½ tsp. salt

½ batch raw *Classic Meatballs* (p. 112)

1½ Tbs. flour

1 Tbs. *parve* margarine or avocado oil (other vegetable oil can be used)

⊛ Step 1 Combine first 6 ingredients and sauté in pot or 2 quart glass casserole dish and cook until onion is tender.

⊛ Step 2 Add Italian seasoning, black pepper, tomatoes, water, and salt.

⊛ Step 3 Simmer uncovered 30 minutes, or microwave 10 minutes (stirring after 5 minutes), until vegetables are tender.

⊛ Step 4 While mixture is cooking, put flour in a bowl and coat meatballs with flour.

⊛ Step 5 Put margarine or oil in a frying pan and add coated meatballs, sautéing until browned on all sides.

⊛ Step 6 Gently add meatballs to vegetable mixture and cook uncovered 5 more minutes.

This delicious recipe was from my gourmet-inspired Uncle David "*alav hashalom*" [may he rest in peace] that he fixed one night when visiting. I'll never forget his Julia Child impersonation as he prepared it. Makes 6-8 servings.

(veggies)   **Sirloin Tips in Burgundy Sauce**

"Beef" =
  D- 4 cups imitation beef chunks or *Seitan Beef Roast* (opposite p.).
  P- 4 cups *parve* soy beef chunks or *Seitan Beef Roast* (opposite p.).
  M- 2 lb. kosher stew meat chunks or kosher steak.

dash fine ground black pepper

4 Tbs. flour

4 Tbs. *parve* margarine (divided)

1 medium chopped onion (½ cup)

1 (4 oz.) can sliced mushrooms (drained), **OR lb. sliced fresh mushrooms**

2 cups kosher burgundy or other kosher red wine

2 tsp. *parve* beef soup mix, OR 1 *parve* beef bouillon or soup cube

1 bay leaf

dash coarse ground black pepper

1 batch *Potatoes Au Gratin* (p. 187)

1 batch *Deluxe Almond Green Beans* (p. 196)

⚙ Step 1   Cut "Beef" into 1-inch chunks, and season with few shakes of fine ground pepper. Coat with flour and set aside.

⚙ Step 2   Put 3 Tbs. margarine in a frying pan and heat to melt, then add onions and mushrooms, sautéing until onion is tender.

⚙ Step 3   Remove onions and mushrooms and put in a large pot.

⚙ Step 4   Put "Beef" and last 1 Tbs. margarine in frying pan and sauté (brown on all sides).

⚙ Step 5   Transfer "Beef" to pot with mushrooms, and add wine, soup mix, bay leaf and coarse pepper, then cook covered, simmering 20 minutes for D or P, or 40 minutes for M.

⚙ Step 6   Heat potatoes and green beans, put on plates, dish out "Beef" and serve hot.

Based on the Armour® Dinner Classics "Sirloin Tips in Burgundy" that came out in the mid-80s. Green beans can be substituted with snow peas or sugar snap peas fixed just like the green beans (which is more like the real thing). If using D or P, a quicker alternative is combine "Beef", the can of mushrooms and 1½ cups *Condensed Golden Mushroom Soup* (p. 159) in a pot and heat through. If using M, Step 4 can be done in a crock pot cooking 5-6 hours on low. This can be served with *Parve Yorkshire Pudding* (p. 214) for an elegant side dish. Makes 4 servings.

Seitan Beef Roast

Beef *Parve Broth* (p. 110)**:** stove- 5 cups, crock- 6 cups, plain- ⅞ cup + 1 Tbs. (divided)

5 Tbs. *parve* mashed potato flakes (divided)

5 Tbs. warm melted *parve* margarine (divided)

¼ cup quick tapioca

2 cups + 2 Tbs. vital wheat gluten

¼ tsp. paprika

¼ tsp. ground black pepper

2 tsp. garlic powder

1½ tsp. onion powder

¼ cup *parve* beef soup mix

¼ cup *parve* mushroom soup mix

2 Tbs. *parve* onion soup mix

½ tsp. liquid smoke

1 Tbs. *Fishless Worcestershire Sauce* (p. 92)

½ cup tomato sauce

2 tsp. microwave browning sauce

¼ cup *Parve Milk* (p. 85)**, OR other *parve* milk alternative**

❀ Step 1   Blend 1 Tbs. each: broth, potato flakes and margarine in a pan. Set aside.

❀ Step 2   In one bowl, combine ¼ cup potato flakes, tapioca, gluten, paprika, pepper, garlic and onion powders, and soup mixes, blending well to make a dry mix. Set aside.

❀ Step 3   In a large mixing bowl, blend liquid smoke, Worcestershire, tomato and browning sauces, milk and ⅞ cup warm broth. Stir in ¼ cup hot margarine. (It's okay if it gets globby.)

❀ Step 4   Stir dry mix into wet mixture quickly. Knead dough, blending well (2-5 minutes).

❀ Step 5   Stretch and compress for that stringy meat texture. Stretch it out on flat surface.

❀ Step 6   Dot on margarine mixture. Roll up jelly roll-style into a long lump. Press together.

❀ Step 7   Put 4¼ cups *Broth* in large pot, or put 5¼ cups in 6 qt. crock pot.

❀ Step 8   <u>To Boil</u>- Bring to boil. Add Seitan and simmer covered 1 hour. Gently flip every 15 minutes. (Broth becomes gravy.) <u>Crock Pot</u>- Add Seitan, cook on Low 6 hours, High 3 hours.

Roast should be tender and juicy with authentic aroma, flavor and texture. Makes about 3½ lb.

🥛 (🥕veggies) **Yankee Pot Roast** 🥛

½ tsp. salt

½ tsp. black pepper

½ tsp. garlic powder

½ tsp. ground thyme

2 Tbs. flour (for M, and D or P chunks only. Omit for D or P *Seitan Beef Roast*)

"Beef" = { **D-** plain *Seitan Roast* (Steps 1-6), OR 1 qt. imitation beef chunks.
P- plain *Seitan Roast* (p. 319 Steps 1-6), OR 1 qt. *parve* beef chunks.
M- 2-3 lb. kosher roast, OR 1-2 lb. 1-inch stew meat chunks.

3 Tbs. avocado oil (use 1 Tbs. for D or P *Seitan Beef Roast* if less fat is desired)

1 small sliced or chopped onion (¼ cup)

1 batch (1½ cups) *Beef or Onion Gravy* (p. 102)

1¾ cups water

"Extras" = { **D-** 2 tsp. oil + 2⅔ Tbs. *parve* beef soup mix + 2½ cups water.
P- 2 tsp. oil + 2⅔ Tbs. *parve* beef soup mix + 2½ cups water.
M- ½ cup water mixed with 3 Tbs. flour.

2 small or 1 large bay leaf

12 very small (cut in half) **or 6 larger red new potatoes** (cut in 2-inch chunks)

at least 1 cup baby cut carrots, OR 6-7 small carrots (cut in 1-inch pieces)

⚜ Step 1   Blend first 4 seasonings. Combine with flour for D or P chunks and M.

⚜ Step 2   Lightly coat "Beef" evenly with seasoned flour and set aside. Add remaining flour to pot. (Skip Steps 2-3 for *Seitan* if desired.) Heat oil in pot, add onions, sauté until brown.

⚜ Step 3   Add "Beef" D or P chunks or M and lightly brown sides.

⚜ Step 4   Combine gravy, water and "Extras" in a bowl, blending well, then add to pot.

⚜ Step 5   Add remaining ingredients to pot. Simmer covered: For D or P *Seitan*- 1 hour 15 minutes, (flip every 20 minutes). For M- 3-4 hours until "Beef" is tender. For all chunks- ½ hour.

This recipe can be made in a 6 qt. crock pot as well. Add ¾ extra cup beef *Parve Broth* (p. 110) to crock. Do Steps 1-4. For Step 5, add all ingredients to crock. (D or P don't need flipping.) Cook on High 3 hours for D or P, 4 hours for M. Cook on Low 6 hours for D or P, 8 hours for M. It can also be cooked overnight on Low if 3 cups extra water are added. Makes 4 servings.

Sefardi Shabbat Stew (Chamin)

(barley) (potato)("Beef")   (barley)

3 Tbs. olive oil

1 small chopped onion (¼ cup)

8 minced garlic cloves (4 tsp.)

"Beef" = {
D- 2 cups imitation beef or steak chunks.
P- 2 cups *parve* soy beef or steak chunks.
M- 1 lb. kosher stew meat cut into 1-inch chunks + 2¼ tsp. salt.
}

3½ tsp. ground cumin

1 Tbs. ground coriander

¼ tsp. ground turmeric

⅛ tsp. cayenne pepper (optional)

6 cups water (add extra for overnight crock pot cooking)

1 large potato (peeled and cut into 1-inch cubes)

½ tsp. baking soda (if using raw beans)

⅓ cup pearled barley, OR 1 cup wheat berries, OR ¾ cup raw white rice

½ cup navy beans (soaked overnight)**, OR 1 (15 oz.) can navy beans**

1 large bay leaf

⅛ tsp. ground oregano

1 tsp. curry powder

¼ cup *parve* beef soup mix (for P & D only)

1-3 whole unbroken eggs (optional)

❀ Step 1   Put olive oil in large pot, add onion, garlic and "Beef", sautéing until brown.

❀ Step 2   Add cumin, coriander, turmeric and cayenne, sauté 3 minutes.

❀ Step 3   Add last ingredients, gently adding whole eggs. Bring to boil and simmer 2 hours. It can be put in crock pot on Low- 8 hours, or High- 4 hours. For overnight on Low as a true Shabbat stew, (all ingredients can be added directly to crock omitting Steps 1-2) using at least a 4 qt. crock and adding 2 cups extra water on long winter nights, or 1 cup extra during short summer nights.

Serve with slices of Tunisian Kukla (p. 211) adding the wrapped packet in Step 3. Added eggs get hard-boiled and brown inside. Makes 4-6 generous servings.

Tender Beef Liver with Onions

3-4 Tbs. avocado oil (other vegetable oil can be used)

1 large sliced or chopped sweet Vidalia onion (more can be used, if desired)

"Liver" = {
D- 1¾ cups *Parve Chopped Liver* (p. 139).
P- 1¾ cups *Parve Chopped Liver* (p. 139).
M- 1 (12 oz.) kosher chopped liver (1¾ cups).

1 small beaten egg

2 Tbs. melted *parve* margarine

¾ cup *All Purpose Breading Mix* (p. 83- optional for breaded version)

⊛ Step 1   Put oil in a skillet heating until hot, add onions and fry until browned.

⊛ Step 2   Remove browned onions from pan. Set aside and keep warm.

⊛ Step 3   Combine "Liver", egg and margarine in a bowl, blending into a paste, and shape into 4 patties. (Set out a few minutes to dry if very moist.)

⊛ Step 4   Optional for breaded version- Put breading mix in a shallow bowl or plate, and dredge "Liver" in breading, pressing it in and repeat to coat thoroughly.

⊛ Step 5   Add liver to oil, gently fry on both sides (if breaded- fry until each side is evenly browned).

⊛ Step 6   Gently remove liver with a spatula, put on plates and top with reserved onions.

For those who love liver, you can still have it– this classic recipe fits the bill! Makes 2-4 servings.

For M only- 1 (12-16 oz.) pkg. kosher pre-broiled, pre-*kashered* liver can be used just like the real thing. Trim away any tough, well-done areas and do Steps 1-2. Continue with the preferred version below:

For the breaded version- Omit egg and skip Step 3. Instead coat liver in melted margarine, then proceed with Steps 4-6.

For non-breaded version- Omit egg, margarine and breading. Skip Steps 3-4. Proceed with Steps 5-6, simply heating through.

Creamed Chipped Beef

2 cups *White Sauce* (p. 101- make with salt)

"Beef" =
- **D-** 1-2 pkg. imitation beef slices, OR 2 pkg. raw imitation bacon.
- **P-** 1-2 pkg. *parve* soy beef slices, OR 2 pkg. raw *parve* soy bacon.
- **M-** 1 lb. sliced kosher pastrami or corned beef.

8 pieces white bread or toast (whole slices, OR torn into 1-2-inch pieces)

Step 1   Heat white sauce, shred "Beef" into strips and add it to sauce, heating through.

Step 2   Put bread on 4 plates and pour sauce evenly over bread. Makes 4 servings.

☆ ☆

(rice)("Meat")

Kielbasa & Rice

2 Tbs. avocado oil (other vegetable oil can be used)

2 medium chopped onions (1 cup)

4 cloves minced garlic (2 tsp.)

2 medium seeded and diced green bell peppers (1½ cups)

"Kielbasa" =
- **D-** 1-1½ pkg. (4-6) imitation Kielbasa or brats.
- **P-** 1½ pkg. (4-6) *parve* soy Kielbasa or brats.
- **M-** 1 lb. kosher Kielbasa, (casing removed, boiled ½-hour, halve).

2 (15 oz.) cans diced tomatoes (undrained)

1 (8 oz.) can tomato sauce

½ tsp. black pepper

¼ tsp. ground thyme

2 cups hot cooked white *Perfect Rice* (p. 205)

Step 1   Put oil, garlic, onions and bell peppers in large pot. Sauté until onions are tender.

Step 2   Add next 4 ingredients, simmer 15-20 minutes, or until peppers are tender.

Step 3   Add "Kielbasa" to tomatoes and green peppers. Heat through at least 5 minutes.

Step 4   Put rice on 4 plates and ladle mixture evenly on hot rice.

Polska Kielbasa is literally "Polish sausage". Makes 4 servings.

Pork Fried Rice

1 batch pre-assembled *Fried Rice* (p. 281)

"Pork" = {
D- 2 cups minced imitation bologna or ham.
P- 2 cups minced *parve* soy bologna or ham.
M- 2 cups minced cooked kosher duck, lamb, or dark meat turkey.

Step 1   Crumble and stir "Pork" into eggs and green onions, blend well and heat through.

Step 2   Heat mixture through in large frying pan or wok.

1½ cups leftover scrambled eggs can be used instead of first 4 ingredients. Makes 4-8 servings.

✿ ✿

Glazed Ham

¼ cup melted *parve* margarine

½ cup brown sugar

6 Tbs. prepared mustard

"Ham" = {
D- 1 (1¼ lb.) batch uncooked ham *Seitan* (p. 111).
P- 1 (1¼ lb.) batch uncooked ham *Seitan* (p. 111).
M- 1 lb. whole kosher smoked turkey breast.

whole cloves

Step 1   Blend first 3 ingredients until smooth, heat until warm and set aside.

Step 2   For D or P, shape into 3 loaves. Spread warm glaze on 3 lightly greased 3 x 5 mini loaf pans for D or P, or a lightly greased baking pan for M.

Step 3   Put "Ham" in pans and spread glaze over entire "Ham".

Step 4   Make criss-cross slashes 1-inch apart in "Ham" top. Preheat oven to 350° F.

Step 5   Firmly press a clove in where slash lines meet (remove before eating).

Step 6   Cover. Bake 1 hour for D or P, or 15 minutes for M until heated through.

Leftover glaze can be served warm with "Ham". All versions come out extremely realistically. (Stacks of sliced *parve* imitation ham for D or P, or smoked turkey slices for M can also be used. Simply heat through in Step 6.) Makes 4-8 servings.

Country Ham with Grits & Red Eye Gravy

(with biscuits or toast)　　　　　　　　(with biscuits or toast)

¼ cup melted *parve* margarine (divided)

"Ham" =
　D- 2-3 pkgs. imitation ham slices (doubled slices).
　P- 2-3 pkgs. *parve* soy or seitan ham slices (doubled slices).
　M- 1 lb. smoked kosher chicken or smoked kosher turkey slices.

1 cup black coffee

1 tsp. *parve* imitation bacon bits

½-1 batch *Country Grits* (p. 207)

4-8 slices of toast or *Simple Biscuits* (p. 217- optional)

¼ cup *parve* margarine (optional)

✸ Step 1　　Put 2 Tbs. margarine in a frying pan, and add "Ham" in single layer (doubled or tripled for P or D).

✸ Step 2　　Lightly fry "Ham" slices on both sides, but don't let it crisp. Remove from pan and keep warm.

✸ Step 3　　Add coffee, stir in last 2 Tbs. margarine and bacon bits.

✸ Step 4　　Bring to boil and simmer 1-2 minutes. (This is real red eye gravy.)

✸ Step 5　　Heat grits and biscuits or toast separately, and put equal portions on 4 plates.

✸ Step 6　　Butter biscuits or toast with margarine if desired.

✸ Step 7　　Place equal amounts of "Ham" on each plate, and pour red eye gravy over each serving of "Ham". Serve hot.

This recipe makes authentic red-eye gravy. If you're fixing this at night, it may be preferable to use decaffeinated coffee to avoid insomnia! Makes 4 servings.

Whole or pressed smoked turkey breasts can be sliced into large ½-inch thick pieces just like real ham steaks, but since they're already cooked they need only to be sautéed.

Fried Pork Chops with Stuffing

"Chops" =
- **D-** 4 imitation chicken patties.
- **P-** 4 *parve* soy or seitan chicken patties.
- **M-** 4 kosher duck or turkey breasts, lamb chops, or chicken patties.

½ cup *All-Purpose Breading* (p. 83- for originally un-breaded "Chops" only)

½ cup *Bread Crumbs* (p. 116- to bread un-breaded "Chops" only).

1 large beaten egg (optional- for breading "Chops")

2 tsp. ground sage, OR 4-8 fresh sage leaves (for non-breaded "Chops" only)

¼ cup avocado oil (other vegetable oil can be used)

1 batch beef *Stove Top® Style Stuffing* (p. 212- double margarine)

2 Tbs. water (if needed)

⊛ Step 1   If using pre-breaded "Chops", skip Steps 2-3, and if using M turkey or duck breasts, pound them until flattened. (If non-breaded chops are preferred, skip 2-3 as well.)

⊛ Step 2   Combine breading and crumbs in a bowl, and put egg in another bowl.

⊛ Step 3   Dip "Chops" in egg, then coat well with crumb mixture and let dry. Repeat this.

⊛ Step 4   Put "Chops" on a plate and sprinkle sage evenly on both sides. (For non-breaded "Chops", rub them with fresh sage leaves.)

⊛ Step 5   Heat oil in a frying pan, and fry all "Chops" on both sides until golden brown (and cooked through for M about 20 minutes). Keep them warm.

⊛ Step 6   Heat stuffing and add water if too dry, mixing until well blended.

⊛ Step 7   Put warm stuffing and "Pork Chops" on plates and serve hot.

A kosher spin on an old classic, and a dead-ringer for the "real McCoy". Makes 4 servings.

Whole or pressed smoked turkey breasts can be sliced into large ½-inch thick pieces just like real chops. Either fix as with Steps 2-4, or rub with fresh sage leaves first for non-breaded "Chops" (Step 4). They only need only to be browned as for D or P, and not cooked as for M.

For the classic baked version, add extra water to stuffing and do Steps 1-5 just until browned, or rub with sage without breading. Place stuffing in mounds in a well-greased casserole and put "Chops" on top. Bake covered at 350º F- 20 minutes for D and P (or M if using sliced smoked turkey breast), or 45 minutes for M or until done and juices run clear.

Hash Brown Scramble

1 batch (2 cups) *Home-Style Hash Browns with Onions* (p. 183)

3½ Tbs. avocado or other vegetable oil

6 eggs

3 cooked *parve* soy bacon strips (crumbled)**, OR 3 Tbs. *parve* bacon bits**

1½ tsp. salt

Step 1   Put hash browns with oil in a frying, and fry until brown on both sides.

Step 2   Break eggs into bowl and beat, add bacon bits and salt, blending well.

Step 3 . Pour into pan and cook stirring until egg is done. Serve hot.

For a different taste treat, substitute ¼ cup crumbled *parve* soy sausage or *Country Sausage* (p. 114) for bacon. Makes 6-8 servings.

☆ ☆

(🥃 on "Hamburger")   ## Fancy Shepherd's Pie

1 batch (1½ cups) *Beef or Mushroom Gravy* (p. 103)

1 (4 oz.) can chopped mushrooms

"Hamburger" = {
D- 1 pkg. (2 cups) imitation hamburger crumbles.
P- 2 cups *Parve Soy Crumbles* (p. 110).
M- 1 lb. kosher ground beef or turkey, (cooked and drained).

1 batch (3½ cups) *Deluxe Whipped Potatoes* (p. 192)

"Cheese" = {
D- 4 slices kosher Swiss or Cheddar cheese.
P- 4 slices *parve* imitation Mozzarella or American cheese.
M- 4 slices *parve* imitation Mozzarella or American cheese.

½-1 tsp. paprika (optional)

Step 1   Mix together gravy, mushrooms, and "Hamburger" in a glass casserole, and heat.

Step 2   Spread mixture flat, spread potatoes evenly on top, put "Cheese" atop potatoes.

Step 3   Sprinkle on paprika, microwave or bake at 350° F until hot. Makes 4-6 servings.

Potato Cheeseburger Casserole

"Hamburger" =
- **D-** 1 pkg. imitation burger crumbles + 3 Tbs. avocado oil.
- **P-** 1 pkg. (2 cups) *parve* soy crumbles + 3 Tbs. avocado oil.
- **M-** 1 lb. kosher ground beef or turkey.

1 medium chopped onion (½ cup), OR ¼ cup soaked minced onion flakes

1 batch (1¼ cup) *Condensed Cheddar Cheese Soup* (p. 151)

⅓ cup water

1 (15 oz.) can sliced potatoes (drained)**, OR 1 large sliced boiled potato**

1¼ tsp. *Italian Seasoning* (p. 434)

⅛ tsp. coarse ground black pepper

Step 1   Combine "Hamburger" and onion in a skillet or casserole dish, cook on stove or in microwave until "Hamburger" is browned and onion is tender.

Step 2   Add remaining ingredients, blend well and bake or heat through.

A fast favorite of Mum's and mine, we affectionately call it "*Cheese Goop*". Makes 2-4 servings.

✿ ✿

(potatoes)   Mary Kitchen® Style Roast Beef Hash

¼ cup *Beef Gravy* (p. 102)

¼ tsp. coarse ground black pepper

¼ tsp. onion powder

"Beef" =
- **D-** 1 pkg. (2 cups) imitation hamburger crumbles + ¼ cup avocado oil.
- **P-** 1 pkg. (2 cups) *parve* soy crumbles + ¼ cup avocado oil.
- **M-** 1 lb. kosher ground beef or turkey, (cooked and undrained).

2 medium potatoes (peeled, diced into ¼-inch tiny cubes, boiled and strained)

Combine ingredients in a skillet or microwave bowl, blend well and heat through. Serve hot.

The tiny potatoes make that special texture and flavor. To fry Southern-style, brown finished hash on each side until crisp. Makes 2-4 servings, or equivalent to 2 (15 oz.) cans.

Fishy Foods

Fish Ingredients

Kosher Oysters

1 cup well-cooked soybeans or garbanzo beans (drained well and pureed)

1 (6 oz.) can tuna in water (undrained)

4 Tbs. parsley flakes

1 egg

2 cups plain *Bread Crumbs* (p. 116)

½ tsp. salt

1 tsp. onion powder

⅛ tsp. black pepper

avocado or other vegetable oil for frying, OR spray oil for baking

⊛	Step 1	Combine beans, tuna, parsley and egg in a blender, blending to make a paste.
⊛	Step 2	Blend bread crumbs, salt, onion powder and black pepper.
⊛	Step 3	Add paste to crumbs, knead well and shape into 1 x 1½-inch oval patties.
⊛	Step 4	Put oil in pan and fry patties on both sides until brown, or put on greased cookie sheet and spray with oil. Bake 15 minutes in preheated 350° F oven until brown. Makes 45-50.

✿ ✿

Crab-Style Fish

¼ cup sugar (no substitutes)

1½ cups hot water

1 lb. fresh or thawed kosher pollock fillets (drained & cut into 1-2-inch chunks)

red food coloring (optional)

⊛	Step 1	Blend sugar and water in a pot. Bring to a boil, stir to dissolve sugar and add fish.
⊛	Step 2	Boil 10 minutes. Pour into a strainer, drain, let cool. Line a pan with paper towels.
⊛	Step 3	Put fish on paper towels. Dot a few pieces with coloring if desired and stir gently to distribute. Set in refrigerator to dry. (Can be used as imitation lobster or shrimp.) Makes 1 lb.

Kosher Clams

1 lb. kosher salt herring

water

✿ Step 1   Rinse herring and put it in a flat layer in a pot or container with enough water to cover herring. Water must be able to touch as much herring as possible. Refrigerator 24 hours.

✿ Step 2   Take herring out of water and let it drain, rinse it and pat it dry.

✿ Step 3   Cut or tear herring into 1-inch pieces or longer strips, and remove all bones.

A kosher equivalent to clams. Use in recipes calling for clams, but treat gently, they're not as tough as real ones. Freeze (gives authentic coloration and texture) or use. Makes 1 lb. or 1 cup.

When dipped in olive oil (for "slippery" consistency) and cut into 2-inch chunks, this recipe is a good substitute for **"Oysters on the Half Shell".** For an authentic color, freeze for a day if desired, then thaw. Serve on real properly *kashered* sea shells (or in individual crocks).

Salt herring can be found in kosher delis, or kosher groceries. Schmaltz herring can be used without soaking, but must be de-boned and isn't quite as authentic.

✡ ✡

Oyster Sauce

4 (6 oz.) cans tuna in water (to yield 1 cup drained tuna liquid)

1½ cups water

2 Tbs. soy sauce

¼ tsp. sugar

¼ tsp. minced garlic

⅛ ground ginger

2 tsp. corn starch

Drain and press tuna liquid through a strainer and into a pot to get ½ cup liquid. Add remaining ingredients, and simmer until thickened. Bottle and refrigerate. Keeps 2-3 weeks. Makes ½ cup.

Used in Chinese cooking. Similar to soy sauce, but richer with more flavor. Use in *parve* dishes.

Fishy Snack Foods and Appetizers

Fishy Snacks

(veggies)   **Chips and Veggies with Clam Dip**

1 cup *Parve Imitation Cream Cheese* (p. 105)

1 batch *Kosher Clams* (p. 330- minced in small pieces)

dash garlic powder

2 tsp. lemon juice

1½ tsp. Worcestershire sauce

dash hot pepper sauce

½ tsp. salt

pinch black pepper

1 (6 oz.) can tuna in water (undrained)

corn chips or potato chips

carrot sticks

celery sticks

❀ Step 1   Set imitation cream cheese out until it reaches room temperature, then put it in a small sealable bowl or container and beat it until smooth.

❀ Step 2   Add next 7 ingredients with cream cheese, and blend well.

❀ Step 3   Put a sieve over bowl and drain tuna liquid through sieve and into a bowl.

❀ Step 4   Squeeze tuna with can lid to get all liquid. (Tuna can be saved and used for other recipes.)

❀ Step 5   Blend thoroughly and put lid on bowl, then refrigerate 1 hour.

❀ Step 6   Put chips or crackers in a bowl, and set it on a large platter.

❀ Step 7   After the hour, set the clam dip bowl on a large platter.

❀ Step 8   Arrange carrot sticks and celery sticks decoratively around bowls.

Can use as dip for just about anything. Makes about 1½ cups dip.

(as snack) (as meal) **Shrimp Egg Rolls** (snack)(meal)

1 cup finely minced kosher imitation shrimp

dash ground ginger

1 tsp. soy sauce

1 Tbs. minced fresh cilantro (Chinese parsley or fresh coriander)

2 finely chopped green onions (¾ cup)

½ cup finely chopped shredded cabbage

½ cup finely chopped bean sprouts

1 batch (24) *Wonton Wrappers* **(p. 116)**

water

cooking oil spray for baking

   ⚘ Step 1   Mix together first 7 ingredients in a bowl, and blend thoroughly.

   ⚘ Step 2   Put a bit of filling in the middle of each wonton wrapper.

   ⚘ Step 3   Seal edges of each wrapper with a bit of water, and pinch edges closed tightly.

   ⚘ Step 4   Place egg rolls on a greased cookie sheet, and spray them with oil.

   ⚘ Step 5   Bake in a preheated 450° F oven 10 minutes on each side, until both sides are lightly browned.

Serve hot, with dipping sauces such as *Sweet & Sour Sauce* (p. 94), and *Hot Chinese Mustard* (p. 440) if desired. Makes 24 rolls.

An alternative is to microwave them. Lay them on a microwave safe plate, and microwave in 1-minute increments, until dough is firm and nearly getting hard. Do not let them burn.

Fishy Appetizers

Broiled Bacon-Wrapped Oysters

olive oil spray

½ batch *Kosher Oysters* (p. 329)

12 slices *parve* imitation bacon (cut in half)

Step 1   Line a small baking sheet with foil and spray it with cooking oil.

Step 2   Carefully wrap a slice of *parve* bacon around each imitation oyster and secure with a toothpick. (If placed seam side down, a toothpick may not be needed.)

Step 3   Place bacon-wrapped oysters on foil and spray thoroughly with oil to coat.

Step 4   Bake in a preheated 450° F about 10 minutes, or broil until *parve* bacon is starting to crisp on edges and stiffen. Serve hot.

These wonderful appetizers were served at a fresh fish restaurant in Florida. Makes 24.

✡ ✡

Garlic Shrimp Balls

1½ cups minced kosher imitation shrimp

¾ cup crushed shredded wheat crackers

2 eggs (beaten)

½ batch (¼ cup) *Papa John's Pizza® Style Garlic Sauce* (p. 99)

Step 1   Combine imitation shrimp with crackers and egg.

Step 2   Roll and squeeze shrimp mixture into 1½-inch balls.

Step 3   Melt garlic sauce in a frying pan on medium-low heat.

Step 4   Sauté balls in margarine until lightly browned on all sides. Serve hot.

This can also be made with imitation crab. Makes about 21 Garlic Shrimp Balls.

Shrimp Cocktail

½ pkg. (1 cup) kosher imitation shrimp or kosher imitation crab

3⅓ Tbs. finely minced horseradish

1½ cups ketchup

Slice shrimp into 1-inch pieces. Combine all ingredients and put into 6 small glasses or crocks. Chill at least ½-hour before serving. The longer it sits, the better the flavor. Makes 4-6 servings.

✡ ✡

Crab Rangoons

1 cup warm *parve* imitation cream cheese

¼ pkg. (or ¼ lb.) finely minced kosher imitation crab

2 Tbs. sugar

¼ tsp. ground white pepper

1½ batches (36) *Wonton Wrappers* (p. 116)

water (for sealing)

avocado or other vegetable oil for frying, OR spray oil for baking

Step 1   Combine first 4 ingredients in a large bowl, blend until mixture is smooth.

Step 2   Chill mixture until firm. Spread wonton wrappers out on a flat surface.

Step 3   Place 1-2 tsp. mixture in the center of each wonton, and wet edges with water.

Step 4   Fold 1 corner to opposite corner (in a triangle), and pinch along edges to seal.

Step 5   As each rangoon is finished, place it on a plate and cover with a paper towel if frying, or place it directly on a well-greased cookie sheet if baking.

Step 6   To Fry- Heat oil ¼ inch in depth in frying pan until hot and fry each rangoon until golden brown on both sides. To Bake- Spray rangoons on cookie sheet heavily with oil and bake 10 minutes at 450º F or until barely starting to brown. Serve hot or keep warm in oven.

A delicious appetizer served in Chinese restaurants. They are good cold too. Makes 36.

A less authentic alternative is to microwave them. Put several on a plate and microwave in 1-minute increments until firm and dry. Do not overcook or insides get crunchy instead of creamy.

Hawaiian Fish Appetizer

6 Tbs. lime juice

½ cup chopped green onions

⅛ tsp. hot pepper sauce (optional)

½ tsp. sugar

1 tsp. salt

1⅛ tsp. cumin seeds or celery seeds

¾ lb. diced kosher salmon fillets

⊛ Step 1   Combine all ingredients except salmon in a mixing bowl, blending thoroughly.

⊛ Step 2   Add salmon and mix thoroughly to coat all pieces, cover and chill 6 hours, stirring once every hour.

⊛ Step 3   Serve chilled in small bowls.

When I first had this in Hawaii, I thought it was smoked salmon, not raw. The odd thing was, the fish had eaten phosphorescent organisms, and the whole thing glowed in the dark! As for flavor, cumin seed gives a richer flavor, and celery seed brings out the lime. Makes 4-6 servings.

✡ ✡

Salmon Rosettes

1 (1 lb.) pkg. lox or smoked salmon (preferably with one side sliced straight)

1 cup room temperature *parve* imitation cream cheese

⊛ Step 1   Lay salmon strips flat on a cookie sheet or counter, and cut in half if very long.

⊛ Step 2   Spread cheese about ⅛ inch thick on salmon, starting 1-inch in on an end of each slice, spreading all the way to other end. (Keep spread ½-inch from irregular side.)

⊛ Step 3   Fold 1-inch plain end in towards the covered part, and roll up the slice "pinwheel" style until it is completely rolled.

⊛ Step 4   Place flat side of rolled salmon down (if there is a flat side), and irregular side up. The fish needs no toothpick, should stay upright on its own, and look rather like a flower.

Can be served on crackers or Melba toasts, if desired. Makes 32 Salmon Rosettes.

Shrimp in Aspic

1 (.33 oz.) pkg. plain kosher gelatin (often called "unsweetened clear diet jell")

1¾ cups water

1 Tbs. *parve* chicken soup mix, OR 1½ tsp. *parve* chicken bouillon powder

1 Tbs. lemon juice

1 Tbs. kosher cooking sherry

1 tsp. celery salt

¼ tsp. garlic powder

⅛ tsp. paprika

¾ pkg. (1½ cups) chopped kosher imitation shrimp

⊛ Step 1   Crush any lumps of gelatin into a fine powder. Combine water and gelatin in a pot or microwave bowl, and stir rigorously with a fork so that gelatin is well dispersed.

⊛ Step 2   Add soup mix, lemon juice, sherry, celery salt, garlic powder, paprika and bring to a boil.

⊛ Step 3   Stir to dissolve soup mix and blend together well, then take off heat.

⊛ Step 4   Add shrimp, stirring it in evenly, then put in small ornate molds or individual bowls.

⊛ Step 5   Chill until firm and gelled. Unmold and serve cold immediately on lettuce leaves, or in bowls.

An elegant appetizer when fancy molds are used. Unlike most of the recipes in this book this recipe does not freeze well. (Do not follow gelatin package directions that state gelatin should be added after boiling.) Makes 4-6 servings.

Parve kosher gelatin (also called "jell" or "gel") can be found at kosher groceries. Do not confuse "unflavored" or "diet" with the sweetened type. Look on the ingredients for sugar or artificial sweeteners.

Fish Soups and Chilis
Fish Soups

Manhattan Clam Chowder

1 Tbs. *parve* chicken soup mix, OR 1½ tsp. *parve* chicken bouillon powder

2½ cups water

1 cup diced potatoes (¼ inch)

1 small chopped onion (¼ cup)

1 small stalk chopped celery (½ cup)

¼ cup diced green bell peppers (seeded)

1 small bay leaf

1½ tsp. imitation *parve* bacon bits (optional)

1¼ cups chopped tomatoes

⅛ tsp. ground thyme

2 Tbs. flour

1½ Tbs. *parve* margarine

¼ lb. *Kosher Clams* (p. 330)

❁ Step 1　In a pot, bring water and soup mix to a boil, then add potatoes, onion, celery, bell peppers, bay leaf, bacon bits, tomatoes and thyme, cooking until vegetables are tender.

❁ Step 2　Reduce heat and slowly add flour and margarine, blending together.

❁ Step 3　Finally, add *Kosher Clams,* raising heat slightly, and stir constantly until slightly thickened.

Serve while hot. Can be served topped with oyster crackers. Makes 4 servings.

337

New England Clam Chowder

(on potatoes)

2 cups water

3 Tbs. *parve* margarine

¼ tsp. salt

2 medium potatoes (diced into ½-inch pieces)

2 cups *Parve Milk* (p. 85), OR other *parve* milk alternative

6 Tbs. flour

¼ tsp. celery salt

¼ tsp. onion powder

¼ tsp. ground thyme

¼ tsp. black pepper

⅜ tsp. ground nutmeg

1 Tbs. *parve* imitation bacon bits (optional)

½ lb. (½ cup) *Kosher Clams* (p. 330)

Step 1   Bring water, margarine and salt to a boil in a pot, then add potatoes and cook 10 minutes.

Step 2   In a bowl, stir together all but last three ingredients until smooth.

Step 3   Reduce heat and add cream mixture, and bacon bits to potatoes, blending together thoroughly.

Step 4   Add *Kosher Clams*, raise heat slightly, and stir constantly until slightly thickened. Serve hot.

This soup is a dead ringer for real clam chowder. It's enough to make you feel guilty! It can be served topped with oyster crackers or chopped green onions. If salty de-boned Schmaltz herring (about 1-1½ pkg.) is substituted for *Kosher Clams*, omit all salts in recipe. Makes 7 cups, about 4-6 servings.

Oyster Stew

2 cups *Parve Milk* (p. 85)**, OR other *parve* milk alternative**

½ cup flour

6 Tbs. *parve* margarine

¼ tsp. celery salt

¼ tsp. onion powder

¼ tsp. ground thyme

¼ tsp. black pepper

½ tsp. ground nutmeg

1 Tbs. *parve* imitation bacon bits (optional)

¼ tsp. salt

2½ cups water

½ lb. *Kosher Clams* (p. 330- Do Not Use *Kosher Oysters!* They will not work)

⊛ Step 1   In a bowl, blend together *parve milk*, flour, margarine, celery salt, onion powder, thyme, pepper and nutmeg until smooth.

⊛ Step 2   In a pot, bring water and salt to a boil, and cook 10 minutes.

⊛ Step 3   Reduce heat and add cream mixture and bacon bits, blending thoroughly.

⊛ Step 4   Add Kosher Clams, raising heat slightly, and stir constantly until slightly thickened.

Serve while hot. Can be served topped with oyster crackers. If a pinkish hue is desired, decrease water by 1 cup, and add 1 cup tomato sauce. Makes 6 cups, about 5-7 servings.

Cream of Shrimp Soup

¼ cup *parve* margarine

4-6 Tbs. flour

¾ cup *Parve Cream* (p. 85)

1¾ cup water

1 tsp. salt

¼ tsp. onion powder

½ tsp. ground nutmeg

dash black pepper (optional)

½ cup minced kosher imitation shrimp

Step 1   Heat margarine over low heat, until melted.

Step 2   Add flour, blending thoroughly, then slowly stir in *parve cream* and water.

Step 3   Stirring constantly, add remaining ingredients and raise heat.

Step 4   Cook until thickened, and serve hot.

Makes 2½ cups soup, or 2 servings.

☺   ☺   ☺

For **"Curried Shrimp Soup"**, add 2 tsp. curry powder and 1 tsp. ginger, heat through. Serve hot. Makes 2½ cups soup, or 2 servings.

(on rice) (on veggies)   **Shrimp Gumbo**

¼ cup chopped celery

¼ cup green bell peppers (seeded and chopped)

¼ cup chopped onion

¼ cup corn

½ (10 oz.) pkg. sliced okra (1 cup)

2 minced garlic cloves (1 tsp.)

⅛ tsp. black pepper (use cayenne pepper instead if you like it spicy)

3 Tbs. melted *parve* margarine or avocado oil (or other vegetable oil)

4 tsp. *parve* chicken soup mix, OR 2 *parve* chicken bouillon or soup cubes

2 cups water

¼ cup flour, OR 1¼ Tbs. quick cooking tapioca

½ (16 oz.) can chopped tomatoes (1 cup)

¼ tsp. ground thyme

¼ tsp. basil leaves

¼ tsp. ground cumin

¼ tsp. salt

½ tsp. hot pepper sauce (add double if you like it spicy)

1 Tbs. Worcestershire sauce

½ pkg. kosher imitation shrimp or imitation crab (chopped)

2 cups hot cooked white rice

✿ Step 1   Combine first 7 ingredients with oil in a pot (or margarine in a 2 quart glass casserole for microwave), cooking until vegetables are tender, then take off heat.

✿ Step 2   In a large bowl, combine soup mix, water, flour, tomatoes, thyme, basil, cumin, salt, hot pepper sauce, and Worcestershire sauce, stirring until thoroughly blended.

✿ Step 3   Add imitation shrimp and tomato mixture to vegetables, and blend well.

✿ Step 4   Bring to a boil and reduce heat, cook until heated through and slightly thickened.

✿ Step 5   Put rice in bowls and serve gumbo hot over rice.

Easiest and tastiest gumbo around. Makes 4 servings.

Lobster Bisque

⅔ cup flour

2½ cups water

¾ (8 oz.) pkg. kosher imitation lobster (diced).

1½ tsp. microwave browning sauce

1 tsp. *parve* chicken soup mix, OR ½ tsp. *parve* chicken bouillon powder

2 Tbs. *parve* margarine

¾ cups *Parve Cream* (p. 85)

pinch ground nutmeg

⅛ tsp. parsley flakes

½ tsp. *Chili Powder* (p. 434)

½ tsp. salt (optional)

⅛ tsp. ground thyme

½ cup tomato sauce

✿ Step 1   Combine flour and water in a large pot or 2-quart casserole dish, stirring until smooth.

✿ Step 2   Stir in remaining ingredients, blending thoroughly.

✿ Step 3   Bring to boil on stove or heat in microwave, and simmer or cook 5 minutes or until slightly thickened. Serve hot.

A gourmet classic made easy. Makes about 1 quart, or 4 servings.

(on asparagus)   **Asparagus Crab Soup**

1 (10 oz.) pkg. frozen asparagus (thawed)**, OR ¾ cup cooked asparagus**

1 (4 oz.) can chopped mushrooms (undrained)

5¼ cups water (divided)

8 tsp. *parve* chicken soup mix, OR 4 *parve* chicken bouillon or soup cubes

¼ tsp. garlic powder

⅛ cup thinly sliced onion

1 (1 lb.) pkg. chopped kosher imitation crab

2 Tbs. corn starch or potato starch

1 large hard-boiled egg yolk, OR 2 small hardboiled egg yolks

½ cup chopped green onions (chopped in 1-inch pieces)

⊛   Step 1   Check asparagus thoroughly for bugs (soak 2 hour in water with a bit of dish soap swished in if needed). Rinse well, chop into bite-size pieces and put in a large pot.

⊛   Step 2   Add mushrooms, 4 cups water, soup mix, onion, and imitation crab.

⊛   Step 3   Stir mixture and bring to boil, simmering 5 minutes.

⊛   Step 4   In a separate bowl, blend corn or potato starch with remaining ¼ cup water.

⊛   Step 5   Add corn starch mixture to pot and stir, blending thoroughly.

⊛   Step 6   Simmer, stirring until slightly thickened and clear.

⊛   Step 7   Crumble egg yolk into a small bowl and add green onions.

⊛   Step 8   Serve soup hot in bowls and garnish with sprinkled egg and green onion on top.

Based on a Vietnamese recipe. Makes 4 servings.

Neo-Classic Bouillabaisse

½ cup olive oil

2 (15 oz.) cans chopped tomatoes

½ cup tomato sauce

1 Tbs. chopped fennel, OR ½ tsp. fennel seeds

10 saffron threads

½ tsp. cayenne pepper

⅛ tsp. celery seeds

3 Tbs. parsley flakes

2 bay leaves

3 minced garlic cloves (1½ tsp.)

1 large onion (½ sliced, ½ minced)

½ (1 lb.) pkg. kosher imitation lobster (cut into 1-inch pieces)

½ (1 lb.) pkg. kosher imitation shrimp (cut into 1-inch pieces)

1 lb. kosher fish fillets (cut into 1-inch pieces)

4 cups hot water

1 (6 oz.) can tuna in water (undrained and nearly pureed)

½ cup kosher white wine

½ tsp. orange extract, OR 2 Tbs. orange juice

1 (1 lb.) loaf baked *parve* store-bought or home-made *Garlic Bread* (p. 213)

Step 1	Put oil in a pot and heat, then add next 10 ingredients (including entire onion).
Step 2	Sauté until onion is tender. Keep heat on, and add lobster, shrimp, fish and tuna.
Step 3	Bring to a boil and add water, continue boiling 20 minutes.
Step 4	Bake garlic bread according to package or make your own, sliced in half.
Step 5	Stir in wine during last few minutes of cooking. Turn off heat and add extract.
Step 6	Cut bread into quarters, place 1 piece in a bowl, and pour bouillabaisse over top.

Serve hot. A French classic fixed in a new way—kosher-style! Makes 8 servings.

Fresh fennel can be found in the produce section of larger supermarkets. Fennel seed and saffron are found in the spice section of larger grocery stores.

(🥕on vegetables)   **Javanese Vegetable Soup**

1 Tbs. avocado or other vegetable oil

½ tsp. minced garlic

¼ cup chopped onion

1 tsp. mashed anchovies

1 bay leaf

1 tsp. ground coriander

½ tsp. ground cumin

1 tsp. salt

3 cups *Imitation Coconut Milk* (p. 86)

2 Tbs. *parve* chicken soup mix, OR 3 *parve* chicken bouillon or soup cubes

2 cups water

1 cup chopped cabbage

1 (15 oz.) can cut green beans (drained)

¾ cup chopped yellow or crookneck squash

½ cup chopped chayote squash (peeled and seeded)

1 small seeded and chopped green bell pepper (¼-½ cup)

¾ cup diced potatoes (peeled)

½ lb. extra firm tofu (cut into ½-inch cubes) **(1¼ cup)**

⊛ Step 1   Put oil in pot for soup add garlic and onions and sauté until transparent.

⊛ Step 2   Stir in anchovies and add remaining ingredients except for tofu.

⊛ Step 3   Bring to a boil and simmer uncovered ½ hour, or until vegetables are tender.

⊛ Step 4   Add tofu and simmer 5 more minutes. Serve hot.

The original recipe uses breadfruit (rarely available in the continental U.S.), which tastes like and is used exactly like potatoes. Makes 4-6 servings.

Chayote squash looks somewhat like a green pear with a cleft chin, and can generally be found in the produce section of larger supermarkets. If it can't be located, extra yellow squash can be substituted for it.

Fish Chilis

(🥕 on beans)   **Red Lobster® Style Seafood Chili**

1½ Tbs. olive oil

⅓ cup chopped onion

2 minced garlic cloves (1 tsp.)

1 small minced stalk celery (½ cup)

½ pkg. kosher imitation shrimp (cut in 1-inch pieces)

¼ lb. kosher white fish fillets (cut into 1-inch pieces)

½ lb. *Kosher Clams* (p. 330)

1 (6 oz.) can tuna in water (undrained)

1½ (15 oz.) cans (3 cups) diced tomatoes (undrained)

1 (4 oz) can tomato paste

½ (15 oz.) can kidney beans

1½ tsp. *Chili Powder* (p. 434)

½ tsp. ground cumin

¼ tsp. ground coriander

1 bay leaf

½ tsp. cayenne pepper

½ tsp. sugar

¾ tsp. salt

½ cup kosher red wine

½ tsp. black pepper

¼ chopped red bell pepper (seeded)

❀ Step 1   Heat oil in a large pot, and add next 7 ingredients, sautéing until no longer transparent, and fish is nearly done.

❀ Step 2   Add remaining ingredients, and bring to a boil, then reduce heat to a simmer.

❀ Step 3   Cover and simmer 15 minutes, stirring often. Serve hot with oyster crackers.

"Seafood Chili"... It sounds a bit weird, but it's actually very delicious! Makes 4-8 servings.

Fish Salads and Side Dishes
Fish Salads

(salad) (crab)   **Taco Bell® Style Crab Taco Bowl Salad**

(if eating bowls)   (on bowls)

1 pkg. kosher imitation crab (shredded)

6 cups shredded prepared tossed salad

2 large diced tomatoes (2 cups)

1 cup sliced black olives (optional)

2 (15 oz.) cans pinto or chili beans (optional)

6 pre-made *Taco Salad Bowls* (p. 117)

1 cup grated *parve* Mozzarella (1 cup)

1 batch *Mexican Restaurant Guacamole* (p. 103- optional)

1½ cups *Parve Creamy Italian Dressing* (p. 89)

⊛	Step 1	In a large bowl, toss together first 5 ingredients.
⊛	Step 2	Divide mixture evenly in 6 portions and put into each taco bowl.
⊛	Step 3	Top each salad with *parve* Mozzarella and guacamole, if desired.
⊛	Step 4	Drizzle Italian dressing over each salad and serve.

A short-lived, yet delicious product from the 1980s. Makes 6 very generous servings.

An easy alternative to using the *Taco Salad Bowls* are to substitute a bag of corn tortilla chips. It isn't authentic, but the taste is similar, although it isn't as fancy or tender. Line the finished salad with plenty of chips, standing upright, and it is still a nice effect.

(or with croutons)   **Anchovy Antipasto**   (croutons)

2 (2 oz.) cans anchovies (drained and diced)

1 pkg. (4 cups) pre-made mixed tossed salad

4 medium chopped tomatoes (2 cups)

3 large seeded and diced green or red bell peppers (about 2¼ cups)

2-3 chopped green onions (about 1 cup)

1 cup *Parve Italian Dressing* (p. 89- or other preferred salad dressing)

1 cup grated *parve* Mozzarella

½ cup *Parve Parmesan Cheese* (p. 108- optional)

2 cups store-bought or homemade *Salad Croutons* (p. 116- optional)

⊛ Step 1   Combine anchovies, salad, tomatoes, bell peppers, green onions and dressing in a large bowl.

⊛ Step 2   Mix ingredients together until thoroughly blended.

⊛ Step 3   Put mixture in individual bowls, and sprinkle with *parve* imitation cheese and walnuts if desired.

⊛ Step 4   Chill until ready to serve, then top with croutons.

Classic Italian salad. Makes 4 generous servings.

Fish Side Dishes

Oyster Dressing

1½ cups water

¼ cup *parve* margarine

8 tsp. *parve* chicken soup mix, OR 4 *parve* chicken bouillon or soup cubes

2 tsp. parsley flakes

3 Tbs. dried minced onion flakes

¼ cup dried minced celery flakes

½ tsp. ground thyme

½ tsp. black pepper

¼ tsp. ground sage

6 packed cups chopped stale bread, OR 4 cups *Salad Croutons* (p. 116)

1 (6 oz.) can undrained tuna (preferably in water, but oil is fine too)

Step 1   Combine first 9 ingredients in a saucepan.

Step 2   Bring to a boil (making sure soup mix is dissolved), and simmer 15 minutes.

Step 3   Add croutons or bread and let sit 5 minutes, then fluff with a fork.

Step 4   Stir tuna in juice and all, breaking up any chunks so that it is indistinguishable. Mix thoroughly.

2 cups *Bread Crumbs* (p. 116) can be substituted for croutons. Do not use store-bought bread crumbs for this recipe, it does not come out right. If moister dressing is desired, add 2-3 Tbs. extra water. If you like a crusty baked texture, put in a 350º F oven 15-20 minutes. It can also be made in the microwave: Do Step 1 and 2 in a glass casserole, cooking 2-3 minutes, then do Step 3. This is also delicious cold. Oyster dressing always was a favorite in my family for Thanksgiving. The only drawback with this, is that you must serve it *before* eating the turkey, but not with it. It's just as good as the real thing, but healthier for you. This can also be made totally in the microwave. Makes 2 cups, or 4-6 servings.

For convenience, all the dry seasonings can be put in a zipper bag, and the croutons in another until ready to make. Then just add water and margarine.

Prawns in Garlic Sauce

½ cup *parve* margarine

16 minced garlic cloves (2⅔ Tbs.)

1 cup minced fresh cilantro (Chinese parsley or coriander)

1 Tbs. lemon juice (more can be added if desired)

1 (1 lb.) pkg. kosher imitation shrimp or crab (minced into ¼-½-inch pieces)

Put first 4 ingredients together in a pan and sauté until garlic is tender. Add imitation shrimp or crab and heat through. Makes 4-8 servings.

Bunches of cilantro can be found in the produce section of larger supermarkets.

✡ ✡

Fish Restaurant Style Hushpuppies

1 batch raw *Corn Bread* (p. 216)

¼ cup finely minced onion

¼ cup (or more) *Fish Restaurant Frying Oil* (p. 363)

Step 1   Combine batter and onion in a mixing bowl, blending thoroughly and let it sit at least 20 minutes.

Step 2   Shape into 1½-inch balls, and set aside on a plate.

Step 3   Heat fish oil in a frying pan until hot, then fry each ball in oil until golden brown.

Step 4   Drain on paper towels and serve hot.

The used fried-fish-oil gives this recipe an authentic flavor. (The same can be done for French fries to make authentic tasting "chips" for fish & chips.) Makes about 2 dozen hushpuppies.

Fish Sandwiches

Cheesy Crab Sandwiches

½ (1 lb.) pkg. kosher imitation crab

1 medium diced tomato (½ cup)

½ cup chopped cucumber (peeled)

½ tsp. salt

⅛ tsp. black pepper

¼ cup mayonnaise

1 cup grated *parve* American or Cheddar

16 slices toast, OR 8 buns

1 cup shredded lettuce

Step 1   Mince imitation crab finely and put it in a bowl.

Step 2   Add next 6 ingredients and blend together thoroughly.

Step 3   Spread crab filling evenly on 8 toast slices or bottom bun halves and place on a cookie sheet (or foil for broiler).

Step 4   Heat crab filling-topped toasts in a warm oven or a under broiler, or heat topped buns in microwave until cheese is melted.

Step 5   Top crab filling with shredded lettuce.

Step 6   Heat other 8 slices toast or upper buns slightly and put them on top of hot sandwiches. Serve warm.

Perfect for a cold night with a cup of soup. Makes 8 sandwiches, 2 per person.

McDonald's® Style Fillet-O-Fish® Sandwich

4 square kosher breaded fish patties

avocado or other vegetable oil for frying (optional)

4 hamburger buns or *Homemade White Buns* (p. 224)

¾-1 cup *Restaurant Tartar Sauce* (p. 92)

4 slices *parve* **imitation American cheese**

❀ Step 1   Fix fish patties according to package directions, especially authentic is to fry them in oil in a frying pan or quickly in a deep fryer. Set aside.

❀ Step 2   Toast bun faces (flat side) lightly, and set them on a platter toasted-sides-up.

❀ Step 3   Spread tartar sauce on bun tops, then put 1 piece cheese on bun bottoms.

❀ Step 4   Place fish atop cheese, and top with upper buns, then place in a heated oven to warm or microwave 10 seconds each.

Serve hot. Goes nicely with *McDonald's® Style French Fries* (p. 180). Makes 4 sandwiches.

✡ ✡

Tasty Tuna Sandwich

2 (6 oz.) cans tuna (drained)

¾ cup mayonnaise

1 tsp. ground thyme

½ tsp. black pepper

2 tsp. tarragon leaves

12 pieces toast

Blend together first 5 ingredients and spread on 6 pieces of toast. Top with remaining toast. Fancier than an average tuna salad sandwich. (Filling is good plain.) Makes 6 sandwiches.

☺   ☺   ☺

For **"Exotic Tuna Sandwich"**, substitute ½ tsp. cayenne pepper for thyme, 1 tsp. ground cumin for tarragon.

☺   ☺   ☺

For **"Zippy Tuna Sandwich"**, use ¼ cup mayonnaise, and add ½ cup creamy horseradish.

Fish Main Dishes

Breaded Kosher Oysters

2 dozen raw *Kosher Oysters* (p. 329)

½ cup corn flake crumbs or matzah (matzo) meal

avocado or other vegetable oil for frying, OR spray oil for baking

✿ Step 1   If making oysters from scratch, halve the recipe, and don't cook. Take each oyster and press into coating, so it's entirely covered. Set aside.

✿ Step 2   For frying method, put ¼-inch oil in pan, and fry oyster on each side until brown.

For baking method, spray a cookie sheet with oil, and place patties on it, then spray oysters, baking in 350° F oven 15-20 minutes or until browned. Makes 2 dozen oysters.

✿ ✿

Fried Kosher Clams

avocado or other vegetable oil for frying

½ lb. *Kosher Clams* (p. 330- cut into strips as oppose to chunks)

½ cup matzah (matzo) meal or *Bread Crumbs* (p. 116)

✿ Step 1   Put oil in a frying pan about ¼ inch deep and heat until hot.

✿ Step 2   Roll clams in bread crumbs or matzah meal to coat thoroughly.

✿ Step 3   Put clams into oil and fry until all sides are golden brown.

✿ Step 4   Drain on a paper towel and serve hot.

The same thing may be done for imitation shrimp to make fried shrimp. For that fish fast-food restaurant taste, use *Fish Restaurant Frying Oil* (p. 363). Makes anywhere from 24-48, depending on how the *Kosher Clams* are cut.

An alternative is to breading is to coat the clams (or imitation shrimp) with the batter used in *Long John's Silver's® Style Battered Fish* (p. 363), and cook in the microwave on 50% power (1 minute at a time), until done. (No oil is needed.)

Clams Oreganata

1½ lb. (1½ cups) minced *Kosher Clams* (p. 330)

1½ cups Italian-style *Bread Crumbs* (p. 116)

½ tsp. basil leaves

2 Tbs. parsley flakes

1½ Tbs. ground oregano

¼ cup *Parve Parmesan Cheese* (p. 108)

1¾ cups *Parve Cream* (p. 85)

1 tsp. garlic powder

½ cup melted *parve* margarine

24 properly *kashered* sea shells or individual crocks for serving in

Combine ingredients, blend well, and put a spoonful of mixture in each shell. Put shells on a cookie sheet and bake 20 minutes in a preheated 350°F oven or microwave 10-15 minutes, or until firm. (Instead of shells or crocks, the mixture can be squeezed into mounds on a greased cookie sheet or microwave safe plate.) Makes 24 clams.

✡ ✡

Clams Casino

1½ lb. (1½ cups) minced *Kosher Clams* (p. 330)

1½ cups Italian-style *Bread Crumbs* (p. 116)

2 Tbs. parsley flakes

2 Tbs. paprika (plus extra for topping)

¼ cup finely ground walnuts

1¾ cups water

1 tsp. garlic powder

6 Tbs. olive oil

24 properly *kashered* sea shells or individual crocks for serving in

Fix exactly as Clams Oreganata, then sprinkle paprika on top before cooking. Makes 24 clams.

Linguini with Clam Sauce

¼ cup *parve* margarine or olive oil

4 minced garlic cloves (2 tsp.)

1⅔ cups water

4 tsp. *parve* chicken soup mix, OR 2 *parve* chicken bouillon or soup cubes

3⅓ Tbs. flour

1 lb. *Kosher Clams* (p. 330- minced)

⅓ cup parsley flakes or chopped fresh parsley

1¼ tsp. ground thyme

1¼ tsp. crushed basil leaves

¼ tsp. black pepper

6½ cups cooked linguini (1 lb. raw)

Step 1   Heat margarine and garlic together in a saucepan, cooking 1 minute.

Step 2   Stir in water and soup mix, bring to boil to dissolve soup mix, and take off heat.

Step 3   Blend in flour until smooth, then slowly bring to a boil stirring constantly.

Step 4   Stir in clams, parsley, thyme, basil, and pepper, simmer stirring 5 minutes.

Step 5   Heat linguini, put it on individual plates, and serve clam sauce over it.

This is a delicious classic dish. The linguini can be made ahead and stored. Cook as for *Perfect Pasta* (p. 208) to keep it from getting mushy or sticking together. Makes 6-8 servings.

Oysters Rockefeller

1 batch (1½ cups) *parve White Sauce* (p. 101- make with soup mix)

1 tsp. *French Dijon Mustard* (p. 440)

1 Tbs. *Parve Imitation Sour Cream* (p. 105)

2 (10 oz.) pkg. frozen chopped spinach (thawed and drained)

1 Tbs. *parve* **imitation bacon bits** (optional)

16-18 *kashered* **sea shells, individual crocks, or foil-lined muffin tins**

1 lb. (about 24 pieces) *Kosher Clams* (p. 330- cut into 2-inch chunks)

2 Tbs. ground walnuts

2 Tbs. parsley flakes

Step 1   Combine first 4 ingredients in a pot on low heat, and blend thoroughly.

Step 2   Add bacon if desired, mix well, heat through, put a bit in each shell.

Step 3   Put a "Kosher Clam" in middle of each, sprinkle walnuts and parsley on top.

Step 4   Broil or bake in preheated 450º F oven until browned. Makes 4 servings.

✿ ✿

Fried Popcorn Shrimp

2 cups *Parve Milk* (p. 85), **OR other** *parve* **milk alternative**

1 cup flour

1 cup *Bread Crumbs* (p. 116)

1 (1 lb.) pkg. kosher imitation shrimp or imitation crab (cut into 1-inch pieces)

avocado or other vegetable oil for frying, OR spray oil for baking

Step 1   Put *parve milk* in a bowl, and mix flour and crumbs in another bowl.

Step 2   Take each shrimp piece, dip it in egg, then coat it with crumbs and set aside.

Step 3   <u>To Fry</u>- Put ¼-inch oil in pan and fry shrimp on each side until brown. <u>To Bake</u>-
Set shrimp on greased cookie sheet and spray well with oil. Bake 15 minutes at 350º F.

For jumbo shrimp, leave whole. Makes 32 popcorn or 8 jumbo.

Shrimp Fried Rice

2 Tbs. *parve* **margarine**

6 large beaten eggs

1 tsp. salt

dash black pepper

⅓ cup avocado or other vegetable oil

1 large chopped onion (¾ cup)

4 minced garlic cloves (2 tsp.)

4 cups cooked white *Perfect Rice* (p. 205)

1 Tbs. soy sauce

1 pkg. kosher imitation shrimp (cut in ½-inch pieces)

2 chopped green onions (1½ cups)

Step 1   Put margarine in a large frying pan or wok and melt, coating pan bottom and sides.

Step 2   Lightly beat together eggs, salt and pepper and add to margarine, cooking until lightly scrambled but moist.

Step 3   Remove eggs from pan and set aside, then put in oil, onion and garlic, cooking until onion is transparent.

Step 4   Add rice to pan and stir fry rice, breaking up any clumps, and add soy sauce.

Step 5   When heated through, stir in eggs, green onions and imitation shrimp, until well blended and heated through.

Serve hot with extra soy sauce if desired. This is a basic recipe and other items can be added as well. Instead of the first 4 ingredients, 1½ cups leftover scrambled eggs can be used. Makes 4-8 servings.

(🧁) (🥕veggies) (🥤shrimp)   **Seafood Paella**

¼ cup olive oil

1 small green bell pepper (cut into strips)

¾ cups raw long grain white or pearl rice

2 minced garlic cloves (1 tsp.)

1 small onion (sliced)

1½ cup *parve* imitation chicken chunks (cut into 1-inch chunks)

1 large tomato (blanched, peeled & chopped), **OR 2 whole canned tomatoes**

½ cup kosher white wine

1½ cups water

1 bay leaf

10 saffron threads

½ tsp. salt

¼ tsp. ground black pepper

4 tsp. *parve* chicken soup mix, OR 2 parve chicken bouillon or soup cubes

½ pkg. kosher imitation shrimp (cut into 1-inch chunks)

1 pkg. kosher schmaltz herring (de-boned, drained, & cut into 1-inch chunks)

1 cup cooked or canned peas

½ (4 oz.) jar pimento slices (¼ cup)

⚜ Step 1   Heat oil in a very large frying pan, add green pepper and rice, stirring constantly.

⚜ Step 2   Sauté until rice starts to brown, and add garlic and onion.

⚜ Step 3   Sauté onions until tender, then add next 11 ingredients blending well.

⚜ Step 4   Bring mixture to a boil. Reduce heat and simmer covered ½ hour, stirring occasionally.

⚜ Step 5   Top with peas and pimentos. Cook uncovered 5 more minutes and serve hot.

Spanish specialty, usually made with pork, shrimp, and clams. Colorful with a delicate flavor. Makes 4 servings.

Shrimp Benihana® Style

2 Tbs. avocado or other vegetable oil

salt

2½ pkg. kosher imitation shrimp

¼ cup hot melted *parve* margarine

⅓ cup *Parve Cream* (p. 85- heated)

¼ cup chopped fresh parsley, OR 1 Tbs. parsley flakes

¼ cup lemon juice, OR 2 lemons (for squeezing)

1 batch (½ cup) *Benihana® Style Ginger Sauce* (p. 93- optional)

Step 1   Heat oil, lightly salt shrimp, then sauté it 2 minutes on each side. Take off heat.

Step 2   Combine margarine, cream and parsley in a pot. Heat, then spread on shrimp.

Step 3   Cook shrimp 2 more minutes, then pour lemon juice on top and serve with warm ginger sauce. Serve hot as-is, or on bed of rice or chow mein noodles. Makes 4 servings.

✡ ✡

Red Lobster® Style Shrimp Scampi

¾ cup *Parve Imitation Butter* (p. 88- liquid version is fine)

12 minced garlic cloves (2 Tbs.)

2 pkg. kosher imitation shrimp

½ cup kosher white wine

2¼ tsp. lemon juice

¾ tsp. *Parve Ranch Dressing Mix* (p. 84)

2 Tbs. ground walnuts

Step 1   Put butter and garlic in a large pan (on medium heat), or in microwave bowl.

Step 2   Cook garlic 1-2 minutes until soft (not brown). Add wine, lemon juice and shrimp.

Step 3   Cook 1-2 minutes, flip then repeat. Add ranch mix and walnuts, blend and reheat.

Serve hot. For a quick version, combine ingredients in a baking dish. Bake 10 minutes at 350° F, and baste shrimp. (Can be garnished with lemon slices or parsley sprigs.) Makes 4 servings.

Lobster Newberg

4 tsp. minced onion

½ cup melted *parve* **margarine**

4-6 Tbs. flour

2 cups *Parve Milk* (p. 85)**, OR other** *parve* **milk alternative**

5 tsp. *parve* **chicken soup mix, OR 2½ tsp.** *parve* **chicken bouillon powder**

⅜ tsp. ground nutmeg

1 Tbs. tomato sauce (optional)

1 pkg. kosher imitation lobster (chopped into bite-size pieces)

¼ cup kosher cooking sherry

4-8 slices toast or bread

Step 1   Sauté onions in margarine in a pot or microwave bowl, until transparent.

Step 2   Put flour in water to make a smooth paste.

Step 3   Add flour mixture, *parve milk*, soup mix and nutmeg to onion pot, stirring until well blended and smooth.

Step 4   Heat on low, stirring constantly until starting to thicken, or microwave in ½-minute increments, stirring each time.

Step 5   Add tomato sauce if desired, imitation lobster and sherry to sauce, blending well and heating through.

Step 6   Put toast on plates, and pour sauce over top in equal portions. Serve hot.

As a delicious alternative, rice can be used in lieu of toast. Makes 4 servings.

Mrs. Paul's® Style Crab Cakes

1 (1 lb.) pkg. kosher imitation crab (finely minced)

¼ tsp. onion powder

2 Tbs. melted *parve* **margarine**

¾ tsp. salt

2 tsp. sugar

2 small beaten eggs

½ cup *parve Parve Milk* **(p. 85), OR other** *parve* **milk alternative**

1 cup *Bread Crumbs* **(p. 116) or matzah (matzo) meal** (divided)

Step 1   Combine first 6 ingredients and ¾ cup crumbs in a bowl and blend thoroughly.

Step 2   Shape mixture into 2-inch round mounds, and coat well with other ¼ cup crumbs.

Step 3   Place mounds on greased cookie sheet and spray with oil to coat thoroughly.

Step 4   Bake 45 minutes in preheated 350º F oven. Makes 8 Crab Cakes (equivalent to 4 pkgs.), or about 4-6 servings.

✡ ✡

Fish Cakes

1¼ lb. kosher boneless fish fillets (patted dry and minced)

2 beaten eggs

1 tsp. salt

¼ tsp. black pepper

1 cup chopped green onions

1 cup *Bread Crumbs* **(p. 116), flour or matzah (matzo) meal**

3 Tbs. avocado or other vegetable oil

Step 1   Put first 6 ingredients in a bowl and blend well. Squeeze, shaping into patties.

Step 2   Heat oil in skillet, fry patties until golden, gently flip and brown other side. Serve.

A great use for remnants of fresh whole fish that come off fillets. Makes 16 cakes, 4-6 servings.

Microwave Salmon Steaks

½ cup *parve* margarine

8 minced garlic cloves (4 tsp.), OR ½ tsp. garlic powder

4 (8 oz.) kosher salmon steaks (¾-inch thick)

	Step 1	Put margarine and garlic in a deep glass baking dish, heat to melt and blend.
	Step 2	Set some garlic butter aside, put steaks in baking dish and coat with some butter.
	Step 3	Cover loosely with plastic, heat 5 minutes on 70% power, flip, rotate and recover.
	Step 4	Heat on 70% power 5 minutes, spoon on remaining butter. Rotate and recover,
	Step 5	Cook 3 minutes on 70% power or until done. Serve hot. Makes 4 servings.

☺ ☺ ☺

For **"Microwave Fish Fillets"**, use same ingredients, but instead use 4 (4 oz.) ½ inch thick kosher fillets, cook on full power 3-5 minutes. Rotate and flip after 2 minutes. Makes 4 servings.

☺ ☺ ☺

For **"Microwave Garlic Crab"**, fix as for *Microwave Fish Fillets* above, using 2 pkg. kosher imitation crab and half the amount of margarine and garlic. Makes 4 servings.

✡ ✡

(rice)(peppers)(fish) Quick Hawaiian Fish

2-4 Tbs. avocado, olive or other vegetable oil

3 large green bell peppers (seeded and chopped in large pieces)

2 medium-large sweet Vidalia onions (chopped in large pieces)

1½ lb. kosher fish fillets or steaks (cut into 1-2-inch chunks)

1 tsp. salt

½ cup lime juice, OR 3 large limes (to squeeze for juice)

2-4 cups cooked white *Perfect Rice* (p. 205)

	Step 1	Put oil in a large frying pan and heat, sauté onions and bell peppers in oil.
	Step 2	Add salt, fish and lime juice (or squeeze every bit of lime juice in) bring to a boil.
	Step 3	Cook until fish and peppers are done and tender, about 5-10 minutes. Serve over hot cooked rice.

Based on a recipe from friends in Hawaii, this has a wonderful unique flavor. Makes 4 servings.

Creamy Tuna Deluxe Casserole

½ cup chopped onions

1 (4 oz.) can chopped mushrooms (drained)

¼ cup *parve* margarine

1 (6 oz.) can tuna

1 batch *Kraft® Style Macaroni & Cheese* (p. 209)

1 batch (1¼ cup) *Condensed Cream of Celery Soup* (p. 148)

Sauté onions and mushrooms in the margarine until onions start to brown slightly. Combine all ingredients together and heat through. Serve hot. Makes 4-8 servings.

✡ ✡

Long John Silver's® Style Battered Fish

1½ cup flour

¼ cup corn starch

½ tsp. baking soda

½ tsp. baking powder

½ tsp. salt

1½ cup water

2 lb. kosher cod or other fish fillets

avocado or other vegetable oil for frying

Step 1   Thoroughly blend first 6 ingredients and dip fillets in batter to coat entirely.

Step 2   Put oil in frying pan ¼ deep (or deeper for more authenticity), heat until hot.

Step 3   Plunge fish into oil, fry on both sides until golden brown. Drain on a paper towel.

Serve with *Fish Restaurant Style Hushpuppies* (p. 350) or French fries. Makes 4-6 servings.

The by-product of this recipe is **"Fish Restaurant Frying Oil"**: When frying the fish, save all leftover oil refrigerated in a jar for future use. This oil creates the authentic "fish restaurant" flavor for fries or hushpuppies. If it gets a "tangy" smell, it may be rancid and must be discarded.

Australian Fried Fish

¼ cup melted *parve* margarine

2 beaten eggs

1½ lbs. (about 6-8) kosher white fish fillets (patted dry)

1 tsp. salt

½ cup flour

2 cups finely chopped or ground macadamia nuts

2 Tbs. avocado or other vegetable oil

Step 1   Combine egg and margarine in bowl and beat until well blended. Set aside.

Step 2   Put flour in one shallow bowl, and macadamia nuts in another.

Step 3   Sprinkle fillets with salt and coat each one in flour, shaking off excess flour.

Step 4   Dip fillets in margarine mixture, coat with nuts then put on racks and chill ½ hour.

Step 5   Heat oil in a skillet until hot. Fry each fillet until brown (about 4 minutes).

Step 6   Flip with a spatula and fry other side until brown. (Shake pan to keep from sticking.)

Step 7   As each fillet is done frying, put it on a baking sheet, cover with foil and keep warm in oven until serving. Serve hot.

Exotic fried fish. Makes 4-6 servings.

✿ ✿

Fish Fillets Au Gratin

1 very small onion (sliced into rings)

¼ cup *parve* margarine

1-1½ lb. fish fillets

½ batch (⅔ cup) *parve Tangy Restaurant Cheese Sauce* (p. 98- heated)

Step 1   Sauté onion rings in margarine until transparent, remove and set onions aside.

Step 2   Put fish in margarine, cook or microwave until done, then set on individual plates.

Step 3   Pour hot sauce over fish, then top with onion rings. Makes 4-6 servings.

Stuffed Flounder

¼ cup minced celery

¾ cup chopped onion

1 minced garlic clove (½ tsp.)

1 Tbs. chopped green onions

6 Tbs. melted *parve* margarine or avocado oil (or other vegetable oil)

1½ Tbs. white wine

½ (1 lb.) pkg. minced kosher imitation crab meat (½ lb. or 1 cup)

1 cup plain *Bread Crumbs* (p. 116)

⅔ cup water

2-3 Tbs. olive oil

1 lb. (4 large) kosher flounder fillets (flattened)

salt

ground black pepper

	Step 1	Combine first 4 ingredients with margarine in a skillet and sauté until tender.
Step 2	Add wine and simmer 5 minutes, add crab and bread crumbs.
Step 3	Add water to crab mixture, blending together to make stuffing, and set aside.
Step 4	Coat a baking dish well with olive oil and place flounder in it in a flat layer.
Step 5	Lightly sprinkle salt and pepper on flounder fillets (stuffed side).
Step 6	Knead stuffing and squeeze it together into 4 separate mounds of equal size.
Step 7	Put stuffing mound in middle of each flounder fillet, and roll flounder around stuffing.
Step 8	Place flounder upside down (seam-side-down) and lightly sprinkle exposed side

of flounder with salt and pepper.

Step 9 Cover baking dish with foil and bake in a preheated 350°F oven 20 minutes.

Step 10 Uncover and bake 10 more minutes or until done. Serve hot.

Those who like lemon on their fish can squeeze a little lemon juice on top in Step 7, and can even put lemon slices on top of the flounder just before Step 8, to make it even prettier. This is even delicious served cold. Makes 4 servings.

Mum's Salmon Croquettes

2 (6 oz.) cans, OR 1 (12 oz.) can red salmon (drained well)

1 beaten egg

dash black pepper

½ cup flour

¼ tsp. salt

1-2 Tbs. avocado or other vegetable oil

Step 1   Mix together salmon, egg and pepper, shape into ovals but flatten on three sides.

Step 2   Put flour and salt in a bowl and mix together. Roll each croquette in flour mixture.

Step 3   Heat oil in a skillet until hot, and fry croquettes on each of flattened sides until browned.

Step 4   Drain on a paper towel lined plate, and serve hot.

These are even good served cold. Makes 7-8 croquettes, or about 3-4 servings.

✡ ✡

Tahitian Marinated Fish

¾ cup lime juice

6 Tbs. chopped onion

1½ tsp. salt

1½ lbs. kosher tuna, whiting or halibut steaks (cut in ¼ x 1½-inch pieces)

2 medium (1 cup) tomatoes (peeled & chopped)

6 Tbs. chopped green onions

3 Tbs. chopped green bell peppers

2 small chopped hard-boiled eggs

1 cup *Imitation Thai Coconut Cream* (p. 86- chilled)

Blend first 4 ingredients well in a bowl, cover and chill 5 hours (or leave at room temperature 3 hours). Stir once an hour. Drain fish (squeeze if necessary), and add remaining ingredients blending well. This recipe valiantly displays the principle of sharp foods. Makes 4 servings.

Fishy Drinks

Clamato® Style Juice

8 (6 oz.) cans tuna in water (to yield 2 cups drained tuna liquid)

3 cups tomato juice

1 tsp. *parve* chicken soup mix, OR ½ tsp. *parve* chicken bouillon powder

½ tsp. Worcestershire Sauce

2 tsp. sugar

⅛ tsp. hot pepper sauce

2 Tbs. lemon juice

⊛ Step 1   Squeeze tuna out with can lid, draining water through a sieve (to remove minute tuna particles) and into a pot or glass casserole dish. (Tuna can be used for other recipes.)

⊛ Step 2   Add remaining ingredients blending well, heat and stir until soup mix is dissolved.

⊛ Step 3   Pour into a pitcher and chill until cold. Makes 4 servings.

✧ ✧

Fishy Spritzer

1 lemon (or 1 Tbs. lemon juice if a lemon is not available)

2 cups *Clamato® Style Juice* (above)

2 tsp. finely grated horseradish (optional)

¼ tsp. hot pepper sauce

¼ tsp. Worcestershire sauce

2½ cups sparkling water, tonic water or club soda

⊛ Step 1   Slice lemon in half, and squeeze one half into a pitcher. (Set lemon half aside).

⊛ Step 2   Put remaining ingredients in pitcher, blend well, and chill if needed.

⊛ Step 3   Pour mixture into 4 glasses, and cut other lemon half into 4 slices.

⊛ Step 4   Make a slit in each lemon slice and garnish each glass by putting it on the edge.

A festive party drink. Alcoholic beverages can be added if so desired. Makes 4-6 servings.

Parve Drinks

Beef-A-Mato® Style Juice

1 qt. tomato juice

1¼ tsp. *Fishless Worcestershire Sauce* (p. 92)

¼ tsp. celery salt

2 Tbs. *parve* beef soup mix, OR 3 *parve* beef bouillon or soup cubes

⅛ tsp. hot pepper sauce

Step 1   Combine all ingredients in a pot or glass casserole.

Step 2   Heat and stir until soup mix is dissolved.

Step 3   Pour in a pitcher and chill until cold.

A different twist on tomato juice. Makes 4 servings.

Savory Vegetable Juice

1 qt. kosher vegetable juice

2 tsp. *Fishless Worcestershire Sauce* (p. 92)

¼ tsp. celery salt

⅛ tsp. cayenne pepper (optional)

½ tsp. hot pepper sauce (do not use Tabasco®, it is much too hot)

Step 1   Combine all ingredients in a pot or glass casserole, blending well.

Step 2   Heat until just starting to boil, allowing flavors to blend, take off heat and let cool.

Step 3   Pour in a pitcher and chill until cold. Serve chilled.

Vegetable juice with a zippy kick. Flavors blend and get spicier over time. Makes 4 servings.

Microwave Hot Cocoa

4 cups *Parve Milk* (p. 85), OR other *parve* milk alternative

8 tsp. cocoa

⅓ cup sugar (16 tsp.)

Combine some liquid with sugar and cocoa in large microwave bowl to make a paste. Add remaining liquid, heat 7 minutes or until desired warmth. Makes 4 servings.

☺   ☺   ☺

For **"Mint Cocoa"**, add a ¼ tsp. mint extract.

☺   ☺   ☺

For **"Mexican-Style Cinnamon Cocoa"** add 1 tsp. ground cinnamon.

☺   ☺   ☺

For **"Nut Cocoa"** add ½ tsp. almond extract.

☺   ☺   ☺

For **"Hot Rum Cocoa"** add 1 tsp. rum extract.

☺   ☺   ☺

For **"Fruity Cocoa"**, add 1 tsp. raspberry or orange extract.

☺   ☺   ☺

For **"Mocha Cocoa"**, add 2 tsp. instant coffee.

☺   ☺   ☺

For **"Cocoa Coffee Twist"**, add 4 tsp. instant coffee, ⅛ tsp. cinnamon, and cut cocoa in half.

✡ ✡

Eggless Eggnog

4½ cups *Parve Milk* (p. 85), OR other *parve* milk alternative

1 (3.4 oz.) pkg. *parve* instant banana or banana cream pudding (½ cup)

4 tsp. sugar

½ tsp. rum extract

dash ground nutmeg (plus extra for sprinkling on top when ready to serve)

❀ Step 1   Put ingredients in a blender or large tight sealing jar. (Do not use real milk!)

❀ Step 2   Mix or shake until well blended, and chill in refrigerator until very cold.

❀ Step 3   Shake well before serving. Serve in glasses and sprinkle nutmeg on top.

Artificial banana apparently shares the same flavor as artificial egg! Makes 4-6 servings.

Arby's® Style Jamocha® Shake

2 cups cold black coffee (average, not extra strong)

2 cups *Parve Milk* (p. 85)**, OR other *parve* milk alternative**

⅛ tsp. salt

6 Tbs. sugar

6 cups *Parve Vanilla Ice Cream* (p. 411)

3 Tbs. *parve* chocolate syrup

- Step 1   Combine first 5 ingredients in a blender. Blend 20 seconds.
- Step 2   Add ice cream and syrup, and blend until smooth.
- Step 3   Pour in 4 tumblers and serve, or freeze 5 hours then take out and stir.

If frozen, it's amazingly realistic, kosher and *parve*! Makes 4 huge (2 cup) shakes.

If a blender is not available, let ice cream soften a bit. Then combine all ingredients in a large well-sealing container and shake well to blend. Do Step 3 as normal.

✿ ✿

Wendy's® Style Frosty®

2 cups *Parve Milk* (p. 85)**, OR other *parve* milk alternative**

2⅔ Tbs. sugar

4 tsp. cocoa

4 cups slightly softened *Parve Chocolate Ice Cream* (p. 412)

- Step 1   Put ingredients in a blender and set on pulse 10 seconds on high until blended.
- Step 2   Pour into 4 large cups and serve right away, or freeze 5 hours, take out and stir.

If frozen, it's amazingly realistic, and kosher! Makes 4 "Biggie®-sized" (large) drinks (6 cups).

For Step 1, this can also be put in a large well-sealing container and shaken well to blend.

Malted Milk Shake

1 cup *Parve Milk* (p. 85)**, OR other *parve* milk alternative**

1 cup *Parve Chocolate Malt Syrup* (p. 123)

4 cups *Parve Vanilla Ice Cream* or vanilla soy ice cream (p. 411- softened)

Put ingredients in blender or well-sealing jar. Blend or shake well and serve. Makes 4 servings.

✡ ✡

Dark Floats

4 large scoops *Parve Vanilla Ice Cream* (p. 411)**, OR vanilla soy ice cream**

4 cups chilled root beer, OR 4 cups chilled cola

Put 2 scoops ice cream in 4 glasses. For Root Beer Float: Pour root beer on top of ice cream. For Black Cow: Pour cola on top of ice cream. Makes 4 servings.

✡ ✡

Pineapple Orange Float

4 scoops *Parve Orange Sherbet* (p. 412- one for each glass)

1⅓ cup chilled pineapple juice

2⅔ cups chilled orange soda (lemon lime can be used as well)

Put 1 scoop sherbet in 4 glasses. Blend juice and soda and pour it over sherbet. Makes 4 cups.

✡ ✡

Sherbet Float

4 large scoops *Parve Sherbet* (p. 412)**, OR *parve* sorbet**

4 cups chilled lemon lime soda, OR ginger ale

Put 1 scoop sherbet in 4 tumblers, and pour soda over sherbet until frothy. (Preferable flavors are raspberry and orange.) Makes 4 servings.

Flavored Cola

4 (12 oz.) cans chilled cola (6 cups)

Cola Flavorings:

Chocolate Cola: ⅔ cup *parve* chocolate syrup

Milk & Cola: 2 cups *parve* soy milk

Rum & Cola: 4½ tsp. rum extract

Stir cola and 1 of the flavors together until well blended and serve cold. Makes 4-6 servings.

Each generation seems to have had its own flavor- in the 40s it was rum, 50s milk, and early 70s chocolate. Nowadays, the manufacturer's make their own blends, but none of these flavors!

✡ ✡

Phosphate Drink

1 cup *Fruit Syrup* or *Flavored Syrup* (p. 122)
4½ cups chilled unflavored sparkling water or seltzer

Blend together well and serve in large clear soda glasses. Makes 4 large servings.

✡ ✡

Chocolate Phosphate

1 cup *parve* chocolate syrup
4½ cups chilled plain sparkling water or seltzer

Blend together well and serve in large clear soda glasses. Makes 4 large servings.

☺   ☺   ☺

For **"Chocolate Mint Phosphate"**, use ½ cup chocolate syrup and ½ cup mint *Flavored Syrup* (see p. 122) with normal amount of water. Makes 4 large servings.

Piña Colada Soda

1 cup + 2 Tbs. chilled pineapple juice

¾ cup + 2 Tbs. chilled *Imitation Cream of Coconut* (p. 124)

2 cups chilled plain sparkling water or seltzer

Blend ingredients together well in a pitcher and serve cold. Makes 4 servings.

✿ ✿

Tropical Sunset Soda

2 (12 oz.) cans chilled lemon lime soda (3 cups)

½ cup chilled tropical punch drink

½ cup chilled orange juice

Combine in a pitcher and serve cold. Pretty color and great flavor. Makes 4 large servings.

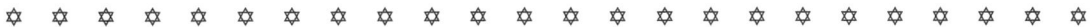

✿ ✿

Sweet & Tasty Lemonade

⅔ cup sugar

4 cups warm water

⅔ cup lemon juice

⅓ cup orange juice

ice (optional)

Step 1   Mix sugar and water together until sugar is totally dissolved.

Step 2   Add juices, blend well and chill until cold.

Step 3   Serve cold with ice, if desired.

This delicious and simple recipe is from Mrs. Ellen Pollock. It has lots of flavor and doesn't leave your mouth puckered! Makes slightly less than 6 cups, or 4-6 servings.

Desserts
Cookies

Thumbprint Cookies

½ cup sugar

2 eggs

⅔ cup *parve* margarine

1 tsp. almond extract

2¼ cups flour

2 tsp. baking powder

¼ tsp. salt

Step 1   Preheat oven to 375º F. Combine ingredients, knead to blend and chill 4 hours.

Step 2   Roll dough ⅛ inch thick, and cut it with a mouth of a jar 2-2½ inches in diameter.

Step 3   Place on a well-greased cookie sheet. Bake 5 minutes, then take out of oven.

Step 4   Press in on center of cookies with your thumb (or back of a spoon).

Step 5   Bake 7 more minutes or until lightly browned. Let cool. Makes 40 cookies.

☺   ☺   ☺

For **"Jelly Thumbprint Cookies"**, top each cookie with a dollop of preserves, jam or jelly, then chill until firm.

☺   ☺   ☺

For **"Iced Thumbprint Cookies"**, top each cookie with a small spoonful of icing made by mixing together 2 Tbs. melted *parve* margarine, 1 cup sifted powdered sugar, ½ tsp. vanilla extract, 1½ Tbs. *Parve Milk* (p. 85) and a few drops food coloring, until smooth. Top cookies, then chill until firm. My grandma, Nana "*aleyha hashalom*" would make these cookies using vanilla extract. She always made 3 colored icings for variety—pink, green, and yellow.

☺   ☺   ☺

For **"Chocolate Iced Thumbprint Cookies"**, top each cookie with a small spoonful of icing made by mixing together 2 Tbs. melted *parve* margarine, 1 cup sifted powdered sugar, ½ tsp. vanilla extract, 5 tsp. *Parve Milk* (p. 85) and 2 Tbs. cocoa. Top cookies, then chill until firm. (Nana would often do an additional batch in chocolate icing.)

Parve Keebler® Style Pecan Sandies®

¾ cup room temperature *parve* margarine

¾ tsp. salt

1 egg white

⅛ tsp. baking soda

2 cups flour

½ cup minced pecans

⅔ cup sugar (divided)

- Step 1   Combine margarine and salt in a large bowl, and beat until fluffy.
- Step 2   Beat in egg white, blending well, and gradually beat in baking soda and flour, blending thoroughly.
- Step 3   Add pecans and ⅓ cup sugar to dough, kneading by hand until well blended.
- Step 4   Add ¼ cup sugar and knead lightly, so that sugar is not totally dissolved.
- Step 5   Roll dough into 36 1-inch balls and place on 2 large well-greased cookie sheets, 1 inch apart. (They should be 1 inch from the edge of cookie sheet.)
- Step 6   Flatten balls with greased bottom of a can or jar so they become a little over ¼ inch thick and 2¼ inches in diameter. (Squeeze jagged edges in, if desired.)
- Step 7   With lightly greased hands, take a little of remaining 4 tsp. sugar and lightly pat it on top of cookies for a light "sandy" coating.
- Step 8   Bake about 10 minutes in a preheated 400° F oven until cookie edges are barely starting to brown. (Do not let them become brown.)

The real thing is indeed kosher, but dairy. These are *parve* and perfect for *Shabbat*. Makes 3 dozen cookies.

For those who like authenticity, the above recipe is just like the real thing.

During experimentation, an alternative, much softer and slightly chewier version was created. It tastes nearly the same, but texture buffs will notice a difference. The "softer" version can be made with one whole egg, ¾ cup *parve* margarine and ½ tsp. baking soda.

Fancy Cream-Filled Cookies

Cookies:

¾ cup room temperature *parve* **margarine**

¾ cup sugar

2 Tbs. *Parve Milk* (p. 85)**, or other** *parve milk alternative*

2 egg yolks

1 tsp. vanilla extract

¼ salt

2¾ cups flour (plus extra for floured surfaces)

powdered sugar (for sprinkling on top)

Filling:

"Milk" = {
D- 1 (8 oz.) can (1 cup) sweetened condensed milk.
P- ½ raw *Parve Caramel* (p. 125) + ¼ cup *Parve Cream* (p. 85).
M- ½ raw *Parve Caramel* (p. 125) + ¼ cup *Parve Cream* (p. 85).

Step 1   To make cookies: Lightly beat margarine, then add sugar and beat until fluffy.

Step 2   Beat in creamer, yolks, vanilla and salt, then gradually add flour until blended.

Step 3   Lightly flour a flat surface and rolling pin, roll out dough to about ⅛ inch thick.

Step 4   Cut out 48 cookies with a 2-2¼ inch round, (preferably fluted) cookie cutter.

Step 5   Put cookies on cookie sheets and bake in a preheated 375° F oven 8 minutes or until lightly browned. Set aside and let cool.

Step 6   To make filling: Put "Milk" into a saucepan and simmer on medium-low heat, stirring constantly 10 minutes or until starting to thicken. Let cool slightly but not completely.

Step 7   Beat filling until smooth if necessary, and take a spoonful of filling and spread it on 24 cookies, then top filling with remaining 24 cookies.

Step 8   Set cookies out flat. Pour a little powdered sugar into a sieve, and sift a little amount of sugar on each cookie just to "dust" it. Keep refrigerated or serve at once.

This is based on a recipe from a friend. Makes 24 cookies.

☺   ☺   ☺

For **"Fancy Jelly-Filled Cookies"**, substitute about ¾ cup raspberry jelly or jam for "Milk" Filling and omit Step 6. Makes 24 cookies.

Gluten-Free Peanut Butter Cookies

1 cup chunky or creamy peanut butter or tahini

¾-1 cup sugar (depending on taste; use at least 1 cup for tahini)

1 room temperature egg (use two eggs for tahini)

1 tsp. vanilla extract (optional)

1 cup parve semisweet chocolate chips (optional- tahini cookies are delicate)

2 Tbs. corn starch (optional; use 4 Tbs. for tahini)

Step 1 Mix first 3 ingredients in a bowl, then stir in vanilla and chocolate chips.

Step 2 Add corn starch and blend. (Chill ½ hour if using tahini.) Preheat oven to 350º F.

Step 3 Drop dough onto greased cookie sheet from spoon, (then crisscross with a fork).

Step 4 Bake in a 7-8 minutes until start to brown. Let cool, gently remove with spatula.

A recipe from an anonymous friend. Tahini can be used in the same amounts as peanut butter, but the cookies are very fragile. They must be laid flat and cannot be stacked. Makes 20-24.

✡ ✡

Parve Girl Scout Cookies® Style Samoas®

1¾ cups coconut

½ batch *Parve Caramel* (p. 124)

2 dozen *Parve Nabisco® Style Lorna Doones®* (p. 378)

1 batch *Parve Dark Chocolate Fudge* (without nuts) (p. 405)

Step 1 Spread coconut on a cookie sheet, bake at 300º F about 20-25 minutes (stirring every 5-10 minutes) until lightly toasted. (Do not let it burn.) Set aside.

Step 2 Heat caramel on low heat to melt stirring constantly, add coconut and blend well.

Step 3 Place cookies on plates, spread caramel on tops and chill until firm.

Step 4 Melt fudge on very low heat, drizzle in stripes over cookies, and chill to harden.

Store in an airtight container. These were an all-time (dairy) favorite as a child, and now they can be eaten with a meat meal on *Shabbat*. (It's well worth it!) Makes about 24 cookies.

Parve Nabisco® Style Lorna Doones®

1½ cup room temperature parve margarine

⅔ cup powdered sugar

1 tsp. vanilla extract

2 tsp. *Parve Milk* **(p. 85), or other** *parve milk alternative*

4 cups flour

½ tsp. baking powder

Step 1   Beat parve margarine in a bowl, add sugar and beat it into margarine.

Step 2   Add vanilla and *Parve Milk* to margarine and blend well until fluffy.

Step 3   Combine flour and baking powder, mixing well then add in small increments to margarine mixture, kneading until well blended.

Step 4   Press into 2 (8 x 16-inch) baking pans until flat and even, then cut into 2-inch squares with a plastic knife.

Step 5   Bake in preheated 325° F oven 20 minutes or until dry and just starting to brown.

Step 6   Let cookies cool when done, serve or keep in airtight container. Makes about 5 dozen.

Normally dairy, these are great for those with egg allergies, as they contain no eggs. Use to make *Parve Girl Scout Cookies® Style Samoas®* on previous page.

☺   ☺   ☺

For **"Orange Shortbread Cookies"**, add 2 tsp. grated orange peel or orange zest and add 4 tsp. orange extract.

☺   ☺   ☺

For **"Mocha Shortbread Cookies"**, double the powdered sugar, add 2 tsp. cocoa, ½ tsp. powdered instant coffee, and 1 tsp. powdered parve non-dairy creamer to dough.

☺   ☺   ☺

For **"Almond Shortbread Cookies"**, add ⅓ cup slivered almonds and 2 tsp. almond extract.

☺   ☺   ☺

For **"Parve Keebler ® Style Fudge Stripes® Cookies"**, use cookies as-is or roll dough out to ¼-½ inch thick, cut cookies into rounds if desired, and gently place on cookie sheets and bake as normal. Melt ½ batch of *Parve Dark Chocolate Fudge* (without nuts- p. 405) on low heat. Spread backs of cookies with chocolate and chill about 5 minutes until hardened. Take cookies out and flip them so that fudge side is down, then drizzle thin parallel stripes of fudge over cookies. Chill to harden.

Chewy-Dewies

½ cup room temperature *parve* margarine

½ cup avocado or other vegetable oil

¼ cup *parve* vegetable shortening

¾ cup light brown sugar

½ cup sugar

1 egg

½ tsp. ground cinnamon

½ tsp. almond extract

½ tsp. vanilla extract

1½ cups flour

3 cups plain uncooked oatmeal

1 tsp. baking soda

½ tsp. salt

⅓ cup raisins

⅓ cup diced dried dates

⅓ cup chopped pecans

Step 1   Combine first 10 ingredients in large mixing bowl and beat together.

Step 2   Mix together flour, oatmeal, baking soda and salt in a separate bowl.

Step 3   Gradually stir dry ingredients into wet ingredients, blending well.

Step 4   Add raisins, dates and pecans, blending thoroughly.

Step 5   Shape into 1½-inch balls and drop about 4 inches apart onto a cookie sheet, then flatten them with a spatula.

Step 6   Bake in a preheated 350° F oven 10 minutes, making sure *not* to brown edges.

Step 7   Let cookies cool. (They will still be extremely soft when fresh out of the oven.)

This recipe was made by Daveed Henn. It was meant to mimic the chewy "Soft Batch" style cookies that came out in the mid to late 80s, but without all the preservatives!

Substitute raisins for dates and pecans to make a soft oatmeal-raisin cookie. Makes 2½-3 dozen cookies.

Archway® Style Wedding Cake Cookies

1½ cups room temperature *parve* margarine

⅓ cup powdered sugar (plus additional powdered sugar for rolling in)

1 egg yolk

½ cup chopped almonds

3½ cups flour

Step 1   Combine first 2 ingredients in a bowl and beat, then mix in next 3 ingredients.

Step 2   Shape into 2 inch balls, gently set on a cookie sheet about 1 inch apart.

Step 3   Bake 30-45 minutes in preheated 300° F oven until fully baked and barely brown.

Step 4   Set aside to cool. Put extra powdered sugar (preferably sifted) into a small bowl.

Step 5   Take each cookie roll and press it into sugar, coating it well and pressing sugar on with your fingers. Makes 2½ dozen.

☺   ☺   ☺

For **"Snow Cap Cookies"**, substitute 1½ cup chocolate chips for almonds. Makes 3 dozen.

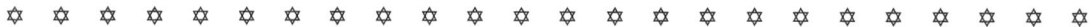

✿ ✿

Pumpkin Cookies

¾ cup room temperature *parve* margarine

1½ cups packed brown sugar

2¾ tsp. *Pumpkin Pie Spice* (p. 434)

1 Tbs. baking powder

1 large beaten egg

1 (15 oz.) can (1¾ cups) mashed cooked pumpkin

2¼ cups flour

Step 1   Put first 5 ingredients in a mixing bowl and beat until fluffy.

Step 2   Stir in pumpkin and flour and blend thoroughly.

Step 3   Drop by large tablespoonfuls 1 inch apart on 2 greased cookie sheets.

Step 4   Bake in a preheated 375° F oven 25 minutes until firm and peaks start to brown.

Step 5   Take out of oven and cool on a wire rack. Makes 4 dozen cookies.

Pastries and Cakes

Taco Bell® Style Cinnamon Crispas®

8 (any size) flour tortillas (cut into quarters)

avocado or other vegetable oil (for frying)

¼ cup *Cinnamon Sugar* (p. 434)

- Step 1   Heat oil, when hot, take a tongs and fry each piece of tortilla in oil until crisp.
- Step 2   Take pieces out of oil and drain on a paper towel on top of a plate.
- Step 3   Put cinnamon sugar in wide bowl and dip each piece to coat both sides.

These can be made in the oven. Brush tortillas with margarine. Put on cookie sheet at 350º F just until crisp, coat with cinnamon sugar. They are best eaten fresh. Makes 8 servings.

☺   ☺   ☺

For **"Crispy Mexican Pastries"**, substitute sifted powdered sugar for *Cinnamon Sugar*. The originals are made of fluted fancy pastry then fried, but for simplicity flour tortillas are used, (yielding the same flavor). They are best eaten fresh. Makes 8 servings, 4 per person.

✡ ✡

Pecan Cinnamon Squares

1½ (packed) cups *Parve Bisquick® Style Mix* (p. 84)

2 tsp. ground cinnamon

6 Tbs. sugar

1 beaten egg

⅓ cup water

½ cup chopped pecans

- Step 1   Heat oven to 350º F, and put ingredients (except nuts) in mixing bowl, blend well.
- Step 2   Pour batter into a greased and floured 8 x 8-inch pan, then sprinkle nuts on top.
- Step 3   Bake 30-35 minutes or until toothpick comes clean. Cool and cut into squares.

Rather like coffee cake, this was my first invented recipe at age 12. Makes 12-15 squares.

Pecan Cinnamon Rolls

Rolls:

1¾ cups flour

1 Tbs. baking powder

1 Tbs. sugar

¼ cup *parve* margarine

½ cup water

½ cup *Parve Milk* (p. 85), or other *parve* milk alternative

¼ cup finely chopped pecans

1 tsp. *Cinnamon Sugar* (p. 434)

Optional Icing:

1 tsp. *parve* margarine

1 tsp. ground cinnamon

⅔ cup powdered sugar

¼ cup finely chopped pecans

Step 1   For rolls- sift together flour, baking powder and sugar.

Step 2   Mix in margarine, *parve milk,* and pecans, blending well.

Step 3   Grease a muffin tin or put in cupcake liners, and spoon batter into cups evenly.

Step 4   Put a bit of cinnamon sugar in the center of each, and gently swirl it into batter with a knife—pinwheel style.

Step 5   Bake in a preheated 450º F oven 12-15 minutes until lightly brown.

Step 6   For Optional Icing- melt margarine and stir in powdered sugar, cinnamon, and pecans.

Step 7   Heat icing lightly, stirring until smooth and then chill.

Step 8   Spread icing on hot rolls after they are removed from tins.

The batter and icing can both be made ahead of time, and refrigerated until ready to bake. Makes 12-15 rolls.

Orange-Iced Sweet Rolls

Rolls:

1¾ cups flour

1 Tbs. baking powder

¼ cup sugar

⅜ tsp. ground cinnamon

¼ cup room temperature *parve* margarine

¼ cup orange juice

¾ cup *Parve Milk* (p. 85), or other parve milk alternative

Icing:

½ tsp. *parve* margarine

1 cup powdered sugar

2 Tbs. orange juice

½ tsp. dried grated orange peel

Step 1   For Rolls- Sift together flour, baking powder, sugar and cinnamon.

Step 2   Mix in margarine, orange juice, water and *Parve Milk*, blending thoroughly.

Step 3   Grease a muffin tin or put in cupcake liners, and spoon batter into cups evenly.

Step 4   Bake in a preheated 450° F oven 12-15 minutes until lightly brown.

Step 5   For Icing- Melt margarine and stir in powdered sugar, juice and orange peel.

Step 6   Heat icing lightly, stirring until smooth and then chill.

Step 7   Spread icing on hot rolls after they are removed from tins.

These are so delicious. Both the batter and the icing can be made ahead of time, and stored in the refrigerator until ready to make. Makes 12 rolls.

Hawaiian Banana-Nut Bread

Bread:

2 cups whole wheat flour

½ cup avocado or other vegetable oil

1 tsp. ground cinnamon

½ tsp. ground nutmeg

¾ tsp. baking soda

½ tsp. salt

1 cup raw sugar or regular granulated sugar

2 beaten eggs

3 large (or 5 small) very ripe mashed bananas (about 1 cup)

½ cup chopped walnuts

Topping:

2 Tbs. *parve* margarine

1 tsp. ground cinnamon

1 Tbs. raw sugar

Step 1   For bread- put ingredients in a mixing bowl, and mix well to blend thoroughly.

Step 2   Pour batter into a greased and floured loaf pan, smoothing it out evenly.

Step 3   Bake 50-60 minutes preheated 350º F oven, then take it out of oven.

Step 4   For topping- combine 1 tsp. cinnamon and margarine in a pot, heat until melted.

Step 5   Spread margarine over top of warm bread, then sprinkle 2 Tbs. raw sugar and sugar over it and put bread back in oven 15 more minutes or until bread is done and inserted toothpick comes out clean. Topping should be slightly crystal-like and crunchy.

Healthy and delicious. I am not a big fan of sweet breads, but this was so good I couldn't get enough! The original was made with fresh duck eggs and small extra-sweet Hawaiian apple bananas, but you don't generally find these too often. Regular bananas are still very good. Makes 1 large loaf, or 4-6 servings (8 if you can restrain yourself!).

Baby Fruit Cakes

(⊗ on cherries)   (▯ on cherries)

- **3 Tbs. dried cherries**
- **3 Tbs. dried cranberries**
- **8 (more if needed) dried apricots** (cut into ¼ inch pieces)
- **6 (more if needed) dried pears** (cut into ¼ inch pieces)
- **10 (more if needed) dried dates** (cut into ¼ inch pieces)
- **1 cup flour**
- **½ cup sugar**
- **⅝ tsp. baking powder**
- **⅛ tsp. salt**
- **⅛ tsp. ground cinnamon**
- **⅛ tsp. ground cloves**
- **⅛ tsp. ground ginger**
- **⅛ tsp. ground nutmeg**
- **⅛ tsp. ground allspice**
- **⅓ cup chopped walnuts**
- **⅓ cup raisins**
- **1 large beaten egg**
- **⅓ cup melted *parve* margarine**
- **2 Tbs. kosher cooking sherry**
- **3 Tbs. water**
- **12 cupcake liners**
- **12 whole dried or maraschino cherries** (stems removed)

	Step 1	Preheat oven to 275° F, combine fruits to make 1 cup total. Set aside.
	Step 2	Combine flour, sugar, baking powder, salt and spices, blending thoroughly.
	Step 3	Add fruits, nuts and raisins, stir to coat well. Add next 4 ingredients and blend.
	Step 4	Place cupcake liners in a muffin tin and spoon into cupcake liners (about ¾ full).
	Step 5	Press dough in to fill liners, top each with a cherry and bake 1 hour.

Bursting with flavor, this is better than using standard candied fruits. Makes 12 cakes.

Parve From-Scratch Brownies

¾ **cup flour**

½ **tsp. baking powder**

dash salt

1¼ **cups sugar** (divided)

¼ **cup cocoa**

½ **cup (1 stick)** *parve* **margarine**

2 **eggs** (beaten with a mixer until foamy)

1 **tsp. vanilla extract**

½ **cup chopped walnuts** (optional)

½ **batch** *Parve Chocolate Ready-To-Use Icing* (optional- p. 120)

Step 1   Sift together flour, baking powder and salt in a mixing bowl, blend and set aside.

Step 2   Mix together cocoa and ½ cup sugar in a separate bowl.

Step 3   Put margarine in a saucepan on low heat to melt. Add cocoa mixture to pot.

Step 4   Bring mixture to a boil 1 minute, take off heat and set aside.

Step 5   Put eggs in a bowl and beat with a hand mixer, add remaining ¾ cup sugar while still beating.

Step 6   Gradually add original flour mixture to eggs, stir by hand to blend, then add cocoa mixture and vanilla as still stirring.

Step 7   Add nuts if desired, stirring together slightly (do not blend thoroughly).

Step 8   Pour batter in a greased 9 x 13 or 7 x 12 inch pan (can be slightly smaller if no nuts are used), and bake ½ hour in a preheated 350º F oven.

Step 9   Let cool completely then frost with icing if desired, and cut into bars.

Delicious chewy-gooey brownies. Based on a recipe from a friend, and well worth the trouble. Makes about 16-20 brownies.

These can also be used for *Fancy Chocolate Mint Brownies* (opposite page).

Fancy Chocolate Mint Brownies

1½ cups powdered sugar

3 Tbs. melted parve margarine

4 tsp. *Parve Milk* (p. 85), or other *parve* milk alternative

¾ tsp. mint extract

green food coloring

1 batch fresh baked non-iced *Parve From-Scratch Brownies* (p. 386)

2 Tbs. *Parve Chocolate Ready-To-Use Icing* (p. 120)

Step 1   Blend first 4 ingredients and coloring drops to desired hue. Spread on brownies.

Step 2   Melt chocolate icing on low, put in pastry tube, squeeze out in lengthwise stripes.

Step 3   Drag knife perpendicular through stripes for wave pattern, then cut. Makes 12-16.

☆ ☆

Ice-Box Cake (Chocolate Wafer Roll)

"Whipped Cream" =
{
D- ⅔ (8 oz.) pkg. (2 cups) thawed dairy whipped cream.
P- ⅔ (8 oz.) pkg. (2 cups) thawed *parve* whipped cream.
M- ⅔ (8 oz.) pkg. (2 cups) thawed *parve* whipped cream.
}

¾ tsp. vanilla extract (optional)

14 *Nabisco® Style Famous Chocolate Wafers®* (p. 119)

Step 1   Gently blend together "Whipped Cream" with extract, if desired.

Step 2   Set 1 wafer flat, spread "Whipped Cream" on it, set 1 wafer on top.

Step 3   Repeat with about 5 wafers, then assemble them together to make a log.

Step 4   Set log sideways in bed of "Whipped Cream" on a plate or loaf pan. Frost with more "Whipped Cream".

Step 5   Chill 4 hours or overnight. Slice diagonally (it makes it prettier) and serve.

Keep refrigerated. The wafers absorb moisture from the "Whipped Cream", and expand to make a tender cake. Unfortunately, the original wafer cookies aren't kosher. However, with the "recreated" recipe it's easy to make this wonderful classic recipe. Makes 4-8 servings.

Pumpkin Muffins

½ cup *parve* margarine

1½ cups brown sugar (packed)

2 beaten eggs

1 cup canned pumpkin

4 Tbs. *Parve Milk* (p. 85), or other *parve* milk alternative

1¾ tsp. *Pumpkin Pie Spice* (p. 434)

2 tsp. baking powder

¼ tsp. baking soda

2 cups flour

½ cup chopped walnuts (optional)

Step 1   Combine margarine and sugar in a mixing bowl and beat together until fluffy.

Step 2   Stir in pumpkin, *Parve Milk* and blend thoroughly.

Step 3   Combine spice, baking powder, baking soda and flour, blending well.

Step 4   Add flour mixture to pumpkin and beat together, then stir in nuts if desired.

Step 5   Line muffin tins with cupcake liners, fill each one up with batter and smooth out the tops.

Step 6   Bake in preheated 375º F oven 20-25 minutes or until inserted toothpick comes out clean, then let cool.

Delightful flavor, and a great way to use up extra pumpkin. Makes 1 dozen large muffins.

Parve From-Scratch Cakes

Basic Cake: (equivalent to 1 pkg. cake mix):

2 cups bleached all-purpose flour (sifted after measuring)

1½ cups sugar

1 Tbs. baking powder

¼ tsp. baking soda

1 tsp. salt

1⅓ cup water

½ cup avocado or other vegetable oil (⅓ cup can be used, but will be drier)

3 large eggs

Cake Flavors:

Chocolate: ¼ cup sugar + ½ cup cocoa + 1 tsp. vanilla extract

Devil's Food: Double "Chocolate" + 1 tsp. baking soda + 3 Tbs. water + 1 tsp. oil

Lemon: 1¼ tsp. dried grated lemon peel + 1½ tsp. lemon extract + 4 drops red
food coloring + 2 drops yellow food coloring

Orange: 1½ tsp. dried grated orange peel + 1 Tbs. lemon extract + 10 drops red
food coloring + 8 drops yellow coloring + substitute orange juice for water

Spice: 2¼ tsp. *Pumpkin Pie Spice* (p. 434)

White: 1 tsp. pure vanilla extract + substitute 4 egg whites for eggs

Yellow: 1½ tsp. pure vanilla extract + 4 drops red food coloring

- Step 1   Grease and flour one or more cake pans, or insert liners in muffin tins; Set aside.
- Step 2   Blend dry Basic Cake and one dry Cake Flavor ingredients in large mixing bowl.
- Step 3   Add all liquid Basic Cake and Cake Flavor ingredients liquid ingredients to bowl.
- Step 4   Beat batter until smooth and well blended. Preheat oven to 350º F.
- Step 5   Pour batter into pans and bake. For each specific pan, times are approximately
as follows: For 24 paper-lined cupcakes, bake about 20-25 minutes.
For 2 (8-inch) round baking pans: 35-40 minutes; 2 (9-inch) round baking pans: 30-35 minutes.
For 1 (9 x 13 inch) rectangular baking pan: 35-40 minutes; 1 Bundt® cake pan: 40-45 minutes.
- Step 6   Bake until inserted toothpick comes out clean or cake starts to separate from
pan. Let cake cool slightly, then remove from pan and cool on racks. Makes 12 servings.

Duncan Hines® Style Tiara Desserts

These came out in the early to mid-1980s, but they were taken off the market. Duncan Hines® was kind enough to provide their customers with the recipes for those who asked.

With permission from Pinnacle Foods Corporation, the following recipes are duplicated here for all the Tiara Dessert variations from their *Duncan Hines® Tiara Dessert Recipes* booklet. The original Duncan Hines recipe will be under D. (Duncan Hines currently makes *parve* cake mixes, but the ingredients in the originals were actually dairy.)

You'll see, Tiaras are delicious, pretty and worth the effort. If the special pan has been used in a *treifah* oven, they can't be *kashered* due to the coatings. However, they can be found brand new online and at kitchen supply stores. Look for a "10-inch torte pan". They are fluted and have the center well exactly like the original Tiara pans. I highly recommend getting one or two.

Baking with the Special Pan: Pour batter (3 cups) into greased pan, (flouring is not needed). (Use extra batter for cupcakes.) Bake as recipes indicate, until inserted toothpick comes out clean. Cool pan on rack 5-10 minutes, then invert cake onto rack after baking. When cool, set on a serving plate well-side-up, and fill.

Making An Imitation: If you can't find a pan, the method below (not nearly as pretty) has to suffice…

✿ ✿ ✿ ✿ ✿ ✿ ✿ ✿ ✿ ✿ ✿ ✿ ✿ ✿ ✿ ✿ ✿ ✿ ✿

Imitation Duncan Hines® Style Tiara Dessert Cake Instructions
1 package cake mix or 1 batch *Parve From-Scratch Cakes* (p. 389)

✪ Step 1   Fix cake mix or *Parve From-Scratch Cakes* according to package or directions.

✪ Step 2   Grease 9-inch round pan thoroughly, do not flour. Pour in batter (about 2¼ cups).

✪ Step 3   Bake as directed, until an inserted toothpick comes out clean.

✪ Step 4   Cool on rack 15 minutes. Put on serving plate rounded-side-down (upside down).

✪ Step 5   Using a sharp knife, insert it into cake ½-inch from edge, about ½ an inch deep. Cut cake ½ inch from edge all the way around to make a perfect circle. Cut center crisscross.

✪ Step 6   Cut hole in crisscross, trim bottom smoothly as possible (don't "saw it"), carefully remove inner part of cake to ½ inch deep. Inside doesn't have to look pretty, but border does.

✪ Step 7   You should now have a cake with a "well" in the middle, which will be used for filling. (Since each recipe is for 1 full-size real Tiara, there may be extra filling when making 1 of these smaller cakes, but not quite enough filling for 2. Extra cut out cake scraps can be eaten.)

Cakes can be frozen until needed, if desired. The type of cake mix needed will be listed within "Tiara" in the recipes for each Tiara Dessert. 1 pkg. cake mix makes 2 small Tiara cakes.

(🧁 (3 berries) **Strawberry Chocolate Mousse Tiara Dessert** 🧁 (3 berries)

1 pint small strawberries

"Tiara" = {
  D- Duncan Hines® Swiss Chocolate Cake.
  P- *Parve From-Scratch Chocolate Cake* (p. 389).
  M- *Parve From-Scratch Chocolate Cake* (p. 389).
}

"Chips" = {
  D- ½ cup milk chocolate chips + 2 Tbs. water.
  P- ½ cup *parve* chocolate chips + 6 Tbs. *parve* liquid creamer.
  M- ½ cup *parve* chocolate chips + 6 Tbs. *parve* liquid creamer.
}

1 (8 oz.) container *parve* non-dairy whipped cream topping (3 cups)

⚜ Step 1   Fix cake mix according to directions. For 9-inch pan- Do Steps 2-7 in *"Imitation Duncan Hines® Style Tiara Dessert Instructions"* (p. 390). For real Tiara ("Torte") pan- Pour into greased pan, bake 21-24 minutes or until an inserted toothpick comes out clean.

⚜ Step 2   Reserve 4 strawberries of similar shape and size, and set them aside for garnish.

⚜ Step 3   Thinly slice enough strawberries (placed flat-side down) to line "well" outer edge.

⚜ Step 4   Halve more strawberries and place flat-side-down to cover entire "well" bottom.

⚜ Step 5   On low in pan, melt "Chips" with liquid, stir until smooth.

⚜ Step 6   Remove 2 Tbs. chocolate and set aside. For D- Chill remainder 10 minutes until thickened but still creamy. For P or M- Add directly to whipped cream.

⚜ Step 7   In medium bowl, fold chocolate into whipped cream for mousse, blending well.

⚜ Step 8   Spread into cool "Tiara's" "well" and chill ½ hour, then drizzle 2 Tbs. warm chocolate over mousse.

⚜ Step 9   Garnish top of "Tiara" with reserved 4 strawberries in symmetrical pattern.

⚜ Step 10   Chill 4 hours, or for best results chill overnight. Serve cold.

☺   ☺   ☺

"Raspberry Chocolate Mousse Tiara Dessert", substitute ½ cup warm red raspberry preserves for strawberries. Omit Steps 2-3, and for Step 4, spread preserves in "Tiara's" "well". Proceed with remaining Steps 5-9 as normal, but omit Step 9 and do Step 10.

Chocolate Amaretto Mousse Tiara Dessert

"Chips" =
- **D-** ½ cup milk chocolate chips + 2 Tbs. water.
- **P-** ½ cup *parve* chocolate chips + 6 Tbs. *parve* liquid creamer.
- **M-** ½ cup *parve* chocolate chips + 6 Tbs. *parve* liquid creamer.

1 (8 oz.) container *parve* non-dairy whipped cream topping (3 cups)

½ tsp. almond extract

"Tiara" =
- **D-** Duncan Hines® Dark Chocolate Fudge Cake.
- **P-** *Parve From-Scratch Devil's Food Cake* (p. 389).
- **M-** *Parve From-Scratch Devil's Food Cake* (p. 389).

¼ cup blanched sliced almonds

⊛ **Step 1** Fix cake mix according to directions. For 9-inch pan- Do Steps 2-7 in *"Imitation Duncan Hines® Style Tiara Dessert Instructions"* (p. 390). For real Tiara ("Torte") pan- Pour into greased pan, bake 21-24 minutes or until an inserted toothpick comes out clean.

⊛ **Step 2** On low in pan, melt "Chips" with liquid, stir until smooth.

⊛ **Step 3** Add extract to chocolate blending well. For D- Chill 10 minutes until thickened but still creamy. For P or M- Add directly to whipped cream.

⊛ **Step 4** In medium bowl, fold chocolate into whipped cream for mousse, blending well.

⊛ **Step 5** Spread mousse evenly into "well" of cooled "Tiara", and chill ½-hour.

⊛ **Step 6** Sprinkle almonds on top of mousse then refrigerate 2 hours. Serve cool.

Chocolate Mousse Tiara Dessert

"Chips" = {
D- ½ cup milk chocolate chips + 2 Tbs. water.
P- ½ cup *parve* chocolate chips + 6 Tbs. *parve* liquid creamer..
M- ½ cup *parve* chocolate chips + 6 Tbs. *parve* liquid creamer.
}

1 (8 oz.) container *parve* non-dairy whipped cream topping (3 cups)

"Tiara" = {
D- Duncan Hines® Swiss Chocolate Cake.
P- *Parve From-Scratch Chocolate Cake* (p. 389).
M- *Parve From-Scratch Chocolate Cake* (p. 389).
}

Step 1 Fix cake mix according to directions. For 9-inch pan- Do Steps 2-7 in *"Imitation Duncan Hines® Style Tiara Dessert Instructions"* (p. 390). For real Tiara ("Torte") pan- Pour into greased pan, bake 21-24 minutes or until an inserted toothpick comes out clean.

Step 2 Melt "Chips" in pan on low, stir until smooth. Set aside 2 Tbs. chocolate. (D- First chill remainder 10 minutes until thick but creamy.) Add chocolate to cream, blend, put in "well".

Step 3 Chill ½ hour. Drizzle 2 Tbs. warm chocolate on top. Chill 4 hours, or overnight.

✡ ✡

(cherries) Black Forest Tiara Dessert (cherries)

½ tsp. almond extract

1 (8 oz.) container *parve* non-dairy whipped cream topping (3 cups)

"Tiara" = {
D- Duncan Hines® Devil's Food Cake.
P- *Parve From-Scratch Devil's Food Cake* (p. 389).
M- *Parve From-Scratch Devil's Food Cake* (p. 389).
}

1 (16 oz.) can cherry pie filling

Step 1 Fix cake mix according to directions. For 9-inch pan- Do Steps 2-7 in *"Imitation Duncan Hines® Style Tiara Dessert Instructions"* (p. 390). For real Tiara ("Torte") pan- Pour into greased pan, bake 21-24 minutes or until an inserted toothpick comes out clean.

Step 2 Add almond extract to cream, blend. Spread evenly in "Tiara" well, chill ½ hour.

Step 3 Spoon cherry pie filling evenly in "well", smoothing it out but having a visible layer of mousse surrounding it. Chill 2 hours then serve. (My personal favorite.)

(3 cherries) Cherries & Cream Cheese Tiara Dessert (3 cherries)

"Cake Mix " =
- **D-** Duncan Hines® Butter Recipe Golden Cake (omit oil).
- **P-** *Parve From-Scratch Yellow Cake* (p. 389, omit oil).
- **M-** *Parve From-Scratch Yellow Cake* (p. 389, omit oil).

"Butter" =
- **D-** 1 stick (½ cup) softened butter or margarine.
- **P-** 1 tsp. *parve* butter extract + ½ cup *parve* softened margarine.
- **M-** 1 tsp. *parve* butter extract + ½ cup *parve* softened margarine.

"Cream Cheese" =
- **D-** ⅓ cup (3 oz. bar) real cream cheese (softened).
- **P-** ½ cup warm *Parve Imitation Cream Cheese* (p. 105).
- **M-** ½ cup warm *Parve Imitation Cream Cheese* (p. 105).

2 Tbs. *parve* margarine (softened)

¾ cup powdered sugar (sifted)

¼ tsp. vanilla

½ tsp. *parve* butter flavored extract

1 (8 oz.) container *parve* non-dairy whipped cream topping (3 cups)

1 (16 oz.) can cherry pie filling

Step 1   Blend "Cake Mix" and "Butter" in bowl, add water and egg amounts as directed.

Step 2   For 9-inch pan- Do *"Imitation Duncan Hines® Style Tiara Dessert Instructions"* (p. 390) Steps 2-7. For real Tiara ("Torte") pan- Pour into greased pan, bake 19-21 minutes or until inserted toothpick comes out clean.

Step 3   In small bowl, beat "Cream Cheese" and margarine until light and fluffy, gradually add sugar and vanilla, blending well, and spread mixture evenly into "well" of cool "Tiara".
(*Parve Cream Cheese Ready-To-Use Icing* (p. 121) can be substituted cream cheese mixture.)

Step 4   In a medium bowl, fold butter extract gently into whipped cream, until well blended and color is uniform to make a mousse.

Step 5   Spread mousse evenly into "well" of "Tiara", and refrigerate ½-hour.

Step 6   Spoon pie filling on top (smooth out keeping an edge of mousse visible).

Step 7   Chill 4 hours, or even overnight for best results. Serve cool.

☺   ☺   ☺

For **"Cherries and Cream Tiara Dessert"**, omit "Cream Cheese", margarine, sugar, and vanilla, skipping Steps 3-5. In Step 7, cake needs to be refrigerated only 2 hours before serving.

Cheesecakes and Pies

Parve Sara Lee® Style Cheesecake

1 pre-baked 8 x 8-inch *Graham Cracker Pie Crust* (p. 118- for cheesecakes)

2½ Tbs. *parve* margarine (divided)

1⅓ cups *Parve Imitation Sour Cream* (p. 105- divided)

1¾ pkg. (1¾ cups) store-bought *parve* cream cheese (don't use homemade)

1½ Tbs. corn starch

¾ cup sugar

1¼ tsp. vanilla extract (divided)

3 Tbs. powdered sugar

☘ **Step 1** Set margarine, sour cream and cream cheese out to become room temperature.

☘ **Step 2** Put 1½ Tbs. margarine, ¾ cup sour cream, cream cheese, corn starch, sugar and ¾ tsp. vanilla in a mixing bowl, and beat well until smooth and sugar is dissolved.

☘ **Step 3** Set a pan of water in the oven (to prevent cracking), and preheat it to 350º F.

☘ **Step 4** Pour mixture into crust, bake 50 minutes (center won't be set). Don't let edges brown. (If homemade "cream cheese" is used, it can take up to ½ hour longer and turns brown!)

☘ **Step 5** Let cool slightly and set aside. Melt remaining 2 tsp. margarine, add last 9 Tbs. sour cream, ½ tsp. vanilla, and powdered sugar. Blend thoroughly to make icing.

☘ **Step 6** Spread icing evenly on cheesecake, then bake 10 minutes or until icing is firm.

☘ **Step 7** Take a knife or spatula and insert it around pie pan rim to loosen (if necessary).

☘ **Step 8** Chill 2-4 hours or overnight for best results. Makes 1 large cheesecake.

☺   ☺   ☺

For **"Parve Sara Lee® Style Cherry Cheesecake"**, after Step 8, top cold *Cheesecake* evenly with 1 (21 oz.) can cherry pie filling. Chill. Makes 1 large cheesecake. 🍪 (☉ cherries) 🍪 (all)

☺   ☺   ☺

For **"Mini Cheesecakes"**, make *Mini Graham Cracker Crusts* (p. 118) for cheesecakes. Do Steps 1-3. For Step 4 bake ½ hour. Let cool. Do Steps 5-8. Makes 12. 🍪 🍪

☺   ☺   ☺

For **"Mini Cherry Cheesecakes"**, after Step 8, top each chilled *Mini Cheesecake* evenly with 1 (21 oz.) can cherry pie filling. Makes 12. 🍪 (☉ cherries) 🍪 (▧ cherries if only they are eaten)

395

Chocolate Cream Slices

"Cream Cheese" =
- **D-** 1 (8 oz.) pkg. cream cheese.
- **P-** 1 cup *parve* imitation cream cheese.
- **M-** 1 cup *parve* imitation cream cheese.

1½ tsp. *parve* margarine

½ cup brown sugar

2 tsp. vanilla extract

3 Tbs. cocoa

½ cup chopped pecans (optional)

2 cups *parve* non-dairy whipped cream (divided)

1 baked *Flaky* (p. 119) or *Graham Cracker Pie Crust* (p. 118- 9-inch)

Step 1 Lightly heat "Cream Cheese" and margarine until softened.

Step 2 Combine brown sugar, vanilla, and cocoa with "Cream Cheese" and margarine in a mixing bowl, and beat or stir until well blended.

Step 3 Stir in pecans if desired, then fold in 1½ cups whipped cream container.

Step 4 Put mixture in pie crust, smoothing it out evenly, then chill until firm.

Step 5 Spread remaining ½ cup whipped cream over top of pie, then chill again.

Step 6 If pie is square, cut into 12-16 small squares, if it is round, cut in 8 traditional pie slices.

Rich and delicious, this can also be garnished with chopped nuts, chocolate shavings or both. Homemade *Parve Cream Cheese* (p. 105) can be used successfully, but the consistency is looser and more like pudding-like than firm like fudge or cheesecake. Makes 8-16 servings depending on how you slice it.

Pretty Orange Pie

½ cup sugar

⅓ cup flour, OR ¼ cup potato starch

2½ cups orange juice (divided)

2½ Tbs. softened *parve* margarine or avocado oil (or other vegetable oil)

2 (11 oz.) cans (2½ cups) Mandarin oranges (drained and divided)

1 pre-baked *Flaky* (p. 119) or *Graham Cracker Pie Crust* (p. 118- 9-inch)

Step 1   Blend sugar, flour and ½ cup orange juice thoroughly and put in a medium pot.

Step 2   Add margarine and last 2 cups orange juice, blend well and heat on medium low.

Step 3   Stir constantly until thickened, and then take off of heat.

Step 4   Mince 1 can oranges, stir into pot and pour into pie crust. Let pie chill 1 hour.

Step 5   Top decoratively with remaining can oranges. (A symmetrical swirl pattern radiating from the center is very nice.) Slice and serve cold or room temperature.

Refreshingly different. Other fruits and juices can be used. If using a 20 oz. can of pineapple chunks, reserve 1 cup for rings on top, and mince only ¾ cup in Step 3. Makes 6-8 servings.

Parve Pumpkin Pie

1⅓ cups canned plain pumpkin or mashed cooked pumpkin

rounded ¼ tsp. salt

¾ cup *Parve Milk* (p. 85), OR other *parve* milk alternative

2 medium eggs (½ cup)

⅓ cup sugar

1 tsp. *Pumpkin Pie Spice* (p. 434)

1 (9 inch) store-bought deep-dish or raw *Flaky Pie Crust* (p. 119)

Step 1   Preheat oven to 425° F. Beat together first 6 ingredients until thoroughly mixed, then pour into pie crust. (Crust can then be lined with foil strips to keep it from getting too dark.)

Step 2   Bake 45-55 minutes or until toothpick inserted 1 inch from crust comes out clean.

Step 3   Place on a cooling rack 2 hours. (Center will set as it cools.) Makes 6-8 servings.

Mincemeat Pie

⅓ cup orange juice

2 tsp. lemon juice

1 cup raisins

2 medium (2 cups) apples (peeled, cored and finely chopped)

⅓ cup apple cider

⅔ cup brown sugar

¼ tsp. ground cinnamon

¼ tsp. ground nutmeg

¼ tsp. ground cloves

2⅔ cup brandy (ginger flavored works really well)

2⅔ cup store-bought or homemade *Parve Soy Crumbles* (p. 110)

1 (9 inch) store-bought or raw *Flaky Pie Crust* (p. 119)

1 raw *Flaky Pie Crust* top (p. 119)

❋ Step 1   Combine first 5 ingredients in a large pot and cook until apples are soft and liquid is reduced (about 15-20 minutes).

❋ Step 2   Stir in next 6 ingredients and take off heat.

❋ Step 3   Line a pie plate with first crust, then put mixture in crust.

❋ Step 4   Cut top crust in 1-inch strips and weave them lattice-style on top.

❋ Step 5   Bake in preheated 400º F oven ½ hour or until crust starts to turn brown.

A British classic. Store refrigerated for longer than a day. This is even better when sitting a day, the flavors blend. If it sits a few more days, it gets very spicy. Best served slightly heated. Makes a single 9-inch pie.

Pecan Pie

4 small or 3 large eggs (slightly beaten)

1 cup corn syrup

2 tsp. molasses

⅓ cup sugar

1 Tbs. lemon juice

2 tsp. vanilla extract

¼ cup melted *parve* **margarine**

1 cup pecan halves and pieces

1 (9 inch) store-bought or raw *Flaky Pie Crust* (p. 119)

Step 1   Combine first 7 ingredients in a bowl and blend thoroughly.

Step 2   Put pecans in crust and pour mixture over top. (Line with foil so as not to burn)

Step 3   Bake in a preheated 350°F oven 50-60 minutes or until a knife inserted an inch from pie crust edge comes out clean. Let cool. (Center gels when cool.) Makes 6-8 servings.

✿ ✿

Arby's® Style Turnovers

½ pkg. puff pastry sheets (thawed 20 minutes & cut into four 6-inch squares)

1 (16 oz.) can apple or cherry pie filling

5 Tbs. powdered sugar

4 tsp. hot water

Step 1   Place 2 Tbs. filling in the center of each square, then brush edges with water.

Step 2   Fold one corner to another to form triangles, press edges with a fork to seal.

Step 3   Place on a well-greased cookie sheet and spray or coat generously with oil.

Step 4   Bake 25 minutes in a preheated 400° F oven or until golden brown.

Step 5   Let cool on wire racks. Meanwhile, blend together sugar and water until smooth, and drizzle it decoratively over turnovers. Let sugar harden and serve.

This recipe uses pre-made filling to make it as "easy as pie". Makes 4 turnovers.

McDonald's® Style Pies

½ pkg. puff pastry sheets (thawed 20 minutes & cut into four 6-inch squares)

1 (16 oz.) can apple or cherry pie filling

4-6 cups avocado or other vegetable oil

water

1 clean chemical-free misting bottle

Step 1   Place about 2 Tbs. fruit filling in the center of each square.

Step 2   Brush edges of dough with water, and fold one end to the other to form rectangles.

Step 3   Seal edges with a fork, put them on plastic wrap and freeze them 45 minutes.

Step 4   Take a misting bottle and spray all surfaces of pies with water then put back in freezer 1 hour.

Step 5   Start heating oil (to 375º F in a deep fryer), meanwhile fill a bowl with cold water.

Step 6   Quickly submerge each whole pie in water and take it out immediately.

Step 7   Carefully and quickly drop pies in deep fryer, making sure that they are submerged. Be extremely careful because they will splatter.

Step 8   Put a strainer or a basket over pies to make sure they stay submerged and cook properly.

Step 9   Fry 5 minutes or until they are golden brown, gently take them out and drain them on paper towel lined plates.

Step 10   Put pies in a pre-warmed oven 10-30 minutes or until ready to serve.

With this recipe, you won't have to miss out on the taste. Remember the warning on the package label- "Caution: Filling is hot". They can be made with thawed store-bought ready-made turnovers. Makes 4 pies.

These can be frozen after Step 6, just put them in zipper bags and seal them. When ready to use, just take them out and fry them.

Kellogg's® Style Pop-Tarts®

3 cups flour (plus extra for rolling on)

1 Tbs. sugar

½ tsp. salt

½ tsp. baking powder

¾ cups *parve* margarine

1 lightly beaten egg

½ tsp. lemon juice

¼ cup water

1 cup favorite flavor jam (divided)

¾ cup powdered sugar

¼ tsp. vanilla extract

1 Tbs. warm *Parve Milk* (p. 85)**, OR other *parve* milk alternative**

colored sugar or decorative sprinkles

	Step 1	Combine first 4 dry ingredients in a mixing bowl, add margarine and blend well.
	Step 2	Add next 3 ingredients and knead together until thoroughly blended.
	Step 3	Divide dough into 8 portions, roll each into a ball and put in zipper bags.
	Step 4	Refrigerate ½ hour. Keep balls refrigerated until ready to use. Flour a flat surface.
	Step 5	Roll 1 dough ball out to 7 x 10 inches (cut and piece together as needed).
	Step 6	Cut dough into 2 rectangles (5 x 3½ inches). Pierce one rectangle with holes.
	Step 7	Evenly spread 1 Tbs. jam ½ inch from edges on solid rectangle.
	Step 8	Put pierced rectangle atop jam coated one, and press all edges together to seal.
	Step 9	Gently roll up onto spatula. Transfer to a cookie sheet or glass baking dish pierced-side-up.
	Step 10	Repeat Steps 5-8 for other dough balls, and let cool when done.
	Step 11	Bake 15 minutes in a preheated 425° F until firm and dry.
	Step 12	Combine sugar, *parve* milk, and vanilla blending well, and spread evenly on tarts.
	Step 13	Sprinkle tarts with sugar or sprinkles. Let glaze harden and put in zipper bags.

Store tarts 1 week at room temperature or refrigerated, or freeze up to 3 months. Makes 8 tarts.

Chocolate icing, or brown sugar mixed with cinnamon and a bit of margarine can also be used.

Candies, Puddings, Jells & Ice Creams

Candies

Coconut Truffles

1 batch *Parve Dark Chocolate Fudge* (without nuts) (p. 405- do Steps 1-2)

¾ cup grated coconut (divided)

1 tsp. rum extract

Step 1   Add 6 Tbs. coconut, and rum extract to fudge.

Step 2   Form into ½ inch balls, roll in remaining 6 Tbs. coconut and place on wax paper.

Step 3   Chill 2 hours. These keep for a very long time when stored in airtight containers.

Delightfully addictive! Makes 2 dozen.

☆ ☆

Nut Truffles

1 batch *Parve Dark Chocolate Fudge* (without nuts) (p. 405- do Steps 1-2)

¾ cup finely chopped nuts

1 tsp. almond extract

⅓ cup *Cinnamon Sugar* (p. 434)

Step 1   Keep fudge on very low heat stirring constantly until melted and smooth.

Step 2   Add nuts and almond extract to fudge blending well. Set aside.

Step 3   Put cinnamon sugar in a separate bowl.

Step 4   Form fudge into ½-inch balls. Roll in sugar mixture and place on wax paper.

Step 5   Chill 2 hours and store in airtight container. These keep a very long time.

These are also very good. For a great gift idea, combine with *Coconut Truffles* (above) for variety. Makes 2 dozen.

Parve Peanut Butter Cup Bars

1 (18 oz.) jar peanut butter or tahini

½ cup + 1 Tbs. *parve* margarine (divided)

2¾ cup powdered sugar (add ¼ cup extra for tahini)

1 bag *parve* semisweet chocolate chips

- Step 1   Combine peanut butter (or tahini) and ½ cup margarine together in a pot.
- Step 2   Put peanut butter on low heat and melt, blending together (Do not blend tahini and margarine with heat, mix by hand.)
- Step 3   Add powdered sugar to mixture and blend thoroughly.
- Step 4   Grease a 9 x 13-inch baking dish, press mixture into it and flatten it out smooth.
- Step 5   Combine chocolate chips and additional 1 Tbs. margarine, heat until melted and blend together.
- Step 6   Spread chocolate mixture evenly on top of peanut butter.
- Step 7   Chill until hardened, and slice with a knife for individual bars.

These are from an anonymous friend. This recipe be eaten at a meat meal, and when made with tahini, these can even be eaten by those with peanut allergies! Makes 4 dozen.

If desired, ½ batch of *Parve Dark Chocolate Fudge* (without nuts- p. 405) can be substituted for chocolate chips.

Tahini can be found at larger supermarkets or health food stores (if there is a good *hechsher*).

Parve Mounds® Style Bars

2 cups shredded coconut

2 Tbs. light corn syrup

¾ cup powdered sugar

2 batch *Parve Dark Chocolate Fudge* (without nuts) (p. 405- do Steps 1-2)

❀ Step 1   Heat fudge on very low heat stirring until smooth and well-blended, keeping it barely warm and stirring often. (If fudge dries out add a few drops of water.)

❀ Step 2   Line a cookie sheet with plastic wrap, and dab a portion of fudge in 24 (about 1 x 2½-inch) spots on plastic (slightly larger than candy would be).

❀ Step 3   Put cookie sheet in refrigerator 5 minutes to harden.

❀ Step 4   Put coconut in mixing bowl, and put corn syrup in a medium sized pot.

❀ Step 5   Heat corn syrup in a until just starting to boil, then pour coconut into corn syrup and blend thoroughly.

❀ Step 6   Gradually add powdered sugar to coconut and blend thoroughly until stiff.

❀ Step 7   Divide coconut mixture into 24 portions, and squeeze each portion together into 24 (½ x 3-inch) finger-like mounds.

❀ Step 8   Take cookie sheet out of refrigerator and place coconut portions on top of dabbed fudge spots, pressing it into place.

❀ Step 9   Put cookie sheet in refrigerator 5 minutes to chill.

❀ Step 10   Take a spoonful of hot fudge, and drizzle it over each mound to coat completely meeting up with the lower dabbed fudge.

❀ Step 11   Chill in refrigerator until hard, and store in an airtight container. Makes 2 dozen "snack size" bars.

☺   ☺   ☺

For **"Parve Almond Joy® Style Bars"**, You'll need 48 plain unsalted roasted almonds. During Step 7, as you squeeze the coconut into place, press 2 almonds into each coconut mound. Continue with last Steps as normal. Makes 2 dozen "snack size" bars. 🥛(🥛almonds only) 🥛

Parve Dark Chocolate Fudge

⅔ cup *parve* margarine

2 tsp. vanilla extract

¾ cup *parve* liquid non-dairy creamer (no substitutions)

1 cup cocoa

7⅓ cups powdered sugar

1 cup chopped walnuts (optional)

Step 1   Combine first 4 ingredients in pot and heat on low stirring constantly.

Step 2   Take off heat and gradually add sugar, blending until completely smooth.

Step 3   Blend in nuts if desired, and pour mixture into a greased 7 x 9 inch pan.

Step 4   Chill several hours until firm, then cut into squares. Keep refrigerated.

In this fudge, soy milk *cannot* be substituted for creamer, as it never firms up and the consistency stays a sticky mess like icing. Makes about 2¼ lbs. fudge, and 35-70 pieces (depending on how you slice it).

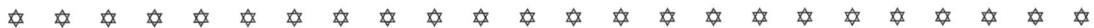

✡ ✡

Parve White Fudge

1 Tbs. *parve* liquid non-dairy creamer or *Parve Cream* (p. 85)

1 cup *parve* imitation cream cheese

1 Tbs. vanilla extract

6⅓ cups powdered sugar (more can be used for firmer fudge, if desired)

½ cup diced dried apricots or candied fruits (optional)

1 cup walnuts (optional)

Step 1   Combine first 3 ingredients in pot. Heat on low, stir until soft and smooth.

Step 2   Take off heat. Gradually add sugar, stir until smooth and completely blended.

Step 3   Blend in nuts and apricots (if desired), blending evenly.

Step 4   Pour mixture into a greased 7 x 9-inch pan and spread top out smoothly.

Step 5   Chill several hours until firm, then cut into squares. Keep refrigerated.

Makes about 2½ lbs. fudge, and 35-70 pieces (depending on how you slice it). White Fudge containing the optional fruits and nuts is often referred to as "Divinity".

Parve Coconut Fudge

Parve White Fudge ingredients (prior page- without optionals, do Step 1)

1½ cups sweetened flaked coconut

Step 1   Add coconut to fudge pot and gradually add sugar. Stir until smooth and blended.

Step 2   Pour mixture into a greased 9 x 12-inch pan and spread top out smoothly.

Step 3   Chill several hours until firm, then cut into squares. Keep refrigerated.

Makes about 3¼ lbs. fudge, and 60-120 pieces (depending on how you slice it).

✿ ✿

Bake-less Oat Fudge

1¾ cup sugar

¼ cup brown sugar

1 Tbs. molasses

½ cup *Parve Milk* (p. 85), or other *parve* milk alternative

¾ cup *parve* margarine

¾ cup cocoa

5 cups plain uncooked oatmeal

1 tsp. vanilla extract

optional garnish: chopped peanuts or candy sprinkles

Step 1   Put first 7 ingredients in pot, boil on medium until sugar melts, stirring constantly.

Step 2   Immediately take off heat, then add oats and vanilla, and blend thoroughly.

Step 3   Roll into 1½-inch balls and let cool or chill. Coat in garnish and refrigerate.

This recipe and its variation below are both from an anonymous friend. Makes 5 dozen.

☺   ☺   ☺

For **"Peanut Butter Bake-less Oat Fudge"**, omit cocoa, decrease margarine to ¼ cup, and add ½ cup warm peanut butter (or tahini) just after Step 2. Blend well. Do the rest as normal.

Puddings

From-Scratch Chocolate Pudding

¾ cup sugar

⅛ tsp. salt

¼ cup cocoa

½ cup flour

4 cups *Parve Milk* (p. 85), or other *parve* milk alternative

2 Tbs. *parve* margarine or avocado oil (or other vegetable oil)

1 tsp. vanilla extract

Step 1   Blend sugar, salt, cocoa and flour thoroughly. Set aside or store for later use.

Step 2   Combine *parve* milk, and margarine or oil in a pot, heat on low heat until hot.

Step 3   Stir cocoa mixture into pot and stir until well-blended and raise heat slightly.

Step 4   Keep stirring until thickened. When it bubbles without stirring, add vanilla and blend.

Step 5   Pour into individual custard bowls or a large container and chill.

Creamy old-fashioned pudding. Makes 4-8 servings.

For nearly "instant" pudding mix, the dry ingredients can be shaken in a sealed jar or container and stored until usage. Better yet, 1⅓ cup powdered milk or a 1 qt pouch (for D), or ⅔ cup powdered non-dairy creamer (for P or M) can be added to the dry mixture, so all you need to do is add 4 cups water, the oil and extract when you make it.

☺   ☺   ☺

For **"Chocolate Mint Pudding"** substitute mint extract for vanilla extract.

☺   ☺   ☺

For **"Chocolate-Almond Pudding"**, substitute ¼ tsp. almond extract for vanilla.

☺   ☺   ☺

For **"Chocolate Rum Pudding"** substitute rum extracts for vanilla.

407

Tapioca Pudding

2 Tbs. quick-cooking tapioca

1¾ cups *Parve Milk* (p. 85), or other parve dairy alternative

⅛ tsp. salt

1 small beaten egg

¼ cup sugar

1 tsp. vanilla extract

⅛-¼ tsp. ground cinnamon or ground nutmeg

Step 1   Combine first 6 ingredients in a pot or microwave safe bowl, and let sit 5 minutes.

Step 2   Heat mixture on stove or in microwave, until it comes to a full boil, (stir often).

Step 3   Take off heat, stir in vanilla and cinnamon (or sprinkle cinnamon on top after being chilled), let stand ½-hour. Serve hot or cold, and keep refrigerated.

Classic tapioca with a hint of spice. It's so easy and it's *parve*! Makes 4 servings.

☺   ☺   ☺

For **"Chocolate Tapioca Pudding"**, omit cinnamon or nutmeg, and add 2 Tbs. each more sugar and *parve* milk, and add ⅓ cup *parve* chocolate chips (melt as cooking) in Step 1.

☺   ☺   ☺

For **"Chocolate Mint Tapioca Pudding"**, fix as *Chocolate Tapioca Pudding*, but substitute mint extract for vanilla extract in Step 3.

☺   ☺   ☺

For **"Chocolate-Almond Tapioca Pudding"**, fix as *Chocolate Tapioca Pudding*, but substitute almond extract for vanilla in Step 3.

☺   ☺   ☺

For **"Chocolate Rum Tapioca Pudding"** fix as *Chocolate Tapioca Pudding*, but substitute 2½ tsp. rum extract for vanilla in Step 3.

☺   ☺   ☺

For **"Butterscotch Tapioca Pudding"**, omit cinnamon, and substitute ¼ cup packed brown sugar for sugar in Step 1, and add an additional ½ tsp. *parve* butter flavored extract in Step 3.

☺   ☺   ☺

For **"Butter-Rum Tapioca Pudding"**, fix as *Butterscotch Tapioca Pudding*, but substitute 1½ tsp. rum extract for vanilla in Step 3.

Rice Pudding

1¾ cup *Parve Milk* (p. 85), or other *parve* milk alternative

⅛ tsp. salt

2 large beaten eggs

¼ cup sugar

½ tsp. vanilla

¼ tsp. ground cinnamon or ground nutmeg

1½ cups plain, unflavored cooked white rice

½ cup raisins

Step 1   Blend ingredients thoroughly and pour into a well-greased 11 x 7-inch baking pan.

Step 2   Bake in a preheated 350º F oven 45 minutes to 1-hour or until firm. Keep refrigerated. Serve chilled or warm. Makes 4 servings.

An old-fashioned egg-custard that is a great use for leftover rice. For some interesting additions, add or substitute some coconut or banana slices in Step 1. Another option is to add *parve* chocolate chips (which melts as cooking) in Step 1.

✿ ✿

Bread Pudding

2½ cups *Parve Milk* (p. 85), or other *parve* milk alternative

⅛ tsp. salt

2 small beaten eggs

¼ cup sugar

½ tsp. vanilla

¼ tsp. ground cinnamon or ground nutmeg

3 cups stale chopped bread (trim off crusts, if desired)

½ cup raisins

Step 1   Blend ingredients thoroughly and pour into a well-greased 11 x 7-inch baking pan.

Step 2   Step 3 Bake in a preheated 325º F oven 45-50 minutes or until firm. Keep refrigerated. Serve chilled or warm. Makes 4 servings.

This is a delicious way to use older stale bread, or better yet, an over-abundance of partial *challot* that can't be used for *HaMotzi* on *Shabbat*. You can't get this great flavor from an instant pudding mix.

Jells and Ice Creams

Jell-O® 1-2-3® Style Dessert

1 (12-16 oz.) container (2 cups) *parve* **non-dairy whipped cream**

3½ cups boiling water (divided)

2 (6 oz.) pkgs. (both the same) *parve* **kosher fruit flavored gelatin** (divided)

"Cream Cheese" =
- **D-** 1 (8 oz.) pkg. cream cheese (melted).
- **P-** 1 cup warm *parve* imitation cream cheese.
- **M-** 1 cup warm *parve* imitation cream cheese.

❀ **Step 1**   Spread whipped cream evenly in either a 9 x 13-inch glass baking dish, or 8 individual glass serving bowls. (Don't use metal.) Put in freezer until firm, while doing next step.

❀ **Step 2**   Combine 1¾ cups boiling water, 1 pkg. gelatin and "Cream Cheese", blend well.

❀ **Step 3**   Pour cream cheese mixture on top of firm whipped cream, and chill until firm.

❀ **Step 4**   Stir together remaining 1¾ cups water and last pkg. gelatin and blend well.

❀ **Step 5**   Pour on top of firm cream cheese, and refrigerate until firm. (Do not freeze.)

Serve chilled but not frozen, preferably in glass. This came out in the early 70s, and was revived shortly in the mid-80s. (1 & 2 alone is good also, without the whipped cream!) Makes 8-9 servings.

✡ ✡

Parve Vanilla Ice Cream

2 (½ pt.) pkg. (2 cups) *parve* **liquid non-dairy whip topping** (shaken)

2 tsp. sugar (varies with other flavors)

1 tsp. vanilla extract

food coloring (optional)

❀ **Step 1**   Pour whip in a chilled mixing bowl and beat about 5 minutes until thick and fluffy.

❀ **Step 2**   Beat in remaining ingredients, put in large sealed container and freeze 24 hours.

Many thanks go to Zipporah Berlove (now Mrs. Zipporah Rosen) for this great recipe. (Taste testing is a must.) Many different varieties are listed on the opposite page. Makes 1 quart.

A unique thing about this recipe is there are no raw eggs in the mixture. For some reason, most parve whip ice cream recipes call for raw eggs. No worry about that here.

For **"Parve Chocolate Ice Cream"**, add ¼ cup cocoa and 1-2 Tbs. sugar. (For a "sour" chocolate, add an additional 2 Tbs. *Parve Imitation Sour Cream* found on p. 105).

☺   ☺   ☺

For **"Parve Coffee Ice Cream"**, add ½ -1 tsp. instant coffee and 1-2 Tbs. sugar.

☺   ☺   ☺

For **"Parve Mocha Ice Cream"**, add 3 Tbs. cocoa, ½ tsp. instant coffee and 1-2 Tbs. sugar.

☺   ☺   ☺

For **"Parve Butterscotch Ice Cream"**, use ½ cup brown sugar, add 6 drops yellow coloring.

☺   ☺   ☺

For **"Parve Strawberry Ice Cream"**, omit vanilla and sugar, add ¾ cup strawberry jam and 8 drops red food color, OR omit vanilla and add 1 (10 oz.) pkg. nearly pureed frozen strawberries.

☺   ☺   ☺

For **"Parve Mint Ice Cream"**, use ½ tsp. mint as vanilla, add 1 Tbs. sugar and 4 drops green.

☺   ☺   ☺

For **"Parve Mint Chocolate Chip Ice Cream"**, add 1 cup chocolate chips to *Mint Ice Cream*.

☺   ☺   ☺

For **"Parve Cookies & Cream Ice Cream"**, add 1½ cups crushed *parve* chocolate cookies.

☺   ☺   ☺

For **"Parve Orange Sherbet"**, substitute 1¼ tsp. orange extract for vanilla, add 1 Tbs. sugar, ⅛ tsp. yellow food coloring and 4 drops red.

☺   ☺   ☺

For **"Parve Lime Sherbet"**, omit vanilla and add ⅓ cup lime juice, ⅓ cup sugar, 8 drops green food coloring and 4 drops yellow.

☺   ☺   ☺

For **"Parve Pineapple Sherbet"**, omit vanilla, add ¼ cup sugar, 1 cup pureed pineapple chunks (without any juice), 1 tsp. lime juice and 1 drop yellow food coloring.

☺   ☺   ☺

For **"Parve Raspberry Sherbet"**, substitute 2 tsp. raspberry extract for vanilla, and add 1-2 Tbs. sugar, ¼ tsp. lemon juice, ⅛ tsp. red food coloring and 8 drops blue.

☺   ☺   ☺

For **"Parve Neapolitan Ice Cream"**, put a little of each of these *Parve Ice Creams* together in the same container either before or after freezing: Vanilla, Chocolate and Strawberry.

☺   ☺   ☺

For **"Parve Rainbow Sherbet"**, lightly swirl together a little of each of these prepared *Parve Sherbets* in a container (preferably before freezing): Lime, Pineapple, Raspberry and Orange.

Fruit Desserts

Pears in Ginger-Almond Sauce

5 fresh firm ripe medium pears (peeled, cored and sliced- about 3¾ cups)

3 cups apple cider

4 tsp. fresh minced ginger root, OR ½ tsp. ground ginger

6 Tbs. flour, OR 3 Tbs. potato starch

1⅓ cup water

½ tsp. almond extract

Step 1   Put pears, cider and ginger in a pot, bring to boil, and simmer 15 minutes

Step 2   Blend flour and water until smooth, add to pears and stir until sauce thickens.

Step 3   Remove from heat and stir in extract. Serve warm or chilled. Makes 4 servings.

✿ ✿

Tahiti-Style Fruit Custard

1 medium ripe mango (peeled, pit removed, and chopped)

1 medium papaya (peeled, seeded and chopped)

1½ (20 oz.) cans pineapple chunks (drained)

¾ lb. ripe bananas (peeled and chopped)

6 Tbs. corn starch or potato starch

½ cup brown sugar

½ tsp. vanilla extract

½ cup *Imitation Thai Coconut Cream* (p. 86- chilled)

Step 1   Put fruits in a blender or food processor and process until nearly pureed.

Step 2   Put a strainer atop a large bowl, gently place fruit in to drain to yield ½ cup juice.

Step 3   Stir corn starch into juice, then add it with sugar and vanilla to fruit, blending well.

Step 4   Spread evenly in greased loaf pan, bake 1 hour at 375° F until starting to brown.

Step 5   Chill covered 4 hours. Put cream in a crock or pour on top. Makes 4-6 servings.

Single-Serve Instant Fruit Dessert

Dessert Base Mix	Topping Mix
2 Tbs. flour	¼ tsp. ground cinnamon
2 Tbs. *parve* kosher fruit gelatin	1 Tbs. brown sugar
1 Tbs. diced dried fruit (match flavor)	1 tsp. graham or matzo crumbs

For Preparation

2 Tbs. boiling water

✿ Step 1   Blend Base Mix ingredients in one custard cup, then Topping Mix ingredients in a separate cup. (For later use, put first cup's ingredients in one small zipper bag, and second cup's ingredients in another. When ready to use, pour contents into a custard cup.)

✿ Step 2   When ready for preparation, stir boiling water into Base Mix in cup.

✿ Step 3   Let sit 2 minutes, then sprinkle on Topping Mix over Base. Serve hot or chilled.

Based on an instant dessert from around 1978. Store until use (Step 2). Makes 1 serving.

✡ ✡

Fried Green Bananas

2½ Tbs. *parve* melted margarine

½ tsp. *Cinnamon Sugar* (optional- p. 434)

3 peeled slightly green bananas (cut in half and sliced lengthwise in half)

Put margarine and cinnamon in a frying pan. Put bananas in flat-sides- down. Sauté on medium heat 7 minutes until lightly browned, flip and repeat. Makes 3-6 servings.

✡ ✡

Fruit Surprises

4 oranges, grapefruits or small cantaloupes (halved and seeded)

4 cups *parve* filling: whipped cream, ice cream or prepared pudding

1 cup garnish: chopped nuts, candy, sprinkles and/or cookie crumbs (divided)

Scoop fruit out of rinds, chop, put in bowl, add filling, blend in ½ cup garnish. Fill 4 fruit halves with mixture, and top with ½ cup garnish. Put other halves on to look whole. Makes 4 servings.

(◊ berries/pears) (🥤 applesauce) **Purple Passion**

½ (15 oz.) can blueberries in syrup (1 cup) (undrained)

2 cups sweetened applesauce or cinnamon applesauce (omit cinnamon)

½ tsp. ground cinnamon (or to taste)

optional: 4 canned pear halves (drained and chopped into ½-inch pieces)

Blend all ingredients thoroughly, including blueberry juice. Chill and serve. Makes 4-6 servings.

✡ ✡

Fancy Applesauce

3 cups applesauce

1 tsp. ground ginger

¾ tsp. ground cinnamon

1 tsp. ground nutmeg

¼ cup raisins

¼ cup chopped walnuts

1 tsp. rum extract, OR ¼ cup kosher wine

Blend ingredients in a bowl. Refrigerate 2-24 hours, the longer the better. Makes 4-6 servings.

✡ ✡

Roasted Luau Pineapples

1 whole medium pineapple

1 tsp. sugar (optional- or to taste)

½ tsp. rum extract (optional)

2 Tbs. melted *parve* margarine

	Step 1	Lay pineapple on its side and slice off ⅓ of side, leaving ⅔ for a shell "bowl".
	Step 2	Preheat oven to 350° F. Remove meat and cut into cubes. (Set both aside).
	Step 3	Blend extract, margarine, cubes and sugar to taste, then put it all in shell.
	Step 4	Put ⅓ side back into place, wrap in foil, and bake 20 minutes. Makes 4 servings.

Creamy Roasted Papaya

2 small-medium ripe papayas (cut in half lengthwise & scoop out seeds)

¼ cup water

¼ cup sugar

1 cup real coconut milk or *Imitation Coconut Milk* (p. 86- room temperature)

Step 1   Grease a baking dish, add water and papayas skin-side-down. Sprinkle on sugar.
Step 2   Bake at 375° F ½ hour. Take out, baste with liquid from bottom. Bake ½ hour.
Step 3   Turn heat to 400° F. Bake 5-10 minutes until liquid is thick. Turn off oven, baste.
Step 4   Pour milk on papayas, then either heat or chill and serve. Makes 4 servings.

Breakfast Papaya

2 large ripe papayas (cut lengthwise in half, seeds removed and)

1 small lime (cut in half)

2 tsp. sugar (optional)

Scoop out meat with a spoon and put in a bowl. Chop it up, and squeeze lime into bowl and add sugar if desired. Toss to coat, and put into shells. Chill ½ hour and serve. Makes 2-4 servings.

(oranges) (pineapple)   Mexican Ambrosia

2 (11 oz.) cans mandarin oranges, OR 3-4 peeled sectioned tangerines

1 cup sweetened shredded coconut

½ (20 oz.) can sweetened pineapple chunks, OR 1 cup chopped pineapple

Combine all ingredients and chill. Makes 4-8 servings.

Mexican Ambrosia was my international recipe project as a kid. So, speaking of projects for kids as well as the whole family, let's have some— *"Fun With Food"*…

Section 5
Fun with Food
Projects & Crafts for Everyone

Kitchen Projects for Kids

Besides cooking, there are all kinds of fun projects that kids can do in the kitchen, which can bring you closer by doing things together. They can give kids a sense of feeling needed, (which cooking together will do), explore the wonders of nature, or even help teach kids about *kashrut*. Most of the projects came from my childhood, either shown to me by my parents or another kid's grandparents. They are real memory-makers. Some are edible and food related, others aren't, but they're all a whole lot of fun. A few may require supervision.

Other projects in this book can be made as well with your children. Any of the *"Herbal Gifts"*, can be done with your child, and they'll love watching and making these unusual things to give as gifts.

Recipe Fun

Learn to Churn

A fun project for kids is actually making real dairy butter (*parve* substitutes *won't* work). It's great for a group of kids, it can be passed around to each child. You'll need 1 half-pint of whipping cream, 2 Tbs. of sour cream and a shaker with a good tight lid. Put them in the shaker, and keep shaking until a ball of butter forms (about 15 minutes- you'll feel it). There will be a big ball of butter resting on the bottom. Gently pour the shaker's contents into a strainer over top of another container for the buttermilk, leaving the butter pat behind in the strainer. Take the pat and put it in its own container. This produces ½ lb. (½ cup) of butter and ¼ cup of buttermilk. It's delicious on fresh baked bread, and can even be turned into "Herbed Butter" in *Herbal Gifts* (on p. 438).

Fashionable Fudge

This project is from an anonymous friend. You'll need 1 cup peanut butter, ½ cup honey, 1 tsp. vanilla extract, and 2 cups of dry powdered milk to bind. Mix the peanut butter, honey and vanilla together, then add the milk, blending well. The dough can be eaten as it's being made, or after being refrigerated or frozen. It can be molded by hand or rolled out and cut with cookie cutters for shapes. Makes rich, delicious dairy fudge that kids love to shape and eat.

Possible substitutions: For the dairy intolerant, *parve* powdered non-dairy creamer can be used. For those allergic to peanuts, tahini [ground sesame seeds or sesame paste], (not to be confused with "tehina"), can be used quite successfully, as long as one is not allergic to sesame.

For a completely *parve*, peanut-free fudge, substitute tahini and *parve* powdered non-dairy creamer for peanut butter and powdered milk. The flavor is still very close to the real thing. Makes 1½ cups of fudge.

Fun with Nature
Growing Garbage

Plants can actually be grown from raw "waste" products in the kitchen. Many can sprout in just 1 day!

Apple Trees can be grown from seeds. Carefully remove the seeds and put them in an old container filled with moist potting soil. Put it in the fridge for 6 weeks. When the time is up, take them out. Within 10 days they should start sprouting. (Don't over-water.) Apple trees grow in cooler climates.

Avocado Trees can be grown from the seed. Carefully remove the seed from a very ripe avocado, and set aside to dry overnight. Remove the paper-like membrane and plant the seed flat side down in a pot with just the tip exposed above the dirt. In 3 months, a root should develop, then a shoot will grow. Avocados will only grow into trees in warm climates.

Potatoes will grow into a leafy plant. Cut a regular potato into pieces so that each piece has an eye. Fill a jar with sand and plant the pieces eyes-up, in the sand. Within about 10 days roots will form and stems will pop up through the sand.

Sweet Potatoes can be cut in half and placed in a jar of water with toothpicks supporting it. After two weeks it will sprout. It can be left as is or planted in a pot.

Ginger Root can be planted (sprout-end up and eyes just above the soil) in spring or summer, (or in a pot) and can have delicate flowers. Ginger grows wild in tropical climates in partial shade.

Horseradish Root segments (9-inch segments) can be planted in any climate, and many people grow it for their Passover Seder. It needs very rich soil and will often get tiny white flowers.

Peanuts can also be planted in a pot in moist sandy soil. Carefully take the peanut out of the shell, but don't disrupt the skin. Put it in dirt about ½-inch from the surface and cover it over. They need very high light to produce yellow flowers. If they flower, a curious thing happens. Unlike tree nuts, the flower part turns *downward* into the soil. Eventually, it develops into a peanut (or "ground nut" as they are called in some countries). This is why peanuts (part of the "legume" or bean family) are the only "nut" with a *brachah* of *HaAdamah*.

Sesame Seeds can be planted in spring (at least 3-months of warm weather) and will produce beautiful flowers if they get enough direct sunlight. Sesame grows in tropical climates in sandy soil.

Bean Plants grow quickly. Put a sponge or cotton ball in an old jar lid or shallow container filled with water. Take a whole bean (or two), put it on the sponge, and it should sprout in a day or so.

Temporary Plants can be made from the tops cut off of your carrots or beets. The carrots look like ferns, and the beets look like broad-leaves. Take a shallow tray and put some potting soil in it. Place the tops on the dirt and fill it with another layer of dirt to cover. Keep it moist, and they'll grow in a week.

Colorful Crystals

This is perhaps the most complex project, better suited for older kids who can truly appreciate its beauty. You'll need a plastic pan or non-metallic flat container at least 6-inches wide, another disposable bowl, non-iodized salt, liquid bluing, water, household ammonia, food coloring, and several pieces of large pine bark nuggets used for landscaping. (Some people use coal or brick.) Look for bluing in mom & pop hardware stores or supermarkets in the laundry detergent area.

Put the nuggets in the container. In a disposable bowl, mix together 4 Tbs. salt, 4 Tbs. bluing, 4 Tbs. slightly warm water and 1 Tbs. ammonia until the salt is dissolved. Pour the mixture over the nuggets so that they are saturated. Be sure that the top of the nuggets are not submerged- they need exposure to air. Drip drops of different colored food coloring in many spots on the tops of the nuggets (unless you want them white). Put the container in the spot where it will sit and don't move it- the crystals disintegrate if they get wet, and jostling makes taller crystals fall over. The pastel, snowflake-like crystals can start forming within 6 hours, and are very pretty after 3 days. They grow rapidly after 1 week, and keep growing even after the solution dries.

I used a large margarine tub and cottage cheese tub for mixing. Leftover solution and a brick were left in the mixing tub. The sides suddenly grew crystals after 1 week. (Note: This project is toxic and stains clothing. Keep away from pets, very young children, and babies. It is a good project for older children.)

Stained Stalks

This project shows how plants take in nutrients. You'll need a small container (such as a small bottle), a thin celery stalk with leaves (some flowers will work as well), and food coloring.

Fill the container with 1 inch of water and add 10 drops of coloring. Slice the celery 5-6 inches from the leafy top and put it in the water. Within 8 hours the leaves will be dyed. (Longer stalks and petal parts turn colors within 24 hours.) Switch colors and it turns that hue with a bit of the old. (Note: Non-toxic, good for younger kids under supervision. Celery can be eaten, and it may get kids to like it!)

Eggs-it In & Out

This is project demonstrates air pressure changes due to temperature, but is also a borderline kitchen magic trick. You'll need a hardboiled egg and a jar or bottle (such as a baby bottle or carafe) with a mouth or neck that is just slightly smaller than the egg.

Carefully shell the egg. The boiled egg must be perfectly smooth and free from cracks. After matching the size, put a small amount of hot water in the bottom of the jar or bottle. Immediately put the egg on top with the bigger end up. The egg will be sucked in! To reverse the process, carefully hold the egg back and dump out the water. Put the bottled egg in the freezer for about ½-hour. Take it out and immediately hold it upside down over a bowl with both hands covering the jar or bottle. The egg should pop out into the bowl as you are holding it. It can also be removed by holding it upside down and blowing on it hard. If it's stubborn, squeeze hard if it's a plastic jar. (Non-toxic. The egg can still be eaten.)

419

Kitchen Tricks
Egg's-Up

You'll need salt, a dry, room-temperature hard-boiled egg, a sturdy, level table, and a steady hand. Pour about ⅛ tsp. in a mound on the table. Carefully place the egg bigger-end-down in the salt to balance. Lightly blow the salt away from each angle. (Carefully clean up excess salt or it gives the trick away.) The egg stays upright, looking like it's standing on end. (Non-toxic. Egg can still be eaten.)

Surprising Rubberizing

You'll need a clean, well-sealing plastic lidded jar, vinegar, and a hard-boiled egg. (A raw egg or a fresh chicken bone may also be used, each with different results).

Gently put the egg in the jar, fill it to the top with vinegar, Put the lid on it for a week and a half. It is highly advisable to set the jar down in a bowl or other container, as the egg will expand, float, and it can cause vinegar to leak out the top.

When the time is up, the now-pickled egg will have no shell. Remove the membrane and it bounces like a crazy ball- but don't bounce it too hard. It will eventually dry out and shrink, and becomes hard after a while.

A whole raw egg can be used too- it becomes a bouncy whitish "water balloon" with a visible yolk inside. (Don't break it or it's a real mess!)

A fresh chicken leg-bone (cleaned of meat) can be used. Ideally, put it in a larger jar with more vinegar. Once it turns dark, the bone gets flexible. Keep in the jar with vinegar. If it dries out, it just gets hard again. Always rinse it before handling. (Nontoxic, but inedible.)

Radical Raisins

All you need is a bottle of seltzer water, raisins, and a clear lidded jar with even sides (no enlarged bottom or the raisins get stuck). Fill most the jar with seltzer (leaving an air gap), then add a few raisins. Seal the lid tightly. In a few minutes raisins will randomly rise to the top, then dive down, and will keep going up and down. They do this for quite a while. (Non-toxic. Both raisins and seltzer can still be eaten.)

Suspended Submarine

Also called a "Cartesian Diver". You'll need a clear 2-liter soda bottle and a rubber squeeze-bulb from an eyedropper or a pen or marker cap. Remove the bottle label and fill it with water. Put the open-end of the rubber bulb in the bottle, squeezing most the air out but not all, so that it barely floats. Make sure the bottle is completely full with no air, and cap it tightly. Squeeze hard on the bottle and the "submarine" dives to the bottom. Let go, and it shoots back to the top. Squeeze gently, and it goes down slowly. A steady hand can keep it suspended in the middle. (Nontoxic, but inedible. Keep bulb or cap away from small children.)

Practical Projects

Scented Citrus

Be it for decoration or air fresheners, pomander balls are a good project for kids. You'll need a toothpick, ribbon, lots of whole cloves, and your favorite (unblemished) fruits. Apples and pears can be used, but more commonly used are citrus fruits, like grapefruits, kumquats, oranges, lemons, limes, tangerines and even an *etrog* [the citron fruit] used on *Sukkot* (see "Sukkot" in Holidays" on pp. 646-647).

For extra fragrance, all or some of these ground spices such as allspice, cinnamon, nutmeg, cardamom or coriander, can be used. If you want to hang it, take a piece of coat hanger or a knitting needle and pierce it through the fruit "shish kebab style" (as the fruit dries, it must be rotated to keep from sticking).

Take a toothpick and make a hole in the fruit skin, then insert a clove. Repeat until the fruit is covered, do it in rows, designs or pretty patterns, or leave some skin showing.

Once done, it can be rolled in ground spices. Set aside at room temperature to dry for a few weeks. Turn now and then so air can get to all sides. They will shrivel and harden. When they have dried, tie a ribbon around it to hang, or wrap it with decorative netting and tie it with a bow. If you had pierced it for tying, thread a ribbon through the hole and tie it.

Pomanders repel moths. They can freshen the air, or the inside of a drawer without using chemicals. They also make good *Sukkah* decorations. These can also be used for *Havdalah* [the ritual to mark the end of *Shabbat*] (see p. 634). (Nontoxic, inedible.)

Birdie Braids

These will feed the birds in the winter, or make nice decorations for a *Sukkah* [temporary dwelling on the holiday of *Sukkot*], as long as it doesn't rain hard and it's put up before the holiday).

You'll need a big batch of plain popcorn, thread, and a dull "crewel" type (needlepoint) needle. Tie a large knot in one end of a thread about 6 feet long. On the other end, thread the needle, and pierce gently through each piece of popcorn. Keep doing this until the whole thread is loosely covered with corn. When you're just about to the end, tie a large knot at the other end. String in trees or bushes for birds to eat, or hang it like paper chains in a *Sukkah* (see "Sukkot" in Holidays" on pp. 646-647). (Popcorn is still edible, but keep needle and thread away from small children.)

Play Paint

You'll need 1 Tbs. sugar, 8 tsp. corn starch, 1 cup water, 2 Tbs. dishwashing liquid, 4 small containers (baby food jars are ideal), and 4 bottles of food coloring (generally they come in blue, green, red and yellow). Blend the sugar and corn starch together in a small pot. Add the water slowly, stirring well to blend and not have any lumps. Cook on low heat, stirring constantly until the mixture thickens into a smooth, jelly-like paste. Take it off the burner and add the dish detergent, stirring very gently as to not make it foam too much. Do not let it cool, or the mixture gets globby and the colors won't mix in properly.

Put some mixture into each container, and quickly stir in food coloring to the desired hues (ideally, about 10 drops of coloring for each of the 4 colors). You now have washable, non-toxic finger paint that can be used on paper (shiny paper doesn't work so well), outside, or even in the bathtub on skin. (It may even encourage kids to take a bath!) It could lightly stain wood or clothing, and tile grout if left to dry- but under normal usage it scrubs off with a toothbrush and dish soap. (Washable, nontoxic, but inedible.)

Professional Place Mats

An important part of keeping kosher is to have designated items such as place mats. You will need several 12 x 15-inch sheets of blue construction paper or poster board (one for each family member, or extra for guests), and several 12 x 15-inch sheets of red construction paper or poster board. (You can even do green for *parve*, if desired.)

Kids can decorate one side as they see fit, with glued-on grocery store sales ad pictures for the foods that match the *kashrut* designation's colors (dairy for blue and meat for red). They can also use crayons, markers, glitter, etc. When they are done, take them to an office or copy store and have them laminated. You now have "professional" kosher place mats, which are easily cleaned. Not to mention a wonderful family keepsake.

Scrupulous Sculptures

For making table decorations, hanging in a *Sukkah*, or making into a mobile, this project mimics ceramics. You'll need 2 cups of flour, 1 cup of salt and 1 cup of water. Food coloring is optional, or a drop can be put in a bit of water for painting-on before baking. (Acrylic or poster paint can be used after baking.) Mix ingredients in a large bowl to form a smooth, stiff dough. (Indeed, this can be used as play-dough if kept in an air-tight, resealable container.) Cut or mold your creation. If it will be hung, put a hole through the top for a string or ribbon. Put on a lightly greased cookie sheet and bake in a preheated 450° F oven 20-30 minutes, or until hardened. Time will depend on size and thickness of the sculpture. Take out of oven if they start to brown, because they are done. Projects can be shellacked or painted with more permanent paint for more durability. Makes 2⅔ cups. (Nontoxic unless shellacked, and too hard to eat. Sculptures of people or especially complete faces should not be made, as it is a *Torah* prohibition.)

Fun & Games
Corny Cuties

You'll need tan thread, scissors, a twist-tie, and 1-2 ears of corn per doll. An adult or older child can cut husk bases (use corn for *Savory Roasted Corn* p. 200). Sort husks (torn pieces can still be used).

1. How to tie all designated spots: Cut a 5-6-inch piece of thread. Pinch area, wrap a twist-tie tightly around the spot (move twist-tie ends aside). Tightly double-tie thread. Remove twist-tie. Trim thread ½-inch from knot.

2. Let's start! Get 4 large same-sized husks. Put 2 husks together (pointed areas together) and lay them flat on table. Place silk on top, place another pair on top like first, then tie pointed ends together 1-inch from top.

3. Fold husk pairs next to silk over thread to cover. Tuck silk in between folded area. "Hair" will stick out.

4. Tie a piece of thread around the husks about 1-inch down from top with silk, tie tightly to make head.

5. Braid 3 very thin husks, and tie each one 1-inch from end- this makes an arm piece that also has hands.

6. Insert arm between husks under head to stick out on either side, then tie just underneath arm for waist.

7. Wrap a long thin husk around back of neck, crisscross around belly, and tie around waist. Repeat for other side. Optional- tie a thin husk around waist for belt. Trim thread or husk pieces. If making a girl, she's done.

8. For a boy, divide husks below waist and tie each part 1-inch from the end for his legs. Keep in warm dry area (such as a sunny window) if not using, to dry and not let it molder. Husks will shrink and dry into place, and exposed thread can be removed. (Non-toxic, *Halachically* correct, because it has no face.)

Kashrut Card Game

This teaches children the basics of *kashrut*, but is fun for the whole family. Kids may have as much fun making the game as playing it! Artistic kids can draw their own pictures, or cut out food pictures and glue them on. For the really initiated with a Hebrew-English dictionary, the Hebrew words for foods can also be added. All games can be adapted to family *minhag*, (such as those who don't eat fish and dairy combined.

To Make the Game: You'll need 36 blank 3 x 5-inch index cards (or 18 blank 4 x 6) For artists- colored pencils, pens or crayons. For non-artists- magazines or grocery sales ads with food pictures.

1. Cut 3 x 5 cards in half (or quarter 4 x 6). (If you have blank business cards, use as-is.) To get 72 cards.

2. Label the tops of the proper number of cards with these words in these colors: 22 cards should have "Dairy" written in blue, 22 red "Meat", 4 yellow "Sharp", and 24 green "*Parve*".

3. Set aside 9 of the "*Parve*" cards, and write in different color (such as pink, black and turquoise) on the bottoms: 5 cards get "Fish", 2 "Meat Equipment" or "ME", and 2 "Dairy Equipment" or "DE".

4. Draw or cut out pictures to put on the appropriate cards:

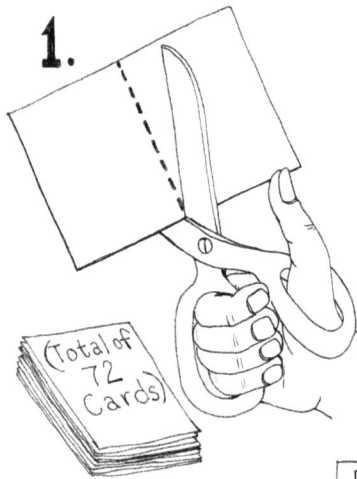

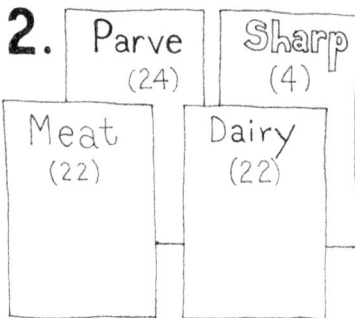

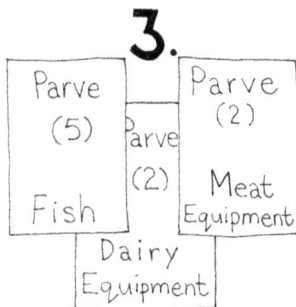

22 "Meat" cards can have meat cuts, chickens or turkeys, or kosher farm animals.

22 "Dairy"- milk, cheese, cottage or cream cheese, or ice cream.

4 "Sharp"- pickles, lemon or lime, onion, hot pepper, garlic or radish.

15 plain "Parve" cards- fruits, vegetables and/or eggs.

5 "Fish"- whole (kosher) fish or fillets.

2 "ME" and 2 "DE" can have any cooked *parve* food. Examples are pudding, cake or cookies. (For durability and cleaning, they can be laminated.)

"The Kashrut Matching Game": This is great for younger kids. Each turn is 1 meal. "*Parve*" and "Sharp" cards are wild cards. The object is to get the most cards. There can be any number of players.

Set up: Put all cards face down on the table in rows of 9 by 8 (or whatever fits the table best).

Rules: Each player turns over 2 cards. If it's a matching pair, a player keeps them and goes again. If the pair is a "Meat" card and a "Dairy" card, it is *treifah* (prohibited), and the player loses their turn. The cards are turned back over. Aside from matching cards 2 "Meat", or 2 "Dairy", pairs can also consist of these combinations: 1 "*Parve*" + 1 "Dairy" or "DE", 1 "*Parve*" + 1 "Meat" or "ME", 1 "Sharp" + 1 "*Parve*", 1 "Sharp" + 1 "Meat" or "ME", 1 "Sharp" + 1 "Dairy" or "DE", or 1 "Fish" + 1 "*Parve*".

After a player gets a "Meat" pair, they must count out loud to 6, (to show they have waited 6 hours) and the player goes again. If a player neglects to count to 6, and then gets a "Dairy" card, that player loses their turn. If a player draws a "Meat" card and a "Fish" or "DE" card, they must turn over a third card, (since you must drink or eat something *parve* between them). If that card is "*Parve*", they keep all 3 cards and go again. If the third card is anything other than "*Parve*", all cards are turned back over, and the player loses their turn. If the third card is another "Fish", they can draw a fourth card. If a family eats dairy with fish, and a "Dairy" and "Fish" are drawn, they keep it and go again. If a family doesn't eat fish with dairy, they should treat it like "Fish" and "Meat". For more challenge, move cards around.

End of Game: When all the cards or possible matches are gone, the player with most cards wins.

"The Kosher Combo Game": The object of the game is to get as many kosher combinations as possible. This game is for any age, and any number of players. "Sharp" cards are wild, becoming what they are paired with. "Meat" and "Dairy" can never be played together. (To have dairy, then *parve*, then meat may be confusing for young children. Advanced players can play this way, but it's less challenging.)

Set up: Shuffle the cards well. Each player is dealt 3 cards. Remaining cards are placed in the middle, face-down. There is a draw pile and a discard pile, and players can draw from either pile (one person's leftovers can be another person's gourmet meal). If one of the two piles is used up, a second pile is made next to the remaining one. Eventually, each player has a personal pile of played combos next to them sitting face-up. (These don't affect the current hand, since they are past meals).

Rules: Each hand represents a meal, and each player gets 1 turn. Pick someone to go first. The game goes clockwise. On the first turn, a player looks at their cards without telling the others what they have and decides what to do. If a player has a kosher combination, they play 2-3 cards face-up in the proper order on their pile for all to see. There can never be a *treifah* combo in a player's hand. If a player has gotten a *treifah* combo, they must discard at least 1 card face-down in the discard pile to keep their hand kosher. One turn consists of drawing the number of cards they lack for a hand of 3, then discarding 1 or more cards in the discard pile or playing a kosher combo on their pile. Discarding cards is 1 turn.

425

Strategies: If one plays their cards right, they often can have a combination of three cards per meal. If a player has a combination such as 2 "Meat" cards and 1 "*Parve*" card, they can choose to play all 3 cards on their pile, or just the 2 "Meat" cards. The advantage to playing all 3 is to get an extra card in their pile. The disadvantage is no extra buffer "*Parve*" card if they need it on the next turn.

Prohibited or *treifah* combos: If a player gets any of these, they must discard one or more cards: 1 "Meat" + 1 "Dairy" + anything else; 2 "Meat" + 1" DE" or 1 "Meat" + 2 " DE"; 1 "Meat" + 1 " DE" + 1 "Sharp"; 1 "Dairy" + 1 " ME" + 1 "Sharp"; 1 "Dairy" + 2 "ME" or 2 "Dairy" + 1 "ME"; 2 "Fish" + 1 "Meat" or 1 "Fish" + 2 "Meat"; 1 "Fish" + 1 "Meat" + 1 "Sharp". (For those that don't eat fish and dairy—2 "Dairy" + 1 "Fish"; 1 "Dairy" + 2 "Fish"; or 1 "Dairy" + 1 "Sharp" + 1 "Fish".)

Permissible combos: 2 "*Parve*" + any; 2 "Meat" + 1 "*Parve*" or "Sharp"; 2 "Dairy" + 1 "*Parve*" or "Sharp"; 3 "Meat"; 3 "Dairy"; 3 "Fish"; 3 "*Parve*" of any type. (If a family does eat fish and dairy together 1 "Fish" + 1 "Dairy", or 1 "Dairy" + 1 "Sharp" + 1 "Fish" are permissible.)

Order of special combos: Players put these on their pile in the proper order or they're out of the game. Combos are played in this order: 1 "Fish" + 1 "*Parve*" + 1 "Meat"; 1 "Fish" + 1 "*Parve*" + 1 "ME" or "DE"; 1 "Meat" + 1 "*Parve*" + 1 "DE"; 1 "Dairy" + 1 "*Parve*" + 1 "ME"; 1 "DE" + 1 "*Parve*" + 1 "ME" or vice versa. (A family that doesn't eat fish with dairy—1 "Dairy" + 1 "*Parve*" + 1 "Fish".)

End of game: If only one more card is left and the next player must draw the last card if they need cards. If they can play it with their other cards, they take their turn. If it is *treifah*, they must discard it or another card, then it's the next player's turn. If all players have done this and no more playable cards are left, the game ends. The last card is turned over and ignored. Add up all cards to get a player's score, but any cards left in their hand are subtracted from their score. The player with the highest score wins.

"The Kosher Cuisine Game": This is similar to the "Kosher Combo Game", but much harder. It can only have up to 4 players and is better for older kids.

Rules: Each player is dealt 5 cards, and each hand consists of 5 cards. There is much more discarding involved, and it is harder to get permissible combinations in a hand to play on your pile. These combinations use all the same rules, but in the end, there are usually no cards left. Strategy and the "luck of the draw" are very important.

End of game: Add up all cards to get a player's score, but any cards left in a player's hand are deducted from the score. The player with the highest score wins.

Funny Food Facts

This is for kids who love fun facts. The world of *kashrut* and food is filled with interesting trivia.

Vicious Veggies: Potatoes leaves are poisonous but not the tuber. Lychee seed is toxic but not the fruit. Rhubarb leaves are deadly but not stems. Cashew shells are toxic, but roasting removes the poison.

Watermatoes: A tomato that is grown strictly in water is called "Hydroponic" and is not considered *"P'ri HaAdamah"* which means "fruit of the ground" by Jewish standards.

Bright Blue Cabbage: If red cabbage is cooked with margarine, it turns a bright blue color. Add lemon juice, and it can turn back into red. (This is much more fun to watch than to eat.)

Yellowfoot: Eating massive amounts of carrots or drinking too much carrot juice can cause a person's skin to temporarily turn yellow or orange (hypercarotinemia) due to the increased amount of beta carotene in a person's system. In some people it only affects the sole of the foot or palm of the hand. (One would have to consume 20 mg or more of beta carotene per day.)

Mango Mouth: Eating too many mangoes (and especially mango skin) can build up toxins resulting in blisters on the mouth. It is particularly irritating to people with poison ivy allergies.

Corny Joke: Corn is the only food item in which you throw out the outside, then cook the inside, then eat the outside, and finally throw out the inside.

Pop Art: Kernels of corn explode when heated due to the high moisture content. The moisture within the starchy inside of the kernel expands and cooks until the shell on the outside explodes. The result is popcorn. Wild rice (a type of grass seed) puffs in its own way, swelling and turning lightly crunchy.

Potato Power: There is enough electrochemical energy in a potato (via a galvanized nail and copper wire stuck into it) to run a small digital clock.

Yam Spoof: Sweet potatoes are often referred to as "yams", but in fact the two are not even related botanically. Most "yams" in the US are really a type of sweet potato. True yams have white meat.

Rays In Celery: Celery was originally white, and still can be when deprived of sunlight.

Going Bananas: Throughout most of the world, bananas are eaten green as a vegetable. When ripe bananas are put in a paper bag with other fruits or vegetables, the bananas give off a gas which causes the other fruits and vegetables to ripen quicker.

Cold Fish: If raw fish is set in a pan of lemon or lime juice, the fish will be fully "cooked" within 3 hours without the use of any heat or microwaves.

Please Pass the Goldfish: Carp, a favorite type of fish used for making *Shabbat* gefilte fish, is in the same family as the goldfish. In fact, the large, colorful koi found in fishponds are Japanese Carp.

Fungus Detectors: There is a gourmet fungus related to mushrooms called "truffles". Pigs are trained to find them growing under the ground. They sniff them out and try to dig them up.

Fungus Among Us: You would never think of eating moldy bread or the stuff that grows on rotten logs, which are a plant-like growth, called fungus. However, there are types of fungus that we do eat, such as mushrooms, truffles, and most particularly yeast, which is used for bread.

Clean Inside & Out: Kosher animals, birds and fish have healthier diets and are good for you when eaten in moderation. Non-kosher animals, birds and fish are generally scavengers, eating dead carcasses or wastes of other animals, and generally have more cholesterol, fat and toxins.

Cat Drugs: Catnip is closely related to mint. It also can make lions and other big cats intoxicated.

Fluffing Flowers: Marsh Mallow is a flower that looks like the hollyhock. Its root was originally used to make the mucilaginous result in the confection marshmallows, now made with gelatin.

Curious Cousins: Quinces are a small delicate fruit that is a member of the rose family, yet it's also a cousin to pears and apples. Brazil nuts are in the same family as tea, blueberries, phlox and kiwi fruit.

Not-A-Nut: Peanuts are not related to other nuts at all— they are closely related to beans and peas. One difference is that after blossoming, the flower's stem goes down into the ground where the nuts form.

Sticky Business: It takes 40 gallons of maple tree sap boiled down to make one gallon of maple syrup.

Busy Bees: Both honey and royal jelly are derived from bees, a non-kosher species. Honey is kosher since bees convert nectar into honey, but royal jelly isn't. It's a glandular secretion from the bee itself.

Forever Honey: Honey is incapable of spoiling since it has little water content and microorganisms can't grow and reproduce in it. Additionally, it was used by Egyptians to embalm their dead.

Sickly Sweet: When the sweetener aspartame is heated above 86° F, it turns into methanol. When broken down by the human body (average temperature 98.6° F) it is converted into formic acid and worse-formaldehyde, a potent chemical used to preserve dead bodies and scientific specimens.

Pickled People: Coroners report that dead bodies last longer before decomposing than they did fifty years ago, due to the large amount of preservatives added to our food.

Counting Sheep: There are more sheep per capita in New Zealand than humans.

Smelly Milk: If a cow or goat eats onion grass before milking, her milk tastes and smells like onions.

Cheese Morphology: The enzyme which changes milk into cheese can be made from an herb called "rennet", but is also commonly derived from a chemical in a cow's stomach. MMMM!

Holey Cheese: As Swiss cheese ferments it produces gas, which bubbles up and makes the holes.

American As Apple Pie: Apple pie is not an American invention, but pizza and chop suey is.

Better Butter Led to Bitter Battle: When margarine first came out, it was originally white, so some companies included a dye packet that turned it light yellow when blended together to make it look more like butter. This threatened the powerful dairy industry, so government regulations prohibited the sale of colored margarine. It was still prohibited until July of 2008 in Quebec, Canada.

Baker's Delight: Originally when instant cake mix came out, the only thing needed to do was add water, mix it and bake it. The product was a bomb because housewives (used to baking from scratch) felt they weren't doing anything. The powdered egg and shortening were dropped, forcing the baker to add eggs and oil. The product was a hit and (unfortunately) has remained the same ever since.

Ancient Documents: Paper can be "antiqued" by tearing along the edges and soaking in tea then letting it dry. For a more authentic look, touch the torn edges lightly with brown permanent marker. (Draw out a treasure map on paper with pencil and hide items for others to find. "X" marks the spot!)

Dye-It: Foods and herbs can be used for color. Before chemicals, clothing was dyed using them. It is easy to see how when blueberries stain your clothes blue, tomatoes- red, grass- green, or mustard- yellow.

Bon Appetit: Warm colored plates and bowls such as red, yellow and orange increase the appetite, whereas cold colored ones such as blue or white decrease the appetite. Color can affect the appetite.

"Mind" Food: Food colorings can also psychologically affect a person. See if people rush to eat green-dyed macaroni and cheese, or drink pink-colored milk. Odds are nobody will want to touch it!

What's In a Name: Popcorn chicken contains no popcorn, doughnuts don't generally have nuts, Jerusalem artichokes are not really artichokes, grilled cheese sandwiches are never grilled, sandwiches ideally should not have sand in them, and kosher dill pickles aren't always kosher.

Cool Food: Foods get freezer burn from self-defrost freezers when food is not well-sealed or has been in the freezer too long. Water molecules escape from the food causing it to dry out (freeze dry), and oxygen molecules flow in, changing the color (and eventually the taste) of the food.

Acid Reigns: It is known that vinegar can dissolve egg shells, but other acids can do damage as well. A tooth soaked in cola will completely dissolve. Stomach acid is a very powerful dissolving agent. That is why heartburn, (stomach acid splashing up on the upper part of the throat called the esophagus) is so painful. Ketchup is also acidic and can be used to clean the tarnish off of copper.

Yummy in the Tummy: In olden days, the intestines of cows or other animals was used for a skin casing in sausage, hot dogs, and the *Ashkenazic Shabbat* flavored dressing "Kishka". It was stuffed into the casing before cooking or smoking. In fact, the word *kishka* means "intestines" in Yiddish.

Leech Lunch: Non-Jews in old Norway prepared a sausage made of congealed blood. I learned this fact from a man of Norwegian descent who saw his grandmother make it. (He was a vegetarian.)

Heavy Metal Breakfast: When cereal that contains nutritional iron is whirled in a centrifuge, tiny pieces of metal will visibly adhere to the magnet. Crush some fortified cereal and stir it up with a magnet, especially on the bottom. You'll see the black iron dust stuck to the magnet.

Hotsy Tots: In emergency situations, the aluminum foil used to bake foods like a turkey or baked potato can also be used as an insulator to wrap around a newborn baby to keep it warm. The foil insulates and reflects the infant's body heat, keeping it toasty warm.

Turkey Talk: Wrapping a turkey in paper towels before roasting makes it extra juicy and tender. It is basically the same principle native Hawaiians used when wrapping food with large elephant ear-like taro leaves before baking in their underground *imu* ovens.

Which Came First: White eggs come from white chickens, and brown eggs come from reddish-brown chickens. (This does not mean that chocolate milk comes from chocolate cows.)

Ancient Eggs: Eggs were buried in China for 100 years and the result was the "Century Egg", which is considered a delicacy there. Nowadays, chicken, quail or duck eggs are packed in a highly alkaline mixture of clay, ash, salt and lime then left to sit for a few months. The result is a strongly aromatic green egg yolk with brown liquid egg white. A popular Chinese meal is a century egg eaten with ham and rice. Perhaps Dr. Seuss visited China before writing his classic book "*Green Eggs and Ham*"!

When Cooks Cry: If you cut an onion, the cells break open and allow formerly separate acids to mix with enzymes which produces a volatile sulfur compound. When this gas reacts with tears, it creates sulfuric acid, which is an irritant that in turn causes the eyes to tear in order to wash it out. Cutting a cold onion helps, and cooking inactivates the enzymes completely.

Pricey Spice: The world's most expensive spice is "saffron". It is the "stigma" (the middle parts of a flower that look like antennae) from a type of fall crocus. It takes 50-80,000 flowers to make a single pound of saffron, which is worth about $500-$5,000.00 on the retail market.

Gimme Some Skin: Cinnamon is made from the tree's outer bark. Mace spice is the ground outer coverings of nutmeg seeds. Black pepper is made from the outer skins, as well as the pepper berries themselves.

Potent Pepper: Black pepper contains an alkaloid which irritates nerve endings in the mucous membrane of the nose when sniffed, causing the reflex of sneezing to remove the irritant.

Hot Stuff: Handling fresh hot peppers can be dangerous without gloves- causing burns to eyes and other sensitive areas, yet when eaten regularly they can aid digestion.

Addictive Drink: The original cola soft drink was made by a pharmacist for medicinal purposes. It contained a small amount of the dangerous illegal drug "cocaine", made from coca. Being made from coca leaves and cola nuts, he called the brand name "Coca Cola". (It's no longer made from coca.)

Tasty Medicine: Many foods have medical properties. To sleep, try drinking warm milk or chamomile tea. To settle upset stomach, eat foods with mint or ginger. (Ginger helps motion sickness.)

The Salsa Solution: Mexican residents are more immune to salmonella poisoning, due to the amount of salsa consumed. The chemical often used to kill salmonella bacteria is "gentamicin". Cilantro in salsa contains the antibiotic "dodecenal", now found to be twice as potent as gentamicin in killing the bacteria. Author's Note: I once had a bad eye infection. After my eye drops ran out, I still had photophobia (sensitivity to light). I ate salsa and the condition improved within minutes. The eye drop chemical was gentamicin! Besides medical treatment, if you get pink eye— it can't hurt to eat salsa!

Herbs & Spices

Basically, the definition of herbs is a "useful" plant. When it comes to cooking, herbs are leaves and flowers, and spices are bark, seeds, pods, woody buds, or roots. Everyone knows how herbs can make wonderful teas, but they can also be made into vinegars, butters, honeys, jellies, sugars, seasoned salts and oils. Whether you grow them yourself indoors or out, or buy them in the produce section at a store, they can come in really handy.

Sometimes all a meal needs to make it more exciting is a little seasoning or garnish. Regardless of the food, herbs and spices can add flavor to foods without using a lot of salt, which makes it healthier in the long-run. Seasonings (especially dried, which are more concentrated) should be used singularly and sparingly until you become familiar with their flavor, but don't combine all of the ones listed in the same category. Not all types go together. For instance, if you put mint and cinnamon together, they cancel each other out and there is no flavor!

Seasoning Guide by Taste

Aromatic: Chinese 5-Spice Powder; Cilantro (fresh Coriander Leaves); Cinnamon (baked); Cloves; Curry Powder; Fenugreek; Garlic; Onion; Saffron.

Bitter: Cloves; Mustard; Paprika; Turmeric.

Hot: Black Pepper; Cayenne Pepper; Chili Powder; Cinnamon; Cloves; Curry Powder (hot); Ginger; Ginger Root (fresh); Hot Peppers; Mustard; Onion (raw); Peppercorns.

Potent: Allspice; Black Pepper; Cajun Seasoning; Cayenne Pepper; Celery Leaves; Celery Seed; Chili Powder; Cinnamon; Cloves; Curry Powder; Dill; Fenugreek; Gremolata Seasoning; Ginger; Ginger Root (fresh); Green Onions; Hot Peppers; Marjoram; Nutmeg; Onion (raw); Oregano; Peppercorns; Rosemary; Saffron; Sage; Turmeric.

Savory: Basil; Bay Leaf; Caraway Seed; Celery Leaves; Celery Seed; Chervil; Chives; Cumin; Fines Herbs; Garlic; Italian Seasoning; Mace; Marjoram; Onion; Oregano; Parsley; Rosemary; Sage; Savory; Sesame Seed; Tarragon; Thyme.

Sweet: Allspice; Anise; Cardamom; Cinnamon; Cloves; Coriander; Fennel; Ginger; Lemon Balm; Lemon Thyme; Licorice; Mace; Mint; Nutmeg; Spice Parisienne.

431

Seasoning Guide for Specific Foods

Asparagus: Chives; Lemon Balm; Sage; Savory; Tarragon; Thyme.

Beef: Basil; Bay Leaf; Black Pepper; Caraway; Chimichurri; Celery Seed; Cloves; Cumin; Curry Powder; Fenugreek; Garlic; Ginger; Marjoram; Onion; Oregano; Parsley; Rosemary; Sage; Savory; Tarragon; Thyme.

Bread: Caraway Seed; Coriander; Cinnamon; Poppy Seed; Saffron; Sesame Seed.

Broccoli: Basil; Dill; Garlic; Lemon Balm; Marjoram; Oregano; Tarragon; Thyme.

Cabbage: Basil; Caraway Seed; Cayenne Pepper; Cumin; Dill; Fennel; Marjoram; Sage; Savory.

Cakes: Allspice; Cinnamon; Coriander; Ginger; Mint; Nutmeg; Poppy Seed; Sesame Seed.

Carrots: Anise; Basil; Chervil; Chives; Cinnamon; Cloves; Cumin; Dill; Ginger; Marjoram; Mint; Parsley; Sage; Savory; Tarragon; Thyme.

Cauliflower: Basil; Caraway; Chives; Cumin; Dill; Garlic; Marjoram; Rosemary; Savory; Tarragon.

Cheese: Basil; Caraway; Celery Seed; Chervil; Chives; Cumin Seed; Dill; Garlic; Hot Pepper; Marjoram; Mustard; Nutmeg; Onion; Oregano; Parsley; Paprika; Peppercorns; Thyme; Turmeric.

Chicken: Anise; Basil; Bay Leaves; Borage; Cajun Seasoning; Chives; Cinnamon; Cumin; Curry Powder; Dill; Fenugreek; Garlic; Ginger; Green Onions; Lemon Thyme; Lovage; Marjoram; Nutmeg; Onion; Oregano; Paprika; Parsley; Rosemary; Saffron; Sage; Savory; Tarragon; Thyme.

Chili: Allspice; Cayenne Pepper; Cinnamon; Cloves; Cumin; Garlic; Hot Peppers; Marjoram; Onion; Oregano; Nutmeg; Paprika; Parsley; Thyme.

Chinese Food: Chinese 5-Spice Powder; Cilantro (Coriander Leaves, also called Chinese Parsley); Garlic; Ginger Root; Green Onions; Hot Peppers; Onion; Sesame Seed.

Cocoa: Allspice; Anise; Cinnamon; Cloves; Ginger; Lemon Balm; Mint; Nutmeg.

Coffee: Allspice; Anise; Cinnamon; Cloves; Ginger; Lemon Balm; Nutmeg.

Cookies: Allspice; Anise; Cinnamon; Cloves; Coriander; Ginger; Lemon Balm; Mint; Nutmeg; Poppy Seed; Sesame Seed.

Corn: Chervil; Chives; Lemon Balm; Onion; Saffron; Sage; Thyme.

Dry Beans: Caraway Seed; Chives; Chili Powder; Coriander; Cumin; Garlic; Hot Peppers; Lemon Thyme; Marjoram; Mint; Onions; Oregano; Parsley; Saffron; Sage; Savory; Thyme.

Duck: Allspice; Cinnamon; Cloves; Garlic; Ginger; Lemon Balm; Marjoram; Nutmeg; Onion; Oregano; Paprika; Parsley; Rosemary; Sage; Thyme.

Eggplant: Basil; Cinnamon; Dill; Garlic; Marjoram; Onion; Oregano; Parsley; Sage; Savory; Thyme.

Eggs: Anise; Basil; Caraway Seed; Cayenne Pepper; Celery Seed; Chervil; Chives; Coriander; Curry Powder; Dill; Fennel; Garlic; Hot Peppers; Marjoram; Mustard Powder; Nutmeg; Oregano; Parsley; Paprika; Peppercorns; Rosemary; Saffron; Sage; Savory; Tarragon; Thyme; Turmeric.

Fish: Anise; Basil; Bay Leaf; Cajun Seasoning; Caraway; Celery; Chervil; Chives; Dill; Fennel; Garlic; Ginger; Gremolata; Lemon Thyme; Lovage; Marjoram; Mustard Seeds; Onion; Oregano; Paprika; Parsley; Peppercorns; Rosemary; Saffron; Sage; Savory; Tarragon; Thyme; Turmeric.

Fruit: Allspice; Anise; Cinnamon; Cloves; Ginger; Lemon Balm; Mint; Nutmeg; Rosemary.

Gravy: Chives; Garlic; Gremolata; Hot Pepper; Marjoram; Onion; Nutmeg; Rosemary; Sage; Thyme.

Green Beans: Basil; Caraway Seed; Cloves; Dill; Marjoram; Mint; Sage; Savory; Thyme.

Green Vegetables: Bay Leaf; Basil; Chives; Dill; Marjoram; Nutmeg; Onions; Savory.

Italian Food: Basil; Caraway; Garlic; Italian Seasoning; Onion; Oregano; Parsley; Red Pepper; Thyme.

Lamb: Basil; Bay Leaves; Cinnamon; Coriander; Cumin; Curry Powder; Dill; Garlic; Ginger; Lemon Balm; Marjoram; Mint; Onion; Parsley; Rosemary; Saffron; Sage; Thyme.

Mexican Food: Black Pepper; Cayenne Pepper; Chili Powder; Cloves; Cilantro (Coriander Leaves); Coriander; Cumin; Garlic; Hot Peppers; Onion; Oregano; Paprika.

Mushrooms: Coriander; Garlic; Marjoram; Oregano; Rosemary; Tarragon; Thyme.

Peas: Caraway Seeds; Chervil; Chives; Rosemary; Tarragon; Thyme.

Pickles: Dill Seed; Dill Weed; Garlic; Hot Peppers; Mustard Seed; Turmeric.

Potatoes: Basil; Caraway Seeds; Chives; Coriander; Dill; Fennel; Lovage; Marjoram; Oregano; Paprika; Parsley; Rosemary; Sage; Tarragon; Thyme.

Rice: Basil; Cumin; Fennel; Garlic; Lovage; Nutmeg; Paprika; Parsley; Saffron; Sazon; Tarragon; Thyme.

Salads: Basil; Borage Leaves; Caraway Seed; Celery Leaves; Celery Seed; Chervil; Chives; Dandelion Greens; Dill Seed; Dill Weed; Fines Herbs; Garlic; Hot Peppers; Italian Seasoning; Marjoram; Mint; Mustard Powder; Onion; Oregano; Paprika; Parsley; Sesame Seed; Tarragon; Thyme.

Smoked Meat: Anise; Caraway; Cardamom; Dill; Garlic; Ginger; Oregano; Rosemary; Sage; Tarragon.

Spaghetti Sauce: Bay Leaf; Cayenne; Garlic; Marjoram; Onion; Oregano; Paprika; Parsley; Thyme.

Spinach: Anise; Basil; Caraway; Chervil; Chives; Cinnamon; Onion; Rosemary; Thyme.

Squash: Allspice; Basil; Caraway Seeds; Cardamom; Cinnamon; Cloves; Dill; Garlic; Ginger; Marjoram; Nutmeg; Onion; Oregano; Paprika; Rosemary; Sage; Savory; Spice Parisienne.

Stew: Bay Leaf; Celery Seed; Cinnamon; Cloves; Cinnamon; Dill Seed; Garlic; Hot Pepper; Marjoram; Mustard Seed; Nutmeg; Onion; Paprika; Parsley; Rosemary; Sage; Thyme; Turmeric.

Stuffing/Dressing: Fennel; Garlic; Marjoram; Onion; Nutmeg; Parsley; Rosemary; Sage; Thyme.

Tea Additions: Allspice; Anise Seeds; Cinnamon; Cloves; Ginger; Licorice; Mint; Nutmeg.

Tomatoes: Basil; Bay Leaf; Chives; Coriander; Dill; Garlic; Lovage; Marjoram; Oregano; Parsley; Rosemary; Sage; Savory; Tarragon; Thyme.

Turkey: Garlic; Marjoram; Nutmeg; Onion; Rosemary; Saffron; Sage; Savory; Thyme.

Yams: Beebalm; Celery Leaves; Cinnamon; Ginger; Lovage; Nutmeg; Thyme.

Homemade Seasoning Combinations

Adobo Seasoning: Blend together 3 Tbs. Garlic Powder, ½ tsp. Black Pepper, and 1 tsp. each: Oregano, Onion Powder, Paprika, and Salt. (Makes about ⅓ cup.)

Bouquet Garni or Pickling Spice: (Can put in a tea ball or bag made of cheese cloth, for soups) Blend equal amounts of these whole spices- Allspice, Bay Leaves, Peppercorns, Cardamom, Cinnamon Stick, Cloves, Coriander Seed, Dill Seed, Mustard Seed, and Red Peppers.

Cajun Seasoning: Blend equal amounts of these ground spices- Black Pepper, Cayenne Pepper, Garlic Powder, Onion Powder, Paprika, and Ground White Pepper.

Chili Powder: Blend equal amounts of ground: Black Pepper, Cayenne, Cloves, Coriander, Cumin, Garlic, Oregano, Turmeric, (+ equal amount Salt) and add 5 times the Paprika.

Chimichurri: Blend 1 Tbs. flakes each: Garlic, Parsley, and Onion, 1 tsp crushed dried leaves each: Basil, Oregano, and Bay, + ¾ tsp each: Red Pepper Flakes and Coarsely Ground Black Pepper. (Makes 5½ Tbs.)

Cinnamon Sugar: Blend together ⅓ cup Sugar and 2 tsp. Cinnamon. (Makes ⅓ cup.)

Cinnamon Powdered Sugar: Blend together ⅔ cup Powdered Sugar and 2 tsp. Cinnamon. (Makes ⅔ cup.)

Fines Herbs: Blend equal amounts of these leaves- Chervil, Parsley, Thyme, and Tarragon.

Gremolata: Blend 2 Tbs. Parsley Flakes, ⅛ tsp. Garlic Powder, and ½ tsp. Grated Lemon Rind. (Makes 2½-3 Tbs.)

Italian Seasoning: Blend equal amounts of Garlic Powder and Onion Powder, and equal amounts of these crushed leaves: Basil, Oregano, Thyme, and Parsley Flakes.

Old Bay Cape Cod Seasoning: Combine these ground spices- 1 Tbs. Bay Leaves, 2½ tsp. Celery Salt, 1½ tsp. Mustard, 1½ tsp. Black Pepper, ¾ tsp. Nutmeg, ½ tsp. Cloves, ½ tsp. Ginger, ½ tsp. Paprika, ½ tsp. Cayenne, ¼ tsp. Mace, and ¼ tsp. Cardamom. (Makes ¼ cup.)

Poultry Seasoning: Blend these ground spices- ¼ tsp. Rosemary, ½ tsp. Sage, and ¼ tsp. Thyme. (Makes 1 tsp.)

Pumpkin Pie Spice: Blend 2½ tsp. Cinnamon, ½ tsp. Cloves, 1 tsp. Ginger, and 1 tsp. Nutmeg. (Makes 1⅔ Tbs.)

Sazon: (Rarely, if ever, found kosher! 1½ tsp. = 1 sazon packet) Blend 1 Tbs each Ground Coriander, Cumin, Turmeric, Salt, and Garlic Powder, + 2 tsp. Oregano, and 1 tsp. Black Pepper. (Makes ⅜ cup.)

Seasoned Salt: Blend together- 1½ Tbs. Salt, 2 Tbs. Sugar, 1 tsp. Paprika, ½ tsp. Turmeric, ¾ tsp. Onion Salt, ¾ tsp. Garlic Salt, and ¼ tsp. Corn Starch. (Makes slightly over ¼ cup.)

Seasoned Salt (Kosher for Passover): Blend spices (must be certified Kosher for Passover)- 2 Tbs. Salt, 2⅓ Tbs. Sugar, 1¼ tsp. Paprika, ½ tsp. Garlic Powder, ½ tsp. Onion Powder. (Makes ⅓ cup.)

Spice Parisienne: Blend equal amounts of ground Cinnamon, Cloves, Ginger, and Nutmeg.

Edible Flowers

Many flowers are edible and are great as garnishes. Rinse flowers very well, and check thoroughly for bugs. Above all else, make sure they have never been sprayed with pesticides.

Edible Garnishes for Salads, Soups, and the Table

The following flowers can be eaten as-is: Beebalm; Borage; Calendula (Pot Marigold); Carnations; Chamomile (unless you are allergic to ragweed); Chive Blossoms; Chrysanthemum; Daylilies; Fuchsia; Geraniums; Hollyhocks; Impatiens; Lavender; Lilac; Mint Blossoms; Nasturtiums; Onion Blossoms; Pansies; Pinks; Redbuds; Rosemary Blossoms; Roses; Safflower Blossoms; Salad Burnet; Snapdragons; Squash Flowers; Violets; Yucca Flowers.

Substitute for Capers

Pick green Nasturtium buds and wash well. Make a mixture of 1 part salt to 8 parts water in a bowl and add buds. If buds try to float, weight them down with a plate. They must be totally submerged for 24 hours. Take buds out of brine and soak in cold water 1 hour. Sterilize jars as for "Herb Honeys". Take buds out of water and put in jars to ½ inch from the top. Bring vinegar to a boil, and pour into the jar until buds are covered. Seal, and refrigerate up to a few weeks.

Stuffed Flowers for Dinner

Pack squash flowers with meat, stuffing or cheese. Fry or baked as any other vegetable.

Drink Decorations

Freeze herbs or flowers in water in ice cube trays or cake molds and freeze. It adds a festive touch of class to tea, juice, carbonated drinks or a plain old punch bowl.

Substitute for Saffron

Seeing as Saffron is considered the world's most expensive spice, it's good to know there's a substitute. Shred some petals of Calendula (Pot Marigold) or Safflower.

For an imitation of the bright yellow Saffron coloring, use a bit of Turmeric.

Herbal Gifts

Herbal foods make great gifts and are really pretty when you put them in decorative containers tied up with a pretty ribbon. These are especially nice, because you've made them yourself. They also are practical, and can be used in many varieties of other foods. Below is a small sampling of what can be done with herbs or spices, and you don't even have to grow them yourself! If you do, just make sure to check for bugs.

Herb Vinegars

These are not only good on salads, but they make great gifts when presented in pretty bottles. (Preferably use a cork or bottles with non-metal caps, as shown above.) Fresh herbs are better, but dried work also. If using fresh herb seeds, bruise slightly before using.

Vinegar: Apple Cider; Red Wine; Rice Vinegar; White Wine. (Any kosher vinegar will do.)

Herbs: Chives; Fennel; Garlic (whole cloves or chopped); Rosemary; Sage; Tarragon. Others make it pretty too: Borage; Cardamom Seed; Chive Blossoms; Cilantro (Coriander Leaves); Dill; Green Onions; Hot Peppers; Mint; Nasturtiums; Oregano; Parsley; Rose Petals; Savory; Violet Petals.

Use 3 fresh herb sprigs (about two inches long) per cup of vinegar. For whole spices such as garlic, hot peppers, or green onions, use 1 piece per cup. If you like highly flavored vinegar, use ¼-cup fresh herb (or 2 Tbs. dried herb) per cup of vinegar. Gently heat the vinegar, but don't get it too hot. Pour it into the bottle. Add the herb, and let it cool. Cap the vinegar and store in a cool, dry place up to a year. Vinegar "pickles", an old-fashioned way to preserve food. It can last nearly indefinitely in the fridge.

Herb Oils

These work well for salads, but the best part is that they add flavor without adding salt. Since oil absorbs the flavor of herbs, it's very potent. Herbs can be used alone or in combinations with other herbs.

Oils: Olive (perhaps the best); Canola; Peanut; Safflower; Sunflower; Walnut. (Although any type will do.)

Herbs: Basil; Cardamom; Celery Leaves; Chervil; Cilantro (Coriander Leaves); Dill; Garlic; Ginger; Green Onions; Hot Peppers; Lemon Thyme; Lemon Verbena; Lovage; Oregano; Saffron; Tarragon; Thyme.

Gently heat the oil, until fragrant but warm (not hot), for about 3 minutes. Put 3 fresh herb sprigs about 2-inches long per cup (or Garlic Cloves, Hot Peppers, or Green Onions—1 piece per cup), into the bottle. Pour oil over top of the herbs into a bottle, and let it cool. Cap the oil. It can now be stored in a cool, dry place for up to six months, (the longer the better). If stored in the fridge, it can keep for years.

Chinese Hot Pepper Oil: All this requires is any type of vegetable oil (except olive oil, which congeals in the cold), dried Red Pepper Flakes, minced Garlic and a sealable bottle or jar. (A squeeze bottle for horseradish sauce works great for this!) Fill the bottle ¼ of the way with Pepper Flakes, ¼ with minced Garlic, then fill the rest of the way with Oil, but not to the top, as oil tends to "creep". Keep refrigerated, and shake before using. Be sure oil is always clear. If it gets cloudy, stringy or fuzzy looking, discard the contents— it's bad.

Herb Salts

Wonderful for potatoes, soups, vegetables or even tomato juice, herb salts are easy to make, and flavors can be made that you can't buy in a store You'll need non-iodized salt or sea salt, and fresh or dried herbs. Virtually any herb or spice can be used. Fresh herbs must go through drying, but dried herbs and spices can be added directly to salt in layers.

Herbs: Basil; Celery Leaves; Chives; Garlic; Marjoram; Oregano; Rosemary; Tarragon; Thyme.

Crush fresh herbs into the salt by using a heavy jar. Put dried herbs and salt in a blender and whirl for a few minutes. Spread it out on a cookie sheet and bake on very low heat about 40 minutes, stirring often.

If you don't want to mess with crushing herbs, take a cookie sheet and put a layer of salt on it, then a layer of herbs, then another layer of salt. Then put it in a medium oven for 10 minutes. Break up any clumps and repeat. Thoroughly blend the salt and herbs, and put in a container to store.

Spices: Allspice; Bay Leaves; Black Pepper; Cardamom; Cayenne; Cloves; Garlic; Ginger; Lemon Peel; Mace; Mustard; Onion Powder; Paprika.

Fish Seasoning Salt: Combine dried lemon peel, ground black pepper, and paprika.

Herb salts will last indefinitely without refrigeration, but some may lose potency after a few years. It will keep indefinitely, as long as it's kept out of sunlight.

Herb Butters

Herb butters (or herbed *Parve Imitation Butter* on p. 84 if you are having a meat meal) are a great accompaniment to fresh baked breads. They also are good on vegetables. Put them in a little crock or a dipping bowl and they can be pretty as well as practical. You can also form them into balls, or put them into candy molds for different shapes and refrigerate them (or you can stick them in the freezer if you need it chilled quickly). It's scrumptious on fresh baked bread. You can also use the real dairy butter made from "*Learn to Churn*" in *Kitchen Projects for Kids* (p. 417).

Herbs Alone in Butter: Basil; Caraway Seed; Chives; Garlic; Parsley; Sesame Seed; Tarragon.

Herb Combinations in Butter for Salty Items: Sesame Seeds + Garlic + Chives; Basil + Oregano + Thyme + Sun-Dried Tomatoes; Garlic + Marjoram. Another combination is called "Fines Herbs", which is made with 1 Tbs. each snipped Chives and Parsley + ½ Tbs. Tarragon + ½ cup butter.

Herb Combinations in Butter for Sweeter Items: Mint + Dill; Lemon Verbena + a bit of Orange Zest.

Set the butter out until it's room temperature, or warm it slightly so that it becomes soft. Beat it, and put the minced herbs right in. (It actually gets better with age, because the flavors have time to blend.) Once it's blended, put it in the refrigerator and keep it chilled until serving. Fresh herbs work well, but dry is okay too. Use 1-Tbs. fresh herb, or 1½ tsp. dried herb (or ½ tsp. crushed seeds) for every ½ cup of butter. Always store herbed butters in the refrigerator. If using fresh herbs they can last for 1-2 weeks and up to a month if kept in an airtight container. If using dried herbs they can last many months. Herb butters can be stored in the freezer for up to 2 years if you are not using them.

Herb Sugars

Sugar is another form of preserving, and either regular granulated white sugar or brown sugar will do (however, brown sugar tends to clump and get hard with moisture). Fresh herbs must be layered, but dried spices can be added directly and blended for immediate use.

Fresh Herbs: Bee Balm; Geranium Leaves; Mint Leaves; Pinks Petals; Rose Petals; Sweet Cicely; Violet Petals. Alternate layers of sugar and herb in a container. Close it tightly and let it sit for a few weeks. Open the container and blend the sugar thoroughly; then store it in an airtight container.

Ground Spices: Allspice; Cinnamon; Cloves; Ginger. Use about 1-tsp. spice to ¼-cup sugar. These can be stored it in an airtight container nearly indefinitely.

Herb Jellies

Apple or other fruit juices are the basics to making flavorful jellies with herbs and spices. Seal in nice jars topped with pretty cloth and tied with ribbon for a different gift. They go well with roasted meat, biscuits or pancakes, and are a good spread for bread or vanilla cookies.

You'll need lots of fruit juice and sugar, a total of 4½ cups fruit juice, and 4½ cups sugar. You also need ½-¾ cup fresh herb (plus extra sprigs too for decoration in the jelly itself, if desired) or 3 Tbs. dried herbs, spices or seeds, 3 Tbs. apple cider vinegar, and ¾ cup kosher-certified fruit pectin.

Juices: Apple; Grape; Orange; Tangerine.

Herbs and Spices: Allspice; Basil; Cinnamon; Cloves; Fennel; Ginger; Mint; Rosemary; Rose Petals; Scented Geraniums; Thyme.

Combinations for Jellies: Apple juice with Mint (known for accompanying lamb dishes); Grape Juice with Tarragon; Orange Juice with Marjoram; Orange (or Tangerine) Juice with Cloves or Cinnamon.

Pick fresh herbs, check for bugs, wash and chop them, or take 4 Tbs. dried herbs or spices (or seeds) and bruise them. Bring 1½ cups juice to a boil, then pour it over the herbs or spices and let it sit about 20 minutes. Strain into a bowl; add vinegar and the rest of the fruit juice. Add sugar and bring it to a boil, then stir in pectin and cook it 1 more minute. Remove from heat and skim off foam.

Sterilize the canning jars and lids as with the Herb Honeys below, and add the decorative herb sprigs, leaves or spices if desired. Pour the boiling hot jelly into the jars to within an eighth an inch from the top. Put the rubber part of the lids on, and then screw the lids on tightly. Invert the jars for a minute and it will seal it completely. Keep it refrigerated after opening.

Herb Honeys

Another item that makes a great homemade gift is herb honey, especially when seen in a pretty jar.

Herbs & Spices: Anise Seed; Bay Leaf; Cardamom; Cinnamon Sticks; Coriander; Candied Ginger; Fennel Seed; Lavender; Lemon Verbena; Marjoram; Mint; Rose Geraniums; Rosemary; Rose Petals; Sage; Thyme; Sweet Violets.

Combinations: Candied Ginger studded with Cloves; Lemon slices with a Cinnamon Stick.

Use about ½ Tbs. fresh herb, (or ½ tsp. dried herb), per cup of honey. Slightly bruise the seeds and or leaves, and put them in a small pot. Pour honey into the pot, and slightly warm it on very low heat for about two minutes. (A safe alternative is to heat it in a double boiler, but it takes so little time to heat it's hardly worth it.) Do not let the honey get hot as this destroys the flavor! Get brand new canning jars and lids and sterilize them by washing them, then pouring boiling water over them. Pour the warmed honey in, and seal it tightly. Store for a week at room temperature, and then they are ready to be used. These are great for adding to tea, putting in salad dressings, or using as a syrup with buttered pancakes. Honey is the only food known to never go bad, so it can last for years without needing refrigeration.

Herb Mustards

Put in small spice jars, these are delectable (or is that "deli"-ctable) gourmet gifts with taste, and there's not all that much to it. Basically, you need dry powdered mustard found with other herbs and spices, and the different liquids used make the distinctive flavors.

Seasonings: Sugar; Salt, pressed Garlic, Tarragon or Vinegar (or anything else you'd like to add) to taste if desired.

Colorings: Paprika yields red, but Turmeric is the traditional mustard additive for that potent yellow coloring. (Uncolored mustard will be the dull color called "maize" in the old crayon sets.)

Cooler Mustard: Hot water makes cooler mustard. Boil the liquid and add it to the powder and blend it into a paste. Then, take more boiling water pouring over the mustard (not blending it) and just let it sit that way for 15 minutes. Then drain off the excess water. You can then add seasonings or colorings to taste if desired. Put the mustard in the little jar and let it cool off for an hour or two, and then put a lid on it to seal. It is preferable to keep mustards refrigerated.

Hotter Mustard: Cold liquids make hotter mustards—add the liquid to the dry mustard per the ratio and blend it. The ratio is generally 2-3 Tbs. liquid to 4 Tbs. Dry Powdered Mustard, and it much better to make it in small quantities until you get the hang of it. If it's too spicy for you, it can be "cooled down" by adding a bit of Olive Oil. Add any additional flavorings or colorings, and then pour it into the jars.

Different variations of mustards can be made simply depending on the type of liquid added:

Cool American-Style Mustard: Hot Water.

English Mustard: Vinegar.

Spicy English Mustard: White Wine.

French Dijon Mustard: Champagne.

Hot Chinese Mustard: Flat Beer.

Extra-Spicy Mustard: Plain Cold Water.

These special types of mustard must be refrigerated, otherwise the flavor starts changing.

It is said by at least 2 sources to put a slice of lemon atop the mustard to keep it fresh, and change it once a week, although I never noticed any difference without it. Always keep any homemade mustard refrigerated, as they contain no preservatives and can go bad. They should keep several months depending on ingredients. Those with vinegar will last longer; those with water and fresh herbs won't last as long.

Now that you can make beautiful food projects, let's learn how to use them for— *"Fine Dining"*...

Fine Dining

Elegant meals start with quality, be it wine and cheese, or kosher meat. This section covers them all.

Kosher Wine & Cheese Pairing Guide

The following charts show what kosher wines and cheeses go together. Both need a reliable *hechsher*.

Wine & Cheese Pairing Chart	
Wine	**Cheese**
Beaujolais	Brie; Feta
Cabernet Sauvignon	Brie; Camembert; Aged Gouda; Camembert; Danablu; Sharp Cheddar
Champagne; Reisling; Sherry	Brie; Cheshire; Colby; Edam; Gouda; Mild Cheddar
Chardonnay	Asiago; Brie; Camembert; Mild Cheddar; Muenster; Provolone
Chenin Blanc	Camembert
Gewürztraminer	Caraway; Goat Cheese; Smoked Gouda; Swiss
Merlot	Aged Gouda; Parmesan; Provolone; Sharp Cheddar
Petite Syrah/Petite Shiraz; Syrah/Shiraz	Asiago; Sharp Cheddar
Pinot Grigio	Ricotta; Provolone
Pinot Noir; Sangiovese	Asiago; Brei; Goat Cheese; Parmesan
Red Bordeaux	Havarti
Red Zinfandel	Asiago; Sharp Cheddar; Aged Gouda; Parmesan
Sauvignon Blanc	Goat Cheese; Feta; Mozzarella; Ricotta
White Zinfandel	Cream; Muenster

Kosher Wine Guide

For kosher wines, it's fairly simple: Buy *mevushal* [cooked] and one doesn't have to worry about how it is handled. "Mevushal" will appear on the label. Since wine and grape juice has a special status, it is treated more stringently. Thankfully, with *mevushal*, the consumer doesn't need to worry about handling.

These are basic wines, not expensive vintage wines. Although older wines are often better, remember the aging process (done in special sealed barrels at a precise temperature) is different than for wine sitting around getting old on the shelf or in the refrigerator. Wine can and does go bad once it has been opened. It is helpful to store it tightly capped in a basement at or around 55° F. Some let wines "breathe" (stay open) for a short time before serving.

Wine Chart			
Wine	**Type**	**Description**	**What Goes with It**
Red (Serve room temperature. Goes with red meat.)	Barbera	Hearty, berry-like	Italian food.
	Beaujolais (Best young.)	Fruity, low alcohol	Red meat.
	Red Bordeaux; Burgundy	Rich, complex	Lamb; Poultry.
	Cabernet Franc	Light, fruity	Italian food; Roasted meats.
	Cabernet Sauvignon	Dry, rich, complex	Roast meat; Heavy stews.
	Chianti; Sangiovese	Hearty	Italian food.
	Malbec; Merlot	Dry, hearty	Pasta; Roasted meats.
	Petite Syrah/Petite Shiraz	Dark, peppery	Strong cheeses; Spicy food.
	Pinot Noir; Côtes-du-Rhône	Dry, earthy	Italian sausage; Lamb; Figs.
	Syrah/Shiraz	Dry, spicy	Spicy food; Strong cheese.
	Red Zinfandel	Dry, Hearty	Poultry; Sausage; Grilled food.
Blush/Rosé (Serve cold.)	White Merlot	Fruity, light pink	Poultry; Fish.
	White Zinfandel	Fruity, light pink	Poultry; Spicy food.
White (Serve cold. Goes with poultry and fish.)	California Chablis	Sweet	Fish.
	Champagne	Sweet, sparkling	Hors d'oeuvres; Cheese; Fish.
	Chardonnay	Dry, crisp, creamy	Poultry; Eggs; Fish; Salads.
	Chenin Blanc; Colombard	Dry, fruity	Fish; Salads; Spicy food.
	French Chablis	Dry, delicate	Fish.
	Gewürztraminer	Sweet, low alcohol	Curry; Spicy food; Fish.
	Johannesburg Riesling	Fragrant, fresh	Smoked fish; Spicy food.
	Late harvest wines	Sweet dessert	Fruit; Less sweet desserts.
	Muscat	Sweet fruity	Spicy food; Fish; Desserts.
	Pinot Grigio/Pinot Gris	Dry, spicy	Fish; Poultry; Italian food.
	Pouilly-Fumé	Dry	Fish; Hors d'oeuvres.
	Riesling; Vouvray	Semi-sweet, semi-dry	Fish; Spicy food.
	Sauternes	Sweet dessert	Blue cheese; Light desserts.
	Sauvignon Blanc	Dry, light, grassy	Fish; Poultry; Citrus fruits.
	Sémillon	Sweet dessert wine	Fruit; Desserts.
	Viognier	Complex, fragrant	Fish; Poultry.

Kosher Cheese Guide

Whether *Chalav Stam* or *Chalav Yisrael*, cheeses types are the same. Aside from the description, the categories they fall into are included for *kashrut* purposes: Hard (aged 6 months— one must wait 6 hours before eating meat), medium or soft (both can be eaten before meat if having washed and eaten *parve*).

The aging process has precise conditions (cultures, temperature) and is not akin to cheese stored in the fridge. "Hard" cheese is dry and grated, unable to be sliced. Domestic Swiss cheese is rarely "aged".

Cheese Chart			
Hardness	**Cheese Type**	**Description**	**What Goes with It**
Hard Generally aged 6 months or longer. (* Some may not truly be "Hard". Read label for "Aged".)	Asiago	Italian grating cheese.	Pizza; Salad; Italian food.
	* Kashkaval	White cheese.	Pizza; Salad; Italian food.
	* Mozzarella/String	Creamy stretchy pizza cheese.	Pizza; Salad; Italian food.
	New York Sharp Cheddar	Orange, very tangy flavor.	Crackers.
	Parmesan; Pecorino; Romano	Nutty-flavor sold pre-grated.	Pasta; Pizza; Popcorn; Salads.
	* Provolone	Smoked yellow-white, round.	Sandwiches; Italian food.
	* Scamorza	Mozzarella-like, often smoked.	Pizza; Salad; Italian food.
	Sharp Cheddar	Orange with a tangy flavor.	Sandwiches; Crackers.
	* Swiss	Pale cheese with large holes.	Sandwiches; Quiche.
Medium Not "Hard" unless "Aged" is stated on package. (Be cautious and read the label.)	American/Process	Blend of many cheeses.	Sandwiches; Sauces.
	Blue; Danablu	Cheese marbled with mold. Served room temperature.	Crackers; Fruit; Salads.
	Cheshire; Colby; Cheddar; Gloucester; Leicester	Orange, slight tang but creamy.	Sandwiches; Crackers; Chili; Mexican food.
	Edam; Gouda	Round, coated in red wax. Creamy, Cheddar-like.	Crackers; Sandwiches; Salads; Fruit.
	Havarti	Buttery. Often flavored.	Crackers.
	Monterey Jack/Jack	Often flavored with jalapeño.	Mexican food.
	Muenster	Creamy white with small holes.	Sandwiches; Quiche; Fruit.
	Port Salut/Port du Salut	Buttery flavored.	Crackers; Fruit; Apple pie.
Soft More aptly called "Fresh", these are never aged.	Brie; Camembert	Buttery, creamy, edible crust.	Crackers; Fruit.
	Cottage	Curds in whey or cream.	Lasagna; Salad; Fruit.
	Cream	Whipped or firm. Often flavored with fruit or herbs.	Bagels; Celery; Dips Cheesecake; Icing.
	Farmer's	Crumbly, like a dry Cottage.	Lasagna; Salad; fruit.
	Feta	Salty, crumbly.	Crackers; Salads.
	Goat; Ricotta; Yogurt	Mild creamy, spreadable.	Lasagna; Pasta filling.
	Neufchâtel	Similar to cream, but less rich.	Bagels; Cheesecake; Icing.

Kosher Meat Cuts

Literally "a cut above the rest", kosher meat is from the front half. All kosher meat, (fresh, packaged or frozen) must be under supervision from a reliable *kashrut* agency. If there is no local butcher or large Jewish community nearby, kosher meat can even be ordered online! For non-kosher recipes, this section can provide kosher substitutes for *treifah* cuts of meat. Cuts come from general regions and very often overlap, such as chuck and neck or shoulder. Kosher cuts will also vary with the butcher, who often improvises. The diagram below shows the general regions of where meat comes from.

Meat Region Diagram

Dotted lines show overlaps. The kosher/*treifah* dividing line is between the 12th and 13th last large rib.

Kosher Meat (Forequarters Only)

A. Breast (*Lamb/Veal*)	C. Chuck	E. Neck	G. Short Plate
B. Brisket	D. Foreshank	F. Rib	H. Shoulder

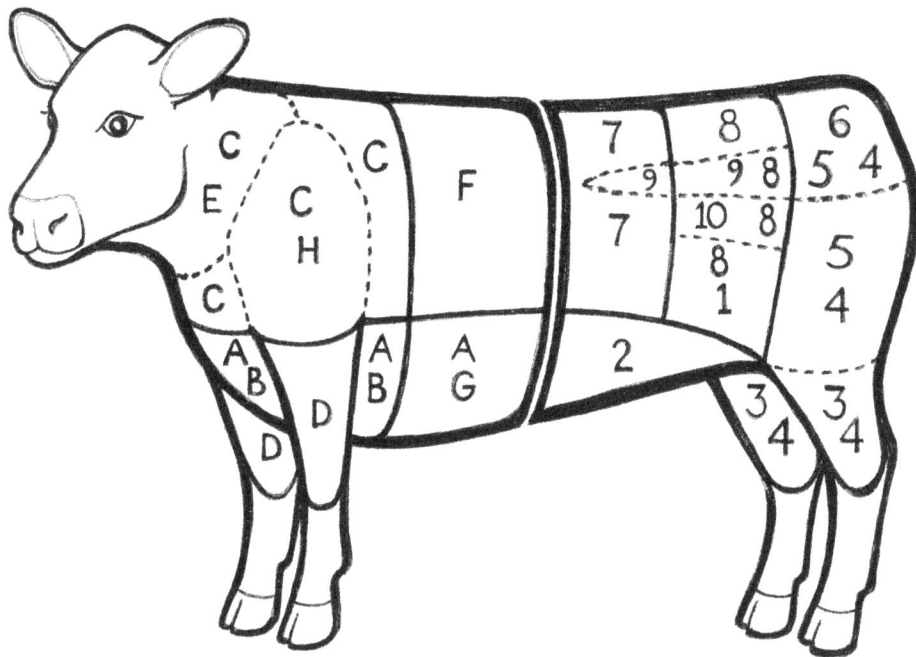

Non-Kosher Meat (Hindquarters)

1. Bottom Sirloin	3. Hind Shank	5. Round	7. Short Loin	9. Tenderloin
2. Flank	4. Leg (*Lamb/Veal*)	6. Rump	8. Sirloin	10. Top Sirloin

Where Various Cuts Come From

Cut names often vary by community, so this is not an exhaustive list. It merely shows the location of common cuts. Ground meat can come from virtually anywhere. Since some cuts of meat overlap into nearby areas, they are listed more than once. Kosher cuts in quotes are imitation *treifah* cuts. Cuts having multiple names are listed first in bold by main name (alternate names are parenthetical). Other cuts (**O**) are individually listed afterward. Lamb or veal cuts are just like beef except for specific cuts listed in italics.

Offal:

Not shown on the chart, some people think these cuts sound just "awful", but these parts are actually kosher!

Feet: (Cooked by long slow simmering.) Many old-timers make calf's foot jelly.

Liver: (Must be broiled to *kasher*, reduce cook time. Pan-fry, broil, grill or broil.) Purchase pre-*kashered*!

Lung: (Cook by boiling or frying.) Purchase pre-*kashered*!

Sweetbreads: (Cooked in any way.) Pancreas and thymus glands. Must be deveined by the butcher.

Tail: (Cooked by long slow simmering, as for soup.) These are most commonly available as "Ox Tails".

Tongue: (Cook by boiling or simmering. See cooking on p. 495) Must be deveined by the butcher.

Kosher Meat Cuts (Forequarters Only)

Brisket: Corned Brisket (Corned Beef); **Deckle Roast** (Dekel); **1st Cut** (Flat Cut, Flat Half Brisket, Thin Cut); **2nd Cut** (Front Cut, Point Cut, Point Half, Point Half Brisket, Thick Cut).

    O- Brisket Strip; Pastrami Roast. *Lamb or Veal: Breast, Riblets.*

Chuck: Arm Roast (Arm Chuck Roast, Arm Pot Roast, Chuck Arm; Round Bone Pot Roast, Round Bone Roast); **Arm Steak** (Arm Chuck Steak, Arm Swiss Steak, Round Bone Steak, Round Bone Swiss Steak); **Chuck Eye Roast** (Apple Roast, Eye Roast, Chuck Fillet, Chuck Tender, Large Kalechal, Mock Tender); **Chuck Eye Steak** (Beauty Roast, Chuck Fillet Steak, Chuck Tender Steak); **Cross Rib Roast** (Boston Cut, English Cut Roast, English Roll, Thick Rib Roast); **7-Bone Roast** (Center Cut Pot Roast, Chuck Roast Center Cut, 7-Bone Pot Roast); **7-Bone Steak** (Center Chuck Steak.); **Middle Chuck Steak** (California Steak). **O-** Chuck Steak; Chuck Roast; "Club Steak"; Flanken-Style Ribs; French Roast; Round Bone Steak; Short Ribs; "T-Bone Steak".

Foreshank: Shank Bone (Marrow Bone, Soup Bone); **Shank Cross Cut** (Kalechal Steak); **Shank Knuckle** (Kalechal Roast); **Shin** (Muscle). **O-** Beef Kalky; Round Kalichel; Stew Meat. *Lamb only: Lamb Ribs (Denver Ribs); Lamb Shank (Lamb Trotter). Veal only: Foreshank. Lamb or Veal: Steak.*

Neck: Brick Roast (if boneless— Rolled Neck); Stew Meat. *Lamb or Veal: Rolled Roast.*

Rib: Flanken (Rib Flanken); **Flanken-Style Ribs** (Brust Flanken, Flanken Short Ribs); **Rib Eye Roast** (Delmonico Roast); **Rib Eye Steak** ("Delmonico Steak", "Fillet Steak", Spencer Steak); **Short Ribs** (Barbecue Ribs, Chuck Short Ribs, Plate Flanken); **Rib Roast** (Boneless Rib Roast, Rolled Rib Roast,

Standing Rib Roast). **O-** Back Ribs; Boneless Rib Steak; "Châteuabriand Steak"; Prime Rib; Rib Steak; Short Ribs; Spare Ribs; Top of Rib Roast; "Triangle Pot Roast". *Lamb only:* ***Riblets (Spareribs); Frenched Rib Chops. Lamb or Veal: Crown Roast; Rack; Rib Chops.***

Short Plate: Flanken-Style Ribs (Brust Flanken, Flanken Short Ribs); **Hanging Tender** (Butcher's Tenderloin, Hanger, Hanger Steak, Hanging Tenderloin, Onglet); **Short Ribs** (Barbecue Ribs, Chuck Short Ribs, English Short Ribs, Plate Flanken); **Skirt Steak** (Fajita Meat, Philadelphia Steak). **O-** "Beef Flank Steak"; "Cubed Steak"; Plate Boiling Beef; Plate Steak Rolls; Rolled Plate; Stew Meat. *Lamb or Veal:* ***Riblets (Spareribs). Breast.***

Shoulder: Blade Roast (Blade Chuck Roast, Blade Pot Roast); **Blade Steak** ("Minute Steak"); **Short Roast** ("Minute Roast"); **Shoulder Roast** (English Roast, Shoulder Pot Roast); **Shoulder Steak** (Clod Steak, English Steak, "Fillet Steak"); **Top Blade Roast** (Top Blade Pot Roast, Flat Iron Roast, Lifter Roast, Puff Roast, Triangle Pot Roast); **Top Blade Steak** (Book Steak, Butler Steak, Flat Iron Steak, Lifter Steak, Petite Steak, Top Chuck Steak); **Under Blade Pot Roast** (California Roast, Under Cut Roast); **Under Blade Steak** (Bottom Chuck Steak, California Steak). **O-** Beef Kalechel; End Roast; End Steak; Kebabs; "London Broil"; "Minute Steak"; Short Roast; Shoulder Fillet Kalecha; Silver Tip Roast. *Lamb only: Arm Lamb Chop; Cushion Lamb Shoulder; Lamb Shoulder Chop; Lamb Stew Meat; Saratoga Lamb Chops. Lamb or Veal: Blade Chops.*

Treifah Meat Cuts (From Hindquarters)

Bottom Sirloin: Bottom Sirloin Steak.

Flank: Flank Steak Fillets, Flank Steak, Flank Steak Rolls, Stew Meat.

Hind Shank: Rear Shank Bone, Stew Meat. *Lamb only:* ***Lamb Leg Chops*** *(Lamb Leg Steak, Lamb Round Leg Steak); Frenched Leg; Leg of Lamb. Veal only:* ***Cutlet*** *(Scallopini); Heel; Veal Roast.*

Round: Eye of Round Steak (Minute Steak, Sandwich Steak); **Top Round Steak** (London Broil). **O-** Bottom Round Roast; Cubed Steak; Eye of Round Roast; Heel of Round; Round Steak; Round Tip Roast; Round Tip Steak; Swiss Steak; Tip Roast; Tip Steak; Top Round Roast. *Veal only: Scallops.*

Rump: Rolled Rump; Rump Roast.

Short Loin: Club Steak (Delmonico Steak); **Strip Steak** (New York Steak, Top Loin Steak). **O-** Pin Bone; Porterhouse Steak; T-Bone Steak; Top Loin Roast; *Lamb or Veal: Loin Chop; Loin Roast.*

Sirloin: Tri-Tip Roast (Beef Loin Tri-Tip Roast, Triangle Tip Roast). **O-** Pin Bone; Tri-Tip Steak; Sirloin Steak; Sirloin Tips; Sirloin Tip Roast. Flat Bone; Round Bone; Wedge Bone.

Top Sirloin: Top Sirloin Cap Steak (Culotte Steak); **Top Sirloin Steak** (Châteuabriand Steak).

Tenderloin: Filet Mignon (Fillet Steak, Tenderloin Steak, Tender Steak, Tournedos); **Tenderloin Roast** (Filet Mignon Roast, Tenderloin Tip Roast). **O-** Tenderloin Steak.

Substituting Meat Cuts

If a recipe calls for a *treifah* cut, simply substitute a kosher cut. A cut known by multiple names goes by the main name in the previous lists for easy identification. Cooking methods should match. Dry heat is baking, broiling/grilling, or pan-frying. Moist heat is boiling/stewing. Microwaving is generally the same as dry heat, but the meat stays moister. (Substitute lamb or veal cuts just like beef, unless noted in italics.)

Treifah Meat Cut Substitute Chart		
Cooking:	For These Treifah Cuts:	Substitute These Kosher Cuts:
Moist Heat Ideal for cooking tougher cuts of meat. Best preceded by browning in oil first- called "braising".	**Areas Suited for Moist Heat:** Flank, Hind Shank or some Round.	**Areas Best Suited for Moist Heat:** Brisket, Neck, Foreshank, Short Plate or Shoulder.
	Bottom Round Roast.	Arm Roast; Cross Rib Roast; Shoulder Roast.
	Cubed Steak; Flank Steak; Round Steak; Tip Steak; Top Round Steak.	Chuck Steak; "Cubed Steak"; "Minute Steak"; Rib Eye Steak.
	Flank Steak.	Hanging Tender; Skirt Steak.
	Rear Shank Bone.	Shank Bone; Shin; Short Ribs.
	Swiss Steak.	Arm Swiss Steak; 7-Bone Steak; Shoulder Steak.
	Top Round Roast; Stew Meat.	Hanging Tender; Skirt Steak; Stew Meat.
	Leg of Lamb.	*Lamb Shoulder; Rack of Lamb.*
	Lamb Leg Chop.	*Lamb Shoulder Chop.*
	Lamb Shank.	*Lamb Neck.*
	Veal Round Steak; Veal Cutlet.	(Chicken Breast pounded flat.)
Dry Heat Best for cooking tender cuts of meat such as steaks. Steaks are best when coated with margarine and seasoned prior to cooking.	**Areas Best Suited for Dry Heat:** Short Loin, Sirloin or Tenderloin.	**Area Best Suited for Dry Heat:** Rib.
	Club Steak; Filet Mignon; Flat Bone; Pin Bone; Porterhouse Steak; Sirloin Steak; Strip Steak; Top Sirloin Steak; T-Bone Steak; Wedge Bone. *Veal Loin Chop.*	Chuck Eye Steak; "Club Steak"; Rib Eye Steak; Rib Steak; "T-Bone Steak".
	Eye of Round Steak (Minute Steak).	"Cubed Steak"; "Minute Steak".
	Sirloin Tips.	Chuck Eye Steak, Rib Eye Steak, Rib Steak or "T-Bone Steak" cut into chunks.
	Tenderloin Roast; Top Loin Roast.	Rib Eye Roast; Rib Roast.
	Tri-Tip Roast; Tri-Tip Steak.	Hanging Tender or Skirt Steak.
	Lamb or Veal Loin Chop.	*Lamb or Veal Rib Chop; Lamb Shoulder Chop.*
	Lamb or Veal Loin Roast.	*Lamb or Veal Shoulder Roast.*
Any Cooking Method Also applies to all Lamb, Veal or Ground Meat.	**Suited for Any Cooking:** Round or Rump.	**Suited for Any Cooking:** Chuck.
	Bottom Round Roast; Eye of Round Roast; Heel of Round; Rump Roast; Tip Roast.	Arm Roast; Chuck Eye Roast; Chuck Roast; Cross Rib Roast; Shoulder Roast; 7-Bone Roast; Top Blade Roast; Under Blade Pot Roast.
	Eye of Round Steak; Round Tip Steak.	Chuck Eye Steak; Top Blade Steak.
	Top Round Steak (London Broil).	Hanging Tender; "London Broil"; Skirt Steak; Top Blade Steak.
	Round Steak.	Chuck Steak.
	Top Round Roast; Top Round Steak.	Hanging Tender; Skirt Steak.
	Veal Rump Roast.	*Veal Foreshank.*
	Veal Round Steak.	*Veal Blade Steak or Arm Steak.*

Fancy Food

This segment can help dress up any meal, be it for entertaining, a romantic dinner with one's spouse, or just for fun and creativity. Fancy food makes the table prettier, whets the most finicky of appetites, and in some cases can often use up small amounts of leftovers. Below are suggestions for those looking for ideas. Other tips can be found throughout this book in Extra Foods (pp. 595-601).

Use colorful and contrasting foods when topping or garnishing to artistically dress up meals. Good examples are black olives set atop shredded cheese, and powdered sugar sifted over chocolate cake.

Topping it Off

Sifting: This is especially suited for sweet desserts. Substances to use are powdered sugar, cinnamon sugar, or cocoa (preferably mixed with a bit of powdered sugar). Hold a strainer over the item to be dusted, and gently put the powdered substance in the strainer a spoonful at a time, rubbing the spoon over it until it is gone. Do it slowly and evenly, and your item will look like professional bakery goods.

If one wants to be very elaborate, they can sift powder in decorative patterns, either on frosted or unfrosted items. Cut out patterns for a stencil from wax paper, such as 3-5 triangles or slightly swirled triangles for round cakes. Place stencil atop the item. Sift, then carefully remove stencil. Some areas will be covered and others bare, and is a dramatic effect.

Sprinkling: Just as candy sprinkles can make a cupcake more decorative, random sprinkling is perhaps the easiest way to make food pretty. Try sprinkling on these items if you need decoration in no time...

For Salty Dairy Dishes Only— Shredded Medium or Hard Cheese; Grated Parmesan or Romano Cheeses. For Salty *Parve*, Meat or Dairy— Grated *Parve* Imitation Cheese; Ground or Chopped Nuts; Toasted Ramen Noodles; Chow Mein Noodles; Mandelin (Soup Croutons); Toasted Crumbs (matzah, bread, corn flake or cracker); Wheat Germ; Chopped Herbs; Chopped Green Onions.

For Sweet *Parve* or Dairy— Candy Sprinkles or Jimmies; Ground or Chopped Nuts; Chocolate Chips; Graham Cracker Crumbs (sautéed in oil); Grated Chocolate; or Tiny Candies (such as cinnamon drops).

Saucing: Pour over foods in random patterns or coat evenly.

For Sweet Foods— Spread on syrup, glazing or icing. Icing can be drizzled on when it is warm, and will harden if chilled, making pretty stripes as it goes over the edge. For flat items, use two different colored icings. Coat the whole surface with the first type, and then put the second color (such as chocolate) in parallel lines. Drag a knife across it perpendicularly for a really neat effect. Napoleons are done this way.

For Salty Meat Foods— Spoon gravy or sauces over the meat, whether a whole bird or roast, or simple slices. It can be further garnished with sprinkled items on top.

Garnishing

Adding: Place herb sprigs around, on top or tucked into food to garnish. (See "Edible Flowers" p. 435.)

Embedding: Serve a main food in a bed of a side dish, a pool of sauce, or atop a garnish.

For Salty Food— Rice; Stuffing; Pasta; Mashed Potatoes; Lettuce; Spinach; Tuna, Egg or Pasta Salad.

For Sweet Food— Whipped Cream; Nuts; Small Candies.

Cutting Edge

Radish Roses: A well-known trick is to cut in half with jagged edges to create roses.

Carved Melons: Another nice idea is to create decoratively-carved produce. (See back cover for my "Jewish Apple".) Perhaps the most common are watermelon baskets. Cut out the handle, remove upper sides, hollow out, and fill with various melon balls. They can also simply be cut in half in a zigzag pattern for speed.

Produce Bowls: Cut produce in half, either straight across, or use a zigzag pattern. Hollow it out and fill it. Fill raw veggie bowls with tuna or egg salads, salsa, dip or sauces. Vegetables to use are bell peppers or avocados. Cooked squashes and eggplants can be halved and used, but if cooked too long they can fall apart, so don't scoop out the meat too close to the skin. Leave at least half an inch to the edge. Fill fruit bowls with whipped cream, syrup, chopped nuts or candy. Fruits to use are citrus or melons.

Naturally Symmetrical Foods

Pears: Set 5 canned pear halves together with the stem end at the center and larger ends facing outward. You now have a flower. The pitted centers can each contain a cherry with one cherry in the middle.

Peaches or Plums: Canned pitted peach or plum halves can be done similarly to pears.

Cherries, Grapes or Cherry Tomatoes: These are very good for topping singularly in the center.

Tomatoes: When sliced, these look like wheels and are great placed in a flower pattern as for pears.

Baby Carrots and Celery: Place like spokes around a round food for a sun beam-like appearance.

Eggs: Halve or slice and put the large end to the outside and the small ends to the center to make a flower. They can be places in a bed of tuna salad with a cherry tomato or half a radish in the center.

Avocado: Cut several in half carefully, and do as for pears above.

Onions: Slice white and or red onions for natural circles. Alternate red and white in pretty patterns.

Orange Sections and Brazil Nuts: These are excellent for making swirl and wave patterns when lined up end to end. For a swirl, alternate the wedges so that the inside is out on one and the one next to it is opposite. It should have an "S" shape. Repeat, making a line. Lines can radiate from the center of round plates, or go along an edge to make a border. Make a wave by putting sections end to end in the same direction like a "W". Any round produce can be used if cut in wedges, or sliced and halved.

Chicken Legs: Set bone-ends to the center and meat ends toward the outside for a flower pattern.

A Set Table

The Kosher Way

Table Decor: Centerpieces should be low, so that guests don't have to look around it to see each other. A lace cloth atop a colored one is a great accent. Try to match colors of centerpiece, tablecloth, napkins, and dishes. Place utensils as shown above, 1-inch from table's edge. (A plastic sheet over a tablecloth makes for easy clean up.)

A = Small Fork. Generally used for fish at a fancy meal, it can be used for salads or dessert.

B = Large Fork. Used for the main meal.

C = Large Plate. Also used for the main meal, this is on the bottom when in place at serving time.

D = Bowl or Small Plate. Generally, a fish and salad plate, or a bowl for soup if in place at serving time.

E = Knife. This is always placed with the cutting edge toward the plate.

F = Spoon. Usually, a larger soup spoon, but if there is no soup it can be a smaller dessert spoon.

G = Glass. This can be a wine goblet, a cup, or whatever one has. A tea cup with saucer can be placed to its right.

H = Dessert Fork or Spoon. I've mostly seen this in kosher homes.

 I = Napkin. Often placed to the left under forks. They can be folded very fancily (see the nice folds shown over the next few pages). Fancy napkins can be placed anywhere– in a plate's center, or even fluted inside of a glass.

Seating: In a kosher home, guests are seated man-man, woman-woman, (as opposed to "boy-girl, boy-girl"), the exception being spouses. A guest of honor (*Kohen* or rabbi) sits at the host's right. A hosting husband and wife may sit at opposite ends if it's a long table. For formal occasions, place cards may be used.

Serving Etiquette: *Always* have serving utensils for each food type, so that guests don't use their own. Never lick your fingers if you get food on them when serving. (Both are unsanitary!) A guest of honor or parent is served first, then it goes by age from oldest to youngest. Guests should wait to eat until the host starts eating. Food passed in a group goes right of the host— counterclockwise. In formal settings, serve food from the left, remove from the right, and serve drinks from the right. One shouldn't scrape or clean dishes at the table.

Pretty Napkins

Nicely folded napkins are a great accent to table décor, and can also serve a practical purpose. The fancy folds seen in entertainment guides are mostly for starched and pressed cloth napkins, but these are designed for ease and speed, and suited for paper napkins. Paper towels that fold into perfect squares can be even better, since they're stiffer and fold well. (Very cheap paper napkins can be too thin, and not cut or folded perfectly.)

One should do these fancy folds before *Shabbat* or major holidays— make the needed number and set aside, otherwise one should really only fold a napkin once to make a simple triangle or rectangle.

Contemporary Rectangular Silver-Holder

1. Start with a square paper napkin, or fold a paper towel precisely in quarters to make one as shown in 1.

2. Position napkin so that a fold-side is to the bottom, and the other fold-side is to the right.

3. Take the upper right corner (point "A") and fold it down about 1-inch, at a perfect 90° angle, and crease it very hard. (Top right corner should now exhibit a square shape.)

4. Fold it over (about 1-inch) 3 more times at the same angle, as though to roll it. (There should be a diagonal 1-inch strip starting at 1-inch from one corner to 1-inch from the opposite corner.)

5. Flip napkin over. Fold "B" over to centerline, and crease very hard.

6. Fold "C" over to centerline, and crease very hard.

7. Flip back over for the completed silverware holder.

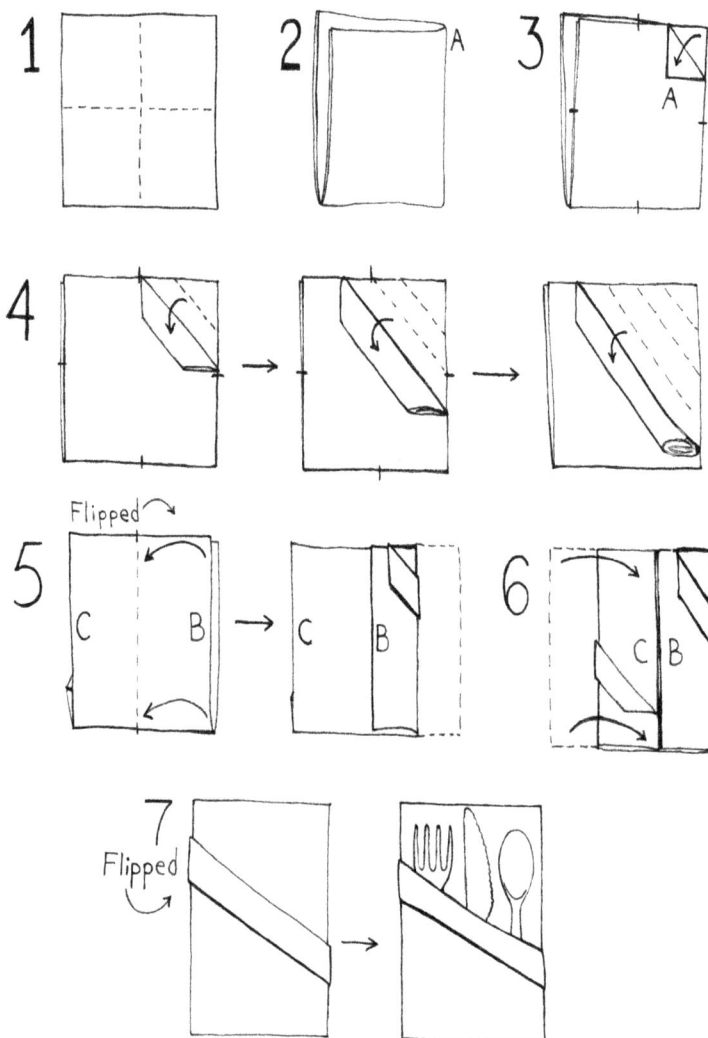

Fancy Diamond Silver Holder

1. Start with a normal square paper napkin, or fold a paper towel precisely in quarters to make one as shown.

2. Turn napkin diagonally to create a diamond, with open corners on top.

3. Fold "A" to centerline 1, and crease (fold hard). (This makes edge "C".)

4. Take "C" and fold it down to "A" on centerline (basically like rolling it). Crease the fold.

5. Flip napkin over. It should look like this in 5.

6. Fold "D" to centerline 2.

7. Fold "E" to centerline 2.

8. It should look like this in 8. Crease folds well.

9. Flip napkin over and you have a diamond.

10. Place silverware in the pouch.

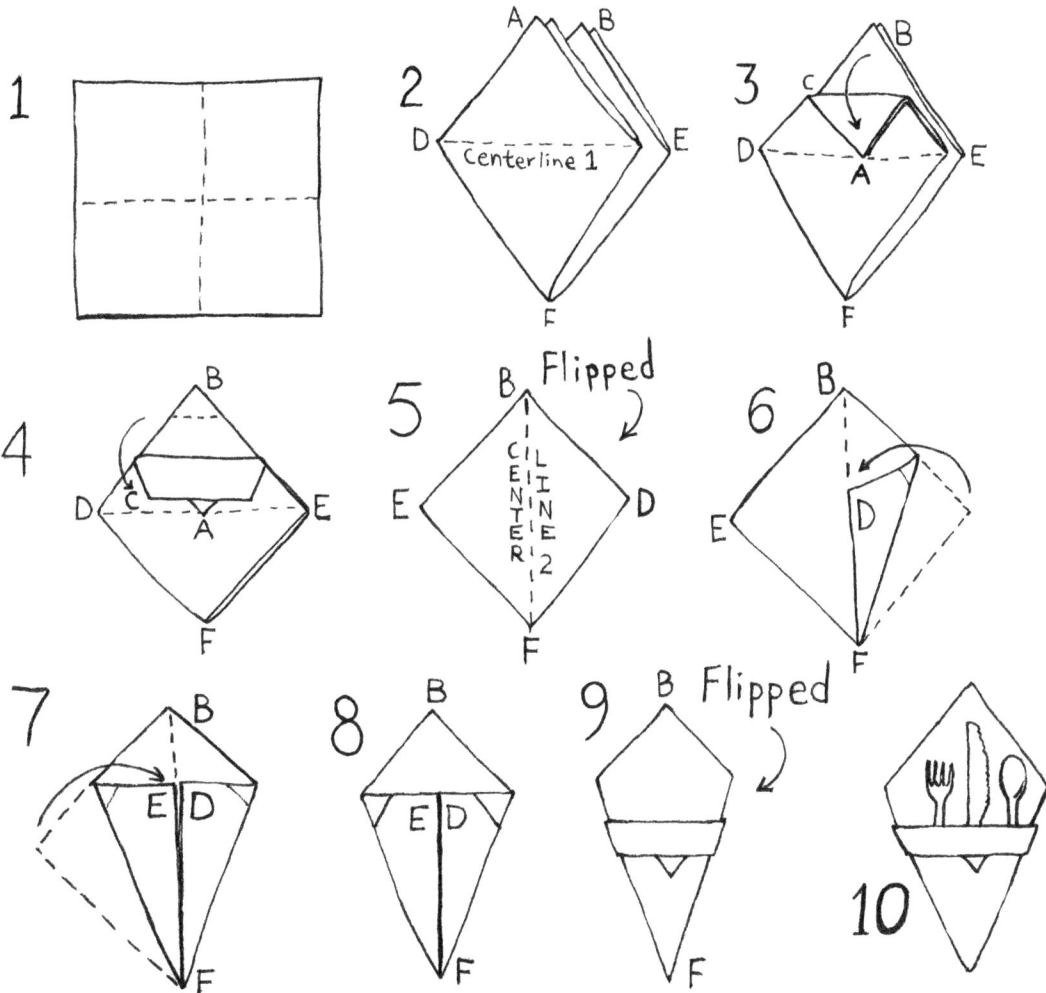

Triangular Fanned Silver Holder

1. Start with a square paper napkin, or fold a paper towel precisely in quarters to make one as shown.

2. Position napkin so that one folded side is to the bottom.

3. Take the upper right corner (point "A") and fold it down ⅓ of the way across at a perfect 90° angle and crease it hard. (The top corner should now exhibit a square shape.)

4. Do the same with the left side taking the upper left corner (point "B") and fold it down ⅓ of the way across. (Top corners should be symmetrical, with the outer napkin should look rather like an arrow.)

5. Fold point "C" down to about ⅔ of the napkin and the fold is about ⅓ from the top.

6. Fold points "D" and "E" over to slightly over the center point of the napkin, as though to roll it. Crease hard.

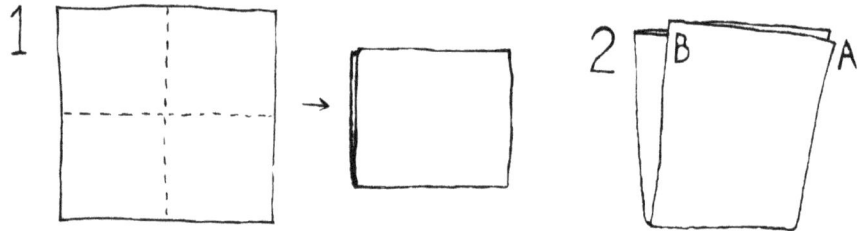

7. Flip napkin over, fold the right side (point "F") over about ⅔ of the way over (bottom should be at center point of napkin), and crease very hard.

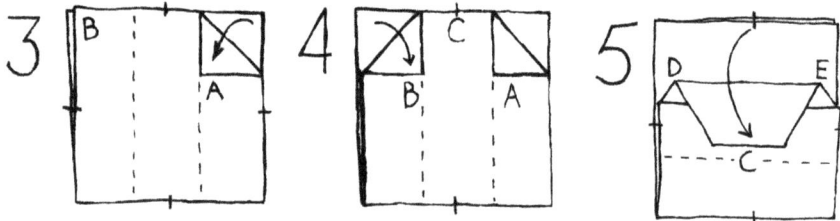

8. Do the same on the other side, folding the left (point "G") over about ⅔ of the way over (covering "F") and crease very hard. (It should be perfectly symmetrical with a point at the bottom.)

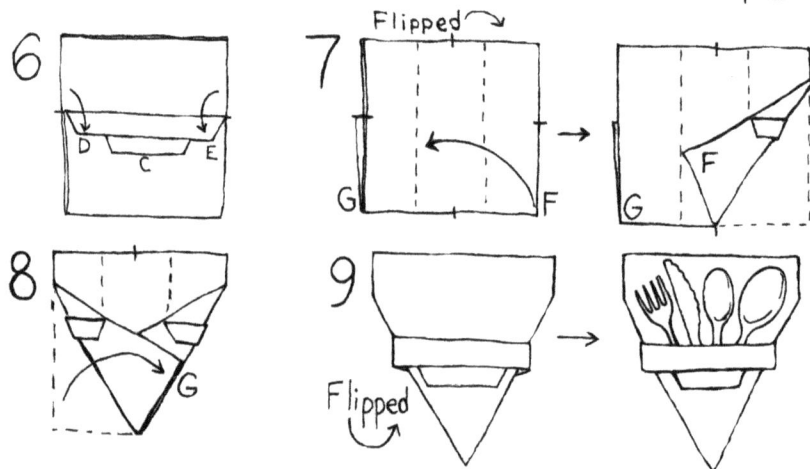

9. Flip it back over for the completed silverware holder, and insert silverware in the pocket, fanning it out to match the napkin.

454

Butterfly Silverware Ring

This is best done with paper towels or large, thicker paper napkins. They should ideally be more rectangular, but square works just as well. Silver rings are semi-functional and add a touch of class.

1. Start with a square paper towel or an unfolded napkin.

2. Fold napkin accordion style (back and forth in even increments). Fold the whole napkin this way.

3. Crease the folds together hard to make it as flat as possible.

4. Fold "A" to "B", crease on center point making "C".

5. Pinch point "D" together. "A" and "B" should be same exact height.

6. Take outer edge of "A" and pull down, opening all the way to touch "C". Crease well at point "D".

7. Do the same with "B", pulling down, open to touch "C". Crease well at "D". You now have a butterfly.

8. Fold it back accordion-style, place silverware in the center, and gently tie the napkin around it.

9. Turn it so that the knot side is down, and place on the center of a plate.

10. Reopen the sides (as shown in 7) to create a bow-like butterfly with silverware "body". It helps to tuck the ends of points "A", "B", "E", and "F" underneath the silver for a little while.

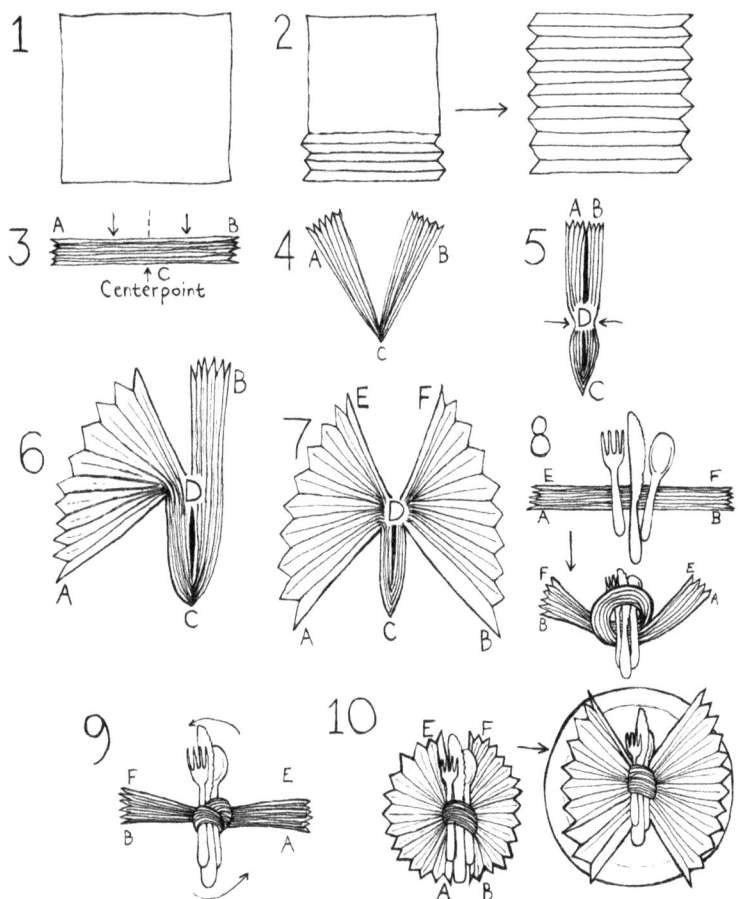

Don't have ingredients for some recipes or projects? For substitutions, equivalencies, plus an endless array of other helpful tips and guides, let's consult the— "*Kitchen Companion*"…

Section 6
Kitchen Companion
A Reference Helper

Practical Pointers
Tips from Saving Money to Cooking and Health

Energy Saving Tips

Freezers & Refrigerators: The air needs to circulate, especially in your freezer where things tend to get shoved in tightly. Always be sure the vents are not blocked or covered by bags. (The vents are those little finned openings that are a nightmare to clean crumbs out of for Passover.) When the freezer is running, put your hand up and ideally you should feel air blowing. If the air doesn't circulate, the freezer could be working twice as hard, and your food is at risk of going bad.

Another tip for either the freezer or refrigerator is to always let your food cool off before putting it in. Not only does it keep the appliance from working harder, it protects the *kashrut* status of the refrigerator or freezer, but also the pot or container that goes in it.

Never leave the door open and just walk away. It is so easy just to close the door and reopen it.

Ovens & Stoves: Ovens, electric stoves and broilers can provide latent heat, if the food item takes a while to cook. Since it takes time for these to cool down, you can turn them off about five minutes early and save the energy. The food cooks even though the stove or oven is off.

Hot Water Heaters: Keep your hot water heater set at a minimum temperature setting. It helps with *kashrut* accidents, protects young children from getting scalded, and saves on your energy bill.

Wrapping the hot water heater and pipes with foam insulation designed just for the purpose can also reduce an energy bill. Since metal dissipates heat easily, If the heater is in a cold basement, the water heater may be working harder than it has to. The hot water ends up being cooled by the pipes. When wrapped, the pipes stay warmer and keep the heat in. Every little bit helps. It is nearly the same principle as with weather-stripping and home insulation.

Crock Pots: In addition to being very low-wattage, they are convenient for time as well. Put all your ingredients in the morning, set on low, and 8 hours later you come back to a fully cooked hot meal. An additional feature they can add that many people utilize on *Shabbat*, is for food warming. Set an aluminum or baking pan upside down on top, and it becomes a perfect food-warmer. Within a short time, bread placed on top will be toasty warm. It is only good for temporary warming, not for cooking. (One must also be careful that it's balanced properly.) It offers heating without using additional electricity.

457

Budget-Stretching Tips

Natural Disposal Freshener: Don't waste your baking soda by dumping it down the drain, let garbage do the work. Put old citrus peels in your disposal and then run it for a fresh clean smell.

No-Dump Pasta: To conserve water and keep the nutrients from pasta in the food, boil it with a minimum of water— 4 cups of water per pound of pasta. Stir throughout the cooking process, and you will be left with no water to have to dump. The pasta absorbs all the water and the nutrients are left in.

Natural Thickeners: Do you want to boil a batch of spaghetti or noodles the usual way? Save the water, it's excellent for adding to soups for natural thickening without adding flour. Save water from boiled potatoes to use in bread dough. It makes home baked bread last longer without preservatives!

Bean Soup: When making a huge batch of plain beans to freeze or use, don't dump the "pot liquor", save it with some of the beans too. Add some seasonings and it will make a delicious bean soup.

Vegetable Soup: Take the *Shabbat* stew *cholent*, add a little water, some beef soup mix, a can of mixed vegetables, and seasonings for a great soup. (See "Extra Foods pp. 595-601. It's designed to save money.)

Well-Done Cookies: Spread icing on the bottoms and place them together as sandwich cookies.

Extra Freezer: It often helps to have a small extra freezer. This is very handy for Passover if and when you sell your *chametz* [leavened products] or store your *kitniyot* [legumes, rice or their derivatives that can be construed as *chametz*]. Store items there, tape up the freezer and mark "sold". Mainly, it helps if you find a sale and stock up, buy in bulk (usually cheaper) or store home-made instant meals (next page).

Buying Food: When buying large quantities of produce such as bananas, buy them singularly. Like bone-in meat, stem weight adds up, causing you to pay for parts you're just throwing out.

Another often misunderstood budget-stretcher is purchasing store-brands. Often, off-brands or store brands are made by brand-name companies. Supermarkets contract with these companies acting as middlemen, still making some profit but offering quality products for a lower price. Consumers get higher quality than generic and save money. The products usually have the same *hechsher* as the name-brand, because it's the same product. The old wives' tale "you get what you pay for" is not always true! In fact, it can be the opposite. Big companies mark up prices so consumers feel they're getting higher quality merchandise (not to mention make more money). In fact, the product may not be as good! Merchandising is an art, not a sign of quality. As for name-brands, "let the buyer beware". It's often the opposite of what one thinks!

Time-Saving & Instant Food Tips

Instant TV Dinners: Make big batches of food and divide them into single-serve portions to make your favorite TV dinners. If that takes too long, put in a piece of chicken from the night before with some of a side dish and half a can of veggies. Now you've got an instant meal ready to freeze for later.

Instant Single-Serving Snacks: Store smaller servings in containers for instant lunches to pop in the microwave. A non-sugary warm snack idea is to fix popcorn in big batches. It's a healthy snack and keeps well. To "doll it up", use some *Popcorn Seasonings* listed on p. 126, or herbs and spices. Put in single serving zipper bags, microwave it 20 seconds and they're ready for kids on the go.

Instant Mashed Potatoes & Gravy: For a snack or lunch, put a heaping spoonful of onion or any other kind of soup mix and ½ cup instant potatoes in a container. Put on a lid and store. When ready to use, pour in 1 cup water, microwave 1 minute and stir. You now have mashed potatoes and gravy.

Instant Hot Cocoa Mix: Find a large sealable container, put in a 1-quart envelope of powdered milk (1⅓ cup), 4 tsp. cocoa, 8 tsp. sugar, and a pinch of salt. Seal the container, shake it for a minute or so, and viola, you have your own instant cocoa mix. Put a bit of water in a cup, add 5 Tbs. of mix, blend into a paste, then add the remaining water. Drink cold, or hot. Mix lasts indefinitely and needs no refrigeration.

Instant Vegetables: Chop up carrots, celery, or green peppers and freeze them in a bag or container. Raw onions can be chopped as well, but be sure to thoroughly coat them with vegetable oil before freezing. (The same goes for refrigerating overnight.) Not only does oil eliminate the overpowering smell of raw onion, but also it keeps them from sticking together, so you can take out the amount you need, and sauté as-is. Use containers and not bags— oil seeps through. Only use olive oil if freezing in specific increments as it freezes solid! Alternately, sauté a big batch and refrigerate up to 1 week, or freeze them in ¼ cup individual increments for quick, flavorful additions to foods (½ cup cooked = 1 cup raw).

Instant Fresh Green Onions: Every time you buy green onions at the store, use only the leaves—stop cutting just before the white part starts. Remove excess skins from the bulbs, and put them in a glass of water. They'll grow this way for a long time (as long as the water is changed periodically). To have them all year long, put them in a pot of dirt in a kitchen window. They even do well there in winter, and seem to enjoy the cold. Harvest outer leaves each time.

Instant Ginger Root: When you buy a ginger root at the store, wash it well and put it in a jar filled with kosher cooking sherry. It lasts indefinitely and is ready to use.

Cooking Tips

Onion Cutting: To keep from crying when cutting onions, refrigerate them or cut them underwater.

Microwave Popcorn: For less un-popped kernels, boil a cup of water in the microwave before popping.

Egg Boiling: Older eggs are better for hard-boiling and peel easier. To avoid green around the yolk, don't cook too long. It helps to plunge the egg into cold water immediately after cooking to cool it down.

No Boil-Over Oats: For creamy oatmeal, instead of all milk, use ⅓ + ⅔ water or add it after cooking.

Potato Cooking: Always cut potatoes at least into quarters. It helps them cook evenly and expose rotten spots inside. Often, I've cut open a host's whole potato in cholent and it was rotten or raw in the middle.

Splatter-less: Use olive oil for sautéing and non-deep-frying. It needs a higher temperature to burn, and only splatters if too hot.

No-Spill Pies: When baking pies, put the pie pan on a cookie sheet to catch spills. It's worth it!

Easy Pie Crusts: Put a bit of flour in an extra-large zipper bag (over 13 inches), zip and shake to coat. Open bag and put dough in. Zip all but a corner. Roll dough out to desired thickness, open bag and gently lift up on top. Loosely roll dough up jelly-roll style and take out. Unroll onto a pie plate.

Gluten-Free Pie Crusts: Line pie tins with ground nuts, such as hazelnuts or blanched almonds.

Fat-Free Baking: Line pans with kosher-certified (silicone-coated) parchment paper instead of greasing them with oil or shortening. Parchment paper cut into small pieces and inserted between rolls can also be used to keep them from baking into each other and connecting.

Double-Wrapping: Put food in foil pan, then wrap the outside with foil. Never line a pan with foil then put in food, especially if the foil is very thin. Foil shreds, can be ingested, and cut the stomach or intestines. Foil is also very thin and cooks into acidic or salty foods, leaving holes in foil and aluminum in food.

Poultry Tips: Remove giblet bag and neck from cavity if applicable. Gizzards (conical-shaped organs) should be rinsed. (Boil with neck for soup or gravy.) If raw livers (*treifah*) are included, remove carefully and discard, or give to someone who regularly *kashers* liver. Rinse bird with water inside and out, pat dry with paper towels and smear cavities with salt. Line roasting pan in foil and spray with oil. Put bird in pan, stuff if desired, tuck wing tips under body, and wrap excess skin over leg tips. Spray with oil, and cover in foil. Bake at 350° F, basting periodically. For brown skin, uncover during last ½-hour, lower heat to 325° F, and baste twice. <u>Unstuffed</u>- ½ hour per lb. <u>Stuffed</u>- Lightly stuff cavity up to ¾ full, bake 1 hour per lb. (Duck or goose may take a bit more time).

Other Helpful Kitchen Tips

Quick Defrosting: Put frozen veggies or chopped cooked meat in a strainer and run hot water over it.

No-Stick Freezing: In various applications, parchment paper cut-to-size is great for keeping individual items separate. Put a layer of parchment, then the food and repeat. Store in zippered freezer bags. Great for pre-seasoned burger patties or dough balls for rolls or pizza. The same is done for candies or cookies in tins.

Non-Stick Cookware: Use silicone, nylon or wooden utensils to stir in non-stick cookware. Metal will scrape the coating. Once scratched it peels, often rusting below. Black flecks will start appearing in food.

Bakeware: Dark-colored and glass bakeware gets hotter. Bake on lower heat or shorter time.

Metal Preservation: Silver- Once goblets and utensils are used, wash off food, polish with a kosher-certified tarnish remover and wash again. Dry well and put them directly into airtight plastic bags. This prevents having to repolish before using. Copper- Polish tarnished items with ketchup, wash and dry.

Stainless Steel: Don't put stainless steel utensils in the refrigerator for long— ironically, it tarnishes.

Calcium Build-Up: Great for tea kettles, plastic hand-washing cups or crock pots. Wet with straight vinegar and let it soak a few minutes. Scrub with a toothbrush or plastic scrub pad, wash and rinse.

Fine Mesh Liquid Strainer: A clean new nylon stocking is far superior to wire strainers. Stretch the opening over the top of a jar or measuring cup, pour in contents and squeeze the remainder through.

Mix-It: For ingredients added at the same time in recipes, blend dry ones together before adding liquid.

Fine-Bristle Scrubber: New toothbrushes are great for vegetable scrubbing, splatter screens or sifters. Gentler than scrub brushes, bristles won't scrape off skins, and clean stuck-on residues on fine screens.

Stainless Tablecloths: If grape juice spills, quickly pour salt around and atop the spill in a mound. Let it dry fully. (Use salt for cooking if desired.) Wash out the tablecloth— it won't stain. (Not for Shabbat!)

Healthy Drains: Put grease in disposable containers and throw it out. Never put it down the drain, even if it's hot or if running hot water. It will hit a cold spot in the pipe and congeal, making a natural "plug".

Unclogging Disposals: Turn on water, run disposal, and dump in a tray of ice cubes.

Stubborn Jar Lids: Method 1: Run under hot water for a few minutes. Method 2: Turn jar upside down so the lid is flat, and hit lid on a flat surface several times. Turn jar over and open. Method 3: As a last resort only! Insert a metal bottlecap opener between the lid and jar. Twist slightly until it audibly sucks or "pops" the safety button.

No-Slip Towels: Here's an easy remedy to keep common woven-style kitchen towels from slipping off handles and falling on the floor. Stick Velcro® patches (loop side) on the door handle front. (Note: This method is not good for fancy terry towels or embroidered towels. They will get pulls or unravel.)

Safe Food and Health Tips

Babies and Honey: Never give honey to an infant under 1-year old, not yet on solid food. Honey contains dormant endospores of "clostridium botulinum". Since a baby's digestive tract is immature and excretions aren't yet acidic, the bacteria can germinate and transform into toxins, causing very dangerous botulism.

Some Like it Black: Charred food (be it fried or grilled) contains carbon, a known carcinogen. For safe grilling, precook meat slightly, then set on foil-covered grill racks to cook. Never eat black parts.

Food Handling: We're careful to make sure we don't cross-contaminate and mix dairy and meat, but how cautious are we about microorganisms? It's common knowledge to wash hands with soap and hot water before handling food. The inverse is also true— wash after handling meat, poultry, fish or eggs.

Using Cutting Boards: Don't cut produce after meat unless cooking immediately. Use separate boards for meat and produce. Clean using a scrub brush, hot water and dish soap, rinse and dry well. To sterilize, wash, then soak 5 minutes in a mixture of 1 tsp. bleach + 1 qt. water. Flip, soak again, then rinse. Dry it.

Rubber Food: If using a rubber scraper "spatula", never use it with hot oily foods. I once used one to scrape a blender and thought the melted margarine was cool enough (the maker said it could withstand 220° F). The tip of the scraper actually melted, leaving tiny bits of semi-molten rubber throughout the food!

Food Temperatures: Bacteria are killed by proper cooking, but survive if food isn't cooked at high enough a temperature. They're particularly present in poultry, eggs and ground meat. Temperature can be measured with a meat thermometer in the thickest part, but don't touch the bone. Be it microwaving, grilling or baking, the internal temperature should be 165° F for poultry, 160° F for ground meat or eggs, and 145° F for fish or cuts of beef, veal or lamb. Stuffed poultry doesn't always reach 165° F, especially in a microwave. Bake stuffing separately— mix in margarine or drippings to flavor, then bake.

If cooking ground meat, be sure it's cooked through. For rare burgers, use a meat thermometer. Contrary to popular belief, what comes out of rare meat isn't blood, it's moisture and juices. Even raw hamburger is considered kosher. (Although nowadays it's not a good idea to eat it due to salmonella.)

Crock pots shouldn't be used on the "Warm" setting to cook food or hold it for long periods of time, such as overnight. Most are just not hot enough. Test your crock pot during the week. If any food ever smells sour or has a whitish or globby film covering it, stay safe and throw it out! Always keep on "Low".

Keep mayonnaise or egg products refrigerated. Unless there's a cooler with ice, don't take these on picnics. Refrigerators should keep food at 35-40° F or less, and freezers should be at 0° F or less.

Safe Water: In an emergency, drinkable water can be made. First filter it through a coffee filter or clean nylon stocking. Boil rapidly 10 minutes, or mix in ¼ tsp. regular bleach (no additives) to 1 gallon water.

Food Nutrients at a Glance

If you closely examine all the nutritional elements that affect one another and enables the body to run smoothly, it is truly amazing to realize the incredible intricacies of Hashem's creations, and how they work.

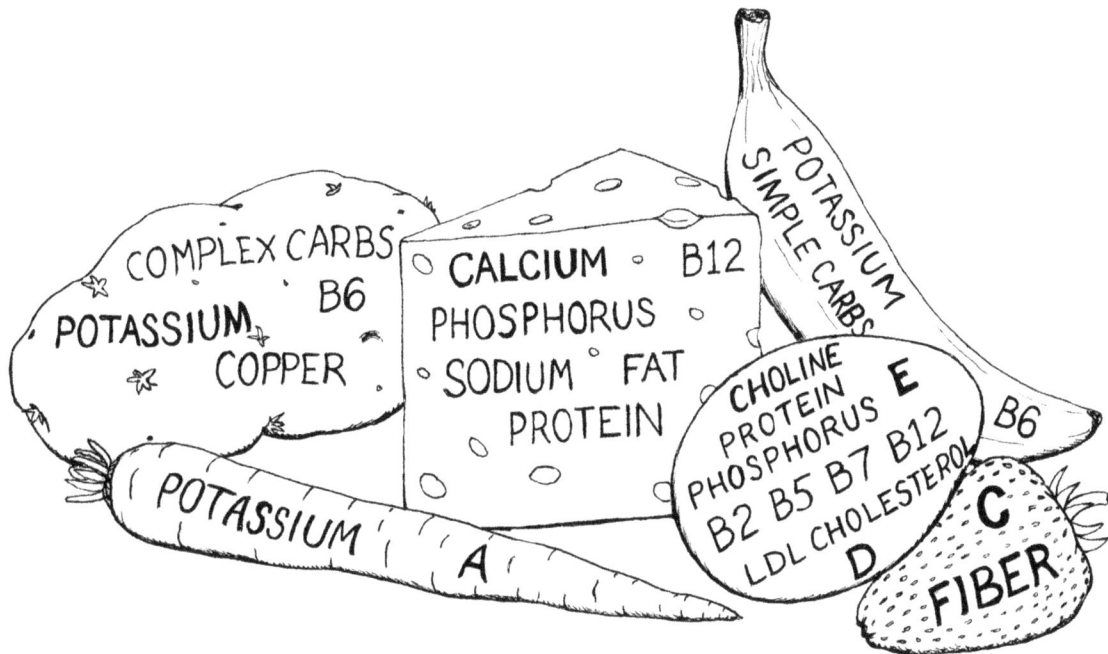

Chesed [kindness] is a major part of Judaism, so people often fix food for others in need or bring food gifts as an invited guest. In joyous times, it could be contributing food to a celebratory event, or providing meals for a woman who has recently given birth. In other circumstances, it could be someone needing kosher food while in the hospital, meals at home after a surgery, when dealing with an illness, and even for those in mourning. This guide was created to help others with this *mitzvah*.

Often, those with medical conditions or food sensitivities may be on special diets, and must avoid certain items. This section shows common components, daily nutrient values, and foods that provide them. It also includes charts covering many health issues. This is strictly a general reference guide, and *does not* replace the advice of a doctor or nutritionist. Nutritional needs vary, depending on age, gender and health.

Nutrient amounts are listed high to low, and based on one average serving unless noted. Recommended Daily Values (RDA or DV) are for an *average adult* on a 2000 calorie diet (amount is averaged if gender differs). These are not the same as for children or pregnant and nursing mothers.

The UL is the "Tolerable Upper Intake Level", or the amount an average person can consume without side effects.

Excess = Do not consume on a regular daily basis; **100%** = 100% RDA or more (+); **Very High** = 50% or +; **High** = 20% or +; **Moderate** = 10% or +; **Low** = usually 5% or less, but these amounts may vary.

Minerals

Minerals are chemical elements required as a nutrient for organisms to thrive. Listed alphabetically.

CALCIUM: An essential mineral for infants and children, calcium strengthens bones and teeth. Women over 50 need extra calcium as they are prone to osteoporosis. Calcium also neutralizes stomach acid.

Oddly enough, the more calcium ingested at one time, the less will be absorbed. If taking calcium supplements, it's preferable to spread out the dosage. Vitamin D is also essential to calcium absorption. Strict vegetarians may not get enough, as certain plants like spinach and rhubarb contain oxalic or phytic acids that decreases absorption. Alcohol can inhibit absorption. Excess salt and protein can cause the body to lose calcium. Caffeine can cause both loss and lack of absorption. Too much calcium may increase risk of heart disease and prostate cancer. The UL is 2500 mg (2.5 g) for adults age 18-50, and 2000 mg (2 g) for adults 51+.

100% (1000 mg) or +: Sardines; Tofu (w/ Calcium Sulfate); Fortified Cereals.

Very High (500-999 mg): Orange Juice (w/ Calcium).

High (200-499 mg): Yogurt; Hard Cheeses; Milk; Milkshake; Eggnog; Soy Milk; Soy Yogurt; 1 tsp. Baking Powder.

Moderate (50-199 mg) Canned Salmon w/ Bones; Spinach; Collard Greens; Ricotta Cheese; Sweetened Condensed Milk; Cottage Cheese; Almonds.

CHROMIUM: Safe when getting from food, this mineral is linked to regulating insulin and glucose in the body, and metabolizing carbohydrates, proteins and fats. Vitamin C and niacin (B3) enhance the absorption of chromium, and cooking with stainless steel increases intake. Soil types affect levels in plants, and animal diets affect levels in meat. It could potentially interact with certain drugs for diabetes, or cause low blood sugar when taken with insulin. There is no set UL for chromium.

High (6 mcg) or +: Broccoli; Red Wine; Grape Juice.

COPPER: Low copper can cause increased cholesterol and anemia (since it is needed for the body to absorb iron). Copper absorption is inhibited by zinc, so take them separately. Soil types affect copper levels in plants. The UL for copper is 10,000 mcg, or 10 mg per day.

100% (.9 mg) or +: Beef Liver; Chocolate (baking); Vegetable Juice; Shiitake Mushrooms.

Very High (.45-.89 mg): Sunflower Seeds; Filberts; Potato Skins.

High (.18-.44 mg): White Mushrooms; Soybeans; Garbanzo Beans; Lentils; Pasta Sauce; Beans.

IODINE: An essential element for thyroid function, and proper bone and brain development fetuses and infants. The body uses iodine to make thyroid hormones, which in turn controls the body's metabolism. Too little can cause hypothyroidism. The UL for iodine is 1100 mcg.

100% (150 mcg) or +: Cod; Haddock; Ocean Perch; Sea Bass; Kombu Seaweed (3½-inch strip); Arame and Wakame Seaweed (½ cup).

IRON: Essential to proper cell function, too little iron causes anemia, weak immune system, feeling cold, and being tired or weak. It is needed to absorb vitamin A. Frequent blood donors should have adequate or extra iron intake. Women need about twice the amount of iron than men. Heme iron (derived from hemoglobin) is readily available in meat, poultry and fish, and is easily absorbed. Less potent non-heme iron (derived from vegetable sources) can contain phytates, which inhibit iron's absorption, unless eaten with foods rich in vitamin C. Soil conditions affect iron levels in plants. Large doses of calcium or antacids can inhibit iron absorption. Excess iron is toxic especially to children. The UL for iron is 45 mg.

100% (13 mg) or +: Instant Corn Grits (enriched).

Very High (6.5-12.9 mg): Chicken Liver; Breakfast Cereals, Hot Wheat Cereals, and Instant Oatmeal (all fortified).

High (2.6-5.6 mg) Giblets; Bagel (enriched); Soybeans (boiled); Beef Liver; Duckling (meat only); Lentils; Spinach (boiled fresh); Tofu; Beef (lean); Pumpkin Seeds; Enriched Rice; Dry Beans (boiled).

MAGNESIUM: Some functions are regulating blood pressure and blood sugar levels. It's thought that magnesium combined with calcium and potassium may help lower blood pressure, and help improve bone density. Some antibiotics negatively interact with it. Crohn's Disease patients and alcoholics need extra. The UL for magnesium is 350 mg.

High (74 mg) or +: Pumpkin Seeds (roasted); Brazil Nuts (raw); Sunflower Seeds (raw); Almonds (roasted); Soybeans (roasted); Baking Chocolate (1-square); Halibut; Cashews; Spinach (boiled/canned); Peanuts (roasted); 100% Bran Cereal; Soybeans (boiled).

MANGANESE: Aiding in metabolism, this is an important trace element for bone formation. It combines with vitamin K to clot blood. Iron decreases manganese absorption and vice versa. The UL for manganese is 11mg.

100% (2.05 mg) or +: Oat Bran Muffin; Pine Nuts; 100% Bran Cereal; Coconut (dry).

Very High (1-2 mg): Whole Wheat Pasta; Filberts; Pineapple (canned); Pecans; Walnuts; Bran Cereals; Oat Bran; Brown Rice; Macadamia Nuts.

High (.41-1 mg): Pecans; Okra (frozen); Oat Bran Bagel; Almonds; Chick Peas; Spinach (cooked); Adzuki Beans; Bulgur Wheat; Tea (fresh); Beans (dry)

MOLYBDENUM: Essential in minute amounts, this is found in tooth enamel. It is needed to process proteins and eliminate toxins. The UL for molybdenum is 2000 mcg.

100% (45 mcg) or +: Navy Beans; Black Eyed Peas (¼ cup is 100% DV); Dry Legumes.

PHOSPHOROUS: Also called "Phosphate", this element helps build strong bones and teeth. Too much can be harmful. Normal kidneys can easily remove the excess, people on dialysis must avoid phosphorous and these: Calcium Phosphate, Phosphoric Acid, Polyphosphates, Pyrophosphate, or Sodium Aluminum Phosphate. The need for phosphorous changes over time. The UL for adults age 19-70 is 4000 mg, and 71+ is 3000 mg.

100% (700 mg): Phosphate Baking Powder (1½ tsp.); Sardines (w/ bones).

Very High (350-360 mg): Bran Cereals (some); Yogurt; Instant Pudding0; Liver.

High (140-310 mg): Salmon (canned); Eggnog; 2% Milk; Roast Poultry; Hot Cocoa; Dry Milk; Brazil Nuts; Buttermilk; Salmon (baked); Romano Cheese; Soy Beans; Haddock; Whole Milk; Ricotta Cheese; Pine Nuts; Halibut (baked); Wheat Germ; Lentils; Ground Beef; Almonds; Cereals (some).

Moderate (70-126 mg): Beans (dry); Ground Turkey; Pistachios; Hard Cheese; Peanuts; Peanut Butter; Egg; Ice Cream; Egg Substitute; Beer.

Low (35 mg): Cola or Pepper-type Soft Drinks (1 cup); Cantaloupe; Strawberries (fresh); Watermelon; Watercress; Coffee; Tomatoes; Lettuce.

POTASSIUM: Necessary for almost every bodily function, especially the kidneys, heart and muscle contraction. It regulates fluids and is needed for proper nerve transmission. Too little can cause weakness, muscle cramps, and irregular heartbeat. Excess salt causes a need for more potassium, and it reduces effects of salt on blood pressure. People on dialysis must stay away from potassium, salt substitutes, or any ingredient with the word "Potassium" in it. For healthy people with good kidney function, there is no UL for potassium.

High (940 mg): Baked Potato (w/ skin).

Moderate (470 707 mg): Prune Juice; Vegetable Juice; Molasses; Potatoes (any w/o skin); Carrot Juice; Beet Greens; Roasted Soy Beans; Adzuki Beans; Sardines; Yogurt; Pomegranate Juice; Hot Cocoa; Beans; Pasta Sauce; Orange Juice; Tuna (baked); Halibut; Sweet Potatoes (baked); Malted Milk; 2% Milk; Soy Beans (boiled); Banana; Grapefruit Juice; Eggnog; Salmon (baked); Lentils; Haddock; Whole Milk; Bok Choy; Spinach (cooked or canned); Split Peas; Turkey; Prunes (dried); Raisins; Sweet Potatoes (canned); Papaya; Mushrooms (cooked White); Pistachios; Tomatoes; Tomato Sauce or Paste; Trail Mix; Winter Squash; Salmon (canned); Citrus Fruit; Almonds; Duck (baked); Parsnips; Kohlrabi; Rutabaga; Tomato Juice; Dates; Peanuts.

Low (60-200 mg): Whole Grain Cereal (some); Filberts; Brussels Sprouts; Peanut Butter; Pine Nuts; Liver; Melons; Tuna (canned); Wheat Germ; Ice Cream; Spinach (raw); Asparagus; Cabbage; Apple; Grapes; Carrots; Broccoli (raw); Chocolate; Buttermilk; Corn; Sauerkraut; Ricotta; Egg Substitute; Cottage Cheese; Beer; Egg; Instant Coffee.

SELENIUM: This is essential for proper thyroid function. Selenium deficiency can cause heart disease and hypothyroidism. Rheumatoid arthritis patients often lack it. It's said 1-2 Brazil nuts a day is better than a supplement! Selenium levels in plants vary depending on region of growth. The UL for selenium is 400 mcg.

100% (55 mcg) or +: Brazil Nuts (2); Halibut; Salmon Fillets (most); Herring (baked); Haddock; Tuna (canned).

Very High (27.5 -54 mcg): Cod; Tuna Steak; Salmon (canned); Lox; Turkey.

High (11 -26 mcg): Whole Grain Bread; Duck; Bread; Couscous; Herring (pickled); Mushrooms (most).

SODIUM: Aka "Sodium Chloride" or table salt, it regulates body fluid volumes and is needed for proper nerve and muscle function. People with high blood pressure and heart problems must avoid it. Potassium reduces effects of sodium on blood pressure. Nearly all processed food contains excess salt (low-fat or non-fat foods often contains more to make up for the loss of flavor). For less sodium, season foods with herbs, rinse canned veggies or buy low-sodium seasoning. Taste-testing can be subjective, what may be too little salt for one person can be too much for another. With this in mind, it is always best to add less salt to a dish without a recipe. It can always be added (and should be) by the individual eating the food. Despite the fact that too much salt can potentially be toxic (although rare), the USDA does not have any UL amount for sodium.

Very High (750 mg) or +: Smoked Turkey; Sour Pickle; Corned Beef; Pizza; Soup (any form); Anchovies; Pasta Sauce; Turkey.

High (300 650 mg): Lox; Sausages; Cold Cuts; Sauerkraut; Hot Dog; Feta Cheese; Rotisserie Chicken; Cottage Cheese; Salmon (canned); Chicken Nuggets; Mushrooms (canned); Dill Pickle (slices); Corn Dogs; Soy Sauce (1 tsp.).

Moderate (150-299 mg): Tomato Sauce; Sweet Pickle (slices); Edam/Gouda Cheese; Olives; Tuna (canned); Hard Cheese; Spinach (canned); Colby/Cheddar Cheese; Worcestershire Sauce; Parmesan Cheese.

Low (75-149 mg): Ricotta Cheese; Goat Cheese; Cream Cheese; Turkey Burger Patty; Chicken; Tomato Paste; Turkey (roasted); Swiss Cheese; Midget Sweet Pickle.

ZINC: This is needed daily for healthy immune system, a proper sense of smell and taste, cell division, protein synthesis, and healing of wounds. When taken with Vitamin C it can potentially help to fight off an oncoming cold. It is primarily found in meat. It can be obtained in some vegetable sources, but unfortunately these contain phytates that inhibit zinc absorption. Vegetarians can take supplements to regain zinc, or eat fluffy baked grain products like bread, as leavenings break down phytates causing more zinc to be absorbed. Legumes can be soaked until they sprout to increase zinc. Alcohol and iron prevent proper zinc absorption. If one uses iron supplements, take zinc at a different time for better absorption. Many with type 2 diabetes lack zinc. Too much zinc can inhibit copper intake, causing anemia. Soil conditions affect zinc levels in plants. The UL for zinc is 40 mg.

100% (9.5 mg) or +: Cereals (fortified); Shoulder Steak; Chuck Roast.

Very High (4.75-9.4 mg): Brisket; Turkey Neck (boiled); Lamb; Ground Beef; Chicken Giblets; Beef Liver; Veal; Roast Turkey (dark meat).

High (1.9-4.6 mg): Beef Tongue; Cereals (non-fortified); Turkey Giblets; Roast Turkey (light meat); Pumpkin Seeds; Baked Beans (canned); Hyacinth Beans; Duck (meat only); Ground Turkey; Adzuki Beans.

Moderate (.95-1.8 mg): Cashews; Sheep's Milk; Lentils; Chickpeas/Garbanzo Beans; White Beans; Chicken Breast (roast skinless); Wild Rice; Milk (All Cow's).

Vitamins

Vitamins are organic substances needed in minute quantities for the nutrition of animals and even plants. They enable growth, maintenance, and repair. They are either fat-soluble or water-soluble. In other words, fat-soluble vitamins (A, D, E, and K) get absorbed when eaten with fatty foods, and they are stored in the fatty tissue and the liver. Water-soluble vitamins (C and the B vitamins) dissolve in water, and for most (but not all) any extra gets flushed out of the body instead of being stored. The vitamins are listed in alphabetical order.

VITAMIN A: This "fat soluble" vitamin is important for maintaining healthy vision (deficiency could cause blindness). It helps regulate the immune system, and promotes healthy skin and membrane linings. Iron is needed to help absorption of vitamin A. Excessive A can counteract the ability of vitamin D to effectively assist in calcium absorption. Vitamin A can be derived from meat or plants, but come in two distinct types: Preformed, and Provitamin. Preformed vitamin A is from meat and is more efficiently absorbed (as Retinol). Provitamin A Carotenoids are from plants, which the body then turns into usable vitamin A. This type is most often in the form of Beta-Carotene, Alpha-Carotene and Beta-Cryptoxanthin. Vitamin A is depleted by alcohol. The UL for preformed vitamin A (most commonly found in supplements) is 3000 mcg, not to be confused with Beta Carotene and other provitamin As. Too much of these can turn the skin orange or yellow (See "Yellowfoot" in Funny Food Facts on p. 427) There is no established UL for the provitamin A carotenoids. The amounts below were listed in IUs as of 2005 when this book was started. Most vitamin supplements are still listed in IUs. They are now measured in mcg retinol activity equivalents (RAE). They can vary greatly with the different types of carotenoids, but the guide below can still be useful for approximations.

Excess (35k-45k IU/10,500-13,500 mcg): Carrot Juice (canned); Turkey Giblets; Beef Liver.

Max (10k-25,500 IU/3k-7,650 mcg) or +: Sweet Potato (boiled skinless); Butternut Squash (baked); Chicken Giblets; Chicken Livers; Carrots (boiled); Pumpkin (canned); Pumpkin Pie (home-made); Spinach; Carrots (raw); Sweet Potato (canned).

100% (5k-9,750 IU/1,500-2,925 mcg): Kale (cooked); Apricots (dry); Collard Greens (cooked); Pumpkin (boiled); Spinach (boiled); Cantaloupe.

Very High (2,500-3k IU/750-900 mcg): Spinach (raw); Vegetable Juice (canned).

High (1k-2k IU/300-600 mcg): Apricots (canned); Papaya; Mango; Red Bell Pepper; Broccoli (boiled); Pink Grapefruit; Oatmeal (instant fortified).

The "B" Vitamins

Originally thought to be a single vitamin, B vitamins were found to be chemically distinct. They are necessary for cell metabolism. Singularly, they are referred to by their proper name, however when they combined in a supplement, they are referred to as "B-Complex". They are listed singularly in numerical order.

VITAMIN B1: Also known as "Thiamin", it is essential for converting sugar into energy. Absorption is dependent on intake of other B vitamins. It is damaged by cooking, and is unstable when exposed to sunlight. Thiamin is found in whole grains. Thiamin hydrochloride is a common additive used to achieve a "meaty" flavor in certain foods. Too little B1 causes weakness and tingling sensations, loss of appetite, and in severe cases nerve damage. Alcoholism can also cause a vitamin B1 deficiency. A lack of thiamin can possibly be caused by overconsumption of coffee or tea. Severe deficiency causes Beriberi, a neurological and cardiovascular disease. The often-fatal "Infant Beriberi" is caused by a nursing mother who is deficient in B1 (even if she has no symptoms of it). Therefore, it is extremely important that mothers get enough thiamin in their diet. There is no UL for thiamine, as it is not harmful in large quantities.

100% (1.15 mg) or +: Soy Burger Crumbles; Fortified Cereals.

Very High (.58-1.14 mg): Malted Milk (fortified); Bagel (enriched); Breakfast Cereals; Fresh Bluefin or Yellowfin Tuna (baked).

High (.23-.52 mg): Sunflower Seeds (dried); Egg Bagel (fortified); Bread (enriched); Oatmeal (fortified); Egg Noodles (enriched); Pasta (enriched); Duck (roasted meat); Soy Beans (boiled); Orange Juice (fresh squeezed); Navy Beans; Black Beans; Black Eyed Peas; Rice (enriched).

VITAMIN B2: Also called "Riboflavin", this helps other B vitamins with their functions. It is also used as a yellow-orange food colorant. Deficiency can cause eye problems, sensitivity to light, cracks in the corner of the lips, bloodshot eyes, anemia, and skin peeling. Riboflavin is unaffected by cooking. Strangely enough, it glows under ultraviolet light, although this actually destroys it. Milk should be kept out of light to ensure it retains B2. There is no UL for riboflavin, one cannot get too much.

100% (1.2-2.2 mg) or +: Beef Liver; Fortified Cereals; Malted Milk (fortified).

Very High (.6-1.1 mg): Turkey Giblets; Sheep's Milk; Pacific Sardines (in tomato sauce); Chicken Giblets; Venison Steaks.

High (.24-.59 mg): Soy Burger Patty; Duck (roasted meat); Eggnog; Eggs; Mackerel; Wild Atlantic Salmon (baked); Soymilk; Milk; Chocolate Milk; Yogurt; Vienna or French Bread; Egg Bread; Soy Beans (dry roasted); Lamb; 1 packet Baker's Yeast; Raisin Bread; Beef; White Mushrooms (stir-fried); Chicken (dark meat); Bluefin Tuna (baked); Beef Tongue; Soy Beans (boiled); Portobella Mushrooms (cooked); Almonds.

VITAMIN B3: This is also known as "Niacin". B3 helps convert foods into energy— especially converting fats, proteins and carbohydrates. It also plays a role in regulating blood sugar and insulin metabolism and helps with the absorption of Chromium. When derived from food and beverages, vitamin B3 is perfectly safe, and by far the best option. There is a UL for B3 for dietary supplements at 35 mg, and after reading this, you'll see why– in the form of "Nicotinamide", 500 mg a day can cause easy bruising, headaches and diarrhea. At 3000 mg daily, it can cause severe side effects, such as nausea, vomiting, and liver damage. Too much, in the form of "Nicotinic Acid" from supplements, 30 mg a day can cause the skin on one's face, arms and chest to tingle, itch, burn, and turn red. At 1000 mg or more daily can cause liver failure.

100% (15 mg) or +: Beef Liver; Fortified Cereals.

Very High (7.5-12 mg): Chicken Breast (roasted- no skin); Halibut (baked); Fried Chicken (white meat); Light Tuna (canned); Malted Milk (fortified); Salmon (baked); Yellowfin Tuna (baked); Trout (baked).

High (3-7.2 mg): Venison (broiled); Tuna Salad; Turkey (roasted meat); Lamb (broiled); Duck (roasted meat); Breakfast Cereals (most); Beef Chuck Pot Roast; Pink Salmon (canned); Turkey Giblets; White Tuna (canned); Sardines in Oil; Ground Beef Patty; White Rice (enriched); Instant Oatmeal; Smoked Salmon; Ground Turkey Patty; Haddock (baked); Peanuts (roasted); Fried Chicken Leg (w/ skin); Bagel (enriched); Mushrooms (cooked); Egg Noodles (enriched).

VITAMIN B5: Also named "Pantothenic Acid", this is needed for many complex chemical processes in the body such as converting carbohydrates into energy and breaking down fats. Lack of B5 can cause weakness, fatigue, numbness, tingling and shooting pain in the feet. There is no UL for pantothenic acid.

100% (5 mg) or +: Beef Liver; Fortified Cereals (fortified).

Very High (2.5-4.5 mg): Breakfast Cereals (most); Shiitake Mushrooms (cooked).

High (1-2 mg): Sunflower Seeds (dry roasted); Giblets (any type); White Mushrooms (cooked); Duck (roasted meat); Eggs; Barley; Egg Substitute; Baker's Yeast (1 packet).

VITAMIN B6: As a supplement, it is called "Pyridoxine". It promotes manufacture of antibodies to aid immune system, and helps proper brain function. Those with autoimmune disorders or on kidney dialysis tend to have lower levels, as do alcoholics, since alcohol destroys B6. Deficiency can cause rashes, scaly skin and anemia. The UL is 100 mg, but B6 from food and drink is not harmful and one can rarely get too much.

100% (1.3 mg) or +: Fortified Cereals; Beef Liver; Malted Milk (fortified).

Very High (.65-1.2 mg): Yellowfin Tuna (baked); Halibut (baked); Cereals (some).

High (.26-.64 mg): Potato (baked with skin); Fried Chicken Breast (w/ skin); Garbanzo Beans (canned); Prune Juice; Beef Steak (broiled); Chicken Breast (roasted); Carrot Juice; Turkey (roasted); Banana; Turkey Giblets (boiled); Instant Oatmeal (fortified); Chestnuts (roasted); Trout (baked); Haddock (baked); Duck (meat); Tomato Juice; Sunflower Seeds; Prunes (stewed); Soy Crumbles; Mashed Potatoes; Pistachios.

VITAMIN B7: Also called "Biotin", this is occasionally called "Vitamin H". It is needed for proper hair, skin, and nail growth. Pregnant women normally have a slight deficiency, and should make sure to get adequate biotin (at least 35 mcg. for nursing mothers). Severe deficiency is rare, but those with alcohol dependency generally have a lack of B7. Deficiency can cause loss or thinning of hair, brittle nails, rashes, pinkeye, and skin infections. There is no UL for biotin.

100% (30 mcg) or +: Chicken Liver; Beef Liver.

High (6-10 mcg): Whole Cooked Egg; Roasted Peanuts (1½ oz.).

Moderate (3-5.5 mcg): Pink Salmon (canned); Ground Beef Patty; Cooked Egg Yolk.

Low (1.5-3 mcg): Fish Sticks; Sunflower Seeds (roasted); Cooked Egg White; Mushrooms (canned); Breaded Chicken Nuggets (fried).

VITAMIN B9: Also known as "Folate" (the natural version), or "Folic Acid" (the synthetic version found in dietary supplements). B9 is used by the body to make DNA and RNA, which are responsible for development of new cell growth. It's especially important for producing healthy red blood cells and preventing anemia. Those with alcohol dependency are generally deficient in B9. It's extremely important for women who are pregnant or want to become pregnant, to get an adequate amount of B9, which is found in all prenatal vitamins. The UL for Folic Acid is 1,000 mcg (1 mg). Any higher, and it can mask any symptoms of a B12 deficiency by correcting the anemia caused by the lack of B12.

The 100% RDA for B9 is 400 mcg for an average adult. However, for nursing mothers it is 500 mcg, and 600 mcg for pregnant women.

100% (400 mcg): Fortified Cereals.

Very High (200-350 mcg): Breakfast Cereals (most); White Rice (enriched); Egg Noodles (enriched); Giblets (boiled); Plain Bagel (enriched).

High (80-180 mcg): Lentils; Black Eyed Peas; Beef Liver; Baker's Yeast (1 packet); Pasta; Raisin Bagel; Beans; Instant Oatmeal (fortified); Grits (enriched); Asparagus; Okra; Spinach (cooked); Flavored Wheat Germ (1½ Tbs.); Soy Burger Patty; Papaya; Orange Juice, (from concentrate); Spinach (canned); Soybeans (boiled); Creamy Wheat Cereal; Dark Greens (cooked); Broccoli (cooked).

VITAMIN B12: An extremely important vitamin, this is alternately named "Cobalamin" (because it contains the metal cobalt) or "Cyanocobalamin". It helps the body to make DNA, and aids in the production of healthy red blood and nerve cells. Stomach acid releases Vitamin B12 from food proteins during digestion.

B12 only occurs naturally in animal-derived foods such as fish, egg and dairy products. Other sources include vitamin supplements, a few enriched products, and 100% fortified breakfast cereals. Contrary to what some believe, nutritional yeast does *not* contain any B12 unless it has been fortified with it.

Vitamin B12 deficiency can be caused by stomach or intestinal disorders, but is most common in strict vegetarians who don't take supplemental B12. Deficiency can result in subtle cognition problems, anemia and nerve damage. Signs of deficiency include fatigue, weakness, loss of appetite, tingling or numbness in extremities, soreness of the mouth or tongue, balance problems, poor memory, confusion, depression, and dementia. An especially important fact for strict vegetarian nursing women— be aware that if no fish, egg or dairy products are consumed, one must take B12 supplements or the infant has a high risk of severe irreversible neurological damage. Consult a doctor or pediatrician for details. All Liver and Turkey Giblets are about the only food that has an excessive amount of B12, but since it is not stored in the body, it doesn't ever reach toxic levels. There is no established UL for B12, due to the body's not storing any excess.

100% (2.4 mcg) or +: Beef Steak; Sockeye Salmon (baked); Sardines; Chicken Giblets; Trout (baked); Fortified Cereals (some); Pink Salmon (canned); Pickled Herring; Pollock (baked); Enriched Soy Milk; Smoked Salmon; Beef Ribs; Flounder or Sole (baked); Light Tuna (canned); Ground Beef Patty.

Very High (1.2-2.2 mcg): Haddock (baked); Halibut (baked); Breakfast Cereals (most)5; Eggs; Tuna Salad; Lamb Shoulder (roasted); Beef Roast; Yogurt; Skim Milk; Lamb Ribs (roasted).

High (.48-1.1 mcg): Turkey; Eggnog; Malted Milk (fortified); Cottage Cheese; 2% Milk; Whole or 1% Milk; White Tuna (canned); Ocean Perch (baked); Cod; Commercial Chocolate Milk; Swiss Cheese; Mozzarella Cheese; Waffle; Buttermilk; Yellowfin Tuna (baked); Camembert Cheese; Feta Cheese.

CHOLINE: Choline is grouped with B vitamins and works together with many of them, such as Folate (B9) to form DNA. It converts excess amino acids into other aminos, preventing heart attack and stroke. Its main function is to regulate mood, memory, muscle control, and it helps to form the membranes surrounding the body's cells. The liver can make small amounts of choline, but most of it is derived from the foods we eat. Choline deficiency is rare, but symptoms can include muscle or liver damage, and non-alcoholic fatty liver disease in the overweight or obese. The amounts of choline needed for the RDA varies vastly with gender. Adult men require 550 mg, and adult women need 425 mg. Nursing mothers require as much as an adult man.

Too much choline can cause fishy body odor, salivating, vomiting, excessive sweating, low blood pressure, and liver damage. The UL for Choline is 3,500 mg. It is not known to interact with other medicines.

100% (487.5 mg): Beef Liver.

Very High (243.75-370 mg): Chicken Liver.

High (97.5-210 mg): Chicken Giblets; Turkey Giblets; Beef Tongue; Cod (baked); Lamb Kebabs (braised); Wild Coho Salmon (baked); Beef Brisket; Fried Egg; Herring (baked); Venison (broiled); Chicken (stewed); Hard-boiled Egg; Flounder (baked); Sole (baked); Sockeye Salmon (baked); Poached Egg; Pink Salmon (canned).

Other Vitamins

Vitamin C: Also called "Ascorbic Acid", it plays a role in healthy immune function and can potentially ward off or shorten the duration of a common cold, especially when taken along with zinc. Vitamin C is also essential for biosynthesis of collagen, aiding in the healing of wounds. Foods rich in C enhance absorption of iron from plant sources. It enables the body to make collagen, the protein required to heal wounds. Vitamin C acts as an antioxidant, protecting the body from harmful compounds that form when the body converts food into energy. It is a water-soluble vitamin that is destroyed by heat and prolonged storage (loss is minimal when foods are steamed or microwaved). Many C-rich foods are best eaten raw. Deficiency can cause swollen gums, slow-healing of wounds, joint pain, and fatigue. Severe deficiency can cause scurvy, which can be fatal if untreated.

The 100% RDA for vitamin C is 90 mg for an average adult man, 75 mg for an adult woman. However, for nursing mothers it is a whopping 120 mg, and 85 mg for pregnant women. The UL for C is 2,000 mg.

100% (82.5 mg) or +: Papaya; Apricot Nectar (canned w/ added C); Orange Juice (fresh squeezed); Peaches (frozen); Sweet Red Bell Peppers (cooked/raw); Pineapple Grapefruit Juice (canned); Green Hot Pepper (whole raw); Cranberry Juice Cocktail; Brussels Sprouts (frozen boiled); Orange Juice (from concentrate); Grapefruit Juice (fresh squeezed) 94; White Grapefruit Juice (from concentrate) 83.

Very High (41.25-80 mg): Grape Drink (canned); Fruit Punch Drink (canned fortified); Kiwi Fruit; Orange; Vegetable Juice; Red Hot Pepper (whole canned/raw); Green Bell Pepper (cooked/raw); Cantaloupe; Mango; Pineapple Orange Juice (canned); Tangerine Juice (canned); Broccoli (cooked; Strawberries; Kohlrabi (boiled); Tomato Juice (canned).

High (16.5-38 mg): Peas in Edible Pods (cooked fresh); Grapefruit; Star Fruit; Lemonade (from powder); Plantain; Broccoli (cooked/raw); Sweet Potato (canned); Malted Milk (fortified); Lemon (1); Honeydew; Sweet Potato (baked w/ skin); Cauliflower (cooked); Pineapple; Grapefruit (canned); Kale (cooked); Cranberry Juice; Cantaloupe; Hungarian Pepper (raw); Mandarin Oranges (canned); Pineapple Juice (canned w/ added C); Cauliflower; Watermelon; Bok Choy (boiled); Raspberries (fresh/frozen); Red Cabbage (raw); Dark Leafy Greens (cooked); Peas in Edible Pods (frozen cooked); Sauerkraut.

Vitamin D: Naturally occurring in few foods, it is common in two supplemental forms– vitamin D3 (Cholecalciferol) and vitamin D2 (Ergocalciferol). D is a fat-soluble vitamin, essential for bone growth and helping the body absorb calcium. It's needed for healthy immune function and can help reduce inflammation. Along with calcium, D helps to prevent osteoporosis. Vitamin D is generally derived from fortified foods, since food is not a natural source of it. Instead, it is produced by bare skin exposed to *outdoor* sunlight (windows block the UVB rays indoors), but the skin limits the intake so there is no way to get too much through sunlight. Vitamin D deficiency can cause rickets (softening of bones) in children. Steroids and certain weight-loss drugs can reduce levels of D. Cholesterol-lowering statins may not be as effective when large doses of D are taken. The UL for all vitamin D is 4000 IU, or 100 mcg. Excess D can cause severe health problems such as dehydration, muscle weakness, kidney stones, kidney failure, irregular heartbeat, and even death.

100% (200 IU/5 mcg) or +: Sockeye Salmon; Cod Liver Oil (1 tsp.); Pink Salmon (canned); Mackerel (cooked); Salmon (cooked); Tuna (canned); Sardines (in oil);

Very High (100-190 IU/2.5-4.75 mcg): Orange Juice (fortified); Vitamin D Milk; Enriched Soymilk (most).

High (40-90 IU/1-2.25 mcg): Yogurt (fortified); Fortified Cereals (some); Eggs (2);

Moderate (20-39 IU/.5-.975 mcg): Cereals (most); Beef Liver; Vitamin D-Fortified Evaporated Milk (1 oz.).

Vitamin E: The most common form is "Alpha-Tocopherol". E is necessary for a healthy immune system function, and helps to create red blood cells keeping the circulatory system healthy. It also aids in healing skin, membranes and other tissues. E is said to have blood-thinning properties- preventing clots. It also helps absorption of vitamin K, so the two should preferably be taken together.

Vitamin E is "fat soluble", which means that fat is required to absorb it. The absorption of Vitamin E can be increased by eating foods containing healthy fats (see "Fats and Oils"). Therefore, people on low-fat diets may have trouble getting enough vitamin E, and should be sure to have an adequate intake of it by eating nuts, seeds, fruits, vegetables and vegetable oils. Alpha-tocopherol doubles as a preservative. The UL for vitamin E supplements is 1,000 mg or 1,500 IU per day. Excess E can increase risk of prostate cancer, and bleeding in general or specifically in the brain (hemorrhagic stroke).

100% (15 mg) or +: Wheat Germ Oil (1 Tbs.).

Very High (7.5-14 mg): Peanut Butter (fortified); Sunflower Seeds (dry or oil roasted); Fortified Cereals; Sunflower Seeds (dry roasted) Almonds.

High (3-6.5 mg): Soy Milk (enhanced only); Safflower Oil; Hazelnuts; Breakfast Cereals (some); Spinach (frozen cooked); Pine Nuts; Molded Potato Snacks; Pasta Sauce; Peanut Butter; Peanuts (dry roasted); Turnip Greens (boiled); Papaya; Peanut Oil; Corn Oil; Potato Chips; Eggs (fried).

Vitamin K: Also called "Phylloquinone", this is needed for proper blood clotting. It's especially prevalent in dark leafy greens. Being "fat soluble", fat is needed to absorb it. Thus, if eaten with butter or oil, the usable Vitamin K is increased. Vitamin E helps the body absorb K, and the two should preferably be taken together. Vitamin K can potentially increase bone mass in those with osteoporosis.

The effectiveness of the blood thinner Warfarin (Coumadin®) to prevent clotting, is diminished by eating large amounts of Vitamin K. Therefore, people on this drug are advised to limit intake of foods with 100% or more of K to 1 serving per day, and those foods very high in K to 3 servings per day. They must keep the daily K intake consistent. (Vitamin E supplements are good for them too— ask a doctor.)

The 100% RDA for vitamin K is 120 mcg for an average adult man, and 90 mcg for an adult woman, including pregnant and nursing mothers. There is no UL for K, as too much is not harmful to most people, with the exception of those on the previously-mentioned blood-thinning drugs.

100% (105 mcg) or +: Kale (boiled); Spinach (boiled); Turnip Greens (boiled frozen); Spinach (canned); Collards (boiled); Beet Greens (boiled); Turnip Greens (boiled); Swiss Chard (boiled); Mustard Greens (boiled); Brussels Sprouts (boiled); Swiss Chard (raw); Parsley (2 Tbs. fresh raw); Broccoli (boiled.

Very High (52.5-102 mcg): Dandelion Greens (boiled); Broccoli (frozen cooked); Spinach Egg Noodles; Sauerkraut; Asparagus (frozen cooked); Spinach (raw); Endive (raw).

High (21-49 mcg): Green Leaf Lettuce; Broccoli (raw); Light Tuna (canned); Cabbage (cooked); Carrot Juice; Rhubarb; Okra (cooked); Plums (stewed); Kiwi; Romaine Lettuce (raw); Bok Choy (boiled); Green Onions (2 Tbs.); Prunes (Dry); Soybean Oil (1 Tbs.); Peas in Edible Pods (boiled); Cabbage (raw); Black Eyed Peas.

Other Food Components

CALORIES: These are simply measurements of the amount of "energy units" stored in food to use as fuel. Since fat or oil is a type of energy, oily or fatty foods are always full of calories. This creates a problem for those who don't get enough exercise to burn off the calories (or in actuality, the fat that contains them).

Unprocessed produce has very few calories and no fat, unlike dairy foods and animal products. Most prepared and packaged foods have more calories. Their processing and ingredients vary so much that an accurate amount cannot be given. Therefore, one must look at a package label to find out exactly how many calories are in a product. If one wants to know basically what foods are high in calories, they merely need to look in "*Fats and Oils*" (pp. 476-478) to see what to avoid.

CARBOHYDRATES: The body can easily turn these into glucose (a sugar the body needs for energy), which is stored in muscles and the liver for later use. Carbs are a type of sugar. There are two types of carbs: Simple- Monosaccharides or single sugars, and Complex- Disaccharides or double sugars. (Also see "*Sugars*" on p. 480.) Prepared foods vary so widely, the amounts are not given below, since the package should list it. Natural foods (produce, meat, etc.) don't come with a label, so their amounts are listed below.

Simple Carbs: Simple carbs are basic sugars that provide instant energy. This can be good if you need power, but it is bad if all you do is just sit around. Fruits with added sugars, sweetened frozen, or canned in heavy syrup have far more carbs than fresh. Canned fruits in light syrup have a bit less, but water-packed canned fruits are nearly like fresh. See package labels for amounts, which would be listed as "Total Carbohydrates".

Prepared Foods: Cake; Candy; Chocolate; Cookies; Doughnuts; Jelly; Licorice; Pudding; Soft Drinks; Sugars (all types); Sweetened Beverages; Syrups (artificial).

Natural Foods (20-30 g): Pears (dried); Prunes; Dates (dried); Pears (fresh); Bananas; Blueberries (frozen sweetened); Cranberries (dried sweetened); Raisins; Peaches (dried); Figs (dried); Apple; Apricots (dried).

(10-19 g): Peach (fresh); Sweet Cherries (fresh); Kiwi; Asian Pear; Honeydew Melon; Orange; Blueberries (fresh); Grapefruit.

<u>**Complex Carbs:**</u> These take longer to break down, but having more healthy fiber, starch, vitamin and mineral content, and they are very good for you.

Prepared Foods: Bagels; Bran Cereals; Cereals; Corn Meal; Couscous; Granola; Macaroni; Oatmeal; Pasta; Pita; Rice Cakes; Shredded Wheat; Tapioca; Tortillas; Wheat Germ; Whole Grain Bread.

Natural Foods (40-60 g): White Rice; Brown Rice; Long Grain White Rice

(18-36 g): Potatoes (whole w/ skin); Sweet Potatoes; Barley; Dry Beans; Lentils; Yams; Bulgur; Buckwheat.

(8-16 g): Corn; Parsnips; Peas; Beets; Wheat Bran; Sunflower Seeds.

CHOLESTEROL: Cholesterol is needed to build and repair cells, and produce hormones. There are two types.

<u>**LDL Cholesterol:**</u> "Cholesterol" usually refers to bad LDL (Low Density Lipoprotein). High blood pressure and heart patients must avoid high levels of LDL, as it can cause heart problems. Saturated fat foods are often high in LDL. Prepared foods vary, so amounts are not given. Packages will state amounts.

Prepared Foods High in Bad LDL: Cake; Ice Cream; Pie Crust; Fried Foods; Doughnuts.

Natural Foods High in LDL: Poultry varies. Skin has more, and dark meat is a bit higher than light.

100% (300 mg) or +: Chicken Liver; Beef Liver; Chicken Giblets.

Very High (150-259 mg): 1 Egg; Turkey Giblets; Veal; Duck (white meat); Beef Tongue; Atlantic Sardines (in oil).

High (60-149 mg): Duck (w/ skin); Corned Beef; Goose; Lamb; Fried Chicken (w/ skin); Turkey (dark meat); Fried Chicken (meat only); Chicken (roasted); Chicken Breast (rotisserie); Ground Turkey; Turkey (light meat); Chicken (stewed); Beef; Sheep's Milk; Ground Beef Patty; Beef Brisket; Hot Dogs/Cold Cuts.

<u>**HDL Cholesterol:**</u> Good cholesterol is "HDL" (High Density Lipoprotein) that actually helps to *reduce* bad LDL, and protects the body from it. Unfortunately, there is little data to provide amounts for HDL. For further information on foods that lower bad LDL and increase good HDL, see "Unsaturated Fats" next.

Natural Foods Containing HDL: Almonds; Apples; Avocado; Barley; Canola Oil; Cashews; Corn Oil; Cottonseed Oil; Fish; Flax Seeds; Kidney Beans; Nuts (tree); Oat Bran; Oatmeal; Olive Oil; Peanut Oil; Peanuts; Pears; Prunes; Safflower Oil; Soybean Oil; Walnuts.

FATS AND OILS: Also called lipids or fatty acids, they're needed for energy, growth, and absorption of fat-soluble vitamins. One should limit fat as the body first burns carbohydrates, next proteins and last fats. One should be aware of three types of fat, trans (very bad), saturated (bad) and unsaturated (good). One's total fat intake (all types of fats combined) should be below 65 g per day. We shall look at the worst to the best.

Trans Fat- Also called "Trans-Fatty Acids", this is the worst type of fat, because not only does it raise bad LDL levels, but it also lowers good HDL (See "Cholesterol" above). High amounts of trans fat are found in foods made with hydrogenated oils such as commercially-baked items. Hydrogenated oils are liquid fat that has been transformed into solid fat (such as those found in shortening and margarine). Partially hydrogenated oils have been thickened (mostly in order to extend shelf life of processed foods), and are the most common sources of trans fat. It's always best to try to avoid foods containing trans-fat. Since the early 2000s, awareness of the harmful effects of trans-fats has led to most commercial foods discontinuing them. Always read the labels, as there may still be a few culprits left over in the forms of the foods listed below.

100% = 0+ g (Any is Too High): Frozen Pies; Microwave Popcorn (some); Cream Pies; Pie Crusts; Graham Cracker Crusts; Imitation Sour Creams (some); Imitation Creams Cheese (some); Solid Shortenings (some); Commercial Soft Cookies; Stick Margarines; Prepared Cake Icings; Chow Mein Noodles; Rice Noodles; Cinnamon Rolls (some); Cheesecake Fillings.

Saturated Fat- This fat is solid at room temperature (such as white beef fat, or the blobs under the skin of chicken). In excess, it's bad for the heart because it causes blood cholesterol to increase. The body must first break down saturated fat into unsaturated fat, and only then can it be turned into energy. One should obviously keep their daily intake of saturated fat below the 100% DV of 20 g.

Very High (10-19 g): Cream Pies; Commercial Chocolate Frosted Doughnuts; Coconut Oil; Ground Beef; Cold Cuts; Pizza; Hardening Ice Cream Topping; Ice Cream.

High (4-9 g): Ground Chuck; Dark or White Chocolates; Butter (stick); Goat Milk; Liverwurst; Malted Milk Balls; Puff Pastries; Cholent; Hard Cheese (all); Hot Dogs (Beef); Eggnog; Cream Cheese; Beef; Cheese Spread; Coconut; Halvah; Whole Milk; Butter (whipped); Salami; Chocolate Chips; Wafers; Doughnuts; Goat Cheese; Filled Wafer Rolls; Chicken Fat; Chicken (w/ skin); Cornish Hen; Duck (baked skinless); Pumpkin Seeds.

Unsaturated Fat- These fats are liquid at room temperature (like olive oil). There are two types— monounsaturated and polyunsaturated. Both help reduce bad LDL and increase good HDL. Of the polyunsaturated, Omega-3 (linolenic acid) is beneficial for arthritis, and Omega-6 (linoleic acid) has anti-inflammatory properties.

Monounsaturated Fat: 100% = 40 g.

High (8-19 g): Macadamia Nuts; Hazel Nuts; White Chocolate; Puff Pastry; Pecans; Avocado Oil; Olive Oil; Almonds; Almond Oil; Canola Oil; Pecan Oil; Peanut Butter.

Moderate (4-7 g): Peanut Oil; Peanuts; Pistachios; Sardines; Hazelnut Oil; Pumpkin Seeds; Rice Oil.

Polyunsaturated Fat: 100% = 24 g.

Very High (12-14 g) Walnuts.

High (4.8-11 g): Safflower Oil; Grapeseed Oil; Pumpkin Seeds; Soybean Oil; Sunflower Oil; Sunflower Seeds; Corn Oil; Cottonseed Oil; Sesame Oil; Pecans; Solid Vegetable Shortening; Peanut Oil; Pecan Oil; Rice Oil.

Moderate (2.4-4.5 g) Pistachios; Mayonnaise; Almonds; Tub Margarine (some).

Omega-3 Fatty Acid: **100% (1.35 g) or +:** Kippers (Herring); Sardines.

High (.27 g) Lox; Pink Salmon (canned); Egg (large).

Moderate (.135-.195 g): Tuna (canned light); Albacore Tuna (canned).

Other Foods Containing Omega-3: Almonds; Canola Oil; Fish Oil; Flax Seed; Flax Seed Oil; Herring; Mackerel; Pumpkin Seeds; Safflower Oil; Sunflower Oil; Sunflower Seeds; Trout; Walnuts.

Omega-6 Fatty Acid: **100% (12.5 g) or +:** The highest by far is Safflower Oil.

Other Foods Containing Omega 6: Corn Oil; Flax Seed Oil; Nuts; Seeds; Sesame Oil; Soybean Oil; Sunflower Oil; Walnut Oil.

FIBER: Also called dietary fiber, this refers to plant matter that cannot be digested. There are two forms—soluble and insoluble. Soluble fiber attracts water, turning gel-like as it goes through the digestive tract, softening the waste matter. It has been proven to lower cholesterol, and can help prevent heart disease. Insoluble fiber is generally thought of as "roughage" or "bulk", and remains relatively intact.

When adding fiber to your diet, do so slowly over a few weeks to avoid abdominal discomfort. Be sure to drink plenty of water. Men tend to need more fiber than women. The 100% RDA for men is 38g, although for women it's 25 g. Somewhere in-between is considered a healthy balance, therefore the DV is averaged and a good guide to use.

<u>**Foods Containing Soluble Fiber**</u> **(2-6 g):** Oat Bran; Pears (raw); Lima Beans (dry); Oatmeal; Psyllium Husk Fiber (dry laxative powders); Apple (w/o skin); Kidney/Navy Beans (dry); Parsnips; Prunes; Strawberries; Sweet Potato.

<u>**Foods Containing Insoluble Fiber**</u> **(2-7.2 g):** Lentils; Split Peas (dry); Wheat Bran; Barley; Beans (most dry); Bulgur; Wheat Germ; Dates; Vegetables (frozen mixed); Whole Wheat Bread; Pears (raw); Walnuts; Corn; Parsnips; Carrots; Prunes; Sweet Potato.

Other High-Fiber Foods (Total Fiber) 100% = 31.5 g

High (6.3-14.2 g): High-Fiber Cereals; Bran-Only Cereals; Pasta (whole wheat); Artichoke; Whole Wheat Cereals; Bran Cereals.

Moderate (3.15-5 g): Raspberries; Winter Squashes; Blackberries; Sweet Potato; Spinach (frozen or canned); Brussels Sprouts; Sauerkraut.

LUTEIN & ZEAXANTHIN: Usually lumped together, these antioxidants help to keep the eyes functioning properly. Although primarily found in greens, they are carotenoids related to vitamin A, and too much can cause yellow skin. They're found in the exact same foods. There is no DV or UL for Lutein or Zeaxanthin.

Foods High in Lutein & Zeaxanthin (6k-12k mcg): (All boiled, fresh or frozen); Spinach; Turnip Greens; Collard Greens.

LYCOPENE: Another antioxidant carotenoid that is found most commonly in red or orange-colored vegetables and fruits, especially tomatoes. Note that foods containing lycopene will stain plastic!

Unlike most nutrients that boil off as they cook, lycopene becomes even more concentrated! It's fat-soluble, and oils help aid its absorption. It is said to possibly help prevent cancer (especially prostate).

There is no DV or UL for lycopene, although it can slow down blood-clotting. Those on anti-coagulant drugs may want to limit their intake of lycopene.

Foods High in Lycopene (13k-24k mcg): Vegetable Juice; Tomato Juice; Pasta Sauce; Tomato Soup.

Fairly High (1k-9k mcg): Tomato Sauce; Salsa; Tomatoes (sun-dried); Watermelon; Tomato Paste; Tomatoes (canned); Vegetable Soup (tomato-based); Tomatoes (cooked); Tomato Puree; Grapefruit (Pink or Red); Ketchup; Tomatoes (raw).

PROTEINS: Proteins are made up of amino acids, the body's "building blocks". The body naturally makes 11 of them. There are 9 more aminos that can't be made by our bodies, called "essential amino acids", and generally these must come from the foods we eat.

Complete protein or high-quality protein sources provide all of the essential amino acids we need. Incomplete protein lacks or is insufficient in one or more essential aminos. Complete proteins are often high in calories and cholesterol. Therefore, one has to have a happy balance, because too much protein can be turned into fat. Too much protein is also not good for those with kidney disorders.

Incomplete proteins are lacking in some of the amino acids. They are generally plant products.

Complementary proteins are two or more incomplete proteins that provide a proper number of essential aminos when combined. If one food lacks certain aminos it can be combined with another that has the missing ones to equal a complete protein, such as beans and rice or a peanut butter sandwich. They don't even have to be eaten at the same meal, but they should at least be eaten on the same day.

Complete Proteins: 100% (50 g)

Very High (25-30 g): Chicken; Beef; Lamb; Tuna Steak (baked); Tuna (canned).

High (10-24 g): The following baked fish- Trout, Perch, Salmon, Bass; Flounder, Mahi-Mahi, Sole, Whitefish, Carp, Haddock, Cod, and Pollock; Liver; Giblets (boiled); Salmon (canned); Hamburger Patty; Eggs (scrambled or fried); Soy Beans; Soy Products; Cottage Cheese; TVP®.

Moderate (5-9 g): Yogurt; Cheese; Milk; Egg (1 hard-boiled); Egg Substitute.

Incomplete Proteins: 100% (50 g)

High (10-24 g): Wheat Germ.

Moderate (5-9 g): Lentils (dry); Split Peas (dry); Beans (dried); Peanuts; Peanut Butter; Seeds; Pasta; Nuts.

SUGARS: Diabetics must avoid most sugars. The more natural or unprocessed a sugar is, the easier it is for the body to process. Sugars are classified as simple carbohydrates. They're broken down into glucose (blood sugar) and used for energy. Monosaccharides (single or simple sugars) include fructose, glucose, galactose and mannose. Disaccharides (double sugars) are sucrose (cane or beet sugar), lactose (milk sugar) and maltose (two glucoses). Invert sugars are sucrose turned into syrups. Ideally one should stay *below* the 100% DV of 40 g. Natural foods are often made up of several different types of sugars.

Other Sugars: Beet Sugar; Brown Sugar; Cane sugar; Corn Sweetener; Corn Syrup; Dextrose; Fructose; Fruit Juice Concentrates; Galactose; Glucose; High-Fructose Corn Syrup; Honey; Invert Sugar; Lactose; Maltose; Malt Syrup; Mannose; Molasses; Raw Sugar; Sucrose; Sugar; Syrup.

Processed Foods: (See package labels for their amounts.) Cakes; Candy; Canned Fruit; Chocolate; Cookies; Honey; Jelly; Licorice; Pudding; Soft Drinks; Table Sugar (Sucrose).

Natural Foods: **100% (40 g):**

Very High (20-25 g): Raisins; Dates; Pear; Figs.

High (8-17 g): Honey (1 Tbs.); Apricots (dried); Prunes; Apple; Banana; Yogurt; Mandarin Oranges (canned); Milk; Buttermilk; Grapefruit; Grapes; Melons; Molasses (1 Tbs.); Orange; Peach; Tangerine.

Moderate (4-7 g): Kiwi; Plum.

Possibly Harmful Food Substances

The following categories are good to be aware of, as some people have no tolerance for them.

CAFFEINE: An aid to keep awake, small amounts aren't a problem. The FDA says that 400 mg (equal to 4 cups of brewed coffee) per day is still safe for most people. The exception is pregnant or nursing mothers, who should limit it to less than 200 mg. Any more may be too much, although it is different for each person, and can depend a lot on body weight. Powdered or liquid caffeine is concentrated, and 1 tsp. pure caffeine (equal to 28 cups of coffee) can even be fatal or cause severe health problems. Many try to avoid caffeine, as too much can increase blood pressure, anxiety, or gives some jitters. For some (not all) migraine sufferers, caffeine helps kill a headache, yet for others it causes a headache. An ENT doctor told me that caffeine can sometimes cause ringing in the ears.

Ingredients Containing Caffeine: Cocoa; Coffee; Green Coffee Bean; Guarana; Kola Nut; Methylxanthine; Tea; Trimethylxanthine; Xanthine; Yerba maté.

Foods with Caffeine: 100% = 400 mg (or +): Brewed Espresso; Chocolate-Coated Coffee Beans (34 beans).

High (80-100 mg): Hot Cocoa; Brewed Coffee; Energy Drinks.

Moderate (40-79 mg): Instant Coffee; Brewed Tea; Yellow Citrus-Type Soft Drinks.

MERCURY: Certain types of fish contain very high levels of mercury (or methylmercury). It occurs naturally, but is more prevalent in some areas due to industrial pollution. Old larger fish have absorbed more mercury, as it accumulates in the body over time, both in humans and the fish they eat. Although it is discarded from the body naturally, it can take over a year for mercury levels to drop substantially. Therefore, the FDA and EPA advise nursing mothers, women who are or may become pregnant, and young children to avoid fish that are high in mercury. It can harm a fetus and cause damage to a young child's nervous system. It is advised to only consume up to 12 ounces of lower mercury fish (such as light tuna) per week, or up to 6 ounces of albacore tuna, tuna steaks, or locally caught non-commercial fish per week for an adult. Portions for young children should be proportionately smaller. If one eats more one week, they can eat less the next week. Since it's eliminated slowly, immediate results are insignificant.

FDA amounts listed below are average mean mercury levels measured in parts per million (PPM).

High (.730-1.450 ppm): Tilefish (from Gulf of Mexico); King Mackerel.

Moderate (.128-.638 ppm): Bigeye Tuna (fresh/frozen); Orange Roughy; Grouper; Spanish Mackerel (Gulf of Mexico); Tuna (other- fresh/frozen); Chilean Bass; White/Albacore Tuna (any); Yellowfin Tuna (fresh/frozen); Halibut; Skipjack Tuna (fresh/frozen); Ocean Trout; Sea Bass; Spanish Mackerel (S. Atlantic); Snapper; Tilefish Atlantic); Carp; Freshwater Perch; Sheepshead.

Low (.01-.118 ppm): Light Tuna (canned); Jacksmelt; Cod; Mackerel (Pacific Chub); Atlantic Croaker; Freshwater Trout; Whitefish; Shad (American); Mackerel (N. Atlantic); Mullet; Flounder; Sole; Herring; Anchovies; Pollock; Haddock (Atlantic); Ocean Perch; Sardines; Hake; Salmon (fresh/frozen); Tilapia; Salmon (canned).

(Most commercial fish sticks are made from fish low in mercury— Cod, Pollock and Haddock.)

ORGANISMS: Harmful or toxic organisms can be found in certain foods. Common symptoms of food-borne illnesses are stomach cramps, nausea, vomiting, diarrhea (often bloody), or occasionally fever. Pregnant women and young children are most susceptible, and the elderly or those with weak immune systems. Salmonella, E. Coli and Listeria can cause kidney damage or death especially in young children.

Drinks: Culprits are untreated water, unpasteurized apple cider, vegetable or fruit juices, and bad milk. Other symptoms are severe stomach cramps or kidney damage in young children. Symptoms occur in days.

One mustn't give brewed tea containing star anise to infants. Severe neurological problems can result.

Eaten Portions: Even infant saliva causes toxins to grow in eaten refrigerated foods! Always heat food.

Honey/Improper Home-Canning: One must never feed honey to a baby under one year old. Some botulism symptoms are double vision, dry mouth or muscle paralysis. Seek immediate medical help.

Fish: Saltwater organisms can affect raw fish. Symptoms can occur within hours if not treated. One strain can be fatal due to shock/dehydration, with symptoms occurring in 1 week or less. It can cause Cholera.

Egg/Meat/Poultry: If eaten raw, undercooked, or left unrefrigerated, symptoms can occur within hours.

Prepared Food: A major cause of Staph infection, Norovirus, and Shigella is due to people making food who don't wash their hands beforehand and touch wounds, pimples, or their nose. Symptoms occur in days. Ideally, food-prep workers should wear rubber gloves.

Perfect Conditions: Organisms thrive, propagate and reproduce when conditions are right. Therefore, one must wash their hands with warm soapy water before handling food after any of the following: Changing diapers or a cat's litter box (outdoor cats or pets on raw diets can carry Toxoplasmosis); Cleaning up after sick people; Gardening; Handling raw eggs, fish, meat, poultry or unwashed produce; Licking fingers; Touching face, hair, money, pets, or wounds (organisms live on the skin); Using the restroom.

SULFITES: Sulfite-sensitivity is not a true food "allergy", and can suddenly develop in those who previously have never had it before. Reactions can happen within minutes or hours, being mild to life-threatening. Sulfite is a sulfur compound that is a naturally occurring by-product of the beer and wine process. Sulfites are often found in wine and grape juice, an essential part of Jewish life. Therefore, one with sensitivity must obtain sulfite-free grape products that are kosher-certified. It's more prevalent in red or sweet wines than white. Up until 1986, sulfites were often put on fresh produce that was eaten raw until the FDA banned this usage. It's still used as a preservative. Sulfites destroy vitamin B1.

Sulfite Ingredients: Sulfur Dioxide; Potassium Bisulfite; Potassium Metabisulfite; Sodium Bisulfite; Sodium Metabisulfite; Sodium Sulfite.

Possible Sulfite-Containing Items: Apple Cider; Baked Goods; Beer; Bottled Lemon Juice; Bottled Lime Juice; Canned Vegetables; Dehydrated Potatoes; Dried Fruit; Grape Juice; Gravies; Guacamole; Jams; Ketchup; Maraschino Cherries; Molasses; Mustard; Peeled Potatoes; Pickled Foods; Potato Chips; Pre-Cut Potatoes; Soup Mix; Sparkling Grape Juice; Tea; Trail Mix; Vegetable Juices; Wine.

Food Allergies

Food allergy is different than intolerance, which is generally minor gastrointestinal discomfort. Allergy or hypersensitivity is an immunological response to certain food proteins. Symptoms can vary from itching, hives, wheezing, swelling of the face, lips or tongue, throat (causing difficulty in breathing or swallowing), to severe-anaphylaxis that can be fatal (shock, low blood pressure and unconsciousness). Symptoms can happen from within seconds to many hours later after having the food.

Allergens are hard to decipher due to chemical names, so unsuspected ingredients are listed as well.

EGG ALLERGY: People with an egg allergy (generally to egg whites) can have instant reactions in severe cases. It is more prevalent in children more than adults. Products ingredient labels must be read.

Egg Items: Dried Egg; Egg Albumin; Egg Powder; Eggs; Egg Solids; Egg Whites; Egg Yolks.

Egg Ingredients: Albumin; Apovitellenin; Baking Powder (containing egg white or egg albumin); Globulin; Livetin; Lysozyme; Ovalbumin; Ovoglobulin; Ovomucin; Ovomuciod; Ovotranferrin; Ovovitella; Ovovitellin; Phosvitin; Silica Albuminate; Surimi (used in imitation seafood); Vitellan.

Foods Containing Egg: Baked Items; Bavarian Creams; Cream Pie; Cream Puffs; Crepes; Custard; Eggnog; Egg Rolls; Fat Substitute; French Toast; Hollandaise Sauce; Ice Cream; Jelly Beans (brushed with egg); Malt Beverages; Mayonnaise; Marshmallows; Meringue; Noodles; Pancakes; Sherbet; Soufflés; Tartar Sauce; Waffles; Whips; Wontons.

Possible Egg Items: Breaded/Batter-Fried Foods; Candy; Cappuccino-Style Drinks; Creamed Foods; Egg Substitute; Root Beer; Sauces; Soft Pretzels; Puddings; Salad Dressings.

FISH ALLERGY: Some people are only allergic to certain types of fish, but in general, most people don't know which type of fish they are allergic to and must avoid all types. If one is ordering a non-fish meal in an establishment that serves fish (like vegan restaurants), food can be contaminated from utensils, grills or fishy oil. Fortunately, *kashrut* laws require fishy items to be labeled as such. All fish items must be avoided completely (some are types of canned fish). Check ingredients for other possible fish items.

Fish Items: Albacore; Anchovies; Caviar; Fish Oils; Imitation Seafood; Kippers; Roe; Sprats; Sushi.

Possible Fish Items: Gelatin; Margarine; Marshmallows; Omega-3 Supplements; Worcestershire Sauce.

GLUTEN AND WHEAT ALLERGY: Gluten (Seitan) is the protein found in wheat, that helps breads rise and become fluffy. This is perhaps the roughest allergy to have since wheat is such a staple. Although they are different disorders, those with wheat allergy, gluten allergy or Celiac Disease must all avoid gluten/wheat products. People with these allergies may benefit from foods containing Magnesium, and vitamins A and B12. Most processed foods contain gluten, so ingredients must be checked well to be absolutely certain.

Naturally High-Gluten Ingredients: All-Purpose Flour; Barley; Barley Flour; Bleached Flour; Bread Crumbs; Bread Flour; Bromated Flour; Bulgur Wheat; Cake Flour; Cake Meal; Cracked Wheat; Cracker Meal; Dry Powdered Mustard; Durum Flour; Durum Wheat; Enriched Flour; Farina; Flour; Glucose Syrup; Gluten; Gluten Flour; Graham Flour; Hydrolyzed Wheat Protein; Malt Flavoring; Malt Vinegar; Modified Food Starch; Matzo Ball Soup; Matzah Meal; Phosphated Flour; Rye; Rye Flour; Seitan; Self-Rising Flour; Semolina; Spelt; Spelt Flour; Triticale; Unbleached Flour; Vegetable Protein; Vegetable Starch; Vital Gluten; Wheat; Wheat Berries; Wheat Bran; Wheat Flour; Wheat Germ; Wheat Gluten; Wheat Starch; White Flour; Whole Grains; Whole Wheat; Whole Wheat Flour.

High-Gluten Processed Foods: Alcoholic Drinks; Barley Water Drinks; Beer; Breads, Breaded Foods; Cereals; Commercial Baked Goods; Graham Crackers; Gravy Mixes; Licorice; Pasta; Matzah (wheat or spelt); Pizza; Pie Crusts; Pumpernickel Bread; Rye Bread; Salad Dressing; Spelt Bread.

Foods Possibly Containing Gluten: Baked Beans; Bouillon Cubes; Brown Rice Syrup; Candy; Chicken Nuggets; Chocolate; Cocoa; Cold Cuts; Hot Dogs; Fish Sticks; French Fries; Gravy; Imitation Seafood; Instant Coffee; Matzah (Matzo); Mouthwash; Pickles; Potato Chips; Pre-packaged Meals; Rice Mixes; Salami; Sausages; Sauces; Seasoned Tortilla Chips; Soup Cubes; Soup (mixes or canned); Soy Sauce (not natural Tamari); Spices; Veggie Patties (Breaded); Vitamin Supplements.

Gluten-Free Flours: Almond; Amaranth; Arrowroot; Beans; Buckwheat (pure); Cassava; Chia Seed; Chickpeas; Corn; Corn Starch; Flax; Garbanzo Bean; Gram Flour (derived from chickpeas); Indian Rice Grass; Kasha (pure); Legumes; Lupin; Millet; Nuts; Oat (certified Gluten-Free); Peas; Potato; Potato Starch; Quinoa; Rice; Rice; Sago; Seeds; Soy; Soybean (Soy Flour); Sorghum (Jowar); Sweet Potato; Taro; Teff; Tapioca (derived from cassava); Wild Rice; Yucca.

MILK ALLERGY: Having a milk allergy is not the same as having lactose intolerance. Reactions can be much more serious, such as swelling of the throat and trouble breathing and can occur quickly. Fortunately, certified kosher foods are always marked "Dairy" if there are milk derivatives in a product.

Milk Ingredients: Casein; Casein Hydrosylates; Caseinates; Ghee; Lactalbumin; Lactalbumin Phosphate; Lactoglobulin; Lactoferrin; Lactose; Lactulose; Milk Solids; Sodium Caseinate; Whey.

Milk Items: Au Gratin Foods; Butter; Butter Fat; Buttermilk; Butter Oil; Cheese; Cheese Powder; Cheese Sauce; Condensed Milk; Cow's Milk; Cottage Cheese; Cream; Cream Candy; Cream Cheese; Creamed/Scalloped Food; Custard; Dry/Powdered/Instant Milk; Evaporated Milk; Goat Milk; Half & Half; Ice Cream; Milk Chocolate; Nougat; Sherbet; Skim Milk; Sour Cream; White Sauces; Yogurt.

Possible Milk Items: Artificial Butter Flavor; Butter Flavor Oils; Cake; Cake Mix; Chocolate; Dry Coffee Creamers; Doughnuts; Malted Milk Syrup or Powder; Margarines (read the label); Mashed Potato Mixes; Non-Dairy Creamer; Puddings; Salad Dressings.

NUT ALLERGY: Nut allergies can be extremely dangerous, and peanut allergies even be deadly, having the highest fatality rate of any food allergen. Since so many products contain nut derivatives, it's extremely important to read ingredient labels each time, as ingredients can change over time. Nut allergies are so serious that only minute trace elements can cause reactions. This includes non-nut items merely having been processed in the same area as nuts, or manufactured on clean equipment that had once processed nuts. People who are allergic to peanuts aren't always allergic to tree nuts and vice versa.

Tree Nut Ingredients: Marzipan; Natural Wintergreen Extract; Nougat; Pure Nut Extracts.

Tree Nut Items: Almonds; Beech Nuts; Brazil Nuts; Cashews; Chestnuts; Ethnic Foods; Filberts (Hazelnuts); Flavored Nuts; Ground/Chopped Nuts; Hickory Nuts; Macadamia Nuts; Mixed Nuts; Nut Butters; Nut Extracts; Nut Flours/Meal; Nut Oils; Nut Pastes; Pecans; Pine Nuts (Pinyon or Pigñon); Pistachios; Walnuts.

Possible Tree Nut Items: Baked Goods; Candy; Cereals; Chili; Ethnic Foods; Frozen Desserts; Granola Bars; High-Energy Bars; Ice Cream; Multi-Grain Breads; Pastries; Salad Dressings; Snack Mixes.

Peanut Ingredients: Beer Nuts; Egg Rolls; Flavored Nuts; Hydrolyzed Plant or Vegetable Protein.

Peanut Items: Atrovent (inhaler); Ground/Chopped Peanuts; Peanut Butter; Peanut Flour; Peanut Oil; Peanuts; "Ground Nuts" (in many other countries, as they grow under the soil).

Possible Peanut Items: Baked Goods; Candy; Cereals; Chili; Chocolate; Ethnic Foods; Frozen Desserts; Granola Bars; High-Energy Bars; Ice Cream; Mixed Nuts; Multi-Grain Breads; Salad Dressings; Snack Mixes.

SESAME ALLERGY: Sesame allergy can affect people of any age. Some may grow out of it, but most do not. Less severe symptoms such as itching, rash or other skin irritation, can occur gradually over hours or days. More severe reactions happen quickly, including hives upon direct contact, or even anaphylactic shock. Some experience allergic reactions to other foods (such as peanuts, filberts and almonds) due to "cross-reactivity", where one chemical substance is similar enough to the initial allergen, that the immune system treats them both alike. Reactions can also extend to skin care and cosmetic products made with sesame oil.

Sesame Ingredients: Baba Ghanoush; Benne Wafers; Falafels; Halvah; Hummus; Sesame Oil; Sesame Seeds; Sesame Sticks; Tahini; Tehina.

Sesame Items: Bagels; Crackers; Ethnic Foods; Hamburger Buns; Pretzels; Snack Mixes; Vienna Bread.

Possible Sesame Items: Energy Bars; Ice Cream; Margarine; Nutritional Supplements; Salad Dressings.

SOY ALLERGY: Often affecting children, a soy allergy can suddenly develop in someone who has previously eaten soy before without any problem. Reactions can happen within minutes or hours, being either as mild as developing itching or hives or as serious as developing breathing problems or swelling of the throat. The latter can be understandable, as soy beans are in the same legume family as peanuts (which has the highest fatality rate of any food allergen).

Some people with soy allergies may still be able to eat Soybean Oil and Soy Lecithin.

Soy Items: Bean Curd; Edamame; Ethnic Foods; Hydrolyzed Soy Protein; Miso; Natto; Shoyu Sauce; Soy; Soya; Soy Albumin; Soy Beans (dry or fresh); Soybean Curd; Soybean Granules; Soybean Oil; Soy Fiber; Soy Flour; Soy Ice Cream; Soy Lecithin; Soy Milk; Soy Nuts; Soy Protein; Soy Sauce; Soy Sprouts; Tamari; Tempeh; Textured Vegetable Protein (TVP®); Tofu (or products made from it).

Possible Soy Items: Artificial Flavoring; Imitation Dairy Products; Imitation Meat Products; Natural Flavoring; Non-Dairy Whip Topping; Vegetable Broth; Vegetable Gum; Vegetable Starch.

Nutrient Data Chart

Nutrient Chart (* should not exceed UL due to health risks)					
Minerals	* UL	RDA Men	RDA Women	**Counteracted By**	**Combine With**
Calcium	*2.5 g	1000 mg	1000 mg	Iron; Salt; Protein; A; Caffeine; Alcohol	D; Magnesium & Potassium
Chromium	*N/A	35 mcg	25 mcg	Simple Sugars	B3; C
Copper	*10 g	900 mcg	900 mcg	Calcium; Zinc; Molybdenum	Iron
Iodine	*1100 mcg	150 mcg	150 mcg	N/A	N/A
Iron	*45 mg	8 mg	18 mg	Calcium; Zinc	Copper; A; C
Magnesium	*350 mg	420 mg	320 mg	N/A	Calcium; Potassium
Manganese	*11 mg	2.3 mg	1.8 mg	N/A	K
Molybdenum	*2 mg	45 mcg	45 mcg	Copper	
Phosphorus	*3-4 g	700 mg	700 mg	N/A	Calcium
Potassium	*N/A	4.7 g	4.7 g	Sodium (Salt)	Calcium; Magnesium
Selenium	*400 mcg	55 mcg	55 mcg	N/A	N/A
Sodium/Salt	*2,300 g	1.5 g (or less)	1.5 g (or less)	N/A	Extra Potassium
Zinc	*40 mg	11 mg	8 mg	Copper; Iron; Alcohol	C (for colds)
Vitamins	* UL	RDA Men	RDA Women	**Counteracted By**	**Combine With**
A	*10,000 IU/3000 mcg	3k IU/900 mcg	2,310 IU/700 mcg	Alcohol	Fat; Iron
B1/Thiamin	*N/A	1.2 mg	1.1 mg	Heat; Sulfites; Alcohol	Water; other Bs
B2/Riboflavin	*N/A	1.3 mg	1.1 mg	Exposure to Light	Water; other Bs
B3/Niacin	*35 mg	16 mg	14 mg	N/A	Water; Chromium
B5/Pantothenic Acid	*N/A	5 mg	5 mg	Heat	Water
B6/Pyridoxine	*100 mg	1.3 mg	1.3 mg	Alcohol	Water
B7/Biotin	*N/A	30 mcg	30 mcg	Excess Raw Egg White	Water
B9/Folate or Folic Acid	*1 mg	400 mcg	400 mcg	Alcohol	Water; other Bs
B12/Cyanocobalamin	*N/A	2.4 mcg	2.4 mcg	N/A	Water; other Bs
Choline	*3500 mg	550 mg	425 mg	N/A	Water; other Bs
C/Ascorbic Acid	*2 g	90 mg	75 mg	Heat	Water; Iron
D	*4000 IU/100 mcg	600 IU/15 mcg	600 IU/15 mcg	Vitamin A	Fat; Calcium
E/Alpha-tocopherol	*1500 IU/1g	22.4 IU/15 mg	22.4 IU/15 mg	N/A	Fat; K
K/Phylloquinone	*N/A	120 mcg	90 mcg	N/A	Fat; E; Manganese
Other		RDA Men	RDA Women	**Energy Equivalents**	
Carbohydrates		300 g	300 g	1 gram = 4 calories	
Cholesterol		Below 300 mg	Below 300 mg	N/A	
Total Fat		Less than 65g of all fats combined		1 gram = 9 calories	
Saturated Fat		Below 20 g	Below 20 g	1 gram = 9 calories	
Monounsaturated Fat		40 g	40 g	1 gram = 9 calories	
Polyunsaturated Fat		24 g or more	24 g or more	1 gram = 9 calories	
Omega-3		1.6 g or more	1.1 g or more	1 gram = 9 calories	
Omega-6		14 g or more	11 g or more	1 gram = 9 calories	
Dietary Fiber		38 g	25 g	N/A	
Protein		50 g	50 g	1 gram = 4 calories	
Sugars		Below 40 g	Below 40 g	1 gram = 4 calories	

Special Health Needs: Food & Nutrients Chart

For those who fix food for others with medical problems, this chart can be used to look up pertinent foods in their categories. Other general categories are listed as well.

Special Health-Needs - Foods and Nutrients		
Those Having:	**Avoid:**	**Try to Eat:**
Anemia	Zinc or Calcium at the same meal as Iron and Copper. Zinc inhibits Copper and Calcium inhibits Iron; Excess Antacids (can inhibit Iron).	Iron & Copper (but do not eat at same meal as Calcium or Zinc); Vitamins B2; B6; B9; B12; Vitamin C (eat in the same meal as Iron-rich vegetables).
Arthritis (Osteoarthritis)	Sugar; Saturated Fat; Refined Carbs	Vitamin B3; B5; Omega-3 Fatty Acids.
Celiac Disease	Gluten; Wheat (see "Wheat Allergy").	Iron; Vitamins A; B12; D.
Crohn's Disease	Accutane (some); High Dietary Fiber.	Iron; Magnesium; Selenium; A; B12; D.
Diabetes	Carbohydrates (unless eaten with fiber); Sugar; Saturated Fat.	Chromium; Magnesium; Zinc; Vitamins B3; B7; C; Soluble Fiber
Dialysis	Phosphorus; Potassium; Excess Salt; Excess Liquid Intake.	Iron; Vitamins A; B9; Some Protein (not excessive).
Food Allergies	(See individual listings on pages 482-485.)	
Heart Problems	Sodium; Cholesterol/Saturated Fat; Lycopene and Vitamin K (if on blood thinner).	Chromium; High-Fiber. Vitamins B-3; C. Vitamin E (if on certain medicines.)
High Blood Pressure	High Sodium Content; High Fat.	Magnesium; Potassium & Calcium; B6; B9; B12; Fiber; HDL (see "Cholesterol").
High Cholesterol	High LDL Cholesterol and Saturated Fat.	Iron & Copper; Chromium; B3; C; Fiber; HDL (see "Cholesterol").
Insomnia	Caffeine; Spicy Foods; Sugar.	Warm Milk; Chamomile Tea; Wine.
Kidney Disorders	Excess Salt; High-Protein; Potassium; Phosphorus; (Too much Calcium Oxalate can cause Kidney Stones).	Iron; Vitamin A; Carbohydrates; Fat.
Lactose Intolerance	Dairy (see "Milk Allergy" p. 484).	Almond, Oat, or Rice Milk; Soy Products.
Liver Disorders	Alcohol; Manganese.	Vitamin B9.
Low Blood Pressure	Carbohydrates (starchy); Caffeine	Sodium; Water.
Migraine	Aged Cheese; Alcohol; Aspartame; MSG; Nitrates; Caffeine (for some).	Caffeine (for some); Feverfew or Rosemary Teas; Water/Liquid.
Nausea	Acids; Dairy Products (for some).	Calcium; Antacids; Ginger Ale; Mint.
Nursing Infants	Molybdenum; Alcohol; Certain Fish.	Zinc; Vitamins A; B12; D.
Obesity	High Cholesterol; Saturated Fat.	Vitamin D; High Fiber.
Osteoporosis	Sodium; Excess Vitamin A; Fat; Alcohol.	Calcium; Magnesium; Phosphorus; Vitamins D; K; Omega-3.
Pancreatic Disorders	Saturated Fat; Sugar.	Vitamin A.
Pregnancy	Molybdenum; Alcohol; Certain Fish.	Iron; Zinc; B7; B9; B12; D; Choline.
Pregnancy/Lactation for Vegetarian Women Only	Molybdenum; Excess Antacids (can inhibit Iron); High-Mercury Fish.	Calcium; Iron; Selenium; Zinc; Vitamins B2; B9; B12; D.
Rheumatoid Arthritis (RA)	Excess Vitamin A; Alcohol (if on certain medications).	Calcium Pantothenate (B5); Iron & Copper; Phosphorus; Selenium; Vitamin B3; B5; B9; B12; Omega-3.
Stomach Disorders	Acidic or Spicy Foods; Caffeine.	Calcium; Vitamins A; B12.
Toothache	Sugar; Cold Foods (like Ice Cream).	Clove Oil; Cloves.
Ulcer (Peptic or Gastric)	Aspirin; Anti-Inflammatory Drugs.	Cabbage; Cabbage Juice.
Ulcerative Colitis	Accutane (in some).	Fish Oils; Oatmeal; Soluble Fiber.

Conversions & Capacities

The following sections are helpful for converting recipes, and seeing how much food will fit in cookware. They can come in very handy. If you ever get recipes from friends, or books from other countries such as Europe or Israel, you'll need these conversions for the U.S. equivalents. The metric system is very precise, but it doesn't matter if your measurements are slightly off. English measures are variable in comparison to metric, except for lengths. They can fluctuate. For instance, ½ cup could be anywhere from 118-125 ml. and 1 lb. could be anywhere from 453-500 grams. There's room for slop. Most recipes aren't so precise that it matters, (except when dealing with very potent spices). (If you keep a calculator in the kitchen, formulas are listed as well as basic conversions.)

The capacity lists are great "cheat sheets". I did this for my own, and was constantly referring back to it. Measurements enables you to divide or multiply recipes at a glance, can sizes help determine how much food is in a can, and container and cookware capacities are good for determining vessel size per amount of ingredients without overflowing or boiling over. (For measuring drops with items such as extracts, a food-grade pipette or medicine dropper works really well.)

Dry Weights

English to Metric Formula: oz. x 28.35 = gr. lbs. x 450 = gr. lbs. x .45 = kg.
Metric to English Formula: gr. x .035 = oz. gr. ÷ 450 = lbs. kg. x 2.2 = lbs.

Basic Equivalencies:

¼ lb. = 125 gr.	½ lb. =250 gr.	¾ cup = 175 gr.	1 lb. = 454 gr.	1½ lb. = 675 gr.
2 lb. = 1 kg.	3 lb. = 1.5 kg.	4 lb. = 2 k.	5 lb. = 2.5 kg.	6 lb. = 3 k.

Liquid Volumes

English to Metric Formula:

tsp. x 5 = ml.   oz. x 30 = ml.   cup x .24 = l.   qt. x .95 = l.   gal. x 3.78 = l.

Metric to English Formula:

ml. x 2 = tsp.   ml. x .032 = oz.   l. x 4.2 = cup   l. x 1.06 = qt.   l. x .26 = gal.

Basic Equivalencies:

¼ tsp. = 1.5 ml.	½ tsp. = 3 ml.	¾ tsp. = 4.5 ml.	1 tsp. = 5 ml.	1 Tbs. = 15 ml.
¼ cup = 60 ml	⅓ cup = 80 ml.	½ cup = 125 ml.	⅔ cup = 160 ml.	¾ cup = 200 ml.
1 cup = 250 ml.	1 pint = 500 ml.	1 qt. = 1.25 l.	½ gal. = 2.5 l.	1 gal. = 5 l.

Temperatures

English to Metric Formula: $^{\circ}F - 32 \times 5 \div 9 = ^{\circ}C$

Metric to English Formula: $^{\circ}C \times 9 \div 5 + 32 = ^{\circ}F$

Basic Equivalencies:

32° F (freezing) 0° C	115° F (simmering) = 46° C	130° F (scalding) = 54° C
212° F (boiling) = 100° C	225° F = 107° C	250° F (very low) = 121° C
275° F (very low) = 135° C	300° F (low) = 150° C	325° F (low) = 165° C
350° F (medium) = 180° C	375° F (medium) = 190° C	400° F (hot) = 205° C
425° F (hot) = 220° C	450° F (very hot) = 231° C	475° F (very hot) = 243° C
500° F (extremely hot) = 260° C	525° F (extremely hot) = 272° C	550° F (broil) = 288° C.

Length, Width or Height Measurements

English to Metric Formula: inches x 2.54 = centimeters.

Metric to English Formula: centimeters x .39 = inches.

Basic Equivalencies:

1 in. = 25 mm. (or 2.5 cm.)	2 in. = 5 cm.	3 in. = 7.5 cm.	4 in. = 10 cm.
5 in. = 12.5 cm.	6 in. = 15.25 cm.	7 in. = 17.75 cm.	8 in. = 20.25 cm.
9 in. = 22.75 cm.	10 in. = 25.5 cm.	11 in. = 28 cm.	12 in. (or 1 ft.) = 30.5 cm.
13 in. = 33 cm.	14 in. = 35.5 cm.	15 in. = 38 cm.	16 in. = 38 cm.
17 in. = 43 cm.	18 in. = 45.75 cm.	19 in. = 48.25 cm.	20 in. = 50.75 cm.

General Capacities

Measurement Equivalencies

dash = a shake	drop = dash	2 dashes = a pinch	20 drops = ⅛ tsp.
3 tsp. = 1 Tbs.	2 Tbs. = 1 oz.	dollop = about 1 Tbs.	4 Tbs. = ¼ cup
¼ cup = 2 oz.	5⅓ Tbs. = ⅓ cup	⅓ cup = 2⅔ oz.	8 Tbs. = ½ cup
½ cup = 4 oz.	10⅔ Tbs. = ⅔ cup	⅔ cup = 5⅓ oz.	¾ cup = 6 oz.
12 Tbs. = ¾ cup	16 Tbs. = 1 cup	1 cup = 8 oz.	1 cup = ½ pint
2 cups = 1 pint	1 pint = 16 oz.	16 oz. = 1 lb.	4 cups = 1 quart
2 pints = 1 quart	1 quart = 32 oz.	2 quarts = ½ gallon	½ gallon = 64 oz.
16 cups = 1 gallon	4 quarts = 1 gallon	1 gallon = 128 oz.	1 gallon = 8 lbs.

Can & Container Capacities

4 oz. can = ½ cup	5 oz. can = ⅝-⅔ cup	6 oz. can = ¾ cup
8 oz. can = 1 cup	10-10.5 oz. can = 1¼ cup	12 oz. can = 1½ cups
15-16 oz. can = 1¾ cup	16-17 oz. can = 2 cups	19 oz.-20 oz. can = 2½ cups
26-28 oz. can = 3-3¼ cups	28-30 oz. can = 3½ cups	46-48 oz. can = 5¾ cups

(* use for cold dry storage only; ** can be used for microwave reheating but not cooking.)

6 oz. Yogurt Tub * = ¾ cup	16 oz. Sour Cream Tub * = 1¾ cups
24 oz. Cottage Cheese Tub * = 2¾ cups	3 lb. Margarine Tub * = 5¼ cups
16 oz. Small Deli Tub ** = 1¾ cup	32 oz. Large Deli Tub ** = 3½ cups
Small Disposable Loaf Pan = 2½ cups	Large Disposable Pie Pan = 4 cups

General Cookware Capacities

Below are examples. Items labeled on the bottom are maximum usable capacity. To prevent spills or boil-overs, ¼ less food should comfortably fit (parenthesized). Brands differ, so these won't be exact.

Small Saucepan = 3 (2½) cups	Medium Saucepan = 6 (5) cups
Large Saucepan = 8 (5) cups	Large Pot = 18 (14) cups
Tiny Biscuit Tins = 2 (1½) Tbs. each	Large Biscuit Tins = ½-⅜ cup each
9 inch Round Cake Pan = 3 (2½) cups	9 inch Glass Pie Plate = 3 (2¼) cups
8 x 4 inch Glass Loaf Pan = 4 (3) cups	8 x 8 inch Square Pan = 5 (4½) cups
11 x 7 inch Glass Baking Dish = 6 (5) cups	11 x 14 inch Baking Dish = 12 (10) cups

Personal Cookware Capacities

To make your own list, do the following: Take a measuring cup and fill it with water to the 1 cup line and pour it into a specific vessel. Do this repeatedly until it is comfortably full, and write down the vessel description and its volume amount in the blank area below for future reference. It may be a hassle at first, but it saves time and trouble in the long run. You'll now have a personalized reference table!

Item: **Volume:**

Food Cooking Guide

The following are listings for fresh foods only. Frozen foods must be completely thawed first. For dry foods see "*Liquid to Dry Ratios*" following this section. Ovens, grills and broilers must be preheated.

Symbol: ▦ = Bake, 🍲 = Boil, 🍳 = Broil/Grill, 🍲 = Crock, 🍳 = Fry, ▨ = Microwave, 🍲 = Stir-Fry.

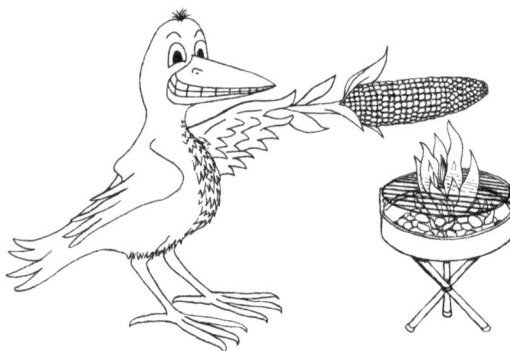

Meat Items

(See *Substituting Meat Cuts* on p. 448 for general tips and the best cooking methods for cuts of meat.)

Bacon (Turkey): ▦ Put on greased sheet. Bake at 350º F 10-15 minutes.

🍳 Fry in a bit of oil about 2 minutes flip, until crisp and juices run clear.

▨ Cover with paper towel. Microwave 1 minute per piece.

Chops & Cutlets: ▦ (Breaded or plain) Bake at 350º F covered 1 hour, uncover after ½ hour.

🍲 Brown if desired, then simmer in broth or water 20-30 minutes.

🍲 Grill or broil 15 minutes flipping halfway through, until desired doneness.

🍲 Put a bit of broth or water in crock with meat. Cook on Low 8 hours or High 4 hours.

🍳 (Breaded) Fry 10 minutes on each side until browned and juices run clear.

▨ Microwave covered 10-12 minutes on 30% power, flip halfway through. Let stand 3 minutes.

Ground Meat (1 lb. Chopped): 🍲 Brown if desired. Simmer in sauce or chili ½ hour.

🍲 Brown. Put in with sauce or chili. Cook on Low 4 hours or High 2 hours (longer for flavor).

🍳 Fry stirring occasionally, on medium heat, about 10 minutes until juices run clear. Drain.

▨ Microwave covered 3 minutes, stir, cook covered 3-4 more minutes until juices run clear.

Hamburgers (4 oz.): ▦ 🍲 🍳 Bake, grill or broil or fry 5-6 minutes on each side until done.

▨ Microwave covered 2-3 minutes per 2 burgers, 3-4 minutes per 4. Flip halfway through.

Hot Dogs: Marinate if desired for dry heat. 🍽 Bake at 350º F 10-15 minutes or until browned.

🍲 Cook in boiling water or steam 15 minutes.

🍳 Broil or grill (turning often) about 5-6 minutes or until browned.

🍲 Put 4 cups water in crock. Cook on Low 1 hour or High 30 minutes.

🍳 Heat a skillet with a bit of oil (a nice addition is chopped onion) and fry about 5-6 minutes or until browned, turning often.

🍱 Cover. Microwave 1 minute per hot dog or 1½ minutes per 4 hot dogs, small sausages 6-8 minutes per lb.

Leg of Lamb: 🍽 Bake uncovered in a preheated 325º F oven 30 minutes per lb.

🍳 Grill 20 minutes, then flip and grill about 35-45 minutes until desired doneness.

🍲 De-bone. Use a large crock, add a bit of liquid. Cook on Low 12 hours, High 6 hours.

🍱 Microwave on high covered 7-10 minutes per pound. Rotate halfway through.

Meat Balls (For 1 lb.): 🍽 Bake at 350º F covered for ½ hour.

🍲 Brown if desired. Simmer in broth or sauce 20 minutes.

🍲 Brown if desired. Put meat balls with some liquid, sauce or broth. Cook on Low 2½-3 hours.

🍳 Fry all meat balls about 3 minutes rotating on all sides until browned and juices run clear.

🍱 Microwave covered 5-6 minutes, rotate halfway through until juices run clear.

Meatloaf: 🍽 Bake at 350º F uncovered for 1 hour, top with sauce 5 minutes before done.

🍲 Shape to fit into crock and top with sauce. Cook on Low 9 hours or High 4-5 hours.

🍱 Microwave 6 minutes on high, top with sauce. Cook 25 minutes on 30% power, rotate halfway through.

Poultry (Chunks): 🍽 Bake covered with liquid at 350º F for ½ hour.

🍲 Cook in boiling water 20 minutes.

🍳 (*Shish Kebabs*): Broil or Grill 10 minutes total or until done, rotate skewers often until desired doneness.

🍲 Put a bit of liquid in crock. Cook on Low 7-8 hours or High 4 hours.

🍳 (Breaded) Fry on each side 6 minutes until juices run clear and breading is browned.

🍱 Arrange with thickest parts to outside. Microwave covered 4 minutes per piece, 6 minutes per 2 pieces, 10 minutes per 4 pieces, etc. turning halfway through, until juices run clear.

🍳 Cut into smaller chunks. Heat a bit of oil in wok or skillet and stir-fry 3-4 minutes.

Poultry (Pieces): (All) Rinse and pat dry with paper towels.

Cover except last 15 minutes. Bake 1 hour at 350º F with some liquid.

Cook in boiling water 30 minutes.

Broil or grill 5 minutes on each side until desired doneness.

Brown if desired. Put liquid or sauce in crock. Cook on Low 6 hours or High 3 hours.

(Breaded) Fry 6 minutes on each side, until juices run clear and chicken is brown.

Grill or broil 5 minutes on each side until desired doneness.

Arrange with thickest parts to outside. Microwave covered 4 minutes per piece, 6 minutes per 2 pieces, 10 minutes per 4 pieces, etc. turning halfway through, until juices run clear.

Poultry (Whole Unstuffed): (Chicken, Cornish Hens, Duck, Goose, Turkey. Also see *Poultry Tips* p. 460 for prep, stuffing and other fowl.) Rinse, pat dry, salt inside cavity, spray with oil and wrap in foil.

Bake at 350º F covered ½ hour per lb., uncover 30 minutes before taking out to brown.

Put a bit of liquid in a large crock pot. Cook on Low 6-8 hours or High 3-4 hours.

Seal in roasting bag or put in covered dish. Cook 7-8 minutes per lb., until juices run clear.

Ribs (3 lb.): Bake 15 minutes covered at 450º F. Add sauce, uncover, bake 1 hour at 350º F.

Cover ribs with water in a large pot and boil 2½-3 hours.

Brown for flavor. Add liquid to crock. Cook on Low 8-9 hours or High 4-5 hours.

Grill or broil ½ hour, coat with sauce and cook 1 hour longer.

Microwave covered on 50% power for 50 minutes. Rotate halfway through cooking time.

Roasts, Brisket & Corned Beef (3 lb.): Brown meat in a bit of oil first for extra flavor. Cover and either bake at 350º F or simmer on the stove in some liquid for 3-4 hours.

Brown for flavor if desired. Add liquid to crock. Cook on Low 10 hours, High 5 hours.

Seal in roasting bag. Microwave on 30% power 40 minutes per lb., rotate every ½ hour.

Sausages (Large): Brats, Chorizo, Italian, Kielbasa, Knockwurst.

Bake at 400º F, or grill (turning often), about 5-6 minutes or until browned.

Cook in boiling water or steam 20 minutes.

Brown if desired. Put in sauce or liquid. Cook on Low 5 hours or High 2½ hours.

Heat a skillet with a bit of oil and fry about 10 minutes or until browned, turning often.

Microwave covered 3-4 minutes per lb., rotate halfway through.

Brown for flavor. Add liquid to crock. Cook on Low 4 hours or High 2 hours.

Steaks (Cubed): 🍳🥘 Broil, grill or fry (breaded or plain) 5 minutes on each side until done.

🍲 Bread if desired, and brown. Add with liquid. Cook on Low 8 hours or High 4 hours.

▦ Microwave covered ½ hour per 4 on 30% power, flip halfway through.

Steaks (Large): 🍳 Broil or grill small steaks 7 minutes on each side until done.

🍲 Brown and add to crock with liquid. Cook on Low 8 hours or High 4 hours.

🥘 Heat a skillet very hot and fry 5-6 minutes on each side until desired doneness.

▦ Microwave covered, 3 minutes per lb. on high, 9 minutes per lb. 30%, flip halfway through.

Steaks (Minute): ▢🍳🥘 Bake, broil or grill 1-2 minutes on each side until desired doneness.

🥘 Heat a skillet and fry 1-2 minutes on each side until desired doneness.

▦ Microwave covered 1-2 minutes per 2 steaks, 2-4 minutes per 4. Flip halfway through.

Steaks (Small- Beef or Lamb): 🍳 Broil or grill 5 minutes on each side or until done.

🥘 Heat a skillet very hot and fry 4-5 minutes on each side until desired doneness.

▦ Microwave covered 2 minutes on high per steak, (longer for well done) flip halfway through.

Stew Meat: Trim away excess fat if desired.

▣ 🍲 Brown in oil for flavor. Cover. Bake at 350º F or simmer in liquid, 3-4 hours.

🍳 (Shish Kebabs) Broil or grill 8-12 minutes total or until done, rotate skewers often.

🍲 Brown for extra flavor. Add liquid to crock. Cook on Low 8 hours or High 4-5 hours.

▦ Microwave covered 5-6 minutes high, 10-12 minutes on 30% power, until juices run clear.

🍲 Cut into smaller chunks. Heat a bit of oil in wok or skillet and stir-fry 5 minutes.

Tongue: 🍲 Cook in boiling water 1 hour per lb. Let cool in broth.

🍲 Add liquid to crock. Cook on Low 10 hours or High 5 hours.

Wings (20 Chicken): Rinse and pat dry with a paper towel unless otherwise stated. Marinate covered in sauce ½ hour in the refrigerator before cooking if desired.

🍲 Simmer in sauce, covered for 30 minutes or until tender.

▣ Cover and bake 45 minutes at 350º F until tender.

🍲 Add to crock after rinsing don't dry. Top with sauce and cook on Low 6 hours, High 3 hours.

🍳 Broil or grill 10 minutes on each side.

▦ Microwave covered 10-15 minutes, (flipping after 5 minutes) until juices run clear.

Parve Items

Apples (Applesauce): Peel, core and quarter to make 6 cups. Add cinnamon sugar if desired.

Cover partially with water in a pot and simmer ½ hour or until tender. Drain, mash or strain.

Put in crock and cook on low 7-8 hours, or high 4 hours. Mash or strain.

Put in large casserole. Cook covered 8-10 minutes until tender (stir after 4). Mash or strain.

Apples (3 Large Cut): Peel and cut into 1-2 inch pieces or slices unless otherwise stated.

Submerge in water and boil ½ hour. Drain and serve with cinnamon sugar if desired.

Coat with margarine, sugar and cinnamon if desired. Bake at 400° F 10-20 minutes.

Put apples and cinnamon sugar in crock. Cook on Low 8 hours, High 4 hours.

Put in margarine and sauté on high heat several minutes until translucent. Top with sugar

Core, cut in half. Place cut-side-up in glass dish and cover. Cook 2-4 minutes until tender.

Apples (Whole): Core, peel bottom third, set in hot water and bake ½ hour at 375° F.

Peel ⅓ way down and submerge in a pot of water. Simmer ½ hour or until tender.

Put a little liquid in bottom of crock. Cook on Low 4 hours, High 2 hours.

Core, cut in half. Place cut-side-up in glass dish and cover. Cook 2 minutes until tender.

Artichokes (Whole): Soak, rinse, check for bugs, cut off bottom stem and leaves.

Fill a baking dish with 1 inch of water, cover and bake at 350° F for 1 hour.

Put ¼ inch water in pot and set artichoke in pot. Cover and boil 45 minutes or until tender.

Put 2 cups water in crock and set stem-down. Cook on Low 4-6 hours or High 3 hours.

Put with ¼ inch water in covered dish. Cook 15 minutes, rotate every 5 minutes until tender.

Asparagus (1 lb.): Soak in soapy water ½ hour, rinse, check for bugs. Cut off bottom stems.

Put ¼ inch cold salt water in pot with asparagus. Boil covered 15 minutes or until tender.

Put 2 cups water in crock and set stem-down. Cook on Low 4-6 hours or High 3 hours.

Put with ¼ inch water in covered dish. Cook 4-6 minutes or until tender.

Bacon (Soy): Put on greased cookie sheet and spray with oil.

Bake 5 minutes at 450° F, flip and bake 2 more minutes.

Fry in a bit of oil about 4 minutes, flip halfway through until crisp.

Spray lightly with oil. Cook 2-3 minutes per 7 pieces, flip halfway through.

Beans (1 lb. Fresh): Green, Runner, Snap, String, Wax. Wash, de-string and snap in pieces.

Simmer covered in water or broth 20 minutes until tender. Drain and add seasoning.

Add with water and seasoning and cook on Low 4-6 hours, High 3 hours.

Microwave about 6-8 minutes (stirring halfway through time) until tender yet crisp.

Beets (1 lb.): Cut off tops and root. Peel before or after cooking. Cut into slices.

Put beets in a greased baking dish with margarine. Bake covered at 400° F for ½ hour.

Put in boiling water. If young, simmer 40 minutes, if older boil 2 hours, or until tender.

Put with a little water in a casserole dish and cook for about 6-8 minutes or until tender.

Broccoli and Cauliflower: Soak in water ½ hour, rinse, check well for bugs. Slash cut stems.

Soak in cold salted water 10 minutes, then boil tightly covered 12 minutes in 1 inch water.

Put a bit of oil in a wok or frying pan, heat and sauté about 3-5 minutes, stirring often.

Put liquid in bottom of crock. Cook on Low 6 hours, High 3 hours.

Put with a little water in a casserole dish and cook for about 8 minutes or until tender.

Brussels Sprouts: Soak ½ hour, rinse, check for bugs. Trim outer wilted leaves, cut off stems.

Soak in cold salted water 10 minutes. Slash cut stem and boil uncovered 10 minutes.

Shred and add with water to crock. Cook 3-4 hours on Low, 2 hours on High.

Put with a little water in a casserole dish and cook for about 6-8 minutes or until tender.

Cabbage: Soak in soapy water ½ hour, rinse, check thoroughly for bugs. Trim outer leaves.

Put in a baking dish with some water and margarine, bake covered 45 minutes at 325° F.

Boil shredded 6-8 minutes until tender. (Simmer a quartered head 15-20 minutes.)

Shred and add with water to crock. Cook 3-4 hours on Low, 2 hours on High.

Shred, put with water in a casserole dish and cook for about minutes.

Carrots: (See Root Vegetables.)

Chayote Squash: (See Squashes- Winter.)

Celery (Chopped): Simmer in a little water 20 minutes or until tender.

Add with water and seasoning to crock and cook on Low 5-6 hours, High 3 hours.

Put a bit of oil or margarine in wok or frying pan, sauté about 3-5 minutes, stirring often.

Put in a bit of water or margarine in covered casserole. Cook 3-5 minutes or until tender.

Corn (Cut): Put in a covered casserole and bake at 325º F for 30 minutes.

Put in a bit of water and simmer covered 3-5 minutes.

Put in a bit of water or margarine in covered casserole. Cook 3-5 minutes or until tender.

Corn on the Cob (4 Ears): Coat in margarine, wrap in foil. Bake at 400º F or grill ½ hour.

Boil water and gently put ears in water. Boil 3-5 minutes.

Coat in margarine and salt, wrap in foil and set in crock. Cook on Low 2 hours, High 1 hour.

Take off outer husk only, remove silks, spread margarine on corn if desired. Leave in inner husk, or wrap in waxed paper. Cook in a covered glass dish 11-13 minutes or until tender.

Cranberries (1 lb.): Submerge berries in boiling water. Cover tightly, cook 3-4 minutes.

Put a little liquid in bottom of crock. Cook on Low 2 hours.

Put in covered casserole with ¼ cup water. Cook (stir often) 5-7 minutes or until skins open.

Edamame (Green Soy Beans in Pods): Boil covered 10-15 minutes until tender, then shell.

To roast, spread in baking pan after boiling, top with margarine. Bake at 350º F until brown.

Eggplant: (Sliced) Drizzle with oil or margarine, or bread it. Bake at 400º F for 15 minutes.

(Halved) Coat cut sides with oil. Place skin-down in casserole. Bake at 350º F 25 minutes.

(Whole Stuffed) Cut off top and scoop out meat leaving a 2 inch thick shell. Put meat in boiling water and cook as desired. Add cooked meat with cooked stuffing and bake about 24 minutes at 400º F or until heated through.

Chop into 1-inch cubes, place in water, simmer 20 minutes or until tender. Drain and mash.

(Breaded Slices) Let dry, add to hot oil in frying pan. Fry 5-10 minutes or until browned.

(Halved or Chopped) Cook with liquid or sauce on Low 8 hours, High 4 hours.

Chop, put with some water in a casserole dish and cook about 10-12 minutes or until tender.

Eggs: Except for hard-boiled, all eggs should be opened and checked for blood spots. Room temperature eggs cook quicker than refrigerated eggs by about 2 minutes.

Baked- Grease muffin tin, gently pour 1 egg in per bowl. Salt, top each egg with margarine. Set tin in a large pan of water. Bake in preheated 350º F oven 5-6 minutes until done.

Hard-Boiled- Gently set in boiling water in odd numbers and cook 15 minutes, then plunge into cold water. Older eggs are much easier to peel.

Soft-Boiled- Gently set in boiling water in odd numbers and cook 3 minutes.

Eggs: *Poached-* Boil water. Stir vigorously and pour egg into vortex. Simmer 4-5 minutes.

Poached- Combine 1 Tbs. vinegar + 1 cup water and bring to boil. In the meantime, put an egg in a bowl and pierce the yolk with a toothpick or sharp knife. Gently pour boiling water over egg and immediately cover and microwave 30-60 minutes. Let stand about 5 minutes afterwards and remove with slotted spoon. For 2 eggs cook 45 seconds to 1½ minutes.

Fried (Sunny-side-up)- Put margarine in a pan and heat it on low heat. Gently pour whole egg out onto warm pan and cook 1-3 minutes. For firm whites, cover until white is firm. For soft whites, sprinkle with water. (If you like the yolk cooked more, flip and cook one minute.)

Scrambled- Put margarine in a pan and heat until the pan is coated. Beat together eggs and seasonings. Pour into pan, raise heat, stir and flip with spatula. Eggs cook in a few minutes.

Scrambled- Melt 1 tsp. margarine per egg in a microwave bowl. Break egg into bowl and add salt and seasonings if desired. Stir well and cover. Heat 1 minute, stirring well after 30 seconds. (For 2 eggs, 1½ minutes, 4 eggs 2-2½ minutes, 6 eggs 3-3½ minutes. Eggs cook outside-in. They will continue to cook after microwaving. Let stand covered a few minutes.

Fish Fillets & Steaks: Fish Fillets can be made in a variety of ways.

Baked- Blend olive oil, water, and seasoning in a baking dish. Add fish, coating with mixture. Cover with foil and bake at 400º F for 20 minutes.

Cook in boiling water 10 minutes.

Broil or grill 3 minutes on each side until desired doneness.

Crock Pot- Put a little liquid in bottom of crock pot. Cook on Low 1½-2 hours.

Fried (Breaded or plain) Put in hot oil, fry on each side 3 minutes until browned or done.

Microwave covered 5 minutes per lb. or until fish flakes easily. Let stand covered 5 minutes.

Fish (Whole 2-3 lb.): Bake at 325º F covered, unstuffed ½ hour, 40 minutes for stuffed.

Place skin-side-down and coat with margarine or oil. Broil or grill 20 minutes, baste often.

For stuffed fish, (if too large, cut to fit) put in a bit of liquid. Cook on Low 1½-2 hours.

Stuffed or unstuffed, microwave covered 10-20 minutes or until fish flakes easily.

Fruits (Stewed Dried): Apples, Apricots, Berries, Cherries, Dates, Figs, Pears. Dates and Figs should be cut open and checked for bugs.

Submerge in water and boil 35 minutes or until tender.

Put a little liquid in bottom of crock. Cook on Low 8-10 hours, High 4-5 hours.

Garlic & Ginger (Chopped): 🍳 Put oil in wok or frying pan, sauté 3-5 minutes, stirring often.

▦ Put in a bit of margarine or oil and cook in covered casserole 3-5 minutes or until tender.

Greens (1 lb.): Beet, Collard, Kale, Mustard, Spinach, Swiss Chard, Turnip. Check for bugs, wash well to remove sand and grit, remove stems or tough ribs.

🍲 Cook covered in boiling water 10 minutes for tender greens, 25-40 for tougher until tender.

▦ Put with a little water in a casserole dish and cook for about 4-6 minutes or until tender.

Hamburgers/Sausage Patties (Soy): 🍳 Spray with oil. Broil or grill 2 minutes until brown.

🍳 Put on greased sheet and spray with oil. Bake at 350º F 10 minutes.

🍳 Fry in a bit of oil about 4 minutes, flip halfway through until brown.

▦ Spray with oil. Microwave 1 minute per burger. If frozen 2 minutes, flip after 1 minute.

Hot Dogs & Sausage Links (Soy): 🍳 ▦ Coat lightly with oil. Cook 30-60 seconds per piece.

🍲 Put in boiling water and cook about 2 minutes.

🍳 Fry in a bit of oil about 5-6 minutes, turning often until evenly browned on all sides.

Kohlrabi: 🍲 Cut off tops, peel knobs. Slice and boil in water uncovered 20 minutes. (Tops too.)

Leeks: 🍲 Put with ¼ inch cold salt water in pot. Boil covered 15 minutes or until tender.

🍳 Put a bit of oil or margarine in frying pan, sauté about 3-5 minutes, stirring often.

🍲 Cut off roots, trim tops. Put with 1 cup water or broth. Cook on Low 3-4 hours, High 2 hours.

Mushrooms (1 lb. Sliced): 🍳 Put a bit of oil or margarine in frying pan, sauté 3-5 minutes.

🍳 (Plain or Breaded) Fry in oil on all sides until browned.

🍲 Coat with oil or margarine. Place in greased broiler and broil stem-side-down 2½ minutes.

🍲 Add with a bit of water or margarine and cook on Low ½ hour.

▦ Put with water or margarine in a casserole, cook covered 4-6 minutes or until tender.

Okra: 🍲 Boil water in pot and drop okra pods in. Simmer 5-8 minutes or until tender.

🍳 (Plain or Breaded) Fry in oil on all sides until browned.

▦ Put 1 lb. with a little water in a casserole dish and cook for about 6-8 minutes or until tender.

Onions: 🍳 (Breaded) Bake at 400º F, rings 12 minutes, whole slashed 35 minutes at 450º F.

🍳 Put (Breaded Rings) Fry in oil on all sides until browned.

🍳 🍳 ▦ In wok, frying pan or covered casserole, add a bit of oil. Cook 3-5 minutes, stir often.

Parsnips: (See Root Vegetables.)

Pears: 🍲 Wash, peel, core and halve. Put in a bit of water and bake covered at 350º F ½ hour.

🍲 Wash, peel and core. Submerge in a pot of water. Simmer ½ hour or until tender.

🍲 Wash, peel and core. Put a some liquid in crock. Cook on Low 4 hours, High 2 hours.

Peas (Fresh in Pods): Sugar Snap, Snow Peas. Wash, trim off ends and remove any strings.

🍲 Simmer covered in water or broth 20 minutes until tender. Drain and add seasoning.

🍲 Add with water and seasoning and cook on Low 4-6 hours, High 3 hours.

🍲 Microwave 1 lb. about 6-8 minutes (stirring halfway through time) until tender yet crisp.

🍲 Put a bit of oil in a wok or frying pan, heat and sauté about 3-5 minutes, stirring often.

Peppers (Chopped or Sliced): *Sweet-* Bell, Pimento, Anaheim. *Mild-* Cherry, Wax, Banana, Poblano. *Hot-* Fresno, Jalapeño. Slice off top, cut open, remove seeds and white membranes.

🍲 🍲 🍲 In wok frying pan or covered casserole, add a bit of oil. Cook 3-5 minutes, stir often.

Peppers (Stuffed): Cut off top, de-seed, gently scrape away pith, rinse. Fill with cooked filling. Green Bells or larger peppers take longer to bake or microwave. They pierce easily when done.

🍲 Replace Bell tops. Put in greased casserole and bake 35 minutes at 350º F until tender.

🍲 For large Hot Peppers- (Anaheim, fresh Jalapeño, Fresno, Poblano.) Slice lengthwise. Coat with breading before stuffing, then sauté 3-5 minutes in oil until tender and browned.

🍲 Replace top on Bells. Put in crock with liquid or sauce. Cook on Low 7 hours, High 4 hours.

🍲 Stuff, put on tops. Cook 2 Bells at a time in covered casserole about 10 minutes until tender.

Potatoes (Small or Pieces): All types including sweet potatoes and yams. Scrub, remove eyes.

🍲 Coat with oil, wrap in foil, bake at 400º F 15 minutes.

🍲 Cook in boiling water 30 minutes. Drain. (Water can be used in soup or bread dough.)

🍲 Put a little liquid or margarine in bottom of crock. Cook on Low 6 hours or High 3 hours.

🍲 Cook in oil 10 minutes on medium heat, stirring frequently.

🍲 Pierce skins, set on paper towel and cook 2 minutes for 1 potato, 3 for 2, 4 for 4 until tender.

Potatoes (Whole Large): All types and yams. Scrub, remove eyes. Pat dry and pierce all over.

🍲 🍲 Coat with shortening or oil and wrap in foil. Bake 1 hour at 400º F.

🍲 🍲 Coat with margarine or oil and cook on Low 8-10 hours, or High 4 hours.

🍲 Microwave 4-5 minutes per potato, 7-8 minutes per 2, 10-12 per 3, flip halfway through.

501

Pumpkins: (See Squash- Winter.)

Quinces: 🔲 Coat with margarine and bake at 350º F 1 hour. Serve hot or cold.

Rhubarb: 🍲 Boil until tender. Time can vary greatly depending on stalks.

🍯 Put a little liquid in bottom of crock. Cook on Low 3 hours.

▦ Chop, put with water in a large casserole and cook on 40% power 30 minutes until tender.

Rutabaga: 🍲 Chop and boil 5-8 minutes or until tender.

▦ Put with a little water in a casserole dish and cook for about 6-8 minutes or until tender.

Root Vegetables: Carrots, Parsnips, Turnips. Cut off tops, wash, peel and chop.

🔲 Slice thinly. Put in a covered baking dish with margarine and liquid. Bake at 350º F 1 hour.

🍲 Put in a pot of boiling water, cook covered 20 minutes or until tender.

🍯 Put a little liquid in bottom of crock. Cook on Low 6 hours, High 3 hours.

▦ Put with a little water in a casserole dish and cook for about 6-8 minutes or until tender.

Spinach & Kale: (See Greens.)

Squash (1 lb. Chopped Summer): Crookneck, Pattypan/Scalloped, Summer, Yellow, Zucchini.

🍲 ▦ Put with some water in a pot or glass dish. Cook for about 6-10 minutes or until tender.

🔲 Bake in pan with a bit of water at 350º F, 25-35 minutes or until tender.

🍳 Put in a bit of margarine or oil and sauté, (or bread and fry), 3-5 minutes or until tender.

🍯 Put a little liquid in bottom of crock. Cook on Low 4 hours, High 2 hours.

Squash (Winter): Acorn, Butternut, Buttercup, Chayote, Hubbard, Pumpkin, Turban.

🔲 Halve or chop. Bake in pan with a bit of water at 350º F, 45-60 minutes or until tender.

🔲 Bread. Put on greased cookie sheet. Bake at 400º F 10 minutes, flip and bake 10 more.

🍲 Put in a pot of boiling water and simmer 45 minutes to 1 hour until tender.

🍯 Put a little liquid in bottom of crock. Cook on Low 5 hours, High 3 hours.

▦ Put with a little water in a casserole dish and cook for about 8-10 minutes or until tender.

Sweet Potatoes & Yams: (See Potatoes.)

Turnips: (See Root Vegetables.)

Zucchini: (See Squash- Summer.)

Dry to Liquid Ratios & Cooking Guide

If dry goods are put in containers to store, in lieu of directions, this guide gives the average cooking and dry to liquid ratios. Special Notes- **Rice**: Rinse. (Add ½ quantity of water for rice cookers.) **Beans**: Rinse, add ¼ tsp. baking soda before cooking. To "quick-soak", boil 3 minutes and let sit covered 1 hour.

Symbol: 🍲 = Boil on Stove Top, 〰️ = Microwave, 🍲 = Simmer in Crock Pot.

1:1 - One Part Dry to One Part Liquid

Baby Cereal: 🍲 〰️ Bring liquid to boil, add cereal. Let sit 5 minutes.

Couscous: 🍲 〰️ Bring liquid to boil, add couscous. (If large, boil 5 minutes.) Let sit 5 minutes.

Pearl Rice: 🍲 Bring water to boil with oil, add rice, simmer 25 minutes, cover after 15 minutes.

Textured Vegetable Protein (TVP®): Needs no cooking. Soak in boiling water or broth.

1:1.5 - One Part Dry to One & One Half Parts Liquid

Mashed Potato Mixes: (Brands requiring more than just water.) Add less liquid to avoid "soup".
🍲 〰️ Bring liquid to boil with margarine and salt, add potatoes, let sit 2-3 minutes and fluff with fork.

1:2 - One Part Dry to Two Parts Liquid

Barley: 🍲 Combine, bring to a boil and simmer 40 minutes.

〰️ Combine with oil, microwave on 50% power in large covered casserole for 15-20 minutes.

Bulgur/Cracked Wheat: 🍲Boil liquid, add bulgur, cover, simmer 15 minutes till liquid absorbs.

Instant/Quick Grits: 🍲 Combine on low heat, cook 5-10 minutes without stirring until tender.

〰️ Combine and cook 1½-2 minutes.

Mashed Potato Mixes: (Brands requiring water only.) Add a bit more liquid to avoid "cake".
🍲 〰️ Boil liquid, add potatoes, let sit 2-3 minutes, then fluff with a fork.

Oatmeal (Instant/Quick): 🍲 〰️ Bring water to boil, add oatmeal, cook 2 minutes.

Kasha (Buckwheat Groats): 🍲Sauté in oil, add to hot liquid, boil 10-15 minutes on medium.

Lentils: 🍲 Rinse, combine with water, cook for 30 minutes to an hour, or until tender.

〰️ Rinse, combine lentils, water and oil, cook covered on 50% power 15-20 minutes.

🍲 Rinse and combine. Low- Cook 6-8 hours; High- Cook 3-4 hours.

Oatmeal (Old-Fashioned): 🍲 ▦ Bring water to boil, add oatmeal, cook 5 minutes on medium.

Orzo: 🍲 Bring liquid to a boil, add orzo, simmer covered 8-10 minutes on low heat.

Quinoa: 🍲 Add to hot liquid, cover, simmer on low 20 minutes, let sit 5 minutes, fluff with fork.

White Basmati/Jasmine Rice: 🍲 Rinse, boil water, add rice, simmer covered 12 minutes, sit 5 minutes.

White Rice (Short or Long Grain): Rinse. Add ¼ cup water extra per 1 cup rice. (Never stir.)

🍲 Bring water, rice and margarine to boil, cook covered on low ½ hour. Let sit 5 minutes.

▦ Add rice to hot water, cook covered 10-15 minutes per cup rice (more, increase time by ¾).

1:3 - One Part Dry to Three Parts Liquid

Brown Basmati Rice: 🍲 Boil liquid, add rice, simmer covered 45-55 minutes, let sit 5 minutes.

Bulgur/Cracked Wheat Cereal: 🍲 Boil liquid, add cereal and simmer 7-10 minutes.

▦ Bring liquid to boil, add cereal and let sit 10 minutes.

Infant Cereal: 🍲 ▦ Bring liquid to boil, add cereal, and let sit 5 minutes.

Most Pre-soaked Dry Beans: 🍲 Rinse beans, combine with water, cook 1-4 hours.

▦ Rinse, combine with water and oil, microwave covered on 50% power 60-70 minutes.

🍲 Rinse, combine with water. Low- cook 10-12 hours; High- Cook 6-8 hours.

Powdered Milk for Whole Milk: No cooking needed, but for extra creamy milk, add creamer.

Quick-Cook Grits: ▦ Blend liquid, grits and salt. Microwave 3-4 minutes per serving until thick.

1:4 - One Part Dry to Four Parts Liquid

Hot Creamy Rice or Wheat Cereal: 🍲 Boil, add cereal and extra liquid. Simmer 1-3 minutes.

▦ Combine and cook in ½ minute increments until thick. Stir between each time.

Flavored Kosher Gelatin: 🍲 ▦ Boil water, add gelatin, stir well, let cool and refrigerate. Note: Kosher Gelatin has directions to have 1 packet gelatin (½ cup) to 2 cups water (1:4). This generally produces a very thin, watery gelatin that tends to disintegrate after a day or so due to excess condensation. It is strongly advised to cut the water down by ¼ cup. This would be 1 packet gelatin (½ cup) to 1¾ cup water. (Actually, a 1:7 ratio.) This consistently produces nice, firm gelatin, that lasts much longer.

Most Dry Peas: 🍲 Rinse, add water, cook 45 minutes to 1½ hours until tender.

▨ Rinse, combine with water. Cook on 50% power in large covered casserole 15-20 minutes.

🍲 Rinse peas, combine with water. Low- Cook 6-8 hours; High- Cook 3-4 hours.

Most Large Dry Beans: 🍲 Combine and cook 3-4 hours until tender.

▨ Combine with some oil, cook on 50% power in large covered casserole 60-80 minutes.

🍲 Low- Combine and cook 10-12 hours; High- combine and cook 6-8 hours.

Most Small Dry Beans: Rinse first, then do either soaking method without discarding water.

🍲 Combine beans with water and cook 1-2 hours until tender.

▨ Combine beans, water and oil, cook covered on 50% power in casserole 50-70 minutes.

🍲 Add beans and water. Low- cook 8-10 hours; High- cook 4-6 hours.

Powdered Milk for Skim Milk or Pudding: No cooking needed. Blend well and refrigerate.

Quick Wild Rice or Brown Rice: Rinse. Sauté rice in oil, add to boiling water never stirring.

🍲 Bring water to boil with oil, add rice, cook 40-50 minutes (brown), or 20 minutes (wild).

▨ Bring water and oil to boil in large casserole, add rice, microwave covered on 50% power 35-40 minutes per cup until tender. If more is desired, increase time by ¾.

Wheat Berries: 🍲 Combine, bring to boil and cook covered 1 hour until tender.

1:5 - One Part Dry to Five Parts Liquid

Quick-Cooking Grits: 🍲 For thicker grits, decrease water slightly, for thicker increase it. Blend liquid, grits and salt, boil 5-7 minutes stirring often, until thickened.

Soups from Pre-soaked Dry Beans or Peas: 🍲 Combine and cook 1-4 hours until tender.

🍲 Low- Combine and cook 10-12 hours; High- Combine and cook 6-8 hours.

1:7 - One Part Dry to Seven Parts Liquid

🍲 For firmer, stronger gelatin. See "Kosher Gelatin" under 1:4 ratio.

1:16 - One Part Dry to Sixteen Parts Liquid

Tapioca: 🍲 Combine with liquid and sugar for 5 minutes. Bring to boil stirring. Cool 20 minutes.

▨ Blend with liquid and sugar for 5 minutes. Cook 10 minutes (stir every 3). Cool 20 minutes.

General Equivalencies

Equivalencies can be helpful for determining the multiplication or division of a recipe. Meant to be a guide, these are close but approximate, as every fruit or vegetable can vary slightly and it will never be exact. Fortunately, most recipes do not have to be too precise.

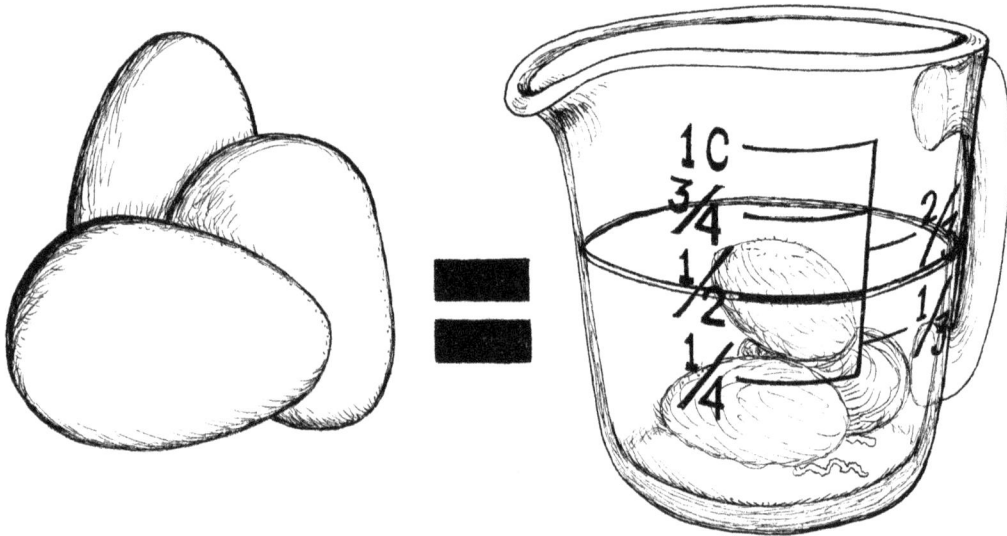

Item	Amount	Equivalency
Acorn Squash	5 oz.	1 cup chopped
Alfalfa Sprouts	1 lb.	6 cups
Allspice	1 oz.	4½ Tbs. (ground)
Almonds	6 oz.	1 cup
Almonds (ground)	1 lb.	2⅔ cups
Almonds (slivered, blanched)	4 oz.	1 cup
Almonds (whole in shell)	1 lb.	1¼ cups shelled
Almonds (whole in shell)	3½ lb.	1 lb. shelled
Ancho Chile (Pasilla) Pepper	1 whole chile	1 oz.
Anchovies (canned)	2 oz.	3 Tbs. mashed
Anchovies (canned)	2 oz.	10-12 anchovies
Anise (Fennel)	1 lb. bulb	3 cups sliced
Apples	1 medium	1 cup sliced apples
Apples	1 lb.	3 medium apples

Item	Amount	Equivalency
Apples	1 lb. whole	3 cups pared
Apples (about 10 fresh)	3½-4 lbs.	1 lb. dried
Apples (dried)	6 oz. pkg.	1 cup dry, OR 2⅔ cups cooked
Apples (fresh)	1 lb.	1¾ cups cooked
Apples (fresh)	2½–3 lbs.	1 qt. cooked
Apricots (canned)	15 oz.	6-8 whole
Apricots (canned)	15 oz.	2 cups (drained)
Apricots (dried)	6 oz. pkg.	1 cup
Apricots (dried)	6 oz. pkg.	1½-2 cups cooked in water
Apricots (dried)	1 lb.	3¼ cups
Apricots (fresh)	2 medium	½ cup slices
Apricots (fresh)	1 lb.	3 cups cooked
Apricots (fresh)	2-2½ lbs.	1 qt. cooked
Apricots (fresh)	5½ lbs.	1 lb. dried
Artichoke Hearts	8-10 oz.	1 medium
Artichokes	1 small	2-3 oz.
Artichokes	1 large	15-20 oz.
Arugula	1 oz.	1 cup leaves
Arugula	1 small bunch	1-2 cups chopped
Asparagus	14½-16 oz.	12-18 spears
Asparagus	1 lb.	16-20 small spears, OR 12-15 large
Asparagus	3 lbs.	1 qt. cooked
Asparagus (fresh)	1 lb.	3 cups chopped
Asparagus (fresh)	1 lb.	2-2½ cups cooked
Avocado	1 medium	½ lb.
Avocado	1 medium	1 cup chopped
Avocado	1 lb.	2 medium
Avocado	1 lb.	2½ cups slices or chopped
Avocado	1 lb.	1½ cups guacamole
Baby Carrots (fresh)	1 cup	16-18 carrots
Baby Cut Carrots (fresh)	1 lb.	24-34 carrots
Bacon (Turkey- whole strips)	2 cooked	2 tsp. bacon bits or crumbles

Item	Amount	Equivalency
Baking Powder	7 oz. tin	1¼ cups, OR 60 tsp., OR 16⅔ Tbs
Bamboo Shoots (canned)	8 oz.	1 cup (drained)
Banana	1 medium	1 cup slices
Banana	1 medium	⅓ cup mashed
Bananas	2 large	1 cup mashed
Bananas	4 medium	1⅓-1½ cups mashed
Bananas	1 lb.	4 small, OR 2 large
Bananas	1 lb.	3 medium
Bananas	1 lb.	2 cups chopped
Barley (Pearl)	1 cup raw	4 cups cooked
Barley (Pearl)	1 lb.	2½ cups raw, OR 8 cups cooked
Basmati Rice	1 cup dry	3 cups cooked
Basil (fresh)	½ oz.	1 cup chopped leaves
Bay Leaf (whole)	1 leaf	¼-½ tsp. broken leaves
Bay Leaf (whole)	1 leaf	⅛-¼ tsp. crushed bay
Beans (canned)	15 oz.	2 cups
Beans (dry)	1 lb.	2-2½ cups dry
Beans (fresh Butter or Lima)	1 lb. shelled	3 cups
Beans (fresh Green)	1 lb.	3 cups raw, OR 2½ cups cooked
Beans (frozen)	10 oz. pkg.	1¾ cups cooked
Beans (Garbanzo/Chickpeas dry)	1 cup dry	2½ cups cooked
Beans (Great Northern dry)	1 lb. (2 cups)	5-6 cups cooked
Beans (Kidney dry)	½ lb. (1 cup)	2½ cups cooked
Beans (Kidney dry)	1 lb.	4-5 cups cooked
Beans (large dry)	1 lb.	2½ cups dry
Beans (large dry)	1 lb.	6 cups cooked
Beans (Lima dry)	½ lb. (1 cup)	1¼ cups or 3 cups cooked
Beans (Lima in pods)	4-5 lb. raw	1 qt. cooked shelled
Beans (Navy dry)	½ lb. (1 cup)	2-2½ cups cooked
Beans (medium dry)	1 lb. (2 cups)	3-4 cups cooked
Beans (small dry)	½ lb. (1 cup)	2-2½ cups cooked
Beans (Snap or Pole)	1½–2 lb. raw	1 qt. cooked

Item	Amount	Equivalency
Bean Sprouts (canned)	15 oz.	2 cups (drained)
Bean Sprouts (fresh)	1 lb.	3-4 cups
Bean Sprouts (fresh)	1 lb.	2 cups cooked
Beef (cooked)	6 oz.	1 cup chopped
Beef (cooked chopped)	1 lb.	3 cups
Beef (dried Chipped)	5 oz. jar	24 slices
Beef (dried Chipped)	5 oz. jar	2 cups shredded
Beef (raw Ground)	1 lb.	2 cups
Beef (raw Ground)	1 lb.	12 oz. cooked
Beets (canned slices)	8 oz.	1 cup
Beets (fresh)	1 lb.	3-5 medium beets
Beets (fresh)	1 lb.	4 cups raw (slices or chopped)
Beets (fresh)	1 lb.	2 cups cooked (slices or chopped)
Beets (fresh)	2½–3 lb.	1 qt. cooked
Belgian Endive	1 medium head	10-16 leaves
Bell Peppers	1 large	1 cup chopped, OR 6 oz.
Bell Peppers	1 small	¼-½ cup chopped
Berries	1 pint	2-3 cups
Berries	1¼-3 lb. raw	1 qt. cooked
Black Beans (dry)	1 lb.	2-2⅓ cups dry
Black Beans (dry)	1 lb.	5 cups cooked
Blackberries	1 pint	2-3 cups fresh or frozen
Blackberries	1 lb.	3½ cups fresh or frozen
Blackberries (canned)	15 oz. can	1¾ cups
Black Eyed Peas (dry)	1 lb.	2-2½ cups dry
Black Eyed Peas (dry)	1 lb.	5-6 cups cooked
Black Olives	15 large	1 cup chopped
Black Olives	36 small pitted	1 cup chopped
Black Olives (sliced)	2¼ oz. can	½ cup
Black Olives (whole)	6 oz. can	55 medium, OR 25 extra-large
Black Olives (whole)	6 oz. can	18 super colossal
Blueberries	1 pint	2-3 cups

Item	Amount	Equivalency
Blueberries	1 qt.	3 cups crushed blueberries
Blueberries	1 lb.	2½-3½ cups fresh or frozen
Blueberries (frozen)	10 oz. pkg.	1½ cups
Bok Choy (fresh)	1 large head	2 lb.
Bok Choy (fresh)	1 large head	5 cups chopped stalks
Bok Choy (fresh)	1 lb.	4-5½ cups shredded leaves
Bok Choy (fresh)	1 lb.	¾ cup cooked
Brazil Nuts (in shells)	2 lb.	1 lb. shelled
Brazil Nuts (in shells)	2 lb.	3 cups shelled
Bread (Commercial White)	2 slices	1 cup soft crumbs
Bread (Commercial White)	11 slices toasted	2 cups coarse dry crumbs
Bread (Commercial White)	1 lb. loaf	14-20 slices
Bread Crumbs (dry)	¼ cup	1 slice bread
Broccoli (florets)	1½ lb.	5 cups
Broccoli (whole)	1 lb. head	2 cups florets
Brown Rice	1 cup raw	4 cups cooked
Brussels Sprouts (fresh)	1 qt.	1¼ lbs.
Brussels Sprouts (fresh)	1 qt.	5 cups raw
Brussels Sprouts (fresh)	1 lb.	4 cups cooked or raw
Brussels Sprouts (frozen)	10 oz. pkg.	18-24 whole
Brussels Sprouts (frozen)	10 oz. pkg.	1½-2 cups cooked
Buffalo/Bison (cooked)	6 oz.	1 cup chopped
Buffalo/Bison (cooked chopped)	1 lb.	3 cups
Buffalo/Bison (raw Ground)	1 lb.	2 cups
Buffalo/Bison (raw Ground)	1 lb.	12 oz. cooked
Bulgur Wheat	1 cup raw	2½-3 cups cooked
Bulgur Wheat	1 lb. raw	2¾ cups raw
Bulgur Wheat	1 lb. raw	8 cups cooked
Butter	1 stick or 4 oz.	8 Tbs.
Butter	1 stick or 4 oz.	½ cup
Butter	1 lb.	2 cups
Butterbeans (canned)	15 oz.	2 cups

Item	Amount	Equivalency
Butterbeans (dry)	1 lb.	2 cups raw
Butterbeans (fresh)	1 lb. shelled	3 cups
Butterbeans (frozen)	10 oz. pkg.	1¾ cups cooked
Butternut Squash	5 oz.	1 cup chopped
Butternut Squash	1 medium	3 lbs.
Butternut Squash	1 medium	4 cups cooked mashed
Butterscotch Chips	12 oz. pkg.	2 cups
Cabbage (fresh)	½ large head	1 lb.
Cabbage (fresh	1 medium head	1¼-1½ lbs.
Cabbage (fresh)	1 lb.	3½-4½ cups shredded raw
Cabbage (fresh)	1 lb.	1½-2 cups shredded cooked
Cabbage (minced)	½ lb.	3 cups packed
Cabbage (Slaw)	1 lb.	6 cups
Candied Fruit	8 oz.	1½ cups chopped
Cantaloupe	1 medium	3 lbs.
Cantaloupe	1 medium	4-4½ cups chopped
Cantaloupe	1 medium	25 balls
Cantaloupe	1 lb.	2 cups balls or cubes
Cardamom Pods	1 pod	18-20 seeds
Cardamom Pods	1 pod	1 tsp. ground
Cardamom Pods	10 whole pods	1½ tsp. ground
Carrots	1 lb.	2½ -3 cups cooked
Carrots ("Baby Cut")	1 cup	16-18 carrots
Carrots (fresh)	1½ medium	1 cup grated
Carrots (fresh)	1-2 medium	½ cup chopped
Carrots (fresh)	2 medium	1 cup slices
Carrots (fresh)	1 lb.	12-14 small, OR 5-7 medium
Carrots (fresh)	1 lb.	2½-3 cups chopped
Carrots (fresh)	1 lb.	2½-3 cups grated
Carrots (fresh)	2½–3 lbs.	1 qt. cooked
Carrots (fresh Baby)	1 lb.	24-34 carrots
Carrots (frozen)	10 oz. pkg.	1½-2 cups

Item	Amount	Equivalency
Cashews	1 oz.	18 medium, OR 14 large cashews
Cashews	1 lb.	3¼ cups
Catsup (bottled)	14 oz.	1½ cups
Cauliflower (florets)	1½ lb.	4 cups raw
Cauliflower (fresh)	1 lb.	1½ cups chopped
Cauliflower (fresh)	1 lb.	7½ oz. cooked
Cauliflower (frozen chopped)	10 oz. pkg.	2 cups
Cauliflower (head)	1 medium	1¾-2¼ lbs.
Cauliflower (head)	1½ lb.	2 cups cooked
Celery	1 large stalk	¾ cup chopped
Celery	1 rib	½ cup sliced
Celery	2-3 medium ribs	1 cup chopped or sliced raw
Celery	1 lb. untrimmed	1 bunch
Celery	1 lb.	2 cups chopped or sliced cooked
Celery Flakes	2 Tbs.	¼ cup chopped celery
Celery Flakes	1 oz.	¾ cups chopped celery
Celery Seed	1 oz.	4 Tbs.
Chayote Squash	1 average	½ lb.
Chayote Squash	½ lb.	1 cup chopped
Cheese (Cheddar)	1 (8 oz.) bar	2 cups shredded
Cheese (Cottage)	½ lb.	1 cup
Cheese (Cream)	3 oz.	6 Tbs.
Cheese (Cream)	8 oz. pkg.	1 cup
Cheese (grated Hard)	¼ lb.	1 cup
Cheese (hard)	1 (4 oz.) bar	1 cup shredded
Cheese (Parmesan or Romano)	4 oz. bar	1½ cup grated
Cheese Slices	2 slices	¼ cup shredded into pieces
Cherries (canned Tart)	15 oz. pitted	1½ cups drained
Cherries (dried Tart)	3 oz.	½ cup
Cherries (fresh pitted)	1¼-2½ lb.	1 qt. cooked
Cherries (fresh Sweet)	1 lb. unpitted	1¾ cups pitted
Cherries (frozen Tart)	1 lb. pitted	2 cups

Item	Amount	Equivalency
Cherries (Maraschino)	10 oz. jar	25 cherries with stems
Cherries (Maraschino)	10 oz. jar	33 stemless cherries
Cherry Tomatoes	1 lb.	1 pint
Chestnuts (canned)	10 oz.	25 whole chestnuts
Chestnuts (dried)	1 lb. shelled	35-40 large whole
Chestnuts (dried)	1 lb. shelled	2½ cups whole
Chestnuts (in shell)	1½ lb.	1 lb. shelled
Chestnuts (peeled)	35-40	2½ cups
Chicken Breast	½ breast	½ cup cooked chopped meat
Chicken (cooked)	6 oz.	1 cup chopped
Chicken (whole)	2-3 lbs.	2-3 cups chopped cooked meat
Chicken (whole)	5 lbs.	2¼ lbs. cooked meat
Chickpeas (dried)	1 cup dry	2½ cups cooked
Chilies (canned chopped Green)	4½ oz.	½ cup chopped
Chilies (canned whole Green)	4 oz.	3 whole chilies
Chipped Beef (dried)	5 oz. jar	24 slices
Chipped Beef (dried)	5 oz. jar	2 cups shredded
Chocolate (Baking)	1 square (1 oz.)	3 Tbs. chopped (chips)
Chocolate Chips	6 oz.	¾ cup
Chocolate Chip	12 oz. bag	1½ cups
Chow Mein Noodles (canned)	5 oz.	2½ cups
Cilantro (fresh)	1 sprig	1 Tbs. minced leaves
Cilantro (fresh)	16 sprigs	1 cup minced leaves
Citron (candied Etrog)	6½ oz. jar	1 cup chopped
Cloves (whole)	1 tsp.	¾ tsp. ground
Cloves (whole)	3 oz.	1 cup
Cocoa	1 lb.	4 cups
Coconut (flakes)	4 oz.	1⅓ cup
Coconut (fresh)	1 whole medium	3-4 cups grated
Coconut (fresh)	1 lb.	1 whole medium
Coconut (shredded)	1 lb.	4 cups
Coconut (shredded sweetened)	1 lb.	5 cups

Item	Amount	Equivalency
Coconut (shredded unsweetened)	3½ oz.	1 cup
Coconut Milk (canned)	15 oz.	1⅞ cups
Coffee (ground beans)	1 lb.	80 Tbs., OR about 40 brewed cups
Coffee (Instant)	3 oz. jar	about 47 cups
Coffee (Instant)	4 oz. jar	2½ cups granules
Cole Slaw	1 qt.	7-8 servings
Collard Greens (fresh)	1 lb.	7 cups raw leaves
Collard Greens (fresh)	1 lb.	1½ -2 cups cooked
Collard Greens (fresh)	2-3 lbs. raw	1 qt. cooked
Collard Greens (frozen)	10 oz. pkg.	1½ cups cooked
Cookies (Sandwich)	10 cookies	1 cup crushed
Cookies (Vanilla Wafers)	22 cookies	1 cup fine crumbs
Coriander (whole seeds)	½ cup	1¼ oz. ground
Corn (fresh)	1 ear	about ⅓-½ cup kernels
Corn (fresh)	7 ears	1 qt. cooked kernels
Corn (fresh whole Sweet)	2 medium ears	1 cup kernels
Corn (fresh whole Yellow)	3-4 ears	1 cup kernels
Corn (frozen)	10 oz. pkg.	1¼ cups
Cornish Hen	1 average	1¼ lbs.
Corn Meal	1 cup	4-4½ cups cooked
Corn Meal	1 lb.	3 cups
Cottage Cheese	½ lb.	1 cup
Couscous	1 cup dry	7 oz. raw
Couscous	1 cup dry	2½-3 cups cooked
Cowpeas (Black Eyed Peas)	1 lb. dry	2-2½ cups dry, OR 5-6 cups cooked
Crab Meat (Imitation)	1 lb. pkg.	2 cups minced or chopped
Cracked Wheat	1 cup raw	3¼ cups cooked
Crackers (Graham)	14 square	1 cup fine crumbs
Crackers (Saltine)	28 crackers	1 cup fine crumbs
Cranberries (dried)	6 oz. pkg.	1⅓ cups
Cranberries (fresh)	12 oz.	3 cups
Cranberries (fresh)	1 qt.	6-7 cups cranberry sauce

Item	Amount	Equivalency
Cream Cheese	3 oz.	6 Tbs.
Cream Cheese	8 oz. pkg.	1 cup
Creamer (frozen Non-dairy)	16 oz. pkg.	1¾ cup thawed liquid
Cream (Heavy or Whipping)	4 oz.	1¾ cup whipped topping
Cream (Heavy or Whipping)	1 cup liquid	2 cups when whipped
Cream of Tartar	1 oz.	3 Tbs.
Crook-neck Squash	¼ lb.	1 cup chopped
Crook-neck Squash	½ lb.	1 large, OR 2 small
Crook-neck Squash	1 lb.	1⅔ cup mashed cooked
Crook-neck Squash	2-2½ lb. raw	1 qt. cooked
Crowder Peas (Black Eyed Peas)	1 lb.	2-2½ cups dry, OR 5-6 cups cooked
Cucumber (fresh whole)	1 small-medium	1 cup chopped
Cucumbers	1 lb.	4 cups chopped
Cumin Seed (whole)	1 tsp.	½ tsp. ground
Currants (dried)	1 lb. pkg.	3 cups
Currants (fresh)	1 qt.	3¾ cups
Dates (minced whole)	1 medium	1¼ tsp.
Dates (pitted)	1 cup (½ pint),	3 cups chopped
Dates (pitted)	8 oz.	54 dates, OR 1¼ cup chopped
Dates (whole pitted)	12 oz.	2 cups
Dates (whole unpitted)	1 lb.	60 dates, OR 2½ cups pitted
Dates (whole unpitted)	1 lb.	1½ cups pitted chopped
Dill (fresh heads)	3 heads	1 Tbs. dill seed
Dill (fresh heads)	½ oz.	½ cup
Dill Weed (dried)	1 oz.	¾ cup
Dried Mushrooms	¼ cup crumbled	¼-½ cup reconstituted
Dried Mushrooms	1 oz. pkg.	1-1⅓ cups, OR ⅔ cup crumbled
Dry Soup Mix (Instant)	1 (4-serving) packet	¼ cup powder (4 cups prepared)
Duck	1 average	7-9 lbs.
Egg (Hardboiled)	1 large	6 slices
Egg White (Hardboiled)	1 large chopped	¼ cup
Egg Yolk (Hardboiled)	1 large chopped	1 Tbs.

Item	Amount	Equivalency
Egg (Hen)	1 large	3 oz., OR 3 Tbs.
Egg (Duck)	1 average	3 oz.
Egg (raw)	2 large	½ cup cooked scrambled
Egg (Whites)	1 cup	9 small, OR 8 medium, OR 7 large, OR 6 extra-large, OR 5 jumbo.
Egg (whole)	1 cup	6 small, OR 5 medium, OR 5 large, OR 4 extra-large, 4 jumbo.
Egg (Yolks)	1 cup	18 small, OR 16 medium, OR 14 large, OR 12 extra-large, OR 11 jumbo.
Egg Noodles	1 cup dry	1⅓ cups cooked
Egg Noodles	1 lb.	6-8 cups cooked
Eggplant	1 medium	1½ lbs.
Eggplant	12 oz.	2 cups chopped
Eggplant	1 lb.	3-4 cups diced
Eggplant	1½ lb.	1 cup cooked
Eggplant	1½ lb.	½ cup mashed cooked
Endive (Belgian)	1 medium head	10 to 16 leaves
Etrog (Citron- candied)	6½ oz. jar	1 cup chopped
Evaporated Milk	5 oz. can	⅔ cup
Evaporated Milk	12 oz. can	1½ cups
Fava Beans (fresh in pod)	1 lb.	1-1½ cups shelled
Fennel (fresh)	1 lb. bulb	2½-3 cups sliced
Fennel (fresh)	1 lb. bulb	2¼ cups cooked
Fennel Seed	1 oz.	4 Tbs.
Figs (canned)	16 oz.	12-16 medium figs
Figs (dried)	1 lb.	40 medium figs
Figs (dried)	1 lb.	2⅔-3 cups chopped
Figs (fresh)	1 lb.	9 medium figs
Figs (fresh)	1 lb.	2½ cups chopped
Filberts or Hazelnuts (in shell)	2¼ lb.	1 lb. shelled
Filberts or Hazelnuts (in shell)	2¼ lb.	3⅓ cups shelled
Fish (fresh fillet)	1	4-6 oz.

Item	Amount	Equivalency
Fish (fresh fillet)	5 oz.	1 cup minced
Flour (All-purpose)	1 cup	5 oz.
Flour (All-purpose)	1 lb.	4½ cups
Flour (Cake)	1 lb.	4¾ cups
French Fried Onions	2.8 oz. pkg.	1⅜ cups
Frozen Vegetables	10 oz. pkg.	1¾ cups
Frozen Vegetables	1 lb.	3 cups
Garbanzo Beans (dried)	1 cup dry	2½ cups cooked
Garlic	1 clove	½ tsp. minced, OR ⅛ tsp. powder
Garlic	3 large cloves	1 Tbs. minced
Gelatin (Flavored)	1 single pkg.	½ cup bulk powder
Gelatin (Flavored)	1 single pkg.	2 cups prepared
Gelatin (Plain Unsweetened)	1 single pkg.	4⅜ tsp.
Gelatin (Plain Unsweetened)	1 single pkg.	2 cups prepared
Goose	1 average	10-12 lbs.
Graham Crackers	14 squares	1 cup fine crumbs
Graham (Whole Wheat or Grain)	1 lb.	3¾-4 cups finely milled
Grapefruit	1 lb.	1 medium
Grapefruit	1 medium	10-12 sections
Grapefruit	1 medium	⅔ cup juice
Grapes (seedless)	1 lb.	2½ cups
Grapes (with seeds)	1 lb.	2 cups
Great Northern Beans	1 lb. dry	2 cups dry
Great Northern Beans	1 lb. dry	5-6 cups cooked
Green Beans (canned)	15 oz.	1½ cups
Green Beans (fresh)	3 cups cut	2½ cups cut cooked
Green Beans (fresh)	1 lb.	3 cups trimmed raw
Green Beans (fresh)	1 lb.	2½ cups cooked
Green Beans (frozen)	10 oz. pkg.	1½ cups cooked
Green Bell Peppers	1 small	¼-½ cup chopped
Green Bell Peppers	1 large	6 oz.
Green Bell Peppers	1 large	1 cup chopped

Item	Amount	Equivalency
Green Cabbage	1 lb. head	4 cups shredded
Green Cabbage	1 medium head	1¼-1½ lbs.
Green Cabbage (cooked)	1 lb.	1½-2 cups shredded
Green Cabbage (fresh)	1 lb.	3½-4½ cups shredded
Green Cabbage (minced)	½ lb.	3 cups packed
Green Onions	1 whole plant	¼-½ cup chopped
Green Onions	1 bunch	5 to 8 leaves
Green Onions	2 medium leaves	2 Tbs. chopped
Green Onions	9 leaves	1 cup sliced
Green Peas (dried Split)	1 lb.	2¼-2½ cups dry
Green Peas (dried Split)	1 lb.	5 cups cooked
Green Peas (fresh in pod)	1 lb.	1 cup shelled
Green Peas (frozen)	10 oz. pkg.	1½-2 cups
Green Peppers	1 small	¼-½ cup chopped
Green Peppers	1 large	6 oz.
Green Peppers	1 large	1 cup chopped
Greens	2-3 lbs. raw	1 qt. cooked
Grits (quick-cooking)	¼ cup dry	1 cup cooked
Hamburger (raw)	1 lb.	2 cups
Hamburger (raw)	1 lb.	12 oz. cooked
Hazelnuts or Filberts (in shell)	2¼ lb.	1 lb. shelled
Hazelnuts or Filberts (in shell)	2¼ lb.	3⅓ cups
Head Lettuce (Iceberg)	1 medium head	1½ lbs.
Hearts of Palm (canned)	14 oz.	5-6 stalks
Herbs	1 Tbs. fresh	1 tsp. dry crumbled
Hominy (uncooked)	1 lb.	2½ cups raw
Hominy (canned)	15 oz.	1¾ cup
Honey	1 lb.	⅓ cup
Honeydew Melon	1 medium	3 lbs.
Honeydew Melon	1 large	4 lbs.
Honeydew Melon	1 large	4 cups chopped or 35 balls
Honeydew Melon	1 lb.	2 cups balls or cubes

Item	Amount	Equivalency
Horseradish (fresh root)	1½ lb.	2¾ cups grated
Horseradish (grated root)	3 oz.	½ cup
Hot Dog	1	⅓ cup chopped, OR ¼ minced
Ice	3 to 4 cubes	1 cup crushed ice
Iceberg Lettuce	1 medium head	1½ lbs.
Iceberg Lettuce	1 medium head	25-30 leaves
Iceberg Lettuce	1 medium head	6-8 cups torn
Iceberg Lettuce	1 medium head	4 cups packed grated or shredded
Jerusalem Artichokes	1 lb.	12 medium
Jerusalem Artichokes	1 lb. peeled	2½ cups sliced
Jícama (Mexican Potato)	1 medium tuber	2 cups chopped
Jícama (Mexican Potato)	1 lb.	1 medium tuber
Jícama (Mexican Potato)	1 lb.	4 cups grated
Jigger	1	1.4 oz. (4.5 cl.)
Kale	1 lb.	6 cups leaves
Kale	1 lb.	1¼ cups cooked
Ketchup (bottled)	14 oz.	1½ cups
Kidney Beans	1 cup dry	2½ cups cooked
Kidney Beans	1 lb. dry	2-2½ cups dry
Kidney Beans	1 lb. dry	4-5 cups cooked
Kidney Beans	15 oz. can	2 cups
Kiwifruit	1 medium	5-6 slices or ½ cup
Kohlrabi	1 lb.	2 medium bulbs
Kohlrabi	1 lb.	1¾ cups cooked chopped
Kumquat	1 lb. small	24 kumquats
Leeks	1 lb.	2 large, OR 3 medium
Leeks	1 lb.	2 cups sliced or chopped bulb
Leeks	1 lb.	1 cup cooked
Lemon	1 medium	2 Tbs. juice
Lemon	1 large	3-4 Tbs. juice
Lemon	1 average	1 Tbs. grated rind
Lentils	1 lb. dry	2¼ cups dry

Item	**Amount**	**Equivalency**
Lentils	1 lb. dry	5 cups cooked
Lettuce (Leaf)	1 medium bunch	4-6 cups shredded
Lettuce (Iceberg or Romaine)	1 medium head	1-1½ lbs.
Lettuce (Iceberg or Romaine)	1 medium head	25-30 leaves
Lettuce (Iceberg or Romaine)	1 medium head	4-6 cups shredded
Lima Beans (canned)	15 oz.	2 cups
Lima Beans (dry)	1 lbs.	2 cups raw
Lima Beans (dry)	2 lbs.	1 qt. cooked
Lima Beans (fresh)	1 lb. shelled	3 cups raw
Lima Beans (fresh in pods)	4-5 lbs. raw	1 qt. cooked shelled
Lima Beans (frozen)	10 oz.	1¾ cups cooked
Lime	1 medium	1½-2 Tbs. juice
Lime	1 average	1 Tbs. grated rind
Macadamia Nuts	5 oz. jar	1 cup
Macadamia Nuts	1 lb. shelled	3⅓ cups
Macaroni (1 inch pieces)	1 cup dry	2-2¼ cups cooked
Macaroni (1 inch pieces)	1 lb.	4 cups raw
Macaroni (1 inch pieces)	1 lb. dry	8 cups cooked
Macaroni (Elbows or Shells)	8 oz. dry	4 cups cooked
Macaroni (Large Elbows)	1 lb. dry	7-8 cups cooked
Macaroni (Small)	1 lb. dry	4-5 cups cooked
Mace (Ground)	1 oz.	4½ Tbs.
Mackerel (canned)	16 oz.	2 cups
Mandarin Oranges	11 oz. can	about 15 large to 32 small sections
Mandarin Oranges	11 oz. can	1¼ cups
Mangoes (fruit)	1 large	2 cups chopped
Mangoes (fruit)	1 medium	¾ cup mashed, OR 1 cup chopped
Mangoes (fruit)	1 small	¾ cup chopped
Maraschino Cherries	10 oz. jar	25 cherries with stems
Maraschino Cherries	10 oz. jar	33 stemless cherries
Margarine	¼ lb.	1 stick
Margarine	¼ lb.	8 Tbs., OR ½ cup

Item	Amount	Equivalency
Margarine	1 lb.	2 cups
Margarine	1 lb.	4 sticks
Marshmallows (large chopped)	10-11	1 cup
Marshmallows (miniature)	1 cup	80 marshmallows
Mayonnaise (jarred)	32 oz.	4 cups
Meat (Chicken Breast)	½ breast	½ cup cooked chopped meat
Meat (cooked)	6 oz.	1 cup chopped
Meat (cooked Beef)	1 lb.	3 cups chopped
Meat (cooked Chicken)	6 oz.	1 cup chopped
Meat (cooked Turkey)	1 lb.	3 cups chopped
Meat (raw boneless)	1 lb.	2 cups ground
Meat (raw Hamburger)	1 lb.	2 cups raw
Meat (raw Hamburger)	1 lb.	12 oz. cooked
Meat (whole Chicken)	2-3 lbs.	2-3 cups chopped cooked meat
Meat (whole Chicken)	5 lbs.	2¼ lbs. cooked meat
Melon	1 medium	3 lbs.
Melons (small)	1 lb.	2 cups balls or cubes
Milk (Powdered)	5 Tbs.-⅓ cup	1 cup reconstituted
Milk (Powdered)	1⅓ cups dry	1 qt. reconstituted
Milk (Powdered)	9.6 oz. pkg.	4 cups dry, OR 3 qt. reconstituted
Milk (Powdered)	1 lb.	6⅔ cups dry, OR 5 qt. reconstituted
Mulberries (fresh)	1 pint	2-3 cups
Mulberries (fresh)	1 lb.	3½ cups
Mushrooms (canned)	4 oz.	⅔ cup
Mushrooms (dried)	¼ cup crumbled	¼-½ cup reconstituted
Mushrooms (dried)	1 oz.	1-1¼ cup, OR ⅔ cup crumbled
Mushrooms (dried)	3 oz. reconstituted	1 lb. fresh
Mushrooms (fresh)	8 oz.	2½ cups chopped, OR 3 cups slices
Mushrooms (fresh)	1 lb.	30-40 small, OR 12-14 large
Mushrooms (fresh)	1 lb.	18-20 medium
Mushrooms (fresh)	1 lb.	6 cups sliced, OR 4 cups chopped
Mushrooms (fresh)	1 lb.	3 oz. dried

Item	Amount	Equivalency
Mushrooms (fresh sliced)	8 oz.	1 cup cooked
Mushrooms (fresh sliced)	1 lb.	2 cups cooked
Mustard Greens (canned)	15 oz.	1¼-1½ cups
Mustard Greens (fresh)	1 lb.	6-7 cups leaves
Mustard Greens (fresh)	1 lb.	1½ cups cooked
Mustard Greens (frozen)	10 oz. pkg.	1¼ cups cooked
Navy Beans	1 cup dry	2-2½ cups cooked
Navy Beans	1 lb.	2½ cups dry, OR 5½ cups cooked
Nectarines	1 lb.	4 small, OR 2 large
Nectarines	1 lb.	2-2½ cups sliced
Nectarines	1 lb.	1¾-2½ cups chopped
Nectarines	1 lb.	1½ cups puréed
New Potatoes	1 lb.	9-12 potatoes
Non-Dairy Creamer (frozen)	16 oz. pkg.	1¾ cups thawed liquid
Non-Dairy Whip Topping (liquid)	8 oz. carton	1 pint thawed and not whipped
Non-Dairy Whip Topping (liquid)	8 oz. carton	2 cups thawed and whipped
Non-Dairy Whip Topping (liquid)	32 oz. can	3⅓ cups thawed and not whipped
Non-Dairy Whip Topping (tub)	8 oz. container	3 cups thawed
Noodles (canned Chow Mein)	5 oz.	2½ cups
Noodles (dry)	1 cup	1⅓ cups cooked
Noodles (Egg)	8 oz.	4-5 cups dry or cooked
Noodles (Egg)	1 lb. dry	6-8 cups cooked
Noodles (medium)	3 oz. dry	3 cups cooked
Nutmeg	1 whole	2 tsp. ground
Nuts (Almonds- in shell)	3½ lb.	1 lb. shelled
Nuts (Black Walnuts- in shells)	5½ lb.	1 lb. shelled, OR 3 cups pieces
Nuts (Brazils- in shell)	2 lb.	1 lb. shelled, OR 3 cups
Nuts (Cashews- shelled)	1 lb.	3¼ cups
Nuts (Chestnuts- shelled)	1 lb. whole	35-40 large, OR 2½ cups whole
Nuts (English Walnuts- in shells)	2-2½ lb.	1 lb. shelled, OR 4½ cups halves
Nuts (Hazel/Filberts- in shell)	1 lb.	1 lb. shelled, OR 3⅓ cups
Nuts (Macadamias)	5 oz. jar	1 cup

Item	Amount	Equivalency
Nuts (Macadamias)	1 lb. shelled	3⅓ cups
Nuts (Peanuts- in shell)	1½ lb.	1 lb. shelled, OR 3 cups
Nuts (Pecans- in shell)	2½ lb.	1 lb. shelled, OR 4½ cups
Oatmeal	1 cup uncooked	1¾ cup cooked
Oatmeal	1 lb.	5⅓ cups uncooked
Okra (canned)	15 oz. can	1¾ cups sliced or chopped
Okra (fresh)	1 lb.	35 pods
Okra (fresh)	1 lb.	1½-2 cups sliced
Okra (fresh)	1 lb.	1 qt. or 4 cups chopped raw
Okra (fresh)	1½–2 lb. raw	1 qt. cooked
Okra (frozen)	10 oz. pkg.	1¼ cups sliced or chopped
Olives (chopped Black)	1 cup	36 small pitted, OR 15 large
Olives (sliced Black)	2¼ oz. can	½ cup
Olives (whole Black)	6 oz. can	55 medium, OR 25 extra-large
Olives (whole Black)	6 oz. can	18 super colossal
Olives (whole Spanish)	7 oz. jar	60-65 olives
Onion	1 small	¼ cup chopped
Onion	1 medium	½ cup chopped
Onion	1 large	¾ cup chopped
Onion	1 extra-large	1 cup chopped
Onion	1 lb.	3 large
Onions	1 cup chopped	½ cup sautéed
Onions (French Fried)	2.8 oz. pkg.	1⅜ cups
Onions (Green)	1 whole plant	¼-½ cup chopped
Onions (Green)	1 bunch	5-8 leaves
Onions (Green)	2 medium	2 Tbs. chopped
Onions (Green)	9 leaves	1 cup sliced
Onion Soup Mix (Instant)	1 (4-serving) packet	¼ cup powder (4 cups prepared)
Orange Peppers	1 small	¼-½ cup chopped
Orange Peppers	1 large	1 cup chopped, OR 6 oz.
Oranges	1 medium	6-8 Tbs., OR ⅓-½ cup juice
Oranges	1 medium	¾ cup diced

Item	Amount	Equivalency
Oranges	1 medium	2-3 Tbs. grated rind
Oranges (Mandarin)	11 oz. can	1¼ cups
Orzo	⅓ cup raw	2 oz. uncooked
Orzo	⅓ cup raw	1 cup cooked
Palm Hearts (canned)	14 oz.	5-6 stalks
Papaya	1 small	1½ cups chopped
Papaya	1 medium	2 cups chopped
Papaya	1 large	2½ cups chopped
Papaya	1 lb.	1 medium papaya
Parmesan Cheese	8 oz.	1½ cups grated
Parsley	1 Tbs. chopped	2 sprigs fresh parsley
Parsnips	1 lb.	4 medium parsnips
Parsnips (fresh)	1 lb.	3 cups chopped raw
Parsnips (fresh)	1 lb.	2 cups cooked chopped
Passion Fruit	1 medium	3 oz., OR 1-1⅓ Tbs. pulp
Pasta	8 oz.	4 cups cooked
Peaches (canned)	15 oz.	6-10 halves
Peaches (canned)	15 oz. can	1¾ cups slices (drained)
Peaches (dried)	2 medium	1 cup slices
Peaches (fresh)	1 lb.	3-4 medium
Peaches (fresh)	1 lb.	2-3 cups sliced or chopped
Peaches (fresh)	2-3 lb. raw	1 qt. cooked
Peaches (frozen slices)	10 oz. pkg.	1 cup drained
Peaches (frozen slices)	10 oz. pkg.	1¼ cups slices with juice
Peanut Butter	18 oz. jar	2 cups
Peanuts (in shell)	1½ lb.	1 lb. shelled or 3 cups shelled
Peanuts (shelled)	1 lb.	3 cups
Peanuts (shelled)	4 cups	3 cups peanut butter
Pearl Barley (quick cooking)	1 lb.	2½ cups uncooked
Pearl Barley (quick cooking)	1 lb.	8 cups cooked
Pears (fresh)	1 medium	4 oz. or ½ cup slices
Pears (fresh)	1 large	1 cup packed slices or chopped

Item	Amount	Equivalency
Pears (fresh)	1 lb. small	2 cups sliced
Pears (fresh)	1 lb.	4 medium
Pears (fresh)	2-3 lb. raw	1 qt. cooked
Pears (canned)	15 oz. can	2-2½ cups slices (drained)
Pears (canned)	15 oz. can	6-10 halves
Peas (dry Split)	1 lb.	2½-3 cups dry
Peas (dry Split)	1 lb.	5 cups cooked
Peas (fresh Green in pod)	1 lb.	1 cup shelled
Peas (fresh in pods)	2-2½ lb. raw	1 qt. cooked
Peas (frozen Green)	10 oz. pkg.	1½-2 cups
Peas (shelled)	4 lb.	1 qt. cooked
Peas (Snow)	4 oz.	1½ cups
Pecan Halves	1 cup	4 oz.
Pecan Halves	1 cup	1 cup chopped
Pecans (in shell)	2½ lb.	1 lb. shelled
Pecans (in shell)	2½ lb.	4½ cups shelled
Peppercorns	1 oz.	3 Tbs.
Peppers (Green Bell)	1 small	¼ cup chopped
Peppers (Green Bell)	1 large	1 cup diced
Peppers (Green Bell)	1 large	6 oz. chopped
Persimmon	1 medium	4 oz. meat
Persimmon	1 lb.	2 cups uncooked
Persimmon	1 lb.	1¾ cups cooked
Pignon (Pine Nuts)	5 oz.	1 cup
Pimentos	2 oz. jar	¼ cup chopped
Pineapple (canned chunks)	20 oz. can	1¾ cups
Pineapple (fresh)	1 medium	2-3 lbs.
Pineapple (fresh)	1 medium	2½-3 cups chopped
Pine Nuts (Pignon)	5 oz.	1 cup
Pinto Beans	3 cups cooked	2 cups refried beans
Pistachios (shelled)	1 lb.	3⅔ cups
Plums (fresh)	1 lb.	8-10 small, OR 5 large

Item	Amount	Equivalency
Plums (fresh)	1 lb.	2½-3 cups chopped pitted
Plums (fresh)	1½-2½ lb.	1 qt. cooked
Pomegranate	1 medium	½ -1⅓ cup seeds
Pomegranate	1 medium	½ cup juice
Pomegranate	5 lbs.	3-4 large pomegranates
Pomegranate	5 lbs.	1 qt. juice
Portabella Mushrooms (fresh)	6 oz. caps	2¼ cups chopped
Potato	1 medium	1 cup diced
Potato	1 large	1 cup mashed
Potatoes	3 medium	2-2¼ cups chopped cooked
Potatoes	1 lb.	3 medium potatoes
Potatoes	1 lb.	2-2¼ cups chopped cooked
Potatoes	1 lb.	1¾ cups mashed
Potatoes	1 lb.	2 cups French fries
Potatoes	1 lb.	3 cups shredded
Potatoes (New)	1 lb.	9-12 potatoes
Potatoes (Red)	1 lb.	7-9 potatoes
Potatoes (sliced)	1 lb.	3½-4 cups raw
Poultry (Chicken)	½ breast	½ cup cooked chopped meat
Poultry (cooked)	6 oz.	1 cup chopped
Poultry (whole Chicken)	2-3 lbs.	2-3 cups chopped cooked meat
Poultry (whole Chicken)	5 lbs.	2¼ lbs. cooked meat
Powdered Milk	5 Tbs.-⅓ cup	1 cup reconstituted
Powdered Milk	1⅓ cup	1 qt. reconstituted
Powdered Milk	9.6 oz pkg.	4 cups dry, OR 3 qt. reconstituted
Powdered Milk	1 lb.	6⅔ cups dry, OR 5 qt. reconstituted
Prickly Pear (Sabra)	1 large	½ cup chopped or puréed
Prunes (canned)	9 oz.	24 whole prunes
Prunes (cooked and drained)	1 lb.	2 cups
Prunes (dried)	1 lb.	2¼ cups pitted
Pudding (Instant)	1 (3.4-3.9 oz.) pkg.	½ cup powder
Pudding (Instant)	1 (3.4-3.9 oz.) pkg.	4 cups prepared

Item	Amount	Equivalency
Pumpkin	1 lb. raw	1 cup cooked mashed or puréed
Pumpkin	5 lbs.	4½ cups cooked
Pumpkin (canned)	16 oz.	2 cups
Quinces	1 lb.	3-4 medium quinces
Quinoa	1 cup raw	2 cups cooked
Quinoa	1 lb.	3 cups raw
Quinoa	1 lb.	6 cups cooked
Radicchio	1 head	8 leaves
Radicchio	1½ oz.	1 cup shredded
Radishes (1 bunch)	12 radishes	1 cup sliced
Radishes	1 lb.	1⅔ cups sliced
Raisins (whole with seeds)	1 lb.	3¼ cups
Raisins (whole seedless)	1 lb.	3 cups
Raspberries	1 lb.	3 cups
Raspberries (fresh)	1 pint	1¾ cups
Raspberries (frozen)	10-oz. pkg.	1 cup undrained
Red Bell Peppers	1 large	1 cup chopped, OR 6 oz.
Red Bell Peppers	1 small	¼-½ cup chopped
Red Cabbage (cooked)	1 lb.	1½-2 cups shredded
Red Cabbage (fresh)	1 medium head	1¼-1½ lbs.
Red Cabbage (fresh)	1 lb.	3½-4½ cups shredded
Red Cabbage (minced)	½ lb.	3 cups packed
Red Potatoes	1 lb.	7-9 potatoes
Rhubarb (fresh)	1 lb.	4-8 stalks
Rhubarb (fresh)	1 lb.	3-4 cups chopped
Rhubarb (fresh)	1 lb.	2 cups cooked
Rhubarb (frozen)	12 oz. pkg.	1½ cups chopped cooked
Rice (Basmati)	1 cup dry	3 cups cooked
Rice (Brown)	1 cup dry	4 cups cooked
Rice (Quick)	1 cup dry	2 cups cooked
Rice (White)	1 cup dry	3 cups cooked
Rice (White)	1 lb. dry	2 cups dry, OR 6 cups cooked

Item	Amount	Equivalency
Rice (Wild)	1 cup dry	3 cups cooked
Ricotta Cheese	8 oz. pkg.	1 cup
Rolled Oat	1 lb.	6½ cups uncooked
Rolled Oats	1 lb. uncooked	8 cups cooked
Romaine Lettuce	1 medium head	1½ lbs.
Romaine Lettuce	1 medium head	25-30 leaves
Romaine Lettuce	1 medium head	4-6 cups shredded
Runner Beans (fresh Green)	1 lb.	3 cups raw
Runner Beans (fresh Green)	1 lb.	2½ cups cooked
Rutabaga	1 medium	2-3 lbs.
Rutabaga	12-16 oz.	2 cups chopped cooked
Rutabaga (fresh)	1 lb.	3½ cups chopped raw
Sabra (Prickly Pear)	1 large	½ cup chopped
Sabra (Prickly Pear)	1 large	½ cup puréed
Salmon (canned)	14¾ oz.	1¾ cups
Saltine Crackers	28 crackers	1 cup fine crumbs
Sauerkraut (canned)	15-oz.	1¾ cups
Scallions	1 whole plant	¼-½ cup chopped
Scallions	1 bunch	5-8 leaves
Scallions	2 medium	2 Tbs. chopped
Scallions	9 leaves	1 cup sliced
Schmaltz Herring	1 (7.5 oz.) pkg.	⅓ cup minced
Schmaltz Herring	1 (8 oz.) pkg.	6 Tbs. minced
Shallots	1 medium	1 Tbs. minced
Shortening	1 lb.	2 cups
Snap Beans (fresh)	1 lb.	3 cups cut
Snap Beans (fresh)	1 lb.	2½ cups cooked
Snow Peas (fresh)	4 oz.	1½ cups
Snow Peas (frozen)	1 lb. pkg.	4½ cups
Soup (canned condensed)	10½ oz.	1¼ cups condensed unprepared
Soup (canned condensed)	10½ oz.	2⅔ cups prepared
Soup Mix (Dry Instant)	1 (4-serving) packet	¼ cup powder

Item	Amount	Equivalency
Soup Mix (Dry Instant)	1 (4-serving) packet	4 cups prepared
Sour Cherries (canned)	15 oz. pitted	1½ cups drained
Sour Cherries (dried)	3 oz.	½ cup
Sour Cherries (frozen)	1 lb. pitted	2 cups
Soy Beans (dry)	1 cup	2¾ cups cooked
Soy Beans (dry)	1 lb.	2 cups uncooked
Soy Beans (dry)	1 lb.	5 cups cooked
Spaghetti	1 lb. dry	5-7 cups cooked
Spaghetti (2-inch pieces)	1 cup dry	1¾ cups cooked
Spaghetti (12-inch pieces)	1 lb. dry	6½ cups cooked
Spaghetti Squash	2 lbs.	4 cups cooked
Spanish Olives	7 oz. jar	60-65 olives
Spinach	1¼ cups cooked	⅔ cup squeezed of liquid
Spinach (canned)	15 oz.	1¾ cups
Spinach (fresh)	6 oz.	4 cups
Spinach (fresh)	1 lb.	6 cups raw leaves
Spinach (fresh)	1 lb.	1¼ cup cooked
Spinach (fresh)	10 oz. bag	6 cups stems and leaves
Spinach (frozen)	10 oz. pkg.	1½ cups cooked
Split Peas (dry)	1 lb.	2¼–2½ cups dry
Split Peas (dry)	1 lb.	5 cups cooked
Strawberries (fresh)	1 pint	3½ cups whole
Strawberries (fresh)	1 qt.	4 cups sliced
Strawberries (frozen sliced)	10 oz. pkg.	1 cup drained
Strawberries (frozen sliced)	10 oz. pkg.	1¼ cups undrained
Strawberries (whole frozen)	20 oz pkg.	4 cups
String Beans (canned)	15 oz.	1½ cups
String Beans (fresh)	1 lb.	3 cups cut or trimmed
String Beans (fresh)	1 lb.	2½ cups cut cooked
String Beans (frozen)	10 oz. pkg.	1½ cups cooked
Sugar (Brown- packed)	1 lb.	2¼ cups
Sugar (Granulated White)	1 lb.	2¼ cups

Item	Amount	Equivalency
Sugar (Powdered)	1 lb.	3½-4 cups
Sugar Snap Peas (fresh)	4 oz.	1½ cups
Sugar Snap Peas (frozen)	1 lb. pkg.	4½ cups
Sunchokes (Jerusalem Artichokes)	1 lb.	12 medium, OR 2½ cups sliced
Sun-Dried Tomatoes	1 oz.	10 tomatoes
Sun-Dried Tomatoes	1 Tbs.	3 whole tomatoes minced
Sunflower Seeds (shelled)	3½ oz. pkg.	¾ cup
Sunflower Seeds (whole)	7 oz pkg.	2½ cups
Sweet Anise (Fennel)	1 lb. bulb	3 cups sliced
Sweet Cherries (fresh)	1 lb. unpitted	1¾ cups pitted
Sweetened Condensed Milk	14 oz. can	1¼ cups
Sweet Peppers	1 small	¼-½ cup chopped
Sweet Peppers	1 large	1 cup chopped, OR 6 oz.
Sweet Potatoes	1 lb.	2 large, OR 3 medium
Sweet Potatoes	1 lb.	2 cups cooked chopped
Sweet Potatoes	1 lb.	1½ cups cooked mashed
Sweet Potatoes	2½-3 lbs. raw	1 qt. cooked
Sweet Potatoes (canned)	15 oz.	1¾-2 cups chopped
Swiss Chard	1 lb.	5-6 cups raw
Swiss Chard	1 lb.	2 cups cooked chopped
Tamarind Seed	¼ cup	2 large pods, OR 4 small pods
Tangerines	1 lb.	4 medium
Tapioca	8-oz pkg.	1½ cups dry
Tart Cherries (canned)	15 oz. pitted	1½ cups drained
Tart Cherries (dried)	3 oz.	½ cup
Tart Cherries (frozen)	1 lb. pitted	2 cups
Tea	1 tsp. bulk	about 1-2 cups brewed
Tea	1 lb. bulk	about 125 cups brewed
Textured Vegetable Protein (TVP®)	1 cup dry	2 cups hydrated
Tofu (firm)	1 (12-16 oz.) cake	2½ cups cubed
Tofu (soft)	1 (12-16 oz.) cake	1¾-2 cups puréed
Tomatillos	1 lb.	12-16 medium

Item	Amount	Equivalency
Tomatillos	1 lb.	1 cup chopped cooked
Tomatoes (Cherry)	1 lb.	1 pint
Tomatoes (diced canned)	15-16 oz.	1½ cups
Tomatoes (fresh)	2-3 medium	1 cup diced
Tomatoes (fresh)	2½-3½ lbs.	1 qt. cooked
Tomatoes (Sun-Dried)	1 oz.	10 tomatoes
Tomato Paste	6 oz. can	¾ cup
Tomato Puree	16 oz. can	2 cups
Tomato Sauce	8 oz. can	1 cup
Tomato Sauce	27-29 oz. can	3-3¼ cups
Tuna (canned)	6 oz.	½-⅔ cup meat (drained)
Tuna (canned)	6 oz.	¼-⅓ cup drained liquid
Turkey Bacon	2 strips	2 tsp. crumbled bits
Turkey (cooked)	6 oz.	1 cup chopped
Turkey (cooked)	1 lb.	3 cups chopped
Turmeric (Ground)	1 oz.	4 Tbs.
Turnip Greens (fresh)	1 lb.	6-7 cups leaves
Turnip Greens (fresh)	2-3 lb. raw	1 qt. cooked
Turnip Greens (frozen)	10-oz. pkg.	1½ cups cooked
Turnips	1 lb.	3-4 medium
Turnips	1 lb.	3½ cups raw chopped
Turnips	1 lb.	2 cups chopped cooked
Turtle Beans (Black Beans- dry)	1 lb.	2-2⅓ cups dry, OR 5 cups cooked
TVP® (Textured Vegetable Protein)	1 cup dry	2 cups rehydrated
Walnuts (Black- in shells)	5½ lb.	1 lb. shelled, OR 3 cups pieces
Walnuts (English- in shells)	2-2½ lb.	1 lb. shelled, OR 2 cups shelled
Walnuts (English- in shells)	2-2½ lb.	4½ cups shelled halves
Walnuts (halves)	3½ oz.	1 cup
Water	2 cups	1 lb.
Water Chestnuts	15 oz. can	15-17 water chestnuts
Watercress	1 bunch	2 cups chopped
Watermelon	20 lbs.	20 cups balls or chunks

Item	Amount	Equivalency
Wax Beans (canned)	15 oz.	1¾ cups
Wax Beans (fresh)	1 lb.	3 cups
Wheat Berries (whole kernels)	1 cup raw	2½-3 cups cooked
Wheat (Bulgur or Cracked)	1 cup raw	3-3¼ cups cooked
Wheat Germ	12 oz.	3 cups
Whipped Cream (frozen)	8 oz. pkg.	3 cups thawed
Whipping Cream (unwhipped)	1 cup (½ pint)	2 cups whipped
White Rice	1 lb. raw	2 cups raw, OR 6 cups cooked
Whole Wheat Graham	1 lb.	3¾-4 cups finely milled
Wild Rice	1 cup raw	3 cups cooked
Wild Rice	1 lb.	3 cups raw, OR 9-10 cups cooked
Yams	1 lb.	2 large, OR 3 medium
Yams	1 lb. cooked	1¾-2 cups chopped or mashed
Yeast (Dry Active)	1 (¼ oz.) pkg.	2¼ tsp.
Yellow Bell Peppers	1 small	¼-½ cup chopped
Yellow Bell Peppers	1 large	1 cup chopped, OR 6 oz.
Yellow Squash	¼ lb.	1 cup chopped
Yellow Squash	½ lb.	1 large, OR 2 small
Yellow Squash	1 lb.	2½ cups chopped
Yellow Squash	1 lb.	1⅔ cup mashed cooked
Yellow Squash	2-2½ lb. raw	1 qt. cooked
Zucchini Squash	1 small	1 cup sliced or chopped
Zucchini Squash	1 lb.	2½ cups chopped, OR 3 cups sliced
Zucchini Squash	1 lb.	1⅔ cup cooked mashed
Zucchini Squash	2-2½ lbs. raw	1 qt. cooked

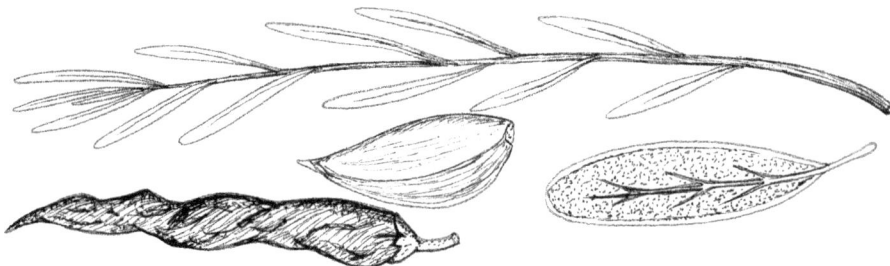

Purchasing Produce

In general, the following rules apply for picking good produce:

Smell: "The nose knows". Ripe produce smells good. Produce with no smell often has little flavor and is usually dry. A rancid or musty smell will often indicate rotting inside.

Weight: Heavier is better. A heavier fruit is more likely to be fresher and juicier.

Firmness: Certain produce should be nicely firm, but not necessarily hard as a rock.

Blemishes: When bruised, produce is susceptible to bacteria or spoilage. Fungal infections can't be seen and make produce rot from the inside out (as with onions and potatoes). Fortunately, one can usually tell by the outside. Be gentle with produce, some damage in the grocery cart or on the trip home.

Coloration: Evenly colored produce is usually better than multicolored, as they have ripened properly.

Other Considerations

Cleanliness: I find that my produce washed with a bit of dish soap and rinsed very well, lasts longer. Other sources say to wash produce with a mixture of water, lemon juice and salt or baking soda (more tips are below). Washing produce with warm water and dish soap eliminates pesticides, chemical fertilizers, artificial colorants, waxes, and gets rid of stuck-on leaves that cause decay. Even organic fertilizer is dirt/dirty. The standard in many organic home gardens is cow's manure. This may be connected to outbreaks of salmonella in certain produce.

Bugs: It helps to check for bugs under natural light. I've found thrips in the heart of clean, closely-knit iceberg lettuce! If there is a tiny brown spot on a vegetable and you can't tell if it's a bug, gently scratch it with a fingernail- bugs will come off. It helps to soak produce for ½ hour in a bowl of water with a drop of dish soap in it. Bugs die and sink. Rinse produce well afterwards. (Produce particularly susceptible to bugs are noted. Although our symbol is a magnifying glass, they only need to be checked by eye.)

Pesticides: Some organophosphate pesticides are known to contain EDCs (see plastics pp. 602-604). Produce is one source for exposure to these. In high amounts, EDCs are linked to obesity, and can cause damage to reproductive systems and mental development- especially in children and developing fetuses.

Produce contaminated with the most pesticides are peaches, apples, bell peppers, celery, nectarines, strawberries, cherries, imported grapes, spinach, and potatoes. Others often containing pesticides are lettuce, pears, kale, carrots, and possibly some fragile berries. Some produce is coated with pesticide or chemicals after harvesting, such as bananas. Bagged salads are pre-washed and should be pesticide-free.

Dealing With Non-Organic Produce: Washing produce helps eliminate most of the chemicals. One should remove outer layers of leafy vegetables and corn, remove root stalks, and peel hard-skinned produce. Even when peeled, and the outer leaves removed, the inner part should still be washed.

Using a scrub brush works well, especially for produce with tough skins and having crevices, such as cantaloupes, potatoes, watermelon, avocados, and bananas (gently). Other easier bruising produce can be rinsed under running water. Small fragile berries can be sprayed with water. An exception to washing are mushrooms that are grown on plant material under specific conditions, and merely need to be brushed off.

Organic Produce: The only sure way to totally eliminate pesticides from the diet is to buy strictly organic produce. With the increased interest in organics, it helps keep the prices lower. However, let the buyer beware, because local farmer's market produce and roadside stands aren't necessarily organic.

Symbols: ◉ = Look For, ⊘ = Avoid, 🌡 = Storage, 🗘 = Season, ⸙ = Susceptible- Check for Bugs.

Fruits

Apples: There are probably more apple varieties than any other fruit. Varieties can vary in color from green, to yellow, to red. Yet others can be multi-colored like the Jonathan with streaks of red. Different varieties have different uses, and some are multi-purpose.

Baking- Fuji, Golden Delicious, Jonagold, and (best) Rome Beauty.

Pies- (Generally more tart.) Granny Smith, Jonathan, Winesap, and (best) Newtown Pippin.

Sauce- Macintosh, Fuji, Newtown Pippin, Golden Delicious, Granny Smith, Jonathan, (best) Gravenstein.

Eating- Most all apples are good for eating, but perhaps the best are Red Delicious and Gala.

- They should be smooth, very firm and unblemished with a delicious smell.

- Avoid blemishes, dents and soft brown spots. When very old, they become mealy and dry.

- They get sweeter once harvested. Keep at cold to moderate temperatures 3-6 months, (don't store too long or they get mealy, dry and tasteless). Apples start to turn brown once peeled and exposed to air.

- Fall, but the season extends through summer.

Apricots: Besides traditional apricots, Apriums are a newer variety (cross between apricots and plums).

- Look for plump, slightly firm, good smelling fruits.

- Avoid those with blemishes, broken skin, and those that are green and hard, or wrinkled.

- They will not ripen once harvested. If overly firm, keep in a paper bag at room temperature for a few days to make softer. Keep at very cool temperatures for 1-2 weeks.

- Spring and summer is the season.

Bananas: Varieties include the Cavendish, (the average available yellow bananas), miniature Baby Bananas (Apple Bananas), the Plantain (a large green cooking banana), and Red Bananas, which have deep reddish-purple skin. Bananas are picked green to endure travel. The *brachah* is *HaAdamah*.

- Pick by smell and sight. Ripe bananas are bright yellow and smell good, should be firm, unblemished and sweet. Tips should not be green. If there is any green, it won't be tasty and will be harder to peel. Green bananas will keep a long time, are slightly tangy and used as a vegetable in many countries.

- Overly ripe are deep yellow and spotted with brown, can smell rancid, and become mushy and extremely fragile. Avoid those with depressions, mold, wetness or cracks in the skin.

- They ripen after harvest. To ripen faster, put in a paper bag at room temperature out of sun or heat. Store at room temperature. If very ripe they can be refrigerated, but the skins turn brown. They might not look pretty, but will taste good. Bananas start to turn brown once peeled and exposed to air.

- There is no special season since they grow in the tropics all year long.

Blackberries: They're very delicate. Use quickly and handle with care. The *brachah* is *HaEtz*.

- Darker berries are riper. Look for firm, plump, unblemished berries, in clean, unstained containers.
- Avoid containers stained with excessive juice, it is a sign of overly ripe or damaged berries.
- Won't ripen after harvest. Store unwashed in a shallow container until eating. Refrigerate 2-3 days.
- Spring through summer is the season.
- Check for bugs (especially wild). If infested, soak ½ hour in dish soap and water, rinse. Check again.

Blueberries: These can be delicate- use quickly. Great in summer when frozen. The *brachah* is *HaEtz*.

- Look for firm, deeply colored, plump unblemished berries, or clean, unstained containers.
- Avoid soft, leaky or moldy berries, and stained containers.
- They do not ripen after harvest. Refrigerate in shallow container 1-2 weeks. Don't wash until eating.
- Spring through summer is the season.

Cherries: These can be sweet or sour (tart). Sweet are sold fresh. Sour ones bruise and are usually dried.

- Look for large, plump, firm cherries with shiny, deep dark coloring and fresh, green stems.
- Avoid small, bruised, soft, split, mushy, moldy, sticky or wrinkled, (and especially stemless) cherries.
- They do not ripen once harvested. They keep at very cool temperature 2-3 weeks.
- Summer is the season.

Coconuts: These have 3 "eyes" and are easier to pick than open! If green, there is little or no meat, but mostly water. As they age, they get dryer until all liquid is gone. Sprouted, the inside is like cotton candy.

- Fresh coconuts should be heavy and have liquid inside when shaken.
- Avoid those that don't have liquid jostling inside, or ones with moldy or wet eyes.
- Keep at room temperature up to 6 months. When opened, keep refrigerated and use within 24 hours. For the Liquid: Puncture 2 of the eyes with a hammer and screwdriver, then drain. Methods For Obtaining the Meat: 1) Drain as for liquid, then (⅓ of the way down from the top) rap with hammer. 2) Don't drain; Bake 20 minutes in a 350° F oven. Let cool, wrap in a towel and split with a hammer.
- Tropical coconuts are always in season.

Cranberries: Perhaps best known for juice or sauce. The *brachah* is *HaEtz*.

- These should be firm with vivid red coloring. Look for clean, unstained containers.
- Avoid wet or soft berries (too old), or lighter-colored berries (too young), or stained containers.
- They don't ripen after harvest. Store refrigerated in shallow container 1 month, or freeze up to 1 year.
- Fall is the season.

Figs: These are many varieties from yellow to green or purple. Some are dried, others are eaten fresh. Figs must ripen on the tree. The "F" of the Israeli P.F.D.O.G. fruits, it always gets the *brachah* of *HaEtz*.

👁 Look for slightly firm, brightly colored, plump figs with smooth skin and stems.

🚫 Avoid rancid smelling, dry, blemished figs, or shriveled ones (except around the stem).

🌡 Figs keep 1 week in the refrigerator. Handle with care as they bruise easily

☙ Summer and fall is the season.

🔍 These must be physically opened and checked for bugs.

Grapefruits: Varieties include White, Red, and Pink, can be seedless or have seeds. Another variety is called Ugli Fruit, and is a cross between a grapefruit and orange.

👁 Look for heavy, evenly colored, smooth and slightly firm. Riper is better and smell will tell.

🚫 Avoid very soft, gray spotted or rancid smelling fruit. Blemishes are okay. Over-ripe fruit can be dry.

🌡 These don't ripen after harvest. Keep at room temperature 1 week, refrigerator 2-3 months.

☙ Winter is the season.

Grapes: Can be Red, White (pale green), Blue (deep purple), with or without seeds. ("G" in P.F.D.O.G.)

👁 Look for large, deep-colored, plump, unspoiled grapes firmly attached to green stems in full clusters. They should be slightly firm and unblemished, although they may have harmless tiny rust spots.

🚫 Stay away from shriveled, brown leaky depressions, moldy, mushy, or sticky grapes.

🌡 They do not ripen once harvested. Keep in an open container in the refrigerator 2-3 weeks.

☙ Fall is the season.

Kiwifruit: Also called Chinese Gooseberry. Under-ripe is tart and ripe is sweet. The *brachah* is *HaEtz*.

👁 They should be plump and smell good. Under-ripe fruit should be firm. Ripe should be slightly soft.

🚫 Stay away from those that are wrinkled, mushy, blemished, or have soft spots.

🌡 They ripen and get sweeter after harvest. To ripen, put in a paper bag at room temperature a few days, but keep out of the sun and heat. They keep refrigerated 2-3 months.

☙ Late fall is the season for California-grown kiwi, and summer through fall for other areas.

Kumquats: A small oval citrus fruit. Some eat the tart rind, others discard it. The *brachah* is *HaEtz*.

👁 They should be shiny and firm with bright coloring.

🚫 Stay away from wet, mushy kumquats with blemishes or wrinkles.

🌡 Keep up to 2 weeks at room temperature, or longer in the refrigerator.

☙ Winter through summer is the season.

Lemons: Types vary mostly by size and shape, and are often picked green and treated with ethylene gas to ripen. Often the outer peel is waxed and shouldn't be used for zest or grating. Lemons are different things to different people. In South America and other areas where they are eaten plain as a fruit, lemons get a *brachah* of *HaEtz*. Those in areas that only use them for juice say *Shehakol*.

- 👁 They should be heavy, slightly firm, somewhat shiny, with even bright yellow coloring.
- 🚫 Avoid those that are very soft, very hard, wrinkled or moldy. Overly ripe fruit can be very dry and won't yield much juice at all.
- 🌡 They do not ripen once harvested. They keep 2-3 weeks in cool to moderate temperatures.
- ☀ Lemons are in season in winter, but are available year-round.

Limes: Limes come in two different varieties, Key and Tahitian. Key Limes are smaller, rounded and more acidic. Tahitian Limes are larger and more yellow-green when ripe. Often the skin is waxed and shouldn't be used for zest or grating. Limes are like lemons with *brachot*. In areas where limes are eaten plain as a fruit, they get of *HaEtz*. Those in areas that only use them for juice, say *Shehakol*.

- 👁 They should be slightly firm, slightly shiny, and brightly colored.
- 🚫 Avoid those that are very soft, very hard, wrinkled or moldy. Overly ripe fruit can be very dry and won't yield much juice at all.
- 🌡 They do not ripen once harvested. They keep 2-3 weeks in the refrigerator.
- ☀ Limes are available year-round.

Loquats: These have golden skin but the meat of different varieties can vary in color from orange to yellow, or can even be white. The *brachah* is *HaEtz*.

- 👁 Look for large fruits without bruises or blemishes.
- 🚫 Avoid those that are bruised or moldy.
- 🌡 They keep well at very cold temperatures for up to 1 week.
- ☀ Summer is the season.

Lychees: Also spelled Litchi, these are small, plump and round fruits. They must be ripened on the tree. (They are also dried in their rinds and available as Lychee Nuts.) Do not eat the skin, and never eat the seed as it is toxic. The *brachah* is *HaEtz*.

- 👁 Look for heavy ones with thin, dark pink skin and a stem attached.
- 🚫 Avoid those that are wet, cracked, green or have no stem.
- 🌡 They do not ripen after harvest. Refrigerate in a plastic bag 3-10 weeks, or freeze 1-2 years.
- ☀ Summer is the season.

Mangoes: They are picked green to prevent damage, and vary in weight. Varieties and colors include: Hadens are yellow and pinkish, Kent and Keitts are green, and Tommy Atkins are red. Those allergic to poison ivy, oak, or sumac shouldn't eat the skin- resins cause rash around the lips. The *brachah* is *HaEtz*.

👁 Mangoes should smell good and be ever-so-slightly soft.

🚫 Avoid wet, wrinkled, mushy, blemished, grayish fruit, loose skin or excessive black spots.

🌡 They get sweeter after harvest. To ripen, put in a paper bag at room temperature until soft, then refrigerate. They keep refrigerated about 1-2 weeks, and if ripe a few days.

🗘 Spring and summer is the season.

Melons: Varieties include the Cantaloupe (Muskmelon), Casaba Melon (don't confuse with Cassava root or Yucca), Crenshaw Melon, Honeydews and Watermelons (can vary in size and some are seedless).

👁 Melons are best picked by smelling and by weight. Ripe, juicy melons smell good and are very heavy. They are best when vine-ripened, indicative of a smooth, well-callused smooth area where the stem was when picked. For ripe melons, look for the following: Cantaloupe- Slightly golden. Casaba- Golden yellow. Honeydew- Light yellow with bright yellow patches, should feel smooth, slick and waxy when ripe, but not hairy, and seeds should rattle and be loose inside. Crenshaw- Should have yellow streaked dark green skin, feel smooth and slick, even waxy when ripe, but not hairy. Watermelons- Should sound hollow if "thumped" with a finger, and should have a yellow area where they sat as they grew. If buying pre-cut (only from a kosher source), look for dark seeds.

🚫 Avoid cracked or blemished melons. Over-ripe can smell rancid. No smell yields no taste. If buying pre-cut watermelon, avoid any with seeds separated from meat, white streaks or cracks in the meat.

🌡 Melons get softer, (but do not ripen) after harvest kept at room temperature (up to 1 week. Ripe, they keep refrigerated 2 weeks. Store Watermelons at room temperature up to 4 weeks. Once cut, wrap in plastic (or put smaller chunks in a zipper bag) and refrigerate up to 1 week.

🗘 Summer is the season for most melons, but winter is best for Crenshaws or Casabas.

Nectarines: Very similar to peaches, (technically a fuzz-less peach) there are a few varieties. The meat comes right off the pit of Freestones. Clingstones hold on tightly to their pits. Semi-Freestone is in-between. Newer types are Mango, and Flying Saucer or Doughnut (that looks like someone stepped on it).

👁 Look for firm, yet slightly soft, with good smell and brightly colored deep yellow and red skin.

🚫 Avoid those that are very hard or green (too young) or very soft, broken or wrinkled (too old).

🌡 They ripen after harvest, get juicier and softer (not sweeter). Put in a paper bag at room temperature, do not refrigerate until ripe.

🗘 Summer is the season.

539

Oranges: There are sweet oranges and sour oranges, seedless or with seeds. Varieties include Blood Oranges, Jaffa, Mandarins, Navels, Tangelos, Temples, and Valencias. Blood Oranges, (not common in the U.S.), have nearly red meat. Mandarin types are Tangerines and Clementines. Navels are seedless and best for eating. Temple oranges are a cross between Mandarin and sweet oranges. Tangelos are a cross between a Tangerine and a grapefruit, and despite this are wonderfully sweet for eating. Valencias have very few seeds and are best for juice. Often outer peels are waxed and shouldn't be used for zest or grating. Jaffa Oranges are imported from Israel and should be kosher certified, due to taking proper tithes.

- All oranges should preferably be heavy, smooth, evenly colored and firm. Blemishes and greenness do not affect the fruit. The riper the better and smell can help tell.
- Avoid bruised or very soft fruit. Overly ripe fruit can be dry yielding little if any juice. Unripe green fruits will not be very sweet or flavorful and don't ripen once harvested.
- All oranges keep up to 2 months in cool to moderate temperatures, however the longer they are stored, the drier they get.
- Winter is the season for most oranges, the exceptions being Blood Oranges and Valencias- spring through early summer is their season.

Papayas: Although they look like a tree and can be very old, papayas have a hollow stem. The *brachah* is *HaAdamah*. They are picked green to prevent damage. Seeds are edible and used as a garnish.

- Should smell good, be slightly soft and starting to turn yellow. If green, look for yellow around stems.
- Avoid hard, green (too young), fermented smell (too old), mushy, wrinkled, dark spots or blemishes.
- They get sweeter once harvested, and can be ripened in a paper bag at room temperature unless very green and hard. Keep in the refrigerator 1-2 weeks, and if ripe about 1 week.
- Summer and fall is the season, but they are available year-round.

Peaches: Some newer varieties are the Saturn, Doughnut, or Jupiter Peach, which looks like it, has been squashed. Meat comes away from Freestone pits. Clingstones hold on to their pits. Semi-Freestone, are in-between. Colors are yellow, or white (lower acid content). They can be delicate, so handle with care.

- Should smell good, be plump, slightly soft, heavy, and lightly colored. Smaller have more flavor.
- Stay away from those that are mushy, bruised or wrinkled, and those that are darker in color, very soft, (too old), or extremely hard with green around their stems (too young). Larger have less flavor.
- They do not ripen after harvest, but can get sweeter. Put upside down in a paper bag to ripen, keep away from heat. Refrigerate 2-4 weeks. (Longer storage yields less flavor.)
- Summer is the season.

540

Pears: Pears are often shipped and sold wrapped in padding to protect them, as they are very thin-skinned, extremely delicate, and must be handled with care. They can be green to golden yellow and anywhere in-between. The brownish Asian Pear tastes and looks more like an apple, and the Forelle has bright red spots. The most common types are the Anjou, Bartlett, Bosc and Comice. Less common are the Asian, Clapp, Forelle, Seckel and Winter Nelis. *For Baking-* Bosc, and especially Winter Nelis. *For Eating-* Bartlett, Seckel, and perhaps the best is Comice. *For Both Baking and Eating-* Anjou Pears.

- 👁 Pears are best picked by smelling and sight. Ripe and juicy smell good and be mildly soft.
- 🚫 Avoid those that are blemished, gashed, have soft areas, or are overly mushy. Also avoid very soft bottoms or wrinkles around the stem. Over-ripe fruit can smell rancid, and no smell yields no taste.
- 🌡 They ripen and get sweeter after harvest. To ripen, keep in a slightly cool area away from heat. Keep open to air- not in a closed plastic bag. Keep refrigerated or at slightly below freezing 2-4 months.
- ☘ Fall is the season.

Persimmons: The two types are yellow-orange Fuyu and dark orange Hachiya. The *brachah* is *HaEtz*.
- 👁 Look for plump, smooth, shiny, even vivid orange color with stem. Soft, wrinkled are ripe but messy.
- 🚫 Avoid cracked, bruised or blemished. Yellow spots are still green and will be tart and not good to eat.
- 🌡 Keep at room temperature to ripen until soft. Refrigerate unripe fruits 1 month, ripe about 1 week.
- ☘ Fall is the season.

Pineapples: There are generally two types, smaller Smooth Cayenne and the larger Sugar Loaf, They are picked and shipped ripe. In the family of bromeliad flowers, their *brachah* is *HaAdamah*.
- 👁 Look for firm, plump, heavy, with good smell and fresh leaves. If ripe, a leaf can easily be pulled out.
- 🚫 Avoid brown or yellow leaves, green fruit or fruit with dark or soft spots, and rancid smelling bottom.
- 🌡 They do not ripen after harvest, but will get soft and juicy at 70° F. Refrigerate up to 1 week.
- ☘ Spring is the season, but they are available year-round.

Plums: Plums can be Freestone or Clingstone, in green, greenish yellow, yellow and red, red, blue, deep purple or black. (Dried are Prunes.) New varieties are Cherry-Plum (hybrid of cherry and plum) and Pluot (hybrid of plum and apricot— "Dinosaur Eggs" are a round speckled type). Never eat the stone.
- 👁 Plums should have bright or deep, even coloring, be plump and slightly firm. Ripe will smell good and be slightly soft. Skin can have a normal (harmless) powdery substance on it. Simply wash it off.
- 🚫 Avoid those that are extremely soft or mushy, have blemishes, wrinkled or split skin.
- 🌡 Put in a paper bag at room temperature to ripen or soften. Refrigerate unripe 3 weeks, ripe less than 1.
- ☘ Summer is the season.

Pomegranates: They are picked and shipped ripe, the rind is not eaten, only seeds and juice. It's often eaten on *Rosh Hashanah* to symbolize plentiful merit because of the numerous seeds. Its juice is very healthy, but stains clothing. "P" in P.F.D.O.G., the *brachah* is *HaEtz*. (Similar— but *HaAdamah*, is the small deep purple Passionfruit, that is ripe when wrinkly. Halve, and spoon out the green juice and seeds.)

👁 Look for heavy fruits with shiny, evenly colored bright or deep red skin.

🚫 Stay away from those that are very hard, cracked or wrinkled.

🌡 Keep whole at room temperature out of sun 1 week, refrigerate 1 month, or freeze 3 months.

🌱 Fall is the season.

Pomelo: Also called Pumelo (and variations of the two spellings) or Chinese Grapefruit. Larger, slightly pear-like in shape, milder and less juicy than grapefruit. They can be green or yellow. The *brachah* is *HaEtz*.

👁 Look for ones that are shiny and smooth.

🚫 Stay away from those with blemishes or gray spots.

🌡 They keep at room temperature 1 week, and very cold temperatures 2 months.

🌱 Winter is the season.

Prickly Pear: A.K.A. "Cactus Pear" and "Sabra". The fruit can taste similar to raspberry or even watermelon due to different types. They have treacherous splinters, but are sold de-thorned. Colors include bright or deep red to green. Peel and discard seeds. There is debate as to whether the *brachah* is *HaEtz* or *HaAdamah*. However, one can't go wrong with the latter *brachah*.

👁 Look for those with even coloration. They can be ever-so-slightly soft.

🚫 Avoid very hard and unevenly colored (too young) very soft, leaky, or wrinkled (too old).

🌡 They will keep in the refrigerator about 1 week.

🌱 Spring through fall is the season.

Quinces: A member of the rose family, the Quince is a cousin to pears and apples, often used for preserves. They look like a fuzzy pear, vary in shape and size (3-6 inches) from round to oval or pear-shaped. When raw they are hard and sour, but turn soft, sweet and red when cooked. They are not as common as they used to be, as they tend to be hard to grow due to susceptibility to pests and parasites. They are delicate, and must be handled with extreme care. The *brachah* is *HaEtz*.

👁 They should be sweet smelling and yellow.

🚫 Avoid those that are brown or wrinkled.

🌡 Ripen at room temperature until it turns yellow and smells good. Keep at or below freezing 2 months.

🌱 Fall through early winter is the season.

Raspberries: A member of the rose family, these can grow wild. The most delicate berry, handle with care. They don't last long. Varieties include black, red, purple and gold or yellow. The *brachah* is *HaEtz*.

- 👁 Look for dry, firm and plump, nicely shaped evenly colored berries, and clean, unstained containers.

- 🚫 Avoid berries that are broken, soft and mushy, wrinkled, have blemishes, mold or browning. Containers with excessive juice can mean over-ripeness or damaged berries.

- 🌡 Store in a shallow container, as they can be crushed from too much weight. Don't wash until ready to eat. Once purchased, use them quickly. They do not ripen after harvest. Keep refrigerated 2-4 days.

- ☙ The season for Black Raspberries is summer, Red or Golden late summer through early fall.

- 🔍 Raspberries should be checked for bugs (especially if wild). Do as for blackberries if infested.

Rhubarb: Best known for tartness, they are usually eaten cooked with sugar or made into pie. The leaves are poisonous and must be removed. Wash the stems well before cooking. The *brachah* is *HaAdamah*.

- 👁 Stalks should be tender and crisp, brightly colored and straight.

- 🚫 Stay away from any that are limp, discolored or have any blemishes.

- 🌡 Wash, dry and cut stems, and store loosely in a plastic bag. Refrigerate 2-4 weeks or chop and freeze.

- ☙ Spring is the season.

Star Fruit: Also "Carambola". There are two varieties, sweet or sour. The sweet is a bit bigger and eaten raw. The sour is smaller and generally cooked. Both skin and meat are edible. The *brachah* is *HaEtz*.

- 👁 Look for large, nicely shaped, firm, plump, crisp with shiny, even colored, golden yellow skin.

- 🚫 Avoid those that are extremely green or have brown spotting.

- 🌡 They do ripen after harvest. Ripen at room temperature in a bag. Refrigerate up to 1 week.

- ☙ Summer through winter is the season.

Strawberries: The least fragile of all berries that you can buy at the store. The *brachah* is *HaAdamah*.

- 👁 Look for firm, dry strawberries that are evenly colored and as deep a red as possible, with fresh, green leafy tops. Smaller can often have more flavor, and smell can indicate ripeness.

- 🚫 Avoid mushy or crushed strawberries and those with blemishes. Also avoid green, white, unevenly colored, or very hard ones (too young), wrinkled, soft, brown, oozing, wet or moldy ones (too old).

- 🌡 They do not ripen after harvest. Store in open containers. Refrigerate for up to 1 week.

- ☙ Spring through summer is the season.

- 🔍 Check for bugs around the leafy tops. If infested, wash tops, cut them off and rinse. A *Shabbat* tip to remove bugs and leaves- push a drinking straw from the bottom of a ripe strawberry through the top.

Vegetables

Artichokes: One could say there's two varieties. One is the Jerusalem, (which is not an artichoke at all). Then there's the Globe, a true artichoke that is actually a type of thistle.

- Globes should be heavy and firm with thick and tightly bundled, firm, bright green leaves.
- Avoid dry, cracked, withered, starting to open, those with holes, many black spots or brown tips.
- To keep fresh, set in a container of water as you would cut flowers, (which is exactly what they are) and put them in the refrigerator. Keep refrigerated about 1 week.
- Spring is the season.
- Artichokes can be infested with aphids, so be sure to check them well. If infested, put a bit of dish soap in a large pot of water and soak ½ hour, then rinse well. Check again. If it still has bugs- discard.

Asparagus: Besides Green, there are White, or purple (Viola) that gets tender and turns green if cooked.

- Asparagus is best small with squeaky, smooth, even-colored stems and tightly closed buds.
- Avoid larger spears and those that are woody, limp or turning brown.
- Will not ripen after harvest. Keep refrigerated in a jar of water up to 2 weeks. (They are better fresh.)
- Spring is the season.
- Check for aphids around the buds. Do as for artichokes if infested.

Avocados: Aside from the rare breadfruit, this is the only "vegetable" that gets a *brachah* of *HaEtz*. (Although technically, both are really a fruit).

- These vary with taste. If you want guacamole, look for soft and ripe for easy mashing (should leave a slight dent if pressed). For salads, they should be very firm. Either way, look for unblemished ones.
- Stay away from ones with bruises, mold, mushy spots or empty pockets that cave in under the skin.
- They ripen after harvest. To ripen, keep in paper bag up to 1 week, or put in sunny window 1-3 days. When ripe, keep refrigerated 1-2 weeks. Avocados start to turn brown if peeled and exposed to air.
- Spring is the season for Californian, fall for Florida, winter from elsewhere. Available year-round.

Beets: Varieties include deep Red, White, Golden, or Candy Stripe (Chioggia). Leaves are also edible.

- Look for dark, small but heavy, hard, smooth beets with crisp leaves and taproot intact.
- Stay away from larger beets that are woody, shriveled, bumpy or have insect holes.
- Cut their leaves cut off a little over 1-inch above the root to prevent bleeding (and ultimately moisture loss). They will keep refrigerated 1-2 months, but the leaves keep for only a few days.
- Summer through fall is the season.

Broccoli: Broccoli can come in Purple or White as well as the traditional Green.

👁 Look for small, tender broccoli with tightly closed, deep colored florets.

🚫 Stay away from larger broccoli with thick stems or yellowed florets, which may be tough with very strong smell and flavor.

🌡 They keep at very cool temperatures about 1-2 weeks.

🗓 Summer and fall is the season.

🔍 Check florets, leaves and stems thoroughly for bugs and worms. Do as for artichokes if infested.

Brussels Sprouts: Mini cabbages on a clustered stem, they also smell like them when cooked.

👁 Look for small, crisp, bright green ones, with compact heads. Cut stems should be white.

🚫 Avoid brown or dirty stems, wilted leaves, and those with bug holes.

🌡 They keep at very cool temperatures 2-3 weeks at most.

🗓 Late fall early winter is the season.

🔍 They must be checked for bugs within the leaves. Do as for artichokes if infested.

Cabbage: Varieties include White (green) and Savoy, but there is also Red, and some fancier varieties such as Napa or Bok Choy (Chinese cabbage), and crinkled decorative types.

👁 Regardless of variety, look for heavy, with firm, crisp, thick leaves and tight, compact heads with bright color. (Bok Choy should be smaller.)

🚫 Avoid those that are limp, yellow or have rust, spotting, gashes, blemishes or foul smell.

🌡 Cabbages keep at very cool temperatures 2 months.

🗓 Fall and winter is the season for all cabbages.

🔍 Bugs can be found in the outer leaves, so examine carefully. Do as for artichokes if infested.

Carrots: Most commonly they are orange, but there are also unusual purple and red carrots. "Baby Cut" carrots sold in bags aren't really young. They're peeled, washed and cut into pieces.

👁 Small are often sweeter with more flavor, and bigger can be dry and tough. Should be deeply colored (green on top is best), firm and crisp, and preferably have leaves attached for sweeter flavor.

🚫 Avoid very large, soft, yellow in color, cracked, bendable, black on top, or sprouting roots.

🌡 Wash and scrub carrots before eating and ideally storing, to avoid annoying crunchy sand. If cut into sticks, store in a container of water in the refrigerator 1-2 weeks. To keep whole (trim off roots or leaves) at very cool temperatures 4-5 months, or refrigerate for 2-3 weeks.

🗓 Fall through spring is the season.

Cauliflower: Besides White, it can be bright Yellow or Green (a hybrid called "Broccoflower").

👁 Look for heavy, firm, tender heads with bright, tightly closed florets, and crisp green leaves.

🚫 Avoid browned or discolored heads with bruises or spots, open florets, or wilted leaves.

🌡 Keep out of the sun or it turns green and refrigerate 2-4 weeks (upside-down for freshness).

🌱 Fall is the season.

🔍 Check thoroughly for bugs and worms. Do as for artichokes if infested.

Celery: Besides green, celery can be white. A close relative is Celeriac, grown for its root.

👁 Look for small celery with firm, crisp, light green stalks and crisp green leaves. Celeriac should be small and heavy.

🚫 Avoid larger celery that is dark green, brown or yellow in color, has gashes or soft spots, and wilted yellow or brown leaves.

🌡 Store in the refrigerator in an unsealed plastic bag and keep stalks attached to the root base. If kept too long and starting to wilt, rehydrate it in a jar of water in the refrigerator. Celery keeps at very cool temperatures 3-5 weeks, Celeriac 3-4 months.

🌱 Fall is the season for Celeriac, and Celery is available year-round.

Chayote Squash: Also called "Vegetable Pears". They're smooth, green, pear-shaped usually with a cleft (don't mistake for wrinkles), and an edible seed. As with any squash, the *brachah* is *HaAdamah*.

👁 Look for firm unblemished fruit, without soft spots.

🌡 They keep at very cool temperatures from 1-2 weeks.

🌱 Summer is the season.

Corn: Varieties include Sweet White, Yellow, or a mixture of both, Blue and decorative non-edible Indian.

👁 All corn should have tightly packed, plump, complete kernels that spurt white juice when punctured. Look for pliable green stalks, ears tightly wrapped in crisp green husks, and moist soft yellow silks.

🚫 Stay away from ears with gaps between kernels, kernels that small and incomplete, or spurt watery liquid. Avoid limp, discolored or moldy, withered, brown or dry husks, stalks that are very light green to white in color, and brown, brittle or moldy silks.

🌡 Corn doesn't ripen once harvested. Keep at very cold temperatures up to 1-2 weeks.

🌱 Summer is the season.

🔍 Corn often harbors caterpillars and aphids. Husk the corn, then wash it well with water and a bit of dish detergent, then rinse it thoroughly.

Cucumbers: They come with or without seeds. English (Burpless) and Israeli types are long, slim with smooth dark skin and sweet flavor (peel waxed skin). Pickling types are bumpy with granules on skin.

👁 Look for firm even, deep green coloring. Heavier is better, and smaller have less seeds.

🚫 Stay away from those with soft or mushy areas, dark areas, bruises, or wrinkled tips

🌡 They do not ripen once harvested. They keep in moderately cool temperatures 1-2 weeks.

🔄 Spring through summer is the season.

Eggplant: Colors include purple, white, or striped in both colors called "Graffiti". Most common is the large Globe, which can be used for stuffing. There is an Asian variety that is smaller, and elongated with less seeds and sweeter flavor, great for frying. Eggplants will stain cutting boards and peelers.

👁 Generally, smaller are less bitter. They should be heavy, well-shaped, plump, firm with even coloring.

🚫 Avoid those that are lighter in weight, sound hollow, have blemishes, light brown areas, scratches, scars, bruises or soft spots, and those with mold on the stems or fruit itself.

🌡 They don't ripen after harvest. Refrigerate up to 1 week. Once peeled, it turns brown if exposed to air.

🔄 Summer is their season.

Green Beans: Most are green. Varieties include Green Beans (String Beans), Snap Beans, Chinese Yard Beans, and yellow Wax Beans. There are stringless, or those with strings needing to be peeled.

👁 Look for straight, velvet-like, crisp pods with bright color. Beans inside shouldn't be visible.

🚫 Avoid flexible pods with rust, or dry, blemished withered or yellow (except Wax Beans) pods.

🌡 They don't ripen once harvested. Keep refrigerated for up to 1-2 weeks.

🔄 Summer is the season.

Greens: *For Cooking-* Beet, Horseradish, Kohlrabi, Mustard and Turnip Greens, Red, Swiss or White Chard, Broccoli Rabe, Chinese Broccoli, Collards, Kale (green, red deep purple, frilly or plain) and Sorrel. *Raw-* Arugula, Belgian, Broad Leaf, Curly (Chicory) or Red Endive, Dandelion greens, and Watercress. Either Cooked or Raw- Escarole, Italian Radicchio (a dark red type of chicory or endive), Purslane, Radish Greens and Red Mustard. (Spinach is in its own listing.)

👁 All should be small, crisp, have bright or deep colored leaves. Swiss Chard- brightly colored stems. Radicchios- large tight heads with crisp white roots. Endive- yellow ends, older are less bitter.

🚫 Avoid large, blemished, slimy, limp, yellow or ones with holes. Wild greens must be pesticide-free.

🌡 Keep greens refrigerated 2-3 weeks (Collards or Kale in plastic), Arugula or Swiss Chard 1 week.

🔄 Spring is the season for most. Belgian Endive, Collards, Kale and Swiss Chard are fall.

💡 All greens must be washed well and checked thoroughly for bugs. Do as for artichokes if infested.

Hot Peppers: These come either fresh or dried. Seeds and veins are the hottest part of fresh peppers. Once cut open, wear gloves- especially if you have sensitive skin. Never touch eyes or other sensitive areas. When done handling, wash hands, utensils or cutting boards with cool soapy water.

Fresh: *Hottest Most Flavorful*- The Habanero, which can come in green, yellow, orange and red.

Extremely Hot- Cayenne and Serrano.

Slightly Milder but Very Hot- The Fresno and Jalapeño (undoubtedly the most common) which come mostly in green, or sometimes mature red.

Relatively Mild- Cherry and Yellow Wax (or Hungarian Wax) peppers.

Mildest- Anaheim (California Green Chile), Banana, Chilaca (a fresh Pasilla), Hungarian and Poblano.

Mild Peppers Used for Stuffing- Both Anaheim and Poblano.

Dried: There are a few varieties of dried peppers sold in bags. Not quite as treacherous to handle, they are hotter.

Hottest- The Habanero.

Extremely Hot- Cayenne.

Slightly Milder, but Very Hot- the Chipotle (Smoked Jalapeño).

Mildest- Ancho (a dried ripe Poblano), Mulato and Pasilla (a dried Chilaca).

- 👁 All fresh hot peppers should be firm and plump, glossy with crisp green stems, heavy with deep, even coloring, and no blemishes. Generally, the smaller the fresh hot pepper or more ripened to red, the hotter it will be. Look for shiny, firm, well-shaped peppers, with fresh green stems. Avoid those with wrinkles, black or soft spots, gashes or cracks. Dried peppers should be deeply colored and whole.

- 🚫 Avoid fresh peppers with wrinkles, cracks, those that have flexible sides, soft spots or blemishes. Avoid dried peppers that are broken, moldy, discolored, or bags with powder or webs (signs of bugs).

- 🌡 They don't ripen once harvested. They keep at moderate temperatures for 2-3 weeks.

- ☘ Summer is the season for fresh hot peppers, dried are available any time.

Jerusalem Artichokes: These are sometimes called Sunchokes, and are not really artichokes at all, but tubers like potatoes. To further lead to the confusion, they are native to North America and not Israel. Fix in any manner that you would a potato, but with one exception- these can actually be eaten raw. They are similar to Jícama listed next. Just as for a potato, the *brachah* is *HaAdamah*.

- 👁 Look for clean, smaller, heavy ones.

- 🚫 Avoid very soft, bruised, sprouting, shriveled or slightly green ones, or scraped-off skin.

- 🌡 Scrub well to clean off dirt before use or storage. If you cut them open, put them in acidic water, as they will start to brown when they hit the air. Ideally, store in a plastic bag or other humid place. They keep 2-5 months- the longer they're refrigerated, the sweeter they get.

- ☘ Fall and late winter is the season.

Jícama: Pronounced **CHee**-ka-ma, (like *Chanukah*) they are also called the Mexican Potato. These are often shipped when larger, as they don't bruise as easily during transport. The brown skin should not be eaten. These look like potato, but taste more like a water chestnut. It can be eaten raw or cooked. The *brachah* is *HaAdamah*.

👁 Look for smaller ones that are smooth and hard.

🚫 Avoid very large ones which are woody or dry, have bruises, cracks, and are soft or sticky.

🌡 Keep them away from moisture. They keep at very cold temperatures 2-4 weeks.

🌱 The season for Jícama is late winter, but is generally available year-round.

Kohlrabi: These can be green, (White Kohlrabi) or purple (Red or Violet). Eat raw or cooked.

👁 Kohlrabi should be small and heavy, firm with evenly colored crisp leaves.

🚫 Stay away from large woody and cracked bulbs, or those having wilted or yellow leaves.

🌡 Keep in sealed plastic bags at very cold to moderately cold temperatures for 2-4 weeks.

🌱 Fall through early spring is the season.

Leeks: Used like onions, these look more like giant scallions.

👁 Look for smaller leeks with firm, unblemished rich green leaves.

🚫 Avoid very large leeks as they will be bitter and tough.

🌡 Leeks should be washed well since dirt will usually be found inside and out due to the way that they are grown. They keep at very cool temperatures for 2-3 months.

🌱 Spring is the season.

Lettuce: Lettuce comes in quite a few varieties. Leaves can be frilly or straight. The most common is the durable and crispy light green Iceberg Lettuce. Romaine Lettuce is more oblong, deeper green, bunches tightly, and smaller is better. In the category of butterheads are Bibb and Boston, which are more delicate with loose leaves.

👁 Iceberg Lettuce should have firm, tightly-packed heads. Smaller Romaine is better. For Iceberg or Romaine, look for those with crisp leaves as opposed to loose and limp. Look for butterheads with firm yet tender, crisp, with medium green colored leaves.

🚫 Avoid lettuce that is slimy, limp, brown or yellowed. Avoid lettuce that has frozen- it simple rots.

🌡 Wash, pat dry and keep refrigerated in a loosely closed plastic bag. Keep leaves attached to root base, harvest outer leaves. Iceberg keeps 1-2 months, Romaine about 2 weeks, and butterhead up to 1 week.

🌱 Spring is the season for all lettuce.

🍖 Be sure to check all lettuce for bugs, especially looser leaf types. Do as for artichokes if infested.

Okra: These look rather like milkweed, and are indeed a pod. The *brachah* is *HaAdamah*.

👁 Look for small, plump, firm, crisp, evenly colored green pods.

🚫 Avoid larger, woody, hard, limp and wrinkled, or yellow or brown pods.

🌡 They don't ripen once harvested. Check thoroughly for bugs. Refrigerate up to 1-2 weeks.

�™ Summer is the season.

♀ Check for aphids around the stems. Do as for artichokes if infested.

Onions: There are various types of onions, some fresh, others are older dry (called "storage" onions) and are available all year. Unless in an area regularly eaten raw, uncooked onions get a *brachah Shehakol*, but if cooked, it is *HaAdamah*. Perhaps the most common, dry onions, others are sweet and fresh. Green Onions are listed under "Other Produce".

Fresh: *Sweet*- Often huge and squatty, the yellow to white Sweet Vidalia (Maui), and the Walla Walla. *Shallots* are in-between with green leafy top and dry papery bulb, but are generally used like an onion.

Dry come in many different varieties, shapes and sizes. Flavors can also vary widely:

Mild- round White or Yellow onions.

Slightly Sweet- Bermuda, the longer oval Spanish with yellow or white skin, and Red Italian. The Pearl onion and Boiling onion are usually white, about only 1 inch in diameter, and not usually available fresh.

Potent- Globe onions, can be yellow, red or white and from 1-4 inches in diameter.

👁 Single- look for firm, heavy, unblemished with shiny, dry skins, and no sprouting leaves. In bags, visually inspect onions- all should look fresh (if one is bad, there are usually more). Note the smell.

🚫 Avoid onions having any hint of a musty or rotten odor, or soft, discolored or moldy spots. Avoid patches of green or black, and skin separated from the top (fungal infection, the core may be rotten).

🌡 Keep out of sunlight and humidity. Onions can keep 1-8 months in a very cold refrigerator as long as there are no blemishes and skins aren't removed. Never keep any onion in plastic bags, whether refrigerated or room temperature, and never store with potatoes.

🌙 Sweet Onion season is spring through summer, Dry Onions fall (always available), Shallots all year.

Parsnips: These look somewhat like a white carrot, but taste like nutty celery.

👁 Look for small, well-shaped roots that are smooth, crisp and firm and cream or yellow color.

🚫 Avoid very large roots, broken, spotty, have gashes, blemishes or soft spots, and an excessive amount of tiny hairy roots. Wrinkled, soft, bendable or rubbery ones are old.

🌡 They should be washed and scrubbed before eating (or storing) to avoid annoying crunchy sand. Store refrigerated in a plastic bag with a bit of water to keep fresh for up to 2-6 months.

🌙 Fall is the season.

Peas: Some peas must be shelled- the common Garden, Green or Sweet peas, and Edamame (Soybeans). Those with edible pods are Sugar Snap peas and Snow peas.

👁 All peas should be crisp, have vivid color and no spots, blemishes, yellowing or wrinkles. Sugar Snaps should be crisp and firm, brightly colored, full and plump, having fully developed sweet peas and pods. Snow peas should be small, crisp, shiny and flat with young undeveloped peas inside tender, well-shaped pods. Of the peas that must be shelled, look for pods that are firm and crisp, shiny, feel like velvet, crisp and plump with soft green tips, stems and leaves (if attached).

🚫 Stay away from pods that look dry, are puffy, limp, or peas that rattle inside when shaken.

🌡 They do not ripen once harvested. Peas keep at very cool temperatures about 1-3 months.

☙ Peas are generally in season in Spring, with pod peas being available year-round.

Peppers: (See Hot Peppers or Sweet Peppers for specific types.)

Potatoes: Varieties can vary in color, the average being reddish-brown as the most common Russet (or Idaho), Yellow or Gold, Red, White, and Blue (or Purple). They come many different shapes and sizes. Some are "new" (young) like little balls, others are thick and stalky, and a few can be long and narrow. Fingerlings are small, waxy, and thin. Russets and Idahos have a network-like skin, and can be medium to very large. Whites can be medium, long oval or small round, with thin, smooth white to light brown skin. Yellow potatoes such as Yukon Gold are golden inside and out and vary in size. Reds are usually round with waxy red skin. Blue or Purple potatoes are less common, vary in size, are oval, thin skinned, and are deep purple inside and out. Of the many different varieties, some have multiple or specific uses:

Mashing- Russets/Idahos, White or Yellow.

Baking- Russets/Idahos, Blue/Purple or Fingerlings.

Boiling or Steaming - Red, White, Yellow, Blue/Purple or Fingerlings.

Frying- White or Yellow.

Roasting- Russets/Idahos, Red, White or Yellow.

👁 Look for clean, smooth skin. If buying in bags, inspect all potatoes and pay close attention to smell.

🚫 Avoid wet, shriveled, large nicks from shovels, cracks or deep crevices. Also avoid those with brown, black soft spongy spots or large dark areas. This could possibly indicate fungal infection, and can be rotten inside. If there is any hint of a musty or rotten odor, don't buy them.

🌡 Do not store in closed plastic bags or they rot. An open paper bag is perfect. Keep out of humidity and sunlight, or they will sprout and turn greenish. Keep room temperature or in cool basement up to 2-9 months, or refrigerate if unblemished. Potatoes start to turn brown once peeled and exposed to air.

☙ Most potatoes are in season any time. New potatoes are in season in spring.

551

Radishes: The most common is the mildly hot, Red Globe Radish. Less common are Black, White, Icicle or Daikon Radishes. White are a long, round Asian type. Daikon are milder, white, long and carrot- like. Black Radish is large and potent, and get a *brachah* of *Shehakol*. All other radishes get *HaAdamah*.

👁 Smaller radishes are more mild. Look for hard, well-shaped radishes.

🚫 Avoid any that very large, cracked, moldy, blemished, shriveled, woody or have insect holes.

🌡 Wash, dry, cut off tops and refrigerate. Most keep 3-4 weeks, Black or Daikon 3 months dry.

🌱 Red and White Radishes are in season in spring, Black and Daikon Radishes in winter.

Rutabagas: These are preserved with wax to keep in moisture. The *brachah* is *HaAdamah*.

👁 Look for smaller yet heavy, firm, rutabagas with wax firmly attached to smooth skin. A lumpy, non-symmetrical shape is normal.

🚫 Avoid those that have blemishes of any kind, mold, and white areas where the wax has separated. Shrinkage can denote old age.

🌡 They must be washed well with soap and water before use. They keep at room temperature 1 week, or at very cool temperatures for 2-4 months.

🌱 Winter is the season.

Spinach: This can be plain (Smooth Leaf or Flat Leaf), crinkled (Savoy), or both (Semi-Savoy).

👁 Look for small whole, firm and crisp, rich green leaves with thin stems. It should smell fresh

🚫 Avoid broken, limp, yellowed, crushed, slimy leaves or bug holes, and rancid or musty smell.

🌡 Spinach will keep when stored loosely in a very cold refrigerator 1-2 weeks.

🌱 Spring is the season.

🔍 They should be checked thoroughly for bugs and washed well. Do as for artichokes if infested.

Summer or Soft Squashes: These generally have edible skin and seeds, and can be served cooked or raw. Varieties include Pattypan or Scalloped, Yellow Crookneck (Summer), Yellow Straightneck, and Zucchini. Pattypan are usually white, but can be green or yellow, are scalloped, flat and round like a puffy plate, and is often stuffed and baked. Yellows are always yellow, and often boiled or fried. Zucchini is smooth, usually is green (or marbled with white), or yellow.

👁 All should be firm, plump, evenly colored, slightly shiny, and the smaller in size the better.

🚫 Avoid those with mold on the squash or stem, soft spots, gashes or blemishes of any kind.

🌡 They don't ripen once harvested. They are delicate, having very thin skin and are easily bruised, so handle with care. Store them open to the air. They keep refrigerated 1-2 weeks.

🌱 Summer is the season.

Sweet Peppers: The most common are the Bell Pepper, (sometimes called mangoes by older people) and come in Green, Yellow, Orange, Red or occasionally Purple. Green are younger and more tart, and Red Bells (actually ripe Green Bells) are very sweet. Yellow and Orange are special varieties and are ripe and mellow. Other Sweet Peppers include Pimentos, which are generally jarred, and California Green Chilies (Anaheims) can become mildly spicy. All are good for stuffing.

- 👁 Even, deep coloration is best in any pepper. They should be very firm, without blemishes, smooth and not shriveled. Green Bell Peppers should be as deep dark green as possible, Red Bells should be as dark red as possible. Lighter red or streaked may not have the full sweet flavor

- 🚫 Avoid soft peppers with blemishes, moldy stems, soft black areas, or uneven coloring. Wrinkles are a sign of very old age.

- 🌡 Peppers do not ripen once harvested. They keep at moderately cool temperatures for 2-3 weeks, (Red Bells 1-2, longer when deep green).

- ☙ Summer is the season.

Sweet Potatoes: U.S. Sweet Potatoes have yellow meat that is drier, in comparison with U.S. yams. The U.S. is the only country that calls Sweet Potatoes "Yams" and vice versa. These and differ from true yams (which are white) in all other countries around the world.

- 👁 Look for heavy, firm and smooth sweet potatoes. Pay special attention to smell.

- 🚫 Stay away from those that are shriveled, have bruises, sticky or oozing sap, cracks, holes or large nicks from shovels, or are sprouting. Be sure they don't have white patches, soft cavities, mold, brown or black soft spongy spots, or they are probably rotten inside. If there is any hint of a musty odor, don't buy them.

- 🌡 The longer they are stored at room temperature, the sweeter they get. Keep out of sunlight and out of humidity. Never store in plastic. They keep 4-6 months at room temperature or in a cool basement.

- ☙ Fall is the season.

Tomatillos: A tart green Mexican tomato, usually used in green salsa. The *brachah* is *HaAdamah*.

- 👁 Choose firm, shiny green tomatillos attached to dry papery husks.

- 🚫 Tomatillos that are yellow, sticky, or without a husk can be old.

- 🌡 They ripen once harvested. They can be ripened by placing them in a paper bag on a warm (not hot) windowsill, but are generally used green. When ready to use, peel off the husk and wash the slightly waxy skin with soap and water. They keep at moderately cool temperatures for about 1 month.

- ☙ Summer and fall is the season.

Tomatoes: Varieties include yellow or orange tomatoes (said to be less acidic), the 1-2 inch Cherry, Grape, or Plum tomatoes for salads, the giant Beefsteak, and oval Roma or Pear tomatoes. Vine ripened are more flavorful. Often tomatoes are picked green and treated with ethylene gas.

👁 Look for heavy, firm but slightly soft, good smelling, evenly colored with smooth, shiny skin.

🚫 Avoid those with bruises or splits.

🌡 They can ripen once harvested, but aren't as good. Ripen by placing in a paper bag on a warm (not hot) windowsill. Ripe will keep refrigerated up to 1-2 weeks, (2 months if green).

🌱 Summer is the season.

Turnips: Turnips are rather pretty for a root, with half purple half white.

👁 Look for firm, heavy, smaller turnips with smooth skin and green leaves (if attached).

🚫 Avoid scars, wrinkles or blemishes. Large woody stemmed ones are older and can be bitter.

🌡 Turnips should be washed dried, their tops cut off before refrigerating, and will keep 1 week.

🌱 Winter is the season.

Winter or Hard Squashes: Winter squashes have dense orange meat with the exception of Spaghetti squash (when cooked, the meat turns stringy yellow like spaghetti). Varieties include Acorn, Buttercup, Butternut, Hubbard, Pumpkin, Spaghetti and Turban. Acorns are small, usually green with a splotch of yellow (the less the better), but can be yellow or white. Buttercup is round and green. Butternut, is light orange and somewhat pear-shaped. Pumpkins are prized for meat and seeds and vary in size. Turbans are green with yellow and orange splotches.

👁 Choose hard, heavy squashes with dull skin and firmly attached stems.

🚫 Beware of gashes, cracks or soft spots.

🌡 They do not ripen after harvest, keep 6 months at room temperature or in a cool basement.

🌱 Fall through winter is the season.

Yams: In the U.S., yams are synonymous with sweet potatoes. Elsewhere a true "Yam" is the tropical yam and has white meat. Here, they're a moister type of sweet potato with orange meat.

👁 They should be firm, heavy and smooth. Pay special attention to the smell.

🚫 Avoid shriveled, bruised, sticky oozing sap, cracks, sprouting, white patches, or mold. Brown or black soft spongy spots may be rotten inside. If there is any musty odor, don't buy them.

🌡 The longer they're stored at room temperature, the sweeter they get. Keep out of sunlight and humidity. Never store in plastic. Keep up to 4-6 months at room temperature or in a cool basement.

🌱 Fall is the season.

Other Produce

Fennel: All parts of fennel can be used, and have a slightly licorice flavor. The *brachah* is *HaAdamah*.

- 👁 Fennel bulbs should be firm and creamy white with straight stalks and large, crisp, frilly green leaves.

- ⊘ Stay away from limp or yellow leaves, those with flowers, and discolored, withered, cracked or blemished bulbs.

- 🌡 Fennel leaves will keep in a plastic bag in the refrigerator 3-4 days, and the bulb 1 week.

- ↻ Fall is the season.

- 🥄 Check for bugs. If infested, put a bit of dish soap in a large pot of cool water and soak ½ hour, then rinse very well. Check again, if it still has bugs- discard.

Garlic: Generally found in White, there are also Green and Purple (Italian) varieties. Unless in an area where it is eaten raw regularly, garlic has a *brachah* of *Shehakol*. If cooked, a whole clove is *HaAdamah*.

- 👁 Look for tight bulbs that are firm and heavy. Choose clean bulbs with dry, unstained white skins.

- ⊘ Avoid bulbs that are loose in their papery skins, moldy, sprouting (bitter), or look water-stained.

- 🌡 Garlic can keep a very long time. Keep garlic out of sunlight and humidity, and don't peel until ready to use. They should easily keep at cool temperatures for 6-7 months. Do not store in plastic bags.

- ↻ There is no special season.

Ginger: Ginger root is the rhizome of a beautiful orchid-like flower.

- 👁 Look for those with tight smooth skin. Smaller is better, and doesn't need peeling.

- ⊘ Avoid sprouting, broken, woody, have wrinkles, cracks, bruises or crumbly spots.

- 🌡 An easy way to store ginger is to wash it and put it in a well-sealed jar of sherry in the refrigerator. It keeps a very long time.

- ↻ Mid-spring is the season.

Green Onions: These are basically young onions, with many different names- Green Onions, Scallions, Spring Onions, and Bunching Onions. Shallots are very similar, but have brown bulbs and are considered a regular onion. The *brachah* is *HaAdamah*.

- 👁 Look for green onions with firm green leaves and small bulbs.

- ⊘ Stay away from large bulbs and limp, withered or yellow leaves (older are very potent).

- 🌡 They keep refrigerated about 1-2 weeks. Better yet, they will grow if kept in a jar of water.

- ↻ Spring is the season.

- 🥄 Check for thrips (especially if growing at home). Wash well with dish soap and water, then rinse.

555

Herbs: There are many different varieties of leafy herbs available fresh at larger supermarkets.

👁 In general, they should be firm, bright green (depending on type), moist and well scented.

🚫 Avoid those that are wilted or have brown leaves.

🌡 Bunches of fresh herbs (parsley and cilantro) keep 1-2 weeks refrigerated in water (changed often).

🔁 Summer is the season.

🔍 Check for bugs in some less aromatic types. Do as for fennel if infested.

Horseradish: When handling, wear gloves, especially for sensitive skin. Never touch eyes or sensitive areas. When done, wash hands and utensils with cold soapy water. Often used at the Passover *Seder*, they normally get a *brachah* of *Shehakol* if eaten raw.

👁 Look for Horseradish roots that are heavy and very hard.

🚫 Avoid those that are green, soft or light weight.

🌡 Do not store near sunlight. It keeps well in very cold temperatures for up to 1 year.

🔁 Fall is the season.

Mushrooms: The White is most common, (when small is called a Button). Another variety is the Cremini, which if left to grow it becomes a Portabella. Most are canned, but others are dried or fresh including Chinese mushrooms such as the Shiitake, Chanterelle (a yellow or golden type), and Porcino. Do not buy fresh for during Passover, as they are often grown on barley. The *brachah* is always *Shehakol*.

👁 They should have firm, smooth, unblemished skin with tightly shut caps. As they age, the gills open and skin browns, developing more flavor. Unless you like small, bigger are better.

🚫 Regardless of type, when buying fresh, stay away from those that are shriveled, moldy, mushy, worm-ridden or bad smelling, have black spots, and containers with excessive liquid.

🌡 All mushrooms are very fragile and don't last long. Refrigerate and keep unwashed in the package, an open container, or paper bag until ready to use, but never tightly wrapped in plastic. Refrigerate up to 1 week, (longer if bought undamaged before gills open). Do not soak, they absorb like a sponge.

🔁 Fall is the season, but they are generally available year-round.

Sprouts: Not just beans. Smaller, hair-like types are Alfalfa (most common) and Clover. Larger types are Adzuki Bean, Daikon Radish, Mung Bean, and Soy Bean. Use sprouts quickly as they don't last long.

👁 Look for crisp, moist sprouts with white roots, yellow to green sprouts (Mung are white).

🚫 Avoid those that smell fermented, are withered, slimy, soft, moldy, or have any brown.

🌡 Refrigerate larger sprouts in a jar of water. Store loosely in the refrigerator for up to 3-5 days.

🔁 Sprouts are available any time of year, as they are not planted crops.

Substitutions

The following are general substitutions that can be used instead of ingredients you may not have, know where to find, or have run out of. Not all substitutes are guaranteed to have perfect results, but those that are truly problematic for certain applications are listed. Many ingredients are good for Passover use. For substituting kosher meat cuts for *treifah* cuts, see *"Treifah Meat Cut Substitute Chart" on p.* 444.

General Substitutes

Item	Amount	Substitute
Acorn Squash	1 cup mashed	1 cup mashed buttercup squash, butternut squash, Hubbard squash, or pumpkin.
Aduki Beans	1 cup	1 cup kidney or red beans.
Alfalfa Sprouts	1 cup	1 cup sprouted lentils, mung bean sprouts, or radish sprouts.
Allspice	1 tsp.	½ tsp. cinnamon + ½ tsp. ground cloves.
Anaheim Chile	3 whole peppers	3 whole canned green chiles, or fresh poblano chile peppers.
Ancho Chile (Pasilla)	1 pepper	1 Mulato chile pepper.
Anchovy Paste	3 Tbs.	1 (2 oz.) can anchovies (mashed).
Anise	1 Tbs. chopped	1 Tbs. chopped caraway leaves or fennel bulb.
Anise Seed	1 tsp.	1 tsp. fennel seeds.

Item	Amount	Substitute
Apple Cider (for drinking)	1 cup	2 tsp. apple cider vinegar + 1 cup apple juice.
Apple Cider (for recipes)	1 cup	1 cup apple juice.
Apple Cider Vinegar	¼ cup	¼ cup white vinegar.
Apple Pie Spice	1 tsp.	½ tsp. cinnamon + ⅛ tsp. cardamom + ¼ tsp. nutmeg.
Apricots (fresh)	4 fruits	4 dried apricots rehydrated in water.
Arrowroot (for thickening)	1½ tsp.	1 Tbs. flour.
Arrowroot (for thickening)	2-3 tsp.	1 Tbs. corn, potato starch, or rice starches.
Artichoke Hearts	1 cup chopped	1 cup chopped Jerusalem artichokes, kohlrabi, or palm hearts.
Artichoke (leaf meat)	1 whole	½ cup mashed asparagus.
Arugula	1 cup leaves	1 cup watercress leaves.
Asian Eggplant	3 whole	1 large globe eggplant.
Asparagus	1 cup cooked	1 cup well-cooked broccoli stems.
Avocado (chopped	1 cup	1 cup chopped chayote squash.
Avocado (mashed)	½ cup	½ cup pureed asparagus, broccoli or peas.
Avocado Oil	2 Tbs.	2 Tbs. grapeseed oil, corn oil or peanut oil.
Baby Spinach	1 cup leaves	1 cup arugula, dandelion greens, or watercress leaves.
Bacon Strips (Turkey)	2	2 turkey bacon strips (for M only).
Bacon Strips (Turkey)	2 crumbled	2 tsp. *parve* imitation bacon bits.
Bagel Chips	2 chips	2 pieces Melba toast, OR 2 thin bagel slices sprayed with canola or other oil and baked in a 350° F oven until crisp.
Baking Powder	1 Tbs.	1 tsp. baking soda + 1½ tsp. cream of tartar + ⅜ tsp. salt, OR ¼ tsp. baking soda + ¼-½ cup molasses, OR ¼ tsp. baking soda + ½ cup yogurt or buttermilk (for D only).
Balsamic Vinegar	1 Tbs.	1 Tbs. sherry or cider vinegar.
Bamboo Shoots (cooked)	1 cup	1 cup cooked Jerusalem artichoke slices, or sliced water chestnuts.
Barley (cooked)	¼ cup	¼ cup cooked wheat berries.

Item	Amount	Substitute
Basil (fresh)	1 Tbs.	1 tsp. dried.
Bay Leaves (crushed)	1 tsp.	1 tsp. ground thyme.
Bay Leaf (whole)	1 leaf	¼ tsp. crushed bay leaves.
Beef Broth	1 cup	1 cup water + 1 *parve* beef bouillon or soup cube, OR 1 cup water + 1-3 tsp. *parve* beef soup mix, OR 1 cup boiling water + 1 beef bouillon or soup cube + 1 Tbs. oil.
Beef Liver (chopped)	1¾ cups	*Parve Chopped Liver* (p. 140).
Beef Liver (cut in pieces)	1 lb.	1 lb. *kashered* chicken livers (for M only).
Beer (liquid in recipes)	1 cup	1 cup apple cider or *parve* beef soup broth.
Beets (chopped)	1 cup cooked	1 cup cooked carrots.
Bell Peppers (fresh)	¼ cup chopped	1 Tbs. sweet pepper flakes.
Bell Peppers (fresh)	3 Tbs. chopped	1 Tbs. dried bell peppers.
Blueberries in Syrup	15 oz. can	2½-3 cups frozen blueberries, cooked with 4 Tbs. sugar until tender.
Bouillon (Cube)	1 cube	1 soup cube, OR 2 tsp. soup mix.
Bouillon (Powdered)	1 tsp.	1 soup cube, OR 2 tsp. soup mix.
Brats	1 lb.	1 lb. cooked kosher beef Kielbasa (M only).
Bread	1 slice	1 sheet matzah, OR 1 oz. matzah farfel.
Bread	4 slices	1 cup matzah meal.
Bread Crumbs	1 cup	1 cup crushed corn flakes, matzah meal or crumbs, cake meal, or cracker crumbs.
Broccoli (florets)	1 cup	1 cup chopped cauliflower.
Broccoli (stems)	1 cup cooked	1 cup cooked turnips or kohlrabi.
Broth	1 cup	1 cup *Parve Broth* (p. 110).
Brown Rice (raw)	3 Tbs.	3 Tbs. raw wheat berries.
Brown Rice	1 cup cooked	1 cup cooked wheat berries or barley.
Brown Sugar	1 cup packed	⅞ cup white sugar + 2 Tbs. molasses or dark corn syrup.
Brussels Sprouts	1 cup	1 cup cooked broccoli tips or cabbage.
Buffalo (ground)	1 cup	1 cup lean ground beef.
Butter	1 cup	⅞ cup olive oil, OR 1 cup *parve* margarine.

Item	Amount	Substitute
Butter	½ cup	½ pint whipping cream + 2 Tbs. sour cream shaken together until butter is formed (for D only)
Butter	1 cup	¾ cup kosher chicken fat (for M only).
Buttercup Squash	1 cup mashed	1 cup mashed acorn squash, butternut squash, Hubbard squash, or pumpkin.
Buttermilk (in baking)	1 cup	1 cup milk + 1 Tbs. lemon juice or vinegar, OR 1 cup milk + 1 tsp. cream of tartar, OR ⅔ cup yogurt + ⅓ cup milk (all for D only).
Butternut Squash	1 cup chopped	1 cup chopped acorn squash, buttercup squash, Hubbard squash or pumpkin.
Cake Flour	1 cup	1 cup all-purpose flour minus 2 Tbs.
Candied Fruit	1 cup	1 cup chopped dried fruits or dried citron.
Candied Ginger	1 cube	½ inch piece ginger root + ½ tsp. sugar.
Cantaloupe	1 large	1 small honeydew melon.
Capers	1 Tbs.	1 Tbs. chopped green olives or pickled nasturtium buds.
Cardamom	2 tsp.	1 tsp. nutmeg, mace or coriander.
Carob Powder	3 Tbs. + 2 Tbs. water	1 oz. chocolate.
Carob Powder	1 cup	1 cup cocoa.
Catsup	¼ cup	¼ cup tomato sauce + 2 Tbs. brown sugar + ¾ tsp. *Spice Parisienne* (p. 434) + dash onion powder + 1 Tbs. vinegar.
Cauliflower	1 cup cooked	1 cup cooked broccoli.
Cayenne Pepper	dash	dash chili powder, hot paprika, red pepper flakes, OR 1 drop hot pepper sauce.
Celery Flakes	¼ cup	½ cup chopped celery cooked until tender.
Celery (fresh)	½ cup	¼ cup frozen or dried celery flakes soaked in ¾ cup water for 5 minutes, then drained.
Cellophane Noodles	2 cups	2 cups rice sticks (in soups or stir frying).
Charoset for Passover	2½ cups	12 oz. (1½ cup) date paste + ½ cup ground walnuts + ½ cup applesauce + 2 tsp. cinnamon + 2 tsp. wine.

Item	Amount	Substitute
Cheese (grated)	½ cup	4 individually wrapped slices, torn in pieces.
Chervil (chopped)	1 tsp. fresh	1 tsp. parsley flakes + ⅛ tsp. dry sage.
Chicken Broth	1 cup	1 cup water + 1 tsp. *parve* chicken soup mix, OR 1 cup boiling water + 1 *parve* chicken soup cube + 1 Tbs. canola oil.
Chicken Liver	1 lb.	1 lb. *kashered* beef liver cut up (M only).
Chicken Liver (chopped)	1¾ cups	*Parve Chopped Liver* (p. 139).
Chili Sauce	1 cup	1 cup ketchup + ⅛ tsp. onion powder + ¼ tsp. *Spice Parisienne* + 1 tsp. *Chili Powder* (both p. 434).
Chinese Hot Pepper Oil	1 Tbs.	1 tsp. pepper flakes + 1 tsp. garlic powder + (optional use) 1 tsp. avocado or other oil.
Chinese Rice Noodles (chopped)	½ cup	¼ cup *mandelin* soup croutons.
Chives (freeze-dried)	1 tsp.	1 Tbs. fresh chives or minced green onions.
Chocolate Coffee Mix	1 cup	4 tsp. sugar + 1 tsp. coffee + 1 tsp. cocoa + dash of cinnamon + 1 cup liquid.
Chocolate (German baking)	4 oz.	¼ cup cocoa + ⅓ cup sugar + 3 Tbs. *parve* margarine or oil. (Not for coatings.)
Chocolate (not for coating)	1 oz.	3 Tbs. carob powder + 2 Tbs. water, OR 3 Tbs. cocoa + 1 Tbs. *parve* margarine or oil.
Chocolate (Semisweet)	6 oz.	¼ cup *parve* margarine or oil + 7 Tbs. sugar + 6 Tbs. cocoa. (Not for coatings.)
Chocolate (Sweet)	4 oz	¼ cup cocoa + ⅓ cup sugar + 3 Tbs. *parve* margarine. (Not for coatings.)
Chocolate (Unsweetened)	1 oz.	3 Tbs. cocoa + 1 Tbs. *parve* margarine or vegetable oil. (Not for coatings.)
Chocolate Chips	3 Tbs.	1 square (1 oz.) chocolate.
Chocolate Chip (Semisweet)	3 Tbs.	1 square bitter chocolate + 1 Tbs. sugar.
Chocolate Milk Mix	1 cup serving	5 Tbs. powdered milk + 2 tsp. sugar + 1 tsp. cocoa. (Add 1 cup water- D only).
Chorizo Sausage	1 lb.	1 lb. *Mexican Chorizo Sausage* (p. 115), OR 2 pkg. soy chorizo sausage.

561

Item	**Amount**	**Substitute**
Chorizo Sausage	1 lb.	1 lb. kosher Kielbasa (for M only).
Cinnamon Sugar	½ cup	½ cup sugar + 1½ tsp. cinnamon.
Citron (Etrog- dried)	1 cup	1 cup candied or dried fruits.
Cloves (ground)	1 tsp.	1 tsp. ground allspice, mace or nutmeg.
Cocktail Sauce	1 cup	1 cup ketchup + 2¼ Tbs. diced horseradish.
Cocoa (from Mix)	1 cup	1 cup water + ⅓ cup powdered milk + 2 tsp. cocoa + 4 tsp. sugar (D only).
Cocoa Powder	1 cup	1 cup carob powder.
Coconut Cream	1 cup	*Imitation Thai Coconut Cream* (p. 86).
Coconut (Cream of)	15 oz. can	*Imitation Cream of Coconut* (p. 124).
Coconut Milk	15 oz. can	1⅞ cups soy, rice, or nut milks, OR 1 cup *Imitation Coconut Milk* (p. 86).
Coconut Milk	15 oz. can	1⅞ milk + 1 tsp. coconut extract (D only).
Coffee (strong brewed)	½ cup	½ cup water and 1 tsp. instant granules.
Cooking Sherry	1 cup	1 cup dry red or dry white wine.
Coriander Seed (whole)	1 tsp.	1 tsp. ground cardamom or coriander.
Corn Starch (in recipes)	1 cup	⅞ cup potato starch.
Corn Starch (to thicken)	1 Tbs.	2 Tbs. flour, OR 2 tsp. arrowroot, OR 4 tsp. quick-cooking tapioca, OR 2 egg yolks, OR 1 Tbs. potato starch, OR 1 Tbs. rice starch.
Corn Syrup	1 cup	1¼ cup sugar + ⅓ cup water boiled together until becoming syrup, OR 1 cup granulated sugar + ¼ cup water.
Cracked Wheat	3½ cups	1 lb. white flour.
Cracker Crumbs	¼ cup	¼ cup matzah meal, bread crumbs, or corn flake crumbs.
Cream	1 cup	1 cup coconut cream. (See note on Milk.)
Cream Cheese (spread)	1 cup	1 cup *Imitation Cream Cheese* (p. 105).
Cream Cheese (in recipes)	8 oz. (1 cup)	(D only) 1 cup cottage cheese + ¼ cup butter pureed together in a blender.
Creamer (Coffee)	1 cup	1 cup *parve* oat creamer.
Creamer (Coffee)	1 cup	1 cup coconut cream. (See note on Milk.)

Item	Amount	Substitute
Cream (Heavy or Whipping)	1 cup	(in recipes other than whipped or baked) ⅓ cup butter + ¾ cup milk (for D only).
Cream (Heavy or Whipping)	1 cup (liquid)	(for whipping) 1 cup evaporated milk + 5½ tsp. lemon juice (for D only).
Cream (Heavy or Whipping)	4 oz. (whipped)	1¾ cup whipped topping (for D only).
Creamer (Liquid Non-dairy)	1 cup	⅓ cup dry non-dairy creamer + ⅔ cups water. (See note on Milk.)
Cream of Tartar	1 tsp.	1 Tbs. lemon juice or vinegar.
Currants (dried)	1 cup	1 cup raisins, OR 1 cup dried cranberries, OR 1 cup dried chopped blueberries, cherries, dates, or soft prunes.
Dandelion Greens	1 cup leaves	1 cup arugula or watercress leaves.
Dark Corn Syrup	1 cup	¾ cup light corn syrup + ¼ cup molasses.
Dill	1 fresh head	1 tsp. dried seed.
Dill	1 fresh head	1 tsp. dried dill weed.
Duck	1 cup chunks	1 cup dark meat turkey or tongue (M only).
Duck (large)	1 whole	1 small goose (for M only).
Egg (for baking)	1 whole	1 Tbs. soy flour + 1 Tbs. water.
Egg (for cookies)	1 whole	2 yolks + 1 Tbs. water, OR ¼ cup egg substitute.
Egg (for custards)	1 whole	2 yolks, OR ¼ cup egg substitute.
Eggplant (chopped)	1 cup cooked	1 cup chopped cooked zucchini squash, Portabella mushrooms or okra.
Evaporated Milk	1 cup	1 cup *parve* liquid non-dairy creamer, OR 1 cup half & half or heavy cream (for D only).
Farfel (Matzah)	1 oz.	1 slice bread, OR 1 sheet matzah.
Fennel Bulb	1 cup chopped	1 cup chopped celery + 1 tsp. fennel or anise seeds.
Fennel Seed	1 tsp.	1 tsp. anise seeds.
Flour (All-purpose)	1 cup	1 cup + 2 Tbs. cake flour.
Flour (Cake)	1 cup	1 cup minus 2 Tbs. all-purpose flour.
Flour (for baking)	1 cup	½ cup matzah meal + ½ cup potato starch, OR 1 cup potato starch or matzah meal.
Flour (for Passover)	1 cup	⅝ cup matzah meal, OR 1 cup potato starch.

Item	Amount	Substitute
Flour (for thickening)	1 Tbs.	1½-2 tsp. potato, corn or rice starch, or arrowroot, OR 1 Tbs. quick-cooking tapioca.
Flour (Self-rising)	1 cup	1 cup all-purpose flour + 1½ tsp. baking powder + ½ tsp. salt.
Flour Tortillas (fried)	2 chopped	1 small bag pita bread chips.
Flour Tortillas (fried)	2 whole	2 plain sheets square matzah (matzo).
Flour (White)	1 lb.	3½ cups cracked wheat.
French Fried Onions	¼ cup	3-5 onion rings (baked until crisp) crumbled.
Garlic Flakes	¼ tsp.	1 minced clove garlic.
Garlic Powder	⅛ tsp.	1 clove minced garlic, OR ¼ tsp. flakes.
Garlic (crushed)	1 clove	¼ tsp. flakes OR ⅛ tsp. garlic powder, OR ½ tsp. garlic salt (reduce salt by ¼ tsp. in recipe).
Garlic Salt	½ tsp.	¼ tsp. salt + ¼ tsp. garlic powder.
Ginger Ale	1 cup	½ cup lemon lime soda + ½ cup cola.
Ginger (Ground)	⅛ tsp.	1 Tbs. grated ginger root.
Ginger Root	1 tsp. minced	¼ tsp. ground ginger.
Goose Meat	1 lb. cooked	1 lb. cooked duck meat.
Graham Cracker Crumbs	1¼ cups	1 cup matzah meal + 1 tsp. cinnamon.
Graham Flour	1 lb.	1 lb. whole wheat flour.
Granola	1 cup	1 cup meusli or muesli.
Grape Seed Oil	2 Tbs.	2 Tbs. avocado oil, peanut oil or corn oil.
Great Northern Beans	1 cup cooked	1 cup cooked navy beans.
Green Beans	1 cup cooked	1 cup cooked wax beans or okra.
Green Bell Peppers	¼ cup chopped	¼ cup chopped orange, red, or yellow bells.
Green Bell Peppers (fresh)	¼ cup chopped	1 Tbs. sweet pepper flakes.
Green Bell Peppers (fresh)	3 Tbs. chopped	1 Tbs. dried bell peppers.
Green Chiles	3 whole	3 Anaheim chiles or poblano chile peppers.
Ground Beef	1 lb.	2 cups rehydrated TVP® (1 cup dry).
Half & Half	1 cup	¾ cup *parve* liquid non-dairy coffee creamer + ¼ cup water. (See note on Milk.)
Half & Half	1 cup	1 cup evaporated milk, OR ⅔ cup low fat or skim milk + ⅓ cup heavy cream. (D only)

Item	Amount	Substitute
Half & Half	1 cup	¾ cup whole milk + ¼ cup heavy cream (D only).
Hamburger (cooked)	1 lb.	2 cups rehydrated TVP® (1 cup dry).
Hamburger (raw)	1 Tbs.	1 Tbs. *Parve Steak Tartare* (p. 140).
Hard-Boiled Egg (chopped)	2 Tbs.	2 Tbs. chopped firm tofu.
Head Lettuce (Iceberg)	1 cup shredded	1 cup shredded Romaine or butter lettuce.
Heavy Cream (Sweetened)	1 cup	1 cup liquid *parve* non-dairy whip topping.
Heavy Cream (Whipping)	1 cup (½ pint)	(for non-whipped or baked recipes) ¼ cup butter + ¾ cup milk (for D only).
Heavy Cream (Whipping)	1 cup (½ pint)	(for whipping) 1 cup evaporated milk + 5½ tsp. lemon juice (for D only).
Herbs	1 Tbs. fresh	1 tsp. dried leaves, OR ¼ tsp. ground herb.
Herbs (chopped)	1½-2 Tbs.	¾-1 tsp. dried loosely crumbled, OR ½ tsp. finely powered or ground dried herbs.
Herb Vinegar	¼ cup	¼ cup vinegar + 1 Tbs. dried herb.
Hoisin Sauce	1 Tbs.	1 Tbs. *Fishless Worcestershire Sauce* (p. 92), OR 1 Tbs. *Oyster Sauce* (p. 330) or Worcestershire sauce (both for Fish only).
Honey	1 cup	1¼ cup sugar + ¼ cup water, OR ¾ cup maple or corn syrup + ½ cup sugar.
Horseradish (fresh grated)	1 Tbs.	2 Tbs. bottled horseradish.
Horseradish Sauce	1 Tbs.	1 Tbs. mayonnaise + ¼ tsp. prepared or grated horseradish.
Hot Cocoa Mix	1 cup	5 Tbs. powdered milk + 2 tsp. sugar + 1 tsp. cocoa. (Add 1 cup hot water- for D only)
Hot Dog (P or M)	1 frank	2-3 tightly rolled pieces P or M bologna.
Hot Oil (Chinese- in recipes)	1 Tbs.	1 tsp. pepper flakes + 1 tsp. garlic powder (optional use) +1 tsp. vegetable oil.
Hot Pepper Sauce	dash	1 drop Tabasco® Sauce, OR dash chili powder, hot paprika, cayenne pepper, pepper flakes.
Hubbard Squash (mashed)	1 cup	1 cup mashed acorn squash, buttercup squash, butternut squash, or pumpkin.
Iceberg Lettuce (chopped)	1 cup	1 cup chopped Romaine or butter lettuce.

Item	Amount	Substitute
Imitation Crab	1 (1 lb.) pkg.	1 lb. *Crab Style Fish* (p. 329), OR 1 pkg. kosher imitation lobster (all Fish only).
Imitation Cream Cheese	1 cup	1 cup *Parve Imitation Cream Cheese* (p. 105- works best for spreads).
Imitation Lobster	1 (1 lb.) pkg.	1 lb. *Crab Style Fish* (p. 329), OR 1 pkg. kosher imitation crab (all Fish only).
Imitation Shrimp	1 (1 lb.) pkg.	1 lb. kosher imitation crab (Fish only).
Imitation Sour Cream	1 cup	1 cup *Parve Imitation Sour Cream* (p. 105).
Instant Cocoa Mix	1 cup serving	5 Tbs. powdered milk + 4 tsp. sugar + 2 tsp. cocoa. (Add 1 cup hot water- D only).
Jalapeño Pepper (minced)	1 medium pepper	½-¾ tsp. red pepper flakes.
Jalapeño Pepper (pureed)	1 medium pepper	¾ tsp. hot pepper sauce.
Jerusalem Artichokes	1 cup chopped	1 cup chopped artichoke hearts, jícama, kohlrabi, palm hearts, or water chestnuts.
Jícama (Mexican Potato)	1 cup chopped	1 cup chopped artichoke hearts, Jerusalem artichokes, kohlrabi, or palm hearts.
Kale	1 cup cooked	1 cup cooked Swiss chard or spinach.
Ketchup	¼ cup	¼ cup tomato sauce + 2 Tbs. brown sugar + ¾ tsp. *Spice Parisienne* (p. 434) + dash onion powder + 1 Tbs. vinegar.
Kidney Beans	1 cup	1 cup red, pink, or pinto beans.
Kidney Beans	1 (15 oz.)	1¾ cups cooked beans with liquid.
Kielbasa (Polish Sausage)	1 lb.	1 lb. *Mexican Chorizo Sausage* (p. 116), OR 1 lb. kosher brats (for M only).
Kiwi Fruit	1 cup slices	1 cup strawberries slices in lime juice.
Kohlrabi	1 cup cooked	1 cup cooked turnips or broccoli stems.
Kohlrabi	1 cup chopped	1 cup chopped artichoke hearts, Jerusalem artichokes, jícama, or palm hearts.
Lamb	1 lb.	1 lb. venison or beef brisket (for M only).
Leeks	½ cup sliced	½ cup sliced green or yellow onions.
Lemon Juice	1 Tbs.	1 Tbs. lime juice or orange juice, OR ½ tsp. lemon extract, OR ½ tsp. vinegar.

Item	Amount	Substitute
Lemon Zest	1 tsp.	1 tsp. lime or orange zest, OR ½ tsp. lemon extract, OR 1 Tbs. lemon juice.
Lime Zest	1 tsp.	1 tsp. lemon or orange zest, OR ½ tsp. lime extract, OR 1 Tbs. lime juice.
Mace (Ground)	½ tsp.	½ tsp. nutmeg or allspice.
Mandarin Oranges (6 oz.)	1 can	1 small fresh tangerine cut in sections.
Mandelin Soup Croutons	¼ cup	½ cup chopped Chinese rice noodles.
Margarine	1 cup	1 cup slightly frozen cottonseed oil.
Margarine	1 cup	⅞ cup canola oil.
Margarine	1 cup	1 cup butter (for D only).
Margarine	1 cup	¾ cup kosher chicken fat (for M only).
Marshmallows (large)	1 whole	8-10 miniature marshmallows.
Marshmallows (miniature)	1 cup	10 large chopped marshmallows.
Matzah	1 sheet	12 soda crackers.
Matzah Meal	1 cup	3 sheets matzah ground in a blender.
Matzah Meal	1 cup	4 slices pulverized toasted bread, OR 1 cup flour, cake meal, or cracker crumbs.
Mayonnaise	1 cup	1 cup sour cream or yogurt, or 1 cup pureed cottage cheese (both for D only).
Meat (cooked Chunks)	1 lb.	1 pkg. soy meat chunks.
Meat (cooked Ground)	1 lb.	2 cups rehydrated TVP® (1 cup dry).
Meat (Sliced Lunch)	2 lb.	1 pkg. soy lunch meat slices.
Melba Toast	2 pieces	2 bagel chips, OR 2 thin slices of French bread baked in a 400° F oven until crisp.
Mexican Potato (Jícama)	1 cup	1 cup water chestnuts or Jerusalem artichoke.

(Note on Milk Substitutes: None of the following parve items can be used when a natural chemical reaction is involved, such as in making butter, cheese, or ice cream, and cold-mixed instant puddings.)

Item	Amount	Substitute
Milk	1 cup	1 cup soy or almond milk (not for salty cooking), OR 1 cup *Parve Milk* (p. 85), OR ⅓ cup powdered soy milk + 1 cup water.
Milk (Whole)	1 cup	1 cup coconut, rice, oat or almond milk.
Milk (Whole)	1 cup	½ cup evaporated milk + ½ cup water (D only).

Item	Amount	Substitute
Milk (Whole)	1 cup	⅜ cup half & half + ⅝ cup skim milk. (D only).
Milk (Whole)	1 cup	1 cup water + ⅓ cup powdered milk (D only).
Milk (Whole in recipes)	1 cup	1 cup water + 1½ tsp. butter (for D only).
Molasses	1 cup	1 cup honey, dark corn or maple syrup, OR 1¼ cup sugar + ⅓ cup water, OR ¾ cup brown sugar dissolved in ¼ cup hot liquid.
Muesli (Meusli)	1 cup	1 cup granola.
Mulato Chile Pepper	1 pepper	1 ancho (pasilla) chile pepper.
Mung Bean Sprouts	1 cup	1 cup alfalfa sprouts.
Mushrooms (fresh)	½ lb.	6 oz. can mushrooms (drained).
Mushrooms (fresh)	⅔-¾ cup	4 oz. can mushrooms (drained).
Mushrooms (fresh)	1 lb.	2½-3 oz. reconstituted dried mushrooms.
Mushrooms (fresh)	1 lb.	12 oz. can mushrooms (drained).
Mustard (Dry)	1 tsp.	1 Tbs. prepared mustard, OR ½ tsp. seed.
Mustard (Prepared)	1 Tbs.	½ tsp. dry mustard + 2 tsp. vinegar.
Navy Beans	1 cup cooked	1 cup cooked great Northern beans.
Oil (Vegetable)	1 cup	1 cup *parve* margarine, or shortening.
Oil (Vegetable)	1 cup	1 cup melted butter (for D only).
Okra	1 cup cooked	1 cup cooked eggplant or asparagus.
Onion (medium chopped)	1 whole	2 Tbs. dried onion flakes.
Onion (chopped raw)	1 small	1 Tbs. dried flakes soaked in 1 Tbs. water.
Onion (chopped raw)	1 cup	¼ cup dry minced, OR 1 tsp. onion powder.
Onion Flakes	1 Tbs.	1 small whole chopped onion.
Onion Powder	1 tsp.	1 cup chopped onion, OR ¼ cup flakes.
Onion Rings (crumbled)	¼ cup	¼ cup French fried onions.
Onion Salt	½ tsp.	¼ tsp. salt + ¼ tsp. onion powder.
Orange Bell Peppers	¼ cup chopped	¼ cup chopped red or green bell peppers.
Orange Bell Peppers (fresh)	¼ cup chopped	1 Tbs. sweet pepper flakes.
Orange Bell Peppers (fresh)	3 Tbs. chopped	1 Tbs. dried bell peppers.
Orange Juice	1 cup	1 cup reconstituted frozen concentrate.
Orange Zest	1 tsp.	1 tsp. lemon or lime zest, OR 1 tsp. finely chopped candied orange peel, OR ½ tsp. orange extract.

Item	Amount	Substitute
Orange Zest	1 tsp.	Tbs. orange juice.
Oregano	1 tsp.	1 tsp. marjoram.
Orzo Pasta	1 cup cooked	1 cup cooked pearl or white rice.
Oyster Plant (Salsify)	1 cup cooked	1 cup cooked Jerusalem artichoke, turnips, artichoke hearts, or asparagus.
Palm Hearts	1 cup chopped	1 cup chopped artichoke hearts, Jerusalem artichoke, jícama, or kohlrabi.
Papaya (chopped)	½ cup	½ cup chopped peach, mango, or nectarine.
Parmesan Cheese	¼ cup	¼ cup Romano cheese (D only).
Parsnips (chopped)	1 cup cooked	1 cup cooked turnips.
Pasilla Chile (Ancho)	1 pepper	1 Mulato chile pepper.
Passover Charoset	2½ cups	12 oz. (1½ cup) date paste + ½ cup ground walnuts + ½ cup applesauce + 2 tsp. cinnamon + 2 tsp. wine.
Peanut Butter	¼ cup	¼ cup tahini [sesame paste], or almond butter.
Peanut Oil	2 Tbs.	2 Tbs. avocado, corn, or grapeseed oil.
Pepitas (Pumpkin Seeds)	¼ cup	¼ cup hulled squash or sunflower seeds.
Pepper Oil (Chinese Hot)	1 Tbs.	(in recipes) 1 tsp. pepper flakes + 1 tsp. garlic powder + (optional use) 1 tsp. oil.
Pepperoni	¼ lb.	1 pkg. *parve* imitation pepperoni or salami.
Pepperoni	¼ lb.	¼ lb. kosher beef pepperoni, salami, brats, or Kielbasa (all for M only).
Pepper Sauce (Hot)	dash	dash chili powder or cayenne pepper.
Pie Crust	any size	Pie tins lined with ground nuts.
Pine Nuts (Pignolis)	¼ cup	¼ cup hulled squash or sunflower seeds.
Pita Chips	1 small bag	2 chopped fried flour tortillas.
Poblano Chile Peppers	3 whole	3 canned green or fresh Anaheim chiles.
Pomegranate	1 fruit	1-3 prickly pear (sabra) fruits.
Potato Starch	1 Tbs.	2 Tbs. flour, OR 1 Tbs. corn starch.
Prickly Pear (Sabra)	1-3 fruits	1 pomegranate, OR 1 cup raspberries.
Pumpkin Seeds (Pepitas)	¼ cup hulled	¼ cup hulled squash or sunflower seeds.
Pumpkin (squash)	1 cup cooked	1 cup cooked acorn, buttercup, butternut, or Hubbard squash.

Item	**Amount**	**Substitute**
Quinoa (cooked)	½ cup	½ cup cooked rice.
Red Beans	1 cup cooked	1 cup cooked pinto or red kidney beans.
Red Bell Peppers (fresh)	¼ cup	¼ cup yellow or orange bell peppers.
Red Bell Peppers (fresh)	3 Tbs. chopped	1 Tbs. dried bell or sweet pepper flakes.
Red Pepper Flakes	½-¾ tsp.	1 medium minced pickled jalapeño pepper.
Red Pepper Flakes	½-¾ tsp.	⅛ tsp. of cayenne pepper.
Red Pop (Soda)	1 cup	1 cup seltzer + 3 Tbs. sweetened cherry or strawberry drink mix.
Rhubarb	1 cup cooked	1 cup cooked cranberries or quinces.
Rice (cooked)	½ cup	½ cup cooked quinoa or orzo pasta.
Rice Noodles (Chinese)	½ cup chopped	¼ cup *mandelin* soup croutons.
Rice Pudding	¼ cup	¼ cup tapioca pudding.
Romano Cheese (grated)	¼ cup	¼ cup Parmesan cheese (D only).
Rum	¼ cup rum	1 Tbs. rum extract + 3 Tbs. water.
Rutabaga (cooked)	1 cup chopped	1 cup chopped cooked kohlrabi bulbs or parsnips, or turnips with ½ tsp. sugar.
Sabra (Prickly Pear)	1-3 fruits	1 pomegranate, OR 1 cup raspberries.
Saffron	1 tsp.	1 tsp. shredded calendula or safflower.
Salami	1 lb.	2½ pkgs. *parve* soy pepperoni or salami.
Salami	1 lb.	1 lb. kosher brats, Kielbasa, or beef pepperoni (all for M only).
Salmon	1 (15 oz. can)	1 (15 oz.) can mackerel.
Salsify (Oyster Plant)	1 cup cooked	1 cup cooked Jerusalem artichoke, turnips, artichoke hearts, or asparagus.
Savory	1 tsp.	1 tsp. thyme.
Self-Rising Flour	1 cup	1 cup all-purpose flour + 1½ tsp. baking powder + ½ tsp. salt.
Sherry (Cooking)	1 cup	1 cup dry red or dry white wine.
Sherry (in baking)	1 cup	1 cup orange juice.
Shortening (Solid Vegetable)	1 cup	1 cup *parve* applesauce (for baking), OR 1 cup margarine + 2 Tbs. water.
Shortening (Solid Vegetable)	1 cup	1 cup butter + 2 Tbs. water (D only).

Item	Amount	Substitute
Snow Peas	1 cup	1 cup sugar snap peas.
Soda (Fruit-Flavored)	1 cup	1 cup seltzer + 3 Tbs. sweetened drink mix.
Soup Cube	1 cube	1 bouillon cube.
Soup Cube	1 cube	1 tsp. soup mix.
Soup Mix	1 envelope	4 soup or bouillon cubes, OR 4 tsp. powdered bouillon.
Sour Cream	1 cup	1 cup *Parve Imitation Sour Cream* (p. 105).
Sour Cream	1 cup	1 cup plain yogurt, OR ⅓ cup butter + ⅔ cup milk, OR ⅓ cup butter + ¾ cup buttermilk or yogurt (all for D only).
Soy Burger	1 lb.	2 cups rehydrated TVP® (1 cup dry).
Soy Burger	1 (14 oz.) pkg.	1 lb. raw ground meat (for M only).
Soy Milk	approx. 1 cup	¾ cup boiling water + ¼ cup soy flour, whisk, simmer 20 minutes, strain and chill.
Soy Milk	1 cup	½ cup *parve* non-dairy creamer + ½ cup water, OR 1 cup milk (for D only).
Spinach	1 cup cooked	1 cup cooked kale or Swiss chard.
Sugar (Brown)	1 cup	⅞ cup granulated sugar + 2 Tbs. molasses.
Sugar Cube	1	½ tsp. granulated sugar.
Sugar (Light Brown)	1 cup	½ cup dark brown or granulated sugar.
Sugar (Powdered)	1 cup	1 cup granulated sugar + 1 Tbs. corn starch (ground in a food processor until it becomes powdery).
Sugar (White or Granulated)	½ tsp. sugar	1 sugar cube.
Sugar (White or Granulated)	1 cup	1 cup firmly packed brown sugar.
Sugar-Snap Peas (in recipes)	1 cup	1 cup snow peas + ½ tsp. sugar.
Sunchokes	1 cup	1 cup water chestnuts or jícama.
Sun-Dried Tomatoes	½ cup	1½ cups drained canned tomatoes, OR 4-6 chopped plum or grape tomatoes.
Sunflower Seeds	¼ cup	¼ cup hulled squash or pumpkin seeds
Sweet Anise	1 Tbs. diced	1 Tbs. diced caraway leaves.
Sweet Anise	1 Tbs. diced	1 Tbs. diced fennel bulb.

Item	Amount	Substitute
Sweetened Condensed Milk	14 oz. can	1 cup nonfat dry milk + 2⅔ cup sugar + ½ cup boiling water + 3 Tbs. melted butter, blended until smooth (not able to be used for thickening by cooking- for D only).
Sweet Peppers	¼ cup chopped	¼ cup chopped yellow, orange or red bell peppers.
Sweet Peppers (fresh)	¼ cup chopped	1 Tbs. sweet pepper flakes.
Swiss Chard	1 cup cooked	1 cup cooked kale or spinach.
Tabasco® Sauce	1 drop	dash chili powder, red pepper flakes, hot paprika or cayenne, OR ¼ tsp. hot sauce.
Tapioca (for thickening)	1 Tbs. quick cooking	1 Tbs. flour.
Tapioca Pudding	¼ cup	¼ cup rice pudding.
Tartar Sauce	½ cup	6 Tbs. mayonnaise + 2 Tbs. pickle relish.
Tehina (Sesame Chickpea Spread)	¼ cup	¼ cup hummus (chick pea spread).
Tahini (Ground Sesame Paste)	¼ cup	¼ cup natural peanut or almond butter.
Tomato Juice	1 cup	½ cup tomato sauce + ½ cup water.
Tomato Paste	½ cup	1 cup boiled tomato sauce (reduced by ½).
Tomato Paste (in recipes)	1 (6 oz.) can	1½ cups tomato sauce reduce amount of liquid in recipe by ¾ cup.
Tomato Sauce	2 cups	¾ cup tomato paste + 1 cup water.
Tomato Soup (condensed)	10¾ oz. can	1 cup tomato sauce + ¼ cup water.
Tomatoes (canned)	1 cup	1⅓ cups chopped cooked tomatoes
Tomatoes (canned for recipes)	1 cup	½ cup tomato sauce + ½ cup water.
Tomatoes (Sun-Dried)	½ cup	1½ cups or 4-6 chopped plum tomatoes.
Tongue (Beef)	1 cup slices	1 cup sliced dark duck meat (for M only).
Turkey Bacon Strips	2 whole	2 *parve* soy bacon strips.
Turkey Bacon Strips	2 crumbled	2 tsp. *parve* imitation bacon bits.
Turkey (Dark Meat)	1 cup slices	1 cup sliced duck meat or tongue (M only).
Turnips	1 cup cooked	1 cup cooked kohlrabi or broccoli stems.
TVP® (rehydrated)	1 cup dry	1 lb. or 2 cups soy crumbles.
TVP® (rehydrated)	1 cup dry	1 lb. or 2 cups crumbled cooked ground beef (M only).

Item	Amount	Substitute
Vegetable Oil	1 cup	1 cup *parve* applesauce (for baking), OR 1 cup melted *parve* margarine or shortening.
Vegetable Oil	1 cup	1 cup melted butter (D only).
Venison	1 lb.	1 lb. lamb (for M only).
Water Chestnuts	1 cup chopped	1 cup jícama.
Watercress	1 cup leaves	1 cup arugula leaves.
Wheat Berries (cooked)	¼ cup	¼ cup cooked brown rice or barley.
Wheat Berries (raw)	¼ cup	3 Tbs. raw barley or brown rice.
Whipped Cream	1 cup	½ cup *parve* non-dairy whip. Beat until stiff.
Whipped Cream	1 cup	1 cup *parve* cream cheese cake icing.
Whipping Cream	1 cup (½ pint)	¼ cup butter + ¾ cup milk (can only use in non-whipped or baked recipes- for D only).
Whipping Cream	1 cup (½ pint)	1 cup evaporated milk + 5½ tsp. lemon juice (use for whipping- for D only).
White Vinegar	¼ cup	¼ cup cider vinegar, lemon or pickle juice.
Wine (for drinking)	1 cup	1 cup non-alcoholic wine or apple cider.
Wine (Red, in recipes)	1 cup	1 cup grape, cranberry or tomato juice.
Wine (Red, in recipes)	1 cup	1 cup kosher beef broth (for M only).
Wine (White in recipes)	1 cup	1 cup apple or white grape juice.
Wine (White in recipes)	1 cup	1 cup kosher chicken broth (for M only).
Worcestershire Sauce	1 Tbs.	1 Tbs. soy sauce + dash of garlic and black pepper.
Yeast (Active Dry)	1 Tbs. powder	1 cake compressed, OR 1 (¼ oz.) pkg. dry.
Yellow Bell Peppers	¼ cup chopped	¼ cup chopped green, orange, or red bell peppers, OR 1 Tbs. sweet pepper flakes.
Yellow Crookneck Squash	1 cup sliced	1 cup sliced zucchini squash.
Yogurt (Plain)	1 cup	(all for D only) 1 cup sour cream, buttermilk, or fresh cream, OR 1 cup heavy whipping cream + 1 Tbs. lemon juice.
Zucchini Squash	1 cup sliced	1 cup sliced yellow crookneck squash.

Opposite Food Substitutes
Tips on Using Parve Substitutions

It should be noted that a *parve* substitute eaten alone by itself is simply not going to taste as good. For example, if one loves a hamburger drenched in mustard, that's great! However, if one eats that same amount of mustard by itself, it's not going to have the same flavor as when it's on the burger. It's going to be a bit less desirable. It might be okay, but it's just not the same. Thus, we have the secret of flavor combinations. As long as an imitation food is eaten with other flavors or fixed in a recipe, it will taste just like the real thing. However, since it is not the real food, it will have slightly different characteristics.

PARVE CHEESE: I always hear how people dislike this product and frankly I think it's psychological. I only say this because even I find myself thinking, "Nah, I'd rather have real cheese". It must have something to do with classical conditioning and dairy being a "comfort" food. I have personally tested all the recipes in this book and know the *parve* cheese foods are as good if not better than the dairy ones!

How to Make It Melt: Keep the "cheese" out at room temperature in order to have it melt easier. Since it is generally soy-based, it lacks the fats in regular dairy cheese that makes it melt so readily.

How to Grate It: For slices, unwrap and stack on a cutting board. Slice in thin strips with a sharp knife and chop a few times. For block, grate on top food to look authentic. If disturbed, it bunches up and looks strange. Finer grating looks less like carrots. Grating when it is frozen gives very good results.

How Long to Keep It: As long as slices are unopened, they keep many months. Once opened, *parve* cheese dries out, or can become moldy after a week. If an unopened package swells up, it's gone bad.

PARVE MEAT: Most real meats don't have as much distinguishable flavor apart from other ingredients.

How to Get a Better Texture: Since it is either wheat or soy-based, it lacks natural fats found in real meat, so often vegetable oil is all it needs. The cooking process causes meat's oily fats to leach into food and give it a certain texture. Therefore, if *parve* meat is used without oil it tends to be dry and doesn't taste as good is it could. The addition of a heart-healthy vegetable oil such as canola gives the appearance, texture and flavor of real meat without saturated fat. Simply mix it the recipe. Whether microwaving or frying, pre-coat or spray soy burger patties with oil to give them a "juicier" texture.

How Long to Keep It: As long as it's unopened, it keeps a few months and can even be frozen. Once opened, it keeps about 1 week. If a new unopened package is swollen like a balloon, it has gone bad.

Listed in the next few pages are items that can be substituted for an opposite food ingredient. They are ideal for turning *treifah* recipes into kosher foods, or cholesterol-filled recipes into heart-healthy ones.

Dairy Substitutes (For Parve or Meat Recipes)

Items cannot be used when a chemical reaction is involved, such as in making butter or ice cream. Soy, nut and rice milks should not be used for salty recipes ore they sometimes turn bitter. They should ideally be used in sweet dishes.

Dairy Item	Amount	Substitute
American Cheese	1 slice	1 slice *parve* imitation American cheese.
Blue Cheese	8 oz.	16 slices *parve* imitation Mozzarella cheese melted and chilled in a square container.
Blue Cheese Dressing 1 cup	1 cup	*Parve Blue Cheese Dressing* (p. 90).
Butter	1 stick	¼ cup *Parve Imitation Butter* (p. 84) or margarine.
Buttermilk (for baking)	1 cup	1 Tbs. lemon juice + ¾ cup *parve* liquid non-dairy creamer + 3 Tbs. water.
Buttermilk (for drinking)	1 cup	1 cup soy, nut, rice or oat milk + 2 tsp. lemon juice or vinegar, OR ¼ cup silken tofu + pinch of salt + ¾ cup water + 1 Tbs. lemon juice or vinegar blended.
Buttermilk (for recipes)	1 cup	1 cup *Parve Imitation Sour Cream* (p. 105).
Cheddar Cheese	8 oz. bar	16 *parve* imitation American cheese slices melted and chilled in rectangular container.
Cheese Slices	12 oz. pkg.	12 oz. pkg. *parve* imitation cheese slices.
Cheese Sauce	8 oz.	1 cup *parve Kraft® Cheez Whiz® Style Sauce* (p.99).
Cheese Spread	6 oz.	¾ cup *parve Smoky Bacon Cheese Spread* (p. 107), OR 6 oz. hummus.
Cottage Cheese	1 cup	1 cup *Parve Cottage Cheese* (p. 109).
Cream	1 cup	1 cup *parve* liquid non-dairy creamer, real or *Imitation Thai Coconut Cream* (p. 86), OR ⅓ cup dry non-dairy creamer + ⅔ cups water.
Cream Cheese	8 oz. bar	8 oz. tub imitation cream cheese, OR 1 cup *Parve Imitation Cream Cheese* (p. 105).
Evaporated Milk	1 cup	1 cup *parve* liquid non-dairy creamer.
Feta Cheese	8 oz.	8 oz. block *Parve Feta Cheese* (p. 109).
Half & Half	1 cup	1 cup *parve* liquid non-dairy creamer.
Heavy Cream (sweetened)	1 cup	1 cup *parve* liquid non-dairy whip topping.
Limburger Cheese	1 cup	1 cup *Parve Blue Cheese Dressing* (p. 90).

Dairy Item	Amount	Substitute
Milk	1 cup	(Can't be used for a catalyst in making butter.) ½ cup liquid non-dairy creamer + ½ cup water, 1 cup *Parve Milk* (p. 85), OR 1 cup nut milks.
Milk (for drinking)	1 cup	⅓ cup powdered soy milk + 1 cup water.
Milk (sweet)	1 cup	1 cup rice milk (use in drinks or sweet foods).
Mozzarella Cheese	1 cup grated	8 slices *parve* Mozzarella torn in pieces.
Mozzarella Cheese	4 slices	8 oz. smoked tofu cut in slices, OR 8 slices *parve* imitation Mozzarella cheese.
Orange/Dark Yellow Cheese	2 slices	2 slices *parve* imitation American cheese.
Parmesan Cheese	¼ cup	¼ cup *Parve Parmesan* (p. 109), OR ¼ cup ground walnuts, OR ¼ cup *parve* kosher nutritional yeast.
Port Wine Cheese	8 oz.	1 cup parve *Port Wine Cheese Spread* (p. 106).
Provolone Cheese	8 oz.	8 oz. smoked tofu.
Romano Cheese	¼ cup	¼ cup *Parve Parmesan* (p. 108), OR ¼ cup ground almonds.
Ricotta Cheese	8 oz.	1 cup *Parve Ricotta Cheese* (p. 109).
Ricotta Cheese (in recipes)	8 oz.	1 cup soft tofu + dash lemon juice, blended slightly.
Skim Milk	1 cup	½ cup *parve* soy or almond milk + ½ cup water.
Skim Milk	1 cup	¼ cup *parve* non-dairy creamer + ¾ cup water.
Sharp Cheddar Cheese	8 oz. bar	16 melted slices *parve* American cheese + 1 tsp. dry mustard + dash cayenne, blend and chill.
Shredded Cheese	1 cup	8 slices *parve* imitation cheese torn into bits.
Soft Cheese (in recipes)	1 cup	1 cup soft tofu + a dash lemon juice.
Sour Cream	1 cup	1 cup *Parve Imitation Sour Cream* (p. 105).
Sweetened Condensed Milk	14 oz. can	1 cup powdered soy milk + ⅔ cup sugar + ½ cup boiling water + 3 Tbs. melted *parve* margarine blended until smooth, OR cream of coconut. This can't be used for thickening caused by cooking.)
Swiss Cheese	2 slices	4 slices *parve* imitation Mozzarella cheese.
Whipping Cream (Sweet)	1 cup	½ pint thawed liquid non-dairy whip topping.
White/Light Yellow Cheeses	2 slices	4 slices *parve* imitation Mozzarella cheese.
Yogurt	1 cup	1 cup *Parve Imitation Sour Cream* (p. 105).

Meat Substitutes (For Dairy or Parve Recipes)

Meat Item	Amount	Substitute
Beef Bacon	2 slices	2 slices *parve* soy imitation bacon.
Beef Bologna	2 slices	2 slices *parve* soy imitation bologna.
Beef Broth	1 cup	1 cup hot water + 1 tsp. oil + 1-3 tsp. *parve* beef soup mix or 1 tsp. *parve* beef bouillon.
Beef Chunks for Stew	1 lb.	1 pkg. *parve* steak chunks or chunk-style soy meat.
Beef Hot Dogs	1 pkg.	1 pkg. *parve* soy hot dogs.
Beef Kielbasa	1 lb.	1 pkg. *parve* imitation pepperoni slices, OR 1 pkg. *parve* imitation Kielbasa or brats.
Beef Liver	1 lb.	1 lb. patties of *Parve Chopped Liver* (p. 139).
Beef Salami	4 slices	8–10 slices *parve* imitation salami or pepperoni.
Bison/Buffalo Meat	1 lb.	1 pkg. *parve* soy steak chunks or seitan chunks.
Brats (sliced)	1 lb.	2 pkg. *parve* imitation brats.
Chicken Breasts	2 breasts	4 soy or vegetable fillets, OR 4 imitation *parve* chicken patties, OR 1 lb. sliced tofu or seitan.
Chicken Broth	1 cup	1 cup hot water + 1 chicken soup cube, OR 1 cup water + 1-3 tsp. *parve* chicken soup mix + 1 tsp. oil.
Chicken Chunks	1 lb.	1 pkg. soy chicken chunks or seitan.
Chicken Fat	about 1 cup	2 large sliced onions sautéed in 2 Tbs. vegetable oil until brown + 2 Tbs. sugar, pureed in a blender.
Chicken Fat (for frying)	2 Tbs.	1 Tbs. olive oil + 1 Tbs. *parve* margarine.
Chicken Livers	1 lb.	1 lb. *Parve Chopped Liver* (p. 139) rolled in balls.
Chicken Nuggets	6 pieces	6 *parve* imitation chicken nuggets or seitan.
Chicken Slices	1 lb.	1 pkg. soy imitation chicken or seitan slices, OR 2 cups pre-soaked chunk-style TVP®.
Chicken Wings	1 lb.	1 pkg. *parve* soy imitation chicken wings, OR 2 cups pre-soaked chunk-style TVP®, OR seitan.
Chopped Liver	1 lb.	1 lb. *Parve Chopped Liver* (p. 139).
Cornish Hens (Chunks)	1 whole	1 pkg. seitan or soy imitation chicken chunks.
Drippings	1 cup	1 cup *Parve Meat Drippings* (p. 85).
Duck (chunks or slices)	1 lb.	1 pkg. soy chicken or seitan chunks + oil.
Giblets (chopped)	¼ cup	¼ cup pre-soaked TVP®.

Meat Item	Amount	Substitute
Goose (chunks or slices)	1 lb.	1 pkg. soy chicken or seitan chunks or slices + oil.
Ground Beef	1 lb.	1 pkg. soy burger, OR 2 cups TVP® (pre-soaked in water or *parve* beef soup broth).
Ground Turkey	1 lb.	1 pkg. soy burger, OR 2 cups TVP® (pre-soaked in water or *parve* beef soup broth).
Hamburger (Raw)	1 Tbs.	1 Tbs. *Parve Steak Tartare* (p. 140).
Hamburgers	1 lb.	1 pkg. prepared soy burgers, OR 1 pkg. soy burger patties, OR 2 cups pre-soaked TVP® in water or *parve* broth.
Kielbasa (thinly sliced)	¼ lb.	1 pkg. *parve* imitation brats, OR 1 pkg. *parve* imitation salami or pepperoni slices.
Lamb	1 lb.	1 pkg. chunk-style soy meat or seitan + 1 Tbs. other vegetable oil, OR *parve* imitation steak chunks + 1 Tbs. vegetable oil.
Meatballs	1 lb.	1 pkg. soy prepared-meatballs, OR make balls from 1 pkg. soy burger or 2 cups pre-soaked TVP® in water or *parve* broth.
Mutton (Older Lamb)	1 lb.	1 pkg. chunk-style soy imitation meat, steak, or seitan + 1 Tbs. canola or other vegetable oil.
Pastrami	4 slices	4 slices *parve* imitation soy pastrami, OR 8 pieces raw soy bacon strips.
Pepperoni	¼ lb.	1 pkg. *parve* soy imitation pepperoni or salami.
Pigeon/Squab	1 whole	½ cup soy imitation chicken or seitan chunks.
Roast Beef Slices	4 slices	8 slices raw soy bacon, OR 4 slices soy pastrami.
Salami	¼ lb.	1 pkg. *parve* soy imitation salami or pepperoni.
Steak	4 strips	4 slices soy steak slice, chunks or seitan, OR 4 sliced style TVP® slices (soaked in *parve* broth).
Stew Meat	1 lb.	2 cups pre-soaked TVP® chunks, OR 1 pkg *parve* imitation steak or seitan chunks.
Tongue	1 lb.	1 pkg. *parve* steak chunks + 1 Tbs. oil.
Turkey	4 slices	4 slices *parve* soy imitation turkey slices or seitan.
Venison	1 lb.	1 pkg. chunk-style soy meat or steak chunks.

<u>*Treifah Food Substitutes That Are Kosher*</u>

The following can be used in recipes or eaten by themselves as-is:

<u>**Treifah Item**</u>	<u>**Substitute**</u>
Bacon	*Parve* soy imitation bacon, OR kosher turkey bacon (for M only).
Bacon Drippings	A little more *parve* margarine than lard amount called for.
Bacon Drippings	Slightly more butter than lard amount called for (for D only).
Bacon Slices (crispy)	Fried *parve* soy bacon, OR fried kosher turkey bacon (for M only).
Bacon Strip (1 crumbled)	1 tsp. *parve* imitation bacon bits, OR 1 crumbled fried strip of *parve* soy bacon.
Bacon Strip (1 crumbled)	1 crumbled fried strip of kosher turkey bacon (for M only).
Baked Ham	*Parve* soy imitation ham slices, OR baked ham *Seitan* (p. 111).
Baked Ham	Kosher smoked chicken or turkey breast (for M only).
Bologna	*Parve* soy imitation bologna, OR kosher beef bologna (for M only).
Brats	*Parve* soy imitation brats, OR kosher beef brats (for M only).
Braunschweiger	*Braunschweiger Sausage* (p. 114).
Braunschweiger	Kosher chopped liver spread (for M only).
Calamari (Squid)	Any mild fish cut in chunks (for Fish only).
Canadian Bacon	*Parve* soy imitation ham or parve soy imitation Canadian bacon, OR kosher smoked turkey slices (for M only).
Chorizo Sausage	*Mexican Chorizo Sausage Filling* (p. 115).
Chipped Beef	*Parve* soy imitation pastrami or raw soy bacon, OR kosher pastrami, corned beef, or salt beef (all for M only).
Clam Juice	*Parve* chicken soup broth, OR kosher chicken broth (for M only), OR drained tuna water, or gefilte fish broth (for Fish only).
Clams	*Kosher Clams* (p. 330), soaked de-boned salt herring, or de-boned unsalted schmaltz herring (all Fish only).
Crab	*Crab Style Fish* (p. 329), OR imitation crab or lobster (Fish only).
Deviled Ham	Smoked whitefish salad (for Fish only).
Frog Legs	*Parve* soy chicken strips, OR kosher white meat chicken (M only).
Goetta	*Goetta Sausage* (p. 113).
Ham	*Parve* imitation ham or Canadian bacon, OR ham *Seitan* (p. 111).
Ham	Kosher boneless smoked turkey breasts (for M only).
Hot Dogs	*Parve* soy hot dogs, or *parve* soy bologna rolled tightly.

Treifah Item	**Substitute**
Hot Dogs	Kosher beef, turkey or chicken hot dogs (for M only).
Italian Sausage	*Parve* soy Italian sausage, OR *Italian Sausage* (p. 112).
Kielbasa	*Parve* pepperoni or Kielbasa, OR kosher beef Kielbasa (M only).
Lard	Slightly more *parve* margarine than lard amount called for, OR a bit more butter than lard amount called for (for D only).
Linguiça Sausage	*Mexican Chorizo Sausage* (p. 115).
Lobster	*Crab Style Fish* (p. 329), OR imitation lobster or crab (Fish only).
Octopus	Any very fishy fish cut in chunks and overcooked (for Fish only).
Ostrich	*Parve* soy imitation steak strips, OR lean kosher beef (for M only).
Oysters	*Kosher Oysters* recipe (p. 329), soaked salt herring, or non-salted schmaltz herring (all for Fish only).
Oysters (mashed)	Crushed tuna (for Fish only).
Oyster Sauce	*Chinese Hoisin Sauce* (p. 93), OR *Oyster Sauce* (p. 330- Fish).
Pepperoni Pizza	Vegan pepperoni cheese pizza, OR *Crisp Crust Pizza* (p. 260).
Pepperoni Slices	*Parve* soy pepperoni slices, OR kosher beef pepperoni (M only).
Polish Sausage	*Parve* soy brats or Kielbasa, OR kosher Kielbasa (for M only).
Pork Chops	*Parve* chicken patties or seitan, OR sliced kosher smoked duck or turkey breast, or kosher lamb chops (all for M only).
Rabbit	*Parve* soy chicken strips, OR kosher chicken strips (for M only).
Rattlesnake	*Parve* soy chicken strips, OR kosher chicken strips (for M only).
Salami	Soy imitation salami or pepperoni slices.
Salami	Kosher beef salami or kosher pepperoni (both for M only).
Salt Pork	*Parve* bacon bits to taste, or chunks of *parve* soy hot dogs.
Salt Pork	Chunks of kosher hot dogs or smoked turkey breast (for M only).
Sausage	*Parve* soy sausage, OR *Country Sausage* (p. 114).
Scallops	Imitation jumbo shrimp sliced into ½-inch chunks and overcooked until tough (for Fish only).
Shrimp	*Crab Style Fish* (p. 329), OR imitation shrimp or crab (Fish only).
Shrimp Paste (Trassi)	Anchovy paste, or ground anchovies (both for Fish only).
Squid	Any mild fish cut in chunks (for Fish only).
Squirrel	*Parve* soy imitation chicken strips, OR chicken strips (for M only).
Trassi (Shrimp Paste)	Anchovy paste, or ground anchovies (both for Fish only).

Food Storage Tips

Keeping Foods Fresh

To keep foods lasting fresher longer (and keep your family healthy), read this section carefully!

Seasonings: Always store herbs and spices in a cool place away from direct sunlight. Not only will sun cause flavors to deteriorate, but it will also bleach delicate herbs. Make sure lids are tightly closed, as the oils evaporate into the air leaving tasteless seasonings. Some spices, such as paprika and chili powder can get infested with bugs.

When adding spices, powdered creamer, or soup croutons to hot foods, pour them into your hand first, or put a small amount in a bowl of that food's designation and then add them to the food. Never put them in straight from the container. Not only will it protect the food item from clumping and spoilage due to condensation, but it protects the *kashrut* of food as well. The reason that cooking food smells good is that as it cooks, it evaporates into the air in the form of steam. Odors contain tiny particles of the food, plus moisture. Put them together, and it can cause bacteria or mold growth in dry foods.

Open Containers: Besides pollen counts, weather reports often include mold counts because their irritating spores float naturally in the air. Never leave food or beverage containers sitting open for any longer than necessary, because these spores deposit onto food. (Part of Hashem's natural clean-up crew.) Be sure that cooked foods stay simmering, and refrigerated or frozen foods are put back soon after using.

Storage Time: Don't keep leftovers in the fridge over 1 week. To store them any longer, freeze them. Use the handy "*Food Freezing Guide*" (pp. 590-594) to see if foods can be frozen, and for how long.

Bacteria Prevention: The main trick to keeping foods fresh is preventing bacteria before it starts. The following tips will help to keep your kitchen as bacteria-free as possible. If you do them, rarely if ever will you smell anything bad or find any spoiled or moldy food in your refrigerator.

Utensils: Always use clean utensils to acquire condiments, jelly and peanut butter, butter, margarine and any type of cheese. Crumbs and residual food develop bacteria. I once saw mold growing in someone's butter, just from a very few crumbs that were left in it. It's helpful to keep a small utensil in the jar.

Eating, Drinking or Tasting: Never drink straight from a bottle of drink, or lick utensils and put them back in a jar or container to get more. Also, don't lick your fingers and then touch food, or cough on food while preparing it. Saliva is replete with germs and bacteria, which causes foods to grow stale, moldy and go bad quickly. The only remedy is cooking. Taste-testing spreads germs, as does coughing or sneezing near food. If you must cough or sneeze during food prep, always do so away from food or into a sleeve. Use a tissue if you must, but be sure to wash hands afterwards. If you're sick, have someone else cook!

Counter Tops: When it comes to food preparation, a clean counter is a must. If you are preparing food, some simple tips will help keep your family and guests healthy. If a counter gets dirty, clean it either with soap and water or some antibacterial cleaner, and then rinse it well. Here are some main culprits: Babies, pets and other items carrying germs, such as school books or money. Although it may be convenient height, never sit a baby on the counter top unless you clean it well afterward, especially if they're sick. Diapers are not foolproof, and carry nasty bacteria, viruses and germs. (Even doctors' offices have protective sheeting that is changed between patients.) I was once invited to eat at someone's house, and the mother (apparently out of habit) sat her baby on the counter to do her hand-washing. A few hours after returning home, I became very ill. I found out later that the baby had been sick with the exact same virus.

Cleanliness: There have been scientific studies done, and you would be amazed at the amount of microbes found on doorknobs and other often-handled items that you normally take for granted as being "clean". When preparing foods, always wash your hands before touching it directly, be it as you're preparing food or serving it. Although it sounds a bit obsessive-compulsive, it also helps to wash cans or bottles before using them. An area of cleanliness that many people don't take into consideration is when purchasing groceries. Rodents can frequent food warehouses, but there are other factors as well. Not only is money at the checkout counter replete with bacteria (and even drugs), but the grocery conveyer belt is full of hidden items too. I was in line at the grand-opening of a supermarket, watching a big package of pork ribs sitting on the new conveyer belt, dripping blood all over it. Understandably pressed for time, the cashier cleaned it up- but not very thoroughly. Over time, that belt would probably be full of bacteria!

Keep It Cool: When at the grocery store, get frozen or refrigerated items last, just before checkout. Frozen meat and liquid items take a while to thaw. However, refrigerated dairy such as milk gets warm fairly quickly and must stay as cold as possible. If you do self-checkout, pack cold items together— they keep each other cool. It's good to keep fresh meats with meats and dairy with dairy in case of leakage.

Bottled or Jarred Items: To keep milk fresher and lasting longer, always wipe the mouth of the plastic jug with a new, small piece of paper towel after every use. It also helps to squeeze the jug slightly to get as much air out as possible. I have had a gallon of milk last a whole month this way! Wiping the mouth of jars or bottles helps keep food fresh. Dried gunk on the mouths of jars not only prevents an airtight seal, but it's also a breeding ground for bacteria. Clean, properly kept food keeps refrigerators bacteria-free and smelling nice. Another tip is when items are out of the fridge and on the table while eating, keep the lids on. Although the open area looks small to us, it's the size of the Grand Canyon to microorganisms.

Can Openers: Whether electric or handheld, always clean your can opener's cutter wheel with a piece of paper towel after each use. If a food has a lot of liquid, it can even get on the feeder wheel and that should be cleaned off as well. Very salty foods can sometimes cause can openers to rust. This quick process of cleaning helps prevent a nasty buildup of old dried-on food, keeping it bacteria-free. It also lengthens the life of your can opener as well.

Refrigerators and Freezers: Set your refrigerator at 40-35° F, and set the freezer at 0° F or less. This prevents bacteria from reproducing and foods turning. Keep all vents unblocked for proper air circulation.

Keeping Foods Bug-Free

How Infestations Start: Often bug infestations occur on their own. The microscopic eggs may already be in food and you would never even know it. They can get in while at the warehouse, or while on the grocery shelves. There can even be stragglers in your home from time to time. If foods are stored properly, you generally don't have to worry about infestations. Once I asked a *shelah* when I had dumped a box of macaroni in the water and found beetles and their larvae floating to the top. I proceeded to pour off the bugs and scoop out any remaining ones, until it was completely clean. It turned out that the bugs did not make the pot *treifah*—which was my main concern, since the bugs do not impart a flavor. To my surprise, the food (no longer containing any bugs), was actually *permissible*, but I just couldn't quite bring myself to eat it!

Identification: It helps to know a little about your enemy when it comes to combat. There are many different bugs and even more varieties, but let's stick to the most common: Meal moths, beetles and Psocids. Indian meal moth larvae are destructive white to yellow or tan caterpillars. The brown moths are often found in pet shops flying around, or in cereals, pasta, corn meal, crackers or other dry grain goods, and pet food. Sometimes you'll see webs or tiny tan cocoons attached to the inside of a box. This is an indication of meal moth infestation. Dermestid beetle larvae are another pest, which are plump, hairy things found in grain products, and they also like wool, fur and dander (skin and hair products, hence the name "derm" or skin). Adult beetles prefer pollen, so they vacate and leave behind dried hairy skins.

Confused flour beetles and red flour beetles are very common. They're long and thin, brown or black. Similar, but longer in appearance is the saw-toothed beetle or merchant grain beetle, both of which can bore into sealed packages or get into food through tiny holes. All of these are often mistaken for weevils, which eat the same diet, but have long snouts. Cigarette beetles or drug store beetles are brown, short and oval, and love nuts, flour, wheat products, macaroni, crackers and dry pet foods. The larvae are found at the bottom or throughout the food. If pasta is infested, they float to the top when put in the water.

The worst pest has to be the very tiny, often nearly transparent white to light brown insects called "Psocids". Often, they are seen crawling on books—hence a common name is "book lice". Unlike most bugs, it only takes one to reproduce and they are particularly prolific, doing so at lightning-fast speed. They're especially fond of paper, cardboard, rice, grain items, especially oatmeal and creamy wheat cereals. They like it hot and humid. Within a short time of infestation, the cereal will literally be moving. It is so creepy! It gives me nightmares and I like studying bugs. Grain mites are tinier, yet similar in tendency and habitat. They often favor animal feed, especially if wet.

Protection & Prevention: Kosher consumers can't eat bugs, and must do all we can to prevent the infestation from happening. Keep foods in cool dry areas (and preferably up off of the floor). Bugs love humidity and warmth- 80°-90° F or so. Anyone who's lived in a tropical climate can attest to the fact that insects like it warm and humid! If foods are stored for a year or more, they should be checked for bugs. (They should also be checked for evidence such as skins, cocoons, or webs and large amounts of powder.)

To keep grain products, beans or nuts from getting bugs, put them in well-sealing jars or airtight containers. Another method I use for just about everything, is to freeze items for 24 hours or longer in a freezer at 0° F, (bug experts recommend 4 days). Then let thaw until room temperature so there is no longer any condensation, and then put the whole package in zipper bags (this also helps prevent flour leakage). Freezing actually kills bugs and their eggs, whereas they merely become dormant in the fridge and wake up later as they warm up. If you have room, store items like creamy wheat cereals and barley in a refrigerator, or better yet freeze them. Put crisp items like crackers in sealed plastic zipper bags at room temperature, otherwise they become soggy. Never leave cereal bags open. Roll them tightly and clip with a clothespin, or twist them shut and secure with a twist-tie. For less-eaten cereals, transfer to an airtight container or zipper bag.

Keep cupboards clean and use natural pest deterrents. Putting bay leaves in cabinets deters pests. Never use pesticides in food areas, they can get into food. (Personally, I won't use them outside either. It not only kills bugs, but wildlife like birds or squirrels, and is can harm pets and kids who may get into it.)

Older Foods

Some foods improve with age, can be repurposed for other things, or even resurrected.

Potatoes: Are potatoes in your fridge or pantry sprouting and shriveled? Don't throw them out— this is when they are the best! Once they start shriveling, they develop a delicious, sweet flavor perfect for hash browns or whatever. Simply take off the sprouts. I intentionally let mine age for a superior flavor.

Bananas: When bananas are overly ripe or stored in the refrigerator may look really disgusting, but they are scrumptious when used in the *Hawaiian Banana-Nut Bread* recipe on p. 384.

Onions: If onions sprout, use the leaves as you would green onions. (The bulb is still good, but strong.)

Grapes: Grapes may shrivel, but unless they're brown or mushy, these "young raisins" are very sweet.

Raisins: If raisins have gotten hard, boil them in water for a few minutes and they'll be as good as new. Raisins and other dried fruits become sweeter and tastier with age. Their natural sugar preserves them.

Drinks: Flat beer is needed for *Beer Batter Tempura* (p. 82). Revitalize flat soft drinks with 2-3 parts soda to 1 part seltzer water. Raisins added to champagne are said to regain the fizz. (I have never tried it.)

Bread & Rolls: The standard thing to do with stale bread was to use it for other foods, such as bread pudding and stuffing. If bread, cake, rolls, or cookies are getting hard or stale, microwave 10-20 seconds to resurrect. (This works for less freezer-burned items. If it smells like plastic, give it to the birds.)

Honey: Is your honey crystallized? Don't store it in the fridge, it will crystallize even more! Honey is one of very few foods that never goes bad. All honey crystallizes eventually, and often it's packed and shipped this way before it is processed and put into jars. To fix it, put honey in a double boiler, or one small pot in a larger pot of water. Heat on low until it melts, stirring the whole time. Pour in a jar and it's as good as new. Literally! (Never heat it in an oven, microwave or boil it. That destroys its flavor).

Rice: As dry rice ages, it gets a stronger flavor (like Basmati rice). Use fresh if you don't like rice flavor.

Eggs: Are your eggs getting old? Actually, freshly hatched raw eggs can be stored unrefrigerated for a short while. Refrigerated store-bought eggs can last a few months. If you are concerned that your raw eggs are getting old, fill a bowl or pot with enough warm water to completely cover the egg. Put the egg in the water. If it stays on the bottom, it's fresh. If it nearly floats it's older. (Older eggs are best for hard-boiling, they peel easily.) If a tested egg pops up above the surface of the water, it may be bad. To discard rotten eggs with no smell, take the egg and smash it underwater in a clean toilet bowl. Flush it away.

Short-Term Food Storage

Generally, most cooked foods will last in the refrigerator for about 1 week, if kept properly. Refrigerators should ideally maintain a temperature of 35-40° F or less. The following are based on proper processing as listed in "*Keeping Foods Fresh*" on pp. 581-583.

Canned Vegetables: Under normal circumstances these will last in a sealed container for 1 week in the fridge. If they have been rinsed with water to remove added salt before being put in a container, they do not last for very long, often only 2 days. Be sure to heat these well before storing.

Raw Foods: Any foods containing raw eggs, cooked eggs or mayonnaise do not last long at all and must be constantly kept cold. Once raw vegetables or fruits are chopped, they start to deteriorate, often lasting 2 days at the most. These must be kept in a sealed airtight container.

Fresh Fruits or Vegetables: With the exception of leafy items, lettuce and celery, don't store fruits and vegetables in plastic bags (especially sealed) unless directed. Just as putting produce in a paper bag helps make it ripen faster, putting produce in plastic bags makes them go bad twice as fast, since it locks the humidity in. If you have grapes, strawberries, or other small berries, after you wash them, put them in an open bowl or container, and do not seal them with a lid. The refrigerated air naturally keeps the fruit drier, preventing spoilage. I've had fresh grapes last a long time keeping them this way.

Cabbage, Lettuce and Celery: Use only the outer leaves or stalks first and as needed, but keep the remainder attached to the plant. They'll last a long time without withering.

Herb Bunches: Parsley, cilantro or other leafy herbs, (whether harvested or bought), stay fresh with minimal wilting when stems are put in water and leaves are loosely covered with a plastic bag.

Potatoes: Wash potatoes and let them dry before they are put in the fridge, it keeps your vegetable drawers much cleaner. Then, when you want to fix potatoes, they're ready to use immediately. The dirt-free potatoes help keep down bacteria and mold spores as well. Never keep them in sealed plastic bags or they will rot.

Box Flaps: For boxes such as baking soda or creamy wheat cereals with that annoying "open here" pouring flap that always seems to get stuck inside, there is an easy solution. Cut the flap open with a knife or razor blade. Then take the flap by the corner, pushing in the blade to force the flap out. Once it's out, here's the trick to keeping it out: Take a piece of paper towel and cut it twice the size of the flap opening. Fold the paper towel over in half (to stiffen) and put the folded edge at the top under the open flap. Gently push the flap down and inward. The towel gets trapped in the opening, creating a perfect seal. The tucking method keeps it fresh and prevents spilling. If a grain product to be stored awhile, refrigerate it in a zipper bag.

Homemade Bread: Bread is said to last longer using boiled potato water as liquid, and peanut oil.

Parve Soy "Meat" Products: If you plan not to use a package soon, they freeze very well and can keep nearly indefinitely (except for cold-cut slices). For tips on these items see p. 574.

Parve Soy Crumbles: When used with pasta meals such as lasagna, some types of parve soy crumbles have food colorant added. these shouldn't sit too long or the noodles can absorb the coloring of the "browned" soy meat. It is still healthy, but looks rather unappetizing.

Pre-Formed Pie Crusts: Crusts such as graham that are bought from the store often have a protective plastic insert on top. Once the pie has been baked, flip the plastic over and place it on top of the filled pie, folding the edge of the aluminum pan back over the plastic. You now have a perfect cover for your pie, high enough that the plastic won't disturb any delicate meringue or decorated tops. It travels well too!

Egg Advice: *Fresh–* Some people refuse to wash their eggs, however, washing eggs before use doesn't hurt them—as long as you use *warm* water (ideally between 110°-115° F). An interesting fact I learned when raising egg-laying ducks, is if they were washed with cold water, the semi-permeable shell could possibly suck impurities in with the water. After all, eggs were meant to be incubated by their mothers. Although it is said that eggs are washed before packaging, some I've seen have not been very clean looking, and with the threat of salmonella, it doesn't hurt. My washed eggs have lasted about 6 months or more. Store pointed-side-down for longer lasting eggs. Interestingly, in some other countries, fresh (raw) eggs are not sold refrigerated. When refrigerated, eggs can last raw 1-3 months or more.

Fresh eggs are best used when room temperature if you want fluffy baked goods or well-blended, smooth sauces. If needed right away, they can be set in a bowl of warm water (not hot) for 5 minutes.

Hard-Boiled– Hard-boiled eggs can last a very long time refrigerated, or about 1 week unrefrigerated. When boiling eggs, boil an odd number. It is good to have a special pot just for eggs. It doesn't have to be fancy. A pot with a raised middle works great, because it keeps the eggs from bumping into each other and cracking, and they are easier to remove from the pot. If you're in a hurry, an easy way to get eggs out of the hot water when they're done is to use a gravy ladle. They roll right in. Put the egg in a bowl of ice-cold water, and they're virtually ready-to-eat. (Using older eggs makes them easier to peel.)

If hard-boiled eggs get mixed up with raw ones, here's a way to identify them: Spin the egg like a top. If it wobbles it's raw, if it spins evenly it's boiled. To avoid this, date your fresh boiled eggs with a pencil.

In times of old, our sages instituted a *Halachah* to never peel a hardboiled egg and leave it overnight, even if it's wrapped up and in the refrigerator. Even more so, never leave opened raw eggs overnight. Salmonella reproduces rapidly in raw eggs. Commercial frozen "egg products" have gone through major processing such as pasteurization, and removing cholesterol. They are totally different from eggs freshly broken and removed from the shell. They may look similar and taste the same, but they haven't just been cracked open and stirred well. The processing takes away any danger of salmonella and other potentially harmful organisms.

Long-Term Food Storage

Some foods can be kept for longer periods of time than others. The following foods are based on proper processing as listed in "Keeping Foods Fresh" on pp. 581-583.

Condiments: These can be refrigerated for very long periods of time, as well as vinegars and oils

Raw Meats & Fish: As long as they are kept well-wrapped and relatively air-tight, these will keep well when refrigerated- but should ideally be used within a few days, (possibly up to 1 week if still wrapped in the original packaging). Wrapped properly they can be frozen up to a year, but for longer periods of time they can dry out. If this happens, they go well in dishes with sauces, or in soups which re-hydrates them.

Cooked Meats & Fish: These will keep in the refrigerator up to 1 week. As long as they are covered with sauce, breading or liquid, they can be frozen up to 1 year. If they aren't covered in these, they will dry out and become freezer burned. How are many "instant" foods made? They use freeze-dried or dehydrated foods.

Bread & Buns: These can be stored in the refrigerator in a sealed plastic bag for 2-4 weeks, depending on handling. Moisture, germs and skin oils from hands can cause bread to go bad faster. For fresh bread, it is good to squeeze the bread out of the bag to the spot where it is to be cut, then hold it with the bag while cutting. Bread and rolls cannot be frozen for very long, (at least in self-defrosting freezers), or they always seem to get that freezer taste or like plastic bag. This is partly due to the fact that plastics can leach out flavor (sometimes even *treifah*) into foods when stored for a long period of time. When well-wrapped, bread and rolls can last many months in manual defrost freezers.

Tortillas: These can be kept in the refrigerator when well-wrapped, for a few months. Flour tortillas can be frozen to remain fresh at all times if well-sealed for a long time. Corn tortillas can freeze up to 1 year.

Flour: Flour and other dry grain products should be put in a large sealed zipper bag, and put in the fridge. This protects them from bugs and keeps them fresh. Flour can be stored in the freezer up to 2 years.

Yeast: If you don't bake bread or rolls often, keep your yeast (and flour) in the freezer. This will keep the yeast alive much longer than just at room temperature. Another tip for when you do use it, is to never use it with water that is over 115° F (*yad soledet bo*) or it can cause the dough to not rise.

Nuts & Seeds: All nuts (except maybe peanuts), and all seeds (including sesame and poppy) should be stored in the refrigerator to keep their oils from becoming rancid.

Oily Items: Most people don't think about these foods as being "fried", but their high oil content makes them susceptible to going rancid. Therefore, always keep these items closed in their original packaging until needed. They may keep up to a year, but usually no longer. Items like Chow Mein Noodles, Rice Noodles, Ramen

Noodles, Potato Chips, Tortilla Chips, Dry Roasted Sunflower Seeds, and Nuts. If any of these items smell like paint thinner or other chemical, don't eat them, throw them out. Even the birds don't usually eat these!

Butters & Margarines: These can be refrigerated for very long periods of time. Butter can even be stored in the freezer for about 2 years.

Hard Cheeses: Mold spores travel in air and cheese is highly susceptible to them. Once opened, cheese either molders or dries out. It can be preserved by freezing. This works great for shredded cheese as long as you occasionally squeeze the bag to keep it from clumping. You'll have instant fresh grated cheese whenever you need it, and it literally takes no time to thaw. Just sprinkle it on your dishes. Chunk cheese freezes indefinitely as well, but will crumble once it has been frozen. This is great if you want to grate it anyway, all you need to do is thaw it out, take it in your fingers and squeeze it slightly. It automatically crumbles as though you grated it without having to clean a grater.

If a bar of cheese isn't used right away, keep it refrigerated but don't open it until needed. When slicing cheese, hold it by the wrapper without touching it directly. Skin oils can cause it to molder

Cottage Cheese: When unopened, cottage cheese will last many months in the refrigerator, and fairly long once it's been opened. It can be kept in the freezer, but the curds get a bit broken up. If you're a real "texture" person", you may not like it, but it is passable for most people.

Cream Cheese: This can be refrigerated unopened for many months, and a week or two once opened. It must be sealed well, or it will dry out. It doesn't store well in the freezer for eating on bagels, as it tends to separate and become partly water and partly curd. However, if it is to be put in recipes to be cooked, it's fine. (With added salt, it can be a good substitute for Ricotta in lasagna.)

Milk: If it is kept constantly refrigerated, and the rim of the top is kept clean, milk can often last up to a month. When frozen, milk tends to separate becoming partly water and partly curdled. It is okay for recipes, but not for drinking unless used in coffee. It tastes good but the texture is lousy.

Potatoes: Whole potatoes store well in a cool basement or the refrigerator, otherwise keep in an open paper bag at room temperature. Never store in plastic- they will rot! Once peeled, they turn brown when air hits them and they must be put in salted water in the fridge. They keep several days, but may still turn brownish. Potatoes do not freeze well, whether raw, cooked, whole or mashed. Due to their cell structure, they get a really strange consistency. They must be commercially processed in order to be frozen. Cooked potato products such as French fries and instant mashed potatoes freeze very well, and both are good in Instant TV Dinners mentioned in *"Time-Saving Tips"* on p. 459.

For a list of different foods and how long they can be kept in the freezer, (or if they should be kept in the freezer at all), see the *"Food Freezing Guide"* on the next few pages (pp. 590-594).

Freezing Foods

When it comes to freezing, old-fashioned manual-defrost freezers are best. Frost-free freezers not only thaw frost over and over (by heating on and off), but thaws the food as well, causing freezer burn. Freezers should be kept at 0° F or less for the best results. (For more advice, see pp. 605-606.)

It's helpful to mark the date and food type as you freeze items, especially if it's an imitation food. The following method doubles as an "inventory" list: Get a magnetic dry-erase board with a magnetic pen (or 3 different colored pens) to put on the freezer door. Number your containers with permanent markers. Each time a container is used, write the number, date and food on the board, and if it's in the fridge or freezer. You'll know exactly what you have without searching. Once a food is eaten, erase the entry.

Non-grain-based foods can be thawed quickly if put in a sieve and water run over them. This removes frost without retaining extra water. If freezing dry foods, be sure to get all the air out of the zipper bag or wrap, as this can cause freezer burn faster. When freezing sauces or other liquids, remember that foods expand when frozen. Never freeze liquids in glass jars. When using plastic jars or bottles, be sure to only fill them ¾ full, leaving an air gap for expansion, or you may have a big mess to clean up. A great way to freeze them is in small zipper bags in 1 cup increments. When ready to use, take the bag and put it in a bowl of hot water. Gradually smooth it through the bag with your hands. It thaws out within minutes without overcooking in the microwave. You'll have fresher sauces and know exactly how much you have. Some foods freeze better and last longer than others, so the following guide can be helpful:

General Food Freezing Guide

Food Item	Freezing Quality & Storage
Avocado	Freezes well only as guacamole or puree, but keeps 5-6 months.
Bagels (Cooked)	Keep very well for many months.
Bananas (Raw)	Peels and freeze in zipper bags as instant "freezer pops". Keep well for a few weeks. Otherwise, they get mushy and separate.

Food Item	Freezing Quality & Storage
Basil (Fresh)	Turns black if frozen as-is. Blanch first by pouring boiling water over it, then let cool before freezing. Keeps several weeks.
Batter (Cookie or Cake)	Do not freeze well.
Batter (Frying)	Keeps very well for many weeks.
Beans (Cooked)	All keep very well for many months.
Beets (Cooked)	Keep very well for many months.
Bell Peppers (Chopped Raw)	Keep very well for many weeks. For better storage, cut in strips. Frozen gets a "cooked" consistency and shortens cooking time.
Bread	Wrapped well in plastic in a zipper bag, it keeps about 1-2 months.
Bread Crumbs	Keeps a very long time in zipper bags.
Bread Dough	(After first rise/punch down.) Keeps 2-4 months if well wrapped.
Butter	Unsalted keeps very well for 1 year. Salted keeps a few weeks.
Cabbage (Raw)	Does not freeze well at all.
Cakes (Pre-baked)	Keep very well for many weeks when wrapped well.
Carrots (Chopped Raw)	Keep for many months, but tend to get a rubbery consistency.
Carrots (Cooked)	Keep very well for many months.
Celery (Chopped Raw)	Keep well for many weeks. Use half as much as fresh in recipes.
Celery (Cooked)	Keep very well for many months.
Cheese (Grated)	Keeps 1-2 years, as long as not melted. Perfect way to store it.
Cheese (Hard)	Becomes crumbly when frozen. For easy shredding, just crumble.
Chicken (Cooked)	Freezes well for many months, although baked tends to dry out unless completely covered in gravy or liquid.
Cholent or Chamin	Keeps well for many months, although large potatoes get mushy.
Cold Cuts	Keep many weeks. For ease, freeze layered with wax paper.
Cookies	Keep well, for several months.
Corn (Cooked)	Keeps very well for many months.
Cottage Cheese	Keeps well and for many months.
Cream Cheese	Tends to separate. Good to use for cooking. Keeps many months.
Cream Soups	Freeze well for many months.
Cream (Whipping)	Doesn't retain whipping quality, freezes well for frozen desserts.
Cucumbers (Chopped Raw)	Don't keep very well and retain a "cooked" consistency.
Dough (Bread or Roll)	Keeps very well for many months.
Dough (Pie Crust)	Keeps very well for many months.

Food Item	Freezing Quality & Storage
Doughnuts	Keep very well for many months.
Dried Fruits	Keep nearly indefinitely.
Egg Rolls	Raw or cooked, keep very well for many months.
Eggs (Hard-Boiled)	Remove from shell and combine with other foods. Keep well.
Eggs (Raw)	Do not freeze well at all, and should never be frozen.
Feta Cheese	Keeps very well for many months.
Fish (Cooked)	Keeps many months if in sauce. Frozen dry, it keeps a few weeks.
Fish (Cooked Gefilte)	Keep many months in container separated by wax paper layers.
Fish (Jarred Gefilte)	Doesn't freeze well. Tends to separate and become like a tasteless mushy sponge full of water.
Fish (Raw)	Keeps very well for many months if kept airtight.
Flour (All Types)	Freezes well and will keep 2 years, but need only be refrigerated.
French Fries (Cooked)	Freeze well for many weeks.
Fried Breaded Foods	Keep very well for many months.
Fruit (Cooked)	Freezes well for many weeks.
Fruit Juice	Freezes well for many weeks.
Fruit (Raw Chopped)	Most freeze well if in water or syrup for many weeks.
Garlic (Raw Chopped)	Put in a plastic container and fill with equal amount of canola or other oil. Sealed well, it keeps nearly indefinitely with no smell.
Garlic (Cooked)	Keep well for many months.
Gelatin	Does not freeze well at all.
Gravies	Keeps very well for many months.
Hamburger Patties	Cooked or raw, keep very well for many months. Freeze in a zipper bag, between wax paper or plastic layers for easy access.
Herbs (Fresh)	For tough-stemmed herbs freeze leaves on flat surface before putting in a bag. Delicate herbs can be frozen whole in sprigs. All keep about 6 months, just as well if not better than dried herbs.
Ice Creams	Keep well 2-3 months, any longer it crystallizes and gets gummy.
Imitation Burgers	Both chub packs and patties freeze well for many months.
Imitation Butter	Keeps very well for several months. It's preferable to store frozen.
Imitation Cheese	Freezes well but slices get soft. Block grates even better frozen!
Imitation Cold Cuts	Freeze for a few months. (Too long they lose flavor and fall apart.)
Imitation Cream Cheese	Freezes well, although package directions usually say not to.

Food Item	Freezing Quality & Storage
Imitation Meats	Sausages, cold cuts and burgers freeze well for many months.
Imitation Sour Cream	Gets a grainy texture but freezes fairly well, especially in recipes.
Jams & Jellies	Keep well for about 6 months.
Lettuce	Do not freeze. It wilts then rots.
Margarine (Stick)	Keeps well for a year.
Meat (Cooked)	Keeps many months if in sauce. Frozen dry, it keeps a few weeks.
Meat (Raw)	Keeps very well for many months if kept airtight.
Milk	Separates slightly, good for cooking. Keeps a few months.
Mushrooms	If raw, they stink! Freeze only after cooking, they keep for a year.
Non-Dairy Creamer	Freeze well can be kept nearly indefinitely.
Nuts	Keep nearly indefinitely, but really only need refrigeration.
Oil	Doesn't freeze unless at 0° F. No need to freeze, just refrigerate.
Olives	Freeze well, but get a bit wrinkled.
Onions (Cooked)	Keep well for many months.
Onions (Raw Chopped)	Put in a plastic container (*not* bags) and fill to cover with avocado or other oil. Sealed well, it keeps nearly indefinitely with no smell.
Parsley (Fresh Whole)	Does not freeze well.
Parve Cottage Cheese	Freezes fairly well for a short period of time.
Pasta (Cooked)	Keeps very well for many months.
Pastries	Keep very well for many months.
Peppers (all types)	Sliced and put in zipper bags, these freeze well for many weeks.
Pickles	Keep well and for many months. (Really only need refrigeration.)
Pie Crusts (Pre-baked)	Keep very well for many months, but are very delicate.
Pie Crusts (Raw)	Keep very well for many months, but are very delicate.
Pies	Baked or raw, they keep very well for many months.
Potatoes (Instant Mashed)	Freezes very well for many months.
Potatoes (Cooked or Raw)	Whether whole or sliced, they do not freeze well at all.
Potatoes (Real Mashed)	Do not freeze well at all.
Poultry	Raw or cooked, it freezes well for many months, although baked tends to dry out unless completely covered in gravy or liquid.
Preserves	Keep well for about 6 months.
Puddings	Keep very well for many months.
Refried Beans	Keep well for a few months. Any longer they lose all flavor.

Food Item	**Freezing Quality & Storage**
Rice (Cooked)	Alone it keeps for well for a few months. If frozen in very oily sauces it keeps many weeks well also. Frozen with other items such as tomatoes, it can separate leaving strange consistency.
Ricotta Cheese	Keeps very well for many months.
Rolls	Wrap well in plastic or foil in a zipper bag. Keeps about 3 months.
Sandwiches	Freeze fairly well for a few weeks, but tend to get soggy.
Sauces	Keep very well for many months.
Seitan (Cooked)	It can keep well for many months if well-wrapped or in gravy.
Seitan (Raw)	Freezes beautifully if well-wrapped. Thaw completely before use.
Sherbets	Keep well 2-3 months, any longer it crystallizes and gets gummy.
Smoked Salmon & Lox	Keep very well for a few weeks, after which they get an off flavor. Freeze between layers of wax paper or plastic for easy access.
Sorbets & Ices	Keep well 2-3 months, any longer it crystallizes and gets gummy.
Soups	Keep very well for many months.
Squash (Chopped Raw)	Does not keep very well, and retains a "cooked" consistency.
Squash (Cooked)	Keeps very well for many months.
Stew	Keeps very well for many months.
Strawberries	Keep well for many months, but do not hold their shape.
Sweet Potatoes (Cooked)	Keep very well for many months.
Tahini (Sesame Seed Paste)	Freezes very well in an airtight container for many months.
Tehina (Chickpea/Sesame Spread)	Does not freeze well.
Textured Vegetable Protein	Rehydrated, keeps nearly indefinitely. Dry doesn't need freezing.
Tofu	Freezes well many months and gives it a better "meatier" texture.
Tomatoes (Chopped Raw)	Keep very well for many weeks, retain a "cooked" consistency.
Tortillas	Corn keep very well for many months. Flour keeps 2-3 months.
Tzatziki Sauce	Can be frozen, but tends to separate. (Flavor is still just as good.)
Vegetables (Chopped Raw)	Keep well for many weeks, some retain a "cooked" consistency.
Vegetables (Oven Roasted)	Eggplant and peppers get mushy but taste okay. Keep for months.
Watercress (Fresh Whole)	Does not freeze well.
Wonton Wrappers (Raw)	Keep very well for many months.
Yams (Cooked)	Keep very well for many months.
Yeast	Keeps up to 2 years in freezer, or 1 year in refrigerator.

Extra Foods & Quick Additions

If you have a little something extra leftover from a meal, don't pitch it! Sometimes all you need in a recipe is a little of something. Often, one ingredient creates a special flavor, or makes the difference between having to run all the way to the store and being able to make a certain dish. "Leftovers" were crucial to help stretch out food bills in the Depression and Wartime era when money was scarce and food was rationed. There's no such thing as food that can't be used (unless it's spoiled). Throwing out leftover food is just plain wasteful! It's a shame because casseroles and other dishes often taste better after having been refrigerated for a day or two. The food "marinates" allowing the flavors to fully blend.

If it weren't for this enterprising attitude of "food recycling", this book may have never been written. It was an "experimental" food that just so happened to taste like a certain other food, which gave birth to an idea that became this book. All due to a tiny bit of leftover tuna added to some falafels! Many "not-enough-for-anything" items can be turned into great dishes. Stale bread is a staple for many recipes and there's a *Halachah* that says we're forbidden to throw out bread (and in general food or anything useful).

"Leftovers" have gotten a bad rap. As long as they're not kept beyond a week in the fridge, are constantly refrigerated or frozen (not left out), and are reheated thoroughly, there's no problem. Microbes only live and propagate under ideal conditions (room temperature or under 165° F).

Extra foods can be eaten as lunches or quick snacks— just pop them in a microwave-safe container and heat. If you hosted a crowd and have surplus food don't toss it! Use it to make something special.

595

Extra Foods Guide

What can I use that for? This guide offers suggestions of what to do with different kinds of foods.

Serving tips for extra or even fresh foods: Use food psychology! Pretty food stimulates finicky appetites. (See "Fancy Food" on p. 449 for more ideas.). Give small portions— leave them wanting more!

Turn your leftovers or surplus into delicious new foods, or add spunk to plain-old weekday dishes…

Dairy Items

Cheese Bricks: Crumble or grate and use on top of refried beans, *parve* spaghetti or chili.

Cottage Cheese: Use in lasagna. Serve with *Hot Pepper Oil* (p. 437) and sunflower seeds.

Cream: Mix with 3 parts water as milk or creamer. Use in *Kraft® Style Cheez Whiz®* (p. 99).

Cream Cheese: Melt on top of asparagus or potatoes, fix *Delectable Asparagus Soup* (p. 153) or *Totally Tubular Appetizers* (p. 141). For a nice spread, heat slightly and add herbs or finely minced olives. Chop into cubes and use as soup garnish for dairy soups.

Croissant: For a great, tasty sandwich, split lengthwise and put 2 cooked soy bacon strips with a slice of pepper-jack cheese in the middle. Heat and eat.

French Onion Dip: Use with soy meat in *Beef Stroganoff* (p. 315), omit onions and sour cream.

Half & Half: Mix with an equal portion of water for a milk substitute.

Ice Cream: Put a little in a glass of milk for shakes, or add to cola or root beer to make floats. Only a scoop or two is required for a delicious old-fashioned banana split— top with syrup and an optional Maraschino cherry.

Liquid "Non-Dairy" Creamer: Stir into cocoa to make it rich and delicious.

Milk: Use milk instead of water for oatmeal or creamy wheat cereals for an extra creamy flavor. Put a bit into cola to make *Flavored Cola* (p. 372).

Oyster Crackers: Crumble and fry in butter, then mix into hot buttered noodles.

Powdered "Non-Dairy" Creamer: Stir into soft margarine to make a low-fat version of butter.

Romano Cheese: Add to buttered spaghetti with garlic salt for a delicious side dish.

Sherbet: Put in lemon lime drinks for a great punch, and add a sprig of mint to make it pretty.

Soups: Dress up with shaped cheese crackers, minced herbs, nuts or sunflower seeds.

Sour Cream: Add a dollop atop soups or chili. Add to soy burger and noodles with gravy to make a dairy Beef Stroganoff. Only 1-2 Tbs. is needed to make homemade butter (p. 417).

String Cheese: Put on top of pizza, refried beans, *parve* chili or spaghetti. Stuff in a parve meatloaf mixed with Italian seasoning and top with spaghetti sauce.

Yogurt: Use like sour cream, or make into salad dressing by adding a bit of lemon and honey.

M*eat* I*tems*

Beef Bologna: Use in recipes calling for pork, or use with imitation cheese on pizzas.

Beef Hot Dogs: Use in *Coney Islands* (p. 174), cut up for baked beans, bean soups or *Chicken Gumbo* (p. 154). They are even good on a baked potato with *parve* imitation cheese.

Chicken: Bread with *Kentucky Fried Chicken® Style Breading Mix* (p. 82) or make *Popeye's® Style Fried Chicken* (p. 293). Cut up in pieces for soups, stir-fry, or casseroles. Chopped chicken goes perfectly in main dishes such as *Chicken Divan* (p. 298), *Chicken à la King* (298), or *Country Chicken Stew with Dumplings* (p. 299).

Chicken (From Soup): Dress up bland soup chicken whether whole or pieces— combine 1 envelope parve dry soup mix (such as ranch or onion), ¼ cup margarine and ¼ cup water. Stir together and heat on medium-low until boiling. Pour over chicken and heat. It's scrumptious and takes only a minute or two to heat through in the microwave.

Chili: Put on spaghetti or rice, burritos, tacos, *Coney Islands* (p. 173) or *Chili Cups* (p. 133).

Cholent or Chamin: Stir into soups or stews to make them more thick and robust.

Cold Cuts: Use with imitation cheese on pizzas or sandwiches. Cut up and use in meat recipes. Roll up with *parve* imitation cream cheese to make *Totally Tubular Appetizers* (p. 141).

Gravy: Serve over rice (sprinkled with green onions) or meat; add to soups or stews to thicken.

Hamburgers: Chop up and put in chili or soup. Cut into pieces for pre-made meatballs.

Meat Balls: Put in soups, stroganoff, or pasta sauce. Chop for chili or taco meat.

Meat Loaf: Break apart and put in recipes calling for hamburger, like spaghetti sauce or chili. Slice in halves and put on a submarine sandwich bun with spaghetti sauce.

Pastrami: Use like chipped beef, or combine with lunch meats to make a super sub sandwich.

Roasts: Cut up in chunks for stews, soups, stir-fry or *Bite-Size Beef Wellington* (p. 305).

Salami: Makes a good substitute for pepperoni on imitation cheese pizzas, or wrap around imitation cream cheese to make *Totally Tubular Appetizers* (p. 141).

Smoked Turkey: 2-inch-thick slices make a perfect ham or pork chop substitute as in *Fried Pork Chops with Stuffing* (p. 326), *Country Ham with Grits and Red-Eye Gravy* (p. 325), or *Glazed Ham* (p. 324). Instead of bacon bits, mince it for *Hash Brown Scramble* (p. 327).

Soups: Garnish with minced raw onion, chopped nuts, or toasted ramen or Chow Mein noodles.

Steaks: Reheat in the microwave to keep moist. Serve with *Blueberry Steak Sauce* (p. 87) for a delicious change of pace. Dress up whole steaks by smothering in mushrooms sautéed in garlic and margarine or onions sautéed until browned. Leftover steak can be cut into chunks for stews, soups, or stir-fry.

Parve Items

Apple Juice: Stir into oatmeal with brown sugar and cinnamon.

Apple Sauce: Dress up with nuts and dessert wine to make *Fancy Applesauce* (p. 414).

Asparagus: Make into a single serving of *Delectable Asparagus Soup* (p. 153).

Baked Potatoes: Scoop out the potato and use for mashed potatoes, saving the skins for *T.G.I. Fridays® Style Potato Skins* (p. 144). Top with cheese, broccoli or mushrooms to doll them up. Make *Superb Potato Patties* (p. 186).

Bananas: Fresh over-ripe bananas can be used in banana bread. Freeze fresh bananas as freezer pops for kids. Green under-ripe ones can be used as a veggie. See pp. 248 and 413.

Beans: There's an endless list for beans, mainly chili and soups, but can be mashed into refried beans or breaded and fried for fritters. Stir in 2 Tbs. taco seasoning per can for chili beans. The broth (pot liquor) from making beans can be diluted, seasoned and used in or as soup.

Black Olives: Slice and serve atop pizza, beans, soup, nachos, and *Chili Cups* (p. 133).

Bread: Stale bread is a staple for *Stove Top® Style Stuffing* (p. 212) *Oyster Dressing* (p. 349) or *Bread Pudding* (p. 409). Make fresh again by microwaving them 20 seconds.

Broccoli: Add cheese sauce, toss together with chicken and sauce, or top a baked potato.

Candy: Add hard candies, lollypops, or other sucking candies to tea water for unusual flavors.

Challah: Use for stuffing/dressing (see Bread), *Salad Croutons* or *Bread Crumbs* (both p. 116). It is delicious when heated and served with *Herb Butters* (p. 438).

Chili: Put in burritos, spaghetti, rice, *Chili Cups* (p. 133) or *Chilaquiles Casserole* (p. 274).

Chocolate Bars: Grate and sprinkle on ice cream, cakes or other sweets for fancy deserts.

Chow Mein Noodles: Sprinkle on top of salads, or use like wheat cereal or snack mixes.

Coffee: Use extra unflavored plain black coffee in *Pumpernickel Bread* (p. 219), *Country Ham with Grits and Red Eye Gravy* (p. 325), or *Arby's® Style Jamocha® Shake* (p. 370).

Corn Flakes: Crush and use as breading for fried chicken.

Corn on the Cob: Cut corn off the ear and use in soups or sauté with onions and peppers in oil.

Couscous: Put in chicken soup as a filler as in *Quick Spicy Chicken Soup* (p. 158), toss with salads, or top with cheese and use like macaroni.

Crackers: Crumble and fry in margarine, then serve mixed into hot buttered noodles.

Cucumbers: Blend with sour cream for delicious *Tzatziki Sauce* (p. 101). Put it in some vinegar with garlic or herbs or hot peppers for custom-flavored pickles.

Eggplant Patties: Put with pasta sauce in a baking pan or glass casserole and top with real or *parve* Mozzarella cheese for a quick eggplant parmesan.

Egg Salad: Use in recipes needing hardboiled eggs, or dress up with curry powder and paprika.

Egg Whites: *Keebler® Style Pecan Sandies* (p. 375) and *From-Scratch White Cake* (p. 389).

Egg Yolks: *Archway® Style Wedding Cake* (p. 380) and *Fancy-Cream-Filled Cookies* (p. 376).

Fish: Mince and use for *Fish Cakes* (p. 361). Use as a treifah seafood substitute.

Fruit: Put on top of ice cream, dip pieces in melted chocolate, or stir into warm gelatin and chill.

Garlic Cloves: Stir minced into potatoes or soup. Make garlic butter for bread or vegetables.

Gefilte Fish: Made from ground fish, it's easily used for the *Fish Cakes* (p. 361) recipe.

Graham Cracker Crumbs: Fry in a little oil for a delicious topping for pies or ice cream.

Hard-Boiled Eggs: Only 1-2 eggs are needed in *Thousand Island Dressing* (p. 86), *Parve Chopped Liver* (p. 139), *Chorizo & Rice* (p. 265), *Asparagus Crab Soup* (p. 343), and *Peruvian Chicken Curry* (p. 296). Chop and use as a garnish for soups or add to salads.

Hard-Boiled Egg Whites: Use to make *Parve Cottage Cheese* (p. 109).

Hard-Boiled Egg Yolks: Use in *Parve Steak Tartare* (p. 140) or *Asparagus Crab Soup* (p. 343).

Hot Peppers: A little goes a long way! Use on *Chili Cups* (p. 133) or chili, in salsa or burritos.

Imitation Crab: Only ½ cup minced crab is needed for scrumptious *Stuffed Flounder* (p. 365).

Imitation Cream Cheese: Chop into cubes to use as soup garnish. (See other uses in Dairy.)

Imitation Sour Cream: Add a dollop on top of soups or chili. (See other uses in Dairy.)

Instant Mashed Potato Flakes: Use it like flour, it also makes great breading.

Jam or Jelly: Stir into plain yogurt. Use as icing for cupcakes or vanilla cookies add sprinkles.

Liquid Parve Non-Dairy Creamer: Stir into cocoa or instant milk to make it rich and delicious.

Maple Syrup: Stir into baked beans for extra flavor, or use to dress up oatmeal.

Mashed Potatoes: Stir into soups for thickening, or make *Superb Potato Patties* (p. 186) or *Simple Potato Pierogies* (p. 184).

Matzah: Use as a substitute for crackers, a base for pizza, or chop and use like bread crumbs.

Mushrooms: Sautéed, they can go in anything. Serve atop steak, potatoes, pizza, or eggs. Put on top of a baked potato with Parmesan cheese and melted margarine for a great meal.

Non-Dairy Creamer (Any): Stir into instant mashed potatoes to make them taste extra rich.

Nuts: Grind and sprinkle on salads or ice cream. A sizable amount can be used as pie crust.

Oatmeal (Dry): Stir into cereals such as granola with milk. (A delicious way to get extra fiber.)

Oatmeal (Prepared): Revive with extra water, juice or milk. maple syrup, nuts, fruit, or applesauce. Add to meat loaf or *Goetta Sausage* (p. 113). Use in *Parve* or *Oat Milk* (p. 85).

Onion Dip: If *parve* imitation, use in *Beef Stroganoff* (p. 315), omit sour cream and onions.

Onion Rings: Make your own *parve* French-fried onions using onion rings- Spread them out flat on a cookie sheet, and bake at 400° F until crisp. Crumble in casseroles or salads.

Onions: Freeze in oil for future use. Put on top of beans, chili, pizza, stir into omelets, or soups.

Onion Soup: Add to a thick dry cholent, stews or dry mashed potatoes.

Onion Soup Mix: Add to cholent, soups stews. Sprinkle on mashed potatoes.

Oyster Crackers: Crumble and fry in margarine, then mix into hot buttered noodles.

Peanut Butter: Add flavorings for flair, or use in the surprising *Southern Belle Soup* (p. 153).

Pickles: Mince to make relish or tartar sauce. Add it to a jar of hot peppers for zippy pickles.

Pizza Sauce: Put on bagels or matzah with cheese. Stir into omelets, or add to tomato soups.

Popcorn: Dress up plain popcorn with seasonings found in *Stovetop-Popped Corn* (p. 126). Mix with marshmallow crème and roll into balls to make tasty treats.

Potatoes: For boiled sliced or chopped potatoes, when just about done, drain most the water and add a few Tbs. parve onion or other soup mix to make delicious flavored potatoes.

Potato Flakes: Use like flour for thickening soups. it makes great breading for fried chicken.

Powdered Parve Non-Dairy Creamer: Stir into margarine to make a low-fat version of butter. Stir into cocoa mixes to make extra-rich hot chocolate.

Preserves: Stir into plain yogurt. Use like frosting for cupcakes and add sprinkles.

Puff Pastry Sheets: Use in *Doggies in a Blanket* (p. 135), or make mini croissants- Cut thawed sheets diagonally in half, slightly stretch corners to make a pie wedge shape. Brush with melted margarine, roll larger end toward smaller end. Put on greased cookie sheet, turn ends inward to form crescent shapes. Bake 25 minutes in a preheated 400° F oven.

Ramen Noodles (Dry): Chop and toast in the oven for a truly delicious salad topping.

Ramen Noodle Soup Base Packets: Use 1 packet as a substitute for 1 tsp. bouillon. Stir into pasta, meatloaf, mashed potatoes or rice for extra flavor.

Ramen Noodle Soups: To get unusual flavors, fix 1 pkg. chicken flavor, plus add the following:

  Chicken Teriyaki- 1½ tsp. brown sugar + ½ tsp. soy sauce + dash garlic powder.

  Chili- 1 Tbs. taco seasoning + 2 Tbs. salsa (for extra spicy add ⅛ tsp. red pepper flakes).

  Creamy Chicken- ⅛ tsp. garlic powder +. 1 Tbs. *parve* dry non-dairy creamer, OR 1 cup soy milk (omit 1 cup water), OR ½ cup *parve* liquid non-dairy creamer (omit ½ cup water).

  Curry- 1 tsp. curry powder + ½ tsp. ground ginger + dash cayenne + ½ tsp. ground cumin.

  Hot N' Spicy: ⅛ tsp. cayenne pepper.

  Mexican- dash red pepper flakes + dash garlic powder + dash ground cumin.

Ramen Noodles (Package): For variety, cook and drain then add seasoning packet.

Refried Beans: If unseasoned, use instead of beans in *Parve Chopped Liver* (p. 139). Top with cheese and taco sauce (I like it with hot peppers) for a single serving dish similar to *Taco Bell® Style Pintos N' Cheese* p. 127).

Rice: Rice keeps a long time. Make *Parve Cottage Cheese* (p. 109), *Rice Pudding* (p. 409) or *Fried Rice* (p. 281, 282, 357), mix with chili and sour cream, top with raw onion. Add to *Indian Curried Bean & Lentil Soup* (p. 170) and reduce water. For rice milk, puree plain rice with equal or greater amount water, adding vanilla and sugar to taste.

Rolls: Chop up and use for *Stove Top® Style Stuffing* (p. 212) *Oyster Dressing* (p. 349) or *Bread Pudding* (p. 409). Make fresh again by microwaving them 20 seconds.

Salsa: Stir into omelets, vegetable soups, stir into hamburger or soy meat to make taco filling. It makes a great substitute for tomatoes in virtually any recipe.

Salt Herring: When soaked, it's a substitute for oysters or clams. See *Kosher Clams* (p. 330).

Saltine Crackers: Crumble and fry in margarine, then mix into hot buttered noodles.

Scrambled Eggs: Combine with rice, onions and soy sauce for *Fried Rice* (p. 281, 282, 357). Dice and add to soups with chopped green onions as a garnish.

Seitan: Chop 2 beef flavored cutlets, combine with *Beef Gravy* (p. 102) and 1 (15 oz.) can mixed veggies to make a delicious and quick stew. Chop up in pieces and add to a stir fry, or coat chicken flavored pieces with breading and fry for popcorn chicken.

Soups: Sprinkle with minced herbs, green onions, nuts, toasted ramen or Chow Mein noodles.

Soy Ice Cream: Add to water and creamer for *parve* malts and shakes, or soda for *parve* floats.

Spaghetti Sauce: Stir into omelets, add to tomato-based soups, or use it as pizza sauce. To make a different meatloaf, combine with some garlic powder, Italian seasoning and burger. Mix in shredded *parve* cheese for M or dairy cheese for D or P. Top with more spaghetti sauce and cook as normal.

Sunflower Seeds: Stir into salads or cottage cheese.

Tahini: Use for sandwiches like peanut butter, or make *Southern Belle Soup* (p. 153). (Not to be confused with "Tehina", a Chickpea and Sesame spread.)

Tomatoes: Chop and add to soups, rice or chili. If you lots of home-grown tomatoes to use, make *Super Salsa* (p. 96). Smother a halved tomato with sour cream and bacon bits.

Tortilla Chips: Crush or use whole for *Chilaquiles Casserole* (p. 274), make a single serving of *Taco Bell® Style Nachos* (p. 128) or *Taco Bell® Style Nachos Bell Grande®* (p. 275). Crushed finely, they can be used as a coating for fried chicken.

Tuna: Use in casseroles, or *Breaded Kosher Oysters* (p. 353), the recipe that started it all.

Vegetables: Any can be used in soups, stews, or stir-fries. Dress up with sauces or garnishes.

Wheat Germ: Mix with yogurt or sprinkle on top of canned veggies for a healthy variation.

Wheat Berries: Use cooked berries like Textured Vegetable Protein (TVP®) in place of meat. Use in place of brown rice in recipes or side dishes.

Wine: Add to long-simmering meat or seitan dishes for a luscious gourmet flavor.

Safe and Unsafe Plastic Usage

In Section 2, we explored how plastics can affect *kashrut*. This guide presents how to safely use kitchen plastics and how to avoid harmful misuse. If one knows the principles that affect *kashrut*, they will easily be able to deal with plastic. The factors were known by our Sages hundreds of years ago: Heat causes leaching of *treifah* (and unsafe chemicals), as does sharpness (acidity), and time (over 24 hours). One realizes how important it is when the Torah states "Be cautious for yourself and greatly cautious of your soul" (*Devarim* 4:9). One who isn't cautious and knowingly refuses to remedy a dangerous situation is said to be judged in the Heavenly Court as having taken their own life. This is why we don't combine fish and meat. Due to life's sanctity, it's more important to avoid risk than even to avoid *treifah* food!

With the exception of plastic wrap, the International Universal Recycling Code is often on the bottom of a container or on a package, and can help determine a plastic's safe or unsafe usage. Its center contains a plastic or resin identification code, (either a number or letters) to designate the specific plastic. If not present on a container or package and there is no mention of being safe for food or microwave use, discard it and don't even think of using it for food! Always use plastic as intended, and follow directions of use when listed. If you reuse containers, be aware that not all plastics can be used for heating food.

Certain plastics are safe for short-term microwave use, dishwashers and food storage. Although not mandatory to display, the international fork and cup symbol is found on some safe kitchenware. Less often, it displays a "safe for microwave use" symbol, or those words. Often, plastics can contain *treifah* ingredients or chemical compounds that can leach into food when heated, so it's important to keep them from getting too hot. Greasy foods often affect plastic and cause chemicals to leach out. Oily tomato products and highly acidic foods can do this and the inverse, leaching into plastic and staining it, especially if hot. Many plastics are kosher and safe, such as Teflon®, some are non-kosher, and others are neither kosher nor safe. There has been concern with chemicals used in processing that contribute to a plastic's flexibility, strength or rigidity. Some can be potentially carcinogenic (causing various cancers), or contain endocrine disrupting chemicals (EDCs) that mimic estrogen, possibly causing reproductive harm. Plastics are listed in order of resin identification code with the actual name or brand. Below the code, the following symbols show information on the particular plastic:

General Products Made of This: Safe Kitchen Usage: Potential Harm:

Recycle # 1 (PETE or PET)- Polyethylene Terephthalate or Polyester:

♳ As thin clear plastic, peanut butter jars, soda bottles and some disposable bowls are made of this. When thicker and opaque, this plastic is used for heatable meal trays. It is commonly used for fabric.

🖒 Safe for food contact. When buying vegetable oil, this is a safe plastic. If clear, it is best if used cold and never heated. If opaque, it can be used for heating food, but not for prolonged microwave cooking. It is considered a single-use plastic and should not be reused for food heating.

🖓 Do not use this in its clear form for heating in microwaves or putting very hot foods or grease in, it shrinks and melts when hot, leaving a big mess!

Recycle # 2 (HDPE)- High Density Polyethylene:

♴ Typically, milk jugs, margarine and cottage cheese tubs are made of this. Due to chemical resistance, it is generally used for strong household chemicals such as ammonia or bleach.

🖒 Safe for food contact with dry or cold food. It is for single-use and should not be reused for heating.

🖓 Don't buy vegetable oils that are contained in this type of plastic, as the oil absorbs non-kosher additives from the plastic. Considered single-use plastic, there is a possibility that heating can draw out non-kosher additives and harmful chemicals into food, especially if the food is oily.

Recycle # 3 (PVC)- Polyvinyl Chloride or Vinyl:

♵ Used in commercial plastic wrap, non-stick cookware utensils, plumbing pipes, toys or upholstery.

🖒 The resin identification code is not listed for plastic wraps. If heating in the microwave, keep at least 1 inch away from food. If meat or cheese is wrapped in it, the oils cause chemicals to leach into food over time, so it's best to store these in zipper bags. The FDA considers any chemical levels to be safe.

🖓 Prolonged food contact should be avoided. PVC can contain possible EDC phthalates including both DEHA and DEHP (also a possible carcinogen), and can contain BPA, a known EDC. BPA leaches into food. PVC is toxic if burned. Most plastic wrap companies have switched to LDPE.

Recycle # 4 (LDPE)- Low Density Polyethylene:

♶ Typically used for plastic zipper bags, mustard or honey squeeze-bottles, and recently plastic wrap.

🖒 Safe for food contact, especially if cold. Can use to reheat food for short durations in the microwave.

🖓 Don't use to cook in for long periods of time in the microwave, and do not use as a boil-in bag for food, (such as for some frozen foods or rice). Do not store highly oily foods in zipper bags, as they become semi-permeable and the oil seeps right through within a day or two, leaving a puddle of oil.

Recycle # 5 (PP)- Polypropylene:

♲ Most plastic microwave-safe kitchenware is made of this, as well as disposables and some margarine tubs. Usually this is the main type of plastic to display the international fork and cup symbol below.

🍴 Generally safe for food contact and food reheating in the microwave, however extremely long durations of cooking should be avoided. Oily foods, or those high in fat or sugar should be reheated for only a short amount of time, as they can get hot enough to melt plastic and become infused into it.

👎 Don't buy vegetable oils that are in this type of plastic, as the oil can absorb non-kosher additives. Do not use it to cook oily foods or dry goods in the microwave. Oily foods can case warping, scoring, melting, chemical leaching, and if too hot, dry or oily foods can cause the container to melt and leave pinholes. When frozen, containers made of this can be very brittle and usually shatter if dropped.

Recycle # 6 (PS)- Polystyrene, Polystyrene Foam, Foam, Styrofoam™ (made of Styrene):

♲ Used for some disposable plastic utensils and containers. Most commonly used for polystyrene foam cups, vegetable and meat trays, egg cartons, packing peanuts and cushioning for delicate items.

🍴 Foam cups and bowls should be kosher certified, and can be used in the microwave to reheat food in short durations. Foods such as soups having foam cups advise cooking the contents in something else.

👎 Do not use PS for microwave cooking- if thin, it can develop holes if too hot. Polystyrene foam is considered "unstable when heated", can melt if it gets too hot, is flammable and never breaks down in the environment. Styrene is a suspected carcinogen.

Recycle # 7 (Other)- Miscellaneous plastics other than 1-6, including Polycarbonate (PC) and ABS Copolymers, Polyurethane, Polymethyl Methacrylate, Nylon, various Epoxy Resins and all unknown plastics:

♲ Some food containers, baby bottles and 5-gallon water bottles are made of PC. Children's dental sealants can contain PC or epoxy resin. Most food and beverage cans are lined with epoxy resins, yet only the metal recycle symbol is displayed on the label, and never the resin identification code. High-temperature Nylon is used for oven baking bags and non-stick kitchen utensils, as well as fabric.

🍴 Nylon is safe and unassociated with health risks. It is best to use other # 7 plastics temporarily for non-heat dry food storage. The FDA considers BPA levels for food containers too low to cause harm.

👎 Never use # 7 plastics in the microwave for heating or cooking food. Bisphenol-A (BPA) is mainly used in PC and epoxy resins, can possibly cause reproductive harm due to EDCs, and is potentially carcinogenic. BPA will leach out of plastics and into food. Baby products containing BPA and PC plastics are banned in Canada.

Kitchen Item Purchase & Usage

For deciding on future purchases, ways to improve energy efficiency, or extending the life of kitchen items, this guide sorts through the details so you can make an intelligent decision and know what to look for. It addresses pros and cons, usage, and common misconceptions of major appliances and items.

Refrigerators or Freezers

General Details: Although refrigerators and freezers do not have many *kashrut* concerns, they can vary when it comes to food storage quality. Refrigerators should keep food at 35-40° F or less, and freezers should be at 0° F or less. Decades ago, all freezers had to be defrosted manually, which took a lot of time. Refrigerator-freezers nowadays are almost always self-defrost or "frost-free", which is a big convenience. Unfortunately, convenience comes with a price tag. Each time the defrost cycle goes on, it heats the area slightly to melt any frost. This also defrosts food and causes freezer burn, especially in items like bread that take little time to thaw. These freezers should be used for short-term storage. If foods are to be stored long-term, it's advisable to get a separate manual-defrost freezer to keep food at sub-zero temperatures at all times. An extra freezer comes in handy for Passover, as well as keeping food fresher for a longer time.

Passover Issues: *Kashering* is not an issue for refrigerators, but models should be easy-to-clean for Passover. Avoid those with many grooves, crevices or hard-to-reach areas where crumbs can hide.

Shabbat Issues: The simpler model the better, unless you get a special fridge with "Sabbath mode". Test during a weekday, or better yet at the store before purchase. Make sure fan motors, digital displays and lights don't go on if the door is opened. Light bulbs should be easily accessible to unscrew for *Shabbat* and *Yom Tov* [Holiday or Festival] (also called a "*Chag*" in Hebrew). Avoid models with buzzers, audio messages, digital displays, or lights that go on when doing certain actions. If you don't want to worry about unscrewing bulbs, there is a handy device that clips onto a refrigerator or freezer's light switch next to the door. It can be slid on and off, allowing the light to stay on for weekdays, and off on *Shabbat*. This is great for hard-to-reach bulbs. (One must remember to slide it on *Erev Shabbat*, and the company advertises they can give you a reminder call.) If you want a refrigerator with an icemaker, be sure it can be turned off before *Shabbat*, or that the hanger bar can be lifted so that if ice is removed it won't make more ice. Ice or water dispenser on a door cannot be used on *Shabbat* or *Yom Tov* since they have electric pumps or motors. (They don't work like plumbing.) Buying a refrigerator with Sabbath mode ensures the devices will be off on *Shabbat* and *Yom Tov*— but only if set properly beforehand.

Stoves

If you must get a new stove for *kashrut* reasons, there are features to look for. Try to get a stovetop (as well as the interior of the oven if buying a freestanding unit) in stainless steel, not porcelain-enamel for easy *kashering*. If at all possible, stay away from glass cooktop stoves. Although easy to clean, they aren't easily *kashered*, and most hold they cannot be kashered at all. Attempting to *kasher* it can risk cracking the glass and ruining it.

Something to note in freestanding stoves, is where the oven vents heat and moisture. Some models vent through the back, others in the front. Some vent through a stove burner, usually located in the rear. This particular burner will affect the *kashrut* of what is on it. If you buy a stove that vents through a burner, never use that burner for an opposite food when the oven is on at the same time. The burner must be *kashered* after each use of the oven, or use it with the same type of food that is baked in the oven.

Shabbat Issues: A stove should ideally have as few features as possible, with knobs, and no lights, digital features, buzzers etc. Research first—buy later! Modern stoves now have a safety device that causes them to go off after 12 hours. For *Shabbat* and holidays, you'll need to keep them on the entire time. Stoves made before the 1990s had few features and did not have the 12-hour safety feature. If you get a new one, make sure it has "Sabbath Mode", which bypasses the safety switch, enabling it to stay on until you turn it off. However, some stoves billed as having "Sabbath Mode", may switch off after 24 hours, which interferes with holiday usage. There are also potential problems due to power failures. A reliable rabbi or *kashrut* agency has a list of stoves that meet the *Halachic* criteria, or you can ask a manufacturer about the safety feature details.

General Cookware: Special glass pots can be used on the stove but be sure it's not too cold or the extreme temperature change could cause it to crack or shatter. For any cookware, be absolutely sure that when you have it on the heat that it contains food or liquid. An empty pot or pan can get so hot that it will melt and can ruin a stove, or the cookware itself. See the specifics on gas and electric stoves later for the vast differences pertaining to metal cookware. Cookware is not usually cheaper or more expensive because of brand or quality, but because it is designed for specific usage.

ELECTRIC STOVES: In general, cooking with electric is more efficient, safer, and usually is much cheaper. The burner element spreads out heat evenly, efficiently, and depending on the cookware used, can reduce cooking time. Electric heat is easily produced from many different sources, and in some cases, it's becoming cheaper to use than gas. It's very safe, efficient, and there are no toxic side effects.

Advantages: Electric is highly efficient in that latent heat from burners will continue cooking with no cost if one plans to turn it off ahead of time. Burners can usually be turned off 5 minutes beforehand and still provide enough heat to cook for the duration. By far, the quickest, easiest item to *kasher* is an electric stove's coil-style burner since they are self-*kashering*. Cookware is much lighter for electric stoves.

Disadvantages: Electric stoves can't be used during a power outage. Burners cannot be adjusted on *Yom Tov*, and temperatures can be hard to determine. Thick or heavy cookware takes longer to heat, isn't as efficient, and also takes a long time to cool, causing food to become overcooked and lose nutrients.

Cookware: Cookware for electric stoves is the total inverse of gas. Thinner pots are made for electric burners, since they heat quickly and need less cooking time. The stove can be turned off early and the latent burner heat used to cook with, which is much more efficient and literally costs nothing. Electric range cookware should have flat bottoms to fit snugly against the burner; otherwise, they won't heat quite as efficiently.

Cheaper and thinner cookware doesn't necessarily mean poor quality! Less metal goes into it, so it is cheaper to produce and is lighter weight. It can be aluminum or stainless steel, which are easily *kashered*. It can also be painted or porcelain-enamel, which can't be *kashered*, but due to the price it is easily replaced. These even come in many colors for easy color-coding. For the types of cookware materials, see the next entry on "Cookware" under "Gas Stoves" for care.

Non-stick cookware is generally made of aluminum. It too comes in a variety of colors but can't be *kashered*. Most manufacturers recommend coating the cooking surface with oil before first used. Most cookware is coated with Polytetrafluoroethylene (PTFE) known as Teflon®, a very safe plastic. It's only problematic if it reaches over 500° F and deteriorates emitting toxic fumes, which have been known to kill small pet birds as they have a low body weight (and obviously aren't good for humans either). Therefore, never leave non-stick cookware unattended while cooking or put it on a hot burner with nothing inside. If cookware is empty, it can reach the toxic temperature and burn the coating. Never use harsh scrub pads such as steel wool for cleaning, and only use nylon, silicone or wooden utensils for stirring. Using metal will scrape the coating, and cookware can then potentially rust. Once this starts it spreads and eventually black flecks will be in your food. Less quality non-stick cookware can deteriorate over time.

If you already have a thick metal pot and food burns on the bottom (rather common), here is a helpful, easy cleaning method: Put an inch of water in the pot or pan (covering the burnt-on food), and heat it. Turn off the burner and let it cool. It now should be fairly easy to clean with a scrubber pad.

GAS STOVES: In general, cooking with a gas stove entails harsh heat directed in one spot. If you have thin cookware, it causes uneven cooking and literally food can be burnt in the center, yet still cold on the outer edges of the pot or pan. Once known for being cheap, with rising fuel costs and depleted natural resources, gas is quickly becoming more expensive in certain areas. Older gas stoves had to be lit manually, and later there were continuously burning pilot lights (unless it blew out and had to be re-lit). Nowadays, most stoves have electronic ignition, making them virtually identical to electric in care.

Advantages: Gas has a very quick response time for adjusting temperatures. The heat is instantly on or instantly off. Another advantage is you can visually see the level of the flame to know how hot it is. You can also adjust the flame up or down on a *Yom Tov*. In the event of a power outage, gas stoves can still be used (via the old-fashioned way), whereas electric burners are not usable.

Disadvantages: Gas leaks can potentially cause an explosion, dangerous carbon monoxide fumes, and have an unpleasant odor, which gas companies add for protection enabling one to smell it if it is leaking. If you are using a gas stove on *Shabbat* or *Yom Tov*, there is a possibility that a pilot light or flame can go out when nobody is home and the house could be filled with deadly fumes. Cookware is very heavy.

If a gas stove has electronic ignition, often the knobs are designed in such a way that if they are turned too far they can hit the ignition sparker, which is an *averah* [sin]. Each time it sparks, a fire is created, much the same as using a car engine. Gas stoves aren't as easy to *kasher*, but are *kasherable*. However, they are much more of a hassle than *kashering* electric stoves, both time and safety-wise.

Cookware: Gas cookware doesn't come in many colors for color-coding a kitchen, and can occasionally be available with non-stick coatings. (For care of nonstick coated pots and pans, see "Cookware" under "Electric Stoves" on the previous page.) Gas cookware is generally much more expensive and very heavy due to the amount of metal used, (a consideration for those who can't lift heavy items). In order to spread out the harsh heat of gas, the cookware is designed to distribute heat evenly and hold heat after the flame has been turned off. Gas heat is instant on, instant off, with little latent heat, and the heavy cookware compensates for this. Thicker gauge cookware, iron skillets, and cookware with heavy bottoms are designed for gas stoves, and are the most efficient means of cooking for them. Cookware is often rounded on the bottom to better fit the gas grates. Other materials are usually the same as electric but thicker.

Cast iron cooking surfaces must be coated with vegetable oil to keep from rusting, building up a barrier of oil and carbon. However, carbon is carcinogenic (can cause cancer). They take a long time to heat, but stay hot. They can react with acidic foods and rust. Some foods turn black if cooked on cast iron.

Carbon steel is used in woks and will rust unless coated with oil, as with cast iron.

Copper heats well and distributes heat evenly. However, it tarnishes easily and will react with acidic foods. Most copper cookware is lined with other metals.

Aluminum is lighter and distributes heat well, although it's generally soft and easily dented. It has been associated with Alzheimer's disease, although this has not been proven. Unless it is anodized, aluminum can react with acidic foods, turning the interior dark colors and changing the flavor of some foods. Anodized aluminum doesn't react, is harder and more durable.

Stainless steel is heavy-duty and very easy to care for. It doesn't react with food or easily dent. Often, stainless steel and aluminum cookware have a thick disk on the bottom to distribute heat evenly.

Ovens

There is not much difference between gas and electric, other than lighting. Older gas ovens had to be lit manually, and later there were continuously burning pilot lights (unless the pilot blew out and had to be re-lit). Nowadays, most gas ovens have electronic ignition, making them virtually identical to electric in care. In the event of a power outage, they can still be used (via the old-fashioned way), whereas electric ovens are not usable. The last difference is that electric freestanding ovens have a drawer for storage (preferably for the type of food the oven is used for), whereas the drawer in a gas oven is the broiler.

A double oven is a nice feature if you don't want to mess with double-wrapping in foil. However, you must make sure that one oven doesn't vent into the other oven, or it defeats the whole purpose!

In a freestanding stove with oven, the oven can vent through a rear stove burner. It is not a problem if you only use your oven for *parve* foods. However, it could potentially affect the *kashrut* status of what is placed on that burner, as it shouldn't be used for an opposite gender food when the oven is on. The burner should be *kashered* after oven use, or it should be used it with the same type food that is baked in the oven.

Before using a new oven for the first time, wash the interior and racks with warm soapy water and rinse well, just as for any new pot, due to oily coatings. The racks needn't be immersed in a *mikvah* (see section on "Immersion" pp. 57-61), since they don't make direct contact with food.

Passover Issues: A self-cleaning oven is always better, as it eliminates a lot of hassle for *kashering*. It is ideal to get an oven with a stainless steel interior instead of porcelain-enamel, but they are expensive and not common. For non-self-cleaning ovens, preferably order a second set of racks or buy an oven insert.

Shabbat Issues: It's best to get an oven with simple old-fashioned dials, and no lights, digital readouts, or buzzers. Check during a weekday to be sure no lights or displays are turned on in the panel if the door is opened. Modern ovens have a safety switch that turns the oven off after 12 hours. (See *Stoves*, p. 606.) For *Shabbat* and holidays, you may need to keep it on the entire time. Pre-1990 ovens are great, they have few features, and don't have the 12-hour safety switch. It may be beneficial to get a new oven with "Sabbath mode" that bypasses the safety switch. Some "Sabbath mode" ovens may switch off after 24 hours, which is a problem for holiday usage. They do pose a potential problem during power failures. Ask a reliable *kashrut* agency for a list of models.

Bakeware: Non-specific to gas or electric. Reduce baking time for glass, ceramic and dark metals.
Glass such as Pyrex or Corningware is easy to care for. Never put foods directly from the freezer into the oven, temperature extremes cause glass to crack. *Kasherability* is debatable. Porcelain-enamel-coated or painted metal is not *kasherable*. It can chip and rust. Metal bakeware comes in steel or aluminum. Bare steel must be washed and dried thoroughly, as it can rust with moisture. Aluminum can dent easily. All are *kasherable* unless they are nonstick. Silicone bakeware has proven to be safe both from chemical dangers and for average baking temperatures (can be heated to over 600° F). It can go directly from freezer to hot oven, has non-stick properties, and baked goods are easily removed. (Set on a metal pan to keep sturdy.) Sharp objects can't be used with it, and it's not *kasherable*.

Baking: Allow ½ hour per lb. at 350° F for solid meat like roasts or whole poultry. Bone-in meats take longer to bake than boneless. Exposed foods will brown, so double-wrapped foods won't brown but still taste just as good, even for broiling. Allow about 15 minutes more baking time for double-wrapped foods. If an oven runs cold, the old-fashioned knob types can be adjusted, otherwise bake items slightly longer.

ELECTRIC: Baking with electric is more efficient. There must be a light that comes on to show when the element is burning, in order remove warm food on *Shabbat*, and to bake on *Yom Tov*.
Advantages: It is very safe and efficient.
Disadvantages: The temperature cannot be adjusted for baking on *Yom Tov*.

GAS: Gas is easier for keeping food warm on *Shabbat*, and doing actual baking on *Yom Tov*.
Advantages: The flame must be on to open and close the door or adjust temperatures on a *Yom Tov*. Gas lets one see and hear when it is on, and also enables food to be removed from the oven on *Shabbat*.
Disadvantages: Potential gas leaks, carbon monoxide fumes and pilot light or flame blowouts.

Sinks

CHINA AND PORCELAIN-ENAMEL: These are often found in older homes, either as inset sinks or part of a huge sink-board. They are regaining popularity as a "chic" item in non-Jewish homes.

Advantages: China and porcelain sinks often come in a variety of colors.

Disadvantages: These chip easily and not *kasherable* according to most opinions. Glass shatters in it when dropped. Unless your rabbi holds porcelain can be *kashered*, it must be lined with foil for Passover.

STAINLESS STEEL: These are very common everywhere, and require no special care.

Advantages: It is easily *kashered*. It is readily available and reasonable. Dropped glasses don't usually break when dropped in stainless steel, as they tend to have a slight bouncing effect to them.

Disadvantages: Cheap grades can rust if concentrated dish soap is left on it. It only comes in one color. High-gloss "polished" style stainless will show scratches very easily.

PURE MARBLE AND GRANITE: Generally found in more affluent homes.

Advantages: If made of pure stone only, and as long as they are smooth and polished, these can be *kashered* for normal year-round and for Passover use. They look elegant and can be many different colors.

Disadvantages: These are very expensive. Glasses will shatter if dropped in them.

COMPOSITE: These are made of plastic and ground stone, and look like granite or marble.

Advantages: They look very elegant and can come in some different colors.

Disadvantages: These cannot be *kashered* for Passover use and must be covered with aluminum foil. They can chip and scratch easily, and are somewhat expensive.

CORIAN: Corian® can be molded into shapes such as scallop shells for an elegant-look.

Advantages: They can look elegant, come in different shades, and are readily available.

Disadvantages: They can chip and scratch easily, and can be expensive. They cannot be *kashered*, and must be completely covered with foil for Passover. Use care with glasses or plates or they will usually shatter if dropped. These sinks scratch easily and can chip.

Countertops

A trivet should ideally put down before placing a hot pot on any countertop. Not only does this keep the counter kosher, but helps preserve it since many can be ruined by heat. Never cut directly on a counter, it will scratch and never the same.

LAMINATES: Perhaps the most common type of countertops, there are many brands (such as Formica®). They may or may not be *kasherable* for general use. Ask your rabbi how he holds.

Advantages: These are available in a wide variety of colors, patterns and textures to match virtually any kitchen décor. They are reasonably priced compared to other countertops.

Disadvantages: According to many opinions, laminates cannot be *kashered* for Passover and must be covered over with foil. When laminates scorch, they can never be brought back to their original condition.

WOOD: These can be very beautiful, but are not very common.

Advantages*:* If smooth and crack-less, they may be *kashered* for Passover or normal use. If they are not smooth, they can be sanded down and then *kashered*.

Disadvantages: Wood is not very practical in a kitchen. It scratches and gouges very easily, can dent if hit too hard, and can absorbs food. If it has cracks or holes there is no way to *kasher* it, and it must be covered with foil for Passover. If scratched, it must be sanded and can make it uneven and less pretty.

PORCELAIN: These are usually found in old homes in the form of a giant sink-board.

Advantages: If you're into nostalgia, you may like an old porcelain-enamel sink-board.

Disadvantages*:* These are not *kasherable* according to most opinions. They chip very easily and when they do, they often rust, and any glasses dropped in them will shatter. The entire surface must be covered with foil for Passover, unless your rabbi holds porcelain can be *kashered*.

STAINLESS STEEL: These are the standard for use in commercial kitchens.

Advantages: Stainless steel is easily *kashered* both for normal use and for Passover.

Disadvantages: It is very expensive. The thicker the gauge of steel, the more expensive it will be. It can dent if hit too hard, and can scratch if cut on directly. It only comes in one color.

ROCK: Pure granite and marble. Generally found in very affluent homes.

Advantages: If they are made of pure stone only, (as long as they are smooth and polished), they can be *kashered* for both normal and Passover use. These are very elegant, and come in a few different colors.

Disadvantages: These can chip and scratch easily and are usually expensive.

COMPOSITE: These are essentially made of plastic and ground stone, and look like granite or marble.

Advantages: They are elegant looking, and come in some different colors.

Disadvantages: These cannot be *kashered* and must be covered over with aluminum foil. They can chip and scratch easily, and are somewhat expensive.

CORIAN: Corian® can be molded into various styles and shapes.

Advantages: These can look elegant, come in different shades and are readily available. They can be *kashered* for general or Passover use by sanding down a layer.

Disadvantages: They can chip and scratch easily. They are not practical to *kasher* for Passover and should ideally be covered over with foil. The method of *kashering* for regular use is extremely messy, must be done by a contractor, and there are no guarantees as to how it will look afterwards.

TILE: This is rarely used for countertops. Tiles are usually embedded in grout on wood.

Advantages: Available in a variety of colors and finishes to match any décor. When installing new, decorative tiles can be added with plain ones for artistic flair. Smooth tile may possibly be *kasherable*, but the grout can be a serious problem. Ask your rabbi how he holds.

Disadvantages: Unless sealed properly with silicone sealer, the grout usually can stain. If any tiles are chipped or rough, they cannot be *kashered* and must be covered with foil for Passover. If a tile is chipped or cracked, it is not easily replaced (if it can be at all), and may not match unless you have leftovers.

Microwave Ovens

Some microwave ovens have a simple timer dial, and others can be very fancy with special buttons for items like coffee, potatoes, or popcorn. The higher the wattage, the faster food cooks. A very high wattage microwave is 1000-1200 watts. High wattage is 800-900, average is 600-800, and very low wattage is 300-500. Recipes in this book are based on average wattage. Cooking in a microwave is quick and efficient. Just as an electric stove's latent heat can be utilized, solid or oily foods continue cooking once the power is off. Never run any microwave when it is empty — the waves have nowhere to go and it can become damaged.

Kashrut Issues: It is advisable not to get an over-the-stove model, unless the microwave is designated the same type of food as what is cooking on the stove. If you have an over-the-stove model, be absolutely sure the door is closed every time you are going to cook, as steam can render the microwave *treifah*.

Shabbat Issues: Since microwaves aren't used on *Shabbat* or *Yom Tov* days, there are no issues of use.

Passover Issues: The only real concern is that it be easy to clean and *kasher* for Passover.

Microwave Cooking: Microwave ovens cook by exciting molecules in food. As the molecules move faster it makes friction, which causes heat and results in cooking. Foods cook from the outside in, so occasional stirring is required for any liquids or foods that are not solid. Foods are easily heated with little or no preparation. Items can go from freezer to microwave with little or nothing done in between. In general, most foods can be cooked very well. Most meat browns automatically and foods with high fat or oil content will heat very fast and continue cooking even after having been microwaved. Baked goods can be made, but don't brown and can't be left unattended— they can burn and possibly ignite if they dry out.

Solid pieces of food should be placed so that the smaller ends are pointing inward and the thicker ends out. It looks quite decorative, but the main idea is that the outer thicker parts get cooked more, leaving the fragile inner parts less done. Although many microwaves have rotating trays, foods must still be rotated occasionally, such as flipping it over, or putting the inside area to the outside for even cooking. This is especially true for large pieces of food. Popcorn is an exception- exploding kernels move around. It's worse to stop a microwave halfway through popping corn, as it loses heat resulting in longer cooking time, and popped kernels will scorch. (The smell of burnt popcorn will permeate the entire house, and is really bad!) Some cooking foods have less aroma but often don't smell bad, with the exception of raw chicken. Cooked uncovered, it smells rather like a wet dog. Bone-in meats will take longer to cook.

A nice aspect is that stale bread or cookies can become like new when heated. Some foods such as rice and pasta take the same amount of time as on a stovetop and don't cook well, so there is no advantage to microwaving them. Whole eggs can't be cooked in the shells. When out of the shell, whole yolks must be pricked. Any foods that are enclosed in a shell, membrane or skin (such as eggs, tomatoes and potatoes) must be pricked or vented, or the steam trapped inside can make food explode. However, foods can still be double-wrapped with zipper bags, or put in a container then double-wrapped with plastic wrap to keep a microwave *parve*. It is not airtight and doesn't seal completely, but it keeps any steam from escaping just enough to affect *kashrut*. Double-wrapping doesn't affect microwave cooking.

Cooking Time: This is affected by the wattage of a microwave oven. (Recipes in this book are based on an average 700-watt microwave oven. Higher wattage microwaves may need less cooking time, and lower wattage may need more.) Unlike conventional cooking, when you increase the amount of food, you must increase cooking time. However, if you double the amount of food, don't double the amount of time. (Decrease doubled time by about ¼.) Cook for a shorter time- if it needs more cooking, you can always cook it more. It helps to take food out and stir it periodically for even cooking, or rotate it. Meats and poultry should be covered, with very little water added. Solid meat takes as long as in an oven or crock pot, and should be on 30% power. Poultry generally can be cooked 7-8 minutes per lb. on full power. Since food cooks via fast-moving molecules, cooking continues after the power is off, as the molecules take time to slow down. This is especially true of dense foods. Residual cooking is called "standing time".

Temperature: Some microwaves come with a temperature probe. Meat can also be measured out of the microwave with a thermometer to be sure the inner temperature is adequate, since food cooks from the outside-in. Foods keep cooking after the microwave has stopped, so be sure to remove it early if it is getting done. As with common cooking, microwaving kills germs and organisms when food gets to a high enough temperature. For foods that are more delicate such as fish or eggs, these are often heated on less than full power. It's rather the same as cooking foods on the stovetop in a double-boiler or on low heat.

Settings: Recipes state what power level to use for certain foods. Settings are thought of as being how a flame would cook (e.g., high, medium, low), but actually are the duration of time that the magnetron tube is on. You can hear it cycling on and off on lower settings. These are the most common settings:

<u>Cooking Level 10</u> = 100% power, also called "Full Power" or "High". It is the most common setting, and in no-frills microwaves, it is often the only setting. Items which are oily (such as meat or cheese), or contain much milk should be watched on this setting, as they heat rapidly and will boil over quickly.

<u>Level 7</u> = 70% power, or Medium High. Good for pretty durable foods that you don't want to get too overdone, yet still need a good amount of heat to cook.

<u>Level 5</u> = 50 % power, or Medium. This is best for somewhat delicate foods, like eggs.

<u>Level 3</u> = 30% power, or Defrost/Low. Best for defrosting, heating oily food, or cooking large solid meat.

Converting Conventional Recipes: Time for cooking should generally be reduced by three quarters. Oils should be used sparingly in recipes, as it makes food cook quicker, and foods can't be fried in oil. If you must sauté vegetables, they can be done nicely in margarine in a lightly covered bowl. Liquids used in cooking should be reduced, and in cases where firmness is needed liquid can often be omitted. If a recipe calls for frequent stirring, the food should be taken out and rearranged or stirred in short increments but equal to the entire cooking time added. If a liquid food is cooking for a long time, it should be in an over-sized bowl to prevent it boiling over.

Cookware: Metal can't be used in a microwave, so be sure food is free of foil (except tiny strips for shielding), twist ties, staples, poultry plumbes (white tags attached to poultry wings designating it kosher), that paper containers have no wire handles, and food is removed from metal trays. Dinnerware cannot have gold rims or trim.

For actual cooking, any of the following can be used in a microwave: Glass (perhaps the best), ceramic or crockery (depending on the glaze used), seashells, bone, wood, bamboo skewers, high-temperature plastics labeled "safe for microwave use" or with the symbol 〰, or when bearing the international cup and fork symbol ⏚, and plain white paper-towels listed as safe for microwave use for baking potatoes. All can be used for long periods of time.

Bakeware, cups, plates or bowls made especially for the microwave are fine to use. Additionally, plastic wax or parchment paper, cloth, paper cups, and paper plates. (Paper products can ignite if microwaved too long, or without food or liquid in the microwave at the same time.)

All above items, plus straw or wooden baskets lined with napkins, plastic coated foam plates, and certified foam can also be used for quick re-heating. However, they shouldn't be used for long durations. Crockery and ceramic can be tested for microwavability by putting the item in with a glass with a cup of water. Microwave on high 1 minute and if the item is cool, it's safe. If an item is hot, do not use it.

Food Reheating: The beauty of a microwave (and perhaps the only reason some people buy one) is the ease of food reheating. Unless double-wrapping for *kashrut* protection, airtight food containers (such as heatable meals) must be vented when they have a plastic seal. Puncture it or open a corner, to prevent bursting. If microwave-safe resealable plastic storage containers are be used, always loosen the lid so that it doesn't have an airtight seal. Paper and many types of plastics can be microwaved for short times, and are great for food reheating. However, not all plastics can safely be used in a microwave. Just because a container may not melt or get hot, it is not an indication that the plastic is microwave-safe. Foam is able to be microwaved but can release harmful chemicals and non-kosher ingredients into food or drinks. For these very important details, see *"Safe and Unsafe Plastic Usage"* on pp. 602-604.

Hot Water Urns

These must be gravity-fed, without electric pumps. The burner, lights, buzzers or signals cannot go on when any water is taken out, and it must stay on over 24 hours. It has to be turned on well before *Shabbat*.

Crock Pots

The moist, slow heat of a crock pot makes meats more tender and brings out the flavors of food as with marinating. Crock pots are great when you don't have time to cook. Basically, all the ingredients can be tossed into the crock in the morning, and after several hours it's ready and waiting to be eaten.

Multiple settings are not needed. Just because it may have many different settings, it doesn't mean it's better. For instance, if a crock pot has a "Warm" setting, pay no attention to it. This feature is only good for temporary use, such as 1-3 hour. It is primarily meant to hold food that has just been pre-cooked and is already hot, and not meant for actual cooking. (If one wants to heat pre-cooked leftovers, it is advisable to set it to low or high first, and once the food is heated through entirely, only then set to warm.) If Warm is used for a long period of time, the food can go bad, since it's not a hot enough to cook food. The beauty of a crock pot is that the food is cooking the entire time. Many people have used the Warm setting, and found their food turned sour. Digital "Smart" pots cook the food either on low or high, then automatically go to the "Warm" setting whether you like it or not. These are not good for *Shabbat*. It's only good if you come home at the particular time the food is done. It can't be left sitting for hours longer, or the food goes bad.

Shabbat Issues: When shopping for crock pots, take your needs into consideration. Look for a crock pot with a removable crock, and the old-fashioned knobs. If a crock is built-into the unit, it cannot be used for *Shabbat*. Avoid those with buttons, digital features, and "Smart" settings. Preferably, try to get one in an oval shape. (This will be discussed in "Shabbat Use" later.)

Passover Issues: Crock pots can't be *kashered* for Passover, but if you don't want to spend time cooking, it is a great idea to just get a special one for Passover. There are no additional issues.

Crock Pot Sizes and Care: If you are by yourself, a simple 3-quart crock pot is great. It's big enough for a 2 lb. roast, and you'll have leftovers for a few meals. If your family consists of 2-3 people, a 3-quart crock pot is fine, and it will be perfect for a meal or two. If you want leftovers, try a 5-6 quart crock. If you have a large family or a lot of guests, the bigger the crock pot the better. There are handy double-bowl metal inserts when you don't want a lot of food, but want to cook two different foods at the same time. The metal inserts can be used with or without a crock. If used by themselves without the crock, metal inserts cook food faster. Used in the crock is just like crock cooking. Only the temperature varies.

Crock Pot Care: Crock pots are easy to care for. If you use them correctly, they will last many years. Follow the manufacturer's directions if it is an unusual crock pot. Never leave an empty crock in the base when it is on, the crock can crack. If your crock pot has removable metal inserts for a double-bowl, the inserts can be used in the base alone, or the inserts can be put inside the crock if the crock has 1 quart of water in it first (double this amount for *Shabbat*). Both inserts must be used simultaneously. A crock can be used in the microwave alone but not the lid or metal inserts. Don't set a crock or metal insert on a stove burner. The crock, lid, and metal inserts can be washed in a dishwasher. Plastic scrub pads work well on the crock (and inserts). If there's calcium on the crock, scrub it with plastic pads and vinegar. Always let the lid and crock cool before running under cool water or washing. Use hot soapy water. The base can be wiped with a damp sponge or cloth. Never use cleanser or steel wool on any crock pot part.

Be sure there's always some liquid in a crock pot when cooking or the sides can scorch. Generally, food doesn't burn or get stuck on the crock if enough water is used. If it does, fill the crock with a hot water, let it sit about 10 minutes, then scrub it out with a plastic scrub pad if needed. Never use metal utensils to stir with. Don't set a crock down or slide it on easy-to-scratch surfaces, as the crock bottom is extremely rough and will scratch it.

Crock Pot Cooking: Browning meat isn't necessary, but can enhance flavor. The longer food cooks (such as on Low), the more tender it gets, and the more flavorful. When making very liquid foods such as soups, leave 2 inches from the top to prevent boiling over. Never use dairy products in a crock pot, they will curdle or separate. Pasta products don't do very well when using the low setting, they tend to disintegrate into the food. Rice is similar but a little more stable, however it tends to split open and look a

617

bit strange. The lid must be on the crock pot the entire time the food is cooking, or it releases too much moisture and dries out the food, but the major issue is that it won't stay hot enough to cook food.

Cooking Times: Small or cut pieces of meat cook faster than large pieces or whole meats. Whole poultry averages an hour per pound on High, 2 hours per pound on Low. Large beef roasts averages 1 hour 15 minutes per pound on High, 2½ hours per pound on Low. If you have metal double-bowl inserts, the time will be cut in half if used in the base. If you use them in a water-filled crock, the time will be the same as if using the crock itself. For details on overnight cooking for *Shabbat*, see "*Shabbat Use*" below.

Converting Conventional Recipes: Virtually anything cooked on a stove or slow roasted in an oven can be cooked in a crock pot. For general use, decrease the liquid in conventional recipes. A little liquid goes a long way. Stirring is a good idea to keep the top of food from scorching, but the moist heat rarely enables food to scorch unless it is cooked too long. If pasta or dumplings are called for in a recipe, add them in last ½ hour of cooking, or they disintegrate, or the soup gets thicker, and you'll have no noodles.

Shabbat Preparation: When preparing the crock pot for *Shabbat*, the temperature knob and the entire inside must be lined with a layer of aluminum foil. Line the foil over the outer edge to cover it, as this part also is hot enough to cook. One might think the heat is only on the bottom, but this isn't true. They actually heat from the side walls. If done using it on *Shabbat*, the whole crock can be taken out, leaving behind the foil. It's not a fire hazard since it's a low wattage, self-contained heater.

Shabbat Use: Always keep a crock pot on Low or food dries out, scorches and becomes bitter. When cooking food overnight for *Shabbat*, be sure to add about 1-2 extra cups of water to the pot no matter how much food is in it. This is the amount of evaporation (about 1 cup per 5 hours) over the roughly 15-hours. (It's longer in winter, and 3 cups may be added.) If there isn't enough liquid in the pot, the food will scorch. If double metal inserts are used, put extra water in the crock before the inserts are put in. If using raw unsoaked beans, barley or rice instead of cooked, add 1-2 extra cups of water as they will absorb it.

If food is on the verge of burning, water can only be added from a hot water urn that had started boiling before *Shabbat*. If you don't have one, here's a nifty trick if your crock pot is an oval shape: Take the crock out and put it sideways on top and inside of the rim. It's still considered being on the flame (since it heats on the sides, not the bottom), and is a permissible way of "reducing heat" without turning it down. Test it on a weekday to be sure it balances properly, and keep it far out of the reach of children or pets.

An inverted metal baking pan can be put atop a cooking crock pot, and food set on it to warm. (Be sure it's balanced properly for safety.) Food can also be set under the pan edges as heat reflects down from it. Neither method is hot enough or normally considered cooking, and are great for warming food. Note that these methods should not be used for a long period of time, as they usually won't keep the food hot enough.

Hot Water Heaters

General Details: Although not generally an appliance in the kitchen, it affects many aspects of life. The temperature must be easily adjustable, to set it below scalding temperature for safety's sake. This also helps the energy bill, and a lower the setting is better for *kashrut*, since heat is a major affecting factor.

Holiday Issues: A water heater is essentially like a large kettle sitting on a burner with a thermostat. As hot water is used, cool water enters the kettle triggering the thermostat to turn on the burner element.

It's best to get gas with a pilot-light. Since the flame is pre-existing, one can use hot water.

Don't get a gas water heater with electronic ignition— each time it is used, it triggers and makes a spark to light. Don't get electric unless you won't be using hot water on a holiday at all. Basically, every time hot water is used the burner is newly lit (just like gas with electronic ignition).

Haven't learned enough and you are wanting to know even more? We'll continue with extra information for those who are— *"Hungering for A Higher Education"* ...

Section 7

Hungering for a Higher Education

Finding Meaning In Practice

Practical Applications of Torah

WHAT ARE THE DETAILS OF CERTAIN LAWS THAT AFFECT FOODS? The following things are affected by agricultural *Halachot* even without the Temple. They are expounded upon below:

Respect for Bread: Food and drink are our sustenance, and are not to be wasted (nor should any useful item be discarded). This is derived from the prohibition of cutting down a fruit-bearing tree (*Devarim* 20:19). Bread has a special status, and was part of the Temple service. Twelve loaves of bread were always present— miraculously staying fresh all week. Bread should always be treated with respect.

⇨ When distributing *challah* after *HaMotzi*, it should be passed politely or set down, never thrown.

⇨ One shouldn't put bread in the garbage. Stale bread can be reused (see "*Extra Foods*" on pp. 595-601).

⇨ If it is partially eaten or has gone bad, it can be fed to wildlife (except on *Shabbat* or holidays) or pets.

⇨ One should not step on crumbs or other food, and if one sees it on the floor, they should pick it up.

New Grain: It's not a new problem— being new *is* the problem! An offering called the *Omer* was brought during Passover, and even though we don't have a Temple now, this day is still special. It makes all previously sprouted B.R.O.W.S. plants, grains, flour and products permissible to eat from that time on. They are then called *yashan* [old] because they were in existence at that moment. Any seed that sprouts after the day of the *Omer* becomes *chadash* [new], literally a new entity. Any resulting food product from *chadash* will be forbidden until the next year's day of the *Omer* has passed (*Vayikra* 23:14). Therefore, the *mitzvah* is called the prohibition of eating *chadash*.

All B.R.O.W.S. products are permitted after any given Passover, and from then through July is time to stock up. Dry products (flour, oatmeal, pearl barley, pasta, cereal, crackers, snack bars, etc.) will stay fresh until the next Passover if stored properly (see "*Keeping Foods Bug-Free*" pp. 583-584). In August, watch out— *chadash* products reach U.S. stores: Oats, then barley and wheat, and lastly durum products (like pasta). U.S. flour can include "winter wheat" (permitted year-round) and "spring wheat" (which requires investigation), making all flour and commercial baked goods suspect after July (unless marked *yashan*).

Observing *chadash* is mandatory in Israel (regardless of whether one is visiting or living there), as the holiness of the land holds the Jew to a higher standard. Some say that crops grown by non-Jews outside Israel are exempt, however, most rabbis agree that it applies to B.R.O.W.S. grown by anyone, anywhere.

To keep this *mitzvah*, get a current copy of the annual "*Guide to Chodosh*", or go to the website "Yoshon.com". There is also a special book to teach people how to keep it called "*Vintage Grain*" by yours truly.) These are guides and have instructions for checking date codes and lot numbers on packaging, to ensure that B.R.O.W.S. products are *yashan*. It is said that those who are strict with this *mitzvah* will be blessed.

The Mitzvah of Challah: We briefly mentioned the background of this important *mitzvah* in Section 2 (p. 28). It's mandatory to do in Israel (one can't eat till it's been taken). Here are the details that apply:

Ingredients: *Challah* can only be taken from B.R.O.W.S. items made with some amount of water. If a dough was made with only fruit juice or oil (no water), *challah* can't be taken.

Amounts: *Challah* is taken on a minimum weight of flour. Freshly sifted flour is fluffy, and more is needed to obtain the same weight as flour measured from a bag. Flour labeled "pre-sifted" has settled with shipping and is considered to be unsifted. Straight-out-of-the-bag amounts are as follows:

a. **Take *Challah* with a *Brachah*-** For an amount of at least 5-lbs. (16½ cups), however, some have the *minhag* of at least 3⅔ lbs. (12¼ cups). Ask your rabbi which custom applies to you.

b. **Take *Challah* without a *Brachah*-** Between 2½ lbs. (8⅔ cups) and your amount for a *brachah*.

c. **No *Challah* is Taken-** On any amount less than 2½ lbs. (8½ cups). Note: One must not plan small batches of bread in order to intentionally avoid taking *challah*.

Combining Batches: Small batches of dough or baked items can be combined in order to reach the specified weight. Tally up the flour amounts you used in the dough or baked items in order to determine if enough has been made for *challah* to be taken with or without a *brachah*. The items cannot be eaten until the portion is separated. Put the items in a large box (or all touching on a tablecloth lifted up over them as if in a container) and take *challah*, as instructed below.

Some maintain that only items made of like-kind dough can be combined. Others allow different types, such as a cake and several loaves of bread. One should ask their rabbi if they can mix dough types.

Non-Baked Items: If a large quantity of dough is made to be cooked (such as for pasta) or fried (like doughnuts), even if over 5 lbs. is being made, *challah* is taken without a *brachah*.

Taking Challah: Ideally, take *challah* from dough after kneading. If *challah* is taken from an item after baking, use a piece of the baked item. *Challah* can never be taken on *Shabbat*. If (outside of Israel) *challah* hadn't been taken and there's no other bread on *Shabbat*, set a bit aside and take it after *Shabbat*.

1. Stand, grasp some of the dough with your dominant hand and say the *brachah* (if applicable).

2. Pull off some dough equal in size to a large olive where you have been holding it.

3. Hold up the olive-sized portion and say the statement found in most *siddurim*, "this is a portion taken from dough" (preferably in Hebrew). (This statement can vary slightly according to *minhag*, but it is said even if no *brachah* is made.) Say the *brachah* if applicable. Some then say additional verses.

4. Burn the olive-sized portion (now called "*challah*") and dispose of it properly. (See next page.)

Burning the Challah Portion: Since we cannot benefit from the portion taken, it must be burnt until totally charred on all sides (but not necessarily all the way through). Various methods work for this:

⇨ Always flatten the dough, or tear apart the baked item— more surface area makes it burn quicker.

👍 A propane torch used outside is perhaps the quickest and most efficient method to burn the portion. Set the portion in a foil pan, or directly on concrete. Point the flame on the portion, which burns quickly with very little smoke. Flip it with a stick or tool to expose unburned areas until the entire piece is completely charred black, usually in less than 2 minutes. (See *"Torching Tips"* on p. 50.)

☞ A gas grill can be used for burning the portion, but the portion must be wrapped in foil so that it doesn't impart flavor to the grill (especially the grates). Nothing else can be roasted while the portion is being burnt because the burning portion becomes "fuel" in the grill, which is considered beneficial. Grill with the lid closed on the highest setting until the portion is charred, which usually takes about 45 minutes because the foil reflects the heat and keeps out the oxygen needed to char the portion.

☞ A small charcoal grill can be used to burn the portion. If the grill is normally used to roast food, the grate must be removed so that the portion being burnt doesn't impart flavor to it. Place the portion directly on the hot coals, and keep the lid off (or open). Never put lighter fluid on the portion because the fluid is toxic and would give it a non-food status (it would have been given to a *Kohen* as food). After the coal ash has cooled, pour it in a bag and put it in the trash (it cannot be used for fertilizer).

☞ A stove or toaster oven can be used for burning the portion, but the portion must be wrapped in foil so that it doesn't impart flavor to the appliance. Nothing else can be baked while the portion is being burnt because the burning portion becomes "fuel" in the oven, which is considered beneficial. Heat the portion on the highest setting until the portion is charred, which takes about 45 minutes because the foil reflects the heat and keeps out the oxygen needed to char the portion. It can also be wrapped in foil and roasted on top of a burner or under the broiler. A disadvantage is that smoke flavor gets out, and can leave a residue that could taint future foods. Indoor burning really stinks up the house!

✋ One must never store the portion with other taken pieces (such as freezing it for a combined burning, for instance, destroying *chametz* at Passover time). It must be burned as soon as possible.

Disposing of the Burnt Portion: Even though the portion is charred, it could still give benefit to a non-*Kohen*, so it must be disposed of as soon as possible. Once burned:

👍 Put the burnt portion (or whatever is left) in a zipper bag or double wrap it and place it in the garbage.

✋ Never throw it "directly" in the garbage— a *mitzvah*-related item should be treated respectfully.

🚫 Do not bury it, as it becomes fertilizer, thus giving benefit to your plants or trees.

🚫 Do not feed it to animals, as nothing should benefit from it (they most likely wouldn't like it anyway).

Mixing Species: In Israel, all species of plants must be grown in separate areas. Outside Israel, only sowing other species of plants in a grape vineyard is prohibited for a Jew. (*Vayikra* 19:19, *Devarim* 22:9.)

Grafting: It is prohibited for anyone to graft different species in order to make a new type of fruit (grafting the same species is permissible). Jews can't buy or take care of hybrid or grafted trees, and must uproot them (despite the prohibition of destroying fruit trees). However, a Jew can buy hybrid or grafted produce (if done by a non-Jew). This law (*Vayikra* 19:19) applies today in any place.

Forbidden Fruit: Fruit from a tree planted or transplanted within three years, is called "arlah" [literally covered up] (*Ashkenazim say* "orlah"), and it must be burned (or possibly buried). The three years start from the time it comes into existence or is placed, whether it's a sprouted seed, potted plant put in the ground, transplanted existing fruit tree, grafted-on branch (of the same species), or new branch which sprouted from the trunk or root. Most orchards have older trees, so buying fruit is not a concern.

Fourth year fruits are holy and similar to *Ma'aser Sheni* (see next page). Fruit is redeemed with a coin and then it can be eaten. However, most *poskim* [rabbis who answer *shelot*] say that grapes are the only fruits outside of Israel that must be redeemed. Fruits from the fifth year on are permissible. These laws are from the *Torah* (*Vayikra* 19:23-25), and valid today everywhere, for Jewish or non-Jewish grown fruit.

Sabbatical Year: Every seven years, Israeli land must rest. No crops may be planted, harvested or pruned on *Sh'mittah* [a Sabbatical year], but anything that grows naturally can be eaten (*Vayikra* 25:2-7). Hydroponic produce is not affected by *Sh'mittah*. The *Torah* promises a big enough crop in the sixth year to last the entire seventh year for all who keep this *mitzvah* (*Vayikra* 25:20-21). Some say this is a proof that the *Torah* is divinely inspired, as no human can control nature to make such a promise. The first Temple was said to be destroyed because Israel neglected this *mitzvah* (as prophesized by Moses in *Vayikra* 26:34-35). As a result, Israel was exiled to Babylon and the land lay desolate for the number of ignored *Sh'mittah* years. The year of this book's first printing, 2021-22 (The Hebrew year of 5782) was a *Sh'mittah* year. Upcoming *Sh'mittah* years are: 2028-29 (5789), 2035-36 (5796), 2042-43 (5803), 2049-50 (5810), 2056-57 (5817), and 2063-64 (5824).

Tithes of Israeli Produce: Like *challah*, a *brachah* is recited for tithes. Excluding hydroponics, any Israeli produce must be certified that all tithes have indeed been taken. No part of produce can be sold or used in any way until tithes have been taken. There are five different types of tithes as follows:

    a. *Terumah* [special tithe], also called *Terumah Gedolah* [large special tithe], is roughly one-fortieth to one-sixtieth of the produce. In Temple times was given to *Kohanim* and their immediate families to be eaten (*Bamidbar* 18:24-32). Nowadays, it can be any amount. It is either double-wrapped, burned or buried, as nobody can benefit from it (just like *challah*— a type of *Terumah* that applies even outside Israel).

b. "*Ma'aser Rishon*" [first tithe] generally called "*Ma'aser*" is one-tenth of produce remaining after *Terumah* is taken. Now, *Ma'aser* is eaten by the owner or given to a *Levi* [one from the Levite tribe]. *Levi'im* [Levites] also had to give a tenth to *Kohanim* before using their *Ma'aser*. (*Vayikra* 27:32-33)

c. "*Terumat Ma'aser*" [special tithe] is one-tenth of produce remaining after *Ma'aser Rishon*. No part of produce can be used until *Terumat Ma'aser* has been taken. As with the other *Kohanic* tithes, it cannot be benefited from. It's double-wrapped and discarded. (*Vayikra* 22:10-16).

d. "*Ma'aser Sheni*" [second tithe] is taken in the first, second, fourth and fifth years of the *Sh'mittah* cycle. It is one tenth of produce remaining after *Ma'aser Rishon*. It was to be eaten in Jerusalem, or exchanged for money to purchase food. It still must be redeemed with a coin and eaten by the owner.

e. "*Ma'aser Ani*" [tithe for the poor] is taken on the third and sixth years of the *Sh'mittah* cycle. It is one tenth of produce remaining after *Ma'aser Rishon*. It was given to the poor, convert, widow and orphan (*Devarim* 14:29). Anyone can eat it nowadays. (*Vayikra* 27:30-31, *Devarim* 14:22-23).

Crossbreeding: It is prohibited for anyone to crossbreed animals, such as a donkey and horse to create a mule. However, one may make use of a non-Jew's crossbreed. This applies anywhere. (*Vayikra* 19:19)

Prohibition of Cruelty to Animals: Although humans can eat, use and work animals, there must be some benefit or it is senseless cruelty and is forbidden. The *Torah* mentions many laws preventing *tza'ar ba'aley chaim* [cruelty to a living creature]. Aside from those mentioned in "*Pets and Kashrut*" other laws are sending a mother bird away from her nest to take her young or eggs for food (*Devarim* 22:6-7). One must help an animal that collapsed from its load (*Shemot* 23:5, *Devarim* 22:4). One can't work a donkey and ox together (*Devarim* 22:10). One can't muzzle animals while working so they can be free to eat (*Devarim* 22:1). One can't slaughter an animal and her young the same day (*Vayikra* 22:28).

Sport hunting and fishing are prohibited as no benefit of food or clothes is derived. Wounded animals can also escape and suffer. Judaism teaches if we're compassionate to animals, how much more so should we be to people! Both Moses and David were chosen to lead the Jewish nation due to their concern for the sheep they tended.

Unfortunately, monetary gain is often a higher priority than animal welfare. Mass production causes crowded, inhumane conditions that result in unhealthy, unhappy animals, whose lives can be worse than death. Although the *Torah* specifically prohibits it, cruelty to animals doesn't affect *kashrut*. However, many rabbis don't permit eating meat of inhumanely treated animals due to principle alone. Information is on the following page for those concerned with cruelty. Sensitive people may not want to read it, but one should really know what they're eating. Demand will only continue the vicious cycle of cruelty. Therefore, those who want to stop the cycle should publicize it, and refrain from buying these products.

Note: The following page contains material that may not be suitable for sensitive readers.

<u>Treatment</u>: There are two meats to be concerned with for inhumane treatment and living conditions:

One meat to avoid is goose liver and "*pâté de foie gras*", or French goose liver pâté. Geese are often force-fed to produce larger livers. Force-feeding causes them great pain, both from the method of feeding, and the liver expanding putting pressure on other organs. Albeit not a common kosher item, it does exist.

A more common meat is white veal, also called "fancy veal" or "milk-fed veal". I knew this issue existed with *treifah* meat, but never dreamed it could affect kosher meat. After much investigation on the subject, a shocking revelation was that the *only* kosher veal is white, and no kosher red veal is available. In order to create white veal this is what is done: Veal calves are taken away from mother cows at an early age. Instead of living a life happily nursing from their mothers, they are usually locked up in a dark barn. Once in the barn, they are always kept in tiny pens, basically unable to move. This is done so they will gain weight, to keep their muscles from developing (developed muscles are tougher), and their delicate bones won't be broken. Sometimes, although not always, they may be fed a diet of milk and meat, which would not be allowed *Halachically* for a Jewish owner, because a benefit is involved. The calves are starved for iron; the meat is white because they are totally anemic. In a desperate attempt to try to get the iron that they lack, calves rub against the wire pens to scrape off hair to eat, and it then becomes hairballs in their stomachs. They live their entire lives this way. Due to the way they are raised, they are very sickly, and only 40% of them even pass as kosher. Non-Jews actually own these farms, as obviously no *Torah*-observant Jew with a conscience could do such a thing to an animal; it totally violates the prohibition of *tza'ar ba'aley chaim!*

<u>Slaughter</u>: Concerning *treifah* meat, when it comes time for the slaughterhouse, there is little care about animal welfare. Methods can involve stun guns, chemicals, regular guns, or even sledgehammers to finish off the job. I shudder to think what the animals must go through.

In general, kosher slaughter is as painless and stress-free as it can possibly be, if done according to *Halachah*. Perhaps the only issue is a method called "Rubashkin", named for the rabbi who devised it. It is used solely by *Lubavitch Chassidim* for *Glatt* kosher meat. An animal is placed in a drum that rotates it upside down making it easier for the *shochet* to painlessly slaughter an animal, but this likely causes it distress. Packages are labeled "Rubashkin", so if you don't approve of this, purchase a different product.

Prohibition of Eating the Limb of a Live Animal: One of the seven *Noachide* laws [Noah's seven laws, followed by non-Jews] is "You shall not eat meat with its soul." *Bereshit* 9:4). Meat must be cut up only after an animal has died and is no longer moving. This ensures that it will not feel any pain. Although twitching can be due to neural reflexes even when an animal is already dead, because the moment that an animal has lost total consciousness is not absolutely known, twitching is the sign we use to determine a precise time of death. Non-kosher slaughterhouses will often start to cut up meat even before the animal has stopped twitching. If this occurs, the meat is not fit for *Noachides*, let alone Jews.

Commercial Baking, Cooking and Maids: Many laws in the Torah concern Jews not intermarrying with idolaters or other nations. Therefore, there are laws stemming from this that are still followed, as the Torah explicitly states its laws are eternal and won't change. (*Devarim* 4:2, 4:40).

Aside from commercially cooked or baked food and restaurants being under reliable *hashgachah*, the following laws only concern foods which are fancy enough to be served at a wedding or king's table. They don't apply to foods that could be eaten raw, or beverages consisting mostly of water (like coffee or tea).

It is extremely important to realize that if these rules are not followed, it could potentially render one's utensils and cookware *treifah* and they may have to be *kashered* or discarded!

Baking: The laws of baking are sometimes a little different than the laws for cooking:

   a. In general— a Jew must light the oven or pilot light for baked items to be kosher for another Jew.

   b. Concerning baked goods from a kosher restaurant or bakery run completely by non-Jews, a Jew must light the flame (or at least a pilot light) if the oven has cooled off, or the flame or pilot went out.

   c. In a commercial plant, a Jew must at least light the pilot light, glow plug, etc. even if by a remote switch or code if the food is to be considered kosher and cooked by a Jew.

   d. Bread made in a commercial plant that has a dairy designation should not be purchased.

Cooking: The laws for cooking are sometimes more stringent than those of baking:

   a. In general— *Ashkenazim*: The same rules apply for cooking as baking- the Jew should have at least lit the initial pilot light, flame (or Sterno® if at a restaurant).

   Sefardim: Cold food must be placed on a hot flame by a Jew, or a Jew must turn on a burner after the cold pot is set on the burner.

   b. Concerning non-Jewish run kosher restaurants, if a flame or pilot went out, a Jew must re-light it.

   c. In a commercial plant (like a cannery), a Jew must at least light the initial pilot light, glow plug, etc. even if by a remote switch or code, if the food is to be considered kosher and cooked by a Jew.

   d. Cold-smoked fish (such as lox) is not a problem, because it isn't "cooked" by heat, but by smoke.

   e. A company that makes plain frozen vegetables may not be problematic since they are steamed.

Maids: If a maid is a Torah-observant Jew, there is no *Halachic* problem. If not, the following apply:

   a. In order for a maid to heat food, all the general rules apply as for "Baking" and "Cooking" above.

   b. A maid can prepare a whole kosher meal if a Jew takes some part in the actual cooking process.

   c. Ideally, a Jew should be in or around the house when the maid is cooking or preparing food.

   d. If a maid uses a microwave to heat food, there's no problem since microwaving isn't considered "cooking" by ordinary means— using a flame for heat. (Neither is pickling, brining or smoking.)

   e. Non-cooked wine or grape juice bottles must be sealed and unopened in order for non-Jewish maids or non-observant Jews to handle them. *Mevushal* wines and grape juices are not problematic.

WHAT IS THE DIFFERENCE BETWEEN LAW, CUSTOM, TRADITION, AND STRINGENCY?

Although seemingly similar, these four practices differ greatly in application. They are defined below:

a. Halachah: Jewish Law derived from the *Torah* and *Talmud*. It applies to every Jew.

b. Minhag: Custom followed by Jews from a general region as a whole (such as *Ashkenazim* or *Sefardim*), or a specific group (like German *Ashkenazim*, *Bobover Chassidim*, or Yemenites).

c. Mesorah: Unbroken tradition. This must be continuously passed from parent to child from a family's country of origin without any interruption in its practice.

d. Chumrah: A stringency beyond *Halachah*. This is something one personally chooses to do of their own free will, or a group decides to take on collectively, and it cannot be forced on anyone else.

Within the scope of *Halachah*, an individual's situation, group affiliation, family customs, and personal preference combine to make each and every Jew unique. We shall discuss the nuances of each category:

Halachah

Halachah is similar to judicial law in the respect that the first case to be presented sets the precedence for all later cases. The older the law, the more weight it carries, which is why we look to the Torah and Talmudic sources for guidance. What makes Jewish law unique, is that all Jews are considered as one collective unit. Once everyone accepts a law, it becomes binding and cannot be tampered with. All Jews unanimously accepted the Torah at Mt. Sinai (*Shemot* 19:8), and confirmed its universal approval again during the Purim incident, therefore, *Halachah* applies to all Jews.

Every Jew is expected to try to follow *Halachah*, and doing each *mitzvah* earns the Jew merit in the World to Come. If one deliberately violates *Halachah*, they are considered to be a *rasha* [wicked person]. However, if a person that doesn't know any better is learning, sincerely trying, or interested in growing, they are not held responsible for things done unknowingly. In fact, when a person takes on a *mitzvah* and continues it, all previous *averot* [transgressions] concerning it are erased (as if they had performed the *mitzvah* all along). This truly shows the depth of Hashem's compassion and forgiveness.

If there is an unusual situation, a person might get a leniency from a *posek* that will apply to that person only. A perfect example is the wife who had to take a medicine containing non-kosher glycerin in order to save her life (see p. 35). The rabbi must take all factors into consideration (even the level a person is on) in order to determine the *p'sak* [decision or verdict].

Minhag

You may wonder why there are so many different *minhagim*. One should remember that Israel came from 12 different tribes, each with a unique personality, no one better than another—just different. The same is true for *minhagim*. Each Jew has a special mission in life, so no two Jews are exactly the same. That's the beauty of *Klal Yisrael* [the whole Jewish nation]. Just as a body can't exist without certain parts, we can't exist without each other. Every Jew is an indispensable part of the whole!

Minhag or custom is much like *Halachah* when it comes to a person's general heritage. Jews have lived all over the world, and an individual *Bet Din* [court of three rabbis] would rule a certain way pertaining to the situation in that country at the time. For example, *Ashkenazim* were a bit more lenient in areas of *Glatt* kosher beef since it was harder to obtain in Europe. Once a ruling is made it becomes similar to a law and must be followed. However, *Sefardim* had sufficient beef and maintained the stricture, therefore the leniency became a *minhag* to *Ashkenazim* instead of a *Halachah* to all Jews. This is why *minhagim* to certain general groups is nearly like *Halachah* to them.

Minhagim can be unique to a specific group or community. Some communities would revere a great rabbi and emulate his ways, which is particularly common amongst *Chassidim*. When a community as a whole unanimously agrees to do something within the limits of *Halachah*, it becomes an acceptable *minhag*. For instance, in Baltimore, Maryland, there are certain Jews who will only eat fish prepared in strictly *parve* utensils. As long as the stricture or leniency does not conflict with the general accepted *Halachah* of all Jews (one can never be more lenient than law allows), then the *minhag* can become an obligation. This is how Jews with common heritage but from different cities can have different *minhagim*.

Although the Jewishness is transmitted by maternal line, the tribal line (which determines *minhag*) is passed down paternally. Therefore, a person should try to keep the *minhagim* of the ancestors on their father's side to honor them. If they have no paternal Jewish lineage, they should follow the general *minhagim* of their nationality, community, or group they identify with. A woman generally takes on the *minhagim* of her husband when she gets married, and she becomes part of his tribe.

Changing *minhagim* can be *Halachically* precarious. When someone does something three times in a row it establishes what is known as a *chazakah* [strong or right of claim], which is like a vow, and can be *Halachically* binding on a person. If this new *minhag* conflicts with an established one, a *shelah* should be asked. It may be possible to remove the obligation (if someone regrets what they inadvertently or mistakenly started) through a *Bet Din* which has the authority to annul certain types of vows.

If one must do a *minhag* different from their own, they can avoid any obligation by making a formal declaration beforehand that they are doing it "*b'li neder*" [without a vow].

Mesorah

Since a *mesorah* is an unbroken tradition, it cannot be taken on by anyone who simply wants a privilege or more convenient way of life. For example, some have a shorter waiting period between eating meat and dairy— this requires a *mesorah* since it drastically affects *Halachah*. Another excellent example is that most *Sefardim* can eat rice on Passover, whereas many years ago, *Ashkenazim* accepted a stringency upon themselves to not eat rice, beans or corn during that time. *Ashkenazim* can't just decide to take on the *Sefardi* custom.

Chumrah

Let's say a person decides to be strict, for instance, not drinking a beverage left uncovered overnight. Once they undertake it, it becomes a *chumrah* for that person. It's like a vow for them. Although it's good to be strict, a person must be able to handle it. Also, one should never impose their personal *chumrot* [stringencies] upon others, especially on family members. When first considering doing a *chumrah*, they may want to do it *b'li neder*.

Differences in Customs

It seems kind of strange, but all views in Torah-true Judaism are correct. Consider an analogy: An artist sketches a person's face from one side, and a second artist draws their hair from the opposite side. Who drew the actual person? Both! It's all a matter of perspective. Each artist sketched a totally different picture, but both views are correct. It is the same way with Judaism as well. Even though there are completely opposite *minhagim*, neither one is right or wrong— just *different*. It is perfectly fine to be proud of one's own ways, but should never feel superior to another. Therefore, nobody should ever criticize another observant Jew for a difference in *minhag*.

Those with different customs can still eat at each other's homes even though there are *Halachic* distinctions. For example, a *Sefardi's* "bread" contains mostly flour, water and yeast, without added fruit or vegetables, and consider an *Ashkenazi's* sweet "bread" as cake. The *Sefardi* can simply say a different *brachah* (*Mezonot* instead of *HaMotzi*), or bring their own "water *challah*". One should explain their *minhag* and the host will likely understand. For minor, non-*Halachic* customs, one should yield to one's host out of respect. For instance, if your *minhag* is to stand for *Kiddush*, but your host sits, you should sit. Someone with a strict *mesorah* might opt to do their own *Kiddush* after their host (with permission).

It should be noted that eating at another's home only applies when the host is actually keeping kosher in accordance to accepted *Halachah*. Jewish law allows room to bend some rules to respect fellow Jews. To illustrate, most *Sefardi poskim* allow a *Sefardi* who only eats the higher level *Bet Yosef* beef to eat at a home of an *Ashkenazi* who eats *Glatt* kosher beef. Even though the *Glatt* kosher beef is on a slightly lower level, it is still normally eaten in a *kashrut*-observant home. However, there are some who still prefer to be strict. As an example, most *Chassidim* will not eat anything from a home that does not keep *chalav Yisrael*. It's always best to check with your rabbi concerning levels of *kashrut*.

Shabbat and the Kitchen

WHAT SHOULD I KNOW FOR SHABBAT? For those new to keeping kosher, it is highly likely that you are new to other aspects of Judaism. Whether new to the concepts, or converting to Judaism, here are some highlights: *Shabbat* is a beautiful holiday vacation that occurs every week. A celebration of creation, it was made for the Jewish people. Since Hashem rested on that day, our own rest signifies to the world that we are His people, "chosen" to emulate His ways, by serving Him with a higher standard of law. Observing *Shabbat* is our acknowledgement that Hashem created the universe, and it affirms the mutual love between Hashem and the Jewish people.

When starting to observe *Shabbat*, take time to be a guest first and you'll gradually ease right into it. As with *kashrut*, start slowly and study about the subject. Ask a local Jewish bookstore, a *Kollel* [place of *Torah* learning], or your rabbi for books on *Shabbat* laws. Due to different *minhagim*, it is best to be guided by your rabbi, as specific customs can vary so greatly. We'll cover many things you need to know.

If a person is converting and not yet Jewish- they cannot keep *Shabbat* completely, since *Shabbat* wasn't meant for Gentiles. This only means that until one is converted, they must do at least one thing to break *Shabbat*. If they are not yet living in a Jewish community, driving to synagogue may suffice. Odds are, if a potential convert is already living in the community (which they should be), a Jew may hint for them to do something, like turning a light on or off. They might say, "the light in this room is so bright it's giving me a headache!" They have to hint, as a Jew is not allowed to directly ask a non-Jew to do anything for them that they can't do themselves. A Jew can't derive personal benefit from *melachah* [creative work].

The Shabbat Experience: *Shabbat* is said to be $^1/$60th of the World to Come. To experience a taste of it, *Shabbat* meals are the place to start! The entire evening is replete with meaning. Family and friends gather to eat a sumptuous meal, as the best foods are saved for this time. Meals are full of wonderful conversation, laughter, spontaneous singing, and hosts often say inspiring *divrei Torah* [words of *Torah*]. The night starts by "accepting" commencement of *Shabbat*, (rather like accepting a gift from Hashem).

631

Lighting Candles: One of the *mitzvot* [good deeds/laws] of women is lighting *Shabbat* candles. It is said to create *shalom bayit* [peace in the home]. The candles (or oil) also set a peaceful atmosphere for a beautiful meal. Some *Chassidic* girls start lighting at age three, but most girls don't light until they are married or away. Wives light with husbands in mind. Single men light their own candles. Two candles are lit, based on the two times *Shabbat* is mentioned the Ten Commandments. (One is to remember it, the other to observe it.) Some women light an extra candle for each child. The *bracha*h for lighting is found in any *siddur*, and is the main formula then "... *Ner shel Shabbat*" {some say "*Ner shel Shabbat* <u>Kodesh</u>"}, "... Who has commanded us in the kindling of the {<u>Holy</u>} *Shabbat* lights". It is done in different orders depending on one's *minhag*:

<u>Sefardim</u>: One first says the *brachah*, then lights the candles, no differently than any other *mitzvah* order.

<u>Ashkenazim and Chassidim</u>: This is one of the few *mitzvot* in which a *brachah* comes *after* an action. The candles are lit, then the eyes are covered with the hands as the *brachah* is recited. The reasoning is, if one said the *brachah* first, they have accepted *Shabbat* upon themselves and then couldn't kindle the fire!

If one's running late, before the lighting *brachah*, they can state that they accept *Shabbat* after *Minchah* [afternoon prayer] (but before sunset). Single men often do this so they can drive to synagogue, leaving the car there until after *Shabbat*. Some husbands pre-light candles for their wives to be part of the *mitzvah*. It helps the wick to ignite easier.

Accepting Shabbat: Women generally accept *Shabbat* by lighting candles at a prescribed time before sunset. Men usually accept *Shabbat* at synagogue with prayer. Once a person accepts *Shabbat*, it is considered *Shabbat* for them, regardless of whether the sun has set or not, and they can no longer do *melachah*. One can't eat or drink anything between accepting *Shabbat* and hearing or reciting *Kiddush*.

Terminology: Just before and all during *Shabbat*: *Sefardim* say, "*Shabbat Shalom*" [Sabbath Peace], *Ashkenazim* say "*Gut Shabbos*" or "*Good Shabbos*" [have a "Good *Shabbat*"]. After *Shabbat* is over, *Sefardim* say "*Shavua Tov*" and *Ashkenazim* say "*Gut Vak*". Both mean have a "Good Week".

Making Kiddush: Most have the *minhag* of blessing their children before or after *Kiddush*. "*Shulchan*" means both "table" and "altar" in Hebrew. Therefore, when we make *Kiddush* and joyously eat our *Shabbat* meal, it is akin to bringing holy offerings on the Altar in the Temple. This is why the *Shabbat* meals are so special; *Kiddush* sanctifies a meal, "dedicating" it to Hashem. *Kiddush* is very important for the first night's meal, as it speaks of the creation of *Shabbat*, and one can't eat or drink until it is recited. A *Kiddush* cup should be nice– complete and unchipped, holding at least ½ cup. It's set on a plate to catch overflowing wine (signifying abundance). Some *Sefardim* add three drops of water to it prior to saying *Kiddush*.

One can't make *Kiddush* with wine or grape juice that had been drunken from— it's considered "spoiled" (one could add a larger amount of fresh). If wine or grape juice is unavailable, almost anything can be used except water, and the *brachah* "*Shehakol*" is used. If there is only enough wine for two meals, wine should be used for the first meal. The remainder is saved for *Havdalah* [separation ending *Shabbat*]. *Kiddush* can be made on *challah* after hand-washing, recited with *HaMotzi* instead of *HaGefen*. The paragraphs to say can be found in a *siddur*. The one who makes *Kiddush* is usually the man of the house, but if there is no man present, anyone can make *Kiddush*. If there is an important guest, such as a rabbi or a *Kohen* [one of priestly lineage], the honor of making *Kiddush* should be deferred to them. The one making *Kiddush* must have everyone else in mind, and drink at least 4 oz. of wine or grape juice. Then the *P'ri HaGefen brachah* is said, and everyone answers "*Amen*". Ideally, they should either have some wine from the *Kiddush* cup, or their own in a small cup. It's meritorious to have wine from the *Kiddush* cup. (Usually, it's poured for each person before drinking, although some pass the cup around.) *Kiddush* is recited Friday nights and at *Shabbat* lunch. For *Kiddush* lunch, extra verses may be added, but only *P'ri HaGefen* is required.

<u>Sefardim</u>: Before saying *P'ri HaGefen,* the host says, "*L'Chaim*" on the cup, and everyone answers "*L'Chaim*".

Shabbat Challah: Two whole *challot* ("*Lechem Mishneh*" [twice the bread]) are used, representing the double portion of *manna* given to prepare for *Shabbat*. Before *Kiddush* is made over wine, the *challot* are covered or put out of sight. *Challot* remaining at the table are placed under a decorative cover. Some put it between two covers, as the *manna* was protected between two layers of dew. Although bread is eaten first on weekdays, the wine is first on *Shabbat*, so it is the custom to cover *challah* as not to "embarrass" it. This is yet another lesson in Judaism of teaching compassion to others. If a loaf has been used for *Lechem Mishneh* once, it can be used for it again as long as it is complete. If a loaf has cracked and part has come off, it cannot be used. However, if less than 2% came off, it's still acceptable, as are *challah* rolls that became attached during baking. (They were intended to be separated.) There are different *minhagim* on *brachot* (see *1. Bread— King HaMotzi* p. 67), and many beautiful, symbolic customs for its presentation. Everyone washes and says *Netilat Yadayim*, then without talking, sit down at the table.

<u>Ashkenazim and Chassidim</u>: *Challah* can be plain, sweet, have raisins (on holidays), or most types of *matzah* can be used. *Ashkenazim* place the loaves one on top of the other, one representing Hashem and the other Israel. The loaf to be eaten at that meal is gently scratched (but not cut) with a bread knife "exposing the best of the bread". A host holds up the *challot*, says *HaMotzi*, and then cuts it up. It's then sprinkled with salt. *Ashkenazim* must have an amount at least the size of an egg (equivalent to if the bread were compressed.)

<u>Sefardim</u>: Plain *challah* is used and it never contains fruit. (A minority of *Sefardim* have 12 small *challot*, representing the original 12 loaves used in the Temple.) Pita bread can be used, as well as hand-made *Shmurah Matzah* since it's like bread and made by hand. Loaves are held side-by-side with all ten fingers touching it, (representing Hebrew letter "*yud*" with a numerical value of 10, found in Hashem's Name). They raise their hands or the *challot*, and recite a verse in Psalm 145 "*Pote-ach et yadecha umasbia lechol chai ratzon*" ["You open your hand and satisfy all living things and their desires"], sometimes with other phrases, then recite *HaMotzi*. Most *Sefardim* tear the *challah* instead of cutting it and some dip it in salt. *Sefardim* must eat at least 1 oz.

For all, after *HaMotzi*, the host immediately takes a bite from the first piece. He divides it up, and adds the salt, since Temple offerings were presented with salt. Next, he distributes it to his wife (or parents, or honored guest), and then it's usually distributed in order of descending age to each guest. Others put it on a plate and pass it down.

Daytime Kiddush at Synagogue: If one hears *Kiddush* in synagogue, they must have the intent that it is *Kiddush* for them, and answer "*Amen*" when hearing *P'ri HaGefen*. (See "*Making Kiddush*".) After that one can drink any beverage without saying *Shehakol* since *P'ri HaGefen* covers all beverages drunken afterwards, and excludes them from their normal after-*brachah*. (However, one can't eat *Shehakol* foods without saying a *Shehakol brachah*.) If wine or grape juice is unavailable or another drink preferred, *Kiddush* can be made on an alcoholic beverage or a national drink, but *Shehakol* is said instead of *P'ri HaGefen*. For a synagogue's *Kiddush* to be valid and "stick", *Mezonot* must be eaten. All the proper *brachot* must be said before and after. See "*The Kingdom of Brachot*" on pp. 64-76.

The Third Shabbat Meal: *Sefardim* call this "*Seudah Sh'lishit*", *Ashkenazim* call it "*Shalosh Seudos*" or "*Shaloshudos*". There's no formal *Kiddush*. It's preferable to have *Lechem Mishneh*, which is done just as for daytime *Kiddush* using the top loaf. If not eating *challah*, one must at least have *Mezonot* or fruit.

Havdalah: *Havdalah* separates the holy *Shabbat* day from the mundane workweek, and can be found in a *siddur*. It's recited well after sundown, "when three small stars are visible". Some hold this is 40 minutes, most 42, and the strictest is 72 minutes. One says a special paragraph in the nighttime prayer that serves to separate *Shabbat* from the rest of the week, in able to do *melachah*. If one forgot to add the paragraph, or a woman doesn't normally say the prayer, one should state "*Baruch hamavdil ben kodesh lechol*" ["Blessed is the separation between the sacred and the secular"] to be able to do *melachah*. In fact, one must state it in order to light the *Havdalah* candle. After *Shabbat* is over, everyone must hear *Havdalah* before working, eating or drinking (with the exception of water). It is preferable for a man to make *Havdalah* for his wife. Most *Ashkenazim* do *Havdalah* standing, and *Sefardim* sit. *Havdalah* is often recited at synagogue after the nighttime prayer.

Havdalah is recited on a *Kiddush* cup containing undiluted wine or grape juice, with a bit is spilled over onto a plate. Some do *Havdalah* on other beverages, but this is not common. A special candle is lit, fragrant spices are smelled, and a *brachah* is made on each item. The special candle is often braided as it must be like "a torch", but two candles can be held together with flames touching. We examine our nails to make use of the light. After the *Havdalah* paragraph is recited, the fire is extinguished with the wine, usually from on the plate. Some dip their fingers in the wine and apply it to the eyelids or nape of the neck for symbolic *kabbalistic* blessings. (There is an unverified custom for one to apply it to their pant pockets as a symbol for gaining wealth.) A man who did *Havdalah* drinks the remainder and says the after-*brachah*, or it's given to a child.

The Fourth Shabbat Meal: Some have the custom of having a fourth meal after *Havdalah*, as a way of extending *Shabbat*, implying that we don't want it to end. Called "*Melaveh Malkah*" [Escorting the *Shabbat* Queen], this "Feast of the King" was celebrated by King David. It's treated like the third meal, preferably eating bread and having warm food. It can only be prepared for, after having heard *Havdalah*. Eating *Melaveh Malkah* is said to nourish the "Luz" bone, which is a specific tiny bone possessed only by Jews.

WHAT ABOUT HAVING GUESTS ON SHABBAT? One should first learn the basic laws to properly observe *Shabbat*. Having guests can be stressful until one is used to it. The following tips are helpful:

⇨ Be a guest first and watch what others do. Ask lots of questions, people will be happy to teach you.

⇨ Read about the *Shabbat* laws. Many laws pertaining to the kitchen are in this book.

⇨ Practice how to do things on a weekday first, to help ensure you won't do anything wrong.

⇨ Try fixing *Shabbat* meals for your family before having guests. Actually "doing" is the best training.

Shabbat observance is the general outward indicator as to one's religious sincerity, (see "What Should I Know for *Shabbat*?" on p. 631), since it the loving sign of commitment between Hashem and the Jewish people. Once a Jew is committed to being "*Shomer Shabbat*" [observant of the laws of *Shabbat*], and keeping kosher, others will feel comfortable to eat at their house.

Before moving to a new neighborhood where one can walk to synagogue, the best thing to do on *Shabbat* is to either to stay at home to say your prayers, or stay with a local observant family overnight. Ask your rabbi or someone you've become acquainted with. If they know of someone you can stay with, odds are that family will be happy to host you. It's a great way to observe how people do things. It can be great fun, a wonderful learning experience, enables you to see the beauty of *Shabbat*, and a means with which to bond and get to know people. Once one understands the principles behind the *Shabbat* laws, it's really not all that hard. It simply takes a little practice. One should know what they're doing on *Shabbat*, because if they accidentally cooked, the food is prohibited to be eaten, due to deriving benefit from *melachah*. If one did turn out to do something wrong, not only might they be sinning, but they could inadvertently cause others to as well.

WHAT ARE THE BEST FOODS FOR SHABBAT? Foods often served at the *Shabbat* meal are– fish as an appetizer, with salad or vegetables and pickles. Sometimes soup is served, and then a full meat meal with dessert. Many people have a hot drink afterward, like tea or coffee.

For practical reasons, the best foods for beginners to serve on *Shabbat*, are *gefilte* fish or other type of boneless fish fillets as an appetizer. It is often served with horseradish or salsa. Pre-bagged salad and pre-sliced pickles are ideal. Meat soups should be prepared ahead of time, and bones or cartilage removed. Rice or potatoes are great side dishes since they stay hot longer. Boneless chicken is perfect for a main meal. Virtually any favorite can and should be served on *Shabbat*, as it's praiseworthy to save the best items for then, from food to clothing. Since the time before *Shabbat* can be very hurried, it's advisable to do most cooking on Thursday. This also allows flavors to blend and taste even better, plus letting the cook relax.

For a hassle-free *Shabbat*, avoid these foods: Chicken, meat or fish having bones, soup containing small bones, whole or sliced fruit which have rinds and seeds, corn on the cob, fruits containing pits or seeds, and unshelled nuts or seeds. Some people don't eat chicken skin, and if not, it is best removed.

WHAT SHABBAT LAWS CONCERN THE KITCHEN? For further knowledge as to the "why's" behind the laws, there are many excellent books on *Shabbat*. The majority of *Shabbat* laws, perhaps more than any other aspects of Judaism, pertain to the kitchen and food. This is due to the prohibition of kindling a fire and cooking food on *Shabbat*. Other areas aren't nearly as involved as the preparation, serving and eating of food.

The following guidelines should take care of most of your general kitchen and *Shabbat* needs. Once one learns more, and why it is that certain things are prohibited, it makes much more sense. It just takes a little patience and practice. Here again, remember to start slowly, and do a little at a time. Some people accomplish this by taking on a new *Shabbat Halachah* each week. It may seem tricky at first but believe it or not, eventually one reaches a stage where it becomes second nature. For now, we'll deal with learning some kitchen-related *Shabbat* laws, since food is essentially what this book is about.

The *Shabbat* laws deal with what is considered *melachah* or "work". This isn't work like a job, it's defined by the different creative works (both constructive and destructive) that went into building the *Mishkan* [the "portable" Temple that Israel used in the desert]. There are 39 *melachot* [the different types of work described above]. For *Shabbat* in the kitchen, some of these are cooking, changing consistency, squeezing or wringing, sorting, separating, kindling a fire, smoothing, creating, tearing, writing, and erasing.

Once one gets used to keeping *Shabbat*, they tend to wonder how they ever survived without it. Within *Shabbat* is a sense of having escaped the mundane world of working and paying the bills. Its meals are truly serene and happy, rewarding and meaningful. Hashem knew the importance of having a rest-day once a week, which helps one cope with the stresses of juggling a job, family and finances. It really is just like taking a vacation every single week! As with any vacation, one just has to make a little advance preparation.

Food Preparation: Food must be prepared beforehand, with the exception of fixing fresh fruit or vegetables that may wither or turn colors. These can be prepared immediately before eating. If one wants to remove a part of a fruit or vegetable, such as cutting off leafy or inedible tops, taking off bad spots, or discarding bugs which are clinging to it, some of the good fruit must be taken with the "bad" part. Some people hold that you can't wash fruit or vegetables on *Shabbat*, and others hold you can't check for bugs, however, not everyone holds this way. In any case, one cannot drown bugs intentionally on *Shabbat*.

Colanders, sieves, graters and peelers are prohibited since they are "specialized tools". So, peeling or paring of fruits or vegetables must be done with a regular knife for immediate use only. Boiled eggs, oranges and whole nuts can be peeled or shelled by hand immediately before consumption, but it is best to place the waste directly into the garbage, (see "Waste Products from Food" on p. 640). Food can be chopped with a knife for immediate use. Grinding is prohibited on *Shabbat*, except when foods were in a powdered state prior to baking, such as cookies or crackers. Cooked foods can be mashed using a *shinui* [doing in an unusual manner], such as with a handle, instead of a fork or masher. If powdered foods are mixed with a liquid, it should be kept on the runny side, because one can't make a thick paste (just like making mortar). Along these lines, thick foods such as mashed potatoes must only be stirred using a *shinui*, such as using one's non-dominant hand, or stirring in a crisscross manner if one normally stirs in circles.

Salting and pickling are actions that preserve food, and are considered preparing for a day other than *Shabbat*. Salting can also change a food's texture (causing beans to soften) and is similar to the action of tanning hides. (Of course, one can season their plate of food with salt for immediate consumption.) One must not put raw vegetables in a jar of pickle juice or vinegar. Remember, sharp liquids like vinegar react just like they are cooking.

Appliances and Cookware: All cooking or warming appliances must be turned on before *Shabbat*. Always have lids on pots prior to *Shabbat*. The pots can't be covered after *Shabbat* has started, since it causes the food to cook or get hotter. Food can be kept warm, so one or two burners or other appliances must be turned on before *Shabbat*. If any burners are on, the stovetop must be covered by a *blech* [a metal sheet covering the stovetop], and the knobs should be covered as well. If you wish to put food on or near the burner on top of a *blech*, it must be done prior to *Shabbat*. (Some rabbis consider a glass cooktop stove like a *blech*.) Any pots of food that are set on the *blech* after *Shabbat* has started, must have been fully cooked beforehand and can't be set directly on a burner underneath the *blech*. Unlike food placed on the stove before *Shabbat*, it must be offset to the *blech* perimeter and can never be moved directly on the flame.

If using a crock pot, (which I highly recommend), it must have a removable crock, and it follows essentially the same principle as your stovetop. Since the food can't be directly on the flame or it would be cooking, a *blech* must be created by lining the interior of the crock pot base with aluminum foil. The entire surface must be covered, including the sides and slightly over the top. The knob should be covered as well. The actual element inside a crock pot base is usually on the sides, not the bottom.

A warming tray without adjustable knobs that stays at a constant temperature can be used without covering, since these are only used to warm food and not cook it.

Ovens on Shabbat: It is preferable not to use an oven on *Shabbat*. If an oven is on over the duration of *Shabbat*, there are several things one must know. Any food inside an oven must be completely cooked, or the oven must have a metal insert (the *blech* principle) and the knobs should be covered. The oven should be on fairly low heat; it is only keeping warm. The oven element or flame must come on before the oven door can be opened and the food removed. Therefore, one must be able to tell when the oven is on before opening the door. One can't put food back into a hot oven unless it has a metal insert, and most people don't bother with it. An oven can ideally be turned off just before *Shabbat*, and food stays warm for that night's meal. These issues are covered in "Ovens" in "Kitchen Item Purchase and Use" on pp. 609-610.

Food Heating: One way of keeping food warm, is to invert the lid of a pot (handle-side-down), on the blech, or a crock pot that contains food, and put a cookie sheet or aluminum foil pan on top of the inverted lid. In this way, the food is not on the flame, but since heat rises the food is kept very warm, rather a "simulated stovetop"! Be careful that the food on top is balanced properly and that most of the weight is in the middle. If it gets too close to the edge, it could fall, and you'd have a real mess on your hands! This and the next method can be used to warm foods that have been cooked prior to *Shabbat*.

Here is an additional nifty method that I learned totally "by accident", which doubled the warming area. I asked a rabbi about this method, and it is perfectly permissible: A large foil pan was placed upside-down on top of an inverted crock pot lid. Next, bowls of food were placed near but not touching the base of a crock pot, beneath the inverted foil pan. The entire foil pan absorbed the heat and then reflected it down onto the bowls, which kept the food in the bowls warm! It was just enough to warm the food so that it was no longer refrigerator temperature. The bowls of food were taken out of the fridge just before leaving for synagogue, and upon returning, the food was slightly warm. This is good for warming food but not making it hot, and can be used for prepared cooked baby foods or formula. If it's a meat crock pot, it is far too risky to put anything dairy underneath, because condensation inevitably develops and can drip into the item below. If one wants to warm something dairy below, only a *parve* crock pot can be used for this application. Although the heat is not hot enough to affect *kashrut*, condensation does. This method should not be used for long periods of time, especially if a food must be kept hot. Since it's not on the flame, food atop the pan and the bowls below can be removed and returned. Food inside a crock pot is on the flame, and requires a different procedure.

When heating food, its consistency must not change. Ideally, precooked/baked food should at least be room temperature before heating, and not refrigerator cold. Even though a food (such as congealed gravy) has been cooked, the consistency changes drastically and it creates a "new entity". Pre-cooked or pre-baked solid foods that don't change consistency (such as bread or meat) can be thawed out at room temperature, in the refrigerator, or can even be heated. However, one must make absolutely sure there are no ice crystals present if the items are heated.

Potential Food Cooking: Once *Shabbat* starts, uncooked or cool water, as well as seasonings can't be added to cooking food. Herbs or spices are merely dried and still raw, so they can't be added to foods hot enough to cook them. Salt or sugar is actually pre-cooked (as is pasteurized milk), and can be added to hot food if it is taken off the heat, or out of a crock pot base.

One cannot stir anything in a pot or crock pot unless it is totally cooked and has been taken off the flame, since stirring causes food to cook hotter. Anything that is to be cooked, whether it's water in a gravity-fed hot water urn, or food in a crock pot, it must be already ½ to ⅔ cooked before *Shabbat* starts, in order to keep cooking. (An exception to this rule according to some, is if one is fixing a meal for the next day's lunch. Food could be put in raw and started before *Shabbat*. Since it is obvious that it the food will still be raw and it won't be ready in time for dinner, no one is tempted to try to eat it or make it cook faster. Not everyone holds this permissible. Ask your rabbi how he holds.)

One cannot use hot water from the water heater, or it is cooking the new water that enters the heater. If hot water is needed for dishes or handwashing, it must have been heated before *Shabbat*. In winter, some people draw super-hot tap water and put it in large containers just before *Shabbat* has started.

Serving Food: If one wants to serve ice on *Shabbat*, to keep from consistency changing problems, put a tiny bit of water in the bottom of the ice container before putting in the ice. The ice is bound to melt some, and in this way, one isn't visibly creating water, since there was already water in the ice container. This same principle goes for putting ice in hot soup, as long as it's not too hot and has been transferred from container to container three times. The ice can't be distinguished from water as a new and separate entity.

If one wants to put ice, water, seasoning, or *mandelin* [soup croutons] in soup, one must transfer soup with a ladle from a pot, to a bowl. It cools the soup off a bit each time as it goes from one vessel to another, for a total of three times, so you won't be cooking what was added. Use this method for serving tea or coffee. To avoid potential *Halachic* problems, brew a strong concentration of tea before *Shabbat* and keep it warm. This "Tea Essence" can then be added to hot water, and avoids the problems of tea bags and separating.

For soups or other very liquid foods, it's a good practice to use a ladle. The original pot is the first vessel, the ladle is second, and the soup bowl is third. Do not keep the ladle in the pot, or it becomes the same status as a first vessel. If one is having second helpings of hot food, one should wash and completely dry the ladle before serving again. (If it were still wet, you would be cooking the water drops.)

Washing Dishes: One shouldn't wash dishes on *Shabbat*, unless they are needed for that night or lunch the next afternoon. (The exception is, that if unwashed dishes make one extremely uncomfortable, either due to the sight or smell, one can wash them for the honor of *Shabbat*.)

If one needs to wash dishes for the next day's lunch, ideally the dish soap should be diluted or added to a full dishpan. Liquid soap dispensers are great for *Shabbat*, but make sure the soap is diluted or flows easily. *Ashkenazim* hold that bar soaps cause smoothing, which are prohibited on *Shabbat*, although certain *Sefardim* do not hold it is a problem since that is not the intention. Either way, liquid soap is less messy to use anyway. (For weekdays, I even use it in the shower, because it doesn't cause soap scum.)

Never use a sponge for washing dishes, since you can't squeeze the water out—wringing is prohibited. Take a little dish soap on your hand and wash the dishes with it or use a plastic wire type scrubber that does not hold water. Squeezing and wringing also applies to food: One should never press on a tea bag, or squeeze any fruit for juice. The exception is squeezing lemon juice onto a solid, such as a fish, but one never squeezes juice directly into liquid.

Separating: Another law is not to sort or separate, which involves things from silverware to food items. There are some simple guidelines to follow: First of all, never use a slotted spoon for serving, or a colander for draining. These separate solid food from a liquid, and are considered "specialized tools". Other specialized tools are graters, choppers, and peelers.

When it comes to food and separating, there is a general rule to remember: "Always take the good from the bad." This is why it is much better to fix boneless chicken for *Shabbat*— it saves a lot of hassle with separation of meat from the bones. This is what prompted the invention of *gefilte* fish. If one must separate something and has trouble taking the good from the bad, it can be done in a slightly different way: Leave some of the good with the bad! For instance, if there's a huge onion in your child's soup and they hate onions, but you dearly love onions, as long as you take some of the soup with the onion in your spoon, it's perfectly permissible. However, the onion alone can't be taken. The same applies to meat and gristle. When fat is cut away, one must leave a bit of meat on it, or it is considered separating.

Waste Products from Food: If chicken containing bones is served, one must eat the meat from the bones and when done with the bones, leave them on the plate, because waste products are considered "*muktza*" [forbidden items that can't be moved directly]. If one was eating something that contained waste (such as a banana in its peel or a chicken leg), as long as they haven't put the item down yet, they can keep holding it and can put the waste directly into the garbage. The same goes for watermelon seeds and rinds. Spit the seeds out onto the plate, if you will have more watermelon, put the rind (with some melon left on it) directly into the garbage to make room. If one is eating the watermelon by hand and no utensils, one merely takes the eaten rind directly to the garbage without setting it down. One can also spit the seeds directly into the garbage, but never spit seeds out on the ground if eating outside. The seeds can and will sprout, so one would be guilty of planting.

If there are pits, egg or nut shells on a table, and the table is needed for *Shabbat*, they can be scraped with another item such as a napkin or utensil onto a plate. The table can then be cleared, but the remnants should be put directly into the garbage as the plate is still held. This is an indirect way of moving *muktza*.

This also applies to used dishes that are needed for *Shabbat* lunch the next day. When collecting the plates with waste on them, keep an item of silverware or an edible piece of food left on the plate, otherwise one can't move the plate. If one doesn't need the plates, but there is still edible food on them, it can either put it in the garbage or the plates stacked—wastes and all, on the counter. If there is no edible food on the plate it's a problem, because the waste is *muktza*. The remedy to this is that silverware or something needed or of value must be on the plate in order to move it. Once the plate containing the valuable item (be it edible food or utensils) is held up in midair, waste can simply be slid into the garbage.

Muktza Items: As discussed above, *muktza* items cannot be moved. Basically, any items that can't be used on *Shabbat*, become "*muktza*", and they can't be moved. *Muktza* is a prohibition enacted by the rabbis many years ago when people started getting lax about *Shabbat* observance. The *muktza* laws helped re-alert people as to what they were doing, and made them have to think before they acted. It is not prohibited to touch a *muktza* item, but most people prefer to be strict and avoid it. Some *muktza* items include candles, fire, markers, and electric can openers.

Food That is Muktza: Food can be *muktza*? Indeed, some non-waste food items are actually considered *muktza*. Any food that one could not eat as-is, is considered *muktza*. This includes items such as plain flour, raw meat, uncooked rice, raw potatoes— any food that can't be eaten and requires cooking. Be sure that if you need the soy ice cream in the freezer, raw meat isn't stored in front of it, since it can't be moved directly!

Lights and Other Items: One can't create or extinguish a fire on *Shabbat*, and a light bulb (the tungsten inside) is actually burning. Electrical current is considered the same. Unscrew the light bulb in your refrigerator or oven (freezer too if applicable) before *Shabbat*. Also, make sure that the fan motor of your refrigerator or freezer isn't activated when the door is opened. The same goes for lights, buzzers, digital displays, etc. Test these during a weekday. If you have an icemaker, lift the hanger bar so that it's off, and when ice is removed, it doesn't make more ice. If you have ice or water dispensers on the door of your fridge, don't use them. They consist of electric pumps and motors.

Well before *Shabbat* starts, turn on any needed lights, especially in the kitchen, and set up timers for lights to go on and off. (Timers can extend to air conditioners if there is a desperate need, but these require special heavy-duty appliance timers.) You'd be amazed at how habitual it is to turn lights on and off. At first it may be hard to remember, but many people who have been observant for years still tape their light switches or put covers on them, since accidents such as leaning against a light switch, do happen.

Holidays and the Kitchen

ARE HOLIDAYS ANY DIFFERENT THAN SHABBAT? Major holidays are considered a type of *Shabbat*, and differ little concerning spiritual atmosphere. They are also ushered in with candles, and *Kiddush* at the start of the meal. A holiday is called a "*Chag*" by *Sefardim* or "*Yom Tov*" by *Ashkenazim*. This too is a time for inviting guests to eat. The biggest distinction between *Shabbat* and holidays is that one can carry for a need of the day, plus kindling, baking and cooking can be done. Another difference is that a non-Jew (or one going through the conversion process) cannot eat at a Jew's house on a major *Chag*, because a Jew can't cook for a non-Jew. If a host were to run out of food, they might try to cook more, and since cooking was a leniency to enhance the *Chag* it is not meant to be taken for granted. This rule helps us not to take advantage of it. However, a non-Jewish guest can be invited on *Chol HaMo'ed* [the in-between days of a major holiday when *melachah* can be done]. Non-Jewish guests can also come if the major *Chag* falls on *Shabbat*. Since it's prohibited to cook then, there is no worry that a Jew will fix more food. What you have is what you get.

There aren't as many *muktza* items on a *Chag*. Candlesticks can be touched, because fire isn't *muktza*. On the *Chag*, one can only light from a flame lit before the *Chag*. Candle lighting is just like *Shabbat*, except one says the formula and "... for kindling the *Yom Tov* lights". If *Shabbat* falls on a *Chag*, one says "... the *Shabbat* and *Yom Tov* lights". *Ashkenazi* women also add the *brachah* of "*Shehecheyanu*" after the candle lighting *brachah*, but *Sefardim* rely on the person making *Kiddush* to say *Shehecheyanu* with them in mind.

Gas hot water heaters with pilot lights enable one to use hot water for dishes and hand washing. A pre-existing pilot light makes this possible. Any of the *Chagim* or *Yomim Tovim* [major holidays], in which candles are lit, have the same rules with *melachah* as *Shabbat* (and have their own form of *Havdalah*). The minor holidays have no rules of *melachah*. The *Chol HaMo'ed* days are similar, but a few restrictions apply.

CAN I REALLY COOK ON A MAJOR HOLIDAY? By far the biggest difference between *Shabbat* and a major *Chag* is that you can actually cook food and light candles, as long as it's from a pre-existing flame. Most commonly, people light a 24-hour (or longer) candle before the holiday starts just for this purpose.

If one has an electric stove, or a gas stove with electronic ignition, it must be turned it on prior to the *Chag*. The drawback for electric is that temperature setting can't be changed. The nice thing about gas stoves, (aside from a pilot light), is you can actually adjust the flame height of the burners. One must have had practice and know how to do it, or they could risk turning the flame off, which is just as prohibited as lighting a fire. Also, if it has electronic ignition, one risks turning it too far, and each click is starting a fire. Practice doing it during the week to get used to how it works.

Ovens are a problem for both gas and electric. If the door is opened and the heat were *not* on, the change in temperature would cause it to go on, which is the same as physically turning on the oven. If one knows when the heat has come on, (often, gas can be heard), the door can be opened. Electric ovens are a bit trickier, as the indicator light may be delayed.

Although one can't start a new fire, all forms of actual food cooking are permitted, except obviously a microwave. The following list is for things that can be done on a *Chag*, but cannot be done on *Shabbat*:

✔ Some "specialized tools" can be used such as vegetable peelers, apple corers, and potato mashers.

✔ Soup and hot water don't need to be transferred any number of times.

✔ A ladle can stay in the pot, as well as water still left in a wet teacup.

✔ Crock pots must be on just as for *Shabbat*, but water and food can actually be added for that day's meal.

✔ One can wash dishes with hot water for that day's use, if they have a gas water heater with a pilot light.

✔ One can take showers and wash their hands with hot water and liquid soap, with gas heater as above.

✔ One could actually use a gas grill, as long as there was a pilot light, the gas was on and fire was transferred from a pre-existing flame, or the fire was started prior to the *Chag*. The flame could not be extinguished, but one still could actually cook on it, or heat food on it.

✔ One doesn't need a *blech* on the stove or in a crock pot, as food can be put directly on the flame.

✔ Food can be defrosted even if it has ice crystals, and gravy can be heated, as long as it's used that day.

WHAT HOLIDAYS APPLY? Before we cover the holidays, one should know a few details. It is a must to get a Jewish calendar, to easily see when the *Chagim* occur. This helps most to plan ahead for time off of work. With the exception of *Rosh Hashanah* and *Yom Kippur*, the country where one lives makes the difference between having a one-day or a two-day *Chag*. If one lives in Israel, a major *Chag* is celebrated for only one day, but anywhere else in the world It is celebrated for two. We'll cover all the major holidays that apply to these rules. Later we'll have an overview of *Chol HaMoed*, minor holidays, and fasts.

Major Holidays

Here is a brief explanation on major holidays when usual *melachah* cannot be done, but carrying and cooking can. Most of the pictured items at the beginning of this portion are of the major holidays. All involve food. In order to be able to light candles, cook, and bake, proper preparation beforehand is very important. Besides cooking, the following is essential for all major holidays:

Prepare A Pre-Existing Flame: Before the *Chag* has started, a long-burning special candle is lit. Not only is it necessary to light the *Shabbat* or *Yom Tov* candles, it is sometimes needed for *Havdalah* as well. One could use a pilot light from a gas stove or hot water heater, but this is usually not so practical. Most people use a memorial candle, available at any Jewish grocery or Judaica stores, or they are even found online. They usually last over 24 hours, but are also available as 2-day, 3-day, and even 1-week candles. They can come in metal, plastic or glass holders, but glass is usually best, as the metal gets very hot, and the plastic ones can even melt. Rarely will a glass one shatter, but it is still always a good precaution to set it in an out-of-the-way place, on a sheet of aluminum foil or on a metal tray, away from anything remotely flammable.

Transferring Fire: It's helpful to purchase long wooden fireplace matches. A tip for transferring file, *never* use the end with the flammable striking material. It combusts so easily that it will blow out the pre-existing flame, and then you will have no fire at all! Just use the plain wooden end, and set it over the flame. Let it catch fire, light your candles, and then set the match down on the foil or tray and it will go out on its own. *Havdalah* for after a *Chag* generally follows one's normal wait time, unless it's going into *Shabbat*. (See "What to Do When" on p. 655-662.)

Now we'll cover the major holidays, when these things must be done...

Rosh Hashanah

1-2 *Tishrei*. (This is sometimes referred to as "*Yom HaZicharon*" [Day of Remembrance] instead of just "*Yom Tov*" when saying various *brachot*. Check your *machzor* [holiday *siddur*] as to what to say.) The "birthday of the world", and the Jewish New Year. It is celebrated two days everywhere. This is the Jewish "New Year", on which every person must hear the *shofar* [ram's horn] being blown. It's the start of a ten-day period of judgment called "the Days of Awe". One's decree of judgment is said to have been written on this day. On the night time meals, special symbolic foods are eaten (see below). On the first day of *Rosh Hashanah*, many people do a nice custom called *Tashlich* [casting away]. (*Ashkenazim* and *Chassidim* won't do *Tashlich* on a *Shabbat*.) Most hold it still can be done until *Yom Kippur* if needed. The *Tashlich* ritual involves one going to a body of water, usually with live fish. (If no body of water is available, anything filled with water will do, but it isn't as special.) Certain prayers are recited, and one may shake out the hem of their garment into the water, symbolically "casting their sins into the depths" where they will be forgotten. Some people bring bread to feed the fish, but this is totally not permitted, since one cannot feed another's pets or wild animals on *Shabbat* or a *Chag*.

Customary Foods: Most people serve symbolic foods before the meal on both nights, such as apples dipped in honey to signify a sweet year. After *Kiddush* and *HaMotzi*, the apple has the *brachah* of *HaEtz* made on it, since this is not formally part of the meal. Other symbolic foods include fish for fertility, pomegranates and carrots concerning merit, gourd or squash to tear up any evil decree, etc. Many foods have names similar to the words they represent. (The American equivalent to this concept could be to combine a raisin with celery and saying, "May we have a raise in salary".) The symbolic foods are generally eaten after a statement in Hebrew. It can be done in English if that is the only language one understands. This can be found in a *siddur*. Some people have a fish head on the table, and a portion is eaten inferring "May we be the head and not the tail".

Typically, a new or unusual fruit is eaten just like on *Tu B'Shvat* (p. 652). Bitter or sour foods are generally avoided, such as horseradish, pickles and green olives. Instead, sweeter foods are eaten. From *Rosh Hashanah* through *Yom Kippur*, many people go out of their way to eat only *pat Yisrael* items. Many people don't eat nuts due to a connotation of sin. Many Israelis avoid red grapes, red raisins, or drinking red wine.

Ashkenazim often make round *challah* with raisins in it. Instead of dipping *challah* in salt as with the rest of the year, it is usually drizzled with honey. *Sefardim* make their *challah* as usual, since if raisins, eggs or sugar would be considered *Mezonot* and not considered bread. Some *Sefardim* dip their *challah* in sugar instead of salt. Honey cake is the typical dessert for *Rosh Hashana*, to ensure a sweet new year.

Yom Kippur

10 *Tishrei.* (This is sometimes referred to as "*Yom HaKippurim*" [Day of Atonement] instead of just "*Yom Tov*" when saying *brachot*, such as for candle lighting. Check your *machzor* [holiday *siddur*] as to what to say.) Celebrated one day only, everywhere. It's a day-long fast, from before sunset to after sunset the next day. On *Erev Yom Kippur*, one eats a large festive meal, complete with washing for bread. It is said that if one eats a lot before *Yom Kippur*, it is counted in merit as though they had fasted for two days. One who didn't fast but was able to, is liable to spiritual excision. Many wear white to look like angels. Generally, one won't be cooking on this day unless they need to feed small children. In such a case, if cooking is absolutely necessary, it is done in the usual holiday manner. If a doctor declared one too ill, they are not allowed to fast because life takes precedence over everything. The same goes for a woman who has just given birth. If one had to eat, they should have only enough food and water to keep them healthy. (Preferably, less than the required amount for an after-*brachah*— it is not a license for a banquet.) One would add the *Yom Tov* insertions in *Me'ein Shalosh* and in *Birkat HaMazon* if bread were eaten.

This is the holiest day of the year, and can even fall on *Shabbat*, when fasting is normally forbidden, but fasting is still done. It is also a joyous time to be with Hashem, and we are considered like angels that don't eat. Toward the end one does tend to be on a spiritual "high", likely much the way Moses was on Mt. Sinai. The day is filled with prayer, introspection and repentance. It is said that one's judgment has been delivered on this day.

The Five Afflictions: *Yom Kippur* and *Tisha B'Av* have what are called the "five afflictions". One must refrain from food and drink, marital relations, wearing leather shoes, washing (including bathing or showering unless for medical or cleanliness), and anointing (wearing any type of creams, lotions or perfumes). The latter gives many people (including myself) a migraine whether fasting or not. Although fasting aggravates this and it becomes more severe as chemicals in the perfume trigger an allergic reaction. One can't eat or drink (except water) when *Yom Kippur* is over until after they hear *Havdalah*, although the five afflictions are lifted after the fast.

Sukkot

15-21 *Tishrei*. *Sukkot* or "The Feast of Booths or Tabernacles", is an eight-day Biblical fall festival, celebrated partially by eating in a temporary dwelling called a *sukkah*. *Sukkot* lasts one week, but the major holiday depends on where one lives. It is on the first day in Israel, and the first two days everywhere else. Technically, the major holidays on the last day are an entirely separate *Chag*, but attached enough to have *Chol HaMo'ed* days in-between. Traditionally, one starts putting up their *sukkah* right after *Yom Kippur* to go directly from one *mitzvah* to another. There are various guidelines for a kosher *sukkah*. It is said that Hashem's presence dwells in the *sukkah*. *Ashkenazi* and *Sefardi* kids have great fun decorating the *sukkot* [temporary dwellings]. *Chassidim* don't decorate theirs, believing that it is *Hashem's* Abode and it doesn't need decorating. We are commanded to "dwell" in the *sukkah*, so we try to do as much as we can, from eating to *Torah* study, games and sometimes sleeping. Great fun for kids, this holiday is almost like camping out. Real die-hards sleep in the *sukkah*, weather permitting of course. *Chassidim* don't sleep in their *sukkot*, as they feel it is disrespectful. A fun activity is to go "*sukkah*-hopping", visiting different families in their *sukkot*. In addition to the *sukkah*, there is a *mitzvah* to take "*Lulav* and *Etrog*" [palm and citron] with a *brachah*. They are also called the *arba minim* [four species] and consist of willow, palm, and myrtle branches, and a citron fruit. They are wave in a certain manner. Although it seems unusual, waving was regularly done in the Temple for many offerings.

Eating on Sukkot: A *sukkah* is a dwelling, and the thing we do best there is eating! Men must eat in the *sukkah* at all times. This means that whenever they have bread or any *Mezonot* (except rice), they must eat it in the *sukkah*. *Chassidic* men eat and drink in the *sukkah* regardless of what is going on. Women are only obligated to eat in the *sukkah* the first night, but can eat or drink in the *sukkah* any time they like. One can only be excused from eating in the *sukkah* if they find it miserable (such as heavy rain or a swarm of bees), but it is preferable to at least do *Kiddush* and *HaMotzi* before moving back into the house. There are additional *brachot* said for the *sukkah* before eating the meals. Each night, some have the custom to invite the "*Ushpizin*" [holy guests] to dinner, as a way of remembering our forefathers. There is a different "guest" each night. Some people use disposables in the *sukkah*, but being like a *Shabbat*, one's finest items should ideally be used unless they may be ruined. One must be careful not to drop watermelon seeds or spill water on the ground if a *sukkah* is sitting on grass. Traditional *Shabbat* foods are served, and the eating of *challah* with honey or sugar is generally carried over from *Rosh Hashanah*. On *Shabbat*, there must be an *eruv*, (an enclosed backyard fence is fine if a *sukkah* is there) to carry one's food and dishes to the *sukkah*.

Flying Insects: Yellow jackets (a type of wasp) are attracted to sweet foods and meat. It's a good idea to place a bowl of raisins, honey or sweet drink outside but far from the *sukkah*. The bees are drawn to the decoy and stay away from the *sukkah*. Sometimes pine or honeysuckle strewn atop the *sukkah* tends to keep them away as well. If one has a swarm of gallinippers (an insect that looks like a cross between a daddy-long-legs and a mosquito) do not panic. These are totally harmless. Unless bugs are bothering a person intensely, one cannot trap them or kill them. One could squirt bug spray *at them*, but not *on them*.

Chol HaMo'ed Sukkot: On these middle days of *Sukkot*, almost anything can be done as on a weekday, with the exception of laundry for adults, and writing, although writing can be done using a *shinui*.

If food or clothing is needed for the last days of the upcoming *Chag*, they can be purchased on *Chol HaMo'ed*. However, one can't purchase items needed for after the *Chag*, unless there is a financial loss.

Hoshana Rabbah: 21 Tishrei. This is the fifth *Chol HaMo'ed* day of *Sukkot*. Willow branches are beaten on the ground, symbolizing the tearing up of any evil decree of judgment. It's the last day for repentance or it's too late, and for some, the last day *Tashlich* can be done. It's said that one's judgment for the year is sealed this day.

Sh'mini 'Atzeret

22 Tishrei. "Eighth Day Assembly". It immediately follows *Hoshana Rabbah*. Although it could technically be considered the eighth day of *Sukkot*, it is actually its own individual holiday. Outside of Israel, some people still sit and eat in the *Sukkah* on this day, but no *brachah* is said. It is only one day in Israel (combined with *Simchat Torah*), and two days everywhere else (although the second day is called "*Simchat Torah*" see below). The prayer for rain is said, and the blessing for rain is said in prayers until *the* second day of *Pesach*.

Simchat Torah

23 Tishrei. "Rejoicing in the Torah". This is celebrated as part of *Sh'mini 'Atzeret* in Israel. Technically, this is still part of *Sh'mini 'Atzeret*, but it's different enough to warrant its own description.

Simchat Torah is an uncharacteristically spontaneous *Chag* celebrating the renewal of the cyclic *Torah* readings. Every Jewish man gets the honor of being called up to the *Torah* and carries a *Torah* scroll when circling in the synagogue. Often, there is dancing, parts of the service are chanted to silly songs, and humorous sermons may be given. During certain times during the service, abundant candy is thrown to the children. Alcohol is often available as it is a festive time, but it is not nearly as prevalent as with *Purim*.

Passover

15-22 *Nissan*. By far the most involved of any holiday. *Pesach* or "Passover" is an eight-day *Chag* occurring in spring. The entire holiday centers on food, in one way or another. The major holiday depends on where one lives- it is on the first and last day in Israel, and the first two and last two days everywhere else. The in-between days are "*Chol HaMo'ed*". *Pesach* commemorates the exodus from Egypt with hints to deliverance from *Mashiach* [Messiah] when he comes. During *Pesach* no *chametz* [leavening] is to be eaten, seen, or possessed the entire time, down to the minutest particle. (See below.) The highlight of the first two nights (only the first in Israel) is a special meal called "the *Seder*" [Order]. It follows a specific order using a book called a *Haggadah* [Saga- the story of the exodus]. In order to prepare and celebrate properly, one should definitely get one. Some stores offer small promotional ones for free. All the preparations of special foods and the order of the meal will be in the *Haggadah*, and is far more complex than this overview. Although not widely known, non-Jews (or those going through the conversion process) are not permitted to attend a *Seder*.

Other Details: Starting on the second night of *Pesach*, the *Omer* is counted, representing the barley offering brought in the Temple. (See *Shavu'ot* next.) Also, the next morning, the blessing for dew is recited until *Sh'mini Atzeret*.

Preceding *Pesach*, the house is thoroughly cleaned to get rid of all possible *chametz*. Any foods containing it that remain, must be given away or sold to a non-Jew via a contract through a rabbi. If it is sold, it must be taped up or covered, or locked away in a room where nobody goes.

There are very few items that do not need special Passover certification: Plain Unflavored Waters (Spring, Selzer), Bagged Ice, Fresh Uncut Vegetables, Fresh Whole Fish, Eggs, and these 100% pure items: Non-Iodized Salt, Baking Soda, Cocoa, Granulated Sugar, Extra Virgin Olive Oil, and Milk (bought before *Pesach*).

Since refraining from eating *kitniyot* is type of *chumrah*, it can be possessed but not eaten unless one is *Sefardi*. *Halachically* speaking, an *Ashkenazi* could eat at that *Sefardi's* home. The *Ashkenazi* simply cannot eat the rice, and the *Sefardi* would have it out of sight for common courtesy. Some people don't eat *gebrokts* [wetted *matzah*] such as *matzah* meal cakes or *matzah* ball soup. There are many families who do not go out to eat at other homes because *minhagim* differ so much. Many people have dishes and cookware just for *Pesach*, but others prefer to *kasher* (see p. 42) or use disposables.

Preparation: The whole house is cleaned, and the kitchen is cleaned thoroughly and *kashered*. What to do with one's *chametz* depends on one's *minhag*– it is either gotten completely out of the home, or it is "sold" to a non-Jew through a legitimate contract with a Rabbi or *kashrut* agency. If sold, it's kept in a special place, (like a closet, out of sight), often with a taped on "Sold" sign.

The night before *Pesach*, the house is customarily searched for *chametz*. It has to be a legitimate search. One should take a few pieces of *chametz*, and hide them throughout the house. (To make it easier: the day before *Pesach*, take 10 pieces of toasted oats cereal, wrap each one in a small piece of paper towel, and secure it with paper-backed masking tape. Store in a small paper bag until hiding time.) Ideally the search is done by candlelight, although some may use a flashlight for safety reasons. A declaration is made (found in a *siddur*) before the search, and then without talking, the search commences. You may find some real *chametz* in the process, and this is great! Some needs to be found for declarations and burning. When the search is complete, say the second declaration, and put the *chametz* pieces in a safe place so they will be burned the next morning. In the morning after prayers, take the *chametz* to be burned (also with a declaration after burning). Some larger Jewish communities have public burning sites. If you do not have access to one, use a disposable aluminum roasting pan. Many burn their *lulav* at the same time to tie the seasonal *mitzvot* of the year together.

Chametz: The Jewish definition of "leavening". Whenever certain grains become wet, fermentation (leavening) starts to take place after eighteen minutes. We take precautions to eat only products that are marked "*Kosher L'Pesach*" or "kosher for Passover". If a product is not marked as such, it is possible it contains prohibited *chametz*. All processed products must be certified "kosher for Passover", with a "P". *Kashrut* agencies will have a list of products, which changes from year to year. The same products are not always "kosher for Passover" every year.

Pet food must not contain any *chametz*, but *kitniyot* can be fed to pets. Having pets on a grain-free diet all year is a great idea. *Kashrut* agencies often have a list of "kosher for *Pesach*" pet foods. Fish food applies too, as it usually contains some *chametz*. Freeze-dried tubifex worms are a good substitute, and some goldfish will eat *matzah*!

Customary Foods: It is preferable to use *Shmurah matzah* ensuring no *chametz*. Regular year-round *matzah* has usually been baked after the allotted time of fermentation has elapsed, and could become *chametz*. Having *Shmurah matzah*, especially made by hand, is considered very praiseworthy.

Aside from *matza*, many symbolic foods are eaten at the *Seder*; four cups of wine are drunken; potato, celery, leek or hard-boiled egg dipped in salt water; *matzah* and non-hydroponic lettuce (usually Romaine) and/or horseradish; "*Charoset*", a mixture of wine, ground fruit and nuts, symbolic of our bitter slavery in Egypt and eventual freedom. A festive meal is served in addition to these special foods.

As a stringency, *Ashkenazim* and *Chassidim* don't eat *kitniyot* [beans, rice or products of them].

<u>*Ashkenazim*</u>: Generally, most *Ashkenazim* eat *gebrokts*. Some will not *eat it the* first day, but will then eat them the remainder of *Pesach*. Most *Ashkenazim* use *Shmurah matzah*, whether machine-made or hand-made. Some may use "18-minute *matzah*" that is machine-made under precise conditions.

<u>*Chassidim*</u>: *Chassidim* use only hand-made *Shmurah matzah* and do not eat any form of *gebrokts*. In fact,

they keep their *matzah* in a separate place away from the dining table to ensure that *matzah* will not get wet. Grape juice is permitted on the dining table at the same time as the *matzah*, but never water or drinks that contain it. On the very last day of *Pesach*, some *Chassidim* make it a point to eat *gebrokts*.

Sefardim: Most *Sefardim* use only hand-made *Shmurah matzah*. Some also use a special soft type of unleavened bread. Some *Sefardim* eat *kitniyot* but not all. *Sefardim* are indeed "kosher for *Pesach*"— it is a total misconception that they aren't, as *kitniyot* is not *chametz*. *Kitniyot* may include mustard seed, corn, and peanuts. Most *Sefardim* eat rice on *Pesach*, which must be triple checked for *chametz* prior to the start of the holiday. It is spread out on a white cloth and gone through to make sure that there's no barley or other grain hiding in it.

Chol HaMo'ed Pesach: Just as with *Sukkot*, nearly anything can be done *melachah*-wise. As long as one had their car cleaned of *chametz* before *Pesach*, they can go out on day trips, or to local attractions and the like.

Shavu'ot

6-7 *Sivan.* Celebrated one day in Israel, two days everywhere else. *Shavu'ot* means "weeks" due to the 7-week period of counting the *Omer* from the second day of *Pesach* (first day in Israel). This is a commemoration of the day the Torah was given on Mt. Sinai. The *Book of Ruth* is read, since she was the first convert to Judaism and accepted the *Torah*, similar to the fact that the Jewish nation accepted the *Torah* on Mount Sinai this day as well. Some synagogues are decorated with sprigs from trees, grass, and flowers, reminiscent of Mount Sinai, where the Torah was given.

When Israel first received the *Torah*, they learned the *sh'chitah* laws, but it was *Shabbat*, so they couldn't prepare meat or *kasher* vessels yet, so they had to have dairy. Since *Torah* is likened to nourishing "spiritual milk", this is yet another reason for eating dairy.

Often, people have a dairy meal at night and meat in the day or vice versa. Some still only have meat for the holiday, and treat it no differently than any other *chag*. There is even a *minhag* (mostly done by some *Chassidim*) to eat some dairy foods first, wash their hands, then have something *parve*, (some wait 30-60 minutes in between) and finally eat a meat meal. Those that do this have two *challot* for the dairy meal, and then two separate ones for the meat meal. Any remainders of the dairy meal *challot*, (even if whole), are never used at the meat meal.

On the first night, many synagogues and *Kollelim* [places of *Torah* learning] offer all-night *Torah* study, individual or one-on-one learning, or lectures on *Torah* topics. To add to the excitement, usually snacks and beverages are included. Some people don't stay up all night, as it can interfere with one's morning prayers. Occasionally, second day *Shavu'ot* can occur on *Shabbat*, so one has to make an extra preparation called the "*Eruv Tavshilin*", which is explained in detail on p. 654.

Customary Foods: Dairy foods are usually eaten, by far the most popular item being cheesecake. Other favorite foods include cheese blintzes, pizza, macaroni and cheese, doughnuts, and ice cream.

Minor Holidays

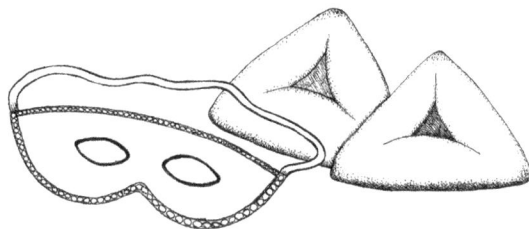

Purim

14 *Adar.* (During a leap year, it occurs in the second *Adar.*) A lively holiday. Children (and some adults) dress up in costume. Purim night and morning, all must hear the *Megillah* [Book of Esther], the only book in which Hashem's name never appears. During the *Megillah* reading, many have the custom to make noise to drown out the wicked Haman's name each time it is mentioned. The general theme is concealment, since Hashem and His miracles were "hidden" and not obvious. *Tzedakah* [charity] is given. Parties, food, skits, and dancing abound. Some have the custom to consume alcohol until they become drunk, as it causes the true nature of a person to be "revealed". On *Purim* day (or Friday if *Purim* is on *Shabbat*), two different ready-to-eat foods ("*Mishloach Manot*") are sent to at least one person. Some send thematic packages to match costumes. The *Seudah* [festive meal] is eaten during the day.

In Jerusalem or any other cities that were surrounded by a wall in the time of Joshua, "*Shushan Purim*" is celebrated a day later. Since the people rested from battle on *Purim* day, the holiday was postponed to the next day on the 15th of *Adar* instead of the 14th. (See "*What to do When*" on "*Shushan Purim on Shabbat*", p. 661.)

Customary Foods: Ashkenazi "*Hamantaschen*" cookies are by far the most common. (See picture above.)

Chanukah

25 *Kislev*-1 *Tevet.* This celebrates victory over the Greek Empire that sought to wipe out Judaism. A miracle occurred when the Temple was recaptured and dedicated, and the last pure flask of oil for the *menorah* [candelabra] which normally lasted one day, lasted eight. Generally, *Sefardim* and *Chassidim* use oil with wicks instead of candles. In some homes, each person has a *Chanukiah* [eight-branched *menorah*]. Spouses share, but husbands light. It's set by a window facing the street to publicize the miracle. Each night a new light is put in (right to left), but it is lit from left to right with an extra light called a *shamash* [attendant]. (On Friday nights, the *Chanukiah* is lit first before *Shabbat* candles.) The *shamash* is lit, *brachot* said, then the actual lights lit one by one. It's customary to sit with the candles ½ hour, and one lights where they sleep. Unlike *Shabbat* candles, one cannot benefit from the *Chanukiah*, except for the *shamash*. Games are played with a four-sided top ("*sevivon*" in Hebrew and "*dreidel*" in Yiddish).

Customary Foods: Jelly doughnuts called "*sufganiyot*" and potato pancakes called "*latkes*" are served. Some eat dairy foods because Yehudit [Judith] used cheese to kill the evil Greek general, and helped win the war. Children often receive gifts, nuts or candy. Throughout the holiday, parties and food abound.

Tu B'Sh'vat

15 Sh'vat. This is the New Year for Trees: The time when the sap starts to flow, a food-related holiday. People eat a new fruit and serve fruits and nuts. When one eats a new fruit for the first time in over 30 days, the *brachah* "*…Shehecheyanu v'kiyemanu v'higi'anu laz'man hazeh*" ["…Who gave us life, sustained us, and brought us to this time"] is recited, next the *brachah* on the fruit, and then eat it.

Lag B'Omer

19 Iyar. First, let's explain what an "Omer" is. For a 49-day period (7 weeks) starting during Passover to the holiday of *Shavu'ot*, the days are counted up from 1 to 49. Each day's count represents the "Omer" barley offering brought to the Temple. Nowadays, without the Temple, the nightly ritual "counting of the *Omer*" takes its place.

In the times of the great Rabbi Akiva, there was a plague that killed 24,000 of his students during the first 33 days of the *Omer*. Lag B'Omer (33rd day of the Omer) marks the anniversary of the end of the students' deaths. Prior to *Lag B'Omer* is a mourning period. No music is played, no haircuts or shaving are permitted (unless one's job requires it), and no weddings allowed until *Lag B'Omer*, (midday the 34th for *Sefardim*). Rabbi Shimon Bar Yochai author of the *Kabbalistic* work *the Zohar*, also died on this day. Per his request it's to be celebrated. During the night, commonly a bonfire is made. The song "*Bar Yochai*" is sung, and mystical stories are told by fireside. During the day, some have archery contests, outings, and community picnics. Grilling and all manner of picnicky foods are eaten.

Fast Days

Besides knowing what foods to eat when, one needs to know when *not* to eat (but one must still feed their young children and pets.) Except for *Yom Kippur* and *Tisha B'Av*, all other fast days are only from dawn to dusk. All the short fast days and *Tisha B'Av* mark the events of tragedies, so we treat them as days of mourning. No food or water can be consumed (unless deemed necessary by a doctor or health condition).

The Fast of Gedaliah

3 Tishrei. A partial fast day, that occurs on the day after *Rosh Hashanah*, this commemorates the assassination of the Jewish governor Gedaliah just before the first Temple was destroyed by the Babylonians.

The Tenth of Tevet

10 Tevet. This day marks the date in which the Babylonians started their siege of Jerusalem. This is the only fast that can occur on a Friday. (See "*Tenth of Tevet Before Shabbat*" in the "'*What to Do When' Guide*" on p. 661-662.)

Fast of Esther

13 *Adar*. (During a leap year, it occurs in the second *Adar*.) The day before *Purim*, this commemorates the fast that Queen Esther instituted in the *Book of Esther*. From *Rosh Chodesh Adar* through *Erev Purim*, the Biblical "half-shekel" per person is given to one's synagogue (about $1.50 or three half-dollar coins). If one could not give their half-shekel, before *Erev Purim*, they can give it any day throughout the month of *Adar*. One must hear the *Megillah* at night, then come home to break the fast. (See also "Purim" on p. 651.)

Fast of the Firstborn

14 *Nissan*. Only for those who were the first offspring of their mother, this is a partial fast on the day before *Pesach*, commemorating the event when the Jewish firstborn were spared from death during the plague of Egypt. Any firstborn man must fast, (some firstborn women do as well), but it is generally avoided by attending a *siyum*, [a celebration of having completed reading a book of *Talmud*], which is most often given at synagogues or a *Kollel*. One must attend this joyous event in order to skip this fast.

Seventeenth of Tammuz

17 *Tammuz*. The date when the walls of the Temple were breached. From this day until *Tisha B'Av* is "the Three Weeks", which is a common time of tragedy for the Jewish people. It's customary not to take risks or go to court. Mourning is observed like the days before *Lag B'Omer*. Just before *Tisha B'Av*, the laws of mourning get stricter. For *Ashkenazim* it's from *Rosh Chodesh Av* until after *Tisha B'Av* ("the Nine Days"). For *Sefardim*, it's the week of *Tisha B'Av*. Meat isn't eaten except for on *Shabbat* or a "*seudat mitzvah*" [meal celebrating a *mitzvah*]. Meat leftovers from these must be frozen until after *Tisha B'Av*.

Tisha B'Av

9 *Av*. This is the most serious and sad day in Judaism, and the anniversary of the destruction of both the first and the second Temples. It is a day-long fast, from before sunset to after sunset. It is literally mourning the Temples' destruction, by fasting, and sitting on the floor or in low chairs (for those of us who can't get down there). It is advisable to drink extra water a day or two before. If it falls on *Shabbat*, the fast is postponed until the next day. One observes the five afflictions and *Tisha B'Av* the ill are treated exactly the same as *Yom Kippur*. Staying cool helps people prone to headaches, as does avoiding perfumes. Fortunately, people aren't allowed to use it, which helps those of us who are sensitive to it.

One should take off their shoes, wear non-leather shoes or slippers, just before and throughout *Tisha B'Av*. Torah isn't studied unless the subject pertains to mourning. Frivolity and joking are avoided. It is customary not to greet others. Some have a *minhag* to sleep less comfortably that night. *Eichah* [Lamentations] is read. Often lectures or films are presented dealing with the holocaust or self-improvement.

One cannot eat until after a certain amount of time after sunset when three stars appear. *Havdalah* isn't recited, because this isn't a *Chag*. *Ashkenazim* and *Chassidim* keep the general mourning restrictions until *Halachic* midday of the tenth of Av. *Sefardim* keep all the mourning restrictions throughout the tenth of *Av* up until three stars can be seen, since that is when the majority of the time the Temple was burning.

Erev Tisha B'Av: Before sundown, one should eat the "*Tisha B'Av* meal" consisting of a small amount of ashes, bread and a hard-boiled egg. (A blackened and crumbled piece of toast works well for ashes, stored in an airtight container will last for years.) This symbolizes mourning and the destruction of the Temples. The egg should be dipped in ashes for *Ashkenazim*. The bread is dipped in ashes for *Sefardim* and *Chassidim*, and the egg eaten cold. When dipping, proclaim "This is the *Tisha B'Av* meal". Preferably eat the meal alone, either on the floor or a low chair. The meal must be completed before sundown. One should have food that does not make them thirsty, although some salt is good, because it helps you retain water. For *Ashkenazim* and *Chassidim*, it should only consist of one cooked food plus other raw foods. One should eat an ample main meal that will last.

If *Tisha B'Av* is observed on Sunday, things are done differently. (See "Tisha B'Av Postponed to Sunday" in the "'*What to Do When' Guide*" on p. 662.) Since mourning is not allowed on *Shabbat*, the *Tisha B'Av* meal is not eaten and eating together is allowed, but one must be certain to stop eating before sundown. *Havdalah* is often recited at synagogue and consists only of the *brachah* for fire.

What Is an "Eruv Tavshilin", and Why Do I Need to Make One? When a *Chag* occurs on a Friday (Thursday night), or, outside of Israel it may be a 2-Day Chag (starting on a Wednesday night), one must make an *Eruv Tavshilin* [mixing of cooked foods] the day before the holiday starts (*Erev Yom Tov*). This simple action enables one to cook, bake, insulate, and light candles in preparation for *Shabbat*. Since normally one cannot prepare for another day besides the *Chag*, it is essential to make the *Eruv* so one can prepare for *Shabbat* on the actual *Chag* itself.

On *Erev Chag* [the eve of the holiday], take a cooked item, (like a hard-boiled egg) and a baked item (such as a bread, or *matzah* on *Pesach*). Hold them together, and make the *brachah* (found in a *siddur*), followed by a short declaration in a language you understand. Set them aside in a safe place so that they won't accidentally be eaten on the *Chag*. Some say the *brachah* and declaration *after* placing the *Eruv* in a safe place. The items have to be eaten sometime during *Shabbat*, it doesn't matter when.

The principle behind the *Eruv Tavshilin* is, that although these foods are designated for *Shabbat*, you had already started to prepare them even before the holiday started. You are just continuing to complete the original work on them during the *Chag*.

What Should I Do When Shabbat & Holidays Are Back-to-Back?

It can be tricky to remember from year to year, what happens when, or how to do certain things, so this is a short, general guide on when to light, fix food, or do certain *mitzvot*. Since one can't prepare for a day other than *Shabbat*, or prepare the second day of *Chag* until the first day is over, there are certain procedures one must do. Just how does one end one day and go into the next? The words and phrases to say should all be found in a *siddur*, but they can be very hard to find! All the unusual times are compiled here together for easy reference. Since days can vary so greatly, where there is a difference in holiday observance, it is noted what area it is for. This guide below should help you be able to know "What to do When" for holidays and events that are back-to-back with *Shabbat*.

The "What to Do When" Guide

Shabbat Before Chag (Israel Only)– 2-Days: <u>Ushering in *Shabbat*</u>: Friday night, a memorial candle is lit just before *Shabbat* candles. One lights and says the formula and candle lighting *brachah*, "...*Lehadlich Ner shel Shabbat*" [...kindling of the *Shabbat* lights]. Normal *Kiddush* is made, *Shabbat* proceeds as normal.

Ending *Shabbat*/Starting the *Chag*: Saturday night (to start *Motza'ei Shabbat*) after sundown, one waits their usual amount of time before *Havdalah*. Before doing any cooking or lighting, one should say "*Baruch Hamavdil beyn Kodesh l'Kodesh*" ["Blessed is the separation between the sacred and the sacred"]. Only *then* can they start to prepare for the *Chag*. Now, one transfers fire from the memorial candle and lights the candles as is their custom, with the *Yom Tov brachah*, "...*Lehadlich Ner shel Yom Tov*" [...kindling of the *Yom Tov* lights]. Some women start preparing the meal, but wait to light after their husbands return from synagogue.

Kiddush/Havdalah: When it is time for the meal, the holiday's *Kiddush* and *brachot* are recited, plus *Shehecheyanu* (except the last day of *Pesach*). Towards the end, the *Havdalah brachah* and a special paragraph is said within *Kiddush*, and the *Shabbat* candles are used as the *Havdalah* flame. The meal and rest of the holiday then continues as usual.

Ending the *Chag*: Before doing any *melachah*, one should say "*Baruch Hamavdil beyn Kodesh l'Chol*" ["Blessed is the separation between the sacred and the secular"] after the normal wait time for *Havdalah*. Actual *Havdalah* is only said on wine with the single last *Brachah* and paragraph. No spices or fire are used.

**Shabbat Before Chag (Outside of Israel)– 3-Days: **<u>Ushering in *Shabbat*</u>: Friday night, a memorial candle (ideally 3-day) is lit before *Shabbat* candles, and all is done the same as above for ushering in *Shabbat*.

Ending *Shabbat*/Starting the 1st Day *Chag*: Saturday night after sundown, one waits their usual amount of time before *Havdalah*. Before doing anything, one must say "*Baruch Hamavdil beyn Kodesh l'Kodesh*". Only *then* can they start to prepare for the *Chag*. Now, one transfers fire from the memorial candle to a new memorial candle (if needed), and then lights the candles with the *Yom Tov brachah* as is their custom. Now she can start preparing or heating the meal, setting the table, etc. Some women light after their husband returns from synagogue.

Kiddush/Havdalah: When it is time for the meal, the holiday's *Kiddush* and *brachot* are recited, (plus *Shehecheyanu* except for the last days of *Pesach*). Towards the end of *Kiddush*, the *Havdalah brachah* "*Baruch Hamavdil beyn Kodesh l'Kodesh*" and a special paragraph are said within *Kiddush*, and the *Yom Tov* candles are used as the *Havdalah* flame. The meal and rest of the holiday then continues as usual.

Ending the 1st Day/Starting the 2nd Day *Chag*: Sunday night, one waits their usual amount of time after sundown. Only *then* can they start to prepare for the *Chag*. Now, one transfers fire from the memorial candle and lights the *Yom Tov* candles as is their custom. Some women wait to light until after their husbands return from synagogue. The *Chag* continues as usual.

Ending the *Chag*: Monday night, after the normal waiting time before doing any *melachah*, one should say "*Baruch Hamavdil beyn Kodesh l'Chol*". *Havdalah* is recited only on wine, with the *brachah* and single *Havdalah* paragraph. No spices or fire are used.

Shabbat Before Pesach (Israel Only)– 2-Days: This requires careful advanced planning. The house must have been cleaned and everything switched over for *Pesach*. However, the day before *Pesach* one does not eat regular *matzah*, and on a non-*Pesach Shabbat*, one should ideally have *challah*, yet one cannot eat *chametz* after a certain time on *Erev Pesach*! What to do? Here is the schedule of events...

Thursday: Any firstborn fast (see Fast of the Firstborn later). The search for c*hametz* is performed after dark.

Friday: All *chametz* is burned. Preparation for *Shabbat*, the *Pesach Seder* and meals is underway.

Ushering in *Shabbat*: Friday evening, a memorial candle is lit before the *Shabbat* candles at the normal candle lighting time with the *Shabbat brachah*. *Kiddush* is done as normal but when it comes time for *HaMotzi*, this is where it gets tricky... Perhaps the majority of people still use *challah*, which can either be eaten outside or in. Carefully spread a napkin out over the plate one will be eating on. One must make sure any crumbs are caught in the napkin, and when done eating, carefully fold the napkin up to contain any crumbs. Bring it to the bathroom and flush it! This gets any *chametz* safely off and out of your property! Now the other alternative used by some *Sefardim*, is to bake or fry *matzah* in oil or egg, which qualifies for the *bracha* of *HaMotzi,* but only in this particular instance, according to Rav Ovadia Yosef z"l. The meal continues with *kosher* for *Pesach* fare.

***Shabbat* Lunch**: Lunch must be eaten extra early before the time to stop eating *chametz*, *Kiddush* is done as normal, and *HaMotzi* is done as described above, being very careful to dispose of the napkin in time. Some people finish and say *Birkat HaMazon*, wait a half hour (go for a walk, nap, etc.), then say *HaMotzi* and eat their *challah* in order to have a third meal for the day. All must be disposed of before the time limit is up.

Ending *Shabbat*/Starting *Pesach*: Saturday night after sundown, one waits their usual amount of time before *Havdalah* then says, "*Baruch Hamavdil beyn Kodesh l'Kodesh*". Only *then* can they start to prepare for the *Chag*. Now, one transfers fire from the memorial candle to a new memorial candle (if needed), and then lights the *Yom Tov* candles as is their custom with the regular *Yom Tov brachah*. Now she can start preparing or heating the meal, setting the table, getting ready for the *Seder*, etc. Some light after their husband returns from synagogue.

Kiddush/Havdalah: When it is time for the meal, the holiday's *Kiddush* and *brachot* are recited, (plus *Shehecheyanu* except for the last day of *Pesach*). Towards the end of *Kiddush*, the *Havdalah brachah* ("*Baruch Hamavdil beyn Kodesh l'Kodesh*") and a special paragraph is said within *Kiddush*, and the *Yom Tov* candles are used as the *Havdalah* flame. The meal and rest of the holiday then continues as usual.

Ending the *Chag*: Sunday night before doing anything, one must say, "*Baruch Hamavdil beyn Kodesh l'Chol*". *Havdalah* is recited only on wine, with the *brachah* and single *Havdalah* paragraph. No spices or fire are used.

Shabbat Before Pesach (Outside of Israel)– 3-Days: This requires careful advanced planning. The house must have been cleaned and everything switched over for *Pesach*. However, the day before *Pesach* one does not eat regular *matzah*, and on a non-*Pesach Shabbat*, one should ideally have *challah*, yet one cannot eat *chametz* after a certain time on *Erev Pesach*! What to do? Here is the schedule of events...

Thursday: Any firstborn fast (see Fast of the Firstborn later). The search for *chametz* is performed after dark.

Friday: All *chametz* is burned. Preparation for *Shabbat*, the *Pesach Seder* and meals is underway.

Ushering in *Shabbat*: Friday evening, a memorial candle is lit before the *Shabbat* candles at the normal candle lighting time, with the *Shabbat brachah*. *Kiddush* is done as normal, but when it comes time for *HaMotzi*, this is where it gets tricky... Perhaps the majority of people still use *challah*, which can either be eaten outside or in. Carefully spread a napkin out over the plate one will be eating on. One must make sure any crumbs are caught in the napkin, and when done eating, carefully fold the napkin up to contain any crumbs. Bring it to the bathroom and flush it! This gets any *chametz* safely off and out of your property! Now the other alternative used by some *Sefardim*, is to bake or fry *matzah* in oil or egg, which qualifies for the *bracha* of *HaMotzi,* but only in this particular instance, according to Rav Ovadia Yosef z"l. The meal continues with *kosher* for *Pesach* fare.

Shabbat Lunch: Lunch must be eaten extra early before the time to stop eating *chametz*, *Kiddush* is done as normal, and *HaMotzi* is done as described above, being very careful to dispose of the napkin in time. Some people finish and say *Birkat HaMazon*, wait a half hour (go for a walk, nap, etc.), then say *HaMotzi* and eat their *challah* in order to have a third meal for the day. All must be disposed of before the time limit is up.

Ending *Shabbat*/Starting 1st Day *Pesach*: Saturday night after sundown, one waits their usual amount of time before *Havdalah*. Before doing anything, one should say "*Baruch Hamavdil beyn Kodesh l'Kodesh*". Only *then* can they start to prepare for the *Chag*. Now, one transfers fire from the memorial candle to a new memorial candle (if needed), and then lights the *Yom Tov* candles with the *Yom Tov brachah* as is their custom. Now she can start preparing or heating the meal, setting the table, getting ready for the *Seder*, etc. Some women wait to light until after their husband returns from synagogue.

Kiddush/Havdalah: When it is time for the meal, the holiday's *Kiddush* and *brachot* are recited, (plus *Shehecheyanu* except for the last days of *Pesach*). Towards the end of *Kiddush*, the *Havdalah brachah* ("*Baruch Hamavdil beyn Kodesh l'Kodesh*") and a special paragraph is said within *Kiddush*, and the *Yom Tov* candles are used as the *Havdalah* flame. The meal and rest of the holiday then continues as usual.

Ending the 1st Day/Starting the 2nd Day *Chag*: Sunday night, one waits their usual amount of time after sundown. Only *then* can they start to prepare for the *Chag*. Now, one transfers fire from the memorial candle and lights the *Yom Tov* candles with the *Yom Tov brachah* as is their custom. Some women wait to light until after their husbands return from synagogue. The *Chag* continues as usual.

Ending the *Chag*: Monday night, after the normal waiting time, before doing any *melachah*, one should say "*Baruch Hamavdil beyn Kodesh l'Chol*". *Havdalah* is recited only on wine, with the *brachah* and single *Havdalah* paragraph. No spices or fire are used.

Shabbat on a Chag (Israel Only)– 1-Day: <u>Ushering in ***Shabbat/Yom Tov***</u>: All preparation and cooking must be already done before candle lighting time on Friday. A memorial candle is lit, then the *Shabbat/Yom Tov* candles are lit at the normal candle lighting time. One says the formula *brachah* with "*Ner shel Shabbat v'Yom Tov*" [the kindling of the lights of *Shabbat* and *Yom Tov*]. *Kiddush* is done with the appropriate insertions for *Shabbat*, the specific *Chag*, and *Shehecheyanu* (except on the last day of *Pesach*).

Ending *Shabbat*/the *Chag*: After one's normal waiting time before doing any *melachah*, one should say "*Baruch Hamavdil beyn Kodesh L'Chol*". *Havdalah* is said on wine with the spices and fire as usual.

Shabbat on First Day Chag (Outside of Israel)– 2-Days: <u>Ushering in ***Shabbat/Yom Tov***</u>: Friday evening, all preparation and cooking must be already done. A memorial candle is lit, then the *Shabbat/Yom Tov* candles are lit at the normal candle lighting time. One says the formula *brachah* with "*Ner shel Shabbat v'Yom Tov*". *Kiddush* is done with the proper insertions for *Shabbat*, the specific *Chag*, and *Shehecheyanu* (except for on the last days of *Pesach*). *Shabbat* continues as normal,

Ending *Shabbat and* 1st Day/Starting the 2nd Day *Chag*: Saturday night after sundown, one waits their usual amount of time before *Havdalah*. Before doing anything, one must say "*Baruch Hamavdil beyn Kodesh l'Kodesh*". Only *then* can they start to prepare for the *Chag*. Now, one transfers fire from the memorial candle and lights the *Yom Tov* candles with the *Yom Tov brachah* as is their custom. Now she can start preparing or heating the meal, setting the table, etc. Some wait to light until the husband returns from synagogue.

Kiddush/Havdalah: When it is time for the meal, the holiday's *Kiddush* and *brachot* are recited, (plus *Shehecheyanu* except for the last days of *Pesach*). Towards the end of *Kiddush*, the *Havdalah brachah* "*Baruch Hamavdil beyn Kodesh l'Kodesh*" is said within *Kiddush*, and the *Yom Tov* candles are used as the *Havdalah* flame. The meal and rest of the holiday then continues as usual.

Ending the *Chag*: Sunday night, after the normal waiting time for *Havdalah* before doing any *melachah*, one must say "*Baruch Hamavdil beyn Kodesh l'Chol*". *Havdalah* is recited only on wine, with the *brachah*, and single *Havdala*h paragraph. No spices or fire are used.

Shabbat on First Day Rosh Hashanah: – 2-Days: <u>Ushering in *Shabbat/Rosh Hashanah*</u>: Friday evening, all preparation and cooking must be already done before candle lighting time. A memorial candle is lit, then the *Shabbat/Yom Tov* candles are lit at the normal candle lighting time. One says the formula *brachah* with "*Ner shel Shabbat v'Yom Tov*". (Some say, "*Shabbat v'Yom HaZicharon*" [*Shabbat* and the Day of Remembrance] instead of *Yom Tov*.) *Kiddush* is done with the appropriate insertions for *Shabbat*, *Rosh Hashanah*, and *Shehecheyanu*. After *HaMotzi*, the special symbolic foods are eaten, and the meal continues.

Ending *Shabbat and* 1st Day/Starting the 2nd Day *Chag*: Saturday night after sundown, one waits their usual amount of time before *Havdalah*. Before doing anything, one should say "*Baruch Hamavdil beyn Kodesh l'Kodesh*". Only *then* can they start to prepare for the *Chag*. Now, one transfers fire from the memorial candle and lights the *Yom Tov* candles as is their custom. One says the formula *brachah* with "*Ner shel Yom Tov*", (or "*Yom HaZicharon*" as mentioned above). Now preparation can start for heating the meal, setting the table, etc. Some women wait to light until after their husband returns from synagogue.

Kiddush/Havdalah: When it is time for the meal, the *Rosh Hashanah Kiddush* and *brachot* are recited, (plus *Shehecheyanu*). Towards the end of *Kiddush*, the *Havdalah brachah* and a special paragraph is said within *Kiddush*, and the *Yom Tov* candles are used as the *Havdalah* flame. The meal continues as usual.

Ending the *Chag*: Sunday night, after the normal waiting time for *Havdalah* before doing any *melachah*, one must say "*Baruch Hamavdil beyn Kodesh l'Chol*". *Havdala*h is recited only on wine, with the *brachah* and single paragraph. No spices or fire are used.

Yom Kippur on Shabbat: Friday still in daytime, one should eat a large festive meal then get ready for the *Chag*. <u>Ushering in *Shabbat/Yom Kippur*</u>: Friday evening, a memorial candle is lit that will burn throughout the *Chag*. (*Ashkenazim* have the custom of its being lit by the husband.) A memorial candle is also lit in merit of the deceased. The *Shabbat/Yom Tov* candles are lit at the normal candle lighting time. One says the formula *brachah* with "*Ner shel Shabbat v'Yom Tov*", but many say "*Ner shel Shabbat v'Yom HaKippurim*" [the kindling of the lights of *Shabbat* and *Yom Kippur*]. *Shehecheyanu* is still said by *Ashkenazi* women, *Sefardim* too if they won't be attending synagogue. *Kiddush* is not made, even if one can't fast due to health. Cooking is not usually done (see overview on p. 645-646). **Ending the *Chag***: After one's normal wait time for *Havdalah* before doing any *melachah*, one must say "*Baruch Hamavdil beyn Kodesh l'Chol*". *Havdalah* is said on wine, usually done at synagogue, but it can be done at home as well. *Sefardim* omit doing the spices, but *Ashkenazim* do the spices as for any other *Shabbat*. The fire is still done as usual, either with the memorial candle itself, or a *Havdalah* candle lit from it.

Shabbat on the Second Day of Shavu'ot (Outside of Israel)– 2-Days: <u>Thursday</u>: Sometime during the day, an *Eruv Tavshilin* is made.

<u>**Ushering in the *Chag***</u>: Thursday night before candle lighting, a memorial candle is lit. One can either light the *Yom Tov* candles then, or wait until later and transfer fire from the memorial candle to light the *Yom Tov* candles. One says the formula *brachah* with "*Ner shel Yom Tov*". The *Yom Tov Kiddush* and *Shehecheyanu* are said.

<u>**Friday**</u>: The *Chag* continues as normal, and one can cook during the day for *Shabbat* as well as the *Yom Tov*.

<u>**Ending the First Day *Chag*/Starting Second Day and *Shabbat***</u>: On Friday evening, at the normal candle lighting time for *Shabbat*, one transfers fire from the memorial candle to light the *Shabbat* candles, and says the formula *brachah* with "*Ner shel Shabbat v'Yom Tov*". The *Shabbat/Yom Tov Kiddush* is done with *Shabbat* and holiday insertions, *Shehecheyanu* is still said, and *Shabbat* proceeds as normal.

<u>**Ending *Shabbat***</u>: After one's normal wait time for *Havdalah* before doing any *melachah*, one must say "*Baruch Hamavdil beyn Kodesh l'Chol*". *Havdalah* is said on wine with spices and fire as usual.

Shabbat After Chag (Israel Only)– 2-Days: <u>Thursday</u>: Sometime during the day, an *Eruv Tavshilin* is made.

<u>**Ushering in the *Chag***</u>: Thursday night before candle lighting, a memorial candle is lit. One can either light the *Yom Tov* candles then, or wait until later and transfer fire from the memorial candle to light the *Yom Tov* candles. One says the formula *brachah* with "*Ner shel Yom Tov*".

<u>***Kiddush***</u>: The *Yom Tov Kiddush* is done with *Shehecheyanu* (except last day *Pesach*), and the meal is eaten.

<u>**Friday**</u>: The *Chag* continues as normal, and one can cook during the day for *Shabbat* as well as the *Yom Tov*.

<u>**Ending the *Chag*/Starting *Shabbat***</u>: Friday evening, at the normal *Shabbat* candle lighting time, one transfers fire from the memorial candle to light the *Shabbat* candles, and says "*Ner shel Shabbat*".

<u>**Ending *Shabbat***</u>: After one's normal wait time before doing any *melachah*, one must say "*Baruch Hamavdil beyn Kodesh l'Chol*", *Havdalah* is said on wine with the spices and fire as usual, even if it is *Chol HaMoed*.

Shabbat After Chag (Outside of Israel)– 3 Days: <u>Wednesday</u>: Sometime during the day on Wednesday, an *Eruv Tavshilin* is made.

<u>**Ushering in the *Chag***</u>: Wednesday night before candle lighting, a memorial candle (preferably a 2-Day) is lit. One can either light the *Yom Tov* candles then, or wait until later and transfer fire from the memorial candle to light the *Yom Tov* candles. One says the formula *brachah* with "*Ner shel Yom Tov*". The *Yom Tov Kiddush* is done with *Shehecheyanu* (except for the last two days of *Pesach*).

<u>**Ending Day-1/Starting Day-2 of the Chag**</u>: Thursday night, one waits their usual amount of time after sundown. Only *then* can they to prepare for the 2nd day of the *Chag*. Now, one transfers fire from the memorial candle and lights the *Yom Tov* candles as is their custom. One says the formula *brachah* with "*Ner shel Yom Tov*". Some women wait to light until after their husbands return from synagogue.

Kiddush: The *Yom Tov Kiddush* is done with *Shehecheyanu* (except last day *Pesach*), and the meal is eaten.

Friday: The *Chag* continues as usual, and one can cook during the day for *Shabbat* as well as the *Yom Tov*.

Ending Day-2 of the *Chag*/Starting *Shabbat*: Friday evening, at the normal *Shabbat* candle lighting time, one transfers fire from the memorial candle, and says the formula *brachah* with "*Ner shel Shabbat*". *Shabbat Kiddush* is done as normal.

Ending *Shabbat*: After one's normal wait time before doing any *melachah*, one must say "*Baruch Hamavdil beyn Kodesh l'Chol*". *Havdalah* is said on wine with the spices and fire as usual, even if it is *Chol HaMoed*.

Purim Before Shabbat: **Thursday**: The Fast of Esther is observed from before sunrise to after sunset. The *Megillah* is read at night, and ideally the fast should be broken after hearing it. (The fast can be broken earlier "when 3 small stars appear", as long as one is going to hear the *Megillah* later that night.)

Friday: The *Megillah* is read at some point during the daytime, gifts given to the poor, *Mishloach Manot* are delivered, and the *Purim* meal must be eaten relatively early and finished about 4-hours before *Shabbat*, so that one can still have an appetite for the *Shabbat* meal.

Ushering in *Shabbat*: Everything else is continued as for any normal *Shabbat*, start to finish.

Ending the Fast/*Kiddush*: One who is fasting cannot eat or drink until they hear *Kiddush*, which would be done after sunset ("after 3 stars are visible").

Ending *Shabbat*: After one's normal wait time before doing any *melachah*, one must say "*Baruch Hamavdil beyn Kodesh l'Chol*". *Havdalah* is said on wine with the spices and fire as usual.

Shushan Purim on Shabbat (Jerusalem, Israel/Walled Cities) Observance of *Shushan Purim* strictly applies to Jerusalem, or any other city that had a wall surrounding it in the time of Joshua. Even though it is not a major holiday, it is still nicknamed "3-Day Purim":

Thursday: The Fast of Esther is observed from before sunrise to after sunset. The *Megillah* is read at night, and ideally the fast should be broken after hearing it. (The fast can be broken earlier but after sunset "when 3 small stars appear", as long as one is going to hear the *Megillah* later that night.)

Friday: The *Megillah* is read at some point during the daytime, and gifts are given to the poor.

Ushering in *Shabbat*/*Kiddush*: Everything else is continued as for a normal *Shabbat*, start to finish.

Ending *Shabbat*: After one's normal wait time before doing any *melachah*, one must say "*Baruch Hamavdil beyn Kodesh l'Chol*". *Havdalah* is said on wine with the spices and fire as usual.

Sunday: *Mishloach Manot* are delivered. and the festive *Purim* meal is eaten during the daytime.

Tenth of Tevet Before Shabbat: **Friday**: The only fast day that can occur on a Friday. One must fast the entire day, up to the time that *Kiddush* is made. One can prepare food for *Shabbat*, but they can't taste-test it.

Ushering in *Shabbat*: Everything else is continued as for a normal *Shabbat*, start to finish.

Ending the Fast/*Kiddush*: One who is fasting cannot eat or drink until they hear *Kiddush*, which would be done at least 40 minutes after sunset (or "after 3 stars are visible").

Ending *Shabbat*: After one's normal wait time before doing any *melachah*, one must say "*Baruch Hamavdil beyn Kodesh l'Chol*". *Havdalah* is said on wine with the spices and fire as usual.

Tisha B'Av Postponed to Sunday: <u>Ushering in *Shabbat*</u>: All is done as for any normal *Shabbat*.

<u>*Shabbat* Day</u>: Eating of the third meal should stop earlier than usual, and well before sunset.

Ending *Shabbat* and Starting *Tisha B'Av*: Saturday night, after the normal waiting time for *Havdalah* one must say "*Baruch Hamavdil beyn Kodesh l'Chol*" in order to do *melachah*. One says the *brachah* over fire only, on a *Havdalah* candle or two regular candles (depending on *minhag*), and no spices are used. (The rest of *Havdalah* is postponed until Sunday night.) At this time, leather shoes are removed, and people start to sit on the floor or in low chairs, and continues through Sunday morning.

Sunday/Ending *Tisha B'Av*: At midday, people can sit on chairs as normal. Men don't wear *Tefillin* until *Minchah*. Sunday night, after the normal waiting time, *Havdalah* is recited without spices or fire. *Sefardim* use wine or grape juice as usual. *Ashkenazim* use a "national beverage" such as beer or tea, with the appropriate *brachah*. It can be done on wine or grape juice, but preferably it is given to a child to drink. Only the last concluding single paragraph with the *brachah* for *Havdalah* is recited.

As they say at the conclusion of the Torah reading for each of the five Books:

"***Chazak, Chazak, V'Nit-chazek*!**" [Be Strong, Be Strong, and May We Be Strengthened!]

Hatzlachah Rabbah [May you have much success!], and I hope you enjoy becoming *Uniquely Kosher*!

Before bidding a final farewell, to make your searching for recipes, food types and Hebrew words easier, here are some more— "*Tools and Resources*"…

Tools and Resources

Staple Items

One can't go wrong with these ingredients in the home! Most can be found in a local grocery or can easily be made. Less common products are noted where they can be obtained.

General Staples

Bread: For sandwiches or croutons. Buy at a supermarket with a *hechsher*, kosher bakery or grocery. Make your own fresh bread with these delicious recipes (pages 219-232).

Bread Dough: For great pizza or calzones (as well as bread or buns). Buy in the frozen section of your supermarket with a *hechsher*, or make *Water Challah* (p. 222) without enhancer.

Broth: Vegan (p. 110) or meat broth adds flavor to veggies. Meat broth is at kosher groceries.

Cheese: Cream, Ricotta, cottage (and yogurt) are readily available as *Chalav Stam*. Harder cheeses and Chalav Yisrael are found in the kosher groceries, or can be ordered online.

Coconut (Flaked): Add to canned fruits or ice cream. A must for *Coconut-Pecan Icing* (p.122).

Eggs: Eat as a meal or add to a cake. Buy anywhere, but avoid eggs from health food stores.

Fish: From canned fish with a hechsher to fresh or frozen fillets, fish makes a healthy meal.

Flour, Potato or Corn Starch: Use for thickening gravies, sauces and soups.

Fresh Produce: Fruits, vegetables and mushrooms are always healthy to keep around.

Herbs: Keep on hand for extra savory flavorings. Store in a cool dark area (see Spices below).

Margarine: *Parve* margarines can now be readily found in supermarkets.

Meat: For carnivores– cold cuts, hot dogs, poultry and beef are found at a kosher butcher shop, fresh or frozen kosher section, or can be ordered online.

Milk: *Chalav Stam* milk can be found with or without a *hechsher* anywhere milk is sold. For *Chalav Yisrael*, one is limited to a kosher refrigerated section or online.

Non-Dairy Creamer: Common as frozen liquid, good substitute for milk when added 1:1 with water.

Oatmeal: Not just a cereal! Add to breads and meatloaf or make into vegan *Parve Milk* (p. 85).

Oil: Avocado and olive oils lend a healthy yet authentic consistency to vegan meats and broths.

Pasta and Rice: Keep your favorites on hand, they are available anywhere.

Potatoes: Great for side dishes or as a main meal when stuffed (pp. 190-191).

Soup Mixes: Parve chicken, beef, onion and mushroom soup mixes add extra flavor to veggies and stews. Some are MSG-free. In the kosher food aisle or order online. A soup staple.

Spices: Collect a wide variety and you'll always be creative. Store in a cool, dark area. (To preserve for long-term use, store in sealed plastic bags as well. They keep fresh for years.)

Sugars or Sweeteners: Not just for desserts. Granulated, powdered and brown are staples.

Tortillas: Use as-is, fry or bake in sauce. Corn and flour are readily available with a *hechsher*.

Gourmet Staples

Chuck Eye or Rib Eye Steak: The most tender cuts. Get at a kosher butcher or buy online.

Cooking Wine: Adds a gourmet touch to simmering recipes. Find in the kosher aisle or online.

Cornish Hens: Mini chickens available frozen at a kosher butcher or grocery, or purchase online.

Dark Chocolate Fudge: Not just good as a candy, warm for a great dessert topping (p. 405).

Dried Tomatoes and Berries: These are great in salads or breads. (Look for a *hechsher*.)

Fresh Herbs: Snipped and added to dishes or salads are a real treat. (Check for bugs!)

Gelatin: Plain kosher gelatin (aka "jell" or "gel") is needed for aspic. Look for unsweetened "diet gel", and check ingredients for sweeteners. This must be unsweetened.

Green Onions: Grow them in water for a quick garnish that adds both color and flavor.

Lamb: Perhaps the only item that has no true *parve* equivalent. Great plain or in *Kosher Gyros* (p. 242). Get at a kosher butcher or purchase online.

Masa Flour: Finely-ground corn flour found in ethnic aisle. Use in Mexican foods; thicken chili.

Nuts and Seeds: More exotic ones like pine nuts and pepitas (hulled pumpkin seeds) can be sprinkled on salads, put in desserts or just about anything. (Look for a hechsher if roasted)

Puff Pastry Sheets: Use in tarts or crust-enclosed meats. Found with pies in the frozen section.

Wonton Wrappers: Versatile for pierogies, egg rolls, ravioli, or potstickers. Found in the refrigerated section or frozen section at grocery stores, or make your own with recipe on p. 116.

Worcestershire Sauce: Condiment made from fermented fish. (Do not use it on meat.) Fishless can be hard to find, but not impossible. You can make your own extremely authentic, easy fishless imitation (see p. 92).

Staples for Quick Meals

Canned Mushrooms: Great pizza topping or soup. Found in the kosher aisle or order online.

Canned Vegetables: Mixed veggies, potatoes, and beans are great for tossing together a meal.

Cheese Soup: Use as a sauce. In the kosher aisle or make your own varieties (pp. 151-152).

Cooked Meats: For those who eat meat, leftover meat can be chopped and frozen for later use.

Condensed Soups: Cheese (pp. 151-152), cream of mushroom, celery, or chicken (p. 147-149) and golden mushroom (p. 159) are staples. Freeze to use as sauces— not just soup.

Frozen Chopped Onion: Frozen in oil, this makes for quick sautéing or is great to top a pizza.

Garlic Powder: Easy, cheap and quick way to add garlic flavor. A little goes a long way.

Gravy: Great for mashed potatoes or to pour on meats. Use in sauces and stews. Buy bottled beef or chicken in the kosher aisle, or make your own in a wide variety of flavors (p. 102).

Instant Mashed Potatoes: A speedy side dish. Use also for thickening and as a breading.

Liquid Smoke: If you don't have a grill but would like to, use this. Found with BBQ sauces.

Microwave Browning Sauce: When you don't have time to brown meat or onions, this adds the color for you! Found in the section with BBQ and Worcestershire sauces.

Onion Flakes: Quickly add chopped onion to moist foods without shedding tears.

Soup Mixes: Parve soup mixes come in many varieties. See "General Staples" above.

Vegetarian Staples

Dairy Alternative Milks: Enriched soy, almond, coconut, or oat milk, and can be used interchangeably. Often found near cereals. Try the delicious *Parve Milk* (p. 85).

Dry Legumes: Protein-packed, available anywhere. Use in soups or Refried Beans (p. 103).

Imitation Cheese: Found in health food stores or larger supermarkets. (Be sure it's *parve*.)

Non-Dairy Whip Topping: Use to make parve whipped cream or ice creams (pp. 411-412). Most often found in the frozen kosher aisle next to ice creams and creamer.

Seitan: Wheat gluten imitation meat. Buy at health food stores or make (pp. 111, 319, 324).

Tofu: Can be used in place of meat or hard-boiled eggs. It can be used to make imitation sour cream or cream cheese (See p. 105). Usually found in the vegetable section.

TVP®: A nearly-instant meat substitute. Often found in the specialty flour aisle, or order online.

Vegan Meat Products: From burgers and sausages to cold cuts, these are a must and can be found in the vegetable section or health food stores. (Look for a reliable *hechsher* or a "D"!)

Vital Wheat Gluten: Used for vegan meats. Found in the specialty flour aisle.

Wonton Wrappers: Use as ravioli or egg roll casings. Found in the vegetarian section.

Menu Ideas

Below are sample menus from simple to fancy of our "Fabulous Food Forgeries". One can also mix, match and substitute. Entire ethnic or fast-food restaurant meals can be planned from the *Quick Specific-Type Recipe Directory* (pp. 671-678).

Casual

Breakfast

Menu:	Classic:		Elegant:	
Main Item:	Sausage & Biscuit Sandwiches, 245		Scramble Cups,	**133**
Side:	Purple Passion,	414	Pears in Ginger-Almond Sauce, 413	

Menu:	Vegan:		Light:	
Main Item:	Eggs Benedict,	251	Microwave Huevos Rancheros,	264
Side:	Fancy Applesauce,	414	Breakfast Papaya,	415

Snacks

Menu:	Classic:		Elegant:	
Snack:	Baked Corn Dogs,	135	Parve Combination Pizza Rolls, 132	
Drink:	Sweet & Tasty Lemonade,	373	Fishy Spritzer,	367

Menu:	Vegan:		Light:	
Snack:	Egg Rolls,	131	Stovetop-Popped Corn (olive oil), 126	
Drink:	Savory Vegetable Juice,	368	Tropical Sunset Soda,	373

Lunch

Menu:	Classic:		Elegant:	
Bread:	Homemade White Buns,	**224**	Pita Bread,	221
Soup:	Cream of Mushroom Soup,	**148**	Golden Mushroom Soup,	**159**
Salad/Side:	McDonald's® Style Fries,	180	Creamy Mushroom-Garlic Pilaf, 208	
Main Item:	Spicy Onion-Burgers,	237	Kosher Gyros, w/ Tzatziki, 242, 101	
Dessert:	Wendy's® Style Frosty®,	369	Chocolate Mint Pudding,	**407**

Casual

Lunch

Menu:	Vegan:		Light:	
Bread:	Whole Wheat Bread,	228	Garlic Bread,	213
Soup:	Teriyaki Noodle,	157	Quick Home-Style Vegetable,	160
Salad/Side:	Salad w/ Thousand Island,	87	Salad w/ Creamy Italian,	89
Main Item:	Fish Cakes,	361	Pasta, 208 w/ Spaghetti Sauce,	100
Dessert:	GF Peanut Butter Cookies,	377	Mexican Ambrosia,	415

Light Supper

Menu:	Classic:		Elegant:	
Bread:	Italian, Cuban Buns,	227 or 229	Herbed Italian-Tomato Rolls,	226
Soup:	Philippine Chicken Soup,	155	Shrimp in Aspic,	336
Salad/Side:	Mum's Creamy Potato Salad,	179	Easy Artichokes,	201
Main Item:	Subway® Style BMT®,	243	Crab Taco Bowl Salad,	347
Dessert:	Mint Chocolate Chip Ice Cream, **412**		Jello® 1-2-3,	410

Menu:	Vegan:		Light:	
Bread:	Italian Rolls,	225	Italian Bread,	**225**
Soup:	Quick Orzo Mushroom Soup,	161	Asparagus Crab Soup,	343
Salad/Side:	Oregano-Basil Veggies,	199	Pepper Surprises,	197
Main Item:	Quick Hawaiian Fish on Rice, 362 205		Kosher BLT Sandwich,	240
Dessert:	Bake-less Oat Fudge,	406	Pretty Orange Pie,	397

Hearty Dinner

Menu:	Classic:		Elegant:	
Bread:	Rye Rolls,	220	Parve Yorkshire Pudding,	214
Salad/Side:	Stuffed Baked Potatoes,	190	Deluxe Almond Green Beans,	**196**
Soup:	Campbell's® Style Bean Bacon,	169	Hearty Italian Sausage Soup,	165
Side:	KFC® Style Fried Mushrooms,	202	Potatoes Au Gratin,	187
Main Item:	Home-Style Meat Loaf,	313	Sirloin Tips in Burgundy Sauce,	318
Dessert:	Parve Cherry Cheesecake,	395	Mincemeat Pie,	398

Fancy

Hors d'Oeuvres & Appetizers

Menu:	Classic:		Elegant:	
Appetizer 1:	Liver Bacon Balls,	140	Shrimp Cocktail,	335
Appetizer 2:	Potstickers	143	Kosher Escargot,	142
Appetizer 3:	Easy Buffalo Wings,	142	Stuffed Mushroom Caps,	146
Appetizer 4:	Doggies in a Blanket,	135	Parve Steak Tartare,	141

Menu:	Vegan:		Light:	
Appetizer 1:	Little Penguins,	136	Jalapeño Poppers®,	138
Appetizer 2:	Potato Skins (*parve*)	44	Mum's Deviled Eggs,	137
Appetizer 3:	Salmon Rosettes,	335	Tomatoes w/ Sour Cream,	144
Appetizer 4:	Garlic Shrimp Balls,	333	Chips & Veggies w/ Clam Dip,	331

Brunch

Menu:	Classic:		Elegant:	
Bread:	Corn Bread,	216	Parve French Toast,	212
Soup:	Home-Style Vegetable Beef,	**160**	Broccoli Cheese,	**152**
Salad/Side:	Green Beans w/ Ham,	196	Classic Italian Antipasto,	178
Main Item:	Country Ham w/ Grits & Gravy,	325	Duck À L'Orange,	287
Side:	Kraft® Style Mac & Cheese,	209	Savory Roasted Corn,	200
Dessert 1:	Ice-Box Cake,	387	Orange Sweet Rolls,	383
Dessert 2:	Pecan Cinnamon Rolls,	383	Parve White Fudge,	405

Menu:	Vegan:		Light:	
Bread:	Garlic Cheese Biscuits,	**217**	Texas Toast,	213
Soup:	Simple Minestrone,	161	Spicy Chicken Noodle Soup,	158
Salad/Side:	Rainbow Pasta Salad,	178	Avocado Bean Salad,	179
Main Item:	Egg-Zucchini Squares,	199	Egg Fu Yung,	280
Side:	Red Beans & Rice,	204	Simple Spanish Rice,	206
Dessert 1:	Baby Fruit Cakes,	386	Pecan Cinnamon Squares,	381
Dessert 2:	Tapioca Pudding,	408	Parve Rainbow Sherbet,	**411**

Fancy

Social Luncheon

Menu:	Classic:		Elegant:	
Bread:	Rye Bread,	220	Mandarin Chinese Pancakes,	215
Fish:	Fried Kosher Clams,	353	Tahitian Marinated Fish,	366
Side:	Fried Okra,	202	Salad w/ Blue Cheese Dressing	90
Soup:	Southern-Belle Soup,	153	Jellied Beef Consommé,	163
Salad/Side:	Quesadilla Spaghetti,	211	Creamed Spinach,	197
Main Item:	Glazed Ham,	324	Practical Peking Duck,	286
Dessert:	Parve Pineapple Sherbet,	**411**	Chocolate Mint Brownies,	387

Menu:	Vegan:		Light:	
Bread:	Parker House Rolls,	232	English Muffins,	**221**
Fish:	Clams Oreganata,	354	Shrimp Benihana® Style,	359
Side:	Eggplant Patties,	194	Yummy Yams,	193
Soup:	Indian Curried Bean & Lentil,	170	Micro-Poached Egg Soup,	155
Salad/Side:	Spaghetti Squash,	198	Oven Roasted Vegetables,	195
Main Item:	Mum's Salmon Croquettes,	366	Microwave Salmon Steaks,	362
Dessert:	Chocolate Pudding,	407	Instant Fruit Dessert,	413

Shabbat or Holiday Lunch

Menu:	Classic:		Elegant:	
Bread:	Water Challah,	222	Fancy Hard Dinner Rolls,	231
Appetizer:	Parve Chopped Liver on lettuce,	139	Hawaiian Fish Appetizer,	335
Salad:	Spinach w/ Parmesan Dressing,	90	Salad w/ Blueberry Vinaigrette,	87
Soup/Stew:	Sefardi Shabbat Stew (Chamin),	321	Scotch Broth,	162
Main Item:	Ginger Beef,	278	Steak & Kidney Pie,	304
Side 1:	Yellow Saffron Rice,	205	Cool Carrots,	203
Side 2:	Tunisian Kukla,	211	Whipped Squash,	198
Dessert 1:	Parve From-Scratch Brownies,	386	Black Forest Tiara Dessert,	393
Dessert 2:	Parve Peanut Butter Cup Bars,	403	Coconut Truffles,	402

Fancy

Elegant Shabbat and Holiday Dinners

Menu:	Classic:		Elegant:	
Bread:	Italian Breadsticks,	230	Pumpernickel Bread,	219
Appetizer:	Oyster Stuffing,	349	Prawns in Garlic Sauce,	350
Salad/Side:	French Green Bean Casserole,	196	Long Grain & Wild Rice,	207
Soup:	Pumpkin Soup,	150	Parve Oxtail Soup,	162
Main Item:	Stuffed Turkey & Trimmings,	289	Stuffed Chicken, 291 w/ Gravy,	102
Side 1:	Deluxe Whipped Potatoes	192	Spinach Quiche ,	249
Side 2:	Broccoli with Cheese Sauce,	198	Scalloped Potatoes,	188
Dessert:	Parve Pumpkin Pie	397	Chocolate Cream Slices,	396

Menu:	Fish:		Meat:	
Bread:	Garlic Bread,	213	French Bread,	223
Appetizer:	Bacon-Wrapped Oysters,	333	Microwave Garlic Crab,	362
Salad/Side:	Anchovy Antipasto,	348	Salad w/ Parve Italian Dressing,	89
Soup:	Neo-Classic Bouillabaisse,	344	Fancy French Onion Soup,	158
Main Item:	Stuffed Flounder,	365	Yankee Pot Roast,	320
Side 1:	Salad w/ Parve Ranch Dressing	88	Savory Stuffed Eggplant,	195
Side 2:	Hushpuppies,	350	Savory Corn Muffins,	216
Dessert:	Parve Samoa® Cookies,	377	Pecan Pie,	399

Menu:	Vegan:		Light:	
Bread:	Honey Oat Buns,	228	Tender White Bread,	224
Appetizer:	Fish Fillets Au Gratin,	364	Oysters Rockefeller,	356
Salad/Side:	Savory Steak Fries,	182	Mum's Baked Beans,	203
Soup:	Easy Egg Drop Soup,	156	Mock Turtle Soup,	164
Main Item:	Ratatouille with (soy) Meatballs,	317	Chinese Cashew Chicken,	284
Side 1:	Crunchy-Cream Potatoes,	193	Spicy Vegetable Curry,	248
Side 2:	Eggplant Casserole,	194	Vegetable Rice,	206
Dessert:	Hawaiian Banana-Nut Bread,	385	Pumpkin Muffins,	388

Quick Specific-Type Recipe Directory

(Variations are bolded.) Whole meals within only one recipe! (Also see Burgers & Sandwiches.)

Complete Meals

Antipasto Salads, 178, 348

Banquet® Chicken Fried Beef Meal, 310

Banquet® Style Salisbury Steak Meal, 309

Banquet® Style Western Meal, 309

Beef Stroganoff, 315

Chicken and rice, 290, 295, 296, 301

Chinese Cashew Chicken, 284

Chorizo & Rice, 265

Country Ham w/ Grits & Red Eye Gravy, 325

Creamy Tuna Deluxe Casserole, 363

Crisp-Crust Pizza, 260

Easy Calzones, 260

Egg Fu Yung, 280

Fancy Shepherd's Pie, 327

Fried rice, 281, 282, 324, 357

Ginger Beef, 278

Gumbos, 154, 341

Hash Brown Scramble, 327

Hearty Chili & Rice, 252

Hong Kong Chicken, 285

Italian pasta, 256-259

Kielbasa & Rice, 323

Kraft® Chicken Applause® Dinner, 296

Neo-Classic Bouillabaisse, 344

Pasta and noodles 253, 254, 255, 300

Peruvian Chicken Curry, 296

Pizza Quiche, 250

Popeye's® Style "Dirty" Rice, 252

Pot pies, 246, 302, 303

Ratatouille with Meatballs, 317

Seafood Paella, 358

Sirloin Tips in Burgundy Sauce, 318

Skyline® Style Chilis, 172, **173**

Steak & Kidney Pie, 304

Stews, 246, 247, 299, 321

Stir-Fry dishes, 279, 283

Stuffed meat, 289, 290, 291, 292, 326, (fish) 365

Super Stuffed Potatoes, 190, **191**

Taco Bell® Taco Bowl Salads, 177, 347

Yankee Pot Roast, 320

Crock Pot Recipes

Calico Bean Soup (13 Bean Soup), 168

Campbell's® Bean w/ Bacon Soup, 169

Campbell's® Split Pea w/ Ham Soup, 169

Columbia® Style Black Bean Soup, 168

Country Chicken Stew w/ Dumplings, 299

Hearty Italian Sausage Soup, 165

Hearty Mexican Meatball Soup, 166

Sefardi Shabbat Stew, 321

Seitan Beef Roast, 319

Scotch Broth, 162

Sirloin Tips in Burgundy Sauce, 318

Yankee Pot Roast, 320

Microwave Recipes

Based on an average 700-1000 watt microwave. (Those merely heated aren't listed.)

Special Non-Allergenic Foods

All recipes in main section can be made with no dairy or meat. Other non-allergen foods are listed here.

Egg-Free

Eggless Eggnog, 369

Girl Scout Cookies® Style Samoas®, 377

Nabisco® Lorna Doone®/Shortbread, 378

Parve Keebler® Pecan Sandies®, 375

Fish-Free

Fishless Worcestershire Sauce, 92

Gluten-Free

Gluten-Free Peanut Butter Cookies, 377

Pie crust substitute, 460, 569

Lactose-Free "Dairy"
(All Fixed Strictly Parve)

Bisquick® Style Mix, 83

Blue Cheese Dressing, 90

Chocolate Malt Syrup, 123

Coconut Fudge, 406

Cottage Cheese, 109

Cracker Jack® Style Snacks, 125

Creamy Parmesan Salad Dressing, 90

Dark Chocolate Fudge, 405

Eggless Eggnog, 369

English Muffins, 221

Feta Cheese, 109

French Toast, 212

Fried Mozzarella Sticks, 137

Girl Scout Cookies® Style Samoas®, 377

Home-Style Pancakes, 215

Ice Creams, 411, 412

Lactose-Free "Dairy" (continued)

Imitation Butter, 84

Imitation Cream Cheese, 105

Imitation Sour Cream, 105

Italian Dressings (& Mix), 89

Keebler ® Style Fudge Stripes®, 378

Mounds® Style Bars, 404

Nabisco Style® Cheese Tid-Bits®, 128

Parmesan Cheese, 108

Parve Milk, 85

Peanut Butter Cup Bars, 403

Pizza Rolls, 132, 132

Pumpkin Pie, 397

Ranch Dressing, 88

Ready-To-Use Icings, 120-122

Ricotta Cheese, 109

Sara Lee® Style Cheesecakes, 395, 395

Sherbets, 411

White Fudge, 405

Yorkshire Pudding, 214

Non-Peanut "Nut" Recipes

(For all, substitute Tahini for peanut butter)

Fashionable Fudge (Kids Project), 419

Gluten-Free Peanut Butter Cookies, 377

Koogle™ Style Peanut Butters, 104

Parve Peanut Butter Cup Bars, 403

Peanut Butter Bake-less Oat Fudge, 406

Southern Belle Soup, 153

Ethnic Foods at a Glance

Combine your favorites ethnic foods and plan entire meals around a theme.

Australian: Australian Fried Fish, 364

Outback Steakhouse® Style:

    Bloomin' Onion®, 201

    Creamy Chili Sauce, 95

British (English): English Mustard, 442

Mincemeat Pie, 398

Parve English Muffins, 221

Parve Oxtail Soup, 162

Parve Yorkshire Pudding, 214

Scotch Broth, 162

Spicy English Mustard, 440

Steak & Kidney Pie, 304

Chinese: Beef Stir Fry, 279

Benihana Ginger Sauce, 93

Cashew Chicken, 284

Chicken Stir Fry, 283

Chinese Hoisin Sauce, 93

Chinese Hot Mustard, 440

Crab Rangoons, 334

Hot Pepper Oil, 437

Easy Egg Drop Soup, 156

Easy Wonton Soup, 156

Egg Fu Yung, 280

Egg Roll & Wonton Wrappers, 116

Egg Rolls, 131, 131, 332

Fried Rice, 281, 282, 357

Ginger Beef, 278

Hong Kong Chicken, 285

Mandarin Chinese Pancakes, 215

Oyster Sauce, 330

Chinese (continued)

Practical Peking Duck, 286

Shrimp Benihana® Style, 359

Stir-Fry Cooking Sauce, 94

Sweet & Sour Sauce, 94

Teriyaki Noodle Soup, 157

Cuban: Columbia® Black Bean Soup, 167

Columbia® Style Cuban Sandwich, 244

Cuban Buns, 229

French: Beef En Croûte, 306

Chicken Cordon Bleu, 291

Duck À L'Orange, 287

Fancy French Onion Soup, 158

French Bread, 223

Jellied Beef Consommé, 163

Kosher Escargot, 141

Neo-Classic Bouillabaisse, 344

Spinach Quiche, 249

German: Banquet® Salisbury Steak, 309

Braunschweiger Sausage, 114

Goetta Sausage, 113

Greek: Kosher Gyros, 242

Tzatziki Sauce, 101

Indian: Curried Bean & Lentil Soup, 170

Curried Shrimp Soup, 340

Curry Sauce, 101

Quick Curried Chicken Soup, 157

Spicy Vegetable Curry, 248

Yellow Saffron Rice, 205

Indonesian: Javanese Vegetable Soup, 345

Malaysian Chicken & Peas, 297

Italian: Anchovy Antipasto Salad, 348

Cheese Ravioli, 259

Chicken Cacciatori, 301

Chicken Parmigiana, 302

Classic Italian Antipasto Salad, 178

Classic Ravioli, 259

Crisp Crust Pizza, 260

Dry Italian Dressing Mix, 89

Easy Calzones, 260

Fettuccine Alfredo, 210

Garlic Bread, 213

Hearty Italian Sausage Soup, 165

Herbed Italian Bread, 226

Herbed Italian Rolls, 226

Italian Bread, 225

Italian Rolls, 225

Italian Sausage, 112

Olive Garden® Style Breadsticks, 230

Parve Italian Dressing, 89

Ratatouille with Meatballs, 317

Simple Minestrone, 161

Smoked Chicken Ravioli in Sauce, 300

Stuffed Manicotti Shells, 256

Three-Cheese Lasagna, 258

Mexican: Burritos, 270, 270

Cheese Enchiladas, 268

Cheesy Spanish Rice, 206

Chorizo & Rice, 265

Crispy Mexican Pastries, 383

Fried Green Bananas, 414

Grilled Fajitas, 277

Mexican (continued)

Hearty Mexican Meatball Soup, 166

Mexican Ambrosia, 416

Mexican Chorizo Sausage, 115

Mexican Restaurant Guacamole, 103

Mexican-Style Cinnamon Cocoa, 369

Microwave Huevos Rancheros, 264

Microwave Tacos, 271

Mild Green Taco Sauce, 97

Neo-Classic Tamales, 273

Quick Quesadillas, 276

Refried Beans, 103

Shredded Chicken Chimichangas, 266

Spicy Mexican Peanut Butter, 104

Super Salsa, 96

Taco Bell® Style (see Fast pp. 677-678)

Tio Sancho® Style Enchilada Dinner, 267

Middle-Eastern: Pita Bread, 221

Sefardi Shabbat Stew, 321

Tunisian Kukla Shabbat Stuffing, 211

Water Challah, 222

Peruvian: Peruvian Chicken Curry, 296

Philippine: Philippine Chicken Soup, 155

Polish: Kielbasa & Rice, 323

Polynesian: Creamy Roasted Papaya, 416

Tahitian Marinated Fish, 366

Tahiti-Style Fruit Custard, 413

Russian: Chicken Kiev, 292

Spanish: Seafood Paella, 358

Simple Spanish Rice, 206

Swedish: Swedish Meatballs, 316

Vietnamese: Asparagus Crab Soup, 343

Regional American Foods at a Glance

Got a hankerin' for food from down yonder? Want to have a *luau*? These are from across the USA.

Cajun: Chicken Gumbo, 154

Popeye's® Style Chicken, 293

Popeye's® Style Dirty Rice, 252

Red Beans & Rice, 204

Shrimp Gumbo, 341

Country/Southern:

Banquet® Style Chicken Fried Beef Steak Meal, 310

Church's Chicken™ Style Fried Okra, 202

Country Chicken Stew with Dumplings, 299

Country Grits, 207

Country Ham w/ Grits & Red Eye Gravy, 325

Country Sausage, 114

Home-Style Hash Browns with Onions, 183

KFC® Style Fried Chicken, 293

KFC® Style Fried Chicken Livers, 139

KFC® Style Fried Mushrooms, 202

KFC® Style Gravy, 101

Parve Home-Style Pancakes, 215

Sausage & Biscuit Sandwiches, 245

Hawaiian: Breakfast Papaya, 416

Hawaiian Banana Bread, 385

Hawaiian Burger Sauce, 91

Hawaiian Coconut Chips, 127

Hawaiian Fish Appetizer, 335

Quick Hawaiian Fish, 362

Roasted Luau Pineapples, 415

North-Eastern:

Arby's® Style Philly Beef & Swiss Sub, 241

Buffalo Wings, 142

Frisch's® Style Chili, 174

Manhattan Clam Chowder, 337

New England Clam Chowder, 338

Skyline® Style Chili, 172, **173**

South-Western/Tex-Mex:

Banquet® Style Western Meal, 309

Texas-Style Chili, 176

Texas Toast, 213

Restaurant & Fast Foods at a Glance

All the favorite fast-food joints in one place! Stick to one restaurant or mix & match for variety.

Arby's® Style:

Beef & Cheddar, 241

Jamocha® Shake, 370

Original Roast Beef Sandwich, 241

Philly Beef and Swiss Sub, 241

Turnovers, 399

Benihana® Style: Ginger Sauce, 93

Shrimp Benihana®, 359

Boston Chicken® Style:

Creamed Spinach, 197

Burger King® Style:

Onion Rings, 200

Chick-Fil-A® Style:

Waffle Fries, 181

Church's Chicken™ Style:

Fried Okra, 202

Bibliography

Some unnoted information was from *shiurim* [Torah classes], general *shelot* to *poskim*, reliable kashrut agencies, and conversations with a variety of Orthodox rabbis. This book is designed to allow one to put *kashrut* into practice quickly. It utilizes an easy-to-understand system, and avoids less relevant issues that can totally confuse newcomers (such as ovens and dry foods vs. moist creating steam). A majority of views are presented.

This book is not a substitute for rabbinic advice. Always consult your own rabbi if you have any questions or there are any confusing issues. Below are sources and references that were consulted or researched to help create this book.

Note: Original website links that are no longer current have been omitted at the time of publishing. These included information on health and nutrition, microwave ovens, plastics, mercury in fish, etc. from the EPA, FDA, and USDA.

Books

Kashrut, Torah and Halachah

Moshe Antebi:
Prayers From the Heart Siddur: A Sephardic Siddur with an English Translation.
Israel Book Shop, 2002.

The Artscroll Mesorah Series:
Siddur Eitz Chaim/The Complete Artscroll Siddur.
Mesorah Publications, Ltd., 1985.

The Artscroll Series/Stone Edition:
The Chumash.
Mesorah Publications, Ltd., 1998, 2000.

The Artscroll Series/Stone Edition:
Tanach.
Mesorah Publications, Ltd., 1996, 1998.

Rabbi Avrohom Blumenkrantz:
The Laws of Pesach: A Digest.
Gross Bros. Printing Co. Inc. (published annually)

Rabbi Simcha Bunim Cohen:
(1) *The Shabbos Kitchen.* 1991.
(2) *The Shabbos Home.* 1995.
(3) *The Laws of Yom Tov.* 1997.
(All) Mesorah Publications

Rabbi Avroham Davis:
Kitzur Shulchan Aruch: A New Translation and Commentary. (vol. 1 and 2)
Metsuda Publications, 1996

Rabbi Binyomin Forst w/ Rabbi Aaron D. Twerski:
The Laws of B'rachos: A Comprehensive Exposition of the Background and Laws of Blessings.
Mesorah Publications, Ltd., 1990.

Rabbi Zev Greenwald:
Sha'arei Halachah: A Summary of Laws for Jewish Living.
Feldheim Publishers, 2000.

Lubavitch Women's Cookbook Publications:
Spice and Spirit: The Complete Kosher Jewish Cookbook.
Bloch, 1990.

Rabbi Eliezer Toledano:
The Orot Sephardic Weekday Siddur.
Orot, Inc., 2000

Hebrew

Hayim Baltsan:
Webster's New World Hebrew Dictionary.
Simon & Schuster, Inc., 1992.

Cooking and Herbs

Introduction to Cooking with the Amana Radarange Microwave Oven.
Amana Refrigeration Company, 1987.

Michelle Evans:
The Slow Crock Cookbook.
Warner Books Inc., 1975.

Norma Jean Lathrop:
Herbs: How to Select, Grow and Enjoy.
H.P. Books, 1981.

James K. McNair:
The World of Herbs & Spices.
Ortho Books, 1978.

Irma von S. Rombauer & Marion Rombauer Becker:
Joy of Cooking.
Scribner, 1995.

Audio

Kashrut Tapes

Star-K Kosher Certification National Kashrus Lecture Series. (Tapes 1 & 2)
Rabbi Moshe Heinemann/Rabbi Dovid Heber/Rabbi Tzvi Rosen. Avrom Pollak, Moderator.
Brooklyn, NY- July 29, 2003, Monticello, NY- July 30, 2003

Computer Software

Food Nutrients

USDA National Nutrient Database for Windows® Search Software.

Web Site Articles

Bug Identification and Insects

What's That Bug?
http://www.whatsthatbug.com/

Food and Cooking

The Cook's Thesaurus (cooking encyclopedia)
http://www.foodsubs.com/

Fruit Seasons (produce guide)
http://www.fruitseasons.com/

Gourmet Sleuth (cooking dictionary)
https://www.gourmetsleuth.com/

Kitchen Charts
https://www.recipegoldmine.com/kitchart/kitchart.html

Meat Charts (*Treifah* meat references)
http://chestofbooks.com/food/recipes/American-Woman-Cook-Book/Meat-Cuts-And-How-To-Cook-Them-Lamb-Chart.html

Health and Illnesses

Federal Government Source for Women's Health
http://www.womenshealth.gov/

Foodborne Pathogens
http://www.fda.gov/Food/ResourcesForYou/HealthEducators

Jewish Holidays and Practices

Chabad.org
https://www.chabad.org/

Rabbi Naftali Silberberg:
Shushan Purim.

Rabbi Eliezer Zalmanov:
How Can the 10th of Tevet Interfere with Shabbat?

Aish.com
Rabbi Shraga Simmons:
Why Dairy on Shavuot?
https://aish.com/48969771/

Wikipedia.org
Days of Week on Hebrew Calendar. ("Four Gates" chart)
https://en.wikipedia.org/wiki/Days_of_week_on_Hebrew_calendar

Kashrut

Chicago Rabbinical Council
https://www.crcweb.org/

Rabbi Sholem Fishbane:
(1) *Slurpees Slurpees Everywhere, Nor Any Drop to Drink?*
(2) *The Kashrus Status of the Popular Latté.*

Rabbi Dovid Cohen:
(1) *Fish and Meat.*
(2) *Fountain Soda: A New Hurdle for the Kosher Consumer.*

Kof-K Kosher Supervision

Rabbi Moishe Dovid Lebovits:
Waiting Between Hard Cheese and Meat. Halachically Speaking, 2009
https://www.kof-k.org/articles/031209090303Doc19.pdf

Orthodox Union/Jewish Action
https://oukosher.org

Rabbi Yisroel Bendelstein:
Compatibility. 2005

Rabbi Dovid Cohen:
Shelled Eggs, Peeled Onions and Garlic Left Overnight: Keeping Products Ruach Ra'ah Free. 2005

Rabbi Avrohom Gordimer:
(1) *Frozen Pizza; Some Hot Kashrus Issues.*
(2) *The Complex Story of Pareve Orange Juice.*
(3) *Say Cheese!*

Dr. Judith Leff:
Do Natural + Wholesome = Kosher?: A Biochemist Takes a Second Look at "Natural" Foods.

Rabbi Yaakov Luban:
(1) *Is Your Oven Kosher? What Every Kosher Cook Must Know.*
(2) *Playing with Fire.*

Rabbi Ari Z. Zivotofsky, Ph.D.:
(1) *What's The Truth About... Giraffe Meat.*
(2) *What's the Truth About... Glatt Kosher.*

Rabbi Moshe Zywica:
Getting the Flavor of Certifying Flavors: A Primer.

UNIQUELY KOSHER

Star-K Kosher Certification/Kashrus Kurrents
https://www.star-k.org/

Rabbi Boruch Beyer:
(1) *It's Kosher on Paper Only.*
(2) *The Kashrus of Tea- With No Strings Attached!*
(3) *Knowing Your Beans: The Kashrus of Coffee.*

Rabbi Zushe Blech:
Industrial Eggs- Not as Simple as It May Seem.

Rabbi Zvi Goldberg:
(1) *Analyzing the Roots: Hydroponics and Halacha.*
(2) *Don't Miss the Boat: Halachic Guidelines of Kosher Cruises.*
(3) *Feeding Your Pet: Barking Up the Right Tree.*

Rabbi Dovid Heber:
(1) *Facts on Wax: Are Vegetable and Fruit Waxes Kosher?*
(2) *Kashrus In Good Taste: Kosher Certifying the Flavor Industry.*
(3) *When You Need to Knead: A Guide to Hafrashas Challah.*
(4) *Meat and Dairy-A Kosher Consumer's Handbook.*

Rabbi Moshe Heinemann:
(1) *Beware: Glatt May Not Always Mean Kosher.*
(2) *Cholov Yisroel: Does a Neshama Good.*
(3) *Food Fit for a King: Reviewing the Laws of Bishul Akum & Bishul Yisroel.*
(4) *Kosher Chickens: From Coop to Soup.*
(5) *Leafing Through Your Vegetables.*
(6) *Oven Kashrus: For Everyday Use.*
(7) *Preparing for Chodosh.*
(8) *The Star-K Pesach Kitchen.*

Avrom Pollak, Ph.D.:
(1) *The Story Behind Kosher Plastics.*
(2) *Yoshon and Chodosh: Something Old Something New.*

Rabbi Tzvi Rosen:
(1) *All Washed Up.*
(2) *The Art of Kosher Wine Making.*
(3) *But What Could Be the Problem With...*
(4) *Can It Be Kosher?*
(5) *Hot Off the Hotline: Kosher is Healthier.*
(6) *Microwaving in the Workplace.*
(7) *On the Road to a Kosher Vacation.*
(8) *Pas Habah B'Kisnin: Pas or Pas Nisht.*
(9) *The Safety of Our Kosher Food.*
(10) *The Secret Ingredient.*
(11) *Ta'am Tov B'Tuv Ta'am: A Flavorful Blend of Kashrus and Spices*

Torah.org
https://torah.org/

Rabbi Doniel Neustadt:
(1) *Selected Halachos Related to Parshas Vaeschanan: Shelled Egg, Peeled Onion, or Peeled Garlic Clove Left Overnight*
(2) *Selected Halachos Related to Parshas Lech Lecha: Mashkim Megulim: What Is It?*

Hebrew Food Term Glossary

בשר = **Basar**. "Meat". A meat or poultry product, or a product containing it.

בית יוסף = **Bet Yosef/*Beys Yoseif*.** (See "*Chalak Bet Yosef*".) Beef lungs are totally free of adhesions.

בהשגחת =**B'hashgachat ... /*B'hashgachas* ...** "Under the supervision of…" {name of Rabbi who's in charge}.

בישול ישראל = **Bishul Yisrael/*Bishul Yisroel*.** "Food cooked by a Jew". (See p. 28 for details.)

ברכתו מזונות = **Birchato Mezonot/*Birchoso Mezonos*.** "Its *bracha* is *Mezonot*". (Dough w/ juice- p. 73.)

חלב = **Chalav/*Cholov*.** "Dairy". (See p. 13 for details.)

חלבי = **Chalavi/*Cholovi*.** "Dairy". (See p. 13 for details.)

חלב ישראל = **Chalav Yisrael/*Cholov Yisroel*.** "Dairy product constantly supervised by a Jew".

חלק בית יוסף = **Chalak Bet Yosef/*Chalak Beis Yoseif*.** "'Smooth' as by Rabbi Yosef Cairo". (See pp. 15-16.)

אין צריך בדיקה = **Eyn Tzarich Bedikah.** "No checking is necessary". (Produce was checked for bugs.)

הופרשה חלה כדין = **Hufr'shah Challah Kadin.** "The laws of taking *Challah* have been fulfilled".

גלאט כשר = *Glatt Kosher*. "Smooth". Kosher beef having had the lungs checked. (See pp. 15-16.)

כשר בשר = **Kasher Basar/*Kosher Basar*.** "Kosher Meat". Meat or poultry product. (See pp. 15-16.)

כשר = **Kasher/*Kosher*.** "Fit for Jewish consumption".

כשר חלב ישראל = **Kasher, Chalav Yisrael/*Kosher, Cholov Yisroel*.** (See "*Chalav Yisrael*".)

כשר חלב = **Kasher, Chalav.** *Kosher, Cholov.* "Kosher Dairy".

כשר למהדרין = **Kasher L'Mehadrin/*Kosher L'Mehadrin*.** "Kosher of extra-fine quality".

חקמ ישן = **Kemach Yashan/*Kemach Yoshon*.** "*Yashan* Flour". (See p. 617 for details.)

כשר לפסח = **Kasher L'Pesach/*Kosher L'Peysach*.** "Kosher for *Pesach*". Fit for Passover use.

כשר לפסח לקידוש ולארבה כוסות = **Kasher L'Pesach L'Kiddush V'L'Arbah Kosot/*Kosher L'Peysach L'Kiddush V'L'Arbah Kosos*.** "Kosher for *Pesach* for *Kiddush* and the Four cups". (See Passover p. 645.)

כשר פארווע = **Kasher, Parve/*Kosher, Pareve*.** "Kosher Neutral", neither dairy or meat.

ללא חשש חדש = **Lelo Chashash Chadash.** "There is no fear of chadash". It is *yashan/yoshon*.

מבושל = **Mevushal.** "Cooked". (See p. 443 for details.)

נעשה מקמח ישן = **Na'aseh M'Kemach Yashan.** "Made of *yashan* flour".

נשחט הודח ונמלח = **Nischat Hodach V'Nimlach.** Meat that has been "Deveined, Soaked and Salted".

פארווע = **Parve or Pareve.** "Neutral", neither dairy or meat. (See p. 9 for details.)

פת ישראל = **Pat Yisrael/*Pas Yisroel*.** "Food baked by a Jew". (See p. 28 for details.)

Glossary of Hebrew Words & Phrases

Below is a list of Hebrew words and phrases to help become familiar with them.

Pronunciations: All stressed syllables are in bold. Generally, all words used in this book are in the common form of *Sefardic* Hebrew, (modern Israeli Hebrew). *Ashkenazic* pronunciations are in *italics* for those who are around many *Ashkenazi* speakers. Anglicized words have no pronunciations listed.

Vowels: O is pronounced as a long "o", as in "hoe". *(Some Ashkenazim say "oy" as in "toy".)*
"A" is "ah" rhyming with "stop". *(Sometimes, Ashkenazim say "o".)*
"E" is "eh" as in "bet". *(Certain "E" sounds are pronounced "ey" by Ashkenazim.)*
"I" is "ee" is as in "beet". *(Sometimes, Ashkenazim say "i" as "ih" as in "big".)*
"U" is "oo" rhyming with "food". *(Sometimes, Ashkenazim say "u" as in "put".)*

Vowel Combinations: "EY" is "ey" as in "whey".
"AI" is "ai" rhyming with "buy" *(Some Ashkenazim say "oy" as in "toy".)*

Consonants: *Sefardim* always pronounce the Hebrew letter ת "Tav" as a "T" sound. *Ashkenazim* pronounce it as an "S" if it has no *dagesh* dot. The most unusual of the Hebrew letters are כ *"Chaf"*, and letter ח *"Chet"*, which are represented as "CH". *Chaf* sound rather like one clearing their throat. *Chet* is similar, but more like a heavy "H" to *Sefardim*. *(For Ashkenazim, Chaf is interchangeable with Chet.)*

Adamah: (Ah-dah-**mah**) *(Ah-**dah**-mah)* Land, soil or earth.
Alav HaShalom: (Ah-**lahv** Ha-Shah-**lom**) May he rest in peace. Literally "May the peace be upon him".
Aleyha HaShalom: (Ah-**ley**-hah Ha-Shah-**lom**) May she rest in peace. "May the peace be upon her".
Al Netilat Yadayim: (Ahl Neh-tee-**lat** Yah-**dai**-yeem) *(Ahl Neh-**tee**-las Yah-**dai**-yeem)* "Title" of the *brachah* for hand-washing. Literally, "for uplifting of the hands".
Amen: (Ah-**men**) *(Ah-**meyn** or less common **Oh**-meyn)* Statement of agreement with what is being said. Acronym of three Hebrew words- a reference to Hashem, King, and faithful.
Arba' Minim: (Ahr-**ba'** Mee-**neem**) *(**Ahr**-ba Mee-**neem**)* Literally, "the four species". Used on the holiday of *Sukkot*, they consist of a citron and branches of willow, palm and myrtle.
Arlah: (Ahr-**lah**) *(**Ohr**-lah)* Fruit from a tree in its first three years, which is sacred.
Ashkenazi: (Ash-ken-ah-**zee**) *(Ash-ken-**ah**-zee)* Literally "Ashkenazite". A European Jew.
Ashkenazic: Pertaining to Jews of European descent. (See below.)
Ashkenazim: (Ash-ken-ah-**zeem**) *(Ash-ken-ah-zeem)* Jews of European descent. There are many different branches, such as Russian, Polish, German, Litvak (from Lithuania). All in all, most are pretty similar. Occasionally, some speak Yiddish, a cross between Hebrew and German. *Ashkenazim* are the most populous of Jews, generally leaning toward the rationalist side as opposed to mystical.
Avar'chah: (Ah-**vahr**-e-chah) Collection of Psalm verses recited by *Sefardim* before *"Grace After Meals"*.

Averah: (Ah-veh-**rah**) *(Ah-**vey**-rah)* A sin.

Averot: (Ah-veh-**rot**) *(Ah-**vey**-ros)* Sins.

Avraham: (**Av**-rah-hahm) Abraham.

Bamidbar: (Bah-meed-**bar**) *(Bah-**mid**-bar)* The Book of Numbers. Literally, "in the desert", or "in the wilderness".

Basar: (Bah-**sar**) Meat or meat products. Literally "flesh".

Benchers: *(**Bent**-shers)* Yiddish for "Birchonim". (Sometimes spelled "Bentchers" or "Bentshers".) Booklets containing *brachot* and *Birkat HaMazon*. "Bench" or "Bentsh" comes from Yiddish for "blessing".

Bet Din: (Bet Deen) *(Beys Deen)* Official Jewish court made up of three Orthodox Rabbis. They are responsible for all judicial matters. Literally "house of judgement".

Bet Yosef: (Bet **Yo**-sef) *(Beys **Yo**-sef)* Highest level of kosher meat eaten by *Sefardim*.

Bereshit: (Beh-reh-**sheet** or Breh-**sheet**) *(**Brey**-shees)* The Book of Genesis.

Birchonim: (Beer-cho-**neem**) *(Beer-cho-nim)* Small booklets containing *brachot*.

Birkat HaMazon: (Beer-**kaht** Hah—Mah-**zon**) Literally "Blessing for the food". A beautiful thanksgiving prayer said after eating bread.

Blech: (Blech) Yiddish for "tin". A metal sheet covering a stovetop, enabling food to be kept warm on *Shabbat*.

B'li Neder: (Be-**lee** Neh-der) Without a vow.

Boreh Nefashot: (Bo-**re** Neh-fah-**shot**) *(Bor-**ey** Neh-**fah**-shos)* Makes or creates souls. "Title" of the after-brachah for general foods.

Brachah: (Brah-**chah**) *(**Brah**-chah or **Bro**-chah)* Blessing. Also written "b'racha", "berachah" or "bracha".

Brachah Acharonah: (Brah-**chah** Ah-chah-roh-**nah**) *(**Brah**-chah Ah-chah-roh-nah)* After-blessing.

Brachah L'vatalah: (Brah-cha Leh-Vah-tah-**lah**) *(**Brah**-cha Leh-Vah-tah-lah)* Blessing "in "vain".

Brachah Rishonah: (Brah-**chah** Ree-sho-**nah**) *(**Brah**-chah Ree-**shon**-ah)* Blessing before.

Brachot: (Brah-**chot**) *(**Brah**-chos)* Blessings. Also written "b'rachot" or "berachot".

Brit: (Breet) *(Bris)* Shortened term for the ritual circumcision or "Brit Milah". Literally "covenant".

Brit Milah: (Breet Mee-**lah**) *(Bris **Mee**-lah)* The circumcision done eight days after a baby boy's birth. Literally "covenant of the circumcision".

Chadash: (Chah-**dash**) *(**Choh**-dosh)* New. Refers mainly to forbidden spring grain.

Chag: (Chahg) Holiday. Generally used by Israelis or *Sefardim*.

Chagim: (Chah-**geem**) Holidays. Generally used by Israelis or *Sefardim*.

Chalak: (Chah-**lak**) Smooth. The Hebrew equivalent to "Glatt", a Yiddish term referring to the checked lung health standard for kosher meat.

Chalak Bet Yosef: (Chah-**lak** Bet **Yo**-sef) *(**Chah**-lak Beys **Yo**-sef)* Kosher meat eaten by *Sefardim*.

Chalav: (Chah-**lahv**) *(**Cho**-lov)* Dairy products. Literally "milk". Also "Chalavi"

Chalav Stam: (Chah-**lahv** Stahm) *(**Cho**-lov Stahm)* Literally "plain milk". Lower level of dairy products, where the USDA is entrusted with enforcing the purity of milk.

Chalav Yisrael: (Chah-**lahv** Yees-rah-**ehl**) *(**Cho**-lov Yis-rah-**eyl**)* Higher level of dairy products supervised by a Jew from milking to packaging.

Challah: (Chah-**lah**) *(**Chah**-lah)* Traditional bread named for the tithe taken from dough. *Challah* is a type of *terumah* meant for only *Kohanim*. See pp. 622-623 for details.

Chamin: (Chah-**meen**) Literally, "hot". Traditional *Sefardi* stew served warm on *Shabbat* lunch.

Chametz: (Chah-**metz**) *(**Chah**-metz)* Leavening not possessed on Passover, extending to grain products.

Chanukah: (**Chah**-noo-**kah**) Literally, "dedication". Holiday celebrating victory over the Greeks, in which an 8-branched *menorah* (candelabrum) is lit.

Chanukiah: (Chah-noo-kee-**ah**) (Chah-noo-**kee**-ah) 8-branched *menorah* used on *Chanukah*.

Charif: (Chah-**reef**) A sharp or pungent item, pertaining to food.

Chassid: (Cha-**seed**) *(**Cha**-sihd)* Literally "a fervent follower". A *Chassidic* Jew.

Chassidic: Pertaining to *Chassidim*. See below.

Chassidim: (Cha-see-**deem**) *(Cha-**sih**-dim)* "Ultra-Orthodox" Jews, often of Polish or Ukrainian descent. They are *Ashkenazim*, but differ so in practice that they are in a category of their own. Groups include Breslover, Bobover, Lubavitch and Satmar, each following a specific *rebbe* (rabbi). Based on the teachings of the Ba'al Shem Tov, they emphasize going beyond the letter of the law. They focus on their particular *Rebbe's* teachings. Many have unusual dress, dangling side-curls and some speak only *Yiddish*.

Chavrutah: (**Chahv**-roo-**tah**) *(Chahv-**roo**-sah)* Study partner, especially in *Torah*.

Chazakah: (Chah-zah-**kah**) *(Chah-**zah**-kah)* Strong right of claim to a continuing custom.

Chesed: (**Cheh**-sed) Kindness, or an act of loving kindness.

Cholent: (***Tsho**-lent* or ***Tshu**-lent)* Pronounced as a normal "CH" in English, it is Yiddish for "hot". This is the traditional *Ashkenazi* stew served warm for *Shabbat* lunch. (Some spell it "Chulent".)

Chol HaMo'ed: (Chol Hah-Mo-'**ed**) *(Chol Hah-**Mo**-ed)* The in-between days of the festivals of *Sukkot* and Passover, when most work can be done.

Chumrah: (**Choom**-rah) *(**Chum**-rah)* An extra stringency that not everyone practices. (*Chumrot* is plural.)

Davar Charif: (Dah-**vahr** Chah-**reef**) A sharp or pungent item, pertaining to food.

Devarim: (Dev-ah-**reem**) *(Deh-**vah**-reem)* The book of Deuteronomy; Literally meaning "words".

Divrei Torah: (Deev-**rey** To-**rah**) *(**Div**-rey **To**-rah)* Words of *Torah*.

Dreidel: (***Drey**-del)* Yiddish word Four-sided Chanukah top, each side has a Hebrew letter corresponding with the words meaning "A great miracle occurred here". (A dreidel is "Sevivon" in Hebrew.)

D'var Torah: (Deh-**var** To-**rah**) *(Deh-**var To**-rah)* A short speech or sermon concerning *Torah*.

Eruv: (Eh-**roov**) *(**Ey**-roov)* Literally "mixing". Designated area enclosing parts of a city, making it like one giant connected courtyard, enabling one to carry on Shabbat.

Eruv Tavshilin: (Eh-**roov** Tahv-**shee**-leen) *(**Ey**-roov Tahv-**shee**-lin)* Literally, "mixing of cooked foods". A process enabling one to prepare on a major holiday on Friday for *Shabbat*.

Eruy Roschin: (Eh-**rooy** Ros-**chin**) (Usually "Eruy" for short.) The pouring method of *kashering*.

Etrog: (Et-**rog**) *(**Es**-rog)* The fruit of the citron tree, used on the holiday of *Sukkot*.

Etz: (Etz) *(Eytz)* Tree.

Fleishig: *(Fley-shig)* Yiddish word meaning "meat".

Gafen: *(Gah-fen)* Vine. Said by *Ashkenazim* and *Chassidim* in *brachot* for wine or grape juice.

Gebrokts: *(Geh-brokts)* From the Yiddish word for "broken", it has come to mean "wetted matzah". On *Pesach*, a *matzah* that comes in contact with liquid, such as *matzah* meal cake or *matzah* ball soup is considered "Gebrokts", which is not eaten by *Chassidim* and others. (Also spelled "Gebrochts".)

Gefen: (**Geh**-fen) Vine. Said by *Sefardim* in *brachot* for wine or grape juice.

Gematria: (Geh-**mah**-tree-**ah**) Numerical value of a Hebrew letter or word.

Ger: (Gehr) A convert to Judaism. Properly said, "*Ger Tzedek*" (righteous convert).

Geeyoret: (**Gee**-yor-et) *(Gee-yor-es)* A female convert to Judaism. Properly said, "*Gerat Tzedeket*" (righteous female convert).

Gerim: (Geh-**reem**) *(Geh-rihm)* Converts to Judaism.

Glatt: *(Glat)* Yiddish for "smooth". Refers to kosher meat having healthy lungs when examined.

Gut Shabbos: (Goot **Shah**-bos) Yiddish, "good Shabbat". *Ashkenazi* greeting for Shabbat.

Gut Vak: (Goot Vahk) Yiddish literally, "good week". *Ashkenazi* greeting after Shabbat is over.

HaAdamah: (**Ha**—Ah-dah-**mah**) *(Ha—Ah-dah-mah)* "The ground". Ground produce *brachah* "title".

HaEtz: (Ha—Etz) *(Ha—Eytz)* The tree. "Title" of the *brachah* on tree fruits.

HaGafen: *(Ha—Gah-fen)* The vine. *Ashkenazi* and *Chassidic* "title" of *brachah* on wine or grape juice.

HaGefen: (Ha—**Geh**-fen) The vine. *Sefardi* "title" of *brachah* on wine or grape juice.

Hagalah: (Hah-gah-**lah**) *(Hah-go-lah)* The boiling method of *kashering*.

Haggadah: (Hah-gah-**dah**) *(Hah-gah-dah)* Literally, "saga". Special book used for the Passover meal which follows a certain order and recreates the saga of the Exodus.

Hak'sharat Kelim: (Hak-shah-**rat** Keh-**leem**) *(Hak-shah-ros Key-lim)* Making items fit for use.

Halachah: (Hah-lah-ch**ah**) *(Hah-lah-chah)* *Torah* Law.

Halachot: (Hah-lah-**chot**) *(Hah-lah-chos)* *Torah* Laws.

HaMotzi: (Hah—Mot-**zee**) *(Hah—Motz-ee)* Blessing made on bread after the hand-washing.

Hashem: (Hah—**Shem**) Literally "The Name", used in general conversation in place of saying the name of our Creator, since His name is Holy and only to be mentioned in prayer.

Hashgachah: (**Hahsh**-gah-**chah**) *(Hahsh-gah-chah)* Supervision for *kashrut*.

Havdalah: (Hav-dah-**lah**) *(Hav-dah-lah)* Official separation to end Shabbat and start the week.

Hechsher: (**Hech**-sher) A *kashrut* supervising agency's certification or "seal of approval" found on a product package, proving that it is kosher.

Hechsherim: (**Hech**-sher-**eem**) *(Hech-sher-im)* Plural of *hechsher*.

Kabbalah: (**Kah**-bah-lah) *(Kah-baw-lah)* Deeper meaning according to Jewish mysticism.

Kasher: (Kah-**sher**) 1. Literally "fit". (The proper Israeli Hebrew pronunciation of "kosher".) (**Kah**-sher) 2. To make fit for use or consumption. Concerning meat: To remove excess blood. Concerning cookware: To make an item like new by way of a specific procedure.

Kashrut: (Kah-**shroot**) *(**Kash**-roos)* "Fitness of". Referring to the Jewish dietary laws.

Kavanah: (Kah-vah-**nah**) *(Kah-**vah**-nah)* Concentration or intention, either for an act or in prayer.

Kelim: (Keh-**leem**) *(**Key**-leem)* Vessels or items used for preparing or holding food or drink.

Kitniyot: (Keet-nee-**yot**) *(**Kit**-nee-yos)* Bean or rice items forbidden to *Ashkenazim* at *Passover*.

Klal Yisrael: (Klahl Yees-rah-**ehl**) The Jewish nation or community as a whole.

K'li: (Keh-**lee** or Klee) A vessel or item that is used for preparing or holding food or drink.

Kohanim: (Ko-hahn-**eem**) *(Ko-**hah**-nim)* Aaron's offspring designated to be Temple priests.

Kohen: (Ko-**hen**) *(**Ko**-heyn)* A descendent of Aaron, designated to give the priestly blessing.

Kollel: (Ko-**lel**) *(**Ko**-lel)* Place of *Torah* learning for men. Literally, "inclusive". ("Kollelim" is plural.)

Kosher: (**Ko**-sher) Fit for consumption. (This is actually the *Ashkenazic* pronunciation of "*kasher*", which has
    ultimately made its way into popular English as meaning "proper", hence the title of this book!)

Lamdeni Chukecha: (Lahm-**den**-ee Choo-**keh**-cha) *(Lahm-**dey**-nee Choo-**keh**-cha)* Literally "Who teaches
    me His laws". Phrase said if one erroneously recited the formula *brachah*.

L'Chaim: (**Lah**–chai-**yim**) *(Lah–**chai**-yim)* "To life!" Exclamation said immediately before saying a *brachah*
    on wine, grape juice or alcoholic beverages.

Lechem: (**Leh**-chem) Bread.

Lechem Mishneh: (**Leh**-chem Meesh-**neh**) *(**Leh**-chem **Mish**-neh)* Literally "double portion of bread". The
    two *challah* loaves used on *Shabbat*, representing the double portion of *manna*.

Levi: (Leh-**vee**) *(**Ley**-vee)* The tribe that Moses descended from. Singers of the Temple.

Levi'im: (Leh-vee-**eem**) *(**Leh**-vee-yihm)* Levites.

Libun Gamur: (Lee-**boon** Gah-**moor**) Absolute or complete heating. The glowing method of *kashering*.

Libun Kal: (Lee-**boon** Kahl) *(**Lee**-boon Kahl)* Light heating. The baking method of *kashering*.

Li'Mehadrin: (Lee–Me-hah-**dreen**) Literally "to the highest quality" referring to the strictest level of *kashrut*,
    especially in Israel. (Also "*Mehadrin*").

Lulav: (Loo-**lahv**) *(**Loo**-lahv)* Palm fronds used on the holiday of *Sukkot*.

Ma'aser: (Ma'-ah-**sehr**) *(**Mah**-sehr)* Tithe.

Ma'aser Ani: (Ma'-ah-**sehr** Ah-nee) *(**Mah**-sehr **Ah**-nee)* Tithe for the poor, taken on the third and sixth
    years of the *Sh'mittah* cycle. It can be eaten by anyone.

Ma'aser Rishon: (Ma'-ah-**sehr** Ree-**shon**) *(**Mah**-sehr **Ree**-shon)* First tithe. One-tenth of produce remaining
    after *Terumah* is taken.

Ma'aser Sheni: (Ma'-ah-**sehr** Sheh-**nee**) *(**Mah**-sehr **Shey**-nee)* Second tithe, taken in the first, second,
    fourth and fifth years of the *Sh'mittah* cycle. The grower could redeem it with a coin.

Marit Ayin: (Mahr-**eet** Ai-yeen) *(**Mahr**-is **Ai**-yihn)* Seemingly doing wrong- something that appears as
    though you might be sinning even if you aren't. Simply put, "It looks bad".

Mashgiach: (Mash-**gee**-ach) Kosher supervisor.

Mashiach: (Mah-**shee**-ach) A king anointed by a High Priest. The man who will return all Jews to Israel.

Matzah: (Mah-**tzah**) *(**Mahtz**-ah or **Mahtz**-oh)* Unleavened bread. Also "*matza*", "*matso*" or "*matzo*".

Matzot: (Mah-**tzot**) *(Mahtz-os)* Sheets of unleavened bread. Also spelled "matsos" or "matzos".

Mayim Acharonim: (**Mai**-yeem Ah-chah-ro-**neem**) *(Mai-yeem Ah-chah-ro-neem)* Waters afterward.

Me'ein Shalosh: (Meh-'**eyn** Shah-**losh**) Literally "three condensed". "Title" of *brachah* said after eating certain grain snacks, wine, grape juice, and certain fruits, named for the three main *brachot* of *Birkat HaMazon*, which are condensed into one after-*brachah*.

Megillah: (Meh-gee-**lah**) *(Meh-gee-lah)* Literally, "scroll". Generally, referring to the Book of Esther.

Mehadrin: (Me-hah-**dreen**) Literally "highest quality" referring to the strictest level of *kashrut*, especially in Israel. (Also "Li'Mehadrin").

Melachah: (Meh-lah-**chah**) *(Meh-lah-chah)* Creative work or task. Generally referred to forbidden activity to be done on *Shabbat*.

Melachot: (Meh-lah-**chot**) *(Meh-lah-chos)* Creative works or forbidden activities on *Shabbat*.

Melaveh Malkah: (Meh-**lah**-veh Mal-**kah**) *(Meh-lah-veh Mal-kah)* Literally "escorting the queen", as in the "*Shabbat* Queen". Also, the feast of the King celebrated after *Shabbat*.

Mesorah: (Meh-so-**rah**) *(Meh-so-rah)* Unbroken tradition. Pertains to a tradition handed down from parent to child from the country of their origin.

Mevushal: (Meh-voo-**shahl**) *(Meh-voo-shahl)* Cooked.

Mezonot: (Meh-zo-**not**) *(Muh-zo-nos)* Literally, "foods". "Title" of the *brachah* said before eating any flour product made of one of the 5 grains: barley, rye, oats, wheat, or spelt.

Mezuman: (Meh-zoo-**man**) *(Muh-zoo-mun)* Literally "summoned". A group of at least three or more men reciting "*Birkat HaMazon*" together, named for the invitation from the leader to others in the group.

Mikvah: (Meek-**vah**) *(Mik-vah)* A special purification pool, containing a specific volume of water that is connected to a source of rainwater or spring water.

Milchig: *(Mil-chig)* Yiddish word referring to dairy or milk.

Miluy V'Eruy: (Mee-**looy** Ve-Ee-**rooy**) Cold-*kashering* method of *kashering* glass. Done by Ashkenazim.

Minchah: (Meen-**chah**) *(Min-chah)* The afternoon prayer.

Minhag: (Meen-**hag**) *(Min-hawg)* A custom.

Minhagim: (Meen-ha-**geem**) *(Min-haw-gim)* Customs.

Mishkan: (Meesh-**kahn**) (**Mish**-kahn) The "portable" Temple used in the desert. Literally, "dwelling place".

Mitzvah: (Meetz-**vah**) *(Mitz-vah)* Usually, one of 613 *Torah* laws. Also can mean a good deed.

Mitzvot: (Meetz-**vot**) *(Mitz-vos)* Plural of *mitzvah*. One of the 613 *Torah* laws. Also good deeds.

Noach: (**No**-ach) Noah, builder of the ark.

Noachides: Non-Jews that follow the seven laws of Noach (above).

Olam Haba: (O-**lahm** Hah-**bah**) *(Oh-lahm hah-bah)* The World to Come.

Omer: (**Oh**-mehr) The barley offering brought in the Temple, it is now stated instead.

Oral Tradition: In Hebrew, it is actually called "*Torah She-Ba'al Peh* [*Torah* that is coming from the mouth]. The oral part of *Torah*, told to Moses on Mt. Sinai. Taught orally from teacher to student, until it was feared it may be lost due to persecution, and it was then written down.

Orlah: (Ahr-**lah**) *(Ohr-lah)* Fruit from a tree in its first three years, which is sacred.

Parve: (**Par**-veh) *(Par-ehv* or ***Par**-vah* or *Par-eh-vah)* (Also spelled "Pareve"). A food or status that is neutral, being neither meat nor dairy.

Pasken: (Pah-**sken**) *(Pahs-ken)* To make a *Halachic* decision in response to a question.

Pat: (Paht) *(Pahs)* Any amount of bread, be it from a crumb to a loaf.

Pat Palter: (Paht **Pal**-ter) *(Pahs **Pal**-ter)* Bread or other grain baked by a non-Jewish commercial bakery.

Pat Yisrael: (Paht Yees-rah-**ehl**) *(Pahs Yis-rah-eyl)* Baked items that a Jew had some part in the baking.

Pesach: (**Peh**-sach) *(Pey-sach)* The major holiday of Passover.

Posek: (Po-**sek**) *(Po-seyk)* A rabbi who is knowledgeable in, deals with and answers *Halachic* questions.

Poskim: (Pos-**keem**) *(**Pos**-kim)* Rabbis who answer detailed, precise *Halachic* questions.

P'ri: (Pree or Pe-**ree**) Fruit.

P'sak: (Pe-**sak**) A Halachic decision or judgement.

Purim: (**Poo**-reem) Literally "lots". Wild holiday in which children dress in costume, and food gifts and charity is given. Based on the Book of Esther.

Rasha: (Rah-**sha'**) *(**Rah**-sha)* A wicked person.

Rav: (Rahv) Rabbi or Posek.

Rosh Hashanah: (Rosh Hah—shah-**nah**) *(Rosh Hah—**shah**-nah)* Literally, "head of the year".

Seder: (**Seh**-dehr) Literally, "order". The special Passover meal having symbolic foods, and following a specific order recreating the Exodus.

Sefarad: (Seh-**fah**-rahd) The Hebrew word for Spain.

Sefardi: (**Seh**-far-**dee** or Sfar-**dee**) *(**Sfar**-di)* Literally "Sefardite". A *Sefardic* Jew. See "*Sefardim*".

Sefardic: Pertains to *Sefardim*. See *Sefardim* below.

Sefardim: (**Seh**-far-**deem** or Sfar-**deem** or Seh-**fahr**-ah-**deem**) *(Seh-**far**-dim* or ***Sfar**-dim)* Jews of Spanish, Asian, African or Middle Eastern descent, from the Hebrew word for Spain "Sefarad". There are many different types, such as Judeo-Spanish, Moroccan, Tunisian, Persian, Iranian, Syrian, Turkish, all with many variations in *minhagim*. Most speak only Hebrew, others Arabic, Spanish, or Ladino, (cross between Spanish and Hebrew). They are known to slant toward the *kabbalistic*.

Seudah: (**Seh**-oo-dah) *(**Soo**-dah)* A festive meal.

Seudah Shelishit: (Seh-oo-**dah** She-lee-**sheet**) Literally "third meal". Third festive meal of *Shabbat*. Also "*Shalosh Seudat*". *Ashkenazim* call it "*Shalosh Seudos*" or "*Shaloshudis*".

Seudat Mitzvah: (**Seh**-oo-**dat** Meetz-**vah**) *(**Soo**-dos **Mitz**-vah)* Meal celebrating a type of *mitzvah* or good deed, such as a *siyum* or *brit milah*.

Sevivon: (Seh-vee-**vohn**) Four-sided Chanukah top, each side has a Hebrew letter corresponding with the words meaning "A great miracle occurred here". (Sevivon is "Dreidel" in Yiddish.)

Shabbat: (Shah-**baht**) *(**Shah**-bos)* The Sabbath, or rest day in which no work is performed.

Shabbat Shalom: (Shah-**baht** Shah-**lom**) *Sefardic* Sabbath greeting. Literally "Sabbath peace".

Shalom Bayit: (Shah-**lom** Bah-**yeet**) *(**Shah**-lom **Bah-yis**)* Peace in the home.

Shalosh Seudos: *(Shoh-losh Se-oo-dos)* Ashkenazi name for third Shabbat meal. Also "*Shaloshudos*".

Shamash: (Shah-**mash**) *(Shah-mash)* Literally "Attendant". Extra light used to kindle *chanukiah* lights.

Shavua' Tov: (Shah-**voo**-ah Tov) Literally, "good week". *Sefardi* greeting after Shabbat is over.

Shavu'ot: (**Shah**-voo-'ot) *(Shah-voo-os)* Literally "weeks". Major holiday 7 weeks after Passover. The day when Israel received the *Torah* on Mt. Sinai.

Sh'chitah: (Sheh-chee-**tah**) *(Sheh-chee-tah)* Kosher slaughter according to Jewish Law.

Shecht: (Shecht) Slaughter in accordance with Jewish Law.

Shehakol: (**She**-hah-**kol**) Literally, "for all", "title" of the *brachah* before for many foods.

Shehecheyanu: (**Sheh**-heh- che-**yah**-noo) Title of the blessing recited on any new item, such as clothing, a house or car— anything a person has received or purchased that makes them happy. It is also said on holidays and on a "new fruit" (one has never eaten or had within 30 days), such as on Tu B'Shvat. The blessing means, "Blessed are You... Who gave us life, sustained us, and brought us to this time".

Shelah: (Sheh-**lah**) *(Shai-lah)* A *Halachic* question asked to a *Posek*.

Shelot: (Sheh-**lot**) *(Shai-los)* *Halachic* questions asked to a *Posek*.

Shemot: (Sheh-**mot**) *(Sheh-mos)* The Book of Exodus. Literally "Names".

Shinui: (Shee-**nooy**) In an unusual manner. Literally "changed" or "altered".

Sh'mini Atzeret: (She-mee-**nee** At-**zeh**-ret) *(She-mee-nee At-zeh-res)* Literally, "eighth assembly". Major holiday on the eighth day after *Sukkot*.

Sh'mittah: (She-**mee**-tah) The seventh year ordained for the land to rest in the agricultural cycle of Israel.

Sh'murah Matzah: (She-moo-**rah** Mah-**tzah**) *(Shmoo-rah Mah-tzah)* Special matzah for Passover that has been watched from harvest through baking.

Shochet: (**Sho**-chet) Kosher slaughterer.

Shomer Shabbat: (Sho-**mehr** Shah-**baht**) *(Sho-mehr Shah-bos)* Observant of the Sabbath.

Siddur: (See-**door**) *(Sid-or)* Jewish prayer book.

Siddurim: (See-door-**eem**) *(Sid-ur-im)* Jewish prayer books.

Simchat Torah: (Seem-**chat** To-rah) *(Sim-chas To-rah)* Wild major holiday when the cycle of the *Torah* reading ends and begins anew. In Israel, it's part of *Sh'mini 'Atzeret*.

Siyum: (See-**yoom**) (**See**-yum) Literally "ending". Celebration of completing reading of a book of *Talmud*.

Sukkah: (Soo-**kah**) *(Soo-kah)* A temporary dwelling used on the holiday of *Sukkot*.

Sukkot: (Soo-**kot**) *(Soo-kos)* The Feast of Booths or Tabernacles, a major holiday celebrated partially by eating in temporary dwellings. Literally "booths".

Talmud: (Tal-**mood**) *(Tal-mud)* The Oral Tradition, written down in book form.

Taref: (Tah-**ref**) "Treifah" or non-kosher.

Tashlich: (**Tash**-leech) Custom the first day of *Rosh Hashanah*, one symbolically casts sins to the water.

Teimani: (**Tey**-mah-**nee**) A Yemenite Jew, or Jew from Yemen.

Terumah: (Teh-roo-**mah**) *(Teh-roo-mah)* Specific tithe always given to *Kohanim*. Since it was meant for *Kohanim*, it cannot be benefited from in any way. *Challah* is a type of *terumah*.

Terumah Gedolah: (Teh-roo-**mah** Geh-doh-lah) *(Teh-**roo**-mah Geh-**doh**-lah)* Largest main tithe supporting the *Kohanim*.

Terumat Ma'aser: (Teh-roo-**mah** Ma'-ah-**sehr**) *(Teh-**roo**-mah **Mah**-sehr)* Special tithe. One-tenth remaining after the first tithe has been taken. As is all *terumah*, it's given to *Kohanim* .

Tevilah: (Teh-vee-**lah**) *(Tuh-**vee**-lah)* Immersion or "to immerse", as for cookware items or a person into a *mikvah*.

Torah: (To-**rah**) *(**To**-rah and sometimes **Toy**-rah)* Referred to as the Jewish "Bible", consisting of the five Books of Moses; can refer to Written Torah, Oral Tradition, and rabbinic teachings.

Treif: (Tref or Treyf) Short for "*trefah*". *Sefardim* say "*taref*".

Treifah: (Tre-**fah** or Trey-**fah**) *(**Trey**-fah)* Literally "torn" as in the prohibition of "torn meat". Unfit for consumption or non-kosher; forbidden by Jewish Law. Also called "*taref*" or "*treif*".

Tzedakah: (Tzeh-dah-**kah**) *(Tzeh-**dah**-kah)* Charity in the forms of money, time, food or help.

Tza'ar Ba'aley Chaim: (**Tza**'-ar **Ba**'-al-**ey** Chay-**eem**) *(Tzar **Bah**-ley **Cha**-yim)* "Cruelty to animals".

Ushpizin: (Oosh-pee-**zeen**) *(Oosh-**pee**-zin)* The holy "guests" who are "invited" to the *sukkah* during the festival of *Sukkot*.

Vayikra: (**Vah**-yeek-**rah**) *(Vai-**yeek**-rah)* The Book of *Leviticus*. Literally, "He called out".

Written Torah: The "Jewish Bible" (Five Books of Moses, Writings, and Prophets).

Ya'akov: (**Ya**'-ah-**kov**) Jacob.

Yad Soledet Bo: (Yahd So-**led**-et Bo) *(Yawd So-**led**-es Bo)* Hand recoiling back due to heat.

Yartzeit: *(**Yar**-tzayeet)* *Ashkenazi* word for the anniversary of death of relative.

Yashan: (Ya-**shan**) *(**Yo**-shon)* "Old". Pertains to "old" grain. Sometimes listed as "*yoshon*" on products.

Yehudit: (Yeh-hoo-**deet**) (Yeh-**hoo**-dis) "Judith". Heroine in the time of the Chanukah miracle, who used salty cheese and milk to put the evil Greek general to sleep. She then killed him, helping win the war.

Yemenites: (Anglicized) Jews native to Yemen- said to be closest to original Jewish tradition and Hebrew pronunciation due to isolation. The fewest of groups, the majority live in Israel. The sects split, one half rationalists, the other *Kabbalistic*. Actually called "*Teimani*".

Yisrael: (Yees-rah-**ehl**) (Yis-rah-**eyl**) Israel. The Jewish nation. Also Ya'akov's other name.

Yom Kippur: (**Yom** Kee-**poor**) *(Yom **Kih**-per)* Literally "Day of Atonement".

Yom Tov: (Yom Tov) Holiday or festival. Literally "good day". Often in Yiddish "Yam Tiff".

Yomim Tovim: (Yom-**eem** Tov-**eem**) *(**Yom**-im **Tov**-im)* Holidays. Literally, "good days".

Zimun: (Zee-**moon**) *(**Zee**-moon)* Literally "invitation". Statement of invitation from the leader of at least three or more men reciting "*Birkat HaMazon* together.

Index

Recipes with bolded numbers are generally variations found at the bottom of a main recipe.

C

D

E

F

H

J

M

N

O

P

S

U

V

W

Extra Recipes

Below is plenty of area for your own personal recipes, so all your favorites can be in one place!

Extra Recipes

UNIQUELY KOSHER

Extra Recipes

Extra Recipes

UNIQUELY KOSHER

Extra Recipes

About the Author

Chasya Katriela Eshkol is the Executive Director and founder of The Yoshon Network Inc., a 501 (c)(3) non-profit organization dedicated solely to the *mitzvah* of keeping *yashan*. TYNI was organized in Cincinnati, Ohio, where she initiated the start of the once rather humble beginnings of the Yoshon.com website. TYNI continues to grow and expand, helping to provide *yashan* information to visitors all over the world.

Chasya has written articles for *Jewish Spirit Magazine* for the Cincinnati Community Kollel, created articles and poetry for the *Cincinnati Jewish Women's Journal*, pen and ink drawings for the Pet Pride Inc. newsletter, and previously created word and crossword puzzles for *The Morris Report* published by Alexander Auerbach and Co.

Other Books by Chasya Eshkol

Can-Do Kosher! A Quick and Concise Guide to Becoming Kosher.

Vintage Grain: The Mitzvah of Keeping Yashan.

Chasya can be reached at WriteChasya@gmail.com.

Tovim Press
TovimPress.com

Quality Books Published by Tovim Press, LLC.

www.ingramcontent.com/pod-product-compliance
Lightning Source LLC
Chambersburg PA
CBHW062015090426
42811CB00005B/860

9 781643 940014